Hedge Funds

Hedge Funds

Insights in Performance Measurement, Risk Analysis, and Portfolio Allocation

GREG N. GREGORIOU
GEORGES HÜBNER
NICOLAS PAPAGEORGIOU
FABRICE ROUAH

WILEY

John Wiley & Sons, Inc.

Published by John Wiley & Sons, Inc., Hoboken, New Jersey.
Published simultaneously in Canada.

For general information about our other products and services, please contact our Customer Care Department within the United States at 800-762-2974, outside the United States at 317-572-3993 or fax 317-572-4002.

Wiley also publishes its books in a variety of electronic formats. Some content that appears in print may not be available in electronic books. For more information about Wiley products, visit our Web site at www.wiley.com.

Library of Congress Cataloging-in-Publication Data:

ISBN-13 978-0-471-73743-8
ISBN-10 0-471-73743-7

Printed in the United States of America

10 9 8 7 6 5 4 3 2 1

Contents

Preface

The idea for this book came about when we realized that our book on Commodity Trading Advisors (CTAs) was so well received. We decided that a hedge fund reader with new chapters dealing with quantitative and qualitative analyses would be a helpful and welcome addition and complementary to the CTA reader. The chapters are intended to introduce readers to some of the issues encountered by academics and practitioners working with hedge funds. They deal with new methods of hedge fund performance evaluation, portfolio allocation, and risk and returns that are imperative in understanding correct selection and monitoring of hedge funds. Although numerous chapters are technical in nature, with econometric and statistical models, by well-known academics and professionals in the field, stress has been put on understanding the applicability of the results as well as the theoretical development. We believe this book can assist institutional investors, pension fund managers, endowment funds, and high-net-worth individuals wanting to add hedge funds to traditional stock and bond portfolios.

Acknowledgments

The editors wish to thank Bill Fallon, senior finance editor, for his enthusiastic support and constructive comments. We also extend sincere and warmest thanks to Alexia Meyers, senior production editor at Wiley, for her wonderful assistance in editing and meticulously reviewing the manuscript. We thank Karen Ludke, editorial program assistant at Wiley, for her outstanding assistance during this process, and Debra Manette, copyeditor, for being very attentive to details in the manuscript.

We also thank Allison Adams, publisher of Institutional Investor Journals, for allowing us to reprint Chapters 1 and 6 from the *Journal of Wealth Management* and Chapter 15 from the *Journal of Alternative Investments*. We also express thanks to Richard E. Oberuc at LaPorte Asset Allocation System (*www.laportesoft.com*) for the use of his software in preparing Chapter 18 and to Josh Rosenberg at Hedge Fund Research (*www.hfr.com*).

The authors further thank Professor Thomas Schneeweis at the Isenberg School of Management/University of Massachusetts and Director/Editor of the Centre for International Securities and Derivatives Markets (CISDM)/*Journal of Alternative Investments* (*JAI*) for allowing the authors of Chapter 18 to reproduce the names the fund of hedge funds in the CISDM database. We kindly thank Raj Gupta, Research Director/Assistant Editor of CISDM/JAI, and Dr. Ellen Yan, Executive Director at CISDM, for her assistance and help with questions regarding the data. We also thank Kevin Hale, an economics and finance student, at State University of New York, College at Plattsburgh for formatting the references.

Nicolas Papageorgiou would like to thank the research office at HEC Montreal.

Finally we thank Tate Haymond at PerTrac (*www.pertrac2000.com*) for the use of his software in preparing Chapter 18.

About the Editors

Greg N. Gregoriou is Associate Professor of Finance and coordinator of faculty research in the School of Business and Economics at State University of New York, College at Plattsburgh. He obtained his PhD (finance) from the University of Quebec at Montreal and is the hedge fund editor for the peer-reviewed journal *Derivatives Use, Trading and Regulation* published by Henry Stewart publications based in the United Kingdom. He has authored over 40 articles on hedge funds and managed futures in various U.S. and U.K. peer-reviewed publications, including the *Journal of Futures Markets, European Journal of Operational Research, and Annals of Operations Research*. This is his third book with John Wiley & Sons.

Nicolas Papageorgiou completed his PhD at the ISMA Centre, University of Reading, United Kingdom in 2002 and has since held the position of Assistant Professor in the Department of Finance at HEC Montreal. His doctoral research focused on the modelling of corporate credit risk, and the empirical evaluation of models for pricing corporate liabilities and credit derivatives. Nicolas Papageorgiou is also interested in alternative fund management, specifically hedge funds and CTAs, and has written several papers and book chapters on performance measurements of these funds. Dr. Papageorgiou's research has been published in leading journals such as *Journal of Futures Markets, Journal of Financial Research, and Journal of Fixed Income*. He has also been invited to present his research at several conferences in North America and Europe.

Georges Hübner holds a PhD in Management from INSEAD. He is the Deloitte Professor of Financial Management at the University of Liège and also teaches finance at Maastricht University and EDHEC (Lille). He has taught at the executive and postgraduate levels in several countries in Europe, North America, Africa, and Asia. He has written two books on financial management and has authored several peer-reviewed research articles in the fields of hedge funds and derivatives, including the *Journal of*

Empirical Finance, the *Journal of Futures Markets,* and the *Journal of Banking and Finance.* He was the recipient of the prestigious 2002 Iddo Sarnat Award for the best paper published in *JBF* in 2001.

Fabrice Rouah is an Institut de Finance Mathématique de Montréal (IFM2) Scholar and a PhD candidate in Finance, McGill University, Montreal, Quebec. Mr. Rouah is a former Faculty Lecturer and Consulting Statistician in the Department of Mathematics and Statistics at McGill University. He specializes on the statistical and stochastic modeling of hedge funds, managed futures, and CTAs, and is a regular contributor in peer-reviewed academic publications on alternative investments. He obtained his BSc in applied mathematics from Concordia University and his MSc in applied statistics from McGill University. This is his second book with John Wiley & Sons.

About the Contributors

Carol Alexander is Professor of Risk Management and Director of Research at the ISMA Centre. Among many industry links, she is Chair of the Academic Advisory Council of the professional Risk Managers International association (PRMIA). Prior to the ISMA Centre, she was a Director and Head of Market Risk Modelling at Nikko Bank, Academic Director of Algorithmics, and for many years, Lecturer in Mathematics at Sussex University. She obtained her PhD (in algebraic number theory) from Sussex, her MSc. (in mathematical economics and econometrics) from LSE, and her BSc. (in mathematics with experimental psychology) from Sussex. Dr. Alexander is the author of a bestselling textbook *Market Models* (John Wiley & Sons, 2001) and editor of 14 books on mathematics and finance. With Elizabeth Sheedy (of MacQuarie University, Sydney) she has recently edited the three-volume *Professional Risk Managers Handbook*. Dr. Alexander is well known for her research in quantitative strategies for fund management and volatility analysis. Her most recent publications include papers in the *Journal of Portfolio Management, Journal of Banking and Finance, Journal of Applied Econometrics,* and *Journal of Financial Econometrics.* She consults as an expert witness and designs commercial software for hedge funds, operational risk, and high-frequency pricing.

Paul Ali is an Associate Professor in the Faculty of Law, University of New South Wales, Sydney, Australia. Mr. Ali was previously a finance lawyer in two of the leading Australian law firms and also in the securitization group of a major U.S. bank. He has, in addition, been a principal of a private investment firm based in Sydney. He has published several books and journal articles on finance and investment law, including, most recently, books on securitization and environmental finance.

Noël Amenc, PhD, is a Professor of Finance at Edhec Graduate School of Business, where he heads the Risk and Asset Management Research Centre. He has conducted active research in the fields of quantitative equity management, portfolio performance analysis, and active asset allocation, resulting in numerous academic and practitioner articles and books. He is an Associate Editor of the Journal of Alternative Investments and Senior Academic Fellow of the Europlace Institute of Finance. He is also a member of the scientific council of the AMF (the French financial regulatory authority). He also is a coauthor of *Portfolio Analysis and Performance Measurement* (John Wiley & Sons, 2004), *La Gestion Alternative* (Economica, 2004), and the Edhec European Asset Management Practices and Edhec European Alternative Multimanagement Practices surveys (2003).

Mark Anson is the Chief Investment Officer for the California Public Employees' Retirement System (CalPERS), which has over $148 billion in assets. He has complete responsibility for all asset classes in which CalPERS invests, including domestic and international equity and fixed income, real estate, corporate governance, currency overlay, securities lending, venture capital, leveraged buyouts, and hedge funds. Dr. Anson earned his law degree from the Northwestern University School of Law in Chicago and his PhD and Master's in Finance from the Columbia University Graduate School of Business in New York City, and his B.A. from St. Olaf College in Minnesota. He is a member of the New York and Illinois State Bar Associations and has earned numerous accounting and financial designations. He is the author of four books on the financial markets and has published over 60 research articles on the topics of corporate governance, hedge funds, real estate, currency overlay, credit risk, private equity, risk management, and portfolio management. Dr. Anson is on the editorial boards of five financial journals and sits on Advisory Committees for the New York Stock Exchange, the International Association of Financial Engineers, AIMR's Task Force on Corporate Governance, the Center for Excellence in Accounting and Security Analysis at Columbia University, and the Alternative Investment Research Centre at the City University of London.

Jean-François Bacmann is a member of the quantitative analysis group for RMF Investment Management, based in Pfäffikon, Switzerland. His key responsibilities are the management of research projects and the implementation of the quantitative in-house software tools. Prior to joining RMF Investment Management in 2002, Dr. Bacmann spent five years as a research and teaching assistant in finance at the Entreprise Institute, University of Neuchâtel, Switzerland. Dr. Bacmann received his Engineering degree in Computer Science and Applied Mathematics from the ENSIMAG, France, a Master's degree in Finance from the University of Grenoble, France, and a PhD in Finance from the University of Neuchâtel. He has published several articles in professional and academic financial journals.

Pierre-Antoine Bares is currently Head of Quant at International Asset Management Ltd, specialists in fund of hedge funds. Pierre-Antoine was formerly Head of Research at Norshield Financial Group, a CTA strategy hedge fund. Prior to that Pierre was a Professor of Physics at the Swiss Federal Institute of Technology in Lausanne, Switzerland, conducting research on risk, hedge funds, and theoretical physics (condensed matter and statistical mechanics) which resulted in many academic publications. He was a risk analyst at UBS, Zurich, a post-doctoral fellow at ILL, Grenoble, France, and at Massachusetts Institute of Technology (MIT), Cambridge, USA. Pierre-Antoine also has a PhD (Erni Medal), Masters, and Undergraduate from the Swiss Federal Institute of Technology, Zurich, Switzerland.

Zsolt Berenyi holds an M.Sc. in Economics from the University of Economic Sciences in Budapest and a PhD in Finance from the University of Munich. His main interest lies in the risk and performance evaluation of alternative investments: hedge funds, CTAs, and credit funds. After working for Deutsche Bank as well as KPMG at various locations for numerous years, he is now working as an independent consultant, heading RISC Consulting.

Keith H. Black, CFA, CAIA is an Assistant Professor in the Stuart Graduate School of Business at the Illinois Institute of Technology. He teaches courses in Global Market Economics, Equity Valuation, Investments, Mutual Funds, Hedge Funds, and Global Investment Strategy. Mr. Black's interest in hedge funds inspired him to write the book *Managing a Hedge Fund* (McGraw-Hill, 2004). He has earned the designations of Chartered Financial Analyst and Chartered Alternative Investment Analyst, as well as an MBA from Carnegie Mellon University. His professional experience includes commodities derivatives trading at First Chicago Capital Markets, stock options research and CBOE market-making for Hull Trading Company, and building stock selection models for mutual funds and hedge funds for Chicago Investment Analytics. He contributes regularly to the *CFA Digest and Journal of Global Financial Markets,* and comments on markets for television and radio financial news shows.

Jean Brunel is the managing principal of Brunel Associates, a firm offering wealth management consulting services to ultra affluent individuals. He spent the bulk of his career in the investment management group of J.P. Morgan, where he worked in the U.S. and abroad from 1976 until his retirement in the spring of 1999. In 1990, he assumed the position of chief investment officer of J.P. Morgan's global private bank, where he focused on the issues of special concern to individual investors, such as tax-efficiency and downside risk protection. Prior to that, he had served in New York, Tokyo, Hong Kong,

Singapore and Melbourne, in various investment and managerial capacities. Upon retiring from J.P. Morgan, he started consulting for wealthy individuals and the institutions that serve them. Thus, he consulted for and then served as chief investment officer of Private Asset Management, at U.S. Bancorp, a position he held until June 2001, when he left to found Brunel Associates. Jean is the editor of the *Journal of Wealth Management,* published by Institutional Investor Journals, is a Trustee of the Research Foundation of The CFA Institute and a Director of Culp, Inc a NYSE listed Textile Company. Further, he authored "Integrated Wealth Management: The New Direction for Portfolio Managers" (a book published in 2002 by Institutional Investors and Euromoney Books) and a number of peer-reviewed articles. A graduate of Ecole des Hautes Etudes Commmerciales in France, Jean holds an MBA from the Kellogg Graduate School of Management at Northwestern University and is a Chartered Financial Analyst.

Daniel Capocci is a PhD candidate at the University of Liège in Belgium and has published extensively on hedge funds in various professional and academic journals, such as the *Journal of Empirical Finance,* the *European Journal of Finance,* as well as for several hedge funds and CTA readers. He has also published a book on the subject titled *Introduction aux Hedge Funds.*

Alain Coën is Associate Professor of Finance at the University of Quebec in Montreal (UQAM). He obtained his PhD in Finance from the University of Grenoble and holds a Master of Arts in Economics with major in Macroeconomics from Laval University. He consults and does research in the areas of asset pricing and portfolio management. His research interests focus on asset pricing, international finance, business cycles and financial econometrics. He has published in several international journals and has written a book on financial management.

Aurélie Desfleurs is Assistant Professor of Finance at the Accounting School of Laval University. She received her Master's and PhD in Finance from Laval University and teaches investment and corporate finance. Her research interests include asset pricing and earnings forecasting, and she has published several papers in the areas of multinational finance and financial forecasting.

Anca Dimitriu is a Visiting Research Fellow at the ISMA Centre. She holds a PhD in Finance from the University of Reading and an MS in Finance from the Doctoral School of Finance and Banking, Bucharest. Her research interests include portfolio optimization, indexing and long/short equity strategies, hedge fund performance and funds of hedge funds portfolio management. She has published many papers in top international academic journals, and she is an active speaker at conferences in many countries.

Dr. Dimitriu has been teaching in Finance MS programs for several years and has also been involved in hedge fund consultancy projects.

Joseph Eagleeye is cofounder and portfolio manager at Premia Capital Management, LLC, in Chicago. As a principal of the Quartile Group, Mr. Eagleeye advises investment companies on hedging strategies, benchmark construction, index replication strategies, and risk management. Prior to joining Premia, Mr. Eagleeye developed programmed trading applications for Morgan Stanley's Equity Division and proprietary computer models for an urban economics consulting firm. From 1994 to 1998 he worked in the Derivative Strategies Group of Putnam Investments. As a member of that group, he researched, back-tested, and implemented relative-value derivatives strategies, which spanned the bond and commodity markets. Mr. Eagleeye holds a degree in Applied Mathematics from Yale University and an MBA from the University of California at Berkeley. He has also contributed chapters to the following edited books: *The New Generation of Risk Management in Hedge Funds and Private Equity Investments* (coauthor, Euromoney, 2003) and *Commodity Trading Advisors: Risk, Performance Analysis, and Selection* (coauthor, John Wiley & Sons, 2004).

Laurent Favre holds a Bachelor's degree in Economics, an MBA in Finance and a Bachelor's in Sports, all from the University of Lausanne. He was high school professor of Economics, Mathematics, and Sports during two years in Switzerland. He has published several papers in the *Journal of Alternative Investments,* is an associate researcher at Edhec School, and he worked for four years for Investment Solutions, UBS Wealth Management (Zurich, Switzerland), as Head of Tactical Asset Allocation. In 2004 he left UBS and founded AlternativeSoft AG (Switzerland). The company specializes in hedge funds screening, portfolio optimization with hedge funds, and hedge fund index returns forecasting.

Barry Feldman, PhD, CFA, is a consultant and the founder of Prism Analytics, a firm started to commercialize the variance decomposition technique he developed and patented. He is also a lecturer at the Kellstadt Graduate School of Business at DePaul University. Prior to founding Prism, he was a senior researcher at Ibbotson Associates, where he designed advanced portfolio optimization methods and other quantitative tools, constructed hedge fund-of-fund portfolios, and conducted research on several topics including hedge funds and behavioral finance. He previously held positions at Scudder Kemper Funds and AT&T. He has spoken widely and published on topics including portfolio construction and risk analysis. In addition being the inventor in the basic patent on cooperative resolution methods, he is the inventor in two pending published applications. He received an undergraduate degree from MIT and a PhD from State University of New York at Stony Brook, both in Economics.

Mohamed Gaber is an Associate Professor and Chair, Department of Accounting at State University of New York, College at Plattsburgh. He received his MBA and PhD from Baruch College (CUNY).

Gregor Gawron is a member of the quantitative analysis group of RMF Investment Management, based in Pfäffikon, Switzerland. He is responsible for the statistical analysis of hedge funds and alternative risk transfer. Prior to joining RMF Investment Management in 2002, Mr. Gawron was a research assistant at the Institute of Statistics and Econometrics at the University of Basel. His main area of research focused on quantitative methods in financial risk management. Mr. Gawron received his Master's degree in Economics from the University of Karlstad, Sweden, and is currently finishing his PhD in quantitative finance at the University of Basel, Switzerland.

Rajna Gibson is Professor of Finance at the University of Zurich, Switzerland since March 2000 and Honorary Professor of Finance at the University of Lausanne. She was a Professor of Finance at Lausanne University from October 1991 to February 2000 and directed its Master in science program in Banking and Finance. She was assistant-professor of Finance at Group HEC, Paris and a visiting scholar at New York University and at John Anderson's graduate school of management at UCLA. She holds a PhD in economic and social sciences and a graduate degree in Business Administration from the University of Geneva. Her papers "Stochastic convenience yield and the pricing of oil contingent claims" (co-authored with Eduardo Schwartz, UCLA) in the *Journal of Finance*, 1990 and "Valuing Swiss default-free callable bonds: theory and empirical evidence," *Journal of Banking and Finance*, 1990 were awarded the Greenwich Capital Markets 1990 Investments prize and the Iddo Sarnat 1990 prize, respectively. She was also a member of the Swiss Federal Banking Commission until December 2004 and is currently a member of the Board of directors at Swiss Re and of the Scientific counsils at the TCIP and FAME, two teaching and reserach organizations located in Switzerland.

Felix Goltz is a Research Engineer at Edhec Risk and Asset Management Research Center, where he is in charge of the production of Edhec hedge fund indices. He holds Master's degrees in Business Administration and Economics and is currently a PhD student in finance at the University of Nice Sophia-Antipolis. His research focus is on the use of derivatives in portfolio management, as well as the econometrics of realized and implied volatility time series.

Sébastien Gyger received his PhD in Physics from the Swiss Federal Institute of Technology in Lausanne (EPFL) in April 2002. His doctorate thesis was focused on the quantitative analysis of hedge funds returns and strategies. Dr. Gyger joined Lombard Odier Darier Hentsch & Cie in June 2002. He is leading the development of the LODH proprietary quantitative approach to third party funds analysis. He is also involved in the research effort on U.S. equity fund managers and comanages two public LODH multimanager funds.

Niclas Hagelin works for the Swedish National Debt Office, where he is a Senior Analyst responsible for developing models for credit risk assessment and pricing. He is also an Associate Professor at the Stockholm University School of Business, from which he received his PhD. Dr. Hagelin previously held senior positions in quantitative trading as well as financial consulting. He has also published numerous articles in scholarly journals on various topics, including corporate risk management and dynamic portfolio allocation.

Ho Ho is Quantitative Portfolio Manager in the Global Equity Unit for CalPERS. Mr. Ho is responsible for research and development of internal active strategies for equity portfolios, hedge fund risk management and designs quantitative models for hedge fund risk attribution, manager monitoring, and quantitative portfolio construction model development. He is a team member of the CalPERS' hedge fund program. He is also responsible for system and model validation of CalPERS' enterprise-wide risk management system. Prior to joining CalPERS, Mr. Ho was Derivative Manager for Transamerica Life Insurance Company. He also worked for KPMG as manager of their Structure Finance Consulting Group. Mr. Ho holds a MBA in finance from the University of Chicago and a BA (Phi Beta Kappa) in Economics from the University of California, Irvine.

Jens Johansen is a Director in UBS's AIS and Flow Research team and has covered alternative investments and equity market flow since 2000. He was recently voted number 4 in the Rising Star category in Extel's Pan-European survey; the team was awarded a number 1 rating in both structured products research and flow research. Prior to that, Mr. Johansen worked at UBS Warburg's investment banking department, specializing in shareholder value and capital structure advisory.

Meredith A. Jones is the Director of Market Research at Strategic Financial Solutions, LLC, a software company founded in 1996 whose mission is to provide solutions relating to the technological needs of the financial industry. She is responsible for researching, speaking, and writing about alternative and traditional investments as well as developing and implementing marketing initiatives and strategic partnerships for SFS. She has written articles for a number of financial publications, including the *Journal of the Alternative Investment Management Association, Alternative Investment Quarterly,* the *Investment Management Consultants Association's Monitor,* and the *Managed Funds Association Reporter.* Her research has appeared in the *Wall Street Journal, Bloomberg Wealth Manager, Hedge Fund Alert, Infovest 21,* and other publications. Prior to joining SFS, Ms. Jones was Vice President and Director of Research for Van Hedge Fund Advisors International, Inc., a global hedge fund consultant with $500 million under management. There she led a staff of 10 research analysts in manager selection, evaluation and ongoing monitoring. Ms. Jones conducted quantitative and qualitative due diligence, on-site visits, and portfolio construction, as well as a number of other research functions.

Harry M. Kat is Professor of Risk Management and Director of the Alternative Investment Research Centre at the Sir John Cass Business School at City University in London. Before returning to academia, Professor Kat was Head of Equity Derivatives Europe at Bank of America in London, Head of Derivatives Structuring and Marketing at First Chicago in Tokyo, and Head of Derivatives Research at MeesPierson in Amsterdam. He holds MBA and PhD degrees in economics and econometrics from the Tinbergen Graduate School of Business at the University of Amsterdam and is a member of the editorial board of the *Journal of Derivatives* and the *Journal of Alternative Investments.* He has (co-)authored numerous articles in well-known international finance journals, such as the *Journal of Financial and Quantitative Analysis,* the *Journal of Financial Engineering,* the *Journal of Derivatives,* the *Journal of Portfolio Management,* and the *Journal of Alternative Investments.* His latest book, *Structured Equity Derivatives,* was published in July 2001 (John Wiley & Sons).

William Kelting is an Associate Professor, Department of Accounting, at State University of New York, College at Plattsburgh. He received his PhD from the University of Arkansas.

Francis C. C. Koh is Practice Associate Professor of Finance at the Singapore Management University (SMU). He is concurrently Director of the MSc in Wealth Management Program. He holds a PhD in Finance from the University of New South Wales and an MBA from the University of British Columbia. Prior to joining SMU, Dr. Koh was working with a multibillion-dollar global investment company based in Singapore.

Winston T. H. Koh is an Associate Professor of Economics at the Singapore Management University (SMU). Prior to joining SMU, Dr. Koh was a General Manager at the Bank of Singapore (a unit of the OCBC Bank Group), where he was responsible for private equity investments. From 1994 to 2000, Dr. Koh held various responsibilities at J.P. Morgan; as Head of the Asian Emerging Markets Strategy team from 1994 to 1998 and as Head of the risk management for Asia ex-Japan from 1998 to 2000. He represented J.P. Morgan as a member of the Bond Market Committee of the Malaysian Monetary Exchange. Dr. Koh received his PhD from Princeton University in 1988. He read Economics at University of Cambridge, where he was a Prize Scholar at Churchill College, from 1982 to 1985. He was awarded a Princeton University Graduate Fellowship for his doctoral studies and also received an Olin Foundation Summer Fellowship in 1987. Dr. Koh is actively involved in consulting and executive development programs. He is an Associate Editor of the *Journal of Restructuring Finance* and a member of the Editorial Advisory Board of *Technological Forecasting and Social Change*. He has also served as an Associate Editor for the *Asia Pacific Journal of Finance*. His publications have appeared in numerous peer-reviewed international journals. Dr. Koh is a recipient of the Lee Kuan Yew Fellowship for Excellence in Research in 2003, at SMU. His current research interests include investment management in global financial markets, economics of information and collective choice, and industry competition and market structure.

Maher Kooli is Assistant Professor of Finance at the School of Business and Management, University of Quebec in Montreal (UQAM). He holds a PhD in finance from Laval University (Quebec) and was a postdoctoral researcher in finance at the Center of Interuniversity Research and Analysis on Organisations. Dr. Kooli also worked as a Senior Research Advisor for la Caisse de Dépôt et Placement de Québec (CDP Capital). His current research interests include alternative investments, initial public offerings, mergers and acquisitions.

Jean-Pierre Langevin is a Partner and Vice-President of Crystalline Management Inc., a Montreal-based hedge fund manager specializing in the Canadian market. Mr. Langevin has spent the last 20 years in the investment management field, during which time he has refined an expertise in financial markets applied mathematics, pursuant to his previous engineering and finance MSc studies at the University of Montreal.

David K. C. Lee is Managing Director and Chief Investment Officer, Ferrell Asset Management. He holds a PhD in Econometrics from the London School of Economics. He is also a guest lecturer specializing in Alternative Investment with the Centre for Financial Engineering and Faculty of Business Administration, National University of Singapore.

Edward Leung joined Standard & Poor's Portfolio Services in 2003 as a Director in the Portfolio Services Group. As a Quantitative Portfolio Analyst, Dr. Leung specializes in applying quantitative techniques to hedge fund indices analysis. Currently he is a Director in the Global Fixed Income Group at Standard & Poor's. Prior to joining Standard and Poor's, he was employed at Knight Trading Group (KTG) as a Quantitative Analyst, focusing on analytical market making and statistical arbitrage. Earlier he was a Senior Associate at Portfolio Management Associate. Dr. Leung is an Adjunct Assistant Professor in Economics at Columbia University. He received his PhD in Economics from University of Pennsylvania and his B.A. in Economics from Northwestern University.

Lionel Martellini, PhD, is a Professor of Finance at Edhec Graduate School of Business and the Scientific Director of Edhec Risk and Asset Management Research Center. Dr. Martellini is a member of the editorial board of the *Journal of Portfolio Management* and the *Journal of Alternative Investments*. He conducts active research in quantitative asset management and derivatives valuation and has been published in leading academic and practitioner journals and featured in *The Financial Times* and *The Wall Street Journal*, among other financial newspapers. He has coauthored reference textbooks on topics related to alternative investment strategies and fixed-income securities, and has served as a consultant for various investments banks and asset management firms both in Europe and in the United States. Dr. Martellini obtained his PhD in Finance from University of California at Berkeley, Haas School of Business, and has four master's degrees in statistics, economics, mathematics, and finance from the University of Paris, École Nationale de la Statistique et de l'Administtation Economique and the École Supérieure de Commerce de Paris.

Jacqueline Meziani has held a variety of product development management, licensing, and marketing positions since joining Standard & Poor's in 1996. Currently she has product management responsibilities for the S&P Hedge Fund Index series and other new, nonequity indices. Previously Ms. Meziani was responsible for marketing the S&P global family of indices, with an emphasis on the non-American indices, to international fund managers, plan sponsors, and consultants. Prior to that, she licensed Standard & Poor's intellectual property and trademarks to insurance companies, asset managers, dealers, and banks for index-based investment products. Ms. Meziani has broad experience in the financial services and technology industries. She was Director of Business Development for an entrepreneurial systems integration consultantcy and Director of Marketing for Tech Hackers Inc., developers of fixed income and options analytics software. She also worked for Chemical Bank (Retail) and Citicorp (Global Fixed Income Research) in a variety of financial communications positions. Ms. Meziani has authored "Exchange-

Traded Funds: A Global Survey" and coauthored "Addressing Risks in Hedge Fund Investments," both published by Institutional Investor in the Risk Guides series, and coauthored "S&P Hedge Fund Index: Structure, Methodology, Definitions, and Practices" in the *Journal of Alternative Investments*. She has presented at numerous conferences on passive management issues. She has an MBA in Finance and International Business from NYU Stern School of Business and a BA in English from the College of St. Benedict (MN).

Kevin McCarthy is a student in the economics and finance department at State University of New York, College at Plattsburgh.

Carlos J. Morales is Assistant Professor in the Department of Mathematical Sciences at Worcester Polytechnic Institute. He specializes in statistics, having earned a PhD from the department of mathematics and statistics at Boston University in 2002. He has been consultant to Edison Mission Marketing and Trading and to New Frontier Advisors in Boston, and advisor to NSF funded projects leading student projects for Deutsche Bank in New York. His expertise is in wavelet-based estimators for nonstationary time series.

Valérie Nevolo obtained her Bachelor's degree from the University of Liège in Belgium in June 2004 in Sciences of Management. She is now working as treasurer at Nagelmackers Management Bank, a subsidiary company of the Delta Lloyd group.

Kok Fai Phoon is Executive Director Designate, Ferrell Asset Management. He holds a PhD in Finance from Northwestern University. Prior to joining Ferrell, he first worked with Yamaichi Research Institute and subsequently at a multibillion-dollar global investment company based in Singapore. He teaches hedge fund, portfolio management, and investment courses at the Centre for Financial Engineering, National University of Singapore, and the Singapore Management University.

Nolke Posthuma is a Researcher at the Investments Research Department of ABP Investments a fully privatized money manager of the pension fund for Dutch public employees and teachers. He joined ABP Investments in 2002. He has worked on quantitative strategies, asset allocation, and hedge funds. He holds an MSc degree in Business Administration from Erasmus University (Rotterdam). He has published peer-refereed book chapters on hedge funds, and his research on hedge funds is often quoted in the international press.

Bengt Pramborg is an Assistant Professor at Stockholm University School of Business. His previous experience includes positions as a Financial Controller in the oil industry, Financial Consultant in banking, and Senior Analyst at the Swedish National Debt Office. His area of interest involves issues concerning corporate risk management, capital budgeting methods, and dynamic portfolio allocations. Dr. Pramborg focuses on empirical research and has published his findings in scientific journals such as the *Emerging Markets Review* and the *Journal of International Financial Management and Accounting*. He holds a PhD in finance and an MSc in mathematical statistics from Stockholm University, as well as an MBA from Yonsei University, Seoul.

François-Éric Racicot is Lecturer in Quantitative Finance at École des Sciences de la Gestion-Université du Québec à Montréal. He holds an MSc in Economics with major in Econometrics from the University of Montreal and received his PhD in Finance from Université du Québec à Montréal. He is also Consultant in Financial Econometrics for various banks and investment firms. His research interest focus on developing econometric methods applied to financial problems. He has also written several books in computational finance and financial econometrics.

Luis Roman is a Visiting Assistant Professor in the Department of Mathematics at Worcester Polytechnic Institute. He holds a PhD in mathematics from the University of Minnesota. His research interests include performance and risk measures under nonconstant volatility and financial models with stochastic volatility.

Milind Sharma is Director and Senior Proprietary Trader at Deutsche Bank. Prior to this, he was Vice President and founding member of Risk & Performance at Merrill Lynch Investment Managers (MLIM). In addition to his investment role on a dozen mutual funds (including the five-star-rated ML Large Cap Series), he was coarchitect of the fixed income and equity risk platforms. Prior to MLIM, he was Manager of the Risk Analytics & Research Group at Ernst & Young, where he was co-architect of Raven™ (their proprietary derivatives & risk engine). He holds MS degrees in Computational Finance and in Applied Mathematics from Carnegie Mellon, where he did research in artificial intelligence while in the doctoral program. He graduated Summa Cum Laude from Vassar College and completed the Honors Moderation curriculum at Oxford University. He has also completed the Professional Development Certificate series from Wharton.

Mark S. Shore is Vice President and Chief Operating Officer of VK Capital Inc. since 1997. Mr. Shore's responsibilities include developing, enhancing and evaluating MSFCM's trading models. Mr. Shore began his career in 1987 with Shearson Lehman Brothers on the floor of the Chicago Board of Trade. In 1989 he became an independent trader to develop models and trade futures and equities. In 1994 Mr. Shore was employed by the University of Chicago's Center for Research in Security Prices as a Senior Research Analyst. He graduated from DePaul University in 1987 with a Bachelor of Science in Finance and an MBA from the University of Chicago in 1998 with concentrations in Finance, Behavioral Science, and Econometrics. Mr. Shore began publishing finance articles in 2000 with current working papers discussing topics on behavioral biases of asset allocation and co-skewness of portfolio diversification.

Kurt W. Silberstein is the Portfolio Manager for CalPERS' Risk Managed Absolute Return Strategies (RMARS) Program, which has invested approximately $900 million of the $2 billion committed. Mr. Silberstein is responsible for overseeing all aspects associated with building the multistrategy hedge fund of funds within CalPERS. Prior to becoming involved with the RMARS Program, Mr. Silberstein was responsible for manager selection and portfolio construction for the $40 billion portfolio managed by CalPERS' external equity managers. Prior to joining CalPERS, Mr. Silberstein was a Vice President with the pension fund consulting firm Strategic Investment Solutions, Inc. As a General Consultant, Mr. Silberstein consulted to public and corporate plan sponsors, high net-worth family offices, foundations, and endowments. Mr. Silberstein served as a member on the Investment Policy Committee and Manager Search Committee during his four years at Strategic Investment Solutions, Inc. Prior to Strategic Investment Solutions, Inc, he spent four years at the Los Angeles County Employees Retirement Association as an Investment Equity Analyst. Mr. Silberstein holds a BS in Finance from California State University, Northridge, and is a Chartered Financial Analyst.

Fredrik Stenberg is a PhD student in mathematics at Mälardalen University. He has worked as a Financial Consultant in banking and as a Software Developer for different financial companies, mostly working with value-at-risk models and asset allocation problems. His research is focuses on stochastic regime processes with applications to finance and insurance. He has published his work in scientific journals such as *Communications in Statistics Theory and Methods* and *Journal of Physics A: Mathematical and General.*

Hilary F. Till is a cofounder of Chicago-based Premia Capital Management, LLC, which specializes in detecting pockets of predictability in derivatives markets by using statistical techniques. Hilary Till is also a principal of Premia Risk Consultancy, Inc. Prior to Premia, Ms. Till was Chief of Derivatives Strategies at Boston-based Putnam Investments. Her group was responsible for the management of all derivatives investments in domestic and international fixed income, tax-exempt fixed income, foreign exchange, and global asset allocation. Prior to Putnam Investments, Ms. Till was a quantitative analyst at Harvard Management Company in Boston, the investment management company for Harvard University's endowment. She holds a BA in Statistics with General Honors from the University of Chicago and an MSc in Statistics from the London School of Economics Ms. Till's articles on derivatives, risk management, and alternative investments have been published in the *Journal of Alternative Investments, AIMA Journal, Derivatives Quarterly, Quantitative Finance, Risk* magazine, and the *Singapore Economic Review*. She has also contributed chapters to the following edited books: *The New Generation of Risk Management in Hedge Funds and Private Equity Investments* (coauthor, Euromoney, 2003), *Intelligent Hedge Fund Investing* (Risk Books, 2004), *The Core-Satellite Approach to Portfolio Management* (forthcoming McGraw Hill, 2004), and *Commodity Trading Advisors: Risk, Performance Analysis, and Selection* (coauthor, John Wiley & Sons, 2004).

Pieter Jelle Van der Sluis is a Senior Researcher who manages the Active Quantitative Strategies team within the Research Department of ABP Investments, a fully privatized money management firm of the pension fund for Dutch public employees and teachers. Dr. Jelle joined ABP Investments in 2000. His team focuses on quantitative strategies for equities, commodities, currencies and GTAA. He is also involved in research on more strategic issues, such as hedge funds, real estate and derivatives. His expertise is on active quantitative investment strategies, asset allocation, asset liability management, forecasting, portfolio construction, risk management and option pricing. Before joining ABP, he was an Assistant Researcher at the Department of Actuarial Science and Econometrics at the University of Amsterdam (1994–1998) and an Assistant Professor of Econometrics, Statistics, and Quantitative Finance and fellow of Center at Tilburg University (1998–2000). He holds an MSc degree in Econometrics and Operations Research from Free University Amsterdam, and a PhD in Economics and Econometrics from the University of Amsterdam. Currently he also serves as an Assistant Professor to the Finance Department at Free University Amsterdam. He has published peer-refereed book chapters and articles in international journals, such as *Studies in Nonlinear Dynamics and Econometrics*, the *Econometrics Journal*, and the *European Finance Review*. He gives guest lectures and is also a frequent speaker at both academic and practitioner's conferences.

Kathryn Wilkens is a Research Associate of the Center for International Securities and Derivatives Markets and Director of Curriculum of the Chartered Alternative Investment Analyst Association. She holds a PhD in finance from the University of Massachusetts at Amherst and is a CAIA member.

Hedge Funds

One

Portfolio Allocation in Hedge Funds

Chapter 1 shows how investors can neutralize the unwanted skewness and kurtosis effects from investing in hedge funds by purchasing out-of-the-money equity puts, investing in managed futures, and/or overweighting equity market neutral and global macro and avoiding distressed securities and emerging market funds. It shows that all three alternatives are up to the job but also come with their own specific price tags.

Chapter 2 investigates the hedge fund industry as it enters a more mature stage. The industry has extended its investor base to institutional investors, who are now faced with a large number of product offerings. These include not only single hedge funds, but also funds of funds and, more recently, investable indexes. Although the existing literature seems to concur on the interest of hedge funds as valuable investment alternatives, a large number of institutional investors still are considering hedge fund investing, but are unsure of which product to choose. This chapter examines the risk factors in hedge fund strategies and assesses the diversification benefits investors can expect from allocating part of their wealth to hedge funds. Different uses of hedge funds are separated into alpha management and beta management. For both of these management issues, indexes that give a true and fair view of particular hedge fund strategies are a necessary tool for the investor. This chapter also examines construction methods for investable hedge fund indexes and how these methods can conserve the properties for a desirable index. Finally, the chapter presents a simplified approach that allows institutional investors to use such indexes to optimally exploit the diversification properties of different hedge fund strategies.

Chapter 3 examines 2,247 individual hedge funds and 647 funds of hedge funds for the period January 1994 to December 2002, investigating whether portfolios of individual hedge funds constructed using a pure momentum strategy can outperform existing funds of hedge funds. Results indicate that neither a momentum nor a contrarian strategy seems appropriate in portfolio construction to beat existing funds of hedge funds. However, the nondirectional individual hedge funds deciles consistently and significantly beat existing funds of hedge funds.

Chapter 4 provides information about investment styles, which is often one of the key ingredients in creating a portfolio of hedge funds. Hedge funds are opportunity driven and therefore change their investment styles at a high rate. The chapter reviews an adaptive technique that tackles the style drift of hedge funds in an optimal way using returns information only. The method gives better insight in the composition of a hedge fund portfolio and may improve its value-at-risk estimates. The method is illustrated with examples from a long-short equity hedge fund and a fund of hedge funds.

Chapter 5 investigates possible gains from diversifying into hedge funds, using a decision function that allows for the inclusion of the higher moments of the return distribution. The results suggest that higher moments are dominated by the first two moments when portfolios are rebalanced on a monthly basis. Further, the findings suggest that inherent biases in hedge fund return indices may overstate the gains from allocating into hedge funds. Finally, through a simple experiment, it is shown that the inability to rebalance the portfolio may seriously impact the benefits that hedge funds appear to offer.

Chapter 6 addresses three important issues that investors need to better understand. First, it discusses the error associated with the classification of hedge fund strategies under one single header—hedge funds—demonstrating that the universe is really quite heterogeneous and should be the broken down into distinct subgroups. Second, the chapter revisits the critical issue of the distribution of hedge fund returns, focusing on the importance of skew and excess kurtosis. And, finally, it suggests that traditional mean-variance analysis takes great pains to construct efficient balanced portfolios incorporating hedge funds.

Chapter 7 develops a synthetic "desirability" index complementing the pursuit for both high risk-adjusted returns and low correlations. It demonstrates that although some hedge fund strategies are less alpha "efficient" than others, their diversification added value with respect to their overall ranking makes them more attractive in portfolios.

CHAPTER 1

Integrating Hedge Funds into the Traditional Portfolio

Harry M. Kat

This chapter shows how investors can neutralize the unwanted skewness and kurtosis effects from investing in hedge funds by purchasing out-of-the-money equity puts, by investing in managed futures, and/or by overweighting equity market neutral and global macro funds and avoiding distressed securities and emerging market funds. All three alternatives are up to the job but also come with their own specific price tags.

INTRODUCTION

Due to their relatively weak correlation with other asset classes, hedge funds can play an important role in risk reduction and yield enhancement strategies. Recent research, however, has also shown that this diversification service does not come for free. Amin and Kat (2003b), for example, show that although the inclusion of hedge funds in a portfolio may significantly improve that portfolio's mean-variance characteristics, it can also be expected to lead to significantly lower skewness and higher kurtosis. This means that the case for hedge funds is not as straightforward as is often suggested and includes a definite trade-off between profit and loss potential.

The sting of hedge funds is literally in the tail because, in terms of skewness, hedge funds and equity do not mix very well. When things go wrong

This chapter originally appeared in the *Journal of Wealth Management* 7, No. 4 (2005): 51–57. This article is reprinted with permission from Institutional Investor, Inc.

in the stock market, things also tend to go wrong for hedge funds, as a significant drop in stock prices is typically accompanied by a drop in market liquidity and a widening of a multitude of spreads. Equity-market-neutral and long/short funds have a tendency to be long in smaller stocks and short in larger stocks and need liquidity to maintain market neutrality. As a result, when the stock market comes down, this type of fund can be expected to have a hard time. Likewise, when the stock market comes down, mergers and acquisitions will be postponed, which will have a negative impact on the performance of risk arbitrage funds. Problems are not limited to funds that invest in equity. A drop in stock prices will often also lead to a widening of credit spreads, which in turn will seriously damage the performance of fixed income and convertible arbitrage funds. Diversification among different funds will not mitigate this.

This chapter discusses a number of ways to solve the skewness problem and the associated costs. We look at the use of out-of-the-money stock index puts, managed futures, and sophisticated strategy selection. Before we do so, however, we briefly discuss the exact nature of hedge fund returns and the associated skewness problem.

EFFECTS OF INTRODUCING HEDGE FUNDS IN A PORTFOLIO

Generally speaking, risk is one word, but not one number. The returns on portfolios of stocks and bonds risk are more or less normally distributed. Because normal distributions are fully described by their mean and standard deviation, the risk of such portfolios can be measured with one number: the standard deviation. Confronted with nonnormal distributions, however, it is no longer appropriate to use the standard deviation as the sole measure of risk. In that case investors should also look at the degree of symmetry of the distribution, as measured by its skewness, and the probability of extreme positive or negative outcomes, as measured by the distribution's kurtosis. A symmetrical distribution will have a skewness equal to zero, while a distribution that implies a relatively high probability of a large loss (gain) is said to exhibit negative (positive) skewness. A normal distribution has a kurtosis of 3, while a kurtosis higher than 3 indicates a relatively high probability of a large loss or gain. Since most investors are in it for the long run, they strongly rely on compounding effects. This means that negative skewness and high kurtosis are extremely undesirable features, as one big loss may destroy years of careful compounding.

Table 1.1 shows the average skewness and kurtosis found in the returns of individual hedge funds from various strategy groups. The average hedge fund's returns tend to be nonnormally distributed and may exhibit signifi-

TABLE 1.1 Average Skewness and Kurtosis Individual Hedge Fund Returns

	Skewness	Kurtosis
Merger Arbitrage	−0.50	7.60
Distressed Securities	−0.77	8.92
Equity Market Neutral	−0.40	5.58
Convertible Arbitrage	−1.12	8.51
Global Macro	1.04	10.12
Long/Short Equity	0.00	6.08
Emerging Markets	−0.36	7.83

cant negative skewness as well as substantial kurtosis. Put another way, hedge fund returns may exhibit low standard deviations, but they also tend to provide skewness and kurtosis attributes that are exactly opposite to what investors desire. It is this whole package that constitutes hedge fund risk, not just the standard deviation. Actually, this is not the whole story as, strictly speaking, we should also include the relationship between the hedge fund return and the returns on other assets and asset classes in the definition of risk. We look at this shortly.

The skewness and kurtosis properties of hedge funds do not come as a complete surprise. If we delve deeper into the return-generating process, it becomes obvious that most spread trading and pseudoarbitrage strategies will generate these features by their very nature as the profit potential of trades is typically a lot smaller that their loss potential. Consider a merger arbitrage fund, for example. When a takeover bid is announced, the share price of the target will jump toward the bid. It is at this price that the fund will buy the stock. When the takeover proceeds as planned, the fund will make a limited profit equal to the difference between the relatively high price at which it bought the stock and the bid price. When the takeover fails, however, the stock price falls back to its initial level, generating a loss that may be many times bigger than the highest possible profit. Spread traders are confronted with a similar payoff profile. They make a limited profit when the spread moves back to its perceived equilibrium value, but when the market moves against them, they could be confronted with a much larger loss. This is why strategies like this are sometimes thought of as akin to picking up nickels in front of a steamroller. Of course, there is no reason why a trader could not get lucky and avoid getting hit by the steamroller for a long time. This does not mean that the risk was never there, however. It always was, but it never materialized so it does not appear from the trader's track record.

Since individual hedge funds carry some idiosyncratic risk, combining hedge funds into a basket, as is standard practice nowadays, substantially reduces the standard deviation of the return on that portfolio. However, it can also be expected to lower the skewness and raise the correlation with the stock market.

Table 1.2 shows the standard deviation, skewness, and correlation with the Standard & Poor's (S&P) 500 of the average individual hedge fund in the various strategy groups as well as an equally weighted portfolio of all funds in each group. From the table we see that forming portfolios indeed leads to a very substantial reduction in standard deviation. With the exception of emerging market funds, the portfolio standard deviations are approximately half the standard deviations of the average individual fund. Apparently, there are many different ways in which the same general strategy can be executed. Contrary to standard deviation, skewness is not diversified away and drops as portfolios are formed. With the exception of equity-market-neutral funds, the portfolio skewness figures are quite a bit lower than for the average individual fund, with especially merger arbitrage and distressed securities funds standing out. Despite the lack of overall correlation, it appears that when markets are bad for one fund, they tend to be bad for other funds as well. Finally, comparing the correlation with the S&P 500 of individual funds and portfolios, we clearly see that the returns on portfolios of hedge funds tend to be much more correlated with the stock market than the returns on individual funds. Although individual hedge funds may be more or less market neutral, the portfolios of hedge funds that most investors actually invest in definitely are not.

So far we have seen that hedge fund returns tend to exhibit a number of undesirable features, which cannot be diversified away. Skewness, kurtosis, and correlation with stocks worsen significantly when portfolios are formed. But we are not there yet, as we have not looked at what happens when hedge funds are combined with stocks and bonds. Although the inclusion of hedge funds in a portfolio may significantly improve that portfolio's mean-variance characteristics, it can also be expected to lead to significantly lower skewness as well as higher kurtosis. Table 1.3 shows what happens to the standard deviation, skewness, and kurtosis of the portfolio return distribution if, starting with 50 percent stocks and 50 percent bonds, we introduce hedge funds (modeled by the average equally weighted random portfolio of 20 funds) in a traditional stock-bond portfolio. As expected, when hedge funds are introduced, the standard deviation drops significantly. This represents the still relatively low correlation of hedge funds with stocks and bonds. This is the good news. The bad news, however, is that a similar drop is observed in the skewness of the portfolio return. In addition, we also observe a rise in kurtosis.

TABLE 1.2 Individual Hedge Fund and Hedge Fund Portfolio Risks

	Individual Hedge Funds			Portfolio of Hedge Funds		
	Standard Deviation	Skewness	Correlation S&P 500	Standard Deviation	Skewness	Correlation S&P 500
Merger Arbitrage	1.75	-0.50	0.47	1.04	-2.19	0.56
Distressed Securities	2.37	-0.77	0.37	1.54	-2.60	0.47
Equity Market Neutral	2.70	-0.40	0.07	1.14	-0.41	0.19
Convertible Arbitrage	3.01	-1.12	0.19	1.64	-1.35	0.38
Global Macro	5.23	1.04	0.14	2.43	0.87	0.37
Long/Short Equity	5.83	0.00	0.35	2.95	-0.29	0.63
Emerging Markets	8.33	-0.36	0.44	6.15	-0.65	0.67

TABLE 1.3   Effects of Combining Hedge Funds with
Stocks and Bonds

% HF	Standard Deviation	Skewness	Kurtosis
0	2.49	−0.33	−0.03
5	2.43	−0.40	0.02
10	2.38	−0.46	0.08
15	2.33	−0.53	0.17
20	2.29	−0.60	0.28
25	2.25	−0.66	0.42
30	2.22	−0.72	0.58
35	2.20	−0.78	0.77
40	2.18	−0.82	0.97
45	2.17	−0.85	1.19
50	2.16	−0.87	1.41

The skewness effect goes far beyond what one might expect given the hedge fund skewness results in Table 1.2. When things go wrong in the stock market, they also tend to go wrong for hedge funds. This is not necessarily because of what happens to stock prices (after all, many hedge funds do not invest in equity), but because a significant drop in stock prices often will be accompanied by a widening of credit spreads, a significant drop in market liquidity, and higher volatility. Since hedge funds are highly sensitive to such factors, when the stock market drops, hedge funds can be expected to show relatively bad performance as well. Recent experience provides a good example. Over the year 2002, the S&P 500 dropped by more than 20 percent with relatively high volatility and substantially widening credit spreads. Distressed debt funds, seen by many investors at the start of 2002 as one of the most promising sectors, suffered substantially from the widening of credit spreads. Credit spreads also had a negative impact on convertible arbitrage funds. Stock market volatility worked in their favor, however. Managers focusing on volatility trading generally fared best, while managers actively taking credit exposure did worst. Equity-market-neutral funds suffered greatly from a lack of liquidity, while long/short equity funds with low net exposure outperformed managers who remained net long throughout the year. As a result, overall hedge fund performance in 2002 as measured by the main hedge fund indices was more or less flat.

So here is the main problem: Individual hedge fund returns tend to exhibit some negative skewness. When combined into portfolios, however, this negative skewness becomes worse. When those portfolios are combined with equity, skewness drops even further. The increase in negative skewness will tend to offset the lower standard deviation that results from the inclusion of hedge funds. In other words, when adding hedge funds, investors' downside risk will largely remain unchanged while at the same time part of their upside potential is diversified away. Unfortunately, this is the opposite of what we want a good diversifier to do.

The next sections discuss three possible ways to reduce this skewness effect, as well as the associated costs, while maintaining the benefits of the lower standard deviation.

PURCHASING OUT-OF-THE-MONEY PUTS

Since the increase in negative skewness that tends to come with hedge fund investing is highly undesirable, it is important to look for ways to neutralize this effect. One solution is to buy hedge funds in guaranteed form only. In essence, this means buying a put on one's hedge fund portfolio so that in down markets, the link between the hedge fund portfolio and the stock market is severed. Unfortunately, the market for put options on (baskets of) hedge funds is still in an early stage. As a result, counterparties for the required contracts are likely to be hard to find as well as expensive. With hedge funds so closely related to the ups and especially downs of the stock market, there is a very simple alternative, though: the purchase of out-of-the-money puts on a stock index. As discussed in Kat (2003a), over the last 10 years a strategy of buying and rolling over out-of-the-money S&P 500 puts would have generated returns with very high positive skewness. It therefore makes sense to use this option strategy to neutralize the negative skewness in hedge funds.

Suppose we added stock index put options to a portfolio of stocks, bonds, and hedge funds with the aim to bring the skewness of the overall portfolio return back to what it was before the addition of hedge funds. Obviously, there is a price tag attached to doing so. Since we are taking away something bad (negative skewness), we will have to give up something good. If we used leverage to keep overall portfolio volatility at the same level as before the addition of the puts (i.e., if we aimed to preserve the volatility benefit of the addition of hedge funds), this means we will have to accept a lower expected return. Economically, this of course makes perfect sense, as the puts that we add will not come for free and, since they are out-of-the-money, are unlikely to pay off (which of course is just another way of saying that the option strategy by itself has a highly negative expected return).

Assuming investors can leverage their portfolio at a rate of 4 percent and the expected returns on stocks, bonds, and hedge funds are equal to their historical 10-year means, Table 1.4 shows the effect of using puts and leverage in a portfolio of stocks, bonds, and hedge funds (always with equal allocations to stocks and bonds). Starting with the situation shown in Table 1.3, adding puts to bring the skewness of the overall portfolio back to what it was before the addition of hedge funds (–0.33), while maintaining the volatility benefit, requires only a small allocation to options. As is also clear from the change in portfolio kurtosis, this small allocation, however, goes a long way in restoring the (near) normality of the return distribution. Unfortunately, the costs in terms of expected return (third column) are quite significant. For example, with a 25 percent hedge fund allocation, investors can expect to lose 61 basis points in expected return. This drop in expected return can be interpreted as the option market's price of the additional skewness introduced by hedge funds.

Of course, this conclusion depends heavily on the assumption that investors can leverage (either directly or through the futures market) their portfolios at 4 percent, which does not seem unrealistic in the current interest rate environment. Obviously, if the interest rate were higher, the costs of the skewness reduction strategy would be higher as well because the difference between the expected return on the unlevered portfolio and the interest rate (i.e., the pickup in expected return due to the leverage) would be smaller. A similar reasoning applies in case of a lower expected return on stocks, bonds, and/or hedge funds.

TABLE 1.4   Effects of Combining Portfolios of Stocks, Bonds, and Hedge Funds with Puts and Leverage

% HF	% Put	Change Mean PA* 50/50 Portfolio	Change Kurtosis	Change Mean PA* 33/66 Portfolio
0	0.00	0.00	0.00	0.00
5	0.12	–0.13	–0.05	–0.22
10	0.24	–0.27	–0.12	–0.48
15	0.36	–0.38	–0.20	–0.87
20	0.48	–0.51	–0.31	–2.26
25	0.60	–0.61	–0.44	–3.20
30	0.71	–0.70	–0.58	–3.43
35	0.80	–0.79	–0.75	–3.52
40	0.86	–0.85	–0.91	–3.41
45	0.88	–0.82	–1.04	–3.20
50	0.87	–0.80	–1.13	–2.83

*PA = per annum

Another important element of the analysis concerns the assumption that the allocations to stocks and bonds are always equal. If we assumed that investors always divided their money in such a way that one-third was invested in stocks and two-thirds in bonds (as opposed to the 50/50 portfolio discussed earlier, we will refer to such a portfolio as a 33/66 portfolio), our results would of course change. Under the assumptions made, a portfolio made up of one-third stocks and two-thirds bonds has a skewness of 0.03. With 25 percent hedge funds, the portfolio's skewness will come down to −0.43, while with 50 percent hedge funds, it will drop to −0.75. Because when hedge funds are introduced, skewness for a 33/66 portfolio drops faster than for a 50/50 portfolio, we will have to buy more puts and apply more leverage. Since the mean of the 33/66 portfolio is substantially lower than the mean of the 50/50 portfolio, however, the increased leverage will not be sufficient to rescue the expected return. As can be seen in the last column of Table 1.4, the costs of the skewness reduction strategy for a 33/66 portfolio are very substantial. With 25 percent hedge funds, the costs of skewness reduction will amount to 3.20 percent, as opposed to only 0.61 percent for the 50/50 portfolio.

In sum, after introducing hedge funds, purchasing out-of-the money puts can restore the (near) normality of the portfolio return distribution fairly easily. However, this may come at a substantial cost to the portfolio's expected return, especially for investors who are overweighted in bonds.

INVESTING IN MANAGED FUTURES

In principle, any asset or asset class that has suitable (co-)skewness characteristics can be used to hedge the additional skewness from incorporating hedge funds. One obvious candidate is managed futures. Managed futures programs are often trend-following in nature. What these programs do is somewhat similar to how option traders hedge a short-call position. When the market moves up, they increase exposure, and vice versa. By moving out of the market when it comes down, managed futures programs avoid being pulled in. As a result, the (co-)skewness characteristics of managed futures programs are more or less opposite to those of many hedge funds.

The term "managed futures" refers to professional money managers known as commodity trading advisors (CTAs) who manage assets using the global futures and options markets as their investment universe. Managed futures have been available for investment since 1948, when the first public futures fund started trading. The industry did not take off until the late 1970s, though. Since then the sector has seen a fair amount of growth, with currently an estimated $50 billion under management.

There are three ways in which investors can get into managed futures.

1. They can buy shares in a public commodity (or futures) fund, in much the same way as they would invest in a stock or bond mutual fund.
2. They can place funds privately with a commodity pool operator (CPO) who pools investors' money and employs one or more CTAs to manage the pooled funds.
3. They can retain one or more CTAs directly to manage their money on an individual basis or hire a manager of managers (MOM) to select CTAs for them. The minimum investment required by funds, pools, and CTAs varies considerably, with the direct CTA route open only to investors who want to make a substantial investment. CTAs charge management and incentive fees comparable to those charged by hedge funds (i.e., 2 percent management fee plus 20 percent incentive fee). Similar to funds of hedge funds, funds and pools charge an additional fee on top of that.

Initially, CTAs were limited to trading commodity futures (which explains terms such as public commodity fund, CTA, and CPO). With the introduction of futures on currencies, interest rates, bonds, and stock indices in the 1980s, however, the trading spectrum widened substantially. Nowadays, many CTAs trade both commodity and financial futures. Many take a very technical, systematic approach to trading, but others opt for a more fundamental, discretionary approach. Some concentrate on particular futures markets, such as agricultural, currencies, or metals, but most diversify over different types of markets.

In this study, the asset class managed futures is represented by the Stark 300 index. This asset-weighted index is compiled using the top 300 trading programs from the Daniel B. Stark & Co. database. All 300 of the CTAs in the index are classified by their trading approach and market category. Currently, the index contains 248 systematic and 52 discretionary traders, which split up in 169 diversified, 111 financial only, 9 financial and metals, and 11 nonfinancial trading programs.

As shown in Kat (2004b), historically managed futures returns have exhibited a lower mean and a higher standard deviation than hedge fund returns. However, managed futures exhibit positive instead of negative skewness and much lower kurtosis. In addition, the correlation of managed futures with stocks and hedge funds is extremely low, which means that managed futures make very good diversifiers. Table 1.5 shows the effect of incorporating either hedge funds or managed futures in a traditional 50/50 stock-bond portfolio.

From the table we again see that if the hedge fund allocation increases, both the standard deviation and the skewness of the portfolio return drop

TABLE 1.5 Return Statistics Portfolios of Stocks, Bonds, and Either Hedge Funds or Managed Futures

	Hedge Funds					Managed Futures			
% HF	Mean	SD	Skew	Kurt	% MF	Mean	SD	Skew	Kurt
0	0.72	2.49	−0.33	−0.03	0	0.72	2.49	−0.33	−0.03
5	0.73	2.43	−0.40	0.02	5	0.71	2.37	−0.28	−0.18
10	0.74	2.38	−0.46	0.08	10	0.71	2.26	−0.21	−0.30
15	0.76	2.33	−0.53	0.17	15	0.71	2.16	−0.14	−0.39
20	0.77	2.29	−0.60	0.28	20	0.71	2.08	−0.06	−0.42
25	0.78	2.25	−0.66	0.42	25	0.71	2.00	0.02	−0.40
30	0.80	2.22	−0.72	0.58	30	0.71	1.95	0.10	−0.32
35	0.81	2.20	−0.78	0.77	35	0.71	1.91	0.18	−0.20
40	0.82	2.18	−0.82	0.97	40	0.71	1.89	0.24	−0.06
45	0.84	2.17	−0.85	1.19	45	0.71	1.89	0.30	0.08
50	0.85	2.16	−0.87	1.41	50	0.71	1.91	0.34	0.19

substantially, while at the same time the return distribution's kurtosis increases. With managed futures, the picture is significantly different, however. If the managed futures allocation increases, the standard deviation drops faster than with hedge funds. More remarkably, skewness rises instead of drops, while the reverse is true for kurtosis. Although hedge funds offer a somewhat higher expected return (assuming future performance will resemble the past), from an overall risk perspective, managed futures appear much better diversifiers than hedge funds.

Now suppose we did the same thing as before: Choose the managed futures allocation such as to bring the skewness of the portfolio return back to what it was before the addition of hedge funds (−0.33), while at the same time preserving the volatility benefit of the addition of hedge funds by the use of some leverage. The results are shown in Table 1.6, which shows that for smaller hedge fund allocations of up to 15 percent, the optimal managed futures allocation will be more or less equal to the hedge fund allocation. Looking at the change in expected return, we see that as a result of the introduction of managed futures, the expected portfolio return increases significantly. With a 25 percent hedge fund allocation, for example, the investor stands to gain 205 basis points in annualized expected return. This of course compares very favorably with the results on out-of-the-money puts. One should, however, always keep in mind that the outcomes of analyses like this heavily depend on the inputs used. A lower expected return for managed futures and/or a higher borrowing rate (used to lever-

TABLE 1.6 Allocations and Annualized Change in Expected Return Portfolios of Stocks, Bonds, Hedge Funds, and Managed Futures

% HF	% MF	Change Expected Return PA*
0	0.00	0.00
5	5.48	0.66
10	9.95	1.15
15	13.60	1.53
20	16.55	1.83
25	18.91	2.05
30	20.80	2.23
35	22.33	2.37
40	23.32	2.46
45	24.04	2.53
50	24.40	2.60

*PA = per annum

age the portfolio volatility back to its initial level) could easily turn these gains into losses.

In addition, although the expected return does not seem to suffer from the use of managed futures to neutralize the unwanted skewness effect from hedge funds, this does not mean it comes completely for free. Investors pay by giving up the positive skewness that they would have had when they had invested only in managed futures.

SMART STRATEGY SELECTION

So far we have modeled the asset class hedge funds as a representative portfolio of 20 different individual funds, a proxy for the average fund-of-funds portfolio. Although this is what most investors currently invest in, it is interesting to investigate how far it is possible to eliminate the skewness effect of hedge funds simply by choosing another hedge fund portfolio (i.e., by allocating differently to the various hedge fund strategies available). This is the approach taken in Davies, Kat, and Lu (2004). Using a sophisticated optimization technique known as polynomial goal programming (PGP), they incorporate investor preferences for return distributions' higher moments into an explicit optimization model. This allows them to solve for multiple competing hedge fund allocation objectives within a mean-variance-skewness-kurtosis framework. Apart from underlining the existence of significant differences in the return behavior of different hedge fund strategies, the analysis shows that PGP optimal portfolios for skewness-aware investors contain hardly any allocations to long/short equity, distressed securities, and emerging markets funds. Equity-market-neutral and global macro funds, on the other hand, tend to receive very high allocations, which is primarily due to their low covariance, high coskewness and low cokurtosis properties. Looking back at Tables 1.1 and 1.2, these conclusions do not come as a complete surprise. The strategies that the optimizer tends to drop are exactly the strategies that exhibit the most negative skewness. Global macro and equity-market-neutral strategies come with much more desirable risk characteristics. Global macro funds primarily act as portfolio skewness enhancers, while equity-market-neutral funds act as volatility and kurtosis reducers (which is especially important given the relatively high volatility and kurtosis of global macro).

An interesting byproduct of the analysis in Davies, Kat, and Lu (2004) is that introducing preferences for skewness and kurtosis in the portfolio decision-making process yields portfolios that are far different from the mean-variance optimal portfolios, with less attractive mean-variance characteristics. This underlines a point made earlier in Kat (2004a) that using standard mean-variance portfolio allocation tools when alternative investments are involved can be highly misleading. It also shows that in hedge fund diversification, there is no such thing as a free lunch. When substantially overweighting global macro and equity-market-neutral strategies, investors can expect more attractive skewness and kurtosis, but at the cost of a less attractive expected return and volatility.

Finally, it is interesting to note that many global macro funds tend to follow strategies that are similar to the strategies typically employed by CTAs. In fact, some of the largest global macro funds have their origins in managed futures. The difference between expanding into managed futures and overweighting global macro funds is therefore probably smaller than one might suspect.

CONCLUSION

The attractive mean-variance properties of typical hedge fund portfolios tend to come at the cost of negative skewness and increased kurtosis. Investors can neutralize the unwanted skewness and kurtosis by purchasing out-of-the-money equity puts, investing in managed futures, and/or by overweighting equity-market-neutral and global macro funds and avoiding distressed securities and emerging market funds. Hedge fund returns are not superior to the returns on other asset classes, they are just different.

CHAPTER 2

Hedge Funds from the Institutional Investor's Perspective

Noël Amenc, Felix Goltz, Lionel Martellini

While an increasing number of institutional investors are investing part of their wealth in hedge funds, many are unsure of the optimal allocation of hedge funds in their portfolios. To address this question, we review the characteristics of hedge fund strategies. This includes examining the risk factor exposure and diversification benefits of hedge funds, as well as their different uses in a core-satellite approach to institutional money management. We then discuss the challenges involved in the practical implementation of a sound investment process that allows institutional investors to optimally exploit the diversification properties of different hedge fund strategies. This approach is based on the construction of investable hedge fund indexes and their use for simplifying the integration of hedge funds in the investor's strategic asset allocation.

INTRODUCTION

Hedge funds have experienced rapid growth over the past decade, and the industry currently holds almost U.S.$1 trillion in assets under management. Arguments in favor of hedge fund exposure are not lacking. In its initial phase, the industry attracted mostly high-net-worth individuals, but it has now become mainstream. Consequently, more and more institutional investors have started allocating to, or at least looking at, hedge funds as a distinct asset class.

Interest from institutional investors comes at a time when they are try-ing to recover from dramatic affects of downturns in equity markets. This is especially true among institutions for which declining interest rates have increased liabilities, at the same time as assets have been reduced. These mar-ket events have not only put into question the investment practices of insti-tutional investors in general, and pension funds in particular, but they also have put emphasis on alternatives to stocks and bonds, such as hedge funds.

Hedge funds are vehicles that allow investors to gain access to the benefits of very active investment strategies, which previously were acces-sible only through the proprietary trading activities of investment banks. Hedge funds are the ultimate organizational form for these activities, since hedge funds have flexible legal structures, they are only lightly regulated, and they offer strong incentives for manager performance. This organiza-tion allows for flexibility in trading, such as using derivatives, employing short selling and leverage, and investing in illiquid securities. The most important characteristic of a hedge fund is that the manager typically does not tie performance to a reference benchmark, such as a market index or a peer group of managers. This is different from most mutual funds. Hedge funds typically use absolute return benchmarks, such as the risk-free rate plus a given number of basis points. Benchmarking of hedge fund returns though peer grouping is becoming common practice.

The classic argument of hedge fund providers is that hedge funds pro-vide investors with access to skilled managers. Sophisticated investors are usually skeptical of this argument, as is anyone who believes that markets are efficient and therefore hard to beat even by skilled money managers. A more widely accepted argument is that, because hedge funds offer risk and return characteristics that are different from traditional investments, they are good portfolio diversifiers. This argument recognizes the different types of risks hedge funds are exposed to as an opportunity for diversification.

Recent academic research has put forward some more subtle arguments in favor of hedge funds. As discussed by Bansal, Dahlquist, and Harvey (2004), hedge funds that periodically shift their holdings between different asset classes allow investors to access the benefits of dynamically con-structed portfolios, but by using static portfolio construction. In addition, hedge funds may allow investors to take risks held by a small number of participants only, and thus perceive high-risk premiums, in accordance with the segmented markets hypothesis. In fact, while a large portion of the pop-ulation holds stock market risk, to a lesser extent in small-cap and emerg-ing market stocks, hedge fund managers have access to less widely held instruments whose risks are more attractively rewarded.

For institutional investors, the reasons behind the benefits of hedge funds are of secondary importance only. Such investors are primarily con-cerned with whether these benefits truly exist and how they can be achieved. These concerns are the focus of this chapter. We therefore investigate how investors can benefit from including hedge funds in their portfolio. In practice, different approaches to hedge fund investing exist. Strategic allocation (inclusion of hedge funds styles in the strategic benchmark), tactical allocation (timing of style exposure), and manager selection are nonexclusive ways of capturing the benefits of hedge funds. Likewise, providers of hedge fund products offer different ways to hedge funds. Investors may invest in one fund, in several funds, or in a fund of funds (i.e., in a managed portfolio of single hedge funds). More recently, these providers have begun to offer investable hedge fund indexes. These indexes are targeting passive institutional investors who are familiar and comfortable with their equity portfolios. Here we attempt to identify the best form of hedge fund investing among the different products offered by providers.

In the rest of the chapter, we examine the five most widely used hedge fund strategies, notably three equity-based strategies—equity market neutral, long/short equity, and event driven—one fixed-income strategy—convertible arbitrage—and one strategy that uses all types of assets, including currencies and commodities—CTA/global macro. According to Credit Suisse First Boston/Tremont (*www.hedgeindex.com*), these five strategies held 91 percent of assets under management in the hedge fund industry at the end of 2003. Likewise, these strategies held 85 percent of total assets under management by single hedge funds in the Center for International Securities and Derivatives Markets (CISDM) database. As a proxy for the return on these hedge fund strategies, we use the Edhec Alternative Indexes (Amenc and Martellini 2003b). Each of these indexes can be thought of as the best one-dimensional summary of information contained in competing hedge fund indexes for the corresponding strategy. The CTA/global macro index is a portfolio that is equally weighted in the indexes for these two strategies. To represent stocks and bonds, and to include the effects of international diversification, we use the MSCI World indexes for equity and for sovereign bonds. Our sample period starts January 1997, which is the starting date for the Edhec Alternative Indexes, and ends August 2004. Monthly returns data over the sample period are collected from the Edhec Web site (*www.edhec-risk.com*) and from DataStream for the MSCI Indexes.

RISKS IN HEDGE FUND STRATEGIES

Characteristics of Hedge Fund Returns

One common claim among promoters of hedge fund products is that these investment vehicles generate absolute returns. This term describes investment strategies that consistently generate positive returns above the risk-free rate, regardless of prevailing economic conditions and without being exposed to major drawdowns of the stock and bond markets. Investors are tempted by strategies that generate absolute returns for two reasons:

1. Because of stable performance, these strategies tend to exhibit low levels of volatility.
2. An absence of exposure to extreme market events (including market rallies) implies that the correlation of returns with stocks and bonds will be low, leading to potential diversification benefits.

Hedge funds, however, are not absolute return investments that deliver positive returns every month. Table 2.1 reports summary statistics for the returns of hedge funds as well as for stocks and bonds. Hedge fund returns show significant dispersion, but this dispersion is lower than for traditional asset classes, and notably stocks. The upper part of the table shows basic performance measures, namely the mean return, volatility, and the Sharpe ratio of each index. The Sharpe ratio measures the expected return in excess of the risk-free rate, per unit of expected risk, where risk is defined as the return standard deviation. All hedge fund indexes have a Sharpe ratio that is superior to that of the stock and bond indexes. In addition, the Sharpe ratio of 1.4 and 1.3 for strategies that are strongly related to the equity market, event-driven, and long/short equity respectively, are lower than that obtained for equity-market neutral and non-equity-related strategies (convertible arbitrage and CTA/global macro). The table also suggests that the low volatility of the hedge fund indexes is partly responsible for their favorable Sharpe ratio. In fact, four of five strategies show volatility below that of bonds, sometimes only half that of bonds.

Table 2.1 also reports downside risk measures. These provide a more direct representation of hedge funds as capital preservers. For hedge funds, the percentage of months with negative returns is substantially lower than for stocks and bonds. The hedge fund indexes have negative returns between 5 to 30 percent of the months over our sample period, while both stocks and bonds show negative returns in almost 50 percent of the months. This paints a different picture of the risk of bonds from that suggested with low volatility. Furthermore, none of the hedge fund indexes suffered from any "crash" months. This is in sharp contrast to stocks, which posted a dramatic −13.8 percent decrease in October 1998. For the equity-market neutral, convertible arbitrage, and CTA/global macro indexes, the worst monthly return is not as low as the worst monthly return for bonds. The Sortino ratio, which replaces the volatility in the Sharpe ratio with downside deviation from a target return, confirms the superiority of hedge funds over traditional assets. The Sortino ratios for hedge fund indexes are

TABLE 2.1 Summary Statistics for Edhec and MSCI Indexes, January 1997 to August 2004

	Equity-Market Neutral	Convertible Arbitrage	CTA/Global Macro	Event Driven	Long/Short Equity	MSCI World Equity	MSCI World Bonds
Annualized Mean Return	10.4%	12.0%	12.0%	11.8%	12.8%	6.7%	6.5%
Annualized Volatility	2.2%	3.8%	4.2%	6.1%	7.6%	16.2%	7.0%
Sharpe Ratio[a]	3.4	2.3	2.1	1.4	1.3	0.2	0.5
% of Months with Negative Returns	5%	14%	18%	21%	30%	45%	46%
Minimum Monthly Return	−1.1%	−3.2%	−2.9%	−8.9%	−5.5%	−13.8%	−3.3%
Sortino Ratio[b]	2.81	0.96	1.22	0.50	0.75	0.16	0.52

[a]Calculated using a risk-free rate of 3 percent.
[b]Calculated using a minimum acceptable return of 3 percent.

superior to the MSCI World index, even though this index is not exposed to drawdowns of stocks in any particular country, but diversifies between the stock markets of all developed economies around the world. In addition, four out of five hedge fund strategies show higher Sortino ratios than the bond index, and one strategy, event-driven, has a Sortino ratio comparable to that of bonds. While the performance measures reported in Table 2.1 are favorable to the different hedge fund strategies, considerable variation in their returns suggests that these strategies did not deliver absolute returns.

A more fundamental reason for the claim that hedge funds deliver absolute returns is that hedge funds are meant to offer positive returns over the risk-free rate but without being exposed to market risk. The rationale is that the excess return generated by hedge funds constitutes a remuneration of manager skill, or alpha, rather than a reward for taking on risks. However, this interpretation depends on specific assumptions that are not necessarily valid. In order for the risk-free rate to be an adequate benchmark of hedge fund performance, a hedge fund investment should have a net zero exposure to market risk, and market risk should be the only risk factor. In other words, the single-factor capital asset pricing model (CAPM) must hold and the investment's beta must be zero. Beta neutrality, however, is not inherent in most hedge fund strategies. Even strategies that claim to be market neutral usually have a low beta, but rarely a beta of zero. More important, there is a consensus among academics and practitioners that multiple rewarded risk factors exist in financial markets, which has led to the development of multifactor models. The most salient additional risk factors are the value and small-cap factors used in the Fama-French three-factor model. In addition, changes in volatility and credit spreads have been found to have an impact on asset returns. Therefore, the excess return above the risk-free rate would be a measure of manager skill only if the given investment has zero exposure to all these risk factors. The growing literature on risk factors of hedge fund strategies suggests that these investments are exposed to a wide range of risk factors (Fung and Hsieh 1997a; Agarwal and Naik 2004). These risk factors tend to be different from the ones traditional asset classes are exposed to. Furthermore, they tend to differ among different hedge fund strategies. It turns out that risk-factor exposure explains some of the favorable properties of hedge funds.

The argument of absolute returns distracts attention away from the risks inherent in hedge fund strategies. This is not helpful for an investor who seeks to understand the precise nature of strategy risks. Funds of hedge funds, for example, typically show low realized volatility or low target volatility. This low volatility is linked more to diversification between different hedge fund strategies and their different underlying risk factors than to low volatility of their components, namely individual hedge funds. Furthermore, simple risk measures, such as volatility, do not account for the dynamic and nonlinear dimensions of hedge fund risks (Lo 2001). Likewise, low correlations do not imply that hedge funds offer absolute returns. The low correlation of hedge fund returns with those of equities and bonds can be linked to exposure of hedge funds to risk factors that are different from the risk factors driving stock and bond returns.

Exposure to Risk Factors

It is instructive to analyze how different hedge fund strategies are exposed to multiple risk factors. The general features of hedge funds include a number of risk/return characteristics that are directly linked to the investment freedom hedge fund managers enjoy. The possibility to invest in derivatives, for example, leads to nonlinear risk exposures. The dynamic nature of the strategies followed by hedge funds leads to the same effect, even if no derivatives are used. Event-driven strategies illustrate this point. Merger arbitrage is probably the best-known example of an event-driven strategy. Merger arbitrage managers bet on the realization of merger deals that have been announced but are not yet concluded. These managers take positions that are similar to a short put position on the equity market (Mitchell and Pulvino 2001). Thus, the returns of merger arbitrage hedge funds depend on the returns of the equity market, but in a nonlinear way. In rising equity markets, the performance of merger arbitrage funds is usually constant and positive, but in adverse equity market conditions, returns can quickly become negative. This is because merger arbitrage strategies collect a risk premium from insuring the risk of deal failure. It is more probable for mergers to not be realized in down markets than in up markets.

In addition to allowing investors to gain nonlinear exposure to risk factors, hedge funds may provide access to additional sources of risk, such as volatility risk. A buy-and-hold position in a stock index will not be exposed to a risk of changes in expected or realized volatility. The value of an option on this index, however, depends on volatility, so the option position is exposed to changes in volatility. The value of a call option on the index will rise with increasing volatility, because the likelihood of obtaining positive outcomes on the index will be higher. That the chance of negative outcomes also increases does not matter to the option holder, as any outcome below the exercise price leads to an option payoff of zero.

To obtain a precise idea of the risks factors underlying each strategy and the nature of the dependency, we look at correlation coefficients of hedge fund index returns with a number of risk factors. We identify 10 factors that constitute sources of risk in financial markets. For factors related to equity markets, we use the change in implied volatility of equity index options as measured by the Chicago Board Options Exchange (CBOE) Volatility Index (VIX). We also use value versus growth and small-cap versus large-cap returns spread. Equity market returns are proxied by returns on the Standard & Poor's (S&P) 500 index. Factors reflecting the conditions in the bond markets are the term and the credit spread, mean, and volatility of treasury bond returns and of treasury bill returns. Finally, we consider exposure to commodity prices. Appendix 2.1 describes the proxies used for each factor in more detail.

Table 2.2 presents the risk factors that influence each strategy. It shows the correlation coefficients for factors for which each hedge fund strategy has significant exposure. The table indicates that most strategies are exposed to the equity market, as proxied by the return on the S&P 500 index. In fact, all strategies except CTA/global macro have a significant and positive exposure to the equity market. Looking at the equity-based strategies, namely equity-market neutral, long/short equity, and event-driven, the small-cap versus large-cap spread has a positive and significant impact, suggesting that part of the returns of these managers comes from holding small-cap stocks and assuming the associated risks. It is more difficult to implement short position on small-cap stocks than for large-cap stocks, so most equity hedge fund managers end up with a long position in the small-cap versus large-cap spread. Likewise, changes in market volatility impact on the returns of all three equity-based strategies. For event-driven, this is consistent with the analogy of these strategies, notably merger arbitrage, to a position in a put option. The sign of the correlation coefficient is negative, as expected, since a short put position loses money when volatility rises. Long/short equity and equity-market-neutral managers have similar exposure to volatility risk. This suggests that short Vega strategies are employed by many equity-market-neutral managers. For long/short equity, there is a negative relation with the value versus growth spread, suggesting that a systematic long/short strategy that buys growth stocks and sells value stocks explains part of the returns of long/short equity managers.

All equity-based strategies are negatively affected by the credit spread (the difference in yield-to-maturity between corporate and treasury bonds). This suggests that managers following these strategies hold long positions in stocks with high exposure to default risk and short positions in stocks with low credit risk, which is consistent with them holding long positions in the small-cap versus large-cap spread. The yield of Treasury bills affects a number of strategies, since these can benefit from an increase in short-term interest rates with their short positions. A number of strategies benefit from flattening of the yield curve, or high bond market returns. Low levels of bond returns volatility usually affect CTA/global macro managers negatively. The returns of CTA/global macro also depend on prices in commodity markets.

The characteristics of hedge fund strategies and their exposure to risk factors suggests that hedge funds, rather than being absolute return vehicles,

TABLE 2.2 Risk Exposures of Hedge Fund Strategies with 10 Risk Factors, January 1997 to August 2004

	Equity Factors[a]				Bond Factors					Others
	Change in VIX	Value vs. Growth	Small Cap vs. Large Cap	S&P 500 Return	Term Spread	Credit Spread	Bond Return	Historical Volatility of Bond Returns	3-month T-Bill	Commodity Index
Equity-Market Neutral	-0.22		0.25	0.42	-0.45	-0.34	0.20		0.48	
Convertible Arbitrage				0.19	-0.18				0.23	
Long/Short Equity	-0.51	-0.21	0.32	0.74	-0.17	-0.32			0.17	
Event Driven	-0.55		0.33	0.65		-0.23				
CTA/Global Macro							0.45	-0.28		0.21

[a]Entries represent correlation coefficients. Only factors significant at the 5 percent level are retained.

show significant exposure to a variety of risk factors. However, rather than being a drawback, investors may actually derive benefits from such multiple risk exposures. Hedge fund strategies offer return characteristics that are different from investments in stocks and bonds. The question for investors is how this can be used to improve the diversification of their portfolio. We analyze the impact of adding hedge fund strategies to a diversified portfolio in the next section.

DIVERSIFICATION BENEFITS

As shown in Table 2.1, the motivation for hedge fund investing stems from favorable risk and return characteristics. Hedge funds exhibit both low volatility and low downside risk, while achieving returns that are considerably above those of bonds. Investors looking for capital preservation would naturally favor investments that generate stable positive returns. The assessment of the stand-alone benefits suggests that investors should replace stock and bond portfolios by a portfolio of hedge funds.

Instead of considering hedge funds as stand-alone investments and discarding stocks and bonds altogether, we address the benefits of hedge fund investing within a portfolio context, namely, as an addition to stocks and bonds. From a practical perspective, investors try to avoid dramatic shifts in allocation, since these lead to high transaction costs. Furthermore, most investors are only beginning to build up experience in hedge fund investing and are thus unwilling to allocate more than a small part of their portfolio to hedge funds. From a theoretical perspective, the choice between investment opportunities must take into account portfolio effects. Adding a stock with low returns and high volatility to a portfolio of stocks may provide benefits if the stock has low correlation with the existing stocks. Our focus is therefore on mixing rather than on choosing between alternatives. Table 2.2 indicates that hedge funds offer a risk exposure that differs from holding stocks and bonds only, and thus have low correlation with these assets. Adding hedge funds to a portfolio composed of traditional assets therefore allows for diversification.

Conditional Correlations

The correlations of financial assets are constant neither in time nor across states of the world. Rather, correlations are both time- and state-dependent. In particular, dependencies tend to be higher in times of market downturns. During market downturns, correlations between equity markets in different countries increases significantly (Longin and Solnik 1995). Therefore, diversification benefits assessed over the whole time period may not reflect the benefits investors expect in times of market turmoil, when those benefits are most valuable. In other words, the unconditional diversification benefits may not hold conditionally. Dependence conditional on down markets may be higher than unconditional dependence.

Table 2.3 assesses the dependence in two states of the equity market, namely negative or positive returns. The results are shown both with hedge fund indexes and with equity market indexes for different countries. The beta with the MSCI World index was chosen as the measure of dependence. This can be justified by the fact that beta indicates the marginal risk of an asset (its contribution to the volatility of a portfolio) and therefore has a more direct interpretation than the correlation coefficient.

Table 2.3 shows betas calculated using the returns of months with positive returns (up) and negative returns (down) of the MSCI World index. The betas of hedge funds with the world equity market are significantly lower than the betas of country indexes with the world equity market. Most betas for hedge fund strategy are lower than 0.1, while the minimum of the betas for country indexes is 0.35. Also, the down market betas of hedge funds stay below 0.4 for all strategies, which is still lower than the up-market betas of international equity. Moreover, for most international equity indexes betas significantly increase in down markets with respect to up-market conditions. However, four out of five hedge fund strategies have remarkably stable betas over the two market states. This suggests that the diversification benefits of hedge funds hold in down markets and that the diversification effects from hedge funds are more stable across different states of the market than those from international equity. In this respect, hedge funds constitute a solution to the unfavorable conditional correlations of stock markets across different countries.

TABLE 2.3 Conditional Betas, January 1997 to August 2004

	Up[a]	Down[b]		Up[a]	Down[b]
Equity-Market Neutral	0.06	0.06	MSCI Japan	0.35	0.55
Convertible Arbitrage	0.09	0.07	MSCI Germany	1.16	1.34
CTA/Global Macro	0.09	0.09	MSCI USA	1.05	0.79
Event Driven	0.13	0.33	MSCI Emerging Markets	0.67	1.22
Long/Short Equity	0.28	0.34	MSCI France	0.99	1.02
			MSCI UK	0.65	0.86

[a]Months with positive returns for the MSCI world index.
[b]Months with negative returns for the MSCI world index.

Higher Moments

Diversification benefits can arise from low correlation or low contribution to the volatility of the final portfolio. Likewise, standard performance measures used to describe hedge fund returns essentially rely on the mean and the volatility. This poses a problem, since asset returns are not fully described by their mean and volatility (the first two moments of the return distribution). It is only under the restrictive assumption of normally distributed returns that the first two moments are sufficient to describe the distribution completely. For a normal distribution, the skewness (the third standardized moment, a measure of asymmetry) is 0 and the kurtosis (the fourth standardized moment, a measure of tail thickness) is 3. Normally distributed returns are symmetric around the mean, and extreme events, such as returns above or below three standard deviations away from the mean, have a very probability of occurring (about 0.1 percent). This is contrary to empirical descriptions of asset returns. For example, asymmetry is especially pronounced for option strategies or hedge funds using options. This asymmetry is reflected by skewness different from zero. Likewise, extreme market events, such as the 1987 stock market crash, have emphasized the importance of considering the kurtosis of the return distribution.

Table 2.4 shows descriptive statistics of the monthly returns of hedge fund, stock, and bond indexes. The values of skewness and excess kurtosis (kurtosis −3) show that asymmetry and fat tails are present in the distribution of returns of all hedge fund strategies. The event-driven index exhibits the most pronounced departure from normality. Returns are left skewed, with a skewness of −2.1, and kurtosis is 10.4 higher than that of a normal distribution. This shows that the annualized mean returns of 12 percent and a standard deviation of 6 percent cannot alone describe the returns distribution. Investors are exposed to the possibility of extreme returns, as indicated by high kurtosis. Moreover, these extreme returns are more likely to be negative than positive, as indicated by negative skewness. From the interpretation of event-driven strategies as a short put position, these distributional properties seem particularly plausible. Table 2.4 also indicates that the excess kurtosis and skewness of hedge fund index returns are more pronounced than those of stock and bond index returns. The Jarque-Bera statistic tests each index for normally distributed returns. Statistically significant departures from normally distributed returns are noted with an asterisk in the Jarque-Bera probabilities. Normality is rejected for three out of five hedge fund strategies, but not for stocks or bonds.

Because investors have preferences over higher moments of the returns distribution, it is crucial to assess how an asset contributes to the different moments of the portfolio's return distribution. We calculate betas for all four moments. The second-moment beta is the contribution of an asset to the second moment (volatility) of the portfolio when a small fraction of this asset

TABLE 2.4 Skewness, Kurtosis, and Jarque Bera-Tests on Edhec and MSCI Indexes, January 1997 to August 2004

	Equity-Market Neutral	Convertible Arbitrage	CTA/ Global Macro	Event Driven	Long/ Short Equity	MSCI World Equity	MSCI World Bonds
Skewness	0.5	−1.1	0.2	−2.1	0.0	−0.6	0.5
Excess Kurtosis	0.6	2.4	1.5	10.4	1.0	0.1	−0.1
Jarque-Bera Statistic	4.0	32.8	7.0	410.3	2.6	5.7	2.9
Jarque-Bera Probability	0.14	0.0*	0.03*	0.0*	0.27	0.06	0.24

*Statistically significant at the 5 percent level.

is added. This corresponds to the standard Capital Asset Pricing Model (CAPM) beta commonly used in investment analysis. The third-moment and fourth-moment betas represent the contribution to the portfolio's third and fourth moments. Table 2.5 presents the different betas for the hedge fund strategies, when adding these to a portfolio of equities or bonds. In general, the lower the beta, the higher the diversification benefit of adding this strategy to a portfolio of traditional assets. Martellini and Ziemann (2004) examine higher-moment beta estimates and the interpretation of these estimates, in the context of portfolio analysis. In particular, they show that the addition of a small fraction of new assets to a portfolio, such as a hedge fund, decreases the portfolio's moments, but only for moment betas less than 1.

Table 2.5 indicates that adding hedge funds to a portfolio of stocks and bonds not only allows volatility to be reduced, because of low correlation, but also improves asymmetry and reduces extreme risks (because of favorable cokurtosis and coskewness). Examining these betas therefore may help investors choose strategies in which to invest, depending on the initial portfolio they hold. For example, long/short equity appears to be a good diversifier for a bond investor, but not so much for a stock investor. These features of diversification indicate that the improvement in terms of risk and return from adding hedge fund strategies can be substantial.

Risk/Return Trade-Off

Broadly speaking, investors may benefit from including hedge funds in a broad portfolio of assets if their returns behave differently from the returns of the assets already included. The conditional betas of Table 2.5 suggest that hedge funds offer more stable diversification than international equity. Examining higher-order comoments showed that hedge funds dispose of risk-reducing properties when skewness and kurtosis are considered, in addition to portfolio volatility.

The chief motivation for investors wishing to include hedge fund strategies in their portfolios is an improvement of their risk/return trade-off. We assess the benefits of including hedge funds in a portfolio comprised of stocks and bonds only. Again, we use the MSCI World indexes as proxies for stock and bond returns. We stress that using world indexes leads to a conservative estimate of the diversification potential of hedge funds, since the stock and bond components of the portfolio are themselves already diversified across countries.

We compute efficient frontiers using a risk measure that takes into account the first four moments of the returns distribution. That is, we compute a modified value at risk (VaR), which yields an estimate of the expected loss at our chosen 99 percent confidence level. The modified VaR is obtained by using a critical value that incorporates the skewness and

TABLE 2.5 Higher Moment Betas of Returns of Edhec and MSCI Indexes, January 1997 to August 2004

	Convertible Arbitrage	CTA/ Global Macro	Event Driven	Long/ Short Equity	CTA/ Global Macro	MSCI World Equity	MSCI World Bonds
2nd Moment Beta with Equity	0.05	0.06	0.26	0.37	0.03	−0.08	1.00
2nd Moment Beta with Bonds	−0.07	0.00	−0.11	−0.05	0.23	1.00	−0.41
3rd Moment Beta with Equity	0.10	0.07	0.46	0.37	−0.09	−0.19	1.00
3rd Moment Beta with Bonds	−0.26	−0.07	−0.47	−0.68	0.42	1.00	−1.68
4th Moment Beta with Equity	0.11	0.07	0.36	0.38	−0.04	−0.11	1.00
4th Moment Beta with Bonds	−0.04	0.03	−0.05	0.06	0.33	1.00	−0.30

kurtosis of the returns distribution via a Cornish-Fisher expansion (Zangari 1996). Figure 2.1 shows the efficient frontiers in the mean/VaR space.

The dashed line shows portfolios that minimize the VaR of portfolio returns for a given mean level of returns. The other lines show this same frontier when hedge funds are included. The risk/return trade-off achieved with hedge funds is more favorable. Indeed, the efficient frontier shifts toward the northwest, suggesting that hedge funds offer diversification benefits. This is chiefly due to their favorable comoments with portfolios of traditional assets. The investor's opportunity set is substantially improved, as can be seen by the magnitude of the shift of the frontier and compared to when only stocks and bonds are considered.

It is also evident from the figure that the different strategies do not offer the same potential for diversification. In fact, some strategies serve as return enhancers in that they allow the investor to achieve higher returns for given levels of risk. This is the case for CTA/global macro, event-driven, and long/short equity strategies. The upper right-hand side of Figure 2.1 indicates that portfolios that include these strategies offer particular high returns for high levels of risk. This may be appealing to investors who seek to enhance their returns. Some strategies, however, allow investors to significantly decrease risk. This is the case for equity-market neutral and convertible arbitrage strategies.

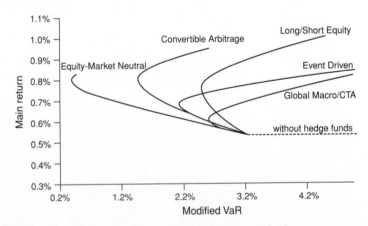

FIGURE 2.1 Efficient Frontiers in Mean Value-at-Risk Plane
Risk-return trade-off when a hedge fund strategy is added to the investor's asset menu of stocks and bonds. Value-at-risk is estimated using a Cornish-Fisher expansion. The indexes used for hedge fund strategies are the five Edhec indexes. Stock and bond returns are proxied for by the returns of the MSCI World Equity and the MSCI World Sovereign Bonds index. Base on monthly returns data for the period January 1997 to August 2004.

SEPARATING ALPHA AND BETA MANAGEMENT

Alpha and Beta Benefits

Hedge funds can provide investors with two types of rewards, just as in the case of any active investment strategy. Modern portfolio theory suggests that returns on a portfolio, in excess of the risk free, can originate from three distinct sources, as described in this relationship:

Excess return on the portfolio = normal return + abnormal return
+ statistical noise

The normal return, or beta benefits, corresponds to the market's reward for the risks to which the portfolio is exposed. It corresponds to a premium for these risks, which can be evaluated with a single-factor model like the CAPM or with a multifactor model. Multifactor models were justified by an equilibrium argument by Merton (1973) and by an arbitrage argument by Ross (1976).

Hedge funds offer three different types of beta benefits:

1. Traditional beta benefits emanating from exposure to stock and bond returns
2. Beta benefits emanating from exposure to other risk factors in equity markets, such as small-cap versus large-cap spread, value versus growth spread, or implied volatility, and in bond markets, such as term spread, credit spread, or bond returns volatility
3. Other alternate beta benefits, such as commodity price levels or currency rates

While the first type of beta benefit does not improve the investor's set of investment choices, the two latter beta benefits expand the investor's risk-taking opportunities. The abnormal return, or alpha benefit, represents the portfolio manager's expertise. Portfolio managers, through superior information or better ability to process commonly available information, sometimes obtain profits that are not due to exposure to rewarded risks. While the existence of alpha is sometimes questioned, alternative betas should be regarded as more reliable because they correspond to a fair reward for exposure to risk factors.

Hedge funds have organizational features that allow their managers to fully exploit their skills, thereby offering ideal conditions for alpha generation. The performance of an active manager, as defined as the information ratio, depends on the quality of the bets the manager takes, the number of bets taken, and the tracking error imposed on the manager (Grinold and

Kahn 2000). The absence of a tracking error constraint allows hedge fund managers to fully exploit their talent and ultimately increases their information ratios. Just as in the case of beta benefits, different sources of alpha may be distinguished, alpha from security selection and alpha from timing the exposure to different risk factors.

Since hedge funds offer both alpha and beta benefits, they constitute a diversification tool for strategic asset allocation decisions, but also a potential source of outperformance. This dual character of hedge funds fits perfectly into the modern investment process that separates management of alphas and betas by organizing the portfolio into a core and a satellite. The core-satellite approach separates beta management, namely choice and construction of a benchmark, and alpha management, namely management of active risk. This approach has three advantages:

1. A passive core and an active satellite involve lower management fees compared to an active global portfolio with tracking error constraints (Amenc, Malaise, and Martellini 2004).
2. The approach permits access to the specific expertise of specialized managers for alpha management, such as boutique managers or specialists, and for beta management, such as index funds or passive mandates.
3. It leads to improved risk management because the asset allocation decision in the core is separated from the alpha generation in the satellite.

Next, we examine how hedge funds can be used for separate beta and alpha management.

Beta Management

The beta exposure seeks to use the portfolio itself as the benchmark. The objective of such a benchmark is not to track a given index, but rather to define over a long horizon the risk and return properties the investor considers optimal. The risk/return profile sought by the investor typically depends on liabilities and on preferences. The construction of a benchmark usually relies on a mix of generic indexes. When dealing with hedge funds and traditional asset classes, investors may be confronted by two situations. First, if investors do not have enough expertise in asset allocation, a global index meant to represent the risk/return characteristics of a given asset class will be selected by investors. Second, if investors wish to identify the portfolio with the optimal risk/return trade-off, an allocation to a subset of indexes will be made. These indexes are meant to represent risks to which investors want exposure over a long investment horizon.

It has been shown that, over long investment horizons, the benchmark or the strategic allocation of an investor constitutes the principal source of performance and of the risk of the portfolio. This is a well-known result for funds investing in traditional asset classes and has recently been confirmed in the case of funds of hedge funds.

Indexes seem to be the natural investment vehicle for beta management. In equity investing, decisions such as transition management or management of cash inflows are usually dealt with by using index products. Likewise, market timing and tactical asset allocation strategies are typically implemented with index futures or tracking funds. It is therefore natural to associate beta management with indexes. However, investors may choose also to capture hedge fund risk exposure by investing in individual hedge funds or in a fund of funds.

It turns out, however, that investors have good reason to use indexes for allocation. By investing in a fund of hedge funds or selecting a portfolio of individual hedge funds, investors necessarily reduce their coverage of the hedge fund universe to a very limited number of products. Typically, this is done deliberately, as investors or fund-of-funds managers hope to select good funds and avoid bad funds. This selection, however, should be separated from the asset allocation decision, since the aim is not to optimize the risk/return trade-off but rather to generate overperformance (i.e., to create alpha benefits).

For investors, the selection of funds is risky. Historically, the returns of hedge funds within a given strategy are quite dispersed. Figure 2.2 illustrates this point for the long/short equity strategy. Choosing only a few funds may leave investors with returns that no longer resemble the aggregate return of managers following that strategy. Investment in hedge fund indexes, however, protects investors from this selection bias. Just like indexes for stocks or bonds, these indexes deliver the anticipated returns of the asset class or investment style.

In addition to selection bias, a fund of hedge funds leaves the investor with hedge fund strategies chosen by the fund of funds manager rather than by the investor. Not only might the resulting allocation be not optimal for a given investor, it likely also varies over time according to rebalancing done by the fund of funds. Therefore, to be in control of the allocation, an investor would prefer using hedge fund indexes.

However, this does not imply that hedge funds belong to the satellite portfolio, while traditional investments belong to the core portfolio. The diversification benefits and the risk-factor exposure of hedge funds suggest that they have their place in the core portfolio. Since hedge funds give access to the betas and risk premiums of additional risk factors, their inclusion is an explicit allocation choice that modifies investor benchmarks and not an attempt to enhance returns above the benchmark by adding a satellite component. In other words, allocation to hedge funds modifies the benchmark but adds no tracking error.

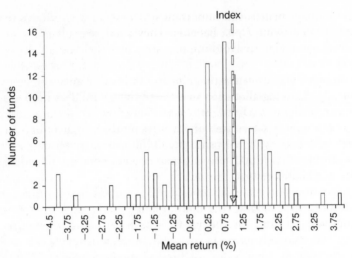

FIGURE 2.2 Cross-Sectional Dispersion of Long/Short Equity Hedge Fund
Returns, January 1998 to December 2003
Distribution of mean return of funds in this strategy. The arrow indicates the mean
return of the Edhec Alternative Index for long/short equity. Based on monthly
returns for the period January 01, 1998–December 31, 2003 of 123 Long/short
equity hedge funds in the CISDM database.

Alpha Management

Hedge funds have a privileged place in the satellite portfolios of institutional investors for a number of reasons. Investors wishing to maximize the
use of the tracking-error budget naturally want funds that are very active
and, above all, that generate positive alpha. In addition, since hedge funds
have low correlation with traditional asset classes, hedge fund portfolios
can be easily transported to a different portfolio; strategic allocation of the
overall portfolio will not be substantially influenced. This is referred to as
the portable alpha benefits of hedge funds (Fung and Hsieh 2004a).

For alpha management, investors frequently turn to funds of funds to
gain exposure to hedge funds. Funds of funds typically justify their fees by
adding value from three sources:

1. By selecting the best individual hedge funds
2. By allocating between different hedge fund strategies
3. By protecting investor capital through due diligence, risk monitoring,
   and reporting

Beta management is still important for funds of hedge funds that concentrate on identifying alpha benefits. They need to manage their strategy exposure when trying to avoid implicit style bets that result from manager selection.

A different way of generating alpha with hedge funds is of focusing on dynamically changing allocation to different hedge fund strategies. Such an investment strategy is a straightforward extension of dynamic allocation between different asset classes or investment styles that is known in the long-only universe as global tactical asset allocation programs. Amenc, El Bied, and Martellini (2003) provide encouraging evidence of predictability in hedge fund index returns through the use of (lagged) multifactor models. With information on the past values of 10-variables that proxy for market risk, volatility risk, default risk, and liquidity risk, a significant amount of predictability is found for six out of nine hedge fund strategy indexes. Investors may take advantage of such predictability by using a timing strategy among various other hedge fund strategies.

Obviously, some features of hedge fund investments prevent investors from actually implementing such a strategy. In particular, the absence of liquidity and the presence of lockup periods pose a problem. Therefore, inter-strategy tactical allocation offerings based on the predictability of hedge fund strategies have experienced little growth in the past. However, the availability of investable indexes that track the returns of different hedge fund strategies has encouraged the emergence of offerings of that kind.

HEDGE FUND INDEXES

For the tasks of strategic allocation and tactical allocation, investors need to rely on hedge fund indexes that are both investable and representative. It has often been argued that two distinct purposes of indexes should be distinguished: an index can be used (1) as a benchmark for investments in specific styles, instruments, or locations, or (2) as an investment vehicle. On one hand, indexes that act as benchmarks have to be unambiguous, verifiable, accountable, and representative. On the other hand, an investable index should enjoy the same properties and, in addition, be investable. It is important to note that these requirements should be achieved at the same time; if an investable index does not have the defining properties of an index (unambiguous, verifiable, accountable, and representative), it should not be called an index but rather a fund of hedge funds.

Representativity

Due to the scarcity of information, representativity through market capitalization is difficult to apply to hedge funds. As a result, finding a benchmark that is representative of a particular management universe is problematic. The different indexes available on the market are constructed from different data, using different selection criteria and methods of construction, and evolve at different paces (Amenc and Martellini 2003b). Because of this heterogeneity, investors cannot rely on competing hedge fund indexes to obtain an accurate picture of hedge fund performance. One serious problem is that existing hedge fund style indexes provide a confusing view of the alternative investment universe, because the collection of these indexes is neither collectively exhaustive nor mutually exclusive. Hedge fund indexes are built from databases of individual fund returns, so they inherit the shortcomings of database, especially in terms of scope and quality of data. Providers of hedge fund indexes use three main competing databases: TASS Tremont, Center for International Securities and Derivatives Markets (CISDM), and Hedge Fund Research (HFR). While all three databases are marred by biases such as survivorship bias, selection bias, and instant history biases, they are far from being homogeneous. For example, HFR excludes managed futures; TASS and Managed Account Reports (MAR) include them. Most hedge funds report to a single database vendor only. Among the 1,162 funds in HFR funds and the 1,627 funds from TASS, only 465 are common to both databases. Fifty-nine percent of the funds that are still active, and 68 percent of the funds that no longer report to HFR are not part of the TASS database. Of the 465 funds found in both the HFR and TASS databases, only 154, or 33 percent, were included in both databases at the same time.

As a result of the incompleteness and heterogeneity of hedge fund data, existing hedge fund indexes suffer from two major shortcomings: They lack full representation, and they are biased.

Existing indexes are not fully representative. During the 1960s and 1970s, a good index was one that was representative of the value-weighted portfolio of all traded assets. The real challenge was to provide investors with the closest approximation of the true market portfolio. This does not easily extend to the alternative investment universe. Hedge funds are not subject to mandatory reporting, so an estimate of the assets under management by the entire industry is difficult to obtain. This is why all existing hedge fund indexes, except CSFB/Tremont, use an equally weighted, as opposed to value-weighted, construction. Besides, because of the lack of regulation on hedge fund performance disclosure, existing databases cover only a relatively small fraction of the hedge fund population. Slightly over half of existing hedge funds choose to self-report their performance to a major hedge fund database. Consider the fact that one of the most popular hedge fund indexes, the Evaluation Associates Capital Markets (EACM) 100, accounts for no more than a tiny fraction of all existing hedge funds (100 selected from among more than 7,000 funds).

The second shortcoming is that existing indexes are biased. Most hedge fund indexes are based on managers' self-reported styles. Given that these managers jealously protect their investment strategies, indexes must rely on managers to accurately self-report their style. This makes sense only when a manager follows a unique investment style and when a manager's self-reported style matches his or her actual trading strategies. None of these assumptions can be taken for granted. In particular, style drift is recognized in the industry. As opportunities eventually disappear in their original strategies, some hedge fund managers commonly start looking at other markets and adopting other strategies.

This diversity in selection criteria and in methods of construction poses serious problems to investors. As an illustration, consider the return differences of competing indexes available on the market, reported in Table 2.6. Significant performance differences within the same strategy are commonly observed between the different competing indexes. This phenomenon is particularly noticeable in periods of crisis, between August 1998 and October 1998. The heterogeneity of the information supplied by the different index providers is spectacular. During October 1998, the performance of the CSFB and Altvest Global Macro indexes differ by over 14 percent. The increasing number of index providers and of construction methodologies highlights the problem of data heterogeneity. Competing hedge fund indexes are not representative and do not provide investors with a consistent pattern of hedge fund performance.

In response to the needs of investors for more representative benchmarks, the Edhec Risk and Asset Management Research Center has proposed an original solution by constructing an index of indexes. Given that

TABLE 2.6 Heterogeneity in Competing Hedge Fund Indexes, January 1998 to December 2003

Hedge Fund Strategy	Max Differences (%)	Date	Lowest Return (%)	Highest Return (%)
Convertible Arbitrage	7.55	Dec 01	EACM (−6.93)	Hennessee (0.62)
CTA	7.50	Dec 00	Barclay (6.00)	S&P (13.50)
Global Macro	14.17	Oct 98	CSFB (−11.55)	Altvest (2.62)
Equity-Market Neutral	5.00	Dec 99	Hennessee (0.20)	Van Hedge (5.20)
Event Driven	5.37	Aug 98	CSFB (−11.77)	S&P (−6.40)
Long/Short Equity	9.51	Feb 00	Altvest (3.50)	CSFB (13.01)

it is impossible to identify the best existing index, we use a combination of competing indexes to identify common information about a given investment style. One straightforward method for obtaining a composite index based on various competing indexes is to compute an equally weighted portfolio of all competing indexes. This would provide investors with a convenient one-dimensional summary of competing indexes. In particular, because hedge fund indexes are based on different sets of hedge funds, the resulting portfolio of indexes would be more exhaustive than any individual indexes. We can push the logic one step further and use factor analysis to extract the best possible one-dimensional summary of a set of competing indexes and can design indexes that can achieve the highest possible degree of representativity. This methodology, which is a natural generalization of the idea of taking a portfolio of competing indexes, was first introduced in Amenc and Martellini (2003b) and has led to the design of the Edhec Alternative Indexes (*www.edhec-risk.com*). Because the Edhec indexes exhibit representativity and stability significantly higher than those of individual indexes, we use them throughout this chapter to proxy the returns on various hedge fund strategies.

Investability

The concern that existing hedge fund indexes are not representative of the universe has been intensified by the recent launch of several investable hedge fund indexes. Indexes provided by Standard and Poor's, Hedge Fund Research, Credit Suisse First Boston/Tremont (CSFB/Tremont), Financial Times Stock Exchange (FTSE), and Morgan Stanley Capital International (MSCI) are among the best-known examples. The objective of these investable indexes is to allow a broad range of investor access to alternative investment strategies at low cost. These indexes do not attempt to be representative of the hedge fund universe. Instead, they choose a limited number of funds that are open to new investors and that guarantee a minimum investment capacity. These indexes are not therefore intended to be used as a reference for the hedge fund market, but rather to provide a convenient and inexpensive way for investors to access hedge funds. Investable hedge fund indexes are even less representative of the universe than noninvestable indexes. This lack of representativity is unsatisfactory for investor beta management and alpha management. For beta management, allocating nonrepresentative indexes implies that the risk and return of the investor's portfolio will depend more on the quality of the provider's fund selection and on the construction biases specific to the index than on the allocation decision of the investor. For alpha management through tactical allocation between hedge fund strategies, the mixture of strategies in a global index means that the investor cannot implement any bets between strategies. Likewise, strategy indexes that suffer from selection bias and do not represent the given strategy deprive the investor of precise control of strategy exposure. The success of investable hedge fund strategy indexes, and their positioning with funds of hedge funds, therefore strongly depends on the capacity of index providers to improve the investability of their indexes without sacrificing representativity. This is not a trivial task, because to be fully representative, an index has to cover the whole universe or a whole strategy, including closed funds.

Reconciling Investibility and Representativity

Given these problems, it is questionable whether designing investable indexes for hedge funds is a feasible task. Goltz, Martellini, and Vaissié (2004) shed some light on this issue by showing that factor-replicating portfolios can be used to construct representative indexes based on a limited number of funds. More precisely, portfolios containing a small number of hedge funds can be made representative by properly selecting funds and designing optimal portfolios. We apply this methodology to an investor who has access to a small database of hedge funds. This is important because, in reality, an investor does not have access to the broad universe of funds included in a large database because many funds are closed for new investment, and others may not be accessible for different reasons. Here we use Lyxor database of 121 managed accounts (*www.lyxor.com*). This platform is widely used in the industry and guarantees high accessibility of its funds, many with daily liquidity.

The first question is how best to represent the common trend for a certain hedge fund strategy. Starting with the CISDM database of returns of 3,500 hedge funds, we extract the combination of individual funds that capture the largest possible fraction of the variability contained in the data. Technically speaking, this amounts to using the first component of a principal components analysis (PCA) of funds returns as a factor. The selection criterion is the loading of individual funds on the first principal component. The higher the loading of a fund on the first principal component, the higher its contribution to the common trend in hedge fund returns following a given strategy. Given that the first eigenvector corresponding to the first principal component is determined so as to maximize the variance of the corresponding linear combination of fund returns, high factor loadings will be allocated to funds that have been highly correlated with their group over the calibration period. Such funds should be the most representative of their group.

Selecting from the Lyxor platform of managed accounts, which is considerably smaller than the universe represented by the CISDM database, we

TABLE 2.7   Representativity of Investable Indexes, October 2001 to September 2004

Investable Index	Correlation with First Principal Component
Convertible Arbitrage	0.912
CTA/Global Macro	0.963
Event Driven	0.866
Equity-Market Neutral	0.626
Equity Long Short	0.937

form factor-replicating portfolios that track the principal component. As suggested by Fung and Hsieh (1997a) in their analysis of hedge fund performance, in the selection stage we retain only those funds in the Lyxor database that are highly correlated to the principal component for which the replica is constructed. Having selected the funds, we optimize their portfolio weights to deliver the maximal correlation of the replicating portfolio returns with the corresponding principal component.

Using monthly returns data from October 2001 to September 2004, for each strategy we choose 8 to 12 funds that are closest to the first principal component extracted from the CISDM database, and we select portfolio weights to maximize correlation with the first principal component. We also constrain weights of individual funds to range from 5 to 20 percent. The correlation coefficients with the factor we attempt to replicate are reported in Table 2.7.

For all strategies except equity market neutral, the correlation of the replicating portfolios with the corresponding first principal component is close to 0.9. The portfolios of managed accounts created in this section can therefore be considered investible indexes that capture the return characteristics of a large set of funds in the universe. This suggests that representativity can be achieved with a very limited number of funds, provided that an adequate method is used to design the portfolio. This method should focus on selecting representative funds, not only high-performing funds. Selecting high performers is an objective for active funds of hedge funds, but not for providers of hedge fund indices.

Hedge Fund Diversification Benchmarks

There are different ways of using investable hedge fund indexes. By their virtue of representativity of the risk exposure and return characteristics of a given hedge fund strategy, these indexes can be used for beta management. Therefore, they are an alternative to funds of hedge funds, which are perceived as alpha management vehicles (i.e., as part of the satellite portfolio and with the aim of enhancing the return of an investor's portfolio with respect to a global benchmark representing the person's strategic asset allocation).

Investable hedge fund indexes may be used in different ways to take advantage of the diversification benefits of hedge funds for strategic asset allocation. One approach would be for each institutional investor to use consultants to define a customized asset allocation on the basis of index products. Another approach would be to design a limited number of benchmarks that can be used by different investors. Here we construct multistrategy hedge fund benchmarks that would exhibit a persistent and robust factor exposure and meet the needs of different classes of investors. The design of these benchmarks again involves two separate steps, a selection stage and an allocation stage.

In particular, we construct two separate portfolios. The Hedge Fund Equity Diversifier and the Hedge Fund Bond Diversifier are benchmarks that are built by selecting investible indexes, with the objective of diversifying an equity portfolio and a bond portfolio, respectively.

Selection

In the selection stage, we investigate the diversification properties of different hedge fund strategies with respect to portfolios of stocks or bonds. When searching for strategies that can properly diversify, it is important to examine moments higher than the first and second moments of hedge fund return distributions. Higher-moment betas can assess the impact of adding a given investable index to the stock or bond portfolio, namely the diversification potential of the index. Motivated by the results of Table 2.5, we select a subset of three strategies to construct the benchmark that diversifies equity portfolios and a subset of four strategies to construct the bench-

TABLE 2.8 Strategies Entering the Equity and Bond Diversifiers

Investable Index	Equity Diversifier	Bond Diversifier
Convertible Arbitrage	Yes	Yes
CTA & Macro	Yes	No
Equity-Market Neutral	Yes	Yes
Event Driven	No	Yes
Long/Short Equity	No	Yes

mark that diversifies bond portfolios. Table 2.8 shows the result of our selection process. The investable indexes that we select are marked "Yes" in the column corresponding to the respective diversifier benchmark.

Optimization

The next step in the construction of global buy-side indexes is to find the optimal allocation of the selected strategy indexes. Our methodology is based on two key principles:

1. Because expected returns are notoriously hard to estimate with any degree of accuracy, we focus on minimizing the risk of an investor's stock or bond portfolio.
2. Because hedge funds are not normally distributed, the measure of risk should be more general than volatility.

We carried out a risk-minimization calculation, where we use the 95 percent value at risk with the Cornish-Fisher correction. Furthermore, we constrain the weight of the hedge fund allocation to 5, 15, 25, and 35 percent of the investor's portfolio and invest the remaining wealth in either in bonds or in stocks. It has been argued that the presence of portfolio constraints, in addition to avoiding corner solutions in optimization techniques, allows one to achieve a better trade-off between specification error and sampling error, similar to what can be achieved by statistical shrinkage (Jagannathan and Ma 2003; Ledoit and Wolf 2003, 2004).

Tables 2.9 and 2.10 show the diversification benefits obtained from adding the diversification benchmarks to a stock and bond portfolio,

TABLE 2.9 Portfolio Performance When Adding an Equity Diversifier to the MSCI World Equity Index, October 2001 to September 2004

Allocation to Hedge Funds (%)	0	5	15	25	35
Annualized Mean (%)	2.0	2.2	2.7	3.2	3.7
Annualized Standard Deviation (%)	15.0	14.2	12.5	10.9	9.4
VaR (95%)	7.6	7.1	6.2	5.3	4.4
Sharpe Ratio[a]	−0.03	0.015	0.057	0.111	0.184
Skewness	−0.56	−0.54	−0.49	−0.41	−0.30
Kurtosis	3.27	3.24	3.17	3.08	2.95

[a]Calculated using a risk-free rate of 2 percent.

TABLE 2.10   Portfolio Performance When Adding a Bond Diversifier to the Lehman Composite Global Treasury Index, October 2001 to September 2004

Allocation to Hedge Funds (%)	0	5	15	25	35
Annualized Mean (%)	−0.3	0.1	0.9	1.8	2.6
Annualized Standard Deviation (%)	3.3	3.1	2.8	2.6	2.4
VaR (95%)	1.7	1.5	1.3	1.1	0.9
Sharpe Ratio[a]	−0.71	−0.61	−0.38	−0.09	0.25
Skewness	−0.26	−0.23	−0.13	0.05	0.25
Kurtosis	2.40	2.51	2.82	3.24	3.65

[a]Calculated using a risk-free rate of 2 percent.

respectively. The first column reports the performance of the stock and bond indexes, respectively. The columns to the right report the same statistics when adding hedge funds with the specified allocation.

These tables indicate that even a small allocation to hedge funds achieves diversification benefits that are economically important. For an equity investor, Table 2.9 indicates that allocating 15 percent to hedge funds in the equity portfolio reduces monthly value at risk and volatility and increases the mean return. In particular, the mean return increases by more than 30 percent (from 2 to 2.7 percent), while the risk is reduced by more than 15 percent, regardless of whether risk is defined as volatility (which reduces from 15 to 12.5 percent) or Cornish-Fisher Value at Risk (VaR) (which reduces from 7.6 to 6.2 percent). For a bond investor, Table 2.10 indicates that a 15 percent allocation to hedge improves the mean return substantially, while the VaR decreases by more than 12 percent and the volatility decreases by more than 15 percent. Figure 2.3 illustrates the diversification benefits in terms of relative improvement of the risk statistics measures. The left figure is based on Table 2.9, and the right is based on Table 2.10. Both indicate the amount of decrease of each risk measure, when hedge funds are allocated to the index.

The results clearly illustrate the diversification benefits of hedge funds. The Cornish-Fisher VaR accounts for higher moments of the return distribution, so the benefits of diversification are robust to extreme risks. Contrary to current studies of hedge fund diversification that employ noninvestable indexes, our approach relies on investable indexes and is therefore more pertinent to investors. The benefits we emphasize stem from the careful two-stage process we employ: the selection of appropriate strategies and the portfolio optimization.

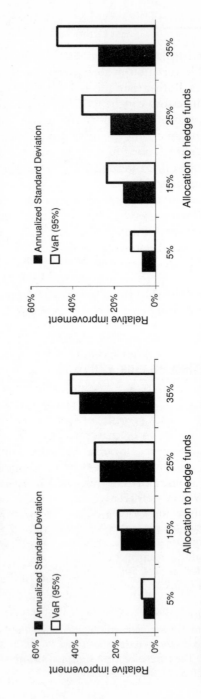

FIGURE 2.3 Diversification Benefits in Terms of Relative Improvement

The bars in the charts indicate the percentage of improvement of two statistics of portfolio risk (annualized standard deviation and monthly modified VaR) in comparison to the case where the portfolio contains no hedge funds. A decrease of the risk measure is indicated by a positive percentage of relative improvement.

CONCLUSION

This chapter argues that hedge funds, rather than being riskless investments, show considerable variation in their returns and are exposed to a wide range of risk factors. Rather than this risk exposure being a weakness, however, institutional investors can benefit from it. This is because the sources of risks driving hedge fund returns are in part fundamentally different from those driving stock and bond returns. Consequently, adding hedge funds to a diversified portfolio offers benefits in terms of an improved risk/return trade-off. Moreover, the diversification properties of hedge funds tend to be more stable than those of international equity, and hedge funds offer risk reduction opportunities even when investors account for higher moments of the returns distribution. We also argue that hedge funds may be useful tools for institutional investors in both beta management and alpha management. Representative hedge fund indexes are applicable in this regard. We present a way of constructing investable and representative indexes of hedge funds and show how these can be used to create diversification benchmarks. These benchmarks are an optimal complement to an investor's existing portfolio of traditional asset classes.

APPENDIX 2.1 DEFINITION OF RISK FACTORS

For all risk factors, end-of-month values are obtained from Datastream for the period January 1997 to August 2004.

Change in Implied Volatility (VIX) The new VIX volatility index obtained from the CBOE. This index measures the implied volatility of Standard & Poor's (S&P) 500 index options. The first difference of this series is calculated in order to obtain the change in VIX as a variable.

Commodity index Monthly returns for the Goldman Sachs Commodity Index.

Credit spread The difference between yields to maturity of the Lehman U.S. Universal High Yield Corporate index and the Lehman U.S. Treasury index for the one to three years' maturity segment.

S&P 500 return Returns for the S&P 500 Composite index.

T-bill 3 months The yield to maturity of the Merrill Lynch Treasury Bill for three months' maturity.

Term spread The difference between yields to maturity of the Lehman U.S. Treasury index for the 5 to 7 years' maturity segment and the Lehman U.S. Treasury index for the 1 to 3 years' maturity segment.

Small cap versus large cap The difference between the returns of the S&P 600 small cap index and the S&P 500 Composite index.

U.S. dollar The U.S. dollar major currency index, calculated by the U.S Federal Reserve Bank. This index expresses the value of the U.S. dollar relative to a basket of major foreign currencies.

Value versus growth The difference between the returns of the S&P 500 Barra Value index and the S&P 500 Barra Growth index.

APPPENDIX 2.2 DESCRIPTION OF HEDGE FUND STRATEGIES

Convertible arbitrage Convertible securities are priced as a function of the price of the underlying stock, expected future volatility of equity returns, risk-free interest rates, call provisions, supply and demand for specific issues, issue-specific corporate/treasury yield spread, and expected volatility of interest rates and spreads. There is therefore much potential for misvaluation of these securities. Convertible arbitrage strategies attempt to exploit price anomalies in convertible corporate securities such as convertible bonds, warrants, and convertible preferred stock. If the financial health of the issuer is good, the convertible bond behaves like a stock; but if it is poor, the convertible bond behaves like distressed debt. Convertible bonds tend to be underpriced because of market segmentation. Indeed, investors discount securities that are likely to change form. Convertible arbitrage hedge fund managers typically buy these securities and then hedge part of the risk by shorting the stock. The primary source of return is the income generated by the arbitrage position. The convertible security pays a coupon, and the short equity position generates interest income on the proceeds of the short sale if the strategy is unlevered. Because both of these return components are stable, convertible arbitrage funds tend to display low volatility. In addition, capital gains can be realized by managing the hedge ratios of these positions. Convertible arbitrage funds are nondirectional.

Equity market neutral These funds also take both long and short positions in equities. Stock positions are usually diversified, so that no single position has a disproportionate effect on the portfolio. Related short positions hedge out much of the systematic risk in the long positions on either a dollar- or beta-adjusted basis, so that the overall portfolio has a limited exposure to market movement. This investment strategy is designed to exploit equity market inefficiencies. It usually involves holding simultaneously long and short matched equity portfolios of the same size within a country. Market-neutral portfolios are designed to be either beta- or dollar-neutral, or both. These funds are therefore nondirectional. Many practitioners of market-neutral long/short equity trading balance their longs and shorts in the same sector or industry. By being sector neutral, they avoid the risk of market swings that can affect certain industries or sectors differently from others. Well-designed portfolios typically control not only for industry and sector, but also for market capitalization, style (growth versus value), and other exposures. Leverage is often applied to enhance returns.

Event driven Also known as corporate life cycle investing. This involves investing in opportunities created by significant corporate events, such as spin-offs, mergers and acquisitions, bankruptcy reorganizations, recapitalization, and share buy-backs. The portfolio of event-driven managers may shift between merger arbitrage, also known as risk arbitrage, and distressed securities. Other managers may adopt a broader scope. Instruments include long and short common and preferred stocks, as well as debt securities and options. Fund managers may hedge against market risk by purchasing S&P put options or put option spreads. Event-driven strategies are usually classified as a separate class alongside directional and nondirectional strategies. Some managers may use leverage.

Global macro and CTAs We group global macro and commodity trading advisor (CTA) funds as one type of strategy, an uncommon practice. We do this because both strategies involve trend-following tactics that use a wide set of assets, such as currencies, interest rate products, and commodities. Global macro strategies make leveraged bets on anticipated price movements of global markets. Macro managers usually employ a top-down global approach in which they benefit from market movements due to shifts in world economies, political fortunes, or global supply and demand forces. Exchange-traded and over-the-counter derivatives are often used to magnify these price movements. Commodity trading advisors are investment funds and managed account programs that take long and short positions in cash and in derivative currency, commodity, or interest rates products. Most funds trade exclusively in spot assets, forwards and futures in currencies, commodities, or fixed income products. Options positions on either class of assets may also be taken. Due to the flexibility of these two strategies, they are difficult to distinguish, which justifies grouping them together.

Long/short equity Long/short hedge managers use a wide range of securities, such as equity and equity derivatives (equity options, equity index options and futures, exchange-traded funds, contracts for difference, and swaps). Managers may attempt to profit from a double alpha strategy, namely generating alpha from both long and short stock positions independently. Managers may also invest in a small number of relative-value trades that attempt to profit from the price movement in one stock versus the price movement in another. In general, the net exposure of equity long/short funds to long positions minus short positions tends to have a positive bias. Therefore, these funds are directional. This is because their managers, most of whom were originally long-only mutual fund managers, usually feel more comfortable with detecting undervalued stocks than overvalued stocks. Similarly, long/short managers, even those who target market neutrality, unintentionally have time-varying residual exposure to a variety of sectors or investment styles (growth or value, small cap or large cap) that can result from their bottom-up stock-picking decisions.

CHAPTER 3

Funds of Hedge Funds versus Portfolios of Hedge Funds: A Comparative Analysis

Daniel Capocci and Valérie Nevolo

Using a comprehensive database made up of 2,247 individual hedge funds, of which 1,346 follow a directional strategy and 877 a nondirectional strategy, and 647 funds of hedge funds over the period January 1994 to December 2002 period, we investigate whether portfolios of individual hedge funds can outperform existing funds of hedge funds. For this purpose, we have built portfolios using Carhart (1997) deciles classification. In regressing each of our individual hedge funds decile portfolios, first against the funds of hedge funds global index, then against each funds of hedge funds decile, and finally against each individual funds of hedge funds present in our database, we find that the best individual and directional hedge funds deciles are those of the middle, which indicates that neither a momentum nor a contrarian strategy seems appropriate in portfolio construction to beat existing funds of hedge funds. Our nondirectional hedge funds deciles consistently and significantly beat existing funds of hedge funds.

INTRODUCTION

The first hedge fund was formed in 1949 by Albert Winslow Jones, a sociologist who had the idea of combining long and short equity positions and applying leverage to magnify the returns of these hedged positions. Hedge funds remained relatively obscure to the investment world until 1966, when it became public knowledge that Jones's fund beat the best mutual funds over 5 and 10 years by 44 and 87 percent, respectively.

The hedge fund industry is largely private and unregulated, which means that the reporting of data is voluntary, creating immediate disclosure problems. Estimating the current size of the market, the growth in the number of funds or the average fund performance is therefore difficult. Despite this, it is generally maintained that over the past decade, the hedge fund business has grown strongly. The number of hedge funds increased from 2,000 to 8,000 and assets under management increased from $190 billion to $1 trillion from 1993 to September 2004. Not surprisingly, the investor base for hedge funds has expanded, from primarily wealthy individuals to pension funds, funds of funds, endowments, and foundations.

Georges Coulon Karlweis, the private bank Edmond de Rothschild's vice-chairman and top investment strategist, established the first fund of hedge funds, Leveraged Capital Holdings, in 1969. The concept was simple: Instead of buying stocks or bonds, he put all the fund's assets into several hedge funds. The idea has made the rarefied world of hedge funds available to smaller investors. The fund of hedge funds industry has grown dramatically in recent years, now controlling U.S.$80 billion in assets. This growth has been driven by the sheer number and diversity of individual hedge funds, coupled with the particularities of hedge fund portfolio management. The fund of hedge funds industry is riding the crest of two major market trends. The first is the interest of institutional investors in hedge fund investments. The total quantity of institutional assets in hedge funds is rising, as are the number of institutions making investments. The second is the general public's tremendous interest in hedge fund investments. This interest has led traditional asset managers to offer hedge fund products and hedge fund managers to partner with traditional financial distribution channels to access individual assets.

LITERATURE REVIEW

Academics have been studying hedge funds since 1997. As more and more studies on performance emerge, the subject becomes more and more precise. Hedge fund performance has been studied in many different ways and results diverge (see, e.g., Agarwal and Naik 2004, Capocci and Hübner 2004). Most nonprofessional investors base their investment decision on past performance, and the funds with good past returns tends to see the bigger inflow: Who will buy a fund that has just lost 10 percent over the last year? On the other side, professional investors, such as fund of funds managers or pension funds, generally perform on-site qualitative due diligence combined with a quantitative analysis to limit their choice not only on past performance. Our objective is to determine if this process helps to create net returns for the final investors once all the fees are taken into account. More precisely, we compare funds of hedge funds managed by professionals with portfolios of hedge funds created simply on the basis of past performance.

Since 1997, the literature on hedge funds has increased dramatically, and today papers on the subject are frequent. From an investor's point of view, diversification is the main reason for investing in a portfolio of hedge funds instead of a single hedge fund. By combining several hedge funds with differing return distributions and risk profiles in a portfolio, investors are able to diversify specific risk away and ensure a more disciplined exposure to the overall hedge fund asset class. Funds of hedge funds were initially diversified across investment styles, sectors, and/or regions. However, more recently, funds of hedge funds that specialize within a single investment style have also emerged; Learned and Lhabitant (2002) call this diversification by judgment. Both types of funds put forward their ability to diversify risks by spreading them over several managers. However, diversifying a hedge fund portfolio also raises a number of issues, such as the optimal number of hedge funds required to achieve diversity, and the influence of diversification on the various statistics of return distribution (typically expected return, skewness, kurtosis, and correlation with traditional asset classes).

One relevant fact is that research within the hedge fund industry is very young. Most of the key papers on this kind of investment were written during the last six years. In this section we have classified hedge fund studies into three categories. The first one concerns studies that are focused on hedge funds performance. The second category is made up of studies where hedge funds investment style is described. The last category reviews various other aspects of the hedge fund industry.

Performance evaluation is essentially concerned with comparing the return earned on a hedge fund with the return earned on some other standard investment assets. Many studies in this category include a comparison of the performance of hedge funds with equity and other indices (see, e.g., Ackermann, McEnally, and Ravenscraft 1999; Brown, Goetzmann, and Ibboston 1999; Edwards and Liew 1999; Amin and Kat 2003a; Capocci and Hübner 2004). Results of these studies are mitigated, depending on the period considered, the data, and the risk-adjusted performance model used.

When the performance of hedge funds is compared with that of mutual funds, most of the studies conclude that hedge funds are the best performers. That is notably the case in Ackermann, McEnally, and Ravenscraft (1999) and in Liang (1999).

Another wave of hedge funds studies concerns persistence in hedge fund performance. Actually, as hedge funds exhibit a much higher attrition rate compared to mutual funds (see Brown, Goetzmann, and Ibbotson 1999; Liang 1999), the issue of performance persistence becomes especially important in the case of hedge funds. The different results obtained are mitigated, but in general the presence of persistence in hedge fund returns is concluded, as in Park and Staum (1998) and in Capocci and Hübner (2004). Yet Brown, Goetzmann, and Ibboston (1999) present evidence that there is no performance persistence among hedge funds, and Agarwal and Naik (2000b) sustain that the persistence among hedge fund managers is short-term in nature.

Finally, many researchers have studied the performance of hedge funds in a portfolio context, notably the diversification benefits of including hedge funds in a traditional portfolio of stock and bonds. As an illustration, we can look at the study of Edwards and Liew (1999), who show that the inclusion of hedge funds in a diversified portfolio raises the Sharpe ratio of the portfolio. Other studies in this field are those of Amin and Kat (2003a,b), Capocci and Hübner (2004) and Learned and Lhabitant (2002).

METHODOLOGY

The aim of this chapter is to determine if built portfolios of hedge funds outperform existing funds of hedge funds. To achieve this objective, we first divide the whole database into four groups. The first one contains all funds of hedge funds present in the starting database and permits us to construct a fund of hedge funds global index. The second one contains all individual hedge funds, both directional and nondirectional. The few individual hedge funds that are neither directional nor nondirectional are also taken into account here. Finally, the third and the fourth groups permit to distinguish directional hedge funds from nondirectional ones.

In each of these four groups, we follow the methodology of Carhart (1997), which is also used in Capocci, Corhay, and Hübner (2005). All funds are ranked based on their previous year's returns. Every January, we put all funds into 10 equally weighted portfolios, ordered from the highest to the lowest past returns. The portfolios are held until the following January and then rebalanced. This yields a time series of monthly returns on each decile portfolio from January 1995 to December 2002, corresponding to 96 mean monthly returns per decile for each of the four groups.

The division in deciles for each year is achieved with Equation 3.1.

$$Decile_{it} = \left[(n-1) \times \frac{10}{n_t} \right] + 1 \qquad (3.1)$$

where $Decile_{it}$ = Decile order attributed to the fund i in year t (i = 1 to n_t).

n = The number attributed to the fund when the database is sorted in descending order on the basis of the previous year mean monthly returns. The best-performing fund of the year $t - 1$ has n equal to 1.

n_t = Number of funds to split between the 10 deciles in year t. It corresponds to funds that existed during the whole year $t - 1$.

The hedge fund deciles constitute our hedge funds portfolios. The idea is not to determine if momentum is present in hedge fund returns, as in Capocci and Hübner (2004), but to construct portfolios of hedge funds in a more subtle and reproducible way than completely randomly. The hypothesis of persistence in performance, namely that hedge funds with an above-average return in one period will also have an above-average return in the next period, will lead investors willing to build on their own a portfolio of hedge funds to choose the previous year's best-performing funds, corresponding to the portfolio of decile 1.

We follow two steps to compare our constructed portfolios of hedge funds with existing funds of hedge funds:

1. We compared the average monthly returns and the Sharpe ratios of each individual (directional, nondirectional) hedge funds decile and its equivalent in the funds of hedge funds deciles.
2. We regress each of the individual hedge fund's deciles against the funds of hedge funds global index. The same regressions are also done taking into account only directional hedge funds on one hand and nondirectional individual hedge funds on the other hand. The regression equation (3.2) used is:

$$R_{dt} = \alpha_d + \beta_d R_{it} + \varepsilon_{dt} \qquad (3.2)$$

where
d = 1 to 16 for the 10 deciles, the three subdeciles of the first decile, and the three subdeciles of the tenth deciles
t = 1 to 96 (months)
R_{dt} = Return of decile d at period t
R_{it} = Return of the FoF index at period t
α_d, β_d, ε_{dt} = intercept, slope, and error term of the regression, respectively

We then turn our attention to the sign and the statistical significance of the alpha obtained (α_d), the measure of out- or underperformance of the decile considered relative to the fund of funds (FoF) global index. The beta is interpreted as a measure of the dependence of the decile's return to the

FoF index. We compute all estimations using Newey and West (1987) standard errors to adjust for autocorrelation in the returns.

To refine this analysis, we took the individual, directional, or nondirectional individual hedge funds deciles as the dependent variables in the regressions, but this time we regressed them against each fund of hedge funds decile instead of against the FoF index. It is indeed also rational for investors eager to invest in funds of hedge funds to look at their previous year's performance. This analysis is in fact more accurate than the previous one in the sense that the funds of hedge funds global index is divided into 10 smaller portfolios, namely our funds of hedge funds deciles. That left us with 100 regressions for each category of individual hedge funds, and the equation (3.3) used each time can be written as:

$$R_{d_{HF}t} = \alpha_{d_{HF}} + \beta_{d_{HF}} R_{d_{FoF}t} + \varepsilon_{d_{HF}t} \tag{3.3}$$

where

d_{HF} = 1 to 10 for the 10 individual hedge funds deciles
d_{FoF} = 1 to 10 for the 10 funds of hedge funds deciles
t = 1 to 96 (months)
$R_{d_{HF}t}$ = return of the individual hedge funds decile d_{HF} at period t
$R_{d_{FoF}t}$ = return of the funds of hedge funds decile d_{FoF} at period t
$\alpha_{d_{HF}}, \beta_{d_{HF}}, \varepsilon_{d_{HF}t}$ = intercept, slope, and error term of the regression, respectively

Finally, the analysis can be pushed a little further by regressing each hedge funds decile (individual, directional, and nondirectional) against each existing fund of hedge funds. This last point will permit us to verify if the results obtained are confirmed for individual funds of funds. The regression equation (3.4) used is:

$$R_{d_{HF}t} = \alpha_{d_{HF}} + \beta_{d_{HF}} R_{FoF_i t} + \varepsilon_{d_{HF}t} \tag{3.4}$$

where

d_{HF} = 1 to 10 for the 10 individual hedge funds deciles
R_{FoF_i} = 1 to 635 for the 635 existing funds of hedge funds
t = 1 to 96 (months)
$R_{d_{HF}t}$ = return of the individual hedge funds decile d_{HF} at period t
$R_{FoF_i t}$ = return of the funds of hedge funds i at period t
$\alpha_{d_{HF}}, \beta_{d_{HF}},$ and $\varepsilon_{d_{HF}t}$ = intercept, slope, and error term of the regression, respectively

DESCRIPTIVE STATISTICS
AND CORRELATION ANALYSIS

The three main existing hedge fund databases are Managed Account Reports (MAR), Hedge Funds Research (HFR) and TASS Management (TASS). We use hedge fund data from MAR, as in Fung and Hsieh (1997b), Schneeweis and Spurgin (1998b), Amin and Kat (2002a), Liang (2003b), and Capocci, Corhay, and Hübner (2005). The data used are exactly the same as those used by the latter study.

The database used gives monthly net-of-fee individual returns and other information on hedge funds during the January 1994 to December 2002 period. To perform the funds of hedge funds analysis, we use the whole database and separate it depending on the classification just reported. Table 3.1 reports the descriptive statistics of the database.

The database used contains 2,894 funds for 1994 to 2002 period. Among those funds, only 1,615 are still living at the end of the period. At first glance we can observe the predominance of individual hedge funds, FoF covering only 22 percent of the whole database. Among the individual hedge funds category, the market timing strategy has the upper hand, standing for 60 percent in the category. As far as the funds of hedge funds category is concerned, funds that allocate capital to a variety of fund types are clearly in the lead, representing 77 percent of this category. The average number of months during which funds in one category continue to report returns is the highest for the FoF category. Over the whole 108-month period, a fund in this category is on average present in the database during 55 months. This result is a little higher but consistent with the 52 months found in Liang (2004).

In the eighth column, we can observe that the highest mean monthly return was achieved by individual funds category (1.08 percent). Inside this category, the market-timing strategy performs better than the nondirectional one, with an average of 1.12 percent per month against 1.01 percent per month. Average returns of FoF are well behind, all at around 0.7 percent per month. The fact that FoF underperform their hedge fund components is also greatly stressed by Liang (2004). Note here that all the monthly returns are significantly different from zero at the 1 percent significance level for all categories and subcategories. With regard to the standard deviation, the most volatile funds category is the individual one, with a 2.28 percent average monthly standard deviation. Funds of hedge funds are less volatile, with 1.77 percent standard deviation. This is certainly due to diversification across different strategies as well as in one particular strategy.

The returns are usually negatively skewed with two exceptions: There are category hedge funds or niche funds of funds. Another point is that the distributions of the returns have fat tails. Kurtosis is higher than 3 for the

TABLE 3.1 Descriptive Statistics on Individual Hedge Funds versus Funds of Hedge Funds, January 1994–December 2002

	No. of Funds	% of Category	% of the Total	No. of Months	Average Months	Living Funds	Dead Funds	Mean Return %
Individual Funds	2,247	100	78	110,888	49.35	1,186	1,061	1.08***
Directional Funds	1,346	60	47	65,914	48.97	647	699	1.12***
Nondirectional Funds	877	39	30	43,891	50.05	533	344	1.01***
No Category Funds	24	1	1	1,083	45.13	6	18	0.93***
Funds of Funds	647	100	22	35,516	54.89	429	218	0.72***
Niche	114	18	4	5,573	48.89	86	28	0.74***
Diversified	501	77	17	29,121	58.13	343	158	0.71***
Other	32	5	1	822	25.69	0	32	0.77***
Global Database	2,894	100	100	146,404	50.59	1,615	1,279	0.99***

	Standard Deviation (%)	Median (%)	Min (%)	Max (%)	Skewness	Kurtosis	Excess Return[a] (%)	Sharpe Ratio[a]
Individual Funds	2.28	1.11	−8.59	7.99	−0.26	2.77	0.71***	0.31
Directional Funds	3.09	1.20	−11.54	11.20	−0.15	2.71	0.75***	0.24
Nondirectional Funds	1.21	0.99	−4.32	4.19	−0.62	2.56	0.64***	0.53
No Category Funds	3.45	0.58	−7.82	12.69	1.17	3.20	0.56*	0.16
Funds of Funds	1.77	0.71	−6.84	6.56	−0.11	3.34	0.35**	0.20
Niche	1.33	0.67	−4.08	5.08	0.22	1.73	0.37***	0.28
Diversified	1.87	0.75	−7.34	6.95	−0.12	3.54	0.34*	0.18
Other	1.69	0.80	−7.35	5.79	−0.89	4.86	0.40**	0.24
Global Database	2.14	1.11	−8.18	7.64	−0.24	3.04	0.62***	0.29

[a]Calculated using a 4.5 percent risk-free rate.
***Significant at the 1 percent level.
**Significant at the 5 percent level.
*Significant at the 10 percent level.

whole database and the FoF category and 2.77 for the individual funds category. When risk and return are considered together through the Sharpe ratio, we are offered a picture that is in line with the mean returns. Accounting for risk, the FoF category (Sharpe ratio = 0.20) underperforms the individual one (Sharpe ratio = 0.31). These observations are consistent with those of Brown, Goetzmann, and Liang (2004). This time, however, the nondirectional funds (Sharpe ratio = 0.53) outperform the directional ones (Sharpe ratio = 0.24). The inclusion of the bear market period starting in April or September 2000, depending on the definition, explains this result.

Directional versus Nondirectional Strategies

Directional strategies use a market-timing approach, which consists of betting on the directions of markets dynamically. These strategies involve either betting on the direction of the asset price movement or betting on the direction of asset price volatility. According to Fung and Hsieh (1999b), global, global/macro, sectors, short-sellers, and long-only leveraged all employ this market timing style. Nondirectional strategies are those that do not depend on the direction of any specific market movement; these strategies aim to exploit short-term pricing discrepancies and market inefficiencies between related securities, while keeping market exposure to a minimum. According to Fung and Hsieh (1999b), the market-neutral category is included in this group. Although they consider event-driven funds as a hybrid style that is more volatile than the nondirectional approach and less volatile than the market timing approach, this strategy is more often considered a nondirectional one, notably in Agarwal and Naik (2000b,c, 2004) and in Bürki and Larque (2001). Therefore, we will consider event-driven funds as being part of the nondirectional category.

Descriptive Statistics for Each Category's Deciles

Table 3.2 reports the descriptive statistics of each decile of our four categories of hedge funds. We compare deciles in each category taken separately, but also between the different categories as a whole.

Panel A of Table 3.2 reports the descriptive statistics of the individual funds. The mean return diminish between decile 1 (1.53 percent) and decile 7 (0.78 percent). It fluctuates to finally reach 0.9 percent at decile 10 afterward. The median indicates the same trend as the mean return. The standard deviation indicates that the previous year's top- and worst-performing decile funds are the most volatile. The standard deviation falls until decile 7 and then increases for worst-performing hedge funds deciles. The minima

TABLE 3.2 Deciles Descriptive Statistics, January 1995 to December 2002

Panel A: Individual Hedge Fund Deciles

	Average No. of Funds	Mean Return	Standard Deviation	Median	Minimum	Maximum	Skewness	Kurtosis	Excess Return[a]	Sharpe Ratio[a]
Ind1	104	1.53%***	5.37%	1.52%	−12.70%	25.26%	0.69	4.53	1.15%**	0.21
Ind2	103	1.33%***	3.74%	1.28%	−12.88%	16.37%	0.03	4.54	0.95%***	0.26
Ind3	103	1.23%***	2.77%	1.31%	−10.50%	11.75%	−0.44	4.69	0.85%***	0.31
Ind4	103	1.22%***	2.16%	1.09%	−9.34%	8.92%	−0.64	6.11	0.84%***	0.39
Ind5	103	1.16%***	2.21%	1.34%	−12.09%	7.05%	−1.90	12.87	0.79%***	0.36
Ind6	103	0.89%***	1.46%	0.94%	−6.87%	4.38%	−1.33	7.41	0.52%***	0.35
Ind7	103	0.78%***	1.45%	0.96%	−6.18%	3.38%	−1.17	4.40	0.40%***	0.28
Ind8	103	0.87%***	1.81%	0.93%	−4.59%	6.42%	−0.09	1.18	0.49%***	0.27
Ind9	103	0.76%***	2.56%	0.92%	−7.77%	6.95%	−0.72	1.39	0.38%	0.15
Ind10	103	0.90%**	3.91%	1.18%	−11.32%	12.74%	−0.28	1.91	0.52%	0.13
Ind1a	35	1.47%***	7.26%	1.31%	−20.24%	34.41%	0.89	4.56	1.10%	0.15
Ind1b	35	1.62%***	5.03%	1.82%	−11.88%	23.64%	0.52	4.23	1.24%**	0.25
Ind1c	35	1.48%***	4.46%	1.59%	−14.96%	17.70%	0.05	3.77	1.10%**	0.25
Ind10a	34	0.90%***	3.11%	0.92%	−6.72%	10.12%	0.18	0.96	0.53%*	0.17
Ind10b	34	0.53%	4.34%	1.20%	−13.21%	12.35%	−0.50	1.47	0.15%	0.04
Ind10c	34	1.30%**	5.17%	1.77%	−15.06%	19.60%	0.09	3.24	0.93%*	0.18

[a]Calculated using a 4.4 percent risk-free rate.
***Significant at the 1 percent level.
**Significant at the 5 percent level.
*Significant at the 10 percent level.

TABLE 3.2 *(continued)*

Panel B: Directional Hedge Fund Deciles

	Average No. of Funds	Mean Return	Standard Deviation	Median	Minimum	Maximum	Skewness	Kurtosis	Excess Return[a]	Sharpe Ratio[a]
D1	62	1.61%**	6.27%	1.59%	−17.27%	29.57%	0.71	4.55	1.23%*	0.20
D2	61	1.33%***	4.48%	1.23%	−13.27%	17.86%	0.22	3.25	0.96%**	0.21
D3	62	1.30%***	3.81%	1.48%	−14.03%	16.55%	−0.19	5.06	0.93%**	0.24
D4	62	1.15%***	3.03%	1.27%	−10.41%	13.03%	−0.34	4.24	0.77%***	0.26
D5	61	1.27%***	3.29%	1.19%	−15.73%	10.96%	−0.94	7.36	0.89%***	0.27
D6	62	1.08%***	2.64%	1.32%	−13.11%	7.57%	−1.34	8.00	0.71%**	0.27
D7	62	0.80%***	2.53%	0.95%	−11.19%	4.79%	−1.29	4.07	0.42%	0.17
D8	62	0.75%***	2.70%	0.99%	−8.82%	6.68%	−0.66	1.03	0.37%	0.14
D9	61	0.66%***	3.20%	0.74%	−8.80%	9.29%	−0.19	1.17	0.29%	0.09
D10	61	0.82%	5.01%	1.56%	−14.48%	18.36%	−0.21	2.13	0.44%	0.09
D1a	21	1.67%*	8.90%	1.52%	−31.74%	38.69%	0.38	4.42	1.30%	0.15
D1b	21	1.49%**	6.06%	1.63%	−14.71%	25.09%	0.25	2.84	1.11%*	0.18
D1c	21	1.64%***	4.93%	1.54%	−11.57%	24.92%	0.83	5.38	1.26%**	0.26
D10a	20	0.86%*	4.66%	1.31%	−13.53%	15.49%	−0.21	1.87	0.48%	0.10
D10b	21	0.31%	4.84%	0.62%	−12.31%	13.70%	−0.27	1.02	−0.07%	−0.01
D10c	20	1.29%*	6.84%	1.80%	−20.10%	26.71%	0.08	2.39	0.91%	0.13

[a]Calculated using a 4.5 percent risk-free rate.
***Significant at the 1 percent level.
**Significant at the 5 percent level.
*Significant at the 10 percent level.

TABLE 3.2 *(continued)*

Panel C: Nondirectional Hedge Fund Deciles

	Average No. of Funds	Mean Return	Standard Deviation	Median	Minimum	Maximum	Skewness	Kurtosis	Excess Return[a]	Sharpe Ratio[a]
ND1	41	1.59%***	2.84%	1.57%	−5.83%	12.29%	0.34	2.32	1.21%***	0.43
ND2	41	1.27%***	1.93%	1.13%	−8.31%	8.58%	−0.81	7.15	0.90%***	0.46
ND3	41	1.10%***	1.55%	1.15%	−8.15%	4.69%	−2.05	12.47	0.72%***	0.47
ND4	41	1.01%***	1.27%	0.97%	−4.48%	4.19%	−1.39	6.02	0.63%***	0.50
ND5	41	0.98%***	1.06%	1.05%	−3.77%	2.91%	−1.05	3.13	0.61%***	0.57
ND6	41	0.79%***	1.00%	0.73%	−4.14%	3.37%	−1.11	6.02	0.41%***	0.41
ND7	41	0.77%***	0.92%	0.90%	−2.13%	2.61%	−0.53	0.30	0.40%***	0.43
ND8	41	0.81%***	0.93%	0.96%	−2.92%	3.26%	−0.82	2.59	0.43%***	0.46
ND9	41	0.94%***	1.49%	0.83%	−4.78%	5.68%	−0.08	2.58	0.56%***	0.38
ND10	40	1.32%***	2.94%	1.14%	−6.22%	15.89%	1.50	6.79	0.94%***	0.32
ND1a	14	1.32%***	4.47%	1.24%	−10.75%	18.95%	0.24	2.40	0.95%**	0.21
ND1b	14	1.55%***	2.74%	1.32%	−4.85%	11.45%	0.56	1.24	1.17%***	0.43
ND1c	14	1.90%***	2.71%	1.84%	−5.08%	10.16%	0.20	0.60	1.53%***	0.56
ND10a	13	1.35%***	4.69%	0.78%	−4.82%	39.12%	5.71	44.42	0.98%**	0.21
ND10b	14	1.33%***	2.82%	1.38%	−5.75%	8.31%	0.10	0.25	0.96%***	0.34
ND10c	13	1.26%***	3.82%	0.95%	−10.52%	19.62%	0.85	5.75	0.88%**	0.23

[a]Calculated using a 4.5 percent risk-free rate.
***Significant at the 1 percent level.
**Significant at the 5 percent level.
*Significant at the 10 percent level.

TABLE 3.2 *(continued)*

Panel D: Funds of Hedge Fund Deciles

	Average No. of Funds	Mean Return	Standard Deviation	Median	Minimum	Maximum	Skewness	Kurtosis	Excess Return[a]	Sharpe Ratio[a]
FOF1	33	0.90%**	3.37%	0.93%	−12.24%	12.75%	−0.10	3.92	0.52%	0.16
FOF2	33	0.94%***	2.40%	0.81%	−7.38%	9.64%	0.17	3.61	0.56%**	0.23
FOF3	33	0.84%***	2.04%	0.78%	−9.00%	7.13%	−0.80	5.77	0.47%**	0.23
FOF4	33	0.95%***	1.90%	0.95%	−7.65%	7.06%	−0.32	5.09	0.57%***	0.30
FOF5	33	0.85%***	1.62%	0.79%	−7.56%	5.97%	−1.00	7.49	0.47%***	0.29
FOF6	33	0.93%***	1.42%	0.78%	−5.06%	4.54%	−0.17	2.98	0.55%***	0.39
FOF7	33	0.82%***	1.34%	0.68%	−3.99%	6.01%	0.39	3.03	0.45%***	0.33
FOF8	33	0.69%***	1.35%	0.67%	−4.12%	4.24%	−0.24	1.37	0.32%**	0.24
FOF9	33	0.64%***	1.66%	0.74%	−4.58%	5.37%	−0.38	1.39	0.26%	0.16
FOF10	32	0.64%**	2.89%	0.53%	−13.04%	13.42%	0.05	8.21	0.26%	0.09
FOF1a	11	0.77%	4.86%	1.33%	−22.88%	14.64%	−0.89	5.78	0.39%	0.08
FOF1b	11	0.99%***	3.59%	0.71%	−10.14%	13.47%	0.16	3.20	0.61%	0.17
FOF1c	11	0.97%***	2.55%	0.95%	−7.88%	11.73%	0.05	4.72	0.60%**	0.23
FOF10a	11	0.94%***	2.68%	0.66%	−6.99%	10.59%	0.52	2.10	0.57%**	0.21
FOF10b	11	0.84%***	2.87%	0.65%	−12.91%	11.49%	−0.37	6.26	0.47%	0.16
FOF10c	11	0.13%	4.15%	0.38%	−19.89%	19.96%	−0.01	9.76	−0.24%	−0.06

[a]Calculated using a 4.5 percent risk-free rate.
***Significant at the 1 percent level.
**Significant at the 5 percent level.
*Significant at the 10 percent level.

indicate no significant differences. The monthly maximum return is the highest for top-performing decile funds, which is not surprising. When returns are adjusted for risk, using the Sharpe ratio with a 0.36 percent monthly risk-free rate, using the risk-free rate from Ibbotson Associates over the January 1995 to December 2002 period, the best-performing funds seem to be those of decile 4. The Sharpe ratio increases from decile 1 to decile 4 and decreases afterward. This is consistent with the fact that the standard deviation is higher for the best- and worst-performing funds deciles. Only funds in decile 1 and 2 have positively skewed performance distribution. The kurtosis is largely positive for all deciles, which indicates that all the distributions of returns have fat tails.

The deciles of directional hedge funds (panel B of Table 3.2) indicate that there is a decreasing trend for the mean return as we go from decile 1 to decile 9 and that the mean monthly returns for funds in decile 10 are slightly higher. The median returns show the same behavior as in the previous category. The standard deviation remains high for best-performing decile funds and is higher still for worst-performing deciles than for those in the middle. The minimum and maximum figures indicate that the worst- and the best-performing results were achieved by funds in the best-performing decile, which is consistent with its high standard deviation. The Sharpe ratio evolves in the same way as in the previous category described, but this time it reaches its peak at decile 5. Distributions continue to have fat tails and to be positively skewed for the first and the second decile only.

Panel C of Table 3.2 reports the descriptive statistics of each decile for the nondirectional hedge funds subcategory. Here the mean returns decrease from decile 1 to decile 7 and then go up until decile 10. The median return continues to follow the same trend as the mean returns, but it reaches its lowest level at decile 6. The standard deviation goes down until decile 7 and increases afterward. What is particular here is that it reaches its highest level at decile 10. As a result, the average Sharpe ratio is the lowest for this decile and is at its best at decile 5. A look at the maximum figures indicates that the highest monthly returns are obtained by the worst decile funds. Return distribution tails are still thick for all funds, but only funds in the worst- and the best-performing deciles have positively skewed distribution.

The funds of hedge funds category is reported in panel D of Table 3.2. The mean monthly returns are more or less stable between decile 1 and decile 6. Then, between decile 7 and decile 10, the decrease is more striking. The median return is the lowest for decile 10 and follows again the same trend as the mean return. The Sharpe measure is the highest where the standard deviation is the lowest, for deciles 6 and 7. It is minimal where the mean return is minimal, decile 10. The minimum and maximum monthly returns are achieved by funds in the worst decile. Finally, we observe that the skewness is negative for all deciles but the second, the seventh, and the tenth ones, and that all distributions have fat tails.

Correlation Analysis

Table 3.3 reports the correlation coefficients between the nine categories listed for the January 1994 to December 2002 period. The table indicates that the categories are highly positively correlated. Fourteen out of 36 intercategory correlation coefficients are above 0.9. These results tally with what is typically reported in the literature, namely that strategies are in general highly correlated when indices are considered (Liang 2003b; Capocci and Hübner, 2004. Capocci, Corhay, and Hübner 2005). The lowest correlation coefficient is obtained between the no category hedge funds and the other funds of funds subcategory of FoF, with a coefficient of 0.29.

The highest correlation coefficients are observed between the whole database and its categories. Moreover, between these eight coefficients, the highest is obtained between the whole database and the individual hedge funds category (0.997). It is important to note here that, whatever the category considered, the directional hedge funds subcategory is more correlated with it than is the nondirectional category, the only exception being with the other funds of funds category.

Next we examine the correlation coefficients between the funds of hedge funds category and the individual (directional, nondirectional) hedge funds categories. The second column of Table 3.3 indicates that the individual hedge funds category is more correlated with funds of hedge funds than its subcategories, the correlation being 0.935. It is slightly higher than the correlation 0.920 of directional hedge funds, than the 0.885 of nondirectional hedge funds, and than the 0.564 of the no category hedge funds.

RESULTS

Decile Analysis

Table 3.4 reports the result of the regression of hedge funds and funds of hedge funds against the FoF global index. Panel A of Table 3.4 indicates that all individual hedge fund deciles, except deciles Ind1, Ind2, Ind9, and Ind10, outperform the FoF index, as evidenced by negative intercepts (alpha). These results indicate that portfolios made up of the previous year's best- and worst-performing individual hedge funds, (the most volatile), underperform the FoF index. Underperformance is not significant, however, except for the subdecile Ind1.a, composed of the previous year's best-performing funds. Deciles Ind4 and Ind6 are the only ones that outperform the

TABLE 3.3 Correlation between Hedge Fund Categories, January 1994 to December 2002

	All Funds	FoF	FoF Niche	FoF Diversified	FoF Others	Individual HF	Directional	Nondirectional	No Category
All Funds	1								
Funds of Funds (FoF)	0.958	1							
FoF Niche	0.854	0.919	1						
FoF Diversified	0.960	0.999	0.904	1					
FoF Others	0.728	0.756	0.693	0.744	1				
Individual Hedge Funds	0.997	0.935	0.827	0.938	0.711	1			
Directional	0.990	0.920	0.812	0.924	0.680	0.995	1		
Nondirectional	0.916	0.885	0.807	0.884	0.733	0.912	0.866	1	
No Category	0.619	0.564	0.444	0.575	0.290	0.625	0.633	0.527	1

TABLE 3.4   Hedge Funds and Funds of Hedge Funds against the Fund of
Hedge Funds Global Index, January 1995 to December 2002

Panel A: Individual Hedge Fund Deciles					
Decile	Mean	Standard Deviation	Alpha	FoF Index	R^2_{adj}
Ind1	1.53%	5.37%	−0.69%	2.60***	0.74
Ind2	1.33%	3.74%	−0.26%	1.87***	0.78
Ind3	1.23%	2.77%	0.05%	1.39***	0.79
Ind4	1.22%	2.16%	0.26%***	1.12***	0.84
Ind5	1.16%	2.21%	0.22%	1.11***	0.79
Ind6	0.89%	1.46%	0.28%**	0.72***	0.76
Ind7	0.78%	1.45%	0.20%	0.68***	0.68
Ind8	0.87%	1.81%	0.17%	0.82***	0.65
Ind9	0.76%	2.56%	−0.08%	0.98***	0.45
Ind10	0.90%	3.91%	−0.19%	1.29***	0.33
Ind1a	1.47%	7.26%	−1.48%***	3.47***	0.72
Ind1b	1.62%	5.03%	−0.32%	2.29***	0.65
Ind1c	1.48%	4.46%	−0.28%	2.07***	0.67
Ind10a	0.90%	3.11%	0.08%	0.97***	0.30
Ind10b	0.53%	4.34%	−0.64%	1.37***	0.31
Ind10c	1.30%	5.17%	0.03%	1.50***	0.26

Panel B: Directional Hedge Fund Deciles					
Decile	Mean	Standard Deviation	Alpha	FoF Index	R^2_{adj}
D1	1.61%	6.27%	−1.01%**	3.07***	0.75
D2	1.33%	4.48%	−0.56%	2.23***	0.78
D3	1.30%	3.81%	−0.31%	1.89***	0.78
D4	1.15%	3.03%	−0.10%	1.47***	0.75
D5	1.27%	3.29%	−0.19%	1.71***	0.85
D6	1.08%	2.64%	−0.01%	1.28***	0.75
D7	0.80%	2.53%	−0.18%	1.15***	0.64
D8	0.75%	2.70%	−0.32%	1.26***	0.68
D9	0.66%	3.20%	−0.33%	1.16***	0.41
D10	0.82%	5.01%	−0.50%	1.54***	0.29
D1a	1.67%	8.90%	−1.93%**	4.24***	0.71
D1b	1.49%	6.06%	−0.86%*	2.76***	0.65
D1c	1.64%	4.93%	−0.27%	2.24***	0.65
D10a	0.86%	4.66%	−0.36%	1.44***	0.29
D10b	0.31%	4.84%	−0.99%**	1.52***	0.30
D10c	1.29%	6.84%	−0.18%	1.73***	0.19

*** Significant at the 1 percent level.
** Significant at the 5 percent level.
* Significant at the 10 percent level.

TABLE 3.4 *(continued)*

		Panel C: Nondirectional Hedge Fund Deciles			
Decile	Mean	Standard Deviation	Alpha	FOF Index	R^2_{adj}
ND1	1.59%	2.84%	0.50%*	1.28***	0.64
ND2	1.27%	1.93%	0.55%***	0.85***	0.60
ND3	1.10%	1.55%	0.51%***	0.69***	0.62
ND4	1.01%	1.27%	0.54%***	0.55***	0.59
ND5	0.98%	1.06%	0.59%***	0.46***	0.58
ND6	0.79%	1.00%	0.42%***	0.44***	0.60
ND7	0.77%	0.92%	0.46%***	0.37***	0.49
ND8	0.81%	0.93%	0.47%***	0.40***	0.58
ND9	0.94%	1.49%	0.48%***	0.54***	0.41
ND10	1.32%	2.94%	0.68%**	0.75***	0.20
ND1a	1.32%	4.47%	−0.08%	1.66***	0.43
ND1b	1.55%	2.74%	0.65%**	1.05***	0.46
ND1c	1.90%	2.71%	0.94%***	1.13***	0.54
ND10a	1.35%	4.69%	0.86%*	0.58***	0.04
ND10b	1.33%	2.82%	0.57%*	0.90***	0.31
ND10c	1.26%	3.82%	0.59%	0.79***	0.13

*** Significant at the 1 percent level.
** Significant at the 5 percent level.
* Significant at the 10 percent level.

global index in a significant way. All deciles are significantly and positively exposed to the global index. The R^2_{adj} obtained are particularly high for each decile, except for deciles Ind9, Ind10, and decile Ind10's subdeciles. This result is certainly due to the high dissolution frequencies across them, which lead to less stable returns compared to other deciles.

Panel B of Table 3.4 reports the same results for the directional hedge funds deciles. All decile portfolios have a negative intercept over the January 1995–December 2002 period considered, but alpha is significantly negative only for subdeciles D1a and D10b and for decile D1. This latter result indicates that a portfolio made up of the previous year's best-performing directional hedge funds significantly underperforms the funds of hedge funds industry as a whole. Another point is that, as was the case for the individual hedge funds deciles, all directional hedge funds deciles are significantly positively exposed to the global index. The R^2_{adj} obtained are also particularly high, the exceptions being the same as the previous panel.

Panel C of Table 3.4 yields very interesting results for nondirectional hedge funds deciles. The alphas indicate that all deciles except ND1a and ND10c are positively and significantly better performers than the global index and that all portfolio standard deviations are very low when compared to those of directional hedge fund deciles. It is also worth mentioning that, relative to the global FoF index, the best-performing decile portfolio is the tenth one, namely the portfolio made up of the previous year's worst-performing funds. The only underperformance we observe, namely for the ND1a subdecile, is not statistically significant. The betas indicate that each decile is also positively and significantly exposed to the index. The R^2_{adj} are lower than they were for the two previous hedge funds categories' deciles. They are below 0.55 for deciles ND7, ND9, ND10, and for all subdeciles.

We also rank funds of hedge funds in deciles each year, based on their previous year's performance. The description of these deciles has already been reported. It is an original way of dividing the funds of hedge funds global index into 10 smaller and more specific portfolios. We regressed each individual, directional, and nondirectional hedge funds' deciles against each funds of hedge funds deciles. This left us with 300 regressions, namely 100 for each of the three hedge fund categories. To make these results more meaningful, we have summarized them by three three-dimensional graphs, which appear in Figure 3.1.

The first graph reports the intercepts obtained when each individual hedge fund decile is regressed against each funds of hedge funds decile. The second and third graphs illustrate the intercepts for the directional and nondirectional hedge fund deciles, respectively. The table below each graph reports the significance level of each regression's alpha shown in the graph. Moreover, the cells of the table are colored in gray when the alpha is negative. The average alphas, betas, and R^2_{adj} obtained when a hedge funds decile is regressed against the 10 funds of hedge funds deciles are reported in the three last columns of these tables. We do not report significance level of the betas, since all hedge fund deciles are positively and significantly exposed to the funds of hedge funds deciles at the 5 percent level.

Panel A of Figure 3.1 illustrates the result of the regressions of individual hedge fund deciles against funds of hedge funds deciles. It indicates that, whatever the FoF decile against which the sixth individual hedge fund's decile is regressed, the alpha is positive, and in a significant way in 80 percent of the cases. These results suggest that decile Ind6, from the individual hedge fund portfolio, significantly outperforms funds of hedge funds, from the previous year's best-performing ones to the previous year's worst-performing ones. Also, the highest average alpha is obtained by regressing the Ind4 individual hedge fund portfolio against each FoF decile and by computing the average of the alphas obtained in these 10 equations. Moreover, the alphas obtained are always positive when we regress the Ind4 individual hedge fund portfolio against FoF deciles, except when regressed against the sixth FoF decile. This is also the case for fifth and the seventh individual hedge fund's deciles. Statistically, we can say that individual hedge funds deciles Ind4, Ind5, and Ind7 portfolios significantly overperform the three

Panel A: Results for the Individual Hedge Fund Deciles

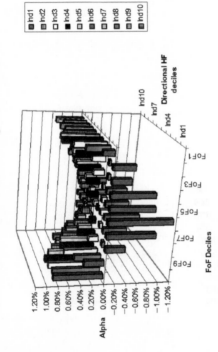

	FoF1	FoF2	FoF3	FoF4	FoF5	FoF6	FoF7	FoF8	FoF9	FoF10	average Alpha	average Beta	average R^2_{adj}
Ind1			*							*	−0.34%	2.240	0.605
Ind2	**		*							***	−0.02%	1.626	0.649
Ind3	***	*	***					**		***	0.22%	1.215	0.658
Ind4	***	***	***	**					***	***	0.38%	1.006	0.715
Ind5	***	**	**					*	***	***	0.33%	1.006	0.680
Ind6	***	**	***		*				***	***	0.35%	0.659	0.662
Ind7	***	**	**			*			**	***	0.27%	0.628	0.600
Ind8	***	**							*		0.25%	0.766	0.568
Ind9							**				0.01%	0.926	0.416
Ind10											−0.08%	1.223	0.321

FIGURE 3.1 Regression of Individual Hedge Funds Deciles against Funds of Hedge Funds Deciles

Panel B: Results for the Directional Hedge Fund Deciles

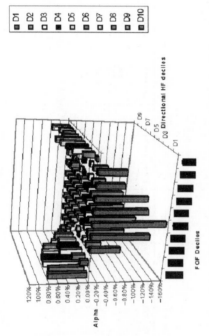

	FoF1	FoF2	FoF3	FoF4	FoF5	FoF6	FoF7	FoF8	FoF9	FoF10	average Alpha	average Beta	average R^2_{adj}
D1		**									−0.60%	2.655	0.6186
D2				*	**	**	**			**	−0.28%	1.937	0.6424
D3	*			*		*				**	−0.07%	1.648	0.6429
D4	**									***	0.08%	1.292	0.6215
D5	**				**	**				***	0.01%	1.525	0.7156
D6	**					**	***			***	0.13%	1.161	0.6363
D7						**	*	*		*	−0.07%	1.056	0.5576
D8						***	***	*			−0.20%	1.162	0.5949
D9						*	**				−0.21%	1.089	0.3710
D10						*	**				−0.35%	1.469	0.2881

FIGURE 3.1 *(continued)*

Panel C: Results for the Nondirectional Hedge Fund Deciles

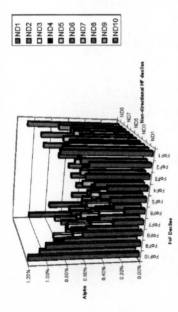

	FoF1	FoF2	FoF3	FoF4	FoF5	FoF6	FoF7	FoF8	FoF9	FoF10	average Alpha	average Beta	average R^2_{adj}
ND1	***	***	***	***	***			**	***	***	0.68%	1.112	0.523
ND2	***	***	***	***	**		***	***	***	***	0.64%	0.768	0.520
ND3	***	***	***	**	**		*	**	***	***	0.58%	0.638	0.548
ND4	***	***	***	***	***	***	***	***	***	***	0.58%	0.513	0.521
ND5	***	***	***	***	***	***	***	***	***	***	0.63%	0.429	0.514
ND6	***	***	***	***	***	**	**	***	***	***	0.46%	0.402	0.522
ND7	***	***	***	***	***	***	**	***	***	***	0.49%	0.345	0.445
ND8	***	***	***	***	**	***	***	***	***	***	0.50%	0.370	0.504
ND9	***	***	***	**	**	*	*	**	***	***	0.52%	0.519	0.379
ND10	***	***	***	**	**			*	**	***	0.74%	0.716	0.182

Legend: ND1, ND2, ND3, ND4, ND5, ND6, ND7, ND8, ND9, ND10

FIGURE 3.1 *(continued)*

This figure reports the alphas (and their significances) of the regressions from the individual hedge funds deciles (directional, nondirectional) to the funds of hedge funds deciles for the January 1995–December 2002 period. T-stats are heteroskedasticity consistent.

***Significant at the 1 percent level.

**Significant at 5 percent level.

*Significant at the 10 percent level. The last columns of each table report the average alpha, beta, and R^2_{adj} obtained when the hedge funds decile of the same line is regressed against funds of hedge funds deciles.

previous years' best-performing FoF portfolios and the two worst-performing ones. It is worth mentioning that three average alphas are negative. The most negative one is the average alpha of the 10 regressions of the first individual hedge fund's portfolios against each FoF decile, but the statistical significance at the 10 percent level is lacking in 60 percent of the cases. We consider the figure in the opposite way, namely by examining a particular FoF decile portfolio and looking at the alphas obtained when individual hedge fund's deciles are regressed against it. All alphas are positive, and significantly so in 70 percent of the cases, when we regress individual hedge fund's deciles against the first or the tenth funds of hedge funds decile. These results indicate that regardless of which portfolio made up of previous year's homogeneous-performing individual hedge funds is considered, it overperforms the best and the worst previous year's FoF deciles. The average R^2_{adj} figures in the table below the graphs show that the proportion of the individual hedge fund's deciles' variances explained by the regressions is relatively high, except for the ninth and the tenth individual funds portfolios, namely those in which the dissolution frequencies are highest.

Panel B of Figure 3.1 reports the regressions of directional hedge fund deciles against each funds of hedge funds decile. This graph speaks for itself. We can see from the graph and from cells colored in gray in the table below that the alphas are mostly negative, but that the directional hedge fund deciles' underperformance is statistically significant in less than one-third of the cases. The most negative average alpha is obtained from the average of the decile D1 directional hedge fund decile with FoF deciles' 10 equations. Moreover, the alpha obtained when the first directional hedge fund portfolio is regressed to a fund of hedge fund decile is always negative (except when regressed against the FoF1, FoF9, and FoF10 deciles). We obtain the same results with the portfolios of the second and the third directional hedge funds, but the statistical significance is stronger for the results of the first one. It is interesting to note that in terms of the number of negative alphas, the worst-performing directional hedge fund portfolios seem to be deciles D8 and D10, the alphas obtained when these two portfolios are regressed against FoF deciles being negative in 80 percent of the cases. Statistically, however, these results leave something to be desired. The best-performing directional hedge fund decile, in terms of the average alpha, when it is regressed against each FOF decile is the sixth one. Moreover, the intercepts obtained are positive when this directional hedge fund portfolio D6 is regressed against the three FoF best-performing and worst-performing portfolios, namely funds of hedge funds deciles FoF1, 2, 3, 8, 9 and 10, but these results are significant only for D1 and D10. We consider again the graph in the opposite way. Regardless of which directional hedge fund decile is regressed against the first and the tenth FoF deciles, the alpha obtained is positive (except when directional hedge fund decile D10 is regressed to the tenth FoF portfolio). Also, our built directional hedge funds portfolios underperform the previous year's middle-performer funds of hedge funds.

Panel C of Figure 3.1 reports the regressions of nondirectional hedge funds deciles against each funds of hedge funds decile. It indicates that all alphas are positive, regardless of which nondirectional hedge funds portfolio is compared to a fund of hedge funds decile. Moreover, the table below the graph indicates that this overperformance is statistically significant in more than 90 percent of the cases, which is striking compared to the previous results. The highest average alpha is obtained by the previous year's worst-performing nondirectional hedge fund portfolio, namely decile ND10. Statistically, however, the results are most significant for the middle deciles (ND4, ND5, ND6, ND7, and ND8). Finally, the average R^2_{adj} obtained are lower than those we obtained for individual and directional hedge funds deciles, indicating that the funds of hedge funds deciles cannot explain the same proportion of the returns of nondirectional hedge funds as they do for individual and directional hedge fund deciles.

HEDGE FUND DECILES AGAINST EACH EXISTING INDIVIDUAL FUNDS OF HEDGE FUNDS

Here our aim is to verify if the results obtained up to now are confirmed at the individual level. After having regressed each of our hedge fund portfolios against the FoF global index, we used the same process by taking our funds of hedge funds deciles as the independent variable in the equations. We regress each hedge fund's decile (individual, directional, and nondirectional) against each existing fund of hedge funds. Each decile is regressed against the 635 funds of hedge funds reporting returns during the January 1995 to December 2002 period. We do not report all the results obtained because we made 6,350 estimations per category. The results are summarized in Table 3.5.

The figures below the +, 0, and – in the alpha distributions indicate the percentage of regressions where alpha is significantly positive, not significantly different from zero, and significantly negative respectively, and that at a 5 percent level. The same convention applies for the beta coefficients. For information, we have also reported the mean alphas and betas obtained in each part of their distributions and in total, as well as the average R^2_{adj} obtained for each decile.

Panel A of Table 3.5 indicates that the first individual hedge fund's decile significantly outperforms 16 percent of existing funds of hedge funds over the period studied. This percentage increases as we turn to middle-decile portfolios, namely deciles Ind4, Ind5, and Ind6. Concerning the average alpha figures, they increase until the fourth decile and decrease

TABLE 3.5 Summary of the Regressions of Individual Hedge Fund Deciles against Individual Funds of Hedge Funds, January 1995 to December 2002

Panel A: Individual Hedge Fund Deciles Regressed against Each Existing FoF

	Average Return	S.D.	Alpha	Alpha Distribution			Beta	Beta Distribution			R^2_{adj}
				+	0	−		+	0	−	
Ind1	1.53%***	5.37%	0.38%	16%	83%	1%	1.653	73%	26%	1%	0.300
			Mean	1.58%	0.20%	−2.75%	Mean	2.096	0.509	−0.699	
Ind2	1.33%***	3.74%	0.51%	26%	73%	1%	1.157	74%	24%	1%	0.314
			Mean	1.13%	0.30%	−1.78%	Mean	1.441	0.370	−0.511	
Ind3	1.23%***	2.77%	0.57%	41%	58%	0%	0.868	76%	23%	1%	0.314
			Mean	0.96%	0.31%	−1.71%	Mean	1.056	0.313	−0.387	
Ind4	1.22%***	2.16%	0.65%	59%	40%	1%	0.733	80%	19%	1%	0.345
			Mean	0.89%	0.34%	−0.98%	Mean	0.865	0.227	−0.304	
Ind5	1.16%***	2.21%	0.58%	49%	50%	1%	0.708	77%	22%	1%	0.318
			Mean	0.92%	0.27%	−1.14%	Mean	0.867	0.200	−0.338	
Ind6	0.89%***	1.46%	0.50%	54%	45%	1%	0.511	78%	21%	1%	0.332
			Mean	0.72%	0.17%	−0.47%	Mean	0.602	0.195	−0.190	
Ind7	0.78%***	1.45%	0.30%	41%	56%	4%	0.473	77%	21%	1%	0.291
			Mean	0.75%	0.08%	−0.65%	Mean	0.564	0.180	−0.240	
Ind8	0.87%***	1.81%	0.30%	41%	56%	3%	0.589	76%	23%	1%	0.270
			Mean	0.78%	0.08%	−0.80%	Mean	0.688	0.287	−0.179	
Ind9	0.76%***	2.56%	0.10%	19%	75%	6%	0.763	70%	28%	2%	0.207
			Mean	1.08%	−0.05%	−1.42%	Mean	0.952	0.352	−0.362	
Ind10	0.90%**	3.91%	0.00%	14%	79%	7%	0.963	60%	38%	2%	0.158
			Mean	1.44%	−0.06%	−2.07%	Mean	1.351	0.428	−0.906	

TABLE 3.5 *(continued)*

Panel B: Directional Hedge Fund Deciles Regressed against Each Existing FoF

	Average Return	S.D.	Alpha	Alpha Distribution			Beta	Beta Distribution			R^2_{adj}
				+	0	−		+	0	−	
D1	1.61%**	6.27%	0.34%	10%	88%	2%	1.885	72%	26%	2%	0.296
			Mean	1.88%	0.22%	−2.74%	Mean	2.414	0.610	−1.055	
D2	1.33%***	4.48%	0.35%	16%	82%	2%	1.354	72%	26%	1%	0.307
			Mean	1.34%	0.20%	−2.02%	Mean	1.723	0.435	−0.562	
D3	1.30%***	3.81%	0.46%	24%	75%	1%	1.175	74%	25%	1%	0.313
			Mean	1.15%	0.27%	−1.74%	Mean	1.451	0.431	−0.528	
D4	1.15%***	3.03%	0.44%	28%	71%	1%	0.929	77%	22%	1%	0.294
			Mean	1.04%	0.23%	−1.38%	Mean	1.111	0.355	−0.437	
D5	1.27%***	3.29%	0.45%	27%	71%	1%	1.075	22%	76%	1%	0.341
			Mean	1.11%	0.24%	−1.37%	Mean	0.361	1.308	−0.423	
D6	1.08%***	2.64%	0.37%	29%	67%	4%	0.827	76%	23%	1%	0.305
			Mean	1.07%	0.15%	−1.01%	Mean	1.012	0.272	−0.410	
D7	0.80%***	2.53%	0.13%	18%	76%	6%	0.733	76%	23%	2%	0.260
			Mean	1.05%	0.01%	−1.05%	Mean	0.889	0.305	−0.517	
D8	0.75%***	2.70%	0.00%	15%	78%	8%	0.883	77%	22%	1%	0.278
			Mean	1.00%	−0.05%	−1.30%	Mean	1.044	0.409	−0.556	
D9	0.66%**	3.20%	−0.10%	13%	80%	7%	0.888	72%	27%	1%	0.189
			Mean	1.05%	−0.13%	−1.86%	Mean	1.077	0.448	−0.666	
D10	0.82%	5.01%	−0.23%	9%	82%	9%	1.116	53%	45%	2%	0.139
			Mean	1.78%	−0.18%	−2.72%	Mean	1.480	0.782	−1.122	

TABLE 3.5 *(continued)*

Panel C: Nondirectional Hedge Fund Deciles Regressed against Each Existing FoF

	Average Return	S.D.	Alpha	Alpha Distribution			Beta	Beta Distribution			R^2_{adj}
				+	0	–		+	0	–	
ND1	1.59%***	2.84%	0.86%	50%	50%	0%	0.970	71%	28%	1%	0.269
			Mean	1.35%	0.38%	-1.48%	Mean	1.178	0.488	-0.357	
ND2	1.27%***	1.93%	0.85%	76%	24%	0%	0.575	78%	21%	1%	0.273
			Mean	0.96%	0.49%	-0.71%	Mean	0.694	0.202	-0.594	
ND3	1.10%***	1.55%	0.70%	72%	28%	0%	0.507	77%	22%	1%	0.286
			Mean	0.85%	0.31%	-0.74%	Mean	0.609	0.181	-0.168	
ND4	1.01%***	1.27%	0.65%	80%	20%	0%	0.437	79%	20%	1%	0.283
			Mean	0.75%	0.25%	-0.53%	Mean	0.517	0.150	-0.154	
ND5	0.98%***	1.06%	0.66%	82%	18%	0%	0.333	23%	76%	1%	0.261
			Mean	0.75%	0.31%	-0.42%	Mean	0.092	0.415	-0.245	
ND6	0.79%***	1.00%	0.49%	71%	29%	0%	0.331	74%	25%	1%	0.282
			Mean	0.62%	0.18%	0.00%	Mean	0.416	0.097	-0.116	
ND7	0.77%***	0.92%	0.49%	68%	30%	2%	0.299	74%	25%	1%	0.220
			Mean	0.66%	0.17%	-0.45%	Mean	0.365	0.126	-0.119	
ND8	0.81%***	0.93%	0.48%	68%	31%	2%	0.326	75%	24%	1%	0.261
			Mean	0.68%	0.09%	-0.49%	Mean	0.398	0.119	-0.122	
ND9	0.94%***	1.49%	0.55%	58%	41%	0%	0.425	65%	34%	1%	0.192
			Mean	0.82%	0.19%	-0.46%	Mean	0.556	0.197	-0.132	
ND10	1.32%***	2.94%	0.68%	41%	57%	1%	0.664	66%	32%	1%	0.126
			Mean	1.39%	0.22%	-1.29%	Mean	0.826	0.367	-0.360	

afterward, but they remain always positive. The right side of panel A indicates that our deciles are rarely significantly negatively exposed to existing funds of hedge funds, a maximum 2 percent of the time for deciles Ind9 and Ind10. The average R^2_{adj} obtained lie between 0.150 and 0.345, the highest ones being those of middle-decile portfolios. As mentioned in Capocci (2004b), these figures may seem low, but R^2_{adj} are always lower for individual estimations than they are for indexes.

Panel B of Table 3.5 reports the summary of the results obtained when regressing each directional hedge fund's decile against each existing fund of hedge funds. Once again, the highest proportions of significantly positive alphas are observed for middle-decile portfolios, but those proportions are lower than those obtained by individual hedge fund's deciles. The average alphas are lower too, and also negative for deciles D9 and D10. The average R^2_{adj} remains relatively low, particularly for the worst-performing deciles. Negative decile exposure to existing funds of hedge funds can be observed in at most 2 percent of the time.

Panel C of Table 3.5 reports the same results for nondirectional hedge fund deciles. What is striking are the extremely high proportions of significantly positive alphas obtained compared with those obtained in the two previous categories. The highest proportions of positive alphas are observed for deciles ND4 and ND5, at more than 80 percent. The tenth decile is the only decile in which the proportion of insignificant alphas exceeds that of significantly positive alphas. Moreover, the average alphas are always higher than those of individual deciles. The proportion of significantly negative alphas and funds of hedge funds exposures remains very low. The R^2_{adj} are slightly lower than in the previous categories, but still higher for middle-decile portfolios.

CONCLUSION

This chapter focuses on the performance of funds of hedge funds. Its objective is to determine if momentum-constructed portfolios of hedge funds under- or overperform existing funds of hedge funds. We have analyzed this using the MAR database, which contains net of fee monthly returns on 2,247 individual hedge funds and 647 funds of hedge funds for the January 1994 to December 2002 period. We divided the hedge fund industry into two categories, directional versus nondirectional hedge funds, and further subdivided into nine individual hedge fund investment strategies.

Funds of hedge funds constitute a tenth investment strategy, which can be further divided, depending on whether the capital is allocated to a variety of individual fund types (diversified) or to a specific type of fund (niche). The fund of hedge funds industry is of great interest for investors. Not only do investors usually benefit from a lower minimum investment, making the hedge fund industry more accessible, but they take advantage of diversification without concerning themselves with manager selection or portfolio management. The disagreeable aspect is that the double fee structure undermines the net-of-fee returns.

The survivorship bias analysis points to a bias of 4.9 percent per year for the whole database. It is much higher for individual hedge funds (5.9 percent) than it is for funds of hedge funds (3.9 percent). This is, above all, due to the diversified funds of hedge funds. Inside the individual hedge funds category, the bias is lower for the nondirectional hedge funds category (4.5 and 1.5 percent) than it is for the directional one (7.3 and 2.7 percent). By the evolution of the three-year rolling period survivorship bias, we have shown that the survivorship bias is on average higher and less stable over time for individual hedge funds than for funds of hedge funds, the latter having the advantage of risk diversification that makes them less volatile. A relative stability is also present concerning the survivorship bias evolution of nondirectional funds, which by definition are less sensitive to market movements.

Our results indicate that despite their low standard deviation compared with their components, because of a poor monthly net-of-fee excess return, funds of hedge funds yield on average a lower Sharpe ratio. Accounting for risk, we find nondirectional hedge funds to be best.

We construct portfolios of hedge funds using the Carhart (1997) momentum decile classification to the individual, directional, and nondirectional hedge funds categories, but also to the funds of hedge funds category. Our results indicate that on the basis of the deciles' mean monthly returns, funds of hedge funds underperform all categories of individual hedge funds, the exceptions being in decile 6 and 7. The nondirectional decile portfolios always show the highest Sharpe ratio, regardless of the decile considered, mainly due to their low standard deviations. The alphas from our regressions indicated that almost all nondirectional hedge funds' deciles significantly outperform fund of funds, that all directional decile portfolios underperform the FoF global index but that these results are significant only for the first decile, and that only middle-decile individual hedge funds significantly outperform the index, but only subdecile Ind1a significantly underperforms it.

To refine these results, we regressed each individual hedge fund's decile against each funds of hedge funds decile. Our results indicated that, again, nondirectional hedge fund's deciles significantly outperform the funds of hedge funds deciles in 90 percent of the cases. The best individual hedge funds deciles are those in the middle. The alphas obtained by directional deciles are negative most of the time, but this underperformance is statistically significant in less than one-third of the cases. The directional hedge funds portfolio, made up of previous year's best-performing funds, namely decile 1, is the worst.

All nondirectional hedge fund deciles consistently and significantly out-perform existing funds of hedge funds, so it would be interesting for investors to build portfolios in this way. For directional and individual hedge funds, neither a contrarian nor a momentum strategy seems appro-priate in portfolio construction for beating existing funds of hedge funds, since the best deciles are those of the middle, namely the less volatile ones. Depending on the investor's underlying objective—to diversify the portfolio or to enhance existing returns—the best way of investing is through a port-folio of the previous year's best-performing directional funds, or funds of hedge funds, respectively.

The next step in analyzing performance of funds of hedge funds could be to apply our decile portfolio construction to individual strategies rather than to our three broad categories. In doing so, we would be able to deter-mine which components of each category, directional or nondirectional, really add value.

APPENDIX 3.1

Although the term "hedge fund" originated from the equally long and short strategy employed by managers like Alfred Winslow Jones, the new definition of hedge funds covers a multitude of different strategies. Database providers and other members of the industry generally define the same basic strategies. The MAR/Hedge database definitions of hedge fund types and subtypes are follow, but it should be noted that there is no industry standard.

Event-driven hedge funds profit from investment opportunities that arise when companies are facing events such as mergers, hostile takeovers, reorganizations, leveraged buyouts, share buybacks, or acquisitions. Dis-tressed securities take positions in corporate bankruptcies and reorganiza-tions, typically through bank debt and high-yield corporate bonds. Risk-arbitrage funds invest in announced mergers and acquisitions, usually by going long the equities of the targets and going short the equities of the acquirers. Merger arbitrage funds seeks to exploit the price disparity from merging companies, typically by taking a long position in the target com-pany and a short position in the acquirer.

Funds of hedge funds allocate capital among a number of hedge funds, providing investors with access to managers they might not be able to dis-cover or evaluate on their own. The mix of underlying strategies and funds can control returns, risk, and volatility. Diversified funds of funds allocate capital to a variety of fund types, while niche funds of funds allocate capi-tal to a specific type of fund. Other funds of funds are neither diversified nor niche.

The term *global funds* refers to a wide category of funds that invest in non-U.S. stocks and bonds. International funds pay attention to economic change around the world, but are more bottom-up oriented in that managers tend to be stock-pickers in markets they favor. Emerging market funds invest in equity or debt of less mature financial markets, which tend to have higher inflation and volatile growth, such as Hong Kong, Singapore, Pakistan, and India. Regional funds focus on specific regions of the world, such as Latin America, Asia, Europe.

The term *global macro funds* commonly refers to those funds that rely on macroeconomic analysis to take bets on the major risk factors, such as currencies, interest rates, stock indices, and commodities. These funds make extensive use of leverage and derivatives, and are usually responsible for most media attention. They include George Soros's Quantum Fund and Julian Robertson's Tiger Fund.

Long-only leveraged funds are traditional equity funds structured like hedge funds. They use leverage and permit their manager to collect an incentive fee.

Market-neutral funds actively seek to avoid major risk factors, but take bets on relative price movements using various strategies. Long/short equity funds use the classic A. W. Jones model of hedge funds, taking long and short positions in equities to limit their exposures to the stock market. Stock index arbitrage funds trade the spread between index futures contracts and the underlying basket of equities. Convertible arbitrage funds buy undervalued convertibles and hedge the position with a short position in the underlying stocks. Fixed income arbitrage funds exploit pricing anomalies in the global fixed income market.

Sector funds are those for which specialists follow specific economic sectors and industries. Their managers use a wide range of methodologies, such as bottom-up, top-down, discretionary, and technical, and a wide range of primary focus, such as large cap, mid cap, micro cap, value growth, and opportunistic.

Short sellers always have a short net position. Managers sell securities short in anticipation of being able to repurchase them at a future date at a lower price. This strategy is also used as a hedge to offset long-only portfolios and by managers who feel that the market is approaching a bearish cycle.

U.S. opportunistic funds are broken into three categories. Value funds focus on assets, cash flow, book value, and out-of-favor stocks. Growth funds invest in growth stocks. Revenues, earnings, and growth potential are key determinants for these managers. Short-term fund manager holds positions for a short time frame only.

No-category funds are those with no stated strategy and funds whose strategy does not correspond to any of the just-listed classifications.

CHAPTER 4

Analyzing Style Drift in Hedge Funds

Nolke Posthuma and Pieter Jelle Van der Sluis

Once you have decided to invest in hedge funds, the main questions are what percentage of the portfolio to allocate to hedge funds and how to construct an optimal portfolio of hedge funds. This issue is often first approached in terms of hedge fund styles instead of individual hedge funds. Knowledge about expected returns and risks combined with dependencies between styles allows one to construct an optimal portfolio of hedge fund styles. Hedge fund styles can be decomposed into various risk premiums. For equities, Fama and French identified two additional risk premiums: the small cap and the value premium. Carhart suggested adding a momentum factor to the model. Today hedge fund researchers attempt to do the same for hedge funds. They model hedge fund styles using factors that proxy credit, liquidity, and insurance premiums. It is suggested that the traditional Fama-French-Carhart factors in combination with some alternative risk premiums are able to explain a large part of hedge fund style returns. By estimating the style exposures to risk factors, one can forecast return and risk characteristics and construct better portfolios. Due to the institutional setup of hedge funds, the style of a particular fund is often unclear. Styles as reported to hedge fund databases or in a prospectus are self-declared by the hedge fund manager. This raises questions on reliability of such a style

---

The views expressed in this chapter are those of the authors and do not necessarily reflect those of our employer and colleagues.

label. Moreover, it is known that hedge funds are opportunity driven and therefore change style over time. A first check of the reliability of the self-assigned style label can be done by Sharpe's return-based style analysis (RBSA). This method has long been used for mutual funds and has recently been applied to hedge funds as well. The drawback of the standard RBSA method is the fact that it cannot deal with the style drift mentioned earlier. That is, the style exposures are assumed to be fixed over time. To overcome this issue, it has been proposed to use rolling regressions instead. However, because the choice of the length of the rolling regression period is subjective and ad hoc and because there are other conceptual problems, we use a more dynamic model that was introduced by one of the authors of this chapter in the context of mutual funds (Swinkels and Van der Sluis 2001). Here we apply this method to the world of hedge funds, where we think it is even more appropriate. Style drift is more severe and the style of the hedge fund is much more opaque than in the case of mutual funds. Our method can be used in several ways. One way is to analyze styles on basis of historical returns from hedge fund databases. This may be useful to identify style changes in response to changing market conditions or to identify interesting hedge fund managers from a database. Another way is to track in real time the style of a particular hedge fund that is in the investor's portfolio. This is useful for a fund of funds manager who wants to keep a certain style allocation over time. Furthermore, estimates of the value at risk can be made more precise and manager structure optimization can be better executed if we are better able to incorporate style drift in the process.

INTRODUCTION

Returns that hedge funds offer are attractive for investors, due to the diversification benefits, and regardless of whether those returns come from carry trading or from the genius of a hedge fund manager. Once it is decided to invest in hedge funds, the first question is how much of the portfolio should be allocated to hedge funds. This issue is not dealt with here but is covered in Amin and Kat (2003b) and Till (2004a), among others. Researchers have documented percentage allocation ranging from 0 percent to 100 percent. The next question is how to create an optimal portfolio of hedge funds. To answer this requires intimate knowledge of the distribution of other assets in the portfolio and the objectives of the investor. As in other areas of portfolio choice, a decomposition of the assets into factors may be of help. Hedge funds can be decomposed in several factors or styles. These factors are located on several risk dimensions of the investment universe. The traditional risk dimensions are equity risk and term spread premiums. Many alternative premiums have been unveiled recently. The bulk of hedge fund returns can be explained by a combination of the traditional and alternative risk premiums. The search for new drivers continues, which should perhaps result in explanation of even more hedge fund returns. Exposure to one of these risk premiums is often called beta. Beta requires no timing or selection skill, but it still requires a fair amount of implementation skill. Alpha, however, is the product of timing and selection skills. Alpha is a scarce good and can be systematically delivered only by the sharpest minds of Wall Street. We believe one should not be obsessed with the alpha, but also value the merits of the alternative betas hedge funds offer. The alternative risk premiums are based on insurance premiums for various risks and a liquidity premium other market participants are willing to pay. Alternative premiums were available through traditional investments only to a small extent. The diversification benefits of adding these alternative risk premiums to an existing traditional portfolio can be huge.

Since the exposures of individual hedge funds and hedge funds style groups change over time to a much higher degree than most other asset classes, we need to adequately measure these changes. One of the authors of this chapter has proposed an adaptive method for dealing with this problem in the context of mutual funds. Swinkels and Van der Sluis (2001) discuss how accounting for time variation in style exposures using rolling regressions is flawed. Because rolling regressions are inefficient due to their ad hoc chosen window size, they propose instead to use the Kalman filter to model time-varying exposures of mutual funds explicitly. This leads to a testable model and more efficient use of the data, because influence of spurious correlation between mutual fund returns and style indices is reduced. Several stylized examples indicate that more reliable style estimates can be obtained by modeling the style exposure as a random walk and estimating the coefficients with the Kalman filter. The differences with traditional techniques are substantial in their stylized examples. The results from their empirical analyses indicate that the dynamic model estimated by the Kalman filter improves style predictions and influences results on performance measurement.

HEDGE FUND INVESTMENT STYLES

There is a vast literature on how to classify hedge funds into styles. Hedge funds use various trading strategies, each having different risk and return characteristics and exposures to traditional asset classes (e.g., equity) that vary strongly from negative to positive. Hedge funds have been labeled and categorized by managers, database vendors, and academics. Because there is no universal style classification, the classifications vary by database vendor. A style classification in a database is often self-assigned. We have found numerous examples of misclassified hedge funds. This does not mean the classification is intentionally wrong. Due to their regulatory freedom, hedge funds are not bound to specific asset classes, a fact that leads hedge funds to invest in a variety of asset classes. Substantial differences between trading strategies of individual managers result in specific risk, return, and correlation patterns.

Classifications can be made with qualitative and quantitative methods. The qualitative method classification type uses characteristics. Examples of characteristics are geographic areas, the balance of long and short positions, the type of asset classes, the degree of systematic trading, and the type of opportunities that are exploited. Quantitative classification can be based on returns and/or holdings. Most risk systems estimate portfolio risk by aggregating all investment holdings. By aggregating the attributes of stocks, such as market cap and region, one can classify the portfolio on size and geographical focus. Performance evaluation based on portfolio holdings can give the most detailed information on attributes. Holdings-based analysis, however, uses information of one single point in time. If portfolio managers do not change holdings, the holdings-based snapshot is useful going forward. However, hedge fund managers add value by active management of positions. It requires more thought to incorporate nonlinear assets and dynamic trading strategies, such as options, into performance evaluation (Glosten and Jagannathan 1994). Managers can also influence reporting quite easily. This problem is called window-dressing; fund managers sell strategically just before the holdings report date. Therefore, we use return-based analysis in which returns are constructed using two points in time. Returns will not only reflect the buy and hold performance, but also performance stemming from the trading strategy activities. Furthermore, window-dressing will not add value to the manager. It probably would lead to lower performance due to costs of the selling before and buying after reporting. Return-based style analysis gives insight in the relationship of hedge fund returns with investment style returns. In this chapter these investment style returns are either buy and hold or dynamic trading strategy returns. The large number of possible investment styles and the relatively small periods of hedge fund returns complicate matters. The model structure is of vital importance for inference. We therefore should choose a parsimonious model. Clues on which factors to use can be found in the style descriptions. If an investor invests in a hedge fund, one should obtain additional information from the hedge fund manager to implement into the model building process.

We briefly define the style classifications and terminology of hedge funds investment styles. We follow the standard classification in relative value and directional strategies. Relative value styles are styles that try to eliminate traditional risks, such as market risk, and try to create value by diversified arbitrage opportunities, such as pairs trading. This type of strategy holds long and short positions at the same time. The returns usually display low volatility and low exposures to the traditional risk premiums. Directional strategies bet on the direction of the market dynamically. These strategies usually hold long or short positions. The long and short positions change over time dynamically. The returns of these strategies have higher volatility and high exposures to the traditional risk premiums. However, when these exposures are measured over a longer horizon, they may be close to zero, because long and short positions may cancel out.

Relative Value

Managers who primarily exploit mispricings between related securities are called relative value managers. As argued earlier, these funds take on directional bets on more alternative risk premiums, while hedging out the more traditional ones. Many relative value strategies can be found in the following substyles.

Long/Short Equity Strategies   This strategies include stock selection, timing, pairs trading, sector rotation, and alternative equity risk premium strategies. For instance, value and small stocks are perceived to carry a specific risk premium for financial distress, which could be exploited. Most long/short strategies have an exposure to the equity market between 0 percent and 100 percent of capital. A special case is *statistical arbitrage,* which is more quantitative than long/short equity. Statistical arbitrage would look more at short-term supply-demand anomalies, whereas long/short equity would also look at valuations, accounting, synergies, and hidden assets. An example of statistical arbitrage is to buy short-term losers and sell short-term winners, hence providing liquidity to other trend-following investors. The portfolios are matched in the sense that the long and short portfolios are of the same size. Hedge funds of this style often try to be cash and/or beta neutral. The sophisticated ones try to control their portfolios on other risk factors in the markets, such as sectors, value, and market capitalization.

Dedicated Short and Equity Market Neutral   In these other equity trading styles, major differences are the amount of equity market exposure. A dedicated short manager attempts to have a negative exposure to the market. An equity market neutral manager attempts to eliminate exposure to the equity market. In general, equity market neutral is more quantitative than long/short equity and has a longer horizon than statistical arbitrage.

Emerging Market   Investing in equity and fixed income securities in emerging markets could deliver returns different from those obtained by investing in developed markets. Market inefficiencies are potentially larger due to less coverage by analysts, lower transparency, less developed investors, different market structures, and government influence. Emerging market hedge fund managers attempt to exploit these opportunities. These hedge funds assume geopolitical and market distress risks, but may also exploit relative mispricings in the emerging markets, similar to long/short equity.

Fixed Income Arbitrage   This category includes bond selection, yield curve timing, term structure arbitrage, and exploiting liquidity and default premiums. Carry trades, whereby long-term bonds are bought and short-term bonds are sold, and swap-spread trades are especially popular among many hedge funds. Variants are the *Asian carry trade* and *gold carry trade*. A simple example of an Asian carry trade is to borrow money in Japan in the local currency and lend in longer-dated assets, for example, Hungarian Treasury bills. In the gold carry trade, gold is leased and then sold in the market. The proceeds are then again invested in longer-dated riskier assets. Most money invested in securities is invested in fixed income securities. These vast markets are influenced by the deliberate deflationary short rate manipulation by governments and central bank politics.

Event Driven   This style classification is reserved for managers who attempt to benefit from events, such as mergers, takeovers, reorganizations, and changes in financial structures. Often a separate style classification is used for *merger arbitrage funds*. These funds systematically sell the bidder and buy the takeover target. The bidder offers a price for the target above the market value. If the merger succeeds, a premium is collected. These hedge funds typically provide insurance against deal break. Another subset of event-driven strategies is *distressed/high yield*. A specific event is a firm becoming financially distressed. Financial distress causes institutions such as banks and regulators to impose restrictions. Banks have larger capital requirements for noninvestment-grade compared to investment-grade loans. Basel II requirements have induced even more limitations on banks to supply capital to distressed firms. The regulatory freedom of hedge funds places managers in a superior position to benefit from investing in distressed firms. This particular event-driven style is called *distressed debt* or *regulation D*. Regulation D of the Securities Exchange Commission allows public firms to sell shares privately to a limited number of accredited investors without formal registration. These shares are usually sold at a discount. The intention of the legislation is to help distressed firms acquire capital and become healthy again. Not all investors act in the spirit of the law. Managers lock in a spread by simultaneously buying the convertible and shorting the stock. Moreover, there is substantial freedom in structuring private equity investments in distressed firms. Structures include *floating rate convertible preferred stock, convertible resets, common stock resets,* and *structured equity lines.* Investors usually negotiate some form of downside protection. Shorting the common stock results in receiving a put option plus a premium, so managers benefit from further distress.

Convertible Arbitrage　　This is another important relative value type strategy that was popular during the 1990s. Convertible bonds can be decomposed in an equity option and a bond. Firms that issue convertibles are often perceived as being more risky than average. Issuing straight bonds would be too expensive, and issuing equity could be unsuccessful for these firms. The convertible is a bond with a relatively low yield, and equity is diluted only if the firm is successful. Convertibles can be cheap relative to the equity or the debt components. Basically, the differences in volatilities of the debt and the equity part, or of the credit spreads, are exploited. Hedge funds are in an excellent position to profit from these arbitrage opportunities. They usually would be long the embedded option from the convertibles and hedge these with the stock.

Equity Debt Arbitrage　　These managers attempt to exploit mispricings between a firm's debt and its equity. High-yield and credit default swaps are fixed income investments with an equity risk part. This equity risk part can be hedged, and if the fixed income market prices the risk differently from the equity market, a premium can be obtained. Hedge funds increasingly exploit the theoretical relationship between the firm's equity and the credit default swap (CDS). If market quotes differ from the theoretical relationships, these hedge funds take positions. They buy or sell a company's CDS and dynamically delta hedge this position with the company's equity or bond. Another name for equity debt arbitrage is *capital structure arbitrage.* This name is sometimes also used to identify the group of *distressed debt, convertible arbitrage,* and equity-debt arbitrage.

Directional Strategies

These styles take directional bets on the more traditional assets such as equity, currencies, and commodities. There are three substyles of directional strategies: global/macro, managed futures, and fixed income directional and equity directional.

Global/Macro　　The macroeconomic status and politics can have substantial impact on fixed income, foreign exchange, and commodity markets. Global macro managers attempt to exploit macroeconomic mispricings. A famous example of a global macro trader is George Soros, who made a fortune attacking the British pound in 1992, forcing it to devaluate below the European Monetary System exchange rate bound. Global macro traders tend to take leveraged directional bets. Exposure to capital markets typically exceeds their capital base, which makes these funds quite volatile. Global macro traders often use forwards and futures.

Managed Futures   Some managers predominantly trade futures. Futures on major market indices, interest rate products, and commodities are most of the time highly liquid and easy to trade. Next to fundamental (macroeconomic) indicators, many traders use indicators for market sentiment and attempt to exploit patterns in prices and volatilities, which is called technical analysis. A trader could further use a judgmental or a systematic approach. Fundamental traders often use judgment, while technical traders (also called commodity trading advisors) use a more rigid trading model. Managers who apply mixtures of these trading styles and select which markets to trade on are labeled discretionary. These strategies can be classified as trend following.

Fixed Income Directional and Equity Directional   These styles take a directional fixed income and equity position and attempt to add some extra return by adding alpha or some risk premiums.

Fund of Funds

Funds of funds are funds of hedge funds. Large institutional investors have the resources to obtain knowledge and operations necessary for direct hedge fund investing and are able to construct diversified portfolios of hedge funds. Funds of funds are invented to deliver smaller investors exposure to diversified portfolios of hedge funds. For their expertise in selecting managers, fund of funds charge fees in excess of the fees paid to underlying hedge funds, resulting in higher fees. The investor pays a management and performance fee first to the individual hedge funds and second to the fund of fund manager. Often the fund of funds itself is regulated, but the funds it invests in are not. A variant is the multistrategy funds, which have different investment styles, managed by the same organization. The advantage of a multistrategy over a fund of funds is a more dynamical allocation among the different strategies.

We conclude that hedge fund strategies are diverse. Hedge funds can apply multiple styles or strategies simultaneously. Diversification over different styles does not necessarily protect investors in market turmoil.

FACTOR MODELS FOR HEDGE FUNDS

Modern portfolio theory offers the capital asset pricing model (CAPM) and the arbitrage pricing theory (APT). Academics and practitioners in the traditional world of equities and bonds have used these models for a long time. For example, in equities the so-called Fama-French model is used in most empirical asset pricing work (Fama and French 1993). In this model the factors are the market, the spread between small- and large-capitalization stocks, and the spread between value and growth stocks. The Fama-French model was extended by Carhart's momentum factor, which is the spread between 12-month winners and 12-month losers (Carhart 1997). In fixed income these factors are usually a parallel shift, steepness and convexity of the yield curve, and the credit spread. In all these models the relation between risk and return is linear. This is a too-tight constraint in the world of hedge funds, where dynamic trading strategies and derivatives are frequently used. These type of strategies give rise to nonlinear relations between risk and return. We need factors that exhibit these nonlinear payoffs. Before we will discuss the type of factor models that have been proposed, we first discuss the model. The model (equation 4.1) can be written as:

$$R_t = \alpha + \sum_{k=1}^{k} \beta_k F_{k,t} + \varepsilon_t \tag{4.1}$$

where R_t = return on a hedge fund at time t
 K = number of factors
 $F_{k,t}$ = return on factor k at time t
 β_k = fund's exposure to factor k
 α = unexplained systematic part of the return
 ε_t = error term, which has expectation zero

Modern portfolio theory teaches us to separate idiosyncratic and systematic risks. The pure active (idiosyncratic) risk is the volatility of the alpha. We can measure the alpha by using the factor model. In this framework, the selection of alpha is independent of the selection of the beta, since the two are independent by construction. This gives rise to a two-step optimization problem. First, the investor determines the right mix of hedge fund betas. Conditional on this choice, the investor can do another optimization where each hedge fund beta is staffed with managers. Research suggests that within a style, at least five managers are needed to diversify away idiosyncratic risk. Of course we want to pick the best manager in each style. The factor models can be used to measure the skill of a manager. This is similar to the Jensen's alpha from the CAPM. We can measure the alpha with respect to the asset-based factors or relative to the peer group–based factors. The active risk is the standard deviation of the error term in the factor model. This error term should be idiosyncratic to the hedge fund manager. This means that the error term should be independent over time and independent of other hedge funds managers. It should also be normally distributed, because if all the noise is idiosyncratic, there should be some form of the central limit theorem at work. If independence and normality are not observed, factors are probably missing from the model.

Researchers have followed three different avenues in defining the factors $F_{k,i}$: Peer group–based factors, return-based factors, and asset-based factors.

Peer Group–based Factors   Lhabitant (2001) proposes to use peer group–based factors, that is, hedge fund indices (e.g., the Hedge Fund Research Index [HFRI] or the Credit Suisse First Boston/Tremont [CSFB/Tremont] hedge fund [style] indices). The problem is that the classification of funds over different databases is not consistent. Moreover, there is the problem of style drift in individual hedge funds. As a consequence, an index may not represent a homogeneous group of funds. Furthermore, the hedge fund indices do not provide information about the underlying fundamental processes. They just show how markets react under normal circumstances. Another problem is the short history available and the biases in the underlying hedge fund data (see Posthuma and Van der Sluis 2004). The peer group analysis is useful for measuring performance relative to peers or to detect style drift.

Returns-based Factors   This method is based on applying statistical methods to a hedge funds database. The returns are clustered by some distance measure, so that a correlation or a *principal components* technique is applied. One advantage is that the method is adaptive, so that the style drift of a fund is automatically taken into account. The outcome of such an analysis is a group of the funds that are correlated with each other. Empirical analysis, shows that the number of common factors ranges from five to nine. One common drawback is that the method is prone to noise fitting. As in the peer group analysis, the short data history and the biases in the data sets are other drawbacks. The interpretation of the factors may also be cumbersome. For an overview of this method, see Brown and Goetzmann (2003).

Asset-based Factors   An asset-based factor is the returns to a replication strategy that systematically follows a certain investment strategy. This approach underlies the Fama-French model. For example, we can form a strategy that systematically follows a carry trade, by shorting short-term Treasury bills and buying long-term strategies. Another example is to systematically buy the acquired and sell the acquirer, mimicking *merger arbitrage;* see Mitchell and Pulvino (2001). Researchers have found that option-type strategies are an important determinant in explaining the variation in hedge fund returns because any dynamic trading strategy employed by a leveraged investor with stop-loss rules displays asymmetric returns. Since the data that are needed for the replicating portfolio are not limited to the history of a particular hedge fund database, asset-based factors allow for a much longer history than the history of hedge funds. Asset-based factors bring insight to the underlying fundamentals. Furthermore, the construction of the factors is independent of the hedge fund returns, which has important theoretical advantages.

We first need to identify the risk and returns drivers of an individual hedge fund. If the exposure of the fund to these risk and returns drivers is stable over time, we can resort to the traditional factor approach to allocation. There are at least two extra difficulties with this approach in hedge funds.

1. Since hedge funds use nontraditional assets and nontraditional instruments, there are many potential factors.
2. Since hedge funds are active investors who employ dynamic trading strategies and are opportunity driven, it is likely they change style more often than traditional money managers.

Factors should be mutually exclusive and exhaustive. "Exhaustive" means that all aspects of the fund should be covered. "Mutually exclusive" means that the factors should not have overlapping return patterns. Overlapping factors could give rise to estimation problems, such as multi-collinearity. Statistical procedures could be used to construct orthogonal factors. Principal components analysis is one way to create orthogonal factors. However, one of the drawbacks of principal components is in their interpretation. The principal component factors are linear combinations of the possible factors, which can be difficult to interpret. Another issue is the rotation of the principal components, since it is possible to apply principal component analysis on different combinations of factors. Due to the interpretation and rotation problems, we opt for the asset-based factors and peer group–based factors. We use only combinations of factors that are at most moderately correlated. Track records of most hedge funds are short and consist of monthly returns. This limits the number of factors that can be included. Randomly picking factors is risky. In choosing the factors, one should also employ some qualitative information about the fund.

A line of research from Agarwal and Naik (2004) and Fung and Hsieh (2001, 2002 a,c) shows how to decompose the hedge fund returns into factor returns. Mainly using asset-based factors, researchers have found exposures to (lagged) equity markets, volatility, credit spreads, the term spread, and option trading strategies. The reported fit of these models (i.e., the R^2) is rather good. Agarwal and Naik used so-called location factors, which are buy and hold investments in traditional instruments such as equity, and bonds to explain hedge fund returns. They added so-called strategy factors, which are returns of dynamic trading strategies. Options can be replicated by dynamically trading the underlying. Dynamic trading rules also can be replicated with options. Therefore, we can view a hedge fund as a portfolio of options. For example, convertible bond arbitrage is similar to a long option. Trend-following strategies, such as managed futures, are long a straddle. A straddle corresponds to buying a put and a call. The holder of the straddle benefits if the underlying moves significantly. It turns out that strategies such as writing monthly out-of-the-money put options on the Standard & Poor's (S&P) 500 explain a large part of the variation in returns of event-driven hedge fund styles. High-yield bonds and emerging market equity and debt are other risk factors on which the event-driven style loads. The convertible arbitrage style can be explained for a significant part by holding (high-yield) bonds, emerging market bonds, and shorting equity. The Carhart momentum factor combined with the traditional Fama-French factors are able to explain most of the long/short equity returns. The amount of variation in returns explained by Fama-French factors, which are very well-known trading strategies, is surprising. Two other well-known strategies are the simple and Asian carry trade. The simple carry trade is often defined by holding long-term government bonds and shorting Treasury bills. The Asian carry trade was constructed by borrowing cheap money in Japan and investing the proceeds in high-yield U.S. investments (e.g., high-yield bonds). The momentum factor, emerging market equity, the Asian and simple carry trade explain a significant part of the global macro returns. Fung and Hsieh explain returns of global macro and managed futures hedge funds with lookback straddles. Asian and simple carry strategies are also present within the fixed income arbitrage style. This style is further explained by mortgage-backed securities and credit spreads.

The nonlinear relationship with underlying markets and the nonnormality of returns have important implications for performance attribution and risk management. Coskewness and cokurtosis between risk premium factors induces phase-locking crash events, such as the liquidity crisis in September 1998 (Lo 2001). The underlying fundamental factor of many strategies is providing insurance and liquidity for risks that other investors fear. We believe that the excess return over investable asset-based factors is a measure that gives better insight in the capabilities of hedge fund managers than absolute returns.

ADAPTIVE STYLE ANALYSIS

The eyes of a predator could be the eyes on the wings of a butterfly. What you see is not necessarily what you get. Managers sometimes change investment style or misclassify themselves, which results in investors being unaware about changing risks. Asset liability management and portfolio construction based on wrongly perceived risk-return patterns could lead to dangerous suboptimal portfolios. Since hedge funds are opportunistic in nature, adherence to a stated investment style may not always hold true in the world of hedge funds, where secrecy and flexibility are key. Hedge funds are predominantly composed of a flexible staff that can swiftly take advantage of market opportunities. There are recurring concerns about the risk posture and risk tolerance of hedge funds over time. This phenomenon is known as style drift. This is a major concern because hedge funds typically have a three-year lockup period. Only against high costs with sufficient advance notice can money be withdrawn from the hedge fund during the lockup period. This makes hedge funds investing more challenging than traditional investing. The investor buys a three-year note in an asset, which can change colors completely. Style drift causes a mismatch risk in the asset allocation process. An investor may have a carefully designed portfolio of hedge funds where the allocation is based on several style factors. It is also important for a fund of funds (FoF) manager to mitigate the impact of a single manager blowup. The FoF manager will therefore diversify across and within styles. Style drift of an individual manager will cause over- and underdiversification across and within styles and inefficient use of the risk budget. To detect style drift, one can demand full position transparency from the hedge fund and have the resources to distill relevant information from these positions. It is also possible to use techniques such as style analysis in which return of the hedge fund is compared to the asset-based or peer-group factors by means of regression. Changes in the coefficients indicate style drift. This is an important aspect of hedge fund modeling that must be dealt with adequately. In this chapter we develop such a procedure. We build on the seminal work on return-based style analysis (RBSA) of Sharpe (1992). Sharpe's framework can be seen as a multifactor extension of the Jensen (1968) single-factor model. It decomposes portfolio returns into style and skill. Style is the part of the returns that can be attributed to market movements. For hedge funds, the "market" should be defined in a broad sense. Skill is idiosyncratic to the manager.

Sharpe's RBSA model (equation 4.2) can be written as a factor model

$$R_t = \alpha + \sum_{k=1}^{k} \beta_k F_{k,t} + \varepsilon_t \qquad (4.2)$$

with constraints $\sum_{k=1}^{k} \beta_k = 1$ and $\beta_k \geq 0$,

where R_t = return on a hedge fund at time t
K = number of factors
$F_{k,t}$ = return on factor k at time t
β_k = fund's exposure to factor k
α = unexplained systematic part of the return
ε_t = error term, which has expectation zero

Sharpe's RBSA model (equation 4.2) can be written as a factor model with constraints:

In the case of hedge funds, the factors $F_{k,t}$ can be asset-based factors and the traditional assets, such as equity and bonds. The constant term α measures manager skill conditional on the traditional assets. The advantages are a bifurcation of the alphas and betas.

The imposed restrictions on the betas are obsolete in many applications. Hedge funds are allowed to maintain short positions and use leverage to increase absolute returns. The application to hedge funds is straightforward and has been shown useful by many authors. In its original form, the exposures are fixed over time and estimated by means of regression or quadratic optimization. Researchers in the mutual fund literature subsequently adopted a rolling regression approach to overcome the style drift. Swinkels and Van der Sluis (2001) scrutinized the rolling regression approach. They developed a superior technique, which does not suffer from the critique. Their technique is adaptive in the sense that changes in the style exposures are picked up automatically from the data. Their method is illustrated for mutual funds. We realized later that this approach was in fact much more powerful for hedge funds. For some time now we have used these tools in our practice to analyze hedge funds. The applicability of our tools was also noticed by Lhabitant (2004, pp. 227–228) in his excellent hedge fund book, from which we quote: "The Kalman filter had originally no particular link with finance. It is only recently that Swinkels and Van der Sluis (2001) suggested applying it to a dynamic model of style analysis."

We first briefly summarize the model of Swinkels and Van der Sluis here. In their paper they adapt the Sharpe model (equation 4.3) by dropping the restrictions and allowing the beta to vary through time:

$$R_t = \alpha + \sum_{k=1}^{k} \beta_{k,t} F_{k,t} + \varepsilon_t \qquad (4.3)$$

$$\beta_{k,t} = \beta_{k,t-1} + \eta_{k,t}$$

Here ε_t and $\eta_{k,t}$ are normally and identically distributed with variance σ_ε^2 and $\sigma_{\eta,k}^2$ respectively. Note that the betas are following a random walk. Unlike the ad hoc rolling regression approach, the time variation in the exposures is explicitly modeled. Simulations in Swinkels and Van der Sluis (2001) show that the random-walk model for beta is fairly robust to misspecification. For example, a sudden style change or block-wave type of exposure are picked up fairly well, although the random-walk model is misspecified here. As in Agarwal and Naik (2000a) to allow for short positions and leverage, no restrictions are imposed on the betas. This model is a statespace model and can be estimated by using standard Kalman filter techniques. No window size of ad hoc chosen length need be used. The Kalman filter procedure chooses the optimal weighting scheme directly from the data. The filter is an adaptive system based on the measurement and updating equations. The time update equations project forward (a priori update). The measurement update equations receive the feedback (a posteriori update). The betas are determined by the Kalman filter procedure. We usually estimate the parameters σ_ε^2 and $\sigma_{\eta,k}^2$ by maximum likelihood, but they can also be prespecified by the user. The statistical properties are well known and model specification tests are well defined. In this chapter we use a straightforward generalization of the R^2 to the dynamic model as our goodness-of-fit statistic. We define R^2 as the percentage of variance of the dependent variable that is explained by the model, that is, $R^2 = 1 - \dfrac{\text{var}(\varepsilon)}{\text{var}(R)}$.
In the case $R^2 = 1$, there is no tracking error, and the style factors fit perfectly. The number $1 - R^2$ can be used as an indicator of the level of active management. This is only valid when the model is correctly specified. An incomplete or inadequate set of factors will lead to a low R^2 and could be misinterpreted as an indication of active management.

Two different filtering procedures exist. The use of the entire data set for each point is the smoothing method, which gives the smoothest pictures of style shift and drift. In the smoothing procedure, the Kalman filter first runs forward through the data then backward and combines the outcomes. The filtering procedure runs only forward through the data. This means that for each point, it employs only historical data to obtain estimates of the exposures. The filtering procedure shows how the exposures were perceived in real time. Constructing time-varying confidence bounds for exposures yields additional information on the relevance of these exposures. The Kalman filter is optimal for a large class of problems and is a very effective and useful estimator for an even larger class. A Bayesian approach easily ties in with the Kalman filter. Here we limit ourselves to using noninformative priors for the parameters. This case corresponds to the classical statistical interpretation. However, incorporation of prior information into the model is easy. It is also relatively straightforward to incorporate additional information, such as holdings information. The use of additional information will improve the precision of the estimations. In our applications we used Ssfpack for Ox by Koopman, Shephard, and Doornik (1999), freely available from www.ssf pack.com. Two important applications of the factor models that could be further improved by our dynamic model could be the in the area of manager structure optimization (MSO) and value at risk (VaR).

Manager Structure Optimization   Since the alpha and the factors are independent by construction, Waring, Whitney, Pirone, and Castille (2000) suggest to split the problem of optimal portfolios in two components.

1. Find the right mix of style exposures (betas).
2. Conditional on this mix, find the best alpha managers.

From the factor model (4.1), we can deduce this expression for the covariance of hedge funds: $V = B'FB + \Omega$. In this expression, B is a matrix of hedge fund exposures to the different factors, F is the covariance matrix of the factor risk premiums, and Ω is a (diagonal) matrix of the residual risks. In constructing a portfolio of hedge funds, one can choose the weights of each fund in such a way that a certain style exposure is obtained. The idiosyncratic risk could be diversified by adding hedge funds. Acknowledging style drift in the estimation of the B matrix can be beneficial to the MSO process.

Value at Risk   A popular measure for measuring tail risk is VaR, which reflects the equity capital (in currency units) that is needed to cover the extreme losses that are experienced. In VaR modeling three parameters should be set:

1. The probability level, which should be chosen very low, since there should be a very low chance that the losses exceed the corresponding VaR.
2. The target horizon, which reflects the time needed to raise additional funds.
3. The accuracy of the VaR number. Of course, the accuracy should be as high as possible. The accuracy is determined by the estimation method, the model, and the data used.

A problem with position-based VaR is that it is static and ignores the dynamic trading in most hedge funds. Furthermore, the use of option-type strategies yields a step function in the payoff function. This is also problematic in the case of a position-based VaR. For example, a hedge fund that writes puts with a probability of 4.99 percent of getting in the money has a very misleading position-based 5 percent VaR. Lhabitant (2001) points out how a factor model can solve some of these problems and provide a more reliable ex-ante assessment of the VaR. Using the factor model in equation 4.1, we can decompose the VaR measure into a value at market risk (VaMR) and a value at specific risk (VaSR) for a portfolio of hedge funds, as shown in equation 4.4:

$$VaR = \sqrt{VaMR^2 + VaSR^2} \tag{4.4}$$

The VaMR is defined as

$$VaMR = \sqrt{\sum_{i=1}^{K}\sum_{j=1}^{K} \rho_{i,j} \beta_i F_i^* \beta_j F_j^*} \tag{4.5}$$

The VaSR equals $\zeta_\alpha \sigma_\varepsilon$, where ζ_α is the α quantile of the normal distribution and σ_ε is the volatility of the error term in (4.1). In equation 4.5, the $\rho_{i,j}$ are the correlation between monthly returns of the hedge fund indices and F_i^* is the α-percentile of the factor returns F_i. This percentile must be estimated with great care. Standard techniques are not sufficient because it is notoriously difficult to estimate tail events, which are rare or might not even happened yet. Often we have too few observations from history to obtain reliable estimates of the tail probabilities. For further details we refer to Chapter 12 of Lhabitant (2004).

EMPIRICAL FINDINGS

Hedge fund managers should be paid for alpha and not for allocating to asset-based style factors. Alpha is the sum of timing and selection skill. However, it is quite complicated to decompose alpha in selection and timing skill (Swinkels, Van der Sluis, and Verbeek 2003). Therefore, we do not attempt to distinguish selection from timing skill. Glosten and Jagannathan (1994) show how the alpha should be interpreted in the presence of timing skill. The upshot of their research is that there is a trade-off between alpha and timing skill in the sense that a contingent claim approach can show the value of timing skill. This value should be compared to the alpha of the manager.

The goal of our analysis is to show the potential benefits of adaptive style analysis with asset-based factors. The adaptive style analysis method is applied on the Credit Suisse First Boston (CSFB)/Tremont long/short equity benchmark, a long/short equity fund, and a fund of funds.

In Figure 4.1, each fund's exposure to the styles with 80 percent confidence bounds are shown in the upper panel. In the bottom panel we show the payoff of the fund and the payoff from the exposure to each of the asset-based factors.

Style Drift in Long/Short Equity Hedge Funds

Most long/short equity hedge funds are not market neutral, but have exposures to the equity market. Goodman, Shewer, and Horwitz (2002), among others, point out that equity hedge funds have exposures to the Fama-French-Carhart style factors (size, value/growth and momentum). By using asset-based factors, we can study the characteristics of these factors over a long period of time. We can examine nonnormality in each of them and see whether these returns tie in with the goals of the investor. There is a caveat to this. Long/short equity funds also have nonlinear payoff patterns. Such patterns can be replicated by an asset-based factor mimicking a portfolio of options. In our example we use a systematic covered call-writing strategy. In order to investigate shifting style exposures of long/short equity funds, we apply the Kalman filter procedure on the monthly returns of the CSFB long/short equity style over the period 1994 to 2004. The risk factors we use consist of the standard market, size, value, and momentum factors plus a covered call trading strategy return factor. With these factors we are able to explain 83 percent of the variation in the long/short equity style. The exposures are displayed in Figure 4.1. The upper panel indicates a positive and significant exposure to the momentum factor over the whole sample period. Furthermore, long/short equity returns in 1994 look similar to returns from writing covered calls, investing in the market index and overweighing growth stocks. In 1995 the focus shifted toward growth and small-cap stocks. We also note that the net long exposure to the market and the covered call strategy declined since 1999. During the last year of the Nasdaq bull market, long/short equity managers were on average exposed to growth and large-cap stocks. Part of this substantial move can be explained by the fact that small information technology companies turned into large-cap companies with growth characteristics, due to the amount of money pouring in these stocks. Exposures to the momentum and the market factor are most significant. The significance of the value factor changes through time. Timing did deliver value, as evidenced, for example, by the lower exposure to the market since 2000. The R^2 calculated from the residuals is 83 percent. The degree of explanation is high for an investment strategy that is supposed to deliver absolute returns, which are not correlated with fundamental market factors.

Figure 4.2 presents the analysis of individual long/short equity hedge funds. We use the Kalman filter to obtain the time varying exposures to five

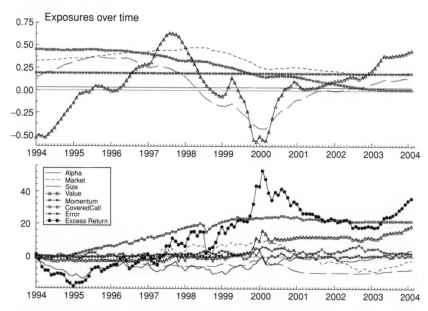

FIGURE 4.1 Style Analysis CSFB/Tremont Long-Short Equity
The upper panel shows the exposures of the CSFB/Tremont long/short equity index to risk factors. The risk factors are the market, size, value, and momentum factors plus a covered call trading strategy return factor. In the lower panel, the cumulative payoff of the index in excess of the risk-free rate is shown together with the returns from the exposures to the factors (the explained part). The alpha and error term express the part of the excess return of the index, which is not explained by the exposures to the factors. Together the explained and unexplained part sum up to the excess payoff line.

risk factors. We use the same risk factors as in the previous example and the same period under consideration. The R^2 calculated from the residuals is 81 percent, which is rather high. The patterns of the individual fund are different from the style index. Exposures vary over time except for the momentum strategy. Most of the time the exposures are significantly different from zero. During the whole period, the exposure to the market was positive. The fund built up exposure to the market during the bull time of the Nasdaq bubble in 1999 and decreased exposure in 2000. The fund gradually shifted from growth in 1994 to value stocks in 1998. The value position was decreased during the period from 2000 to 2003. In 2004 a net growth position remains. The exposure to the covered call strategy decreased in 1998 and 1999 and stayed positive until 2003. During the

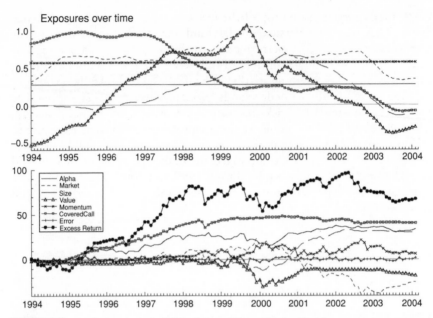

FIGURE 4.2   Style Analysis Individual Long-Short Equity Funds

The upper panel shows the exposures of an individual long/short equity fund to risk factors. The risk factors are the market, size, value, and momentum factors plus a covered call trading strategy return factor. In the lower panel, the returns of the index in excess of the risk-free rate are shown together with the returns from the exposures to the factors (the explained part). The alpha and error express the part of the excess return of the index, which is not explained by the exposures to the factors. Together the explained and unexplained part sum up to the excess payoff line.

sample period the fund switched from large cap to small cap and back again. This shift paid off during the period from 2000 to 2002, as can be seen from the lower panel of the figure. The exposure to the market costs money during the bear market running from 2000 to 2002. The alpha is positive, although not statistically significant from zero.

Analysis of Fund of Funds

Most investors in funds of funds do not know with certainty what they are investing in, simply because they never see the funds' actual holdings. This blind way of investing is chosen by investors who are less able or willing to invest directly in hedge funds. FoF managers are specialists who move money in and out of hedge funds for their clients. For their expertise and costs, they charge a fee on top of the fees charged by the underlying hedge funds. They may even persuade hedge fund managers to move out of their comfort zone to enhance performance. In this study we analyze a fund of funds from a larger family of fund of funds. We use these factors: emerging market equity and emerging market debt. Figure 4.3 shows the exposures and returns of a fund of hedge funds specialized in the Asian region. The excess return above the risk-free rate is negative over the total period. The fund especially lost money in the period before 1999. The exposure to emerging market equity is positive, but changes. In 1998 and 1999, after the liquidity crisis, the fund leveraged the equity component, which paid off. The fund deleveraged equity during 1999 and 2000. The fixed income component was held constant during the whole period but did not add much value.

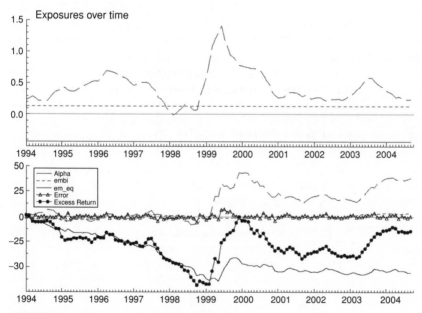

FIGURE 4.3   Style Analysis Fund of Funds

The upper panel shows the exposures of a fund of hedge funds to risk factors. The risk factors are emerging market debt (embi) and emerging market equity (em eq). In the lower panel, the returns of the index in excess of the risk-free rate are shown together with the returns from the exposures to the factors (the explained part). The alpha and error express the part of the excess return of the index, which is not explained by the exposures to the factors. Together the explained and unexplained part sum up to the excess payoff line.

CONCLUSION

The growth in hedge fund assets, number of funds, and investment styles has been enormous. Fund managers hungry for fees exploit every alternative risk premium besides the ones on traditional bonds and stocks. Several strategy fields have already been exhaustively grazed by herds of managers. Capacity limits have been met and new pastures are sought after. Hedge fund managers continue to discover and develop new alternative fields, pushing the financial frontier forward. Even if returns are not high, most investors will benefit from the diversification benefits of hedge funds on traditional portfolios. The free and flexible nature of the hedge fund industry together with the lockup period often imposed by its constituents is its key asset, and a challenge for traditional institutional investors. The lack of transparency and the freedom to apply virtually every imaginable trading style, combined with organizational risks, result in an overall risk-return profile that is difficult to assess. Hedge funds are opportunity driven and therefore change style over time. Asset liability management and portfolio construction becomes more difficult when managers are able to switch styles. With our adaptive return-based style analysis, it is possible to estimate the time-varying exposures of hedge funds to risk factors in an efficient way. The advantage is that the method only requires a time series of historical returns. Our method can be used in several ways. One way is to analyze styles on the basis of historical returns from hedge fund databases. This may be useful to identify style changes in response to changing market conditions or to identify interesting hedge fund managers from a database. Another way is to track in real time the style of a particular hedge fund that is in the investor's portfolio. This is useful for a fund of funds manager who wants to keep a certain style allocation over time. Moreover, risk management measures, such as VaR, and allocation tools, such as manager structure optimization, benefit from a timely detection of style drift.

CHAPTER 5

Hedge Fund Allocation under Higher Moments and Illiquidity

Niclas Hagelin, Bengt Pramborg, and Fredrik Stenberg

This chapter investigates possible gains from diversifying into hedge funds. The study shows that gains from allocating into hedge funds occur even when possible effects of deviations from normality in the hedge fund return data are taken into account. Using a decision function that includes all higher moments of the return distribution produces portfolios that are very similar to those constructed using a mean-variance approximation. This finding is interesting and suggests that higher moments are dominated by the first two moments, at least when portfolios are rebalanced on a monthly basis. Further, the results indicate that the gains from including hedge funds in the portfolios remain (although smaller) when the effects of "stale pricing" are taken into consideration. Finally, the existence of lockup periods hampers the possibility of rebalancing the allocation to hedge funds. This predicament may cause the portfolio to deviate from the targeted "optimal" portfolio. Through a simple experiment we show that the inability to rebalance the portfolio may seriously impact the benefits that hedge funds appear to offer.

INTRODUCTION

In the last decade, the number of existing hedge funds and the value of the assets of these funds under management have witnessed tremendous growth. The attractiveness of hedge funds may be explained by their good performance in terms of relatively high returns, low volatility, and low correlation to other assets. However, recent research has robbed hedge funds of some of their luster as an asset class. The reason for this is that hedge funds are more complicated than traditional assets (i.e., common stocks and bonds) and their benefits are more difficult to evaluate. This complexity arises from the way hedge funds are administrated as well as from the quality and the statistical properties of the return data itself.

It is well known that existing vendor databases provide an incomplete picture of the hedge fund universe and that even this incomplete picture is marred by biases such as survivorship, instant history, and selection. Recent research highlights the care needed in handling the subtleties arising from the lack of quality data (Ackermann, McEnally, and Ravenscraft 1999; Brown, Goetzmann, and Ibbotson 1999; Fung and Hsieh 2000; Liang 2000; Posthuma and Van der Sluis 2004). Failure to account for these deficiencies would lead investors to be grossly overoptimistic about the benefits of hedge funds. This failure may not only cause investors to experience some very unpleasant surprises in the future, but also lead them (on false premises) to allocate too many resources to hedge funds.

Hedge fund return data often depart from normality. Amin and Kat (2003b) and Kat (2004a), among others, show that hedge fund returns exhibit significant negative skewness and excess kurtosis, both undesirable to a risk-averse investor (Rubinstein 1973; Kraus and Litzenberger 1976; Scott and Horvath 1980). Because of this departure from normality, the usual application of the standard tools of portfolio analysis, such as mean-variance portfolio optimization, may lead to wrong conclusions and suboptimal decisions. In response to this, research is emerging that tackles the problem of optimization of asset allocation to hedge funds, taking into account nonnormality in hedge fund returns. This research includes Bacmann and Pache (2004), Davies, Kat, and Lu (2004), and Hagelin and Pramborg (2004b).[1]

Bacmann and Pache (2004) and Davies, Kat, and Lu (2004) construct optimal hedge fund portfolios incorporating possible effects from skewness and kurtosis. Specifically, Bacmann and Pache (2004) assume that investors choose either a portfolio to minimize the risk that returns will fall below a

---

[1] Lee and Lee (2004) and Sharma (2004) are examples of other studies investigating the possible effects from higher moments on hedge fund performance. While Lee and Lee develop an alternative Sharpe ratio, Sharma constructs a performance metric that computes the certainty equivalent gain from hedge funds.

threshold level at some future date or a portfolio to maximize the ratio of the expected gains above a threshold level to the expected losses below that threshold level. They find that mean-variance portfolios usually overweight hedge fund indices with negative skewness and high kurtosis relative to portfolios constructed with the methodology they propose. These results are broadly the same for both in-sample (static optimization) and out-of-sample experiments and point in favor of their proposed methodology. Davies, Kat, and Lu (2004) incorporate investor preferences into a polynomial goal programming optimization function. This approach allows them to solve for multiple competing hedge fund allocation objectives within the mean-variance-skewness-kurtosis framework. Their analysis shows that equity market–neutral funds are risk and kurtosis reducers while global macro funds are skewness enhancers.

Hagelin and Pramborg (2004b) evaluate returns to portfolios that include hedge fund investments, where the investor is assumed to allocate optimally among asset classes (common stocks, bonds, a risk-free asset, and hedge funds) and to rebalance those allocations regularly. They use the discrete-time dynamic investment model proposed by Grauer and Hakansson (1985) that provides an interesting alternative to the standard mean-variance analysis since it focuses on capital growth.[2] Because the capital growth rate is affected by the higher moments of the return distribution, optimizing capital growth given a certain risk tolerance implicitly takes all moments of the return distribution into account. Hagelin and Pramborg (2004b) show that investors will optimally choose to allocate wealth to

---

[2]Grauer and Hakansson (1986) employed the model to construct and rebalance portfolios of U.S. stocks, corporate bonds, government bonds, and a risk-free asset. The results revealed that the gains from active diversification among the major U.S. asset categories were substantial, especially in the case of highly risk-averse strategies. In a later study, Grauer and Hakansson (1987) found that additional diversification could be obtained from including non-U.S. asset categories in the portfolios. Further, Grauer and Hakansson (1995) compared the investment policies and returns on portfolios of stocks and bonds, with and without real estate. Their principal findings were that the gains obtained by adding real estate to portfolios of U.S. financial assets using an active strategy were rather large, especially in the case of highly risk-averse strategies, but that the gains from adding U.S. real estate to portfolios of global assets were mixed. In a recent paper, Hagelin and Pramborg (2004a) used the model to investigate the gains from including emerging equity markets in the investment opportunity set. They found that gains accrued from diversifying into emerging equity markets were modest.

hedge funds, even when they take into account deviations from normality in hedge fund returns. In addition, they show that the optimal allocations result in portfolio returns that have, in some cases, statistically significantly greater returns compared to the cases where hedge fund investing is not permitted.

This study uses the same utility maximization procedure as Hagelin and Pramborg (2004b) to analyze the possible gains from diversifying into hedge funds. We extend their analysis in two principal directions. First we explicitly compare the returns and allocations of portfolios that are optimally constructed using the discrete-dynamic investment model (i.e., taking all moments into consideration) with portfolios that are constructed using a mean-variance approximation. This is interesting since it facilitates a direct analysis of the effect, and possible importance, of considering higher moments when hedge funds are included in the investment opportunity set. Second, we examine the possible effects from illiquidity on the return and risk of portfolios that allocate resources to hedge funds and rebalance these allocations regularly. Illiquidity is usually defined in terms of the costs incurred to enter and exit an investment. This affects the evaluation of hedge fund allocations in at least two ways.

First, illiquidity exists in the lockup periods and advance notice periods that are standard requirements among hedge funds. Singer, Staub, and Terhaar (2003) suggest this may be important since these lockup periods make hedge fund investments illiquid and consequently hamper the possibility of rebalancing the portfolio. Since the investment model used in this study and that of Hagelin and Pramborg (2004b) implicitly assumes that monthly rebalancing is possible, the benefit from inclusion of illiquid assets, such as hedge funds, may be overstated. However, the investment model used in this study, assuming monthly rebalancing, provides a good setting for investigating the possible effect of lockup periods on portfolio return and risk.

Second, a signature of many hedge funds is that they undertake investments in illiquid assets, which results in valuations that are not completely up-to-date (Asness, Krail, and Liew 2001). This "stale pricing effect" induces positive serial correlation in hedge fund returns and underestimation of their true standard deviations (Brooks and Kat 2002; Getmansky, Lo, and Makarov 2003). In accordance with Davies, Kat and Lu (2004), this study adapts the approach proposed by Geltner (1993) to account for this deficiency in the return data.

The results of this study show, similar to Hagelin and Pramborg (2004b), that gains from allocating into hedge funds occur even when the possible effects of deviations from normality in the hedge fund return data are taken into account. In fact, using a decision function that includes all higher moments of the return distribution produces portfolios that are very similar to those that are constructed using a mean-variance approximation. This finding is interesting and suggests that higher moments are dominated by the first two moments, at least when portfolios are rebalanced on a monthly basis. Further, the results indicate that the gains from including hedge funds in the portfolios remain (although smaller) when the effects of stale pricing are taken into consideration. Finally, the existence of lockup periods hampers the possibility of rebalancing the allocation to hedge funds. This predicament may cause the portfolio to deviate from the targeted optimal portfolio. Through a simple experiment we show that the inability to rebalance the portfolio may seriously impact the benefits that hedge funds appear to offer.

METHODOLOGY

Discrete-Time Dynamic Investment Model

Utility Functions and Higher Moments of Returns   The dynamic investment model used in this chapter, based on the multiperiod portfolio theory of Mossin (1968), Hakansson (1971, 1974), Leland (1972), Ross (1974), and Huberman and Ross (1983), and applied by, among others, Grauer and Hakansson (1985, 1986, 1987, 1995, 2001), assumes investors with power utilities. That is, the utility function (Equation 5.1), may be written

$$u(1+r) = \frac{1}{1-\gamma}(1+r)^{1-\gamma}, \ \gamma \geq 0, \ \gamma \neq 1 \tag{5.1}$$

where r is the one-period return
       γ is a parameter for risk aversion

Higher values of γ imply more risk aversion, while $\gamma = 0$ represents the risk-neutral investor. A special case is when $\gamma \to 1$, in which case the utility (Equation 5.2) is logarithmic:

$$u(1+r) = \ln(1+r), r > -1 \tag{5.2}$$

The logarithmic utility implies, and is implied by, a strategy to maximize capital growth, and this utility is therefore often referred to as the growth-optimal strategy. (For a comprehensive account of capital growth theory, see Hakansson and Ziemba 1995.) The utility functions differ from the standard mean-variance framework in that all moments of the return distribution affect the utility of the investor.

The significance of higher moments is supported by a growing number of studies, such as Kraus and Litzenberger (1976), Scott and Horvath (1980), Harvey and Siddique (2000), and Harvey, Liechty, Liechty, and Müller (2003). Harvey and Siddique (2000) show that systematic skewness in asset returns is economically significant and commands a risk premium. Harvey, Liechty, Liechty, and Müller (2003) show empirically that portfolios of assets may display large positive or negative skewness. They illustrate that, unlike the variance of a portfolio, there is no guarantee that the portfolio skewness will be smaller than the linear combination of the stocks' skewness. It may be larger or smaller, and they observe a variety of behaviors when portfolios are assembled from different types of assets.

However, as Grauer and Hakansson (1993) found, with more frequent reallocations, the mean-variance (MV) model may approximate the power utility quite well. They argue that, for well-diversified asset categories and holding periods of one quarter or less, the first two moments appear to leave little room for the higher moments to assert themselves. The MV approximation (equation 5.3) to the utilities in (5.1) and (5.2) is

$$f(1+r) = \frac{1}{\gamma}(1+\mu) - \frac{1}{2}\sigma^2 \tag{5.3}$$

where μ = expected return
   σ^2 = variance

We assume that investors behave myopically. For power-utility investors, the use of myopic decision rules assumes that returns are independent from period to period (but not that they are stationary). The growth-optimal investor behaves myopically even if returns are not independent from period to period. For more on intertemporal portfolio choice, see, for example, Ingersoll (1987, Chapter 11) and Campbell and Viceira (2002, Chapter 5).

Practical Implementation Using the power or logarithmic utility (or the MV approximation) in a multiperiod framework involves solving a constrained nonlinear optimization problem. For this purpose, the investor is required to choose a risk-aversion parameter γ. In this study, γ is set to 0, 0.5, 1, 2, 3, 5, 10, 20, 30, 40, and 60, respectively, indicating investors' risk attitudes ranging from risk neutral ($\gamma = 0$) to very risk-averse ($\gamma = 60$), and where $\gamma = 1$ corresponds to the logarithmic utility in equation 5.2.

At the beginning of each period t, the investor chooses a portfolio, φ_t, on the basis of some member γ of the family of utility functions (equation 5.1) subject to the relevant constraints faced by the investor. For the power investor, this is equivalent to solving this problem (equations 5.4 to 5.7) for each period t:

$$\max_{\phi_\tau} E\left[\frac{1}{1-\gamma}(1+r_t(\varphi_t))^{1-\gamma}\right] = \max_{\phi_\tau} \sum_s \pi_{ts}\frac{1}{1-\gamma}(1+r_{ts}(\varphi_t))^{1-\gamma} \qquad (5.4)$$

subject to

$$\phi_{it} \geq 0, \phi_{Lt} \geq 0, \phi_{Bt} \leq 0, \forall i, \qquad (5.5)$$

$$\sum_i \phi_{it} + \phi_{Lt} + \phi_{Bt} = 1, \qquad (5.6)$$

$$\sum_i m_{it}\phi_{it} = 1, \qquad (5.7)$$

where $r_{ts}(\varphi_t)$ = the (ex ante) return on the portfolio in period t if state s occurs,

$$r_{ts}(\varphi_t) = \sum_i \phi_{it}r_{it} + \phi_{Lt}r_{Lt} + \phi_{Bt}r_{Bt}$$

γ = the risk-aversion parameter which remains fixed over time
ϕ_{it} = the proportion of wealth invested in risky asset i in period t
ϕ_{Lt} = the proportion lent in period t
ϕ_{Bt} = the proportion borrowed in period t
ϕ_t = the vector of weights $(\varphi_{1t}, \ldots \varphi_{nt}, \varphi_{Lt}, \varphi_{Bt})'$
r_{it} = the anticipated total return for asset i in period t
r_{Lt}, r_{Bt} = the interest rate on lending and borrowing at the beginning of period t
m_{it} = the initial margin requirement for asset i in period t expressed as a fraction
π_{ts} = the probability of state s at the end of period t

Constraint (5.5) rules out short sales and (5.6) is the budget constraint. Constraint (5.7) serves to limit borrowing. Here this constraint is applied by setting the margin requirements, Mit, equal to unity, which, in effect, rules out borrowing. For the MV investor in equation 5.3, we simply replace the goal function (5.4), with the empirical equivalent of equation 5.3.

The inputs to the model are based on the estimation method to be described, and at the beginning of each period, t, system (5.4) to (5.7) is solved by a sequential quadratic programming method, using returns from the estimation period preceding period t. At the end of the first estimation month, t, the realized returns on the risky assets are observed, along with the realized borrowing rate. Using the weights selected at the beginning of the month, the realized return on the portfolio chosen for month t is recorded. The cycle is then repeated for all subsequent months.

Estimation

To implement the model we need a method to estimate the distribution of future asset returns (i.e., the r_{it} and π_{ts}). One estimation procedure used by, among others, Grauer and Hakansson (1985, 1986, 1987, 1995, 2001), is the empirical probability assessment approach (EPAA). With this approach, estimation is based on looking back at past realized returns. An estimation window is formed that looks back T periods. With an estimation window of 36 months $(T = 36)$, contemporaneous realized asset returns for each past month, $\mathbf{r}_{t-j}$ $(j = 1,\ldots,36)$, are used, and the set of realized returns for each past month is given the weight $1/T$ $(\pi_{ts} = 1/T)$ for each possible future state). We assume 36 possible future states at the end of the subsequent month, each equally likely, and each corresponding exactly to one of the actual past observed sets of monthly asset returns. The estimate of returns for period t is then $E_{t-1}[\mathbf{r}_t] = \frac{1}{36}\sum_{j=1}^{36}\mathbf{r}_{t-j}$. Thus, using EPAA, estimates are obtained on a moving basis and used in their raw form without adjustments. Since the objective function (utility function) requires that the entire joint distribution be specified and used, there is no information loss: All moments and correlations are implicitly taken into account.

DATA

The data collecting process by data vendors and the fact that reporting is voluntarily gives rise to a variety of biases in hedge fund data. These biases include survivorship bias, instant history bias, and selection bias (Ackermann, McEnally, and Ravenscraft, 1999; Brown, Goetzmann, and Ibbotson 1999; Fung and Hsieh 2000; Liang 2000; Posthuma and Van der Sluis 2004). We obtain monthly observations for the Hedge Fund Research (HFR) fund weighted composite index, the HFR equity hedge index, the HFR merger arbitrage index, the HFR macro index, and the HFR distressed securities index for the period January 1990 to October 2002. To account for the impact of survivorship bias, we adjust the indices in accordance with the evidence presented by Liang (2000).[3] All results in this study refer to indices that have been adjusted for survivorship bias.

To represent stocks we use the Morgan Stanley Capital International (MSCI) World index (containing 23 developed countries), the MSCI USA index, the MSCI Europe index, and the MSCI Japan index. All returns are expressed in U.S. dollars and represent total returns, since both dividends and capital appreciation, or depreciation, are taken into account. The 10-year U.S. Government Bond Return Index and the Dow Jones Corporate Bond Return Index are used as proxies for investments in government and corporate bonds, respectively. The Dow Jones Corporate Bond Return Index includes bonds with sub-AAA ratings and has an average maturity of 20 years. The risk-free asset is assumed to be the one-month Treasury bill rate. Table 5.1 presents the abbreviations of each asset being used, while Table 5.2 presents descriptive statistics on the assets.

RESULTS

Here, we examine the gains accrued from diversifying into hedge funds under two different settings. In the first setting, equities are approximated by the MSCI World index (WORLD) and hedge funds by the HFR fund weighted composite index (HFRI). The second setting uses three equity sub-indices (the MSCI USA index [USA], the MSCI Europe index [EUR], and the MSCI Japan index [JAP]) to proxy for equities and four hedge fund sub-indices (the HFR Equity hedge index [EQ HEDGE], the HFR Merger arbitrage index [MERGER], the HFR Macro index [MACRO], and the HFR Distressed securities index [DISTRESSED]) to proxy for the hedge fund

---

[3]In detail, we subtract 0.17 percent per month from the HFR fund weighted composite index, which equals 2 percent on a yearly basis. Admittedly, this is a relatively crude technique to adjust for the biases inherent in the hedge fund return data. However, Hagelin and Pramborg (2004b) used a fee-adjusted HFR fund of funds index to proxy for the "true" return of the hedge fund universe (see Brown, Goetzmann, and Liang 2004). Fung and Hsieh (2000) argue that index data on funds of hedge funds are almost free of the many biases contained in databases of individual hedge funds. The use of the adjusted HFR fund weighted composite index and the adjusted HFR fund of funds index provided qualitatively similar results in Hagelin and Pramborg (2004b), and we direct the reader to their study for a comparison of the results from using these two indices.

TABLE 5.1 Asset Categories

Symbol	Asset Category
Rf	U.S. one-month T-bill rate
GovB	10-year Treasury Bond Total Return Index
CorpB	Dow Jones Corporate Bond Total Return Index
WORLD	MSCI World Gross Return Index
USA	MSCI USA Gross Return Index
EUR	MSCI Europe Gross Return Index
JAP	MSCI JAPAN Gross Return Index
HFRI	HFRI Composite Index*
EQ HEDGE	HFRI Equity Hedge Index*
MACRO	HFRI Macro Index*
DISTRESSED	HFRI Distressed Securities Index*
MERGER	HFRI Merger Arbitrage Index*

*All hedge fund indices are adjusted for survivorship bias (see note 3).

TABLE 5.2 Descriptive Statistics of Monthly Returns for Included Assets,
January 1993 to October 2002

	Mean	Standard Deviation	Skewness	Kurtosis
Rf	0.36	0.11	−0.65	2.55
GovB	0.69	1.99	−0.08	3.05
CorpB	0.59	1.32	0.02	4.03
WORLD	0.64	4.20	−0.66	3.56
USA	0.87	4.49	−0.57	3.44
EUR	0.77	4.45	−0.62	3.98
JAP	−0.02	6.41	0.41	3.17
HFRI	0.88	2.20	−0.57	5.75
HFRI desmoothed	0.88	2.85	−0.50	5.24
EQ HEDGE	1.14	2.77	0.20	4.57
MACRO	0.93	2.44	0.23	3.64
DISTRESSED	0.78	1.66	−1.59	11.47
MERGER	0.79	1.09	−2.55	14.79
EQ HEDGE desmoothed	1.14	3.23	0.23	4.27
MACRO desmoothed	0.92	2.90	0.16	3.76
DISTRESSED desmoothed	0.75	2.98	−1.66	12.60
MERGER desmoothed	0.78	1.28	−2.41	14.15

universe. The first subsection examines the possible impact from higher moments while the second setting explores the possible impact from illiquidity in hedge fund investments.

Importance of Higher Moments

Figure 5.1 plots the geometric means and standard deviations of the realized annual returns from January 1993 to October 2002, a total of 118 months, using the MV and the power models with values of γ ranging from 0 (risk neutral) to 60 (very risk averse). Strategies are run with and without the inclusion of the HFRI.

Among the asset categories, the HFRI has the highest geometric mean return (10.8 percent), comparing favorably with the equity market geometric mean return (6.8 percent), as represented by the WORLD index. As evidenced from Figure 5.1, hedge fund returns also compare favorably with the returns from holding U.S. government bonds (GovB) or corporate bonds (CorpB). This suggests that resources should be allocated into hedge funds.

From Figure 5.1 it is apparent that the strategies produce very similar results, independently of which of the two decision functions is applied (the MV or the power model). This finding is interesting and may be interpreted as evidence that portfolio allocation can be made without considering the effect of nonnormality in the return data. There are at least two possible explanations for this: The gains from incorporating higher moments into the analysis are offset by estimation errors, or the possibility of reallocating resources on a monthly basis mitigates the effects of higher moments on capital growth. To explore this, we investigate how resources are allocated under the two alternative decision functions. This examination shows that the two decision functions typically generate very similar allocations for our choice of assets and time period. In fact, the correlation between weights is above 99 percent for almost every asset and strategy.[4] This suggests that the similarity in capital growth is due to the fact that the two first moments dominate the effects of higher moments, which is in accordance with the findings of Grauer and Hakansson (1993).

The evidence in Figure 5.1 shows that the presence of hedge funds as an investment opportunity, as represented by the HFRI, tends to increase

---

[4] Only in three cases is the correlation below 99 percent, and for these three cases (γ = 30, 40, and 60 for the case based on the WORLD without inclusion of the HFRI) is the correlation is above 90 percent.

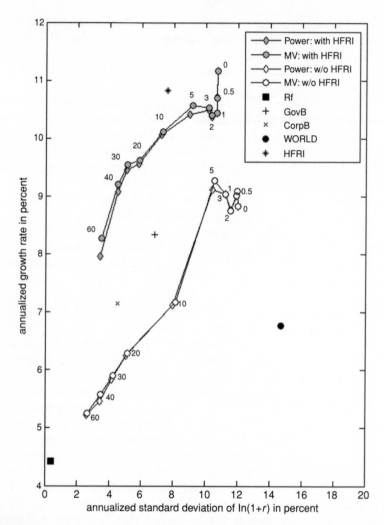

FIGURE 5.1 Annual Realized Returns for Portfolios with and without Hedge Funds (1)

Annualized geometric mean returns and standard deviations for portfolios including the equity markets of developed countries (WORLD), with and without survivorship-adjusted hedge funds (HFRI) included in the investment opportunity set. Strategies include power investors (Power) and mean-variance investors (MV). Monthly rebalancing over the period from January 1993 to October 2002.

the annual geometric returns for all investigated strategies. The average increase in geometric mean returns is 2.4 percent and achieved at little or no expense of increased standard deviations. (For consistency with the geometric mean, the standard deviation is based on the log of 1 plus the rate of return.)

There are a number of commonly accepted ways of testing for abnormal investment performance. We follow the example of Grauer and Hakansson (1995) by using a paired *t*-test of the difference in investment returns. We direct the reader to Grauer and Hakansson (1995) for a detailed description of the test. Table 5.3 displays one-sided *t*-tests for the Power model. The tests indicate that inclusion of the HFRI increases the geometric mean return significantly for 5 out of the 11 strategies investigated, at the 5 percent level. Significance is indicated for the more risk-averse strategies. We note that this result corroborates the finding in Hagelin and Pramborg (2004b) and suggests that hedge funds should be included in the portfolio even when possibly adverse effects on capital growth from higher moments are considered.

Figure 5.2 presents a similar analysis to that presented in Figure 5.1, but allows for diversification into three equity subindices (USA, EUR, and JAP) and four hedge fund subindices (EQ HEDGE, MACRO, DISTRESSED, and MERGER). The choice of hedge fund indices is to some extent arbitrary, but the EQ HEDGE index represents, in terms of assets under management, the single largest hedge fund category. The results are representative of other combinations of indices that we have tested. We examine subindices because they typically exhibit statistical properties that deviate more from normality than the properties of the broader index (see Table 5.2). Hence the likelihood of capturing any possible impact from higher moments on capital growth should be enhanced when the sub-indices are used. Similarly, the possibility of encapsulating any differences resulting from the choice between the two decision functions employed should also increase.

Overall, the results in Figure 5.2 are similar to those presented in Figure 5.1. The inclusion of hedge funds as an additional investment opportunity increases the average geometric returns for all strategies. The average annual increase is 5.4 percent, and significant at the 5 percent level for all 11 strategies (see Table 5.3). The geometric return and standard deviation of portfolios constructed using the alternative decisions functions are very similar. Pairwise correlations (per asset) in weights between the power utility investors and the MV investors are never less than 90 percent. This corroborates the finding in Figure 5.1 that higher moments are of little importance when constructing portfolios that are rebalanced on a monthly basis.

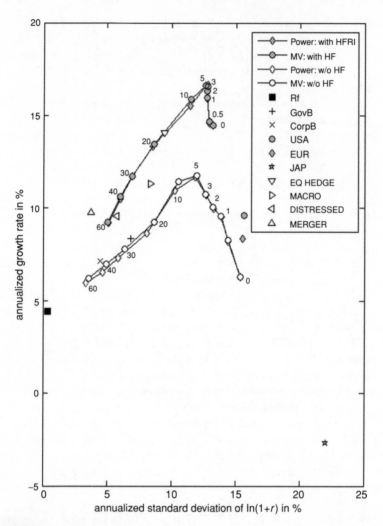

FIGURE 5.2 Annualized Realized Returns for Portfolios with and without Hedge Funds (2)

Annualized geometric mean returns and standard deviations for portfolios including the equity markets of developed countries (USA, EUR, and JAP), with and without survivorship-adjusted hedge funds (HF) included in the investment opportunity set. Strategies include power investors (Power) and mean-variance investors (MV). HF includes diversification among four hedge funds: EQ HEDGE, MACRO, DISTRESSED, and MERGER. Monthly rebalancing over the period from January 1993 to October 2002.

TABLE 5.3 Geometric Mean Returns and Standard Deviation with and without Hedge Funds for Power-Utility Investors

Panel A: WORLD with and without HFRI

	WORLD only		HFRI included (1) survivor bias adjusted			(2) desmoothed			(3) lockup 12 months		
	Mean	Std	Mean	Std	Diff	Mean	Std	Diff	Mean	Std	Diff
0	8.8	12.0	11.2	10.8	2.3	10.5	11.3	1.6	9.9	11.6	1.1
0.5	9.1	12.0	10.7	10.7	1.6	9.9	11.2	0.8	7.9	11.0	-1.2
1	9.0	11.9	10.4	10.7	1.4	10.0	11.2	1.0	7.8	10.9	-1.2
2	8.8	11.6	10.4	10.4	1.6	10.0	10.9	1.2	8.0	10.7	-0.7
3	9.0	11.2	10.5	10.2	1.4	10.3	10.8	1.3	8.3	10.2	-0.7
5	9.1	10.4	10.4	9.0	1.3	10.3	9.8	1.2	9.1	9.3	-0.1
10	7.1	8.0	10.1	7.2	3.0*	9.5	8.1	2.4	9.3	8.0	2.1
20	6.3	5.1	9.6	5.8	3.3*	9.2	6.1	3.0*	8.6	6.1	2.3*
30	5.8	4.1	9.5	5.1	3.6*	8.6	5.1	2.8*	8.1	5.1	2.3*
40	5.5	3.5	9.1	4.5	3.6*	7.6	4.2	2.2*	7.2	4.3	1.7*
60	5.2	2.6	8.0	3.4	2.7*	6.6	3.0	1.4*	6.2	3.2	1.0*

The table contains the *geometric* mean returns (Mean) and standard deviation of $\ln(1+r)$ (Std) for strategies for which portfolios are formed with and without hedge funds, expressed as yearly growth rates and standard deviations. Statistical tests for differences in geometric mean returns between strategies including hedge funds in the investment opportunity set and strategies without hedge funds in the investment opportunity set are also included. Panel A contains values for the case including WORLD as representing stocks and HFRI as representing hedge funds. Panel B contains values for the case including USA, EUR, JAP as representing stocks and EQ HEDGE, MACRO, DISTRESSED, and MERGER representing hedge funds. For each panel the first case displayed is without hedge funds in the investment opportunity set (the first two report columns). Report columns 3–11 display (1) survivorship-adjusted hedge fund indices included; (2) survivorship-adjusted and desmoothed hedge fund indices included; and (3) survivorship-adjusted, desmoothed hedge fund indices with lockup constraint. For each case 1 to 3, the differences in geometric mean returns as compared to the case without hedge funds are shown, using a paired t-test. Significance at the 5 percent level using a one-sided test is indicated with *.

TABLE 5.3 *(continued)*

Panel B: USA, EUR, and JAP with and without Hedge Funds

	USA, EUR, and JAP		Hedge funds included (1) survivor bias adjusted			(2) desmoothed			(3) lockup 12 months		
	Mean	Std	Mean	Std	Diff	Mean	Std	Diff	Mean	Std	Diff
0	6.3	15.4	14.5	13.2	8.2*	14.5	14.1	8.2*	12.7	13.9	6.4
5	8.2	14.4	14.6	12.9	6.4*	14.5	13.8	6.3*	12.7	13.9	4.5
1	9.5	13.9	15.9	12.8	6.4*	15.3	13.7	5.7*	12.7	13.9	3.2
2	10.0	13.3	16.3	12.8	6.4*	15.9	13.6	5.9*	12.5	13.8	2.5
3	10.7	12.7	16.7	12.8	6.0*	15.9	13.6	5.2	12.2	13.6	1.5
5	11.7	11.9	16.6	12.7	4.9*	15.8	13.5	4.1	13.8	13.2	2.1
10	10.9	10.3	15.5	11.5	4.6*	14.8	11.9	3.9	12.2	11.1	1.3
20	8.6	8.1	13.4	8.6	4.7*	11.3	8.8	2.6	9.8	7.9	1.2
30	7.3	5.9	11.7	6.9	4.4*	9.9	7.2	2.6	8.8	6.4	1.5
40	6.5	4.7	10.5	6.0	4.0*	8.9	6.2	2.3	8.5	5.5	1.9
60	6.0	3.4	9.2	5.1	3.3*	7.8	5.1	1.8	7.8	4.7	1.8

The table contains the *geometric* mean returns (Mean) and standard deviation of $\ln(1+r)$ (Std) for strategies for which portfolios are formed with and without hedge funds, expressed as yearly growth rates and standard deviations. Statistical tests for differences in geometric mean returns between strategies including hedge funds in the investment opportunity set; strategies without hedge funds in the investment opportunity set are also included. Panel A contains values for the case including WORLD as representing stocks and HFRI as representing hedge funds. Panel B contains values for the case including USA, EUR, JAP as representing stocks and EQ HEDGE, MACRO, DISTRESSED, and MERGER representing hedge funds. For each panel the first case displayed is without hedge funds in the investment opportunity set (the first two report columns). Report columns 3–11 display (1) survivorship-adjusted hedge fund indices included; (2) survivorship-adjusted and desmoothed hedge fund indices included; and (3) survivorship-adjusted, desmoothed hedge fund indices with lockup constraint. For each case 1 to 3, the differences in geometric mean returns as compared to the case without hedge funds are shown, using a paired *t*-test. Significance at the 5 percent level using a one-sided test is indicated with * .

To shed light on the usefulness of hedge funds as active diversifiers, we examine the portfolio allocations. Because of the great similarity between the allocations that are made under the two alternative decision functions, we present detailed results using only the power utility decision function.

Figure 5.3 depicts, for each active strategy investigated, the portfolio allocation when the HFRI is used to proxy for the hedge fund universe. The figure reveals that substantial allocations are made to hedge funds for all investigated risk appetites. In fact, average allocations range from 38 percent up to 68 percent. These high allocations are in contrast with how investors typically allocate resources in reality, but are roughly in line with the results of earlier studies (Edwards and Caglayan 2001a; Hagelin and Pramborg 2004b). Figure 5.3 also shows that investors who accept more risk include more equities and less of the risk-free asset in their portfolios than more risk-averse investors do.

Figure 5.4 displays the allocation to hedge funds using the four hedge fund subindices (EQ HEDGE, MACRO, DISTRESSED, and MERGER). When these subindices are used to proxy hedge funds, risk-averse investors allocate even more resources to hedge funds than suggested by Figure 5.3. Interestingly, risk-averse investors rely on DISTRESSED and MERGER while less risk-averse investors prefer to allocate resources to EQ HEDGE

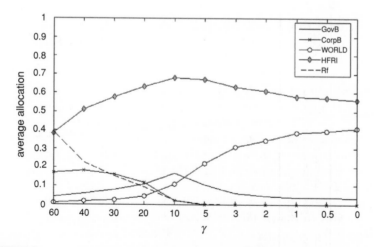

FIGURE 5.3 Average Allocation to Asset Categories for Power-Utility Investors
Average allocation to asset categories for power-utility investors with risk-aversion parameter ranging from 60 to 0. Stocks are represented by the WORLD index and hedge funds by the HFRI index.

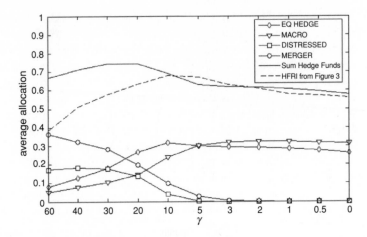

FIGURE 5.4 Average Allocations to Hedge Funds for Power-Utility Investors
Average allocation to hedge funds for power-utility investors with risk-aversion parameters ranging from 60 to 0. Stocks (not reported) are represented by the USA
index, the EUR index, and the JAP index. Hedge funds are represented by the EQ
HEDGE index, the MACRO index, the DISTRESSED index, and the MERGER
index. The sum of weights allocated to hedge funds is shown, as well as the allocation to HFRI from Figure 5.3.

and MACRO. This result is natural considering that EQ HEDGE and
MACRO are characterized by higher standard deviation and returns than
DISTRESSED and MERGER (see Table 5.2).

Figure 5.5 plots the proportions of wealth allocated into HFRI and
equities (as represented by WORLD) over the sample period, for an
investor with a power utility with $\gamma = 10$. From the plots it is evident that
the allocations change drastically over time. This is common for strategies
using a rolling window for estimates (Chopra, Hensel, and Turner 1993;
Hagelin and Pramborg 2004b). For the first half of the evaluation period,
the investor invests roughly 100 percent of wealth in hedge funds. From
September 1998 until December 1999 the investor chooses to allocate no
resources to hedge funds at all. Instead, the investor allocates roughly half
the resources to equities, the remaining being mostly allocated to government bonds. From January 2000 and onward the investor goes in and out
of hedge funds. To conserve space, we do not present any detailed results
for investors with other γ values but note that the propensity to choose
drastic portfolios solutions, in Figure 5.5, is shared with other investors as
well. However, more risk-averse investors tend to choose more diversified
portfolios than less risk-averse investors do.

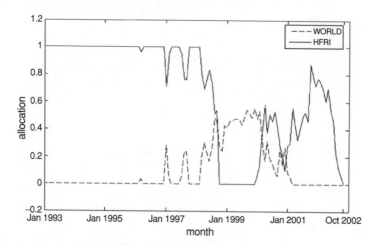

FIGURE 5.5 Allocations for the $\gamma = 10$ Power Investor
Allocations to the WORLD index and to the HFRI index from January 1993 to
October 2002 for a power-utility investor with a risk-aversion parameter, γ,
equaling 10.

Importance of Illiquidity

Here we explore the impact from illiquidity in hedge funds on portfolio
allocations and capital growth. Specifically, we investigate two aspects of
illiquidity in hedge fund investments, one that is induced by serial correlation in hedge fund returns and one that comes from lockup periods and
advance notice periods.

Serial correlation in hedge fund returns is caused by hedge fund managers' difficulty in obtaining accurate values of the many illiquid positions
that the hedge fund has taken (Asness, Krail, and Liew 2001; Getmansky,
Lo, and Makarov 2003). The illiquidity in these positions produces a systematic smoothing valuation error effect that tends to not be diversified
away. This "smoothing" translates into serial correlation and underestimation of the hedge fund's true standard deviations. Brooks and Kat (2002)
adapt the approach proposed by Geltner (1993) to reconcile stale price
problems in hedge fund returns. In accordance with these authors, and
with Davies, Kat, and Lu (2004), we use this approach to unsmooth hedge
fund returns.

For brevity, we direct our presentation to the results for the setting
using the broader indices (HFRI and WORLD) and the power models. Figure 5.6 plots the annual geometric means and standard deviations of the

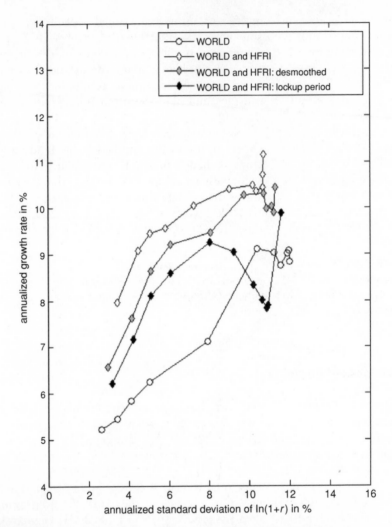

FIGURE 5.6   Annualized Realized Returns for Power-Utility Investors
Annualized geometric mean returns and standard deviations (for power investors)
for portfolios including the equity markets of developed countries (WORLD), with
and without hedge funds (HFRI) included in the investment opportunity set. The
HFRI is adjusted for survivorship bias and also (1) by desmoothing and (2) by desmoothing and imposing a 12-month lockup constraint. Monthly rebalancing over
the period from January 1993 to October 2002 for all assets, except for the HFRI
when the lockup constraint is in effect.

portfolios. As evident from the plot, using desmoothed hedge fund returns produces portfolios with somewhat less tractable features. Specifically, the use of desmoothed hedge fund data results in portfolios with lower geometric returns for all 11 strategies and higher standard deviations for eight of the strategies. Still, the inclusion of hedge funds results in higher geometric returns for all 11 strategies, and significantly so among four of them (see Table 5.3).

Panel A in Figure 5.7 displays the impact from desmoothing on allocations to hedge funds. As expected, use of desmoothed hedge fund returns results in reduced allocations to hedge funds. In particular, allocations decrease with investors' willingness to accept risk. In fact, the most risk-averse investor ($\gamma = 60$) reduces the average allocation to hedge funds from 38 percent to 22 percent, while investors who accept more risk make modest changes in their allocations. From panel B it can be seen that the

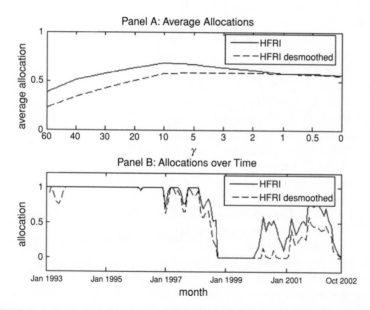

FIGURE 5.7 Average Allocations for Different Power Investors and Allocations for the $\gamma = 10$ Investor over Time

Panel A displays the average allocation to the HFRI for power-utility investors with risk-aversion parameters ranging from 60 to 0, when the HFRI is survivorship adjusted only and when it is also desmoothed. Panel B displays allocations to the HFRI index from January 1993 to October 2002 for the $\gamma = 10$ investor when the HFRI is survivorship adjusted only and when it is also desmoothed.

decrease in hedge fund allocations is not necessarily evenly distributed over the evaluation period.

Illiquidity is induced by the lockup periods and advance notice periods that are standard requirements among hedge funds. These two features hamper the possibility of rebalancing the portfolio. To explore the possible impact of this form of illiquidity, we perform a simple experiment. We introduce a lockup period in the implementation of hedge funds allocations into our model. (For simplicity, we do not impose an advance notice period.) Specifically, the investor undertakes the same optimization procedure as in the previous section to decide each month which assets to include in the portfolio and in what proportions. However, with regard to hedge funds, the investor is able to decide the optimal allocation only once a year, and this allocation is then fixed for one year. For the remaining 11 months, the investor allocates resources to other assets conditioned on the amounts that have (or have not) been locked up in hedge funds. Note that this simple procedure for analyzing the effect of lockup periods cannot capture the true effect from lockup periods. A detailed model, which would include individual funds' specific terms, is not possible with the limited data we have access to. We therefore keep this experiment simple. However, it sheds light on the possible problems that lockup periods constitute in terms of rebalancing the portfolio regularly. The results from the experiment are displayed in Figures 5.6 and 5.8, as well as in Table 5.3.

It is evident from Figure 5.6 that the inclusion of lockup periods into the analysis leads to lower geometric returns. For power investors, the geometric return increases by less than 1 percent when the HFRI is included in the investment opportunity set. While 4 out of the 11 strategies still experience significantly higher capital growth after the inclusion of lockup periods to the analysis, the returns for 5 of the strategies decrease with the inclusion of hedge funds in the opportunity set.

Figure 5.8 displays, for the $\gamma = 1$ investor, the portfolio growth (panel A) and the weights allocated to the HFRI (panel B) when the HFRI is desmoothed only and when it is also subject to the 12-month lockup period constraint. The HFRI is a very attractive investment during the first part of the period; indeed, the allocation equals 1.0 up until 1996, and the lockup constraint does not have any effect. However, panel B reveals that the weights differ quite substantially from this point on. From 1996 until early 1998, the lockup constraint results in no allocation to hedge funds at all, where the unconstrained investor allocates large amounts into HFRI at several intervals. Also, notably around the years 1998 and 2001, and at the very end of the sample period, the lockup constraint affects the investor trying to increase or decrease the stake in hedge funds, with negative consequences.

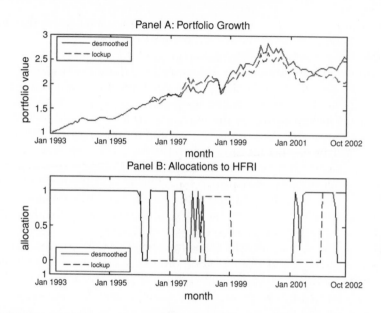

FIGURE 5.8 Capital Growth and Allocation for a Power-Utility Investor with $\gamma = 1$
Panel A displays the growth of portfolios from January 1993 to October 2002 for a
power-utility investor with a risk-aversion parameter, γ, equaling 1 when the HFRI
index is desmoothed and when it is desmoothed and the lockup constraint is imposed,
respectively. Panel B displays the corresponding allocations to the HFRI index for the
period.

We interpret the results in Figure 5.6, Figure 5.8, and Table 5.3 as evidence that lockup periods force investors to have portfolios that, because of
the problem with rebalancing, deviate from their targeted optimal portfolios, which in turn may result in lower capital growth. The higher return
that comes from the inclusion of hedge funds in the portfolio could be a
required compensation for carrying the risk and discomfort of illiquidity.

CONCLUSION

In this study we use the discrete-time dynamic investment model to evaluate the gains from including hedge funds in the investment opportunity set.
This model allows investors to care about all the properties of the return
distribution and to rebalance their portfolios regularly. In short, our results

show that investors will optimally choose to allocate wealth to hedge funds even when they take into account deviations from normality in hedge fund returns. These optimal allocations result in portfolios that have greater capital growth compared to the case in which hedge fund investing is not permitted. We also find that investors who form portfolios on a monthly basis, taking all moments of the return distribution into account, construct portfolios that are very similar to the portfolios being constructed by investors who care only about the expected return and the standard deviation. This suggests that the two first moments of the return distribution dominate higher moments, at least when portfolios are rebalanced on a monthly basis. Our results suggest that the positive effect on capital growth from including hedge funds into the portfolios remains (although smaller) when the so-called stale pricing effect is taken into account. Finally, the lockup periods and advance notice periods may force investors to have portfolios that deviate from their targeted (ex ante optimal) portfolios. This inability to rebalance hedge fund allocations toward the targeted level may seriously reduce the gains that hedge fund allocations appear to offer.

CHAPTER 6

Revisiting the Role of Hedge Funds in Diversified Portfolios

Jean Brunel

Hedge funds have become one of the most important building blocks in diversified portfolios over the last several years. This study examines the error associated with the classification of hedge funds strategies under one single header (hedge funds). We demonstrate that the hedge fund universe heterogeneous and should be the broken down into distinct subgroups. We revisit the critical issue of the difference in the return distribution experienced by hedge funds in general: the skewness of many return series, the survivorship bias inherent in these series, the dangers associated with self-reporting, the excess kurtosis that affects many strategies, and their general lack of tax-efficiency. Finally, we address the role of hedge fund strategies in a diversified portfolio and find that a traditional mean-variance optimization model is not likely to produce a successful allocation.

INTRODUCTION

Hedge funds have become one of the most important building blocks in diversified portfolios. Ineichen (2004) suggests that hedge funds may

This chapter originally appeared in the *Journal of Wealth Management,* Volume 7, Number 3 (2003), pp. 35–48. This article is reprinted with permission from Institutional Investor, Inc.

become the preferred strategy for investors who do not see performance relative to an index as the relevant measure. Yet this segment of the investment universe remains somewhat clouded in mystery, misconceptions, and at times even plainly erroneous views.

In this chapter we address three important issues that need to be better understood by investors. First, as discussed in Brunel (2003), we examine the error associated with the classification of hedge fund strategies under one single header. We demonstrate that the hedge fund universe quite heterogeneous and should therefore be broken down into distinct subgroups. We identify at least two general subsets: absolute return strategies on one hand, and semidirectional strategies, managed futures, and global macro on the other.

Second, we revisit the critical issue of the difference in the return distribution experienced by hedge funds in general. Numerous authors have pointed to the fact that hedge funds tend to offer less readily analyzable performance characteristics. Kat (2003b), for instance, discusses a number of relevant issues, such as the skewness of many return series, the survivorship bias inherent in these series, the dangers associated with self-reporting, and the excess kurtosis that affects many strategies. For investors with tax concerns, hedge funds often tend to be somewhat tax inefficient, although Gordon (2004) discusses how to make them more tax efficient.

Third, we address the question of the role of hedge fund strategies in a diversified portfolio and suggest that a traditional mean-variance optimization model is not likely to produce a successful allocation. One of the most critical issues faced by wealth managers when dealing with hedge funds is deciding how to incorporate them into the portfolio optimization process. The statistical issues related to their performance history make the standard optimization approach at best suboptimal if not completely faulty, because of three important failings.

1. Using historical return and risk statistics for each strategy is unacceptable given the survivorship bias and self-reporting features of most databases (Amin and Kat 2003c).
2. Mean-variance optimizers do not recognize higher statistical moments such as skewness and kurtosis, and thus do not realize that the unusually high Sharpe ratio often shown by hedge funds may simply be a way of paying for negative skewness and high kurtosis.
3. Hedge fund strategies should be placed on a continuum with higher-manager-risk traditional strategies (i.e., long only), to allow total portfolio exposure to manager risk to be well understood.

HEDGE FUNDS ARE NOT A SIMPLE OR EVEN A SINGLE ASSET CLASS

Table 6.1 compares individual and aggregated hedge fund strategies to selected traditional capital market indices for the longest possible period (January 1990 to June 2004) and for the last five years. The Hedge Fund Research (HFR) Index database from which the raw hedge fund data is sourced only goes back to January 1990. Many industry specialists attach relatively little validity to data collected prior to 1994. To have as long a period to review as possible, we elect to stay with that full data set, but recognize that our conclusions are somewhat hampered. For each time period, the data are ranked in order of ascending volatility to allow us to focus on a very important element of the problem, namely where individual hedge fund strategies fit in the overall alternative risk spectrum. Our study has four important ramifications:

1. In either time period, it is clear that individual hedge fund strategies can be found across the full risk spectrum, suggesting that one cannot cover all strategies under a single header such as hedge funds. Indeed, if hedge funds were to be a specific asset class, alongside cash, bonds, or equities, they would have to have certain common risk or return characteristics (Horvitz 2000). In fact, the data seem to suggest that the risk spectrum associated with the full variety of "hedge fund" strategies is about as wide as the spectrum covered by the traditional asset or sub-asset classes, ranging from home currency cash at the low end of the scale to emerging market equities at the higher end.

2. Although there is some variability in the specific strategy rankings across the two periods under consideration, there is still a high degree of consistency in the risk inherent in each of these strategies. This is not surprising, since the risk inherent in each strategy is a function of both the area of the capital market on which each manager focuses and the nature of the bets typically made. Variations in observed return volatility might arise as a result of success in markets or changes in leverage or market exposure levels driven by perceived opportunities, or lack thereof.

3. Looking at the data more closely, we can identify hedge fund strategy clusters. They encompass approaches that would be expected over time to produce return and risk statistics falling within a similar range. At least two such clusters can be identified: strategies whose risk profiles fall in the same range as traditional fixed income strategies and those whose risk profiles exceed fixed income and approximate equities. The first

TABLE 6.1 Hedge Fund Strategies and Traditional Assets, Ranked by Volatility

	1/90 to 6/04			7/00 to 6/04	
	Return	Volatility		Return	Volatility
90-Day T-Bills	4.50%	0.57%	90-Day T-Bills	2.67%	0.60%
Equity Market Neutral	9.14%	3.22%	Relative Value	7.15%	1.81%
International Bonds—Hedged	7.37%	3.27%	Fixed Income Arbitrage	6.73%	2.43%
Fixed Income	5.47%	3.30%	International Bonds—Hedged	5.52%	2.65%
Convertible	10.64%	3.40%	Fixed Income Total	8.33%	2.87%
Fixed Income Total	10.36%	3.51%	Equity Market Neutral	4.79%	2.96%
Relative Value	11.89%	3.67%	Merger Arbitrage	4.27%	3.01%
Salomon BIG Index	7.53%	3.93%	Convertible	8.51%	3.07%
Statistical Arbitrage	8.65%	3.98%	Funds of Funds	4.00%	3.25%
Fixed Income Mortgage Backed	7.83%	4.26%	Statistical Arbitrage	1.86%	3.87%
Merger Arbitrage	10.17%	4.32%	Fixed Income Mortgage Backed	11.38%	4.02%
Fixed Income Arbitrage	8.33%	4.41%	Salomon BIG Index	7.41%	4.16%
Funds of Funds	9.76%	5.69%	Fixed Income High Yield	7.59%	4.26%
Sector Real Estate	6.93%	6.08%	Fixed Income	10.53%	4.53%
Distressed	14.60%	6.20%	Distressed	12.37%	5.11%
Fixed Income High Yield	9.47%	6.48%	Macro	9.50%	5.80%
Event Driven	14.13%	6.66%	Fund Weighted Composite	5.72%	6.00%
Market Timing	12.44%	6.76%	Market Timing	4.66%	6.23%
Fund Weighted Composite	13.72%	7.03%	Event Driven	9.23%	6.37%
High Yield Bonds	9.22%	7.27%	Sector Real Estate	10.55%	6.89%
Macro	15.78%	8.55%	Equity Hedge	4.21%	7.43%

TABLE 6.1 (continued)

Equity Hedge	16.94%	9.01%	Sector Miscellaneous	1.76%	8.81%
Managed Futures	8.56%	9.63%	Emerging Market Global	8.44%	9.05%
Sector Miscellaneous	14.94%	10.65%	**High Yield Bonds**	6.55%	9.85%
Sector Financial	16.16%	11.05%	Managed Futures	10.98%	10.18%
Fixed Income Convertible	8.64%	11.26%	Sector Financial	17.87%	10.69%
Real Estate	12.25%	13.05%	Emerging Market Total	10.72%	11.28%
Emerging Market Asia	10.51%	13.78%	**Emerging Market Bonds**	11.17%	11.86%
Sector Total	18.78%	13.82%	Emerging Market Asia	6.41%	12.02%
Emerging Market Global	13.14%	13.95%	Sector Total	0.43%	13.25%
Equity Nonhedge	16.19%	14.41%	Sector Energy	13.04%	13.75%
Emerging Market Bonds	8.44%	14.78%	**Real Estate**	17.33%	14.42%
U.S. Large Cap Equities	11.40%	14.82%	Equity Nonhedge	4.80%	14.91%
Emerging Market Total	15.13%	15.16%	Fixed Income Convertible	1.67%	16.10%
Sector Energy	15.90%	16.68%	EAFE Equities	-2.16%	16.33%
EAFE Equities	5.07%	16.87%	Sector Technology	-6.27%	16.57%
U.S. Small Cap Equities	12.03%	18.95%	U.S. Large Cap Equities	-3.11%	16.95%
Sector Technology	18.18%	19.01%	Sector Healthcare—Biotech	7.93%	17.22%
Emerging Market Latin America	17.59%	20.07%	Emerging Market Latin America	3.36%	17.31%
Sector Healthcare—Biotech	15.35%	20.70%	Short Selling	12.08%	20.94%
Short Selling	3.93%	21.82%	U.S. Small Cap Equities	6.91%	21.14%
EM Equities	9.93%	23.23%	EM Equities	4.27%	22.50%

group typically comprises approaches where managers seek to hedge all market risk and whose returns should thus be viewed as combinations of some risk-free bond (whose duration would be equal to the average holding period in each strategy) and manager alpha generated through the successful identification of arbitrage opportunities. Table 6.2 displays a possible listing of these absolute return strategies. The second group compromises strategies whose risk profiles exceed fixed income and approximate equities, typically approaches where managers seek to generate alpha from both individual security selection decisions and some market exposure (which may be driven by top-down or bottom-up processes). They should thus be viewed as combinations of some average or structural net market exposure and manager alpha generated through security selection or net market exposure variations. Table 6.3 displays a possible listing of these directional and semidirectional strategies.

4. Although the risk across most hedge fund strategies appears relatively constant in both time periods, the returns seem considerably lower in the most recent time interval. Although it is tempting to attribute all of the difference to greater market efficiency—itself brought about by the exponential growth of funds managed by hedge funds—the data do not

TABLE 6.2   Return and Volatility Statistics, Absolute Return Strategies

	1/90 to 6/04		7/00 to 6/04	
	Return	Volatility	Return	Volatility
Equity Market Neutral	9.14%	3.22%	4.79%	2.96%
Fixed Income Diversified	5.47%	3.30%	10.53%	4.53%
Convertible Arbitrage	10.64%	3.40%	8.51%	3.07%
Fixed Income Total	10.36%	3.51%	8.33%	2.87%
Relative Value Arbitrage	11.89%	3.67%	7.15%	1.81%
Statistical Arbitrage	8.65%	3.98%	1.86%	3.87%
Fixed Income Mortgage Backed	7.83%	4.26%	11.38%	4.02%
Merger Arbitrage	10.17%	4.32%	4.27%	3.01%
Fixed Income Arbitrage	8.33%	4.41%	6.73%	2.43%
Distressed	14.60%	6.20%	12.37%	5.11%
Fixed Income High Yield	9.47%	6.48%	7.59%	4.26%
Event Driven	14.13%	6.66%	9.23%	6.37%
Market Timing	12.44%	6.76%	4.66%	6.23%
90-Day T-Bills	4.50%	0.57%	2.67%	0.60%
International Bonds—Hedged	7.37%	3.27%	5.52%	2.65%
Salomon BIG Index	7.53%	3.93%	7.41%	4.16%
High Yield Bonds	9.22%	7.27%	6.55%	9.85%

TABLE 6.3 Return and Volatility Statistics, Directional and Semidirectional Strategies

	1/90 to 6/04		7/00 to 6/04	
	Return	Volatility	Return	Volatility
Sector Real Estate	6.93%	6.08%	10.55%	6.89%
Macro	15.78%	8.55%	9.50%	5.80%
Equity Hedge	16.94%	9.01%	4.21%	7.43%
Managed Futures	8.56%	9.63%	10.98%	10.18%
Sector Miscellaneous	14.94%	10.65%	1.76%	8.81%
Sector Financial	16.16%	11.05%	17.87%	10.69%
Fixed Income Convertible Bonds	8.64%	11.26%	1.67%	16.10%
Emerging Market Asia	10.51%	13.78%	6.41%	12.02%
Sector Total	18.78%	13.82%	0.43%	13.25%
Emerging Market Global	13.14%	13.95%	8.44%	9.05%
Equity Nonhedge	16.19%	14.41%	4.80%	14.91%
Emerging Market Total	15.13%	15.16%	10.72%	11.28%
Sector Energy	15.90%	16.68%	13.04%	13.75%
Sector Technology	18.18%	19.01%	−6.27%	16.57%
Emerging Market Latin America	17.59%	20.07%	3.36%	17.31%
Sector Healthcare—Biotech	15.35%	20.70%	7.93%	17.22%
Short Selling	3.93%	21.82%	12.08%	20.94%
Real Estate	12.25%	13.05%	17.33%	14.42%
Emerging Market Bonds	8.44%	14.78%	11.17%	11.86%
U.S. Large Cap Equities	11.40%	14.82%	−3.11%	16.95%
EAFE Equities	5.07%	16.87%	−2.16%	16.33%
U.S. Small Cap Equities	12.03%	18.95%	6.91%	21.14%
EM Equities	9.93%	23.23%	4.27%	22.50%

support this contention. Indeed, funds classified in the fixed income universe tend to earn a return that can be broken down into two major components: a risk-free rate and the manager's alpha. By contrast, funds classified in the equity universe tend to earn a return that should be broken down into three components: the manager's alpha, the fund's typical average equity market exposure, and the residual short-term fixed income exposure associated with the equity market risk hedged away. Computing implied overall alphas for both broad segments suggests that the alpha earned by managers has declined. Yet Table 6.4 shows that the most recent period, which was affected by less favorable financial market environments, saw some erosion in the basic return available to managers.

TABLE 6.4 Comparison of Basic Return between 1/90–6/09 and 7/00–6/04

	1/90 to 6/04	7/00 to 6/04
Risk-free Return	4.50%	2.67%
Fixed Income Return	7.53%	7.41%
U.S. Overall Equity Return (65/35)	11.62%	0.40%
Absolute Return Strategies Return	10.24%	7.49%
Semidirectional Strategies Return	13.68%	6.91%
Implied Absolute Return Alpha	5.75%	4.83%
Implied Semidirectional Alpha	4.31%	2.66%

In short, rather than looking at hedge funds as a homogeneous group of investments, it is more sensible to classify them according to their underlying risk profiles. At a minimum, a number of market-neutral strategies could be viewed as related to the fixed income universe, while the balance can be viewed as more like equity-risk.

One might ask whether the excess return earned by hedge fund managers could not simply be attributable to the leverage present in many strategies, whether the returns earned by absolute return strategies could be replicated by applying leverage to traditional fixed income returns, and whether those of semidirectional strategies could be replicated by applying some leverage to traditional equity returns. Evidence suggests that such an approach would not work. Indeed, except for absolute return strategies during the January 1990 to June 2004 period, during which 20 percent leverage would have raised traditional fixed income risk to the same level as absolute return strategy volatility while still experiencing a significant return shortfall, hedge fund strategies produced higher returns and lower risk than comparable traditional alternatives. Thus, the higher returns must be attributable in large part to manager skills and the lower risk to the partial or total market risk hedge inherent in most of these hedge fund–type strategies.

AN IMPORTANT CAVEAT: DIFFERENT RETURN DISTRIBUTIONS

While the observed risk of various hedge fund strategies does appear to allow the foregoing classification, one should immediately note that there are important differences between traditional and nontraditional investment strategies. Brunel (2003) proposes a methodology for dividing total strategy risk between market and manager risk components based on the assumption of zero correlation between manager and market risk. Despite the questions raised by that assumption, the results of the compilations provided demonstrate that traditional strategies are principally market-risk driven, while nontraditional strategies are considerably more dependent on manager risk.

We propose a simple method to differentiate traditional and nontraditional investment strategies. Traditional strategies draw most of their risk and return characteristics from the markets in which the underlying securities are traded. Indeed, traditional managers use index-based investment strategies with important constraints to manage tracking error—the risk taken by the manager by deviating from the relevant index. Thus, total strategy risk principally comprises market risk and only secondarily manager risk. By contrast, nontraditional strategies draw most of their risk and return characteristics from the decisions made by managers. These decisions are driven both by the strategy typically employed by the manager, such as the strategies presented in Table 6.1, and the way in which the manager implements that strategy. Thus, total strategy risk comprises manager risk, and to a certain extent, market risk.

The importance of strategy and manager risk relative to broad market risk helps explain the fact that nontraditional strategies tend to be exposed to less desirable statistical moments, as discussed in Anson (2002a) and Amin and Kat (2003b).

Indeed, certain strategies, particularly those where the number of investment opportunities is somewhat limited, will tend to display negative skewness. This is especially true if the trades carried out within that investment process tend to offer payoff patterns characterized by a large number of small positive outcomes and an occasional poor result. Merger arbitrage would be a good example of such a strategy. Typically, merger arbitragers trade in announced mergers, most of which eventually come to fruition. The risk premium available to the arbitrager is thus fundamentally limited, explaining why most managers employ leverage to bring the expected returns to an acceptable level. However, occasionally an announced merger will fail. In that case, the trade can prove very unprofitable, in part because of the leverage applied to it. Thus, the distribution of expected returns comprises a number of small profitable trades and a very small positive tail. By contrast, when an anticipated merger fails to take place, an important negative tail will appear.

Similarly, manager risk tends to be associated with a higher kurtosis. This makes sense because high kurtosis implies that the tails of the return distribution will be fatter than if returns were normally distributed. Consider the activity of a manager who makes bets away from the index. The fewer the bets, the more likely the returns will differ from those of the underlying index, thus causing either tail to comprise more observations than would normally be predicted. Kurtosis will therefore tend to rise when traditional managers (managers using only long security positions) make a small number of large bets, thus creating concentrated portfolios. By contrast, the kurtosis of a highly diversified fund of hedge funds might actually be lower than that of a highly concentrated traditional manager, if the resulting number of individual underlying bets is so large as to create sufficient diversification.

Table 6.5 presents an analysis of skewness over the last 5 and 15 years for all the individual hedge fund strategies together with selected traditional market indices. The strategies are ranked from the most negative to the most positive skewness. Traditional indices are represented in bold, while absolute return strategies are in italics and directional and semidirectional strategies are in plain font. Averages for each group of strategies are shown and similarly ranked at the bottom of the table. Although the classification is far from perfect, traditional strategies tend to be found in the middle of the distribution, absolute return strategies have the most negative skew, and directional and semidirectional strategies have the least negative skew. This reflects the intuition expressed earlier, in that absolute return strategies will typically be those where the number of opportunities is most finite and the distribution of expected outcome the most regular with the occasional adverse outlier.

Table 6.6 presents a similar analysis of kurtosis for the same sample of strategies, with the same formatting convention—directional and semidirectional strategies appear in normal type, absolute return strategies appear in italics, and traditional strategies appear in bold type. The table indicates that traditional strategies tend to have minimal kurtosis, while hedge fund strategies tend to have significant excess kurtosis. This reflects the observation that manager risk is most important in the determination of total strategy risk for nontraditional strategies. As a group, absolute return strategies tend to have a higher kurtosis than those that incorporate more significant an exposure to market risk.

Our classification, however, is somewhat unfair. Indeed, we compare nontraditional strategies where manager activity is quite significant to unmanaged indexes for which there is, by definition, no manager role. It is reasonable to assume that indexes of actively but traditionally managed portfolios would fall somewhere within the range we create here. The most active managers would tend toward the outcomes associated with nontraditional managers, while the managers most seeking to replicate an index would tend toward the results associated with indexes.

Our cursory analysis confirms the findings of Kat (2003a), among others, and demonstrates that nontraditional strategies incorporate certain risks or

TABLE 6.5 Ranked Skewness for Hedge Funds and for Traditional Assets

	Skew	
	7/00 to 6/04	1/90 to 6/04
Fixed Income Mortgage Backed	−2.99	−3.83
Merger Arbitrage	−1.33	−2.71
Emerging Market Bonds	−0.20	−2.05
Emerging Market Global	−0.20	−1.87
Fixed Income Arbitrage	−0.47	−1.71
Event Driven	−0.75	−1.36
Sector Financial	0.42	−1.22
Convertible Arbitrage	−0.27	−1.19
Relative Value Arbitrage	0.07	−0.92
Emerging Market Total	−0.53	−0.80
Fixed Income High Yield	−0.87	−0.77
EM Equities	−0.30	−0.71
Distressed	−0.10	−0.68
Fund Weighted Composite	−0.31	−0.62
High Yield Bonds	−0.64	−0.53
U.S. Small Cap Equities	−0.44	−0.52
Equity Nonhedge	−0.28	−0.51
Salomon BIG Index	−1.23	−0.46
U.S. Large Cap Equities	−0.18	−0.46
Fixed Income Total	−0.06	−0.34
International Bonds—Hedged	−0.26	−0.31
Funds of Funds	−0.23	−0.26
Real Estate	−1.29	−0.24
90-Day T-Bills	1.03	−0.24
Fixed Income Diversifed	0.88	−0.23
Fixed Income Convertible Bonds	0.17	−0.19
EAFE Equities	−0.25	−0.16
Statistical Arbitrage	−0.72	−0.10
Sector Real Estate	−0.42	−0.09
Sector Total	−0.43	0.06
Market Timing	0.06	0.13
Equity Market Neutral	0.87	0.13
Short Selling	0.19	0.13
Equity Hedge	−0.16	0.17
Emerging Market Asia	−0.27	0.18
Macro	0.39	0.29
Sector Technology	−0.57	0.35
Emerging Market Latin America	−0.16	0.59
Managed Futures	−0.09	0.75
Sector Energy	0.44	0.89
Sector Miscellaneous	−0.84	1.74
Sector Healthcare—Biotech	0.37	2.24
Average Absolute Return	−0.44	−1.04
Average Traditional	−0.38	−0.57
Average Directional and Semidirectional	−0.13	0.12

TABLE 6.6 Ranked Kurtosis for Hedge Funds and for Traditional Assets

	Kurtosis	
	7/00 to 6/04	1/90 to 6/04
90-Day T-Bills	−0.34	−0.57
Fixed Income Diversified	1.34	−0.57
Market Timing	−0.86	−0.48
Equity Market Neutral	1.98	0.25
International Bonds—Hedged	−0.75	0.26
EAFE Equities	−0.18	0.40
Macro	0.94	0.41
Statistical Arbitrage	−0.20	0.51
Equity Nonhedge	−0.58	0.57
U.S. Large Cap Equities	−0.51	0.59
Salomon BIG Index	2.16	0.75
U.S. Small Cap Equities	0.21	0.89
Emerging Market Asia	−0.75	1.00
Short Selling	0.14	1.34
Equity Hedge	−0.31	1.35
Real Estate	3.35	1.38
EM Equities	−0.52	1.76
Sector Technology	0.57	1.93
Sector Energy	1.56	2.46
Convertible Arbitrage	0.07	2.52
Fund Weighted Composite	−0.39	2.77
Managed Futures	−0.58	2.85
Emerging Market Latin America	−0.48	2.91
Sector Total	0.30	2.96
Sector Real Estate	2.91	3.27
High Yield Bonds	1.37	3.53
Emerging Market Total	−0.63	3.75
Fixed Income Convertible Bonds	1.56	3.94
Funds of Funds	−0.57	4.23
Fixed Income Total	2.07	4.70
Event Driven	1.06	4.89
Distressed	−0.40	5.49
Fixed Income High Yield	1.39	6.34
Sector Financial	2.10	8.55
Fixed Income Arbitrage	1.25	9.82
Relative Value Arbitrage	0.29	10.74
Merger Arbitrage	2.76	11.96
Emerging Market Bonds	−0.15	12.99
Sector Miscellaneous	2.02	13.15
Emerging Market Global	−0.44	13.84
Sector Healthcare—Biotech	0.36	13.94
Fixed Income Mortgage Backed	15.77	26.22
Average Absolute Return	2.04	6.34
Average Directional and Semidirectional	0.41	4.48
Average Traditional	0.42	2.20

nondesirable attributes that are not taken into consideration when carrying traditional mean-variance optimizations.

NONTRADITIONAL STRATEGIES IN DIFFERENT MARKET ENVIRONMENTS

The next step in our review is to torture the data to illustrate further the fundamental fallacy of using traditional tools to construct portfolios comprising both traditional and nontraditional strategies. We call this "torture" because this analysis is meant to extract information from the data series. We re-create time series that suit our desired market environment, but do not correct for the resulting loss of serial correlation. Therefore, while our analysis does present interesting results, it has no predictive ability. We revisit the return distribution characteristics of various portfolios and confirm that traditional mean-variance analysis tends to overemphasize hedge fund strategies because the negative attributes associated with skew and kurtosis are not taken into consideration. A reasonable observer would conclude that these negative attributes must by definition be offset in the real world, by higher returns, by lower volatility, or by some combination of both.

In this analysis, we follow a three-step process, still applied to the January 1990 to June 2004 period:

1. We create an efficient frontier using a selection of both traditional and nontraditional strategies by dividing the investment universe into "fixed income–like" and "equitylike" groups.
2. We reconstruct the data series to reflect specific market environments. In the fixed income portion of the analysis, we simply divide the time period among months when the Salomon Broad Investment Grade Index produced positive returns and those when it produced negative returns. In the equity portion of the analysis, we create three different groups, those months when the Standard & Poor's (S&P) 500 posted negative returns, those when it posted substantially positive returns (more than 15 percent annualized), and those in between.
3. We then re-create efficient frontiers for each set of market conditions.

Table 6.7 and 6.8 present the fixed income and equity-efficient frontiers derived using return and risk characteristics calculated over a period encompassing all kinds of market environments. They show that a traditional mean-variance optimizer will seek to use as much nontraditional exposure as possible at any given risk level. Our absolute return proxy is a proprietary

TABLE 6.7 Efficient Frontier Portfolio Characteristics, Fixed Income–like Universe

Expected Return	4.53%	6.61%	9.28%	11.71%	11.92%
Expected Risk	0.56%	1.00%	1.99%	2.99%	3.11%
Target Risk	0.56%	1.00%	2.00%	3.00%	4.00%
Portfolio Composition					
Cash	100%	70%	31%	0%	0%
Bond	0%	3%	9%	5%	0%
Absolute Return Strategies	0%	27%	60%	95%	100%
Total	100%	100%	100%	100%	100%

index calculated using a linear combination of individual absolute return strategies. It is constructed with two goals in mind:

1. It must approximate the kind of portfolio composition generally found among the most reputable and successful funds of funds managers.
2. It aims to minimize correlation between its returns and those of the S&P 500 index.

In both instances, portfolios have minimal exposure to traditional strategies. Only in the fixed income–like universe do traditional strategies play a role, but this simply reflects the fact that cash is a risk-free asset and is thus chosen when the goal is to minimize total risk.

TABLE 6.8 Efficient Frontier Portfolio Characteristics

Expected Return	15.62%	16.64%	16.65%	16.65%	16.65%
Expected Risk	8.59%	9.00%	9.05%	9.05%	9.05%
Target Risk	8.59%	9.00%	10.00%	11.00%	12.00%
Portfolio Composition					
Equity	0%	0%	0%	0%	0%
Equity Hedge	0%	99%	100%	100%	100%
Equity Nonhedge	0%	0%	0%	0%	0%
Managed Futures	0%	0%	0%	0%	0%
Global Macro	100%	1%	0%	0%	0%
Total	100%	100%	100%	100%	100%

TABLE 6.9a Efficient Frontier Portfolio Characteristics with the Salomon BIG Producing Positive Returns, Fixed Income–like Universe

Expected Return	4.58%	8.12%	13.08%	13.62%
Expected Risk	0.60%	1.00%	2.00%	2.54%
Target Risk	0.60%	1.00%	2.00%	3.00%
Portfolio Composition				
Cash	100%	60%	3%	0%
Bond	0%	26%	62%	100%
Absolute Return Strategies	0%	14%	35%	0%
Total	100%	100%	100%	100%

Tables 6.9a and 6.9b show the efficient frontiers derived within the fixed income–like universe, when fixed income returns are positive and when fixed income returns are negative. Predictably, the model seeks to minimize exposure to bonds when they generate negative returns, but increases exposure when negative return periods are eliminated. Clearly, absolute return strategies do have a diversification role to play, but their unusual return distribution characteristics (negative skewness and high kurtosis) prevent them from taking the lead role when the impact of these characteristics is negated by eliminating negative bond return months.

TABLE 6.9b Efficient Frontier Portfolio Characteristics with the Salomon BIG Producing Negative Returns, Fixed Income–like Universe

Expected Return	4.16%	4.96%	6.09%	7.10%	8.07%	8.87%
Expected Risk	0.72%	1.00%	2.00%	3.00%	4.00%	4.83%
Target Risk	0.72%	1.00%	2.00%	3.00%	4.00%	5.00%
Portfolio Composition						
Cash	100%	83%	60%	38%	17%	0%
Bond	0%	0%	0%	0%	0%	0%
Absolute Return Strategies	0%	17%	40%	62%	83%	100%
Total	100%	100%	100%	100%	100%	100%

TABLE 6.10a Efficient Frontier Portfolio Characteristics in a High Equity Return Environment, Equity-like Universe

Expected Return	32.55%	22.54%	42.98%	42.83%	42.83%
Expected Risk	6.76%	7.75%	8.75%	8.94%	7.58%
Target Risk	6.76%	7.75%	8.75%	9.75%	10.75%
Portfolio Composition					
Equity	63%	37%	3%	0%	100%
Equity Hedge	0%	0%	0%	0%	0%
Equity Non-Hedge	0%	0%	97%	100%	0%
Managed Futures	37%	63%	0%	0%	0%
Global Macro	0%	0%	0%	0%	0%
Total	100%	100%	100%	100%	100%

Tables 6.10a, 6.10b and 6.10c present a similar analysis for the equity-like universe. They suggest similar, but not identical, conclusions. The sample of strategies we selected incorporated traditional equities (S&P 500), long/short equities, concentrated equity portfolios with very significant residual equity market exposure, managed futures, and global macro, the latter two in part because of their traditional equity-diversification characteristics. The model tends to prefer equity nonhedge to traditional equities in all but the most favorable equity market environments.

TABLE 6.10b Efficient Frontier Portfolio Characteristics in a Modest Equity Return Environment, Equity-like Universe

Expected Return	8.51%	15.17%	18.29%	17.45%	16.94%
Expected Risk	1.02%	3.50%	6.00%	8.50%	10.60%
Target Risk	1.02%	3.50%	6.00%	8.50%	11.00%
Portfolio Composition					
Equity	100%	20%	0%	0%	0%
Equity Hedge	0%	68%	0%	0%	0%
Equity Non-Hedge	0%	10%	76%	25%	0%
Managed Futures	0%	0%	0%	0%	0%
Global Macro	0%	2%	24%	75%	100%
Total	100%	100%	100%	100%	100%

TABLE 6.10c Efficient Frontier Portfolio Characteristics in a Negative Equity Return Environment, Equity-like Universe

Expected Return	1.09%	−12.01%	−16.20%	−22.30%	−27.83%
Expected Risk	7.37%	8.49%	9.75%	11.00%	12.24%
Target Risk	7.37%	8.48%	9.73%	10.98%	12.23%
Portfolio Composition					
Equity	0%	0%	0%	0%	0%
Equity Hedge	0%	0%	58%	30%	6%
Equity Non-Hedge	0%	44%	42%	70%	94%
Managed Futures	0%	0%	0%	0%	0%
Global Macro	100%	56%	0%	0%	0%
Total	100%	100%	100%	100%	100%

We conclude that nontraditional strategies have a meaningful role to play in diversified portfolio construction and that such a role needs to be carefully analyzed, but without using traditional mean-variance optimization. Nontraditional strategies are most useful in negative traditional market environments, but lose most if not all of their attractiveness when traditional markets do very well. A simple strategy of that chooses only nontraditional strategies will lead to substantial portfolio underperformance in favorable market conditions.

A SIMPLE APPROACH TO PORTFOLIO OPTIMIZATION

Our initial conclusion that traditional mean-variance optimization is not sufficiently powerful begs the question of whether an alternate method exists. Although traditional finance has argued that incorporating higher statistical moments in the optimization process does not produce better results, a different view is adopted once we accept that one crucial issue faced by individual investors is their sensitivity to intermediate stages. For many individuals, decision risk, defined here as the risk of changing strategy at the point of maximum loss, is so important that they need to be satisfied that the selected strategy is both efficient over time and acceptable at all intermediate points in time (Brunel 2003). Investors will therefore reduce a portfolio's exposure to negative skew and high kurtosis, as the combination of these two increases the probability of bad surprises, which are most likely to induce a strategic change at the worst possible time. This

TABLE 6.11 z-Score Based Efficient Frontier Portfolio Characteristics, Fixed Income–like Universe, with $\lambda = 0.01$ and $\gamma = 0.01$

Return	0.37%	0.46%	0.52%	0.55%	0.63%
Volatility	0.16%	0.41%	0.66%	0.81%	1.13%
Skewness	−0.24	−0.46	−0.47	−0.47	−0.46
Kurtosis	−0.57	1.01	0.90	0.84	0.75
Target Risk	*0.16%*	*0.41%*	*0.66%*	*0.81%*	*1.13%*
Portfolio Composition					
Cash	100%	67%	44%	30%	0%
Bond	0%	33%	56%	70%	100%
Absolute Return Strategies	0%	0%	0%	0%	0%
Total	100%	100%	100%	100%	100%

contrasts with many institutional investors who focus solely on utilities based on terminal values at certain points in time.

We design a simple optimization process based on the goal of maximizing a z-score to test the changes in allocation that could occur once higher statistical moments are taken into consideration. Our analysis defines an objective function as: Maximize (Expected Return − Volatility + Skewness − Kurtosis). Skewness and kurtosis are scaled to reflect investor preferences or aversions. To keep the analysis simple, we choose kurtosis rather than excess kurtosis. Table 6.11 shows the result of one such optimization in the fixed income–like universe using the same data as in previous exhibits for the sake of consistency. Note that if one simply scales skewness and kurtosis (by dividing each by 100) to the same order of magnitude as return and risk, and performs the optimization with monthly data, the model will finds no room for absolute return strategies. If λ denotes the scaling constant for skewness and γ the scaling constant for kurtosis, both of which reflect investor aversion to negative skewness and positive kurtosis, then the objective function becomes Maximize (Expected Return − Volatility + $\lambda \times$ Skewness − $\gamma \times$ Kurtosis).

We next investigate how the results would change under higher preference for first two moments (expected return and volatility), and lower preference for the next two moments. Table 6.12 shows the results of a similar optimization, halving the relative importance of the roles of skewness and kurtosis in the objective function. Note that an important exposure to absolute return strategies ensues in the appropriate risk category.

TABLE 6.12 z-Score Based Efficient Frontier Portfolio Characteristics, Fixed Income–like Universe, with $\lambda = 0.005$ and $\gamma = 0.005$

Return	0.37%	0.46%	0.52%	0.79%	0.63%
Volatility	0.16%	0.41%	0.66%	0.81%	1.13%
Skewness	−0.24	−0.46	−0.47	−0.57	−0.47
Kurtosis	−0.57	1.01	0.90	0.47	0.75
Target Risk	0.16%	0.41%	0.66%	0.81%	1.13%
Portfolio Composition					
Cash	100%	67%	44%	0%	0%
Bonds	0%	33%	56%	55%	100%
Absolute Return Strategies	0%	0%	0%	45%	0%
Total	100%	100%	100%	100%	100%

Table 6.13 and 6.14 present a similar analysis in the equitylike universe. These results are comparable to what we found in the fixed income universe. Exposure to traditional strategies tends to rise as the model is made more adverse to negative skewness and high kurtosis. In particular, the allocation to traditional equities falls dramatically when the sensitivity

TABLE 6.13 z-Score Based Efficient Frontier Portfolio Characteristics, Equity-like Universe, with $\lambda = 0.01$ and $\gamma = 0.01$

Return	1.03%	1.01%	0.99%	0.97%	0.95%
Volatility	2.47%	2.92%	3.37%	3.83%	4.28%
Skewness	−0.09	−0.32	−0.41	−0.45	−0.46
Kurtosis	0.90	0.65	0.59	0.58	0.59
Z-Score	−0.02	−0.03	−0.03	−0.04	−0.04
Target Risk	2.47%	2.92%	3.37%	3.83%	4.28%
Portfolio Composition					
Equity	42%	58%	73%	86%	100%
Equity Hedge	13%	9%	6%	3%	0%
Equity Unhedge	5%	4%	3%	2%	0%
Managed Futures	23%	16%	11%	5%	0%
Global Macro	17%	12%	8%	4%	0%
Total	100%	100%	100%	100%	100%

TABLE 6.14 z-Score Based Efficient Frontier Portfolio Characteristics, Equity-like Universe, with $\lambda = 0.01$ and $\gamma = 0.01$

Return	1.16%	1.17%	1.16%	1.15%	0.95%
Volatility	2.48%	2.93%	3.39%	3.85%	4.28%
Skewness	0.00	−0.39	−0.57	−0.65	−0.46
Kurtosis	0.65	0.55	0.60	0.66	0.59
Z-Score	−0.02	−0.02	−0.03	−0.03	−0.04
Target Risk	2.47%	2.92%	3.37%	3.83%	4.28%
Portfolio Composition					
Equity	4%	20%	35%	49%	100%
Equity Hedge	10%	7%	4%	1%	0%
Equity Unhedge	43%	46%	47%	47%	0%
Managed Futures	26%	16%	8%	1%	0%
Global Macro	16%	11%	6%	2%	0%
Total	100%	100%	100%	100%	100%

to skewness and kurtosis is halved. In fact, the main difference between the sets of portfolios presented in Tables 6.13 and 6.14 is the shift from traditional to concentrated equities (equity unhedged), when the aversion to negative skewness and positive kurtosis is halved. Note also that both sets of results provide a reasonable and intuitively predictable set of exposures to the more highly diversifying (low correlation) strategies such as managed futures or global macro.

The "efficient frontier" generated by the model, however, is unusual in terms of the risk return trade-off in both negative skewness and kurtosis aversion scenarios: The higher the risk defined in standard deviation terms, the lower the expected return. This is a reflection of unusual features of the data series. The traditional relationship between volatility and return does not hold, with certain strategies, such as equity hedge (long/short portfolios) or global/macro tending. These strategies tend to offer the highest returns and lowest volatility simultaneously. Although accounting for skewness and kurtosis corrects for these obvious shortcomings (in terms of capital market theory), the experiment still produces results that should be further verified with a more powerful model that covers many more sets of asset classes or strategies.

CONCLUSION

Our work suggests that there is indeed a role for nontraditional, hedge fund–type strategies in diversified portfolios, although we have admittedly not expanded the analysis to issues of tax efficiency, which are well covered in the literature. We believe that rather than considering hedge funds as one single asset class, investors should allocate certain strategies to the portfolio's equity exposure and other strategies to its fixed income component. This would allow a more reasonable allocation where comparable risk levels are contained in the appropriate pockets.

Since these strategies typically provide exposure to less desirable return distribution characteristics, we conclude that a traditional constrained mean-variance analysis is insufficient. Thus, we introduce a simple model that attempts to incorporate all four statistical moments. This approach is inherently imperfect, at least to the extent that it generates portfolio weightings based on actual return distributions. It belongs more in the simulation family of models than in the broader solver family. It is different from traditional solvers in that it cannot generate portfolio weights when only the usual statistical properties of return distributions for various asset classes or strategies are given. Thus, it can be used only on historical return distributions, unless it is possible to generate simulated distributions based on the complete set of statistical properties, which includes the four first statistical moments (average, standard deviation, skewness, and kurtosis) and their respective correlation, coskewness and cokurtosis matrices. In short, it represents only one possible path and is much too sensitive to the dependency of future performance on past performance.

Recent work by Davies, Kat, and Lu (2004) constitutes a very important step forward. They develop a model that incorporates investor preferences for return distributions' higher moments into polynomial goal programming (PGP) optimization, which allows them to allocate hedge funds in a mean-variance-skewness-kurtosis framework. This model, which belongs to the solver family of models, has a similar architecture to our z-score in that it incorporates skewness and kurtosis in the same manner, together with scaling or preference variables that correspond to investor utility. It would be interesting to use such a model to build diversified portfolio-efficient frontiers with various hedge fund strategies and to contrast the characteristics of these portfolios with those of alternatives constructed using a traditional mean-variance optimizer.

CHAPTER 7

Hedge Fund Selection: A Synthetic Desirability Index

Jean-Pierre Langevin

Benefits stemming from the addition of a hedge fund component in any portfolio should be twofold: more alpha (positive returns under various conditions) and lower global portfolio risk (through little or no correlation). In this chapter, we develop a synthetic Desirability Index, which balances the need for both high risk-adjusted returns and low correlations. By applying this indicator to the Credit Suisse First Boston (CSFB)/Tremont subindexes from 1994 to date, we illustrate that although certain strategies are less alpha "efficient" than others, their ability to diversify is such that their overall ranking nonetheless makes them more desirable in a portfolio.

INTRODUCTION

Many institutional investment committees have opted to enter the hedge fund asset class because of its recognized absolute return component, namely its ability to generate alpha. In doing so, however, investors sometimes disregard one important characteristic of hedge funds: the near absence of correlation of their returns with their current institutional portfolios.

The inclusion of hedge funds in a portfolio of assets, be it traditional long-only or fund of hedge funds, ought to be based on the very basic principles elaborated 50 years ago by Markowitz (1952). Each addition should be viewed in the context of increased return (α generation) and global portfolio risk reduction (diversification). The latter is a direct function of asset correlations and appears to be seldom considered to its full extent, especially in the case of hedge funds.

Some institutional investors (specifically funds of hedge funds and large pension plans) make use of both variables through software optimization. Recent theoretical developments have overcome the limitations of mean variance optimization and allow the use of additional statistics to find a set of roughly optimal portfolios. These statistics include the third and fourth moments (skewness and kurtosis) of hedge fund return distributions. These distributions are usually not normal.

The majority of pension plans have chosen funds of hedge funds, viewed as less risky than individual hedge funds. Moreover, funds of funds require less supervision and offer more or less the same benefits, although at a cost equivalent to the fees charged by the fund of funds (FoF) manager. However, with over 7,000 hedge funds and funds of funds available world-wide, representing more than US$1 trillion, selecting a group of strategies, funds, or merely a few funds of funds, can rapidly become a daunting task.

In this chapter we develop a simple technique that institutional investors can use to assess the potential added value of each hedge fund product. Our synthetic Desirability Index (D-Index) takes into account the quest for both high positive marginal risk-adjusted returns (RAR) and low correlation (COR) with any current portfolio. It recognizes the fact that even though a hedge fund product might present a lower RAR than that of the current portfolio, its correlation profile could be attractive enough to make it worth including.

THEORETICAL FRAMEWORK

The approach is developed around investors' preference sets and utility functions. Since both RAR and COR variables can have a significant impact on an institutional portfolio return/risk profile, each of these two characteristics is assumed to generate a certain level of utility to the investor in relation with a current given portfolio. However, utilities induced by these two variables must be considered in a "unit utility" framework.

Assume the following:

RAR_p = Expected risk-adjusted return of current institutional port-
          folio p
RAR_i = Expected risk-adjusted return of hedge fund i
$\Delta R_{(i,p)}$ = $RAR_i - RAR_p$ = Difference between the expected risk-adjusted
          return of hedge fund i, and that of portfolio p
$\rho_{(i,p)}$ = Expected correlation between the returns of hedge fund i and
          those of portfolio p

$\Delta R_{(i,p)}$ and $\rho_{(i,p)}$ can be seen as having the domains Φ in Equations 7.1 and 7.2:

$$\Phi\left[\Delta R_{(i,p)}\right] = \left(-\infty; +\infty\right)$$

(7.1)

$$\Phi\left[\rho_{(i,p)}\right] = \left[-1; +1\right]$$

(7.2)

When examining a potential investment in hedge fund i, the investor naturally wishes that $\Delta R_{(i,p)}$ be as high as possible and that $\rho_{(i,p)}$ be as low as possible. Accordingly, these axioms of preference sets are postulated for $\Delta R_{(i,p)}$:

> More $\Delta R_{(i,p)}$ is always preferred to less (7.2a)
> Positive $\Delta R_{(i,p)}$ has positive utility (7.2b)
> Negative $\Delta R_{(i,p)}$ has negative utility (7.2c)

For $\rho_{(i,p)}$ we postulate that:

> Utility derived from correlation is always nonnegative (7.3)
> Small values of $\rho_{(i,p)}$ are always preferred over large ones (7.4)
> Investors show correlation-aversion over $\Phi[\rho_{(i,p)}]$ (7.5)

Axiom 7.5 states that, as correlation increases, its utility becomes less valuable. To allow for the processing of the two utilities $U(\Delta R_{(i,p)})$ and $U(\rho_{(i,p)})$ in a unit utility framework, this constraint must imposed: Utility U derived from both $\Delta R_{(i,p)}$ and $\rho_{(i,p)}$ must be limited to the domain $[-1;+1]$. This condition is already met in the case of correlation (Equation 7.2), but not for the differential risk-adjusted return, as can be seen from Equation 7.1.

ON THE CORRELATION

In the case of correlation, Equation 7.3 imposes $\Phi[U(\rho_{(i,p)})] = [0;+1]$, which is a subset of the domain constraint $[-1;+1]$ imposed earlier. The expected correlation domain $\Phi[\rho_{(i,p)}] = [-1;+1]$ must therefore be transformed through a utility function whose domain is defined as $\Phi[U(\rho_{(i,p)})] = [0;+1]$, while meeting the requirements of Equations 7.3, 7.4, and 7.5.

Equation 7.4 implies that, $\delta' = \dfrac{\delta\left[U(\rho_{(i,p)})\right]}{\delta\rho_{(i,p)}} < 0$, and Equation 7.5 implies that $\delta'' = \dfrac{\delta}{\delta\rho_{(i,p)}}(\delta') < 0$.

Assuming a general polynomial utility function $U(x) = c_0 + c_1 x + c_2 x^2$ $+ \ldots + c_n x^n$, a unit utility function can transform the correlation domain and meet the concavity requirements specified above. This results in Equation 7.6:

$$U(\rho_{(i,p)}) = 1 - \left(\left(\frac{\rho_{(i,p)}}{2}\right) + 0.5\right)^2 \qquad (7.6)$$

Applying the correlation domain limits, it is easily verified that $U(\rho_{(i,p)}) = 1$ when $\rho_{(i,p)} = -1$ and that $U(\rho_{(i,p)}) = 0$ when $\rho_{(i,p)} = +1$. These two cases correspond to the return series of hedge fund i and portfolio p being perfectly negatively correlated and being perfectly positively correlated, respectively. The proposed correlation unit utility function is illustrated in Figure 7.1.

The unit utility is respectful of the investor's preference sets and intuitively appealing. It assigns maximum correlation utility to any hedge fund product showing perfect inverse correlation with the current portfolio. As correlation increases and approaches zero, correlation utility also decreases at an increasing rate, to the point where for $\rho_{(i,p)} = +1$, no correlation utility is generated. Indeed, no diversification benefit would be gained from adding an asset perfectly correlated to a given portfolio. With $\rho_{(i,p)} = 0$, an enviable characteristic available from only a few products and strategies, the correlation utility (0.75) is much closer to that of $\rho_{(i,p)} = -1$ than it is for $\rho_{(i,p)} = +1$. This functional asymmetry rapidly rewards lower correlations.

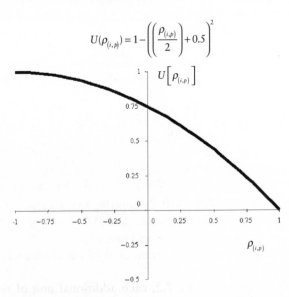

FIGURE 7.1 Utility of Correlation between Hedge Fund i and Porfolio p, as a Function of $\rho(i,p)$.

ON THE DIFFERENTIAL OF RISK-ADJUSTED RETURN

The case for the differential of risk-adjusted return, $\Delta R_{(i,p)}$, is trickier. One may argue that, both technically and intuitively, Equations 7.2b and 7.2c, which describe investors' preference set, could be complemented with two more axioms: that investors like positive $\Delta R_{(i,p)}$ and that they dislike negative $\Delta R_{(i,p)}$. The first suggests $\delta'' = \dfrac{\delta}{\delta \Delta R_{(i,p)}}(\delta') > 0$ with $\delta' = \dfrac{\delta\left[U(\Delta R_{(i,p)})\right]}{\delta \Delta R_{(i,p)}}$

for $\Delta R_{(i,p)} > 0$, while the second implies $\delta'' = \dfrac{\delta}{\delta \Delta R_{(i,p)}}(\delta') < 0$ for $\Delta R_{(i,p)} < 0$,

changing sign at $\Delta R_{(i,p)} = 0$. However, as explained earlier, the original domain $\Phi[\Delta R_{(i,p)}] = (-\infty; +\infty)$ is bounded by -1 and $+1$, once transformed by the unit utility function. No continuous function satisfying Equation 7.2a can accomplish this while simultaneously preserving the asymptotic character of the upper and lower limits imposed to the domain and centered on zero. Instead, we assume that for each gain in $\Delta R_{(i,p)}$, the gain in utility generated by the next gain increases until $\Delta R_{(i,p)}$ reaches 0, after which point it decreases until the investor becomes indifferent to extreme values of positive $\Delta R_{(i,p)}$. Equation 7.2a, however, must still be satisfied.

One utility function that can transform the original domain $\Phi[\Delta R_{(i,p)}] = (-\infty; +\infty)$ into $\Phi[U(\Delta R_{(i,p)})] = (-1; +1)$ asymptotically while meeting the requirements specified by Equations 7.2a, 7.2b, and 7.2c is given by Equation 7.7:

$$U(\Delta R_{(i,p)}) = \frac{\Delta R_{(i,p)}}{\sqrt{1 + \Delta R_{(i,p)}^2}} \tag{7.7}$$

Its first derivative, $\delta' = \dfrac{\delta\left[U(\Delta R_{(i,p)})\right]}{\delta \Delta R_{(i,p)}} = \dfrac{1}{\left(1 + \Delta R_{(i,p)}^2\right)^{3/2}}$, is always positive,

while its second derivative, $\delta'' = \dfrac{\delta}{\delta \Delta R_{(i,p)}}(\delta') = \dfrac{-3\Delta R_{(i,p)}}{(1 + \Delta R_{(i,p)}^2)^2}$ is negative for

$\Delta R_{(i,p)} > 0$ and positive for $\Delta R_{(i,p)} < 0$. By applying the differential risk-adjusted return domain limits, it is easily verified that $U(\Delta R_{(i,p)}) \to 1$ when $\Delta R_{(i,p)} \to +\infty$, that $U(\Delta R_{(i,p)}) \to -1$ when $\Delta R_{(i,p)} \to -\infty$, and that $U(\Delta R_{(i,p)}) = 0$ when $\Delta R_{(i,p)} = 0$. The unit utility function for the differential risk-adjusted return is illustrated in Figure 7.2.

As can be seen from Figure 7.2, each additional unit of risk-adjusted return differential brings a positive contribution to utility. As long as this risk-adjusted return differential is negative—that is, as long as the hedge fund has a lower risk-adjusted return than that of the portfolio—utility will always be negative. Conversely, each positive unit of risk-adjusted return differential will always be rewarded by a positive utility, up to unity when the risk-adjusted return differential reaches $+\infty$. As for the correlation utility, even a small positive risk-adjusted return differential (e.g., $\Delta R_{(i,p)}=5$) can generate nonnegligible utility (0.447).

COMBINING THE TWO UTILITIES IN AN INDEX

At this point, we have two unit utility functions for each of $\Delta R_{(i,p)}$ and $\rho_{(i,p)}$, for hedge fund i. Each of these two functions emphasizes the investor's desire, on one hand, for the largest $\Delta R_{(i,p)}$ values and, on the other hand, for the lowest possible $\rho_{(i,p)}$ to a given portfolio. By adding these two unit functions, we create the Desirability Index appearing in Equation 7.8:

$$
\begin{aligned}
\text{D-Index} &= U\left(\rho_{(i,p)}\right)+U\left(\Delta R_{(i,p)}\right)\\
&= 1-\left(\left(\frac{\rho_{(i,p)}}{2}\right)+0.5\right)^{2}+\frac{\Delta R_{(i,p)}}{\sqrt{1+\Delta R_{(i,p)}^{2}}}
\end{aligned}
\tag{7.8}
$$

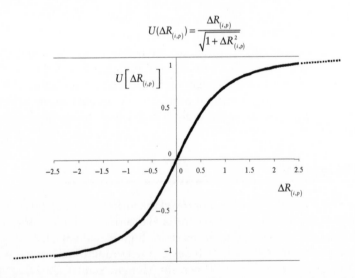

FIGURE 7.2 Utility of Risk-Adjusted Return Differential between Hedge Fund i and Portfolio p, as a Function of $\Delta R(i,p)$.

The index's domain, $\Phi[\text{D-Index}]$, will therefore be the sum of the two utility functions' domain limits (Equation 7.9):

$$\begin{aligned}
\Phi\left[\text{D-Index}\right] &= \Phi\left[U(\rho_{(i,p)})\right] + \Phi\left[U(\Delta R_{(i,p)})\right] \\
&= \left[0;+1\right] + \left[-1;+1\right] \\
&= \left[-1;+2\right]
\end{aligned} \tag{7.9}$$

All possible combinations of $U(\rho_{(i,p)})$ and $U(\Delta R_{(i,p)})$ will therefore be contained within -1 and $+2$. Since $U(\rho_{(i,p)})$ is always positive or nil, only a negative differential risk-adjusted return can induce a D-Index less than zero. However, if a negative differential risk-adjusted return is accompanied by an amount of correlation utility that more than compensates the loss of differential risk-adjusted return utility, the D-Index will be positive. To illustrate, the Figure 7.3 displays the possible domain of the D-Index as a function of differential risk-adjusted return.

The domain of the D-Index is delimited by the bold upper and lower bounds defined by correlation values of -1 and $+1$. As expected, lowering the correlation induces a higher index level. A D-Index isoline, shown in bold strike, illustrates the different possible combinations of correlations and differential risk-adjusted returns to obtain a level of 0.5 in this case. A fund showing a differential risk-adjusted return of $+0.6$, coupled with perfect correlation $(+1)$ with the current portfolio, will have the same D-Index value as one with a differential risk-adjusted return of $+0.09$ but with a correlation of 0.5. A differential risk-adjusted return of -0.3, coupled with a correlation of zero, would yield the same D-Index value.

The idea is not so much to examine the D-Index value in absolute terms but to form a basis with which an investor can rank potential candidates. By mixing both the added value brought on by differential risk-adjusted returns with the expected decrease in total portfolio risk brought on by correlation inferior to one, investors can rapidly detect which funds deserve further analysis.

AN ILLUSTRATION

Assume that a pension plan has approved the inclusion of hedge funds as an asset class in its portfolio. The question is to determine which fund strategies have the greatest added value, in terms of higher risk-adjusted returns or lower total portfolio risk. The D-Index can help rank opportunities.

In this example, a mix of 40 percent Morgan Stanley Capital International (MSCI) (total return in U.S. dollars) and 60 percent J.P. Morgan Global Government Bond index, rebalanced every month, serves as a proxy

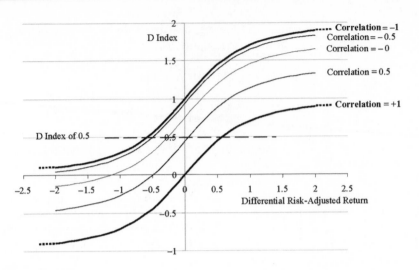

FIGURE 7.3 Desirability D-Index, as a Function of Differential Risk-Adjusted Return, for Various Levels of Correlations between Fund *i* and Portfolio *p*.

for the current global institutional portfolio. The CSFB/Tremont Hedge Fund Index and 14 strategy subindices are used to proxy hedge fund strategies. The reference period covers December 1993 to November 2004, which represents the entire CSFB/Tremont database history. The expected correlations between our global portfolio and the different strategies are proxied by the actual value of the correlation coefficients between the return series during the reference period. The expected risk-adjusted return of the current portfolio is proxied by the Sharpe ratio of the simulated world portfolio. Finally, the risk-free rate is the U.S. three-month Treasury rate. The expected risk-adjusted return of the strategies and funds considered is proxied by the Sharpe ratios of the 14 different strategies, substrategies, and main index reported by CSFB/Tremont. The expected differential risk-adjusted return of each strategy is therefore calculated by subtracting the portfolio's actual Sharpe ratio from each strategy's actual Sharpe ratio.

Table 7.1 shows, for the CSFB Hedge Fund main index and each of the 14 strategies and substrategies, the annualized return, volatility (standard deviation), risk-adjusted return, differential risk-adjusted return, correlation versus global portfolio during the period, and the value of the D-Index. The rank occupied by each strategy/substrategy appears in parentheses.

Despite some strategies showing negative differential risk-adjusted returns, all strategies show a positive D-Index. In other words, the lack of

TABLE 7.1 Statistical Measures and D-Index Values, CSFB/Tremont Universe versus JPM–MSCI Global Portfolio, December 1993 to November 2004

Strategy	Annualized Return	Volatility	Sharpe ratio	Differential Risk-adjusted Return (rank)	Correlation with Portfolio (rank)	D-Index (rank)
3-month Treasury	3.96%		–	–	–	–
Global Portfolio	7.11%	5.88%	0.54	–	–	–
CSFB Hedge Fund Index	10.91%	8.18%	0.85	+0.29 (09)	+0.52 (11)	0.72 (10)
Convertible Arbitrage	9.70%	4.68%	1.23	+0.69 (05)	+0.14 (02)	1.24 (03)
Dedicated Short Bias	–3.18%	17.67%	–0.40	–0.94 (14)	–0.70 (01)	0.29 (13)
Emerging Markets	7.51%	17.10%	0.21	–0.33 (13)	+0.48 (10)	0.14 (14)
Equity Market Neutral	10.26%	3.03%	2.08	+1.55 (01)	+0.40 (07)	1.35 (01)
Event Driven	11.54%	5.85%	1.30	+0.76 (03)	+0.55 (12)	1.00 (05)
Distressed Securities	13.51%	6.73%	1.42	+0.88 (02)	+0.55 (13)	1.06 (04)
Multistrategies	10.46%	6.19%	1.05	+0.51 (06)	+0.47 (09)	0.92 (06)
Risk Arbitrage	8.08%	4.35%	0.95	+0.41 (07)	+0.42 (08)	0.88 (09)
Fixed Income Arbitrage	6.80%	3.85%	0.74	+0.20 (11)	+0.08 (03)	0.90 (07)
Global Macro	13.97%	11.64%	0.86	+0.32 (08)	+0.28 (06)	0.90 (08)
Long/Short Equity	11.94%	10.63%	0.75	+0.21 (10)	+0.61 (14)	0.56 (11)
Managed Futures	6.96%	12.25%	0.24	–0.29 (12)	+0.00 (02)	0.47 (12)
Multistrategy	9.49%	4.40%	1.26	+0.72 (04)	+0.14 (04)	1.26 (02)

performance above the current portfolio appears to be more than compensated for by the correlation profile of that strategy. For example, the negative differential risk-adjusted return value of −0.94 for Dedicated Short Bias (rank 14) is accompanied by an impressive correlation of −0.70 (rank 1). Though the resulting D-Index ranking is near the bottom, at 13, and its value is very low, the diversification effect of this strategy in the global portfolio can be expected to compensate for a significant portion of the global portfolio performance decrease that its inclusion would induce.

The main CSFB index is ranked only 10 out of 14 possible, which means that two-thirds of the strategies have the potential to bring a higher added value in the global portfolio than the main index. Fixed-Income Arbitrage, for example, although not very value additive in terms of differential risk-adjusted return at +0.20 (versus +0.29 for the CSFB index), shows a correlation near zero. Combined, these two numbers bring its total D-Index score to 0.90, corresponding to rank 7.

Some strategies hold their original differential risk-adjusted return rank through the D-Index. Others find a higher level (midpoint ranking) because of favorable correlation structure. Some, such as Multistrategy, go from rank 4 on both variables to rank 2 on the D-Index. In this latter case, the combination of high differential risk-adjusted return and low correlation is responsible for the overall attractive ranking.

HOW MEANINGFUL IS THE D-INDEX?

For the D-Index to be meaningful, it needs to provide the practitioner with a valuable filter that can help determine the best subgroup of funds or strategies for a given portfolio.

To answer this question, 14 portfolios are simulated over the same period and rebalanced at each month-end. Each portfolio is composed of 80 percent of the same global equity and bond portfolio and an arbitrary level of 20 percent of each CSFB strategy. The new annualized returns, volatilities, and Sharpe ratios are then obtained and compared to the original no-hedge fund component values appearing in Table 7.1. The change in Sharpe ratio is used as a base to rank the added value of each strategy included in the world portfolio. The last column on Table 7.2 shows the rank expected by the D-Index, as per Table 7.1.

Of 14 strategies, 11 show the Sharpe ratio ranking very close (within two ranks) to the one predicted by the D-Index. In fact, of the first 5 (approximately 35 percent of the sample) top-ranking strategies expected by the D-Index—Convertible Arbitrage, Equity Market Neutral, Event Driven, Distressed Securities, and Multistrategy—four belong to the same

TABLE 7.2 Statistical Measures, Simulated Portfolios with 80 Percent World Portfolio and 20 Percent CSFB/Tremont Strategy, December 1993 to November 2004

Strategy	Annualized Return	Change in Annualized Return	Volatility	Change in Volatility	Sharpe ratio	Change in Sharpe ratio (rank)	Rank Expected by the D-Index
3-month Treasury	3.96%						
World Portfolio, without hedge funds	7.11%		5.88%		0.54		
CSFB Hedge Fund Index	7.91%	+0.79%	5.73%	−0.15%	0.69	+0.15 (08)	10
Convertible Arbitrage	7.67%	+0.55%	4.93%	−0.95%	0.75	+0.22 (05)	03
Dedicated Short Bias	5.38%	−1.74%	3.38%	−2.50%	0.42	−0.12 (14)	13
Emerging Markets	7.39%	+0.28%	7.01%	+1.13%	0.49	−0.05 (13)	14
Equity Market Neutral	7.76%	+0.65%	4.98%	−0.90%	0.76	+0.23 (04)	01
Event Driven	8.01%	+0.90%	5.44%	−0.44%	0.75	+0.21 (06)	05
Distressed Securities	8.40%	+1.28%	5.56%	−0.32%	0.80	+0.26 (02)	04
Multistrategies	7.81%	+0.69%	5.39%	−0.49%	0.71	+0.18 (07)	06
Risk Arbitrage	7.33%	+0.22%	5.13%	−0.75%	0.66	+0.12 (10)	09
Fixed Income Arbitrage	7.09%	−0.02%	4.83%	−1.05%	0.65	+0.11 (11)	07
Global Macro	8.57%	+1.45%	5.80%	−0.08%	0.79	+0.26 (03)	08
Long/Short Equity	8.12%	+1.01%	6.24%	+0.36%	0.67	+0.13 (09)	11
Managed Futures	7.24%	+0.12%	5.30%	−0.58%	0.62	+0.08 (12)	12
Multistrategy	7.88%	+0.76%	4.83%	−1.05%	0.81	+0.27 (01)	02

group that contributes to the largest positive changes in Sharpe ratios. The largest discrepancy between the rankings is with Global Macro, expected to rank 8 while it actually ranked 3. The D-Index appears to underestimate the importance of the absolute level of return of a given strategy, that is, without taking into account the volatility component. Nonetheless, the index appears to fulfill the main objective of helping investors determine the most promising pool of funds and strategies susceptible to produce favorable return/risk profiles.

CONCLUSION

The Desirability Index is not an absolute measure of utility, nor does it pretend to capture in a single number all subtleties of covariance. It merely tries to combine two important descriptive characteristics of investments that are too often examined independently. The D-Index is a tool for ranking each investment opportunity according to its combined return increase and risk reduction effects.

The example used in this chapter was built around a limited set of opportunities, namely the CSFB/Tremont Hedge Fund Index and its 14 strategies. The problem faced by practitioners is much larger and involves sorting, analyzing, comparing, interviewing, and finally selecting among hundreds of hedge funds and hedge fund products. The methodology presented in this chapter should help investors identify the pool of most promising funds and products. The greater dispersion of D-Index values expected in the case of individual hedge funds, compared to indices, would most likely yield better differentiation between products. By narrowing choices, investors can focus in greater detail on the critical issues of mathematical simulation and due diligence.

This chapter is a first examination of the D-Index as applied to hedge funds and, as such, needs further refinement. More work is needed to avoid potential alpha errors that can arise when a product is assigned a lower rank than deserved. Furthermore, it should be emphasized that the differential risk-adjusted return and correlation inputs should be expected values. Long-term history is not necessarily a valid proxy for these two variables, especially in the case of the differential risk-adjusted return.

TWO

Hedge Fund Management

Chapter 8 explores the increased interest in hedge fund index investing. It extends several index tracking models that are commonly used for equity portfolios to construct hedge fund index tracking portfolios. These portfolios are designed to observe the usual constraints for funds of funds, such as lock-in periods and minimum capital invested. Empirical results demonstrate that it is relatively easy to track a hedge fund index with only few funds and that the availability of different models grants increased flexibility for the design of the tracker fund.

Chapter 9 takes a look at the last five years in which hedge fund assets under management have soared while average returns have fallen significantly. As the hedge fund industry has become more competitive, many management companies have been raising their fees. This chapter explores how some common incentive fees may not be in the investor's best interest. Funds that offer investor-friendly fee structures may have a competitive advantage in attracting and retaining assets.

Chapter 10 provides three analyses of hedge fund profiles against conventional asset markets. These profiles—of daily hedge fund indexes, short selling indexes, and managed futures indexes—provide new insight into the relationship between hedge funds and conventional asset markets and illustrate both consistency and diversity in hedge index properties.

Chapter 11 profiles the technology developed by banks to securitize their corporate loans that has recently been adopted by hedge funds, creating a new financial product known as collateralized fund obligations. These CFOs provide considerable benefits to both hedge fund managers and investors. CFOs enable managers to obtain relatively low-cost, long-term, investment financing for their hedge funds; for investors, CFOs offer diversification benefits in form of credit-rated debt instruments. This chapter explains the structure of CFOs and examines the key legal issues arising out of the application of this new technology to hedge funds.

Chapter 12 analyzes monthly fund returns, and the authors show that volatility persistence in hedge fund returns increases the likelihood of larger maximum drawdowns relative to the case where hedge fund returns are random. The return behavior of various classes of hedge funds, including single-strategy funds, fund of funds, and commodity trading advisors, indicate that volatility persistence and an accompanying increase in the likelihood of larger maximum drawdowns are present in about 30 percent of the sample of over 2,000 funds. Interestingly, while average kurtosis and volatility persistence statistics are similar across funds, the relationship between these statistics and maximum drawdown statistics is stronger for less diversified the funds.

CHAPTER 8

Hedge Fund Index Tracking

Carol Alexander and Anca Dimitriu

This chapter reviews some important innovations in quantitative strategies for investment management. We summarize the advantages and limitations of applying cointegration and principal component analysis to portfolio construction. Empirical examples show that by exploiting the presence of common factors, both models can significantly enhance traditional optimization strategies. More important, such strategies can be used successfully both for traditional investments such as equities and for optimizing more complex portfolios such as funds of hedge funds.

INTRODUCTION

In addition to offering considerable alpha opportunities, hedge funds present very attractive diversification opportunities due to their low correlation with traditional asset classes and also within their peer group. The benefits of adding hedge funds to traditional asset classes portfolios have long been illustrated through the use of hedge fund indexes as investable instruments (Schneeweis and Spurgin 1998a; Schneeweis, Karavas, and Georgiev 2002; Indjic 2002). To this end, investors have the choice of selecting one of the readily investable hedge funds indices (e.g., the ones provided by Standard & Poor's (S&P), Hedge Fund Research (HFR), Credit Suisse First Boston (CSFB)/Tremont, or Morgan Stanley Capital International (MSCI)) or constructing a custom-made index tracking portfolio. The main advantage of the latter scenario is the possibility to control both the fund selection and the portfolio management as to include the investor's preferences.

Hedge funds portfolio optimization is a somewhat controversial topic, with the majority of research on alternative investments still focusing on the absolute performance portfolios (see Favre and Galeano 2002; Krokhmal, Uryasev, and Zrazhevsky 2002; Amenc and Martellini 2003c). Despite the significant enhancements brought to portfolios in traditional asset classes, Liew (2003) argues that hedge fund indexing might not be optimal, given that after adjusting for market exposure and nonsynchronous trading, the majority of hedge funds exhibit negative performance. However, hedge fund alpha estimation is prone to considerable specification and sampling errors, which makes the construction of absolute performance portfolios rather complex. As demonstrated recently (Amenc and Martellini 2003a; Alexander and Dimitriu 2004a), the absolute alpha benefit of hedge fund investing is very difficult to measure with any reasonable degree of accuracy. Due to the myriad of strategies employed by hedge funds, their highly dynamic nature, and the extensive use of derivatives and leverage inducing nonlinear relationships of their returns with the traditional asset classes, models for hedge fund returns are inherently complex (Fung and Hsieh 1997a; Schneeweis and Spurgin 1998b; Agarwal and Naik 2000c; Amenc and Martellini 2003a).

There seems to be considerable interest in hedge funds indexing models. Martellini, Vaissié, and Goltz (2004) review the issue of hedge fund indices in an attempt to reconcile investability with representativity. Their solution follows the methods of Fung and Hsieh (1997a) for constructing portfolios to replicate the principal components of hedge fund returns. However, the range of models available for indexing is considerably larger. In the equity world, many index tracking models have been developed (Roll 1992; Rudolf, Wolter, Zimmermann 1999; and Alexander and Dimitriu 2005), and practitioners now use them extensively. In the alternative investment universe, the portfolio management process has significant particularities, and no hedge fund indexation models have been studied in the extant research literature. In a realistic portfolio management setting, one should attempt to gain exposure to the hedge fund universe with a portfolio comprising a reasonably small number of funds and optimized to replicate a broad index without frequent rebalancing. There are at least two predominant considerations for any hedge fund indexation model:

1. There are significant operational restrictions to actively trading hedge funds, such as minimum investment limits, long lockup periods and advance notice, regular subscriptions and redemptions as rare as once per year, and sales and early redemption fees. To include these in the optimization model constraints on the general objective of tracking accuracy must be added.
2. The optimization model should result in a stable portfolio structure since we are aiming for a passive investment in an alternative asset class.

With these properties in mind, this chapter examines three popular indexing models that are commonly employed for standard equity strategies: the classic tracking error variance minimization model (Roll 1992), the cointegration-based index tracking model (Alexander 1999), and the common factor replication model (Alexander and Dimitriu 2004a). As the name suggests, the third model is more than an indexing model, focusing on replicating only the common trends affecting fund returns rather than tracking a traditional benchmark. If there is a strong common movement in fund returns, their first principal component will be highly correlated to traditional benchmarks, and explain them to a large extent.[1] The use of principal component analysis for indexing purposes in alternative investments has been recently promoted by Amenc and Martellini (2003b), as providing the best one-dimensional summary of the information conveyed by several competing indexes. Fung and Hsieh (1997a) have examined the performance of portfolios of hedge funds constructed to replicate the first principal components of fund returns, noting the similarity between the first principal components portfolio (PC1) and a broad index.

Given the predominant considerations just mentioned, for hedge fund indexing, these models need to be implemented with constraints such as no short sales, and minimum investment limits, and the rebalancing frequency should be set to no less than six months. Our out-of-sample results show that it is possible to obtain fair replicas of hedge fund benchmarks, which preserve most of their features and comprise a relatively small number of funds. Of the models investigated, the standard tracking error variance minimization model produced a reasonable replica of the benchmark, with the lowest turnover. The cointegration portfolio was the most accurate tracker, but at the expense of additional transaction costs. Funds of funds seeking absolute outperformance of a hedge fund index would be well advised to employ a common factor replication framework. All these models produce portfolios that are highly correlated with the benchmark, and more attractive in terms of higher moments.

MODELS FOR INDEX TRACKING

Classic Tracking Error Variance Minimization

Fueled by the increased interest in indexing and the practice of evaluating managers' performance relative to a benchmark, an extension of classical

---

[1]In a perfectly correlated system, the first principal component will be in fact the equally weighted index of all the system components.

mean-variance analysis was made to accommodate a tracking error optimization of equity portfolios (Rudd 1980; Rudd and Rosenberg 1980; Roll 1992; Rudolf, Wolter, and Zimmermann 1999).[2] In this setting, the problem faced by the investor is formulated in terms of expected tracking error and its volatility, rather than expected absolute return and its volatility. As emphasised by El-Hassan and Kofman (2003), the tracking error can be either the investment goal for a passive strategy that seeks to reproduce accurately a given benchmark or an investment constraint for an active strategy that seeks to outperform a benchmark while staying within given risk limits defined by the benchmark.

A general form of indexing model minimizes the tracking error variance for a given expected tracking error. (In the case of a pure index fund, this would be zero.) The intuition behind it is that a fund that meets its return target consistently has no volatility in the tracking error. The analytic solution derived by Roll (1992) is not applicable for portfolios comprising only a subset of the stocks in the benchmark. Instead, the following numerical optimization in equation 8.1 needs to be implemented:

$$\min_{w_k} \sum_{t=1}^{T} \left(r_{index,t} - \sum_{k=1}^{N} w_k r_{k,t} \right)^2 \ s.t.$$

$$\sum_{t=1}^{T} \left(r_{index,t} - \sum_{k=1}^{N} w_k r_{k,t} \right) = 0$$

$$\sum_{k=1}^{N} w_k = 1 \tag{8.1}$$

$$L < w_k < U$$

where $r_{index,t}$ = the return on the index

$r_{k,t}$ = the return on the kth fund, both measured at time t

w_k = the weight assigned to the kth fund

The model minimizes the variance of the tracking error subject to the constraint of zero expected tracking error, and unit sum of weights. Given the specifics of hedge funds investing, we need to impose a positive lower bound L on portfolio weights. The upper bound U is needed for diversification so that the tracking portfolio is not concentrated in just a few hedge funds.

---

[2]The tracking error is defined as the difference between portfolio returns and benchmark returns.

Every financial professional needs the bare essentials.

Institutional Investor magazine provides reliable, unbiased coverage of the events, issues and people who have an impact on the world of business and finance.

Request your FREE TRIAL online at: www.iitrial.com/card

Optimization models based on tracking error are known to have some drawbacks, which limit their applicability to a passive investment framework. One is that the attempt to minimize the in-sample tracking error with respect to an index that, as a linear combination of stock prices, comprises a significant amount of noise may result in large out-of-sample tracking errors. This is a result of the well-known trade-off between the in-sample fit and the out-of-sample performance of a model. An optimization based on tracking error will attempt to overfit the data in-sample, but this is done at the expense of additional out-of-sample tracking error. Moreover, the in-sample overfitting may result in an unstable portfolio structure that is unsuited to passive investments as it implies frequent rebalancing and significant transaction costs.

Classic tracking error models are optimized using a covariance matrix of asset or risk factor returns; these models have additional weaknesses generated by the very nature of correlation as a measure of dependency: It is a short-term statistic, which lacks stability; it is only applicable to stationary variables, such as asset returns. It requires prior detrending of level variables and has the disadvantage of losing valuable information (the common trends in level variables); and its estimation is very sensitive to the presence of outliers, nonstationarity, or volatility clustering, which limit the use of a long data history. All these exacerbate the general problems created by optimization and small sample overfitting.

We therefore examine two other models that are specifically designed to suit a passive investment framework: a variant of the cointegration-based index tracking (Alexander 1999) and the common factors replication (Alexander and Dimitriu 2004b). Both models have been shown to produce, in the equity universe, stable portfolios having strong relationships with either the benchmark itself or with only one of its components (i.e., the common factors affecting stock returns). Their enhanced stability results in a low amount of rebalancing and, consequently, reduced transaction costs.

Cointegration-Based Index Tracking

The most general form of cointegration model allows the replication of any type of index. The rationale for constructing portfolios based on a cointegration relationship with the market index rests on two features of cointegration:

1. The value difference between the index and the portfolio is, by construction, stationary, and this implies that the tracking portfolio will be tied to the benchmark in the long run.
2. The portfolio weights are based on the history of prices rather than returns, and as a result they have an enhanced stability.

As pointed out in the introduction, the issue of transaction costs is central for passive investments. Along with the absolute tracking error and its variance as performance criteria, the amount of transaction costs incurred in managing the tracking portfolio also plays an important role. In these circumstances it seems sensible to include a proxy for the transaction costs in the optimization model.

The most general form of the cointegration model for index tracking (Alexander 1999) is minimizing the variance of the log price spread between the tracking portfolio and the benchmark, subject to zero sum of price spreads (equivalent to zero in-sample tracking error), unit sum of weights that also lie within a lower bound and an upper bound, and, finally, stationary series of price spreads. Instead of minimizing the variance of the price spread, an alternative objective function minimizes the number of trades required to adjust the portfolio weights from one period to another, subject to the same set of constraints, of which the most important is the cointegration with the benchmark. Starting with an initial tracking portfolio cointegrated with the benchmark, the model identifies the new portfolio structure that is closest to the current one, thus involving a minimum number of rebalancing trades, and that preserves the feature of cointegration with the benchmark.

The new optimization problem can be written as:

$$\min_{w_{k,t}} \sum_{k=1}^{N} \left| w_{k,t} - w_{k,t-1} \right| P_{k,t} \ \ s.t.$$

$$\sum_{k=1}^{N} w_{k,t} = 1$$

$$L < w_{k,t} < U \tag{8.2}$$

$$\text{ADF}(\ln(index_t) - \sum_{k=1}^{N} w_{k,t} \ln(P_{k,t})) < \text{critical value}$$

where $index_t$ = the value of the index,
$P_{k,t}$ = the value of the kth fund, both measured at time t
w_k = the weight assigned to the kth fund

Common Factors Replication

The third indexing model investigated is a general portfolio construction model based on principal component analysis. From all possible portfolios containing all the assets in the benchmark and subject to the unit norm constraint on the weights, this model identifies the portfolio that accounts for the largest amount of the total joint variation of the asset returns. Such a property makes it the optimal portfolio for capturing only the common factors driving asset returns, thus filtering out a significant amount of variation that can be ascribed to noise.

The ith principal component, where $i = 1, \ldots,$ k, may be written as:

$$P_i = w_{1i}r_1 + w_{2i}r_2 + \ldots + w_{ki}r_k \qquad (8.3)$$

where $r_1, \ldots, r_k$ = the returns on the hedge funds in the portfolio
$(w_{1i}, \ldots, w_{ki})'$ = the ith eigenvector of the returns covariance matrix

In Alexander and Dimitriu (2004b) the portfolio replicating the first principal component is constructed directly from the normalized eigenvectors of the covariance matrix of asset returns. However, the sampling in the hedge funds universe is an essential feature to preserve, so we will use the first eigenvector as a selection criterion. The higher the loading of a fund on the first principal component, the higher will be its contribution to the common factor. Given that the first eigenvector is determined so as to maximize the variance of the corresponding linear combination of fund returns, high factor loadings will be allocated to funds that have been highly correlated with their group over the calibration period. Such funds should be the most representative in their groups. Having selected the funds according to their loading on the first principal component, the portfolio is optimized to have maximum correlation with that principal component, subject to the usual constraints: nonnegativity and an upper bound on individual weights. The optimization problem can be written as:

$$\max_{w_{k,t}} \; (w_{k,t}P_{k,t}, PC1_t) \; s.t.$$

$$\sum_{k=1}^{N} w_{k,t} = 1 \qquad (8.4)$$

$$L < w_{k,t} < U$$

HEDGE FUND DATA AND BACKTESTING PROCEDURE

Hedge fund data are subject to several measurement biases caused by the data collection process and by the nature of the industry: survivorship bias, when a database does not include the performance of funds that ceased operating during the sample period; selection or self-reporting bias, when the hedge funds in the database are not representative of the population of hedge funds; instant history bias, when the funds entering the database are allowed to backfill their results; and multiperiod sampling bias, when the analysis is restricted to funds having a minimum amount of history available. Fung and Hsieh (2000c) provide an extensive analysis of biases in the TASS hedge fund database. They estimate a survivorship bias of approximately 3 percent per annum. Regarding the instant history bias, they found an average incubation (backfilled) period of one year with an associated bias of 1.4 percent per annum while the multiperiod sampling bias was negligible.

Our fund data comes from the Hedge Fund Research (HFR) dead and alive funds databases, from which we select the period December 1992 to May 2003. We restrict our analysis to U.S.-domiciled funds reporting net of all fees in U.S. dollars, having funds under management above $10 million, and not using leverage. Additionally, to minimize the sample bias of alpha estimates, we require that each fund has at least five years of reporting history. After imposing these selection criteria, our database comprises 282 funds.

To determine the impact of the instant history bias in our database, for each fund we examine the difference between the monthly average of the excess return (over Standard & Poor's [S&P] 500 index) in the first year and the monthly average of the excess return in the first five years. The difference is equivalent to 3.97 percent, and the standard deviation of the difference is 1.01 percent per annum so there is a clear first-year bias in the reported fund performance. In order to eliminate the instant history bias on alpha, we use dummy variables for the first year of reporting in all factor models. The estimated multiperiod bias is negligible, at .33 percent per annum. Selection and survivorship biases are addressed by including dead funds that have sufficiently long reporting history. But this is still not sufficient to ensure that the portfolio performance is identical to the experience of an investor in these funds, because there is no information on the performance of individual funds after having ceased reporting. Statistics show that some funds stopped reporting to HFR because of extraordinarily good performance, but some also because of negative performance. If some funds were liquidated, their investors probably recovered only part of the net asset value last reported. To deal with all these potential biases, we con-

---

[3]A more realistic alternative would be to construct a value-weighted index of all funds. However, the net asset value data are missing for some funds and are discontinued for some others. In order to preserve the number of funds in the selected database, we can only construct the index based on an equal-weighting scheme. Still, as demonstrated by Larsen and Resnick (1998), equally weighted indexes are the most difficult to replicate, and our results can therefore be interpreted as minimal for the case of more commonly value-weighted indexes of hedge funds.

struct an equally weighted index of all funds in our selected database.[3] This will be affected by the same biases. An indexing model needs to be evaluated on a relative basis; with this equally weighted benchmark its performance measurement is bias free, as both the tracking portfolios and their benchmark are affected by the same biases.

In order to test the out-of-sample performance of these models, we use a rolling sample of 60 months prior to the portfolio construction moment for calibration purposes. The first index tracking portfolios are set up in December 1997 and left unmanaged for the next six months as this is the typical lock-in period for hedge fund investments. The portfolios are then rebalanced every six months, reselecting funds based on the relevant criterion and optimizing them according to the indexing model used. We impose a nonnegativity constraint and a 15 percent upper bound constraint on portfolio weights.[4]

OUT-OF-SAMPLE PERFORMANCE ANALYSIS

In order to construct realistic hedge fund portfolios, we need to restrict the number of funds selected. Considering the evidence of maximum diversification benefits with around 30 funds, we use a relevant selection criterion to pick, at each rebalancing moment, approximately 30 funds that are the most likely to support the index tracking objective. Given that several fund allocations will not satisfy the lower bound constraint, the indexing portfolios will contain less than 30 funds. In fact, our indexing portfolios generally contain no more than 10 percent of the total number of funds in the benchmark. Figures 8.1 to 8.4 plot the evolution of each portfolio weights over the sample period. In general, the index tracking portfolios invest in no more than 10 percent of the funds in the universe. Note that the moments when the portfolio structure changes significantly are not the same for the four models.

Tracking Error Variance Minimization Model (TEV)

Since the objective of this model is to minimize the tracking error variance (TEV), a natural candidate for a selection criterion is the correlation of the fund returns with the equally weighted index returns. That is, at each

---

[4]In order to accommodate the minimum investment constraint in our hedge funds portfolio, we eliminate all portfolio holdings of less than 0.5 percent and renormalize the remaining ones. Given the fact that this applies to very small holdings, the differences between the optimized portfolio and the renormalized version are minimal.

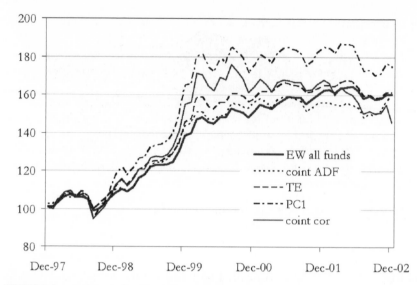

FIGURE 8.1 Performance of Tracking Portfolios versus Equally Weighted Benchmark
(Dec 97 = 100)

rebalancing moment, we select the funds that had the highest correlation
with the index returns over the calibration period.

The out-of-sample performance results are summarized in Table 8.1.
The TEV portfolio is very highly correlated with the equally weighted portfolio of all funds (correlation coefficient 0.94), but it has a slightly lower

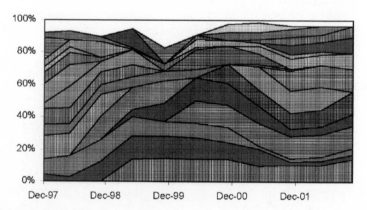

FIGURE 8.2 Weights in TEV Portfolio

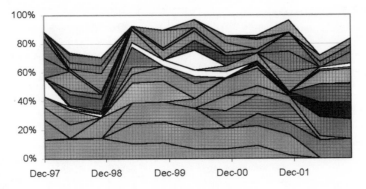

FIGURE 8.3 Weights in ADF Cointegration Portfolio

information ratio (1.26 as compared to 1.48), mostly due to higher volatility. This comes as no surprise, given that the number of funds included in the TEV portfolio is less than 10 percent of the total number of funds, and because they are selected to have high correlation with the index they also have high correlation with each other. Apart from volatility, in terms of higher moments, the TEV portfolio is very similar to the equally weighted benchmark.

Figure 8.5 plots the evolution of a $100 investment in this portfolio, alongside an investment in the equally weighted index. The TEV portfolio outperforms the equally weighted benchmark until mid-2001. Since then

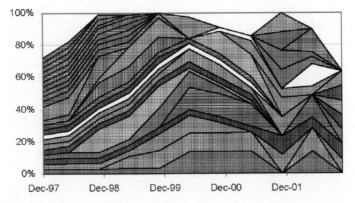

FIGURE 8.4 Weights on Correlation Selected Cointegration Portfolio

TABLE 8.1 Performance of Portfolios Designed to Replicate the Equally Weighted Portfolio of All Funds (Equally Weighted Portfolio of All Funds Included for Comparison)

	TEV Portfolio	ADF Cointegration Portfolio	Correlation Selected Cointegration Portfolio	Common Factors Portfolio	Equally Weighted Portfolio
Annual returns	9.72	10.24	9.34	12.10	10.16
Annual volatility	7.73	7.46	12.07	11.85	6.85
Skewness	0.32	−0.38	0.04	−0.21	−0.18
Excess kurtosis	2.99	1.86	1.01	2.08	2.10
Information ratio[a]	1.26	1.37	0.77	1.02	1.48
Turnover	5.83	10.74	8.91	7.10	4.92
Correlation EW	0.94	0.88	0.94	0.94	1.00

[a]The information ratio is computed as average annual portfolio returns divided by annualized returns volatility.

it has underperformed, but over the five-year horizon it still remains above the benchmark.

Cointegration-Based Index Tracking Portfolio

As an alternative to the TEV model for constructing index-tracking hedge fund portfolios, we implement the cointegration tracking model described in the previous section. Under the constraint of a cointegration relationship between the value of the portfolio and the value of the benchmark, the opti-

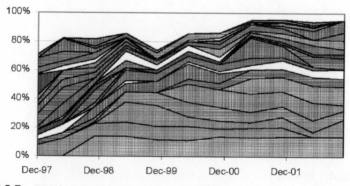

FIGURE 8.5 Weights in Common Factors Portfolio

mization target now focuses on the stability of the portfolio structure, rather than the correlation with the benchmark. The weight constraints are the same as for the TEV model.

In order to control the number of funds in the tracking portfolio, we implement a selection criterion that is consistent with the cointegration constraint. We select the funds according to the degree of cointegration of their cumulative returns with the cumulative returns of the equally weighted index. We note that it is by no means necessary for each individual fund to be cointegrated with the benchmark in order to be able to find a linear combination of them that is cointegrated with the benchmark. However, selecting funds that are individually cointegrated with the benchmark is likely to facilitate the task of finding portfolios that are cointegrated with the benchmark.

As a proxy for the degree of cointegration, we use the augmented Dickey-Fuller (ADF) statistic for the residuals of univariate regressions of index cumulative returns on each individual fund cumulative returns. At each rebalancing moment, we select the 33 funds having the lowest ADFs (highest degree of cointegration with the benchmark) and optimize the portfolio so as to generate the minimum amount of trades subject to the cointegration constraint on the portfolio-index values relationship.

The out-of-sample performance summary is presented in Table 8.1 In terms of both returns and volatility, the cointegrated tracking portfolio outperforms the TEV model, being only slightly more volatile than the equally weighted portfolio of all funds. Again, this performance is remarkable, because it is achieved with only 10 to 15 percent of the funds in the benchmark universe. As expected, the correlation with the equally weighted benchmark is lower than in the case of the TEV model, but remains very high (0.88). One respect in which the cointegrated portfolio is less attractive is turnover, which at 10.7 is much higher than in the TEV model. Thus, the additional feature of cointegration appears to be costly particularly in terms of transaction costs. This can be due to three reasons:

1. The cointegration constraint is very strong, and it requires significant changes to the portfolio structure from one period to another.
2. The ADF fund selection criterion does not result in a stable group of funds to be further optimized under the cointegration constraint.
3. The ADF fund selection criterion is not consistent with the cointegration constraint, which is not well supported by the data on the selected funds.

The last alternative is the most unlikely.

In order to identify the cause of the portfolio instability, we have replaced the ADF fund selection criterion with the correlation criterion used in the TEV model. Even though this criterion is less consistent with the cointegration constraint than the ADF criteria, it produced a relatively stable portfolio structure for the TEV model. When implementing the correlation-based selection criterion in conjunction with the cointegration model, we find that the turnover is significantly reduced (8.9, as compared to 10.7 for the ADF selection). As expected, the correlation with the benchmark is very high (0.94). However, the drawback is the increase in volatility, which results in a lower information ratio (0.77, as compared to 1.37 for the ADF selection and 1.26 for the TEV model).

Clearly, the increased instability of the ADF based cointegration model has to do with the features of the hedge fund returns. The average of the lowest 33 ADF statistics computed on the residuals of univariate regressions of the benchmark cumulative returns on the individual fund cumulative returns is approximately 2.7, which is well above the critical value for the Engle-Granger test for cointegration (usually less than −4, depending on the number of funds in the portfolio and the length of the data sample). Despite the fact that at each rebalancing moment we manage to find a portfolio of hedge funds that is cointegrated with the equally weighted index, the stochastic common factors driving fund returns are weaker than in the case of equities, and cointegration relationships are more difficult to find.

Of all the portfolios analyzed, the ADF cointegration portfolio was the most accurate tracker of the index for the largest part of the sample period, (until September 2001). Over the next six months it underperformed the benchmark, and from mid-2002 to the end of the sample it outperformed it. Overall, it matched the return over five years of the equally weighted index of all funds. Note that from mid-2002 to the end of the sample, the performance of the ADF and the TEV portfolios was not synchronized. Hence one may consider combining them to produce a more accurate replica of the benchmark and to reduce the portfolio volatility.

Common Factors Replication Portfolios

As expected, the portfolio replicating the first principal component is much more volatile than the equally weighted portfolio of all funds. However, its returns are also significantly enhanced to 12 percent per annum, as compared to 10 percent for the benchmark. Overall, the information ratio of this portfolio is less than the one of the benchmark, but their correlation remains very high (0.94). The turnover of this portfolio is between those of the TEV model and the ADF models. In terms of higher moments, the first principal component 1 (PC1) portfolio is the most similar to the benchmark of all three portfolios.

The common factors portfolio clearly outperformed the equally weighted index of all funds until February 2000. Given that during the five years prior to this moment technology funds were very popular front runners and were highly correlated as a group, the portfolio replicating the first principal component was overweighting them relative to the benchmark, and hence it made significant gains. When the technology bubble burst, this portfolio became much more volatile than the benchmark, despite the fact that in terms of returns, the difference between them did not changed dramatically.

CONCLUSION

Despite the modeling complexity caused by biases present in data, noisy correlation structure, alphas that are difficult to estimate, and institutional limitations to trading, alternative investments represent attractive opportunities. The diversification potential of investments in hedge funds has long been advocated, and the next natural step is to look for models to replicate the performance of hedge funds indices. Such models can be a valuable tool for managing funds of hedge funds portfolios. Aiming to develop such a fund selection and optimal allocation process for funds of hedge funds, we have analyzed the out-of-sample performance of a number of index-tracking models that were originally designed for equity portfolios and have adjusted them to fit the special features of alternative investments.

We have shown that it is possible to obtain fair replicas of hedge fund benchmarks that preserve most of their features and comprise only a small number of funds. Each of the models investigated appears to suit a different investment profile: The TEV portfolio generates a reasonable performance associated with low turnover; the ADF cointegration portfolio represents a more accurate replica of the benchmark, but during turbulent periods of regime changes its turnover can be high; finally, the PC1 portfolio represents the model of choice for investors aiming at enhancing index returns while keeping a high correlation with the benchmark and a reasonable turnover.

CHAPTER 9

Designing a Long-Term Wealth Maximization Strategy for Hedge Fund Managers

Keith H. Black

It is no secret that hedge fund fees can be lucrative for fund managers, averaging two to four times those found in mutual funds trading similar securities. Until now, hedge fund managers have been in a seller's market, being able to charge whatever fees they choose, as investors have had an insatiable demand for hedge funds, evidenced by hedge fund assets that increased by U.S. $600 billion in just the last six years. However, as competition rises in the hedge fund industry, we would expect returns to decline and the power in the industry shift to investors. Hedge fund managers who offer fee structures that are better aligned with investor objectives will find themselves growing assets at a faster rate than those managers whose fee structures have more perverse incentives. This chapter suggests several investor-friendly fee structures that can improve the asset-gathering and retention skills of hedge fund managers in an increasingly competitive market.

INTRODUCTION

Hedge fund managers are typically compensated by a combination of a fixed management fee and an incentive fee that increases with the returns of the fund. This structure can be inappropriate for risk-averse investors, as it encourages hedge fund managers to manage high-volatility funds in order to maximize their potential incentive fee income. This myopic structure may have the perverse effect of maximizing current-year income, while potentially reducing the longevity of the fund and, therefore, the lifetime income of the fund manager. Managers who seek to maximize current-year fee income may be managing volatile funds that are prone to large losses and investor defections. While managers of volatile funds may earn a high fee income in a given year, their volatile strategies may cause their fund to have a short life. It is possible that fee income over the life of the manager could be higher when the fund focuses on a lower-volatility strategy that allows the manager to maintain investor assets for a longer period of time. Several fee structures are suggested that can reduce the volatility of the fee income earned by a hedge fund manager, while offering less conflict between the goals of the investor and the hedge fund manager.

Hedge funds are lightly regulated investment pools that can invest in equities, commodities, and/or fixed income securities, often adding leverage, derivatives, and short selling. Their goal is to provide positive returns, regardless of market direction. Investors find hedge funds attractive as portfolio diversifiers when their returns are uncorrelated to traditional investments, as this lack of correlation improves the risk/reward ratios of their portfolios, often reducing total portfolio volatility without sacrificing much return. Hedge fund managers have a different incentive, as they desire to attract assets in order to earn large investment management fees.

The Center for International Securities and Derivatives Markets (CISDM) manages a proprietary database that contains information on the fees, returns, and strategies of the managers of hedge funds and managed futures funds. As of January 2004, the database contained information on 577 managed futures funds and 1,441 hedge funds with stated fee structures and current operations. At that date, the average hedge fund charged an annual management fee of 1.10 percent, while managed futures funds averaged 2.02 percent. The management fee is an annual fee that is charged regardless of the level of return of the fund.

Hedge funds had an average incentive fee of 17.51 percent of profits, while managed futures funds charged a mean 19.41 percent of profits. In a period when the fund is earning profits for investors, the fund managers share in the profits to the extent stated by the incentive fee. When the fund's investors are losing money, however, the managers earn a zero incentive fee. Once incentive fees are paid, the fund has established a high-water mark with their highest-monthly closing net asset value (NAV). When the value of the fund declines below the high-water mark, due to trading losses, no incentive fees are earned until the fund NAV increases beyond this level. The purpose of a high-water mark is to ensure that managers earn incentive fees only once for earning a particular gain. Black (2004) quotes a study by Van Hedge Fund Advisors that states that 89 percent of hedge funds (at the end of the first quarter of 2003) had fee structures that contain a high-water-mark provision. The same study shows that only 18 percent of funds have a hurdle rate; 82 percent of funds have no hurdle rate. With a hurdle rate, the incentive fee is not earned until a minimum return is earned, frequently designated as the risk-free rate or a fixed return. The total incentive fees earned by a fund decline with the size and existence of a hurdle rate. For example, assume that a fund earns an incentive fee of 20 percent of profits, which are 10 percent in a given year. Without a hurdle rate, the manager earns an incentive fee of 2 percent of assets, which is 20 percent of the 10 percent return. With a 4 percent hurdle rate, the manager only earns an incentive fee of 1.2 percent, which is 20 percent of the 6 percent return (10 – 4 percent) above the 4 percent hurdle rate. Evidently, manager income declines and investor returns increase with the size and the existence of a hurdle rate.

A 20 percent incentive fee is the most common in the industry, and 51 percent of hedge funds in the CISDM database charge a 20 percent incentive fee combined with a management fee of 1, 1.5, or 2 percent. Managed futures funds typically have a higher fee structure, where nearly 40 percent of funds charge a management fee of 2 percent with an incentive fee of 20 percent ("2 plus 20"). We find, however, that fees can vary widely across funds. In extreme cases, managed futures funds have charged fees of 6 percent plus 25 percent of profits or 1 percent plus 35 percent of profits. The largest fee structures found among hedge funds range from 2 percent plus 40 percent of profits to 4.8 percent plus 20 percent of profits. We would hope that hurdle rates are most prevalent among funds with the largest incentive fees.

While most actively managed U.S.-focused mutual funds earn a total management fee of less than 1.5 percent per year, the fee potential of hedge funds can be significantly higher. Assuming a 15 percent annual performance, the average total fee of all hedge funds in the CISDM database (assuming no hurdle rates) is 3.72 percent of assets each year, while managed futures funds earn an average of 4.93 percent of assets. The distribution is skewed, as 71 percent of managed futures funds earn over 5 percent of assets, with a theoretical maximum of 9.75 percent of assets in a year of gross returns of 15 percent. Using the same example, we find that 56 percent of hedge funds earn greater than 4 percent of assets, while the fund with the most lucrative fee structure can earn 8 percent of assets for providing investors gross returns of 15 percent. This lucrative fee structure attracts significant talent to the hedge fund industry, but managers' behavior may not be in the best interest of long-term investors, especially when managers can earn more than one-half of the gross returns in a given year. If hedge fund managers seek to maximize their current fees, they may increase the volatility of their fund returns beyond the level desired by fund investors who often are seeking to invest in hedge funds to reduce the volatility of their portfolio.

It may seem that a high-water-mark (HWM) provision protects investors, as investors pay no incentive fee in times when the performance of the fund has receded from recent highs. Goetzmann, Ingersoll, and Ross (2003), however, believe that the high-water mark can be costly to investors. If hedge funds increase the risk of their trading strategies at times when incentive fees are zero and performance is below the high-water mark, these funds become less attractive to investors, even though fees are lower in the current period. This increased risk is a temptation to fund managers who may find it more attractive to "swing for the fences" rather than accept the realization of a zero incentive fee in the current period.

Ennis and Sebastian (2003) explain the trade-offs created when using incentive fees relative to the flat management fees that are prevalent among hedge fund managers. Flat management fees give fund managers the incentive to attract and retain assets, but not to maintain a level of performance. These fees can give perverse incentives when the large asset size of the fund leads to weaker performance, as the manager gets paid more while the investors earn less. Incentive fees could be appropriate for hedge funds, as these fees give managers the incentive to deliver large levels of performance, while preserving the incentive to stop accepting assets at a point where returns decline. Black (2004) gives examples of how a fund can earn a larger total management and incentive fee revenue by managing a smaller amount of assets while maintaining a large return than managing a larger asset base with reduced returns.

Coleman and Siegel (1999) and Anson (2001) explain that there are two agency issues with incentive fees. Anson (2001) describes the similarities between the incentive fees earned by hedge fund managers and call options.

Per Share Incentive Fee = Max (20% × (End NAV − Beginning HWM NAV), 0)

Dollar Incentive Fee = Max (20% × ($ Profits Earned on Total Assets), 0)

The potential size of the incentive fee is similar to the payoff formula of a call option. When investors place assets with a hedge fund manager, they are granting the manager a free call option on the increase in the value of their assets. By understanding the Black-Scholes options valuation model, we can see that the potential incentive fee increases with the amount of assets under management, the length of time the hedge fund manager controls the assets, and the volatility of the fund's investment strategy. As the manager is able to retain investor assets for longer periods of time, the potential value of their incentive fee increases.

While investors may be better served with low-volatility strategies that are relatively uncorrelated to traditional investments, hedge fund managers earn the highest potential payday by pursuing the most volatile strategies.

With the lack of transparency that many hedge funds offer investors, managers may change strategies and volatilities without informing their investors. While hedge fund investors may be risk averse, they have given hedge fund managers the incentive to be risk seeking.

The second agency problem is that of asymmetry. When the fund has large positive returns, both the investor and the fund manager earn large profits. However, the investor suffers much more than the manager during times of losses, as the manager does not earn negative fee income or give back any prior fees at this time. We can assume that the losses are more painful for investors than a lack of incentive income is for hedge fund managers, especially when the manager is still earning the management fee.

Anson (2001) believes that fund managers have the simple incentive to maximize the volatility of fund returns in order to maximize the potential size of the current-year incentive fee. Coleman and Siegel (1999), however, refute this idea. They believe that the manager is risk seeking, increasing volatility when fund returns are below the high-water mark, in order to increase the probability of earning a positive incentive fee. However, fund managers may become more risk averse when returns are far above the high-water mark, as they may reduce volatility, or even stop trading, in order to ensure that they do not lose the incentive fees already earned in the current period.

These fee structures, combined with six problems, serve to make the current standard fee structures difficult for investors. Surprisingly, some investor-friendly fee structures may also improve the risk/reward trade-offs of managing a hedge fund.

PROBLEMS

Problem 1: Is There a Hedge Fund Bubble?

Even though many hedge fund strategies are said to have a limited capacity to manage assets, TASS Research (quoted in Barreto [2004]) estimates that investors contributed over $100 billion to hedge funds in the first nine months of 2004. Brandon (2004) quotes Hennessee Group estimates that the hedge fund community managed $795 billion in January 2004, taking the year-end total in 2004 to over $900 billion. Assets have increased nearly 300 percent since January 2000, when hedge funds managed only $324 billion. Hedge funds managed less than $100 billion as recently as January 1996.

Unfortunately, this increase in hedge fund assets may have contributed to the decline in returns to hedge funds. From 1994 to 1997, the Credit Suisse First Boston (CSFB)/Tremont Hedge Fund Index returned an average of 16.37 percent, earning between 21 percent and 26 percent each year from 1995 to 1997. From 1998 to 2003, the average return fell to only 8.47 percent, exceeding 5 percent only in 1999 (23.43 percent) and 2003 (15.46 percent).

If investors view this trend toward lower returns as permanent, they may question the skill of hedge fund managers and the high fees that they earn. While the large inflows continue to make hedge funds a manager's market, where the fund can dictate the fee structure, a time may come where the lower returns and increasing number of hedge fund managers make for an investor's market, when investors will demand lower or more investor-friendly fee structures. It is clear that 2004 was still a manager's market, as the standard fee structure moved from 1 plus 20 to 2 plus 20.

Problem 2: Manager Incentive Fee Income Goes to Zero When Fund Returns Are Below the High-Water Mark

Benjamin (2003) explains that managers may be tempted to close their fund when their performance is far from the high-water mark. If it is difficult to earn incentive fees, then some managers simply would like to close the fund and start over with new investors. CSFB/Tremont estimates that 73 percent of the 2,000 hedge funds in their database failed to earn incentive fees in 2002, as their declining fund values failed to exceed previous high-water marks. When a fund earns no incentive fee, managers gain only a 1 to 2 percent management fee, which is barely sufficient to pay their fixed costs.

According to the president of CSFB/Tremont, over 20 percent of hedge funds were liquidated in 2003. Recent performance of many hedge funds leaves managers far below their high-water mark, so many managers assume that there is little probability of earning incentive fees in the near future. Once a fund falls 25 to 30 percent below its high-water mark, the manager gives serious thought to closing and reopening the fund, as the high-water marks in the current fund may seem unattainable. It seems that hedge fund managers are eager to give up their free options granted by their original investors by closing down the fund. After liquidating their original fund, hedge fund managers will seek to open a new fund, thereby repricing their free options using the assets of new investors, while terminating the opportunity of their original investors to regain their losses. This short-term mentality can give the industry a bad reputation, because it seems that managers are more worried about their own bonuses than earning high returns for, and building a long-term relationship with, their investors.

While this may not seem fair to investors in the previous fund, there are claims that managers far from their high-water mark (who continue to serve their original investors) would have the perverse incentive to increase the volatility of their returns in order to more quickly regain their incentive fees. While managers may be tempted to liquidate a fund and reopen with a new name and new investors, there can definitely be risks and costs to this strategy. While there are direct expenses, such as the legal costs to design a new fund entity and marketing costs to find new investors, the indirect expenses can be even larger. As managers are taking time to start the new fund, they may have little or no assets under management, which means that they will be earning no management or incentive fees during this time. Perhaps the largest cost could be the cost to a manager's reputation, as potential investors in future funds sponsored by this manager may decline to invest given the managers' lack of respect to the investors in the previous fund. Investors may not appreciate paying large fees to the manager when performance is positive, while not having the chance to make up losses in a time where there is a reduced fee burden.

Problem 3: Investors May Have an Aversion to High Fees, Especially When Their Objective Is Diversification and Risk Reduction Rather than High Returns

The 2003 Greenwich Associates survey describes the attitudes of institutional investors toward hedge funds. Institutional investors that do not currently invest in hedge funds cite the lucrative fee structures of hedge funds as their main barrier to placing assets with alternative investment managers. Funds that make their fee structures more attractive to investors, provided that investors do not assume that lower fee funds have lower-quality management or lower potential returns, may be able to increase their assets under management faster than funds with less investor-friendly fee structures.

However, institutional allocations to hedge funds continue to grow, even in the face of rising fees. Many of these institutions may believe that it is the net returns that matter, not just the size of the fees. Investors may also continue to allocate assets to hedge funds, regardless of the fee structures, in a time where hedge fund returns are expected to be larger than equity market returns. Should equity markets enter a large bull market, we can expect that funds without large equity exposures would find it difficult to attract and retain assets.

Problem 4: Managers of Extremely Volatile Funds May Earn Large Incentive Fees Right before the Fund Loses a Large Portion of Investor Capital

Sender and Singer (2003) describe the rapid demise of the Eifuku master fund, a $300 million Tokyo-based long-short equity hedge fund. After returning 18 percent in 2001 and 76 percent in 2002, the fund lost nearly all of its value in seven trading days in January 2003. This fund was extremely risky, making highly leveraged bets on concentrated positions in small, illiquid Japanese equity securities. In fact, the fund's positions were so large that some investors speculated that the demise of this fund could increase the level of systemic risk in the Japanese markets.

Despite the fact that the fund lost nearly all of the investors' money, the manager likely earned a 2002 incentive fee exceeding $20 million, much of which may have been paid before the demise of the fund. John Koonmen, the young manager, lived a posh lifestyle of sports cars, luxury vacations, and penthouse condos while taking large and risky bets with investors' money.

If the private placement memorandum was well written, investors consciously agreed to accept the risks of leverage, illiquidity, and concentrated positions. If leverage and hubris were Koonmen's only sins, he may have no legal or criminal liability, and may be able to keep the incentive fees, despite the massive losses of his investors.

This makes us wonder if the manager was lucky or skilled. Clearly, investors would like to invest with skilled managers, even though it is difficult to separate the two types of managers in a short time period.

Problem 5: There Is Persistence in Hedge Fund Risk, but Not Hedge Fund Return

Herzberg and Mozes (2003) present a statistical study that concludes there is little persistence in hedge fund returns. Simply knowing that a fund has had high returns in the past does not allow an investor to correctly predict that the fund will have high returns in the future. Funds with recent high returns frequently are high-volatility funds that are correlated with traditional investment markets. High-return funds are likely to increase their assets under management, which can lead to new challenges for the hedge fund manager, whose strategy may work well with small amounts of assets yet struggle to profit with sharply higher asset levels that can lead to declining liquidity and inefficiencies and increased trading costs.

However, there is persistence in hedge fund risk and correlations to traditional investment returns. Funds with a lower historic volatility of returns tend to remain low-volatility funds in the future, while funds with a volatile history tend to remain volatile. Funds with a recent low correlation to underlying markets tend to remain uncorrelated in the future. This observation leads to a credible trading strategy, where an investor chooses hedge funds based on a 36-month trailing Sharpe ratio. Investors who buy the funds with the highest recent Sharpe ratio—defined as the fund return in excess of the risk-free rate divided by the volatility of the fund—are likely to own funds with average future returns and very low future volatility. Can we conclude, then, that more hedge fund managers are skilled at managing risk than at managing returns? If so, we may wish to compensate managers who best manage risk, rather than the current fee structure that encourages managers to take more risk.

Problem 6: While Competition Between Hedge Funds Continues to Grow, Top Managers Continue to Increase Fees

The distribution of assets and performance between hedge funds is quite uneven. Brandon (2004) quotes research by the Hennessee Group that there were 7,000 hedge funds managing nearly $800 billion in assets in January 2004. Of the managers surveyed, 34 percent managed less than $100 million in assets, while 67 percent managed less under $500 million. There were fewer funds that were very large, with 25 percent controlling over $1 billion in assets, with only 3 percent larger than $5 billion. These numbers are quite different from those in a study by Van Hedge Fund Advisors quoted by Black (2004). At the end of 2002, this study suggests that the median hedge fund manages only $33 million, with 77.4 percent of funds managing less than $100 million and only 3.5 percent of funds managing more than $500 million. Given that institutional investors now constitute the majority of new asset flows to hedge funds, we can expect continued consolidation of assets into the largest fund companies.

Many of these smaller funds may find it difficult to attract assets. This difficulty could come from a short track record, undistinguished performance, underdeveloped infrastructure, or the idea that institutions typically contribute assets to the largest funds. If an institution has allocated $1 billion to hedge funds it is likely to contribute $50 million to 20 different fund managers. Most institutions will place this amount of assets to an individual fund only after the fund is already managing over $200 million, as many large investors do not desire to be the largest customer of a very small fund.

The largest funds, and those with the best performance, may be able to continue to attract new assets, despite the trend toward higher fees. However, the smaller funds and those with average historical returns may need to distinguish themselves in other ways to attract assets in this competitive environment. These funds may want to focus on investor-friendly fee structures in order to survive and attract higher levels of new asset flows. How do hedge fund managers maximize their personal wealth? We believe that a long-term relationship with investors that leads to continually growing asset levels and moderate returns can earn much higher total fees than a fund that has a phenomenal year or two of performance before failing in a volatility-induced death spiral.

An innovative fee structure recently introduced by Steve Mandel, manager of the Lone Pine Capital funds, shows the current pricing power of star managers. Jenkins (2004) explains how some of the largest and most powerful management companies have been able to do away with the high-water mark, which has been one way to protect investors from volatility. The "Mandel fee structure," as it has been called by one fund of funds manager, allows the hedge fund manager to earn an incentive fee even when performance is below the high-water mark. When making new highs, the fund earns a 20 percent incentive fee. When recovering from a drawdown, but below the previous high-water mark, the fund earns a reduced 10 percent incentive fee, effectively earning fees multiple times for earning the same profits. The fund continues to earn this 10 percent incentive fee until it has earned back 150 percent of the drawdown amount. After that point, the incentive fee reverts to 20 percent. This fee can be sold as a positive to investors, even as it may increase the total fees paid in a given period. Because this fee reduces the volatility of the fee revenue of the manager, the manager may be less likely to liquidate the fund during a time of poor performance. Should good performance reappear in the future, investors can benefit from the longevity of their fund. We can see the power of these fund managers, as investors are paying incentive fees on the same gain multiple times, while the fund managers maintain a stream of incentive fees even after a period of investment losses.

SOLUTIONS

Implications and Possible Solutions

This leads us to assume that many institutional investors may be conducting a buy versus build decision when deciding how their alternative investment portfolio should be managed. The higher the fee structure, the lower the transparency, and the higher the volatility of fund trading strategies, the more likely institutions may be to build their own in-house alternative asset management capabilities. It seems that the short-term greed and hubris of hedge fund managers may work against them, serving to maximize their short-term wealth but to minimize their probability of building a long-term business franchise.

Out of nearly 7,000 hedge funds, there are, at most, several hundred funds that are run by star managers who can command whatever fees they request. Institutional investors are attracted to funds with high returns, low standard deviation of returns, high transparency, and a long track record of success. For this reason, most institutions invest with the largest and most established funds. While many top managers will retain the power to charge whatever fees the market will bear, the vast majority of hedge fund managers only charge "1 and 20" because that has historically been the standard hedge fund fee structure.

When the majority of institutional investors realize that their potential investment size gives them the leverage to negotiate fee structures, especially with smaller or younger hedge funds, hedge fund managers will need to negotiate fees with these investors. These small and/or new funds will be more likely to attract institutional investment and increase the longevity of their funds by adopting investor-friendly policies, including more rational fee structures and a covenant to continue to serve existing investors, even during adverse market conditions.

Hedge fund managers need to align incentives to alleviate the principal/agent problem. These managers must somehow become more risk averse, or be willing to earn the rewards of their risky behavior over longer periods of time.

Of course, investors must be willing to place their assets with the funds for longer periods of time. Many hedge fund managers feel pressured to deliver large gains in short periods to quell the threat of investor defections. If investors make short-term decisions when they allocate assets to or withdraw assets from hedge funds, managers cannot be criticized for short-term thinking. However, if investors are willing to commit assets to a specific fund for longer periods of time, the hedge fund manager should reciprocate with a fee structure designed to maximize the length of the relationship, and not simply maximize their current-year compensation. Reducing the volatility of returns clearly reduces the threat of investor withdrawals when those withdrawals are correlated to the percentage of assets lost in a given year.

Institutions should consider pressing for one or more of the four modified fee structures in order to better align the manager's incentives with the investor's need for low-risk, absolute return hedge fund performance:

1. Increase the use of hurdle rates
2. Redesign incentives/fees to resemble a deferred compensation plan
3. Introduce capped incentive fees
4. Compute incentive fees based on risk-adjusted returns

Increase the Use of Hurdle Rates

The average annual net return to the CSFB/Tremont Hedge Fund Index was 11.6 percent from 1994 to 2003. Van Hedge Fund Advisors estimates that only 18 percent of hedge funds calculate fees using a hurdle rate. Without a hurdle rate, investors will pay fees totaling 4.17 percent (1 percent plus 20 percent of the gross return of 15.8 percent) to earn this level of performance. Investors would prefer to pay incentive fees only for truly exceptional performance, such as the amount exceeding the risk-free rate or a fixed rate, such as 5 percent. A hurdle rate based on the risk-free rate may be especially warranted when the fund earns a large portion of its return from risk-free securities, such as the collateral used in managed futures funds or the interest earned on the proceeds for short sales.

The return on short-term fixed income instruments is often used as the hurdle rate, which makes sense as this risk-free rate is a key variable in the calculation of the Sharpe ratio, a measure that is often used to evaluate hedge fund managers. For example, assuming that the risk-free rate is 5 percent, the incentive fee would be paid only on the 10.8 percent return in excess of the risk-free rate, for a total fee of 3.16 percent (1 percent + 20 percent of 10.8 percent). The lower fees not only improve investor returns (from 11.6 to 12.6 percent), but also improve the performance history of the hedge fund manager. This improved track record can be another advantage in increasing assets under management.

Redesign Incentive Fees to Resemble a Deferred Compensation Plan

Under current hedge fund contracts, investors typically pay the entire incentive fee at the end of each calendar year (or calendar quarter) in which a new high-water mark is achieved. Therefore, a fund such as Eifuku can earn a large incentive fee and then liquidate in the next year. Similarly, hundreds of other funds have chosen to return capital to their current investors when it is clear that their funds will earn no incentive fees in the current year. Clearly it is not in the best interests of investors to pay a large incentive fee to a manager who will immediately liquidate the fund and terminate the relationship with the investors. Hedge funds may choose to return assets to investors in a time when they do not expect to earn incentive fees, especially when the cost of managing the fund exceeds the income earned from the management fees.

In order to prevent these liquidations that are used simply to reprice the fund manager's free option, a vesting period or a deferred compensation scheme can be defined. Simply stated, the fund manager is rewarded for maintaining a long-term relationship with investors. Perhaps all incentive fees will be paid out over a five-year period, with 20 percent of each year's incentive fee being paid out in each of the next five years. If the manager loses all of the investors' assets or chooses to liquidate the fund before the five years are completed, the fund would forfeit the remaining amount of fees that have not yet vested. After five years, the manager will earn the equivalent of one year's (20 percent times 5 years) incentive fee in each year of continued management, which can be seen as a reward for serving investors in a long-term relationship. Managers may actually find this structure attractive, as it increases cash flow in years where no current incentive fee is earned, which reduces the volatility of their fee income. If the investor terminates the relationship, the manager is immediately entitled to the total incentive fee earned during the entire time of the relationship, which means that all deferred compensation is accelerated to the time of the investor withdrawal.

Introduce Capped Incentive Fees

Because long-term net returns to hedge funds average about 11.6 percent with an annual standard deviation of 8.3 percent, we could place a two-standard-deviation band on hedge fund performance. When a hedge fund returns more than 28.15 percent (or, perhaps, rounded to 30 percent) in a given year, we may predict that this performance is unsustainably high. Perhaps the manager is taking too much risk, or has trades in a market where prices will revert to more normal levels in the future. Alternatively, cynics may conclude that performance spikes for many funds may more likely be in times when the manager was lucky rather than skilled.

What is the implication of capped incentive fees, or incentive fees calculated on longer-term performance? If managers can earn incentive fees only on the first 30 percent of performance in a particular year, they will not be tempted to trade very risky short-term strategies, but may instead focus more on trading strategies that are more likely to produce more sustainable, longer-term returns.

An investor may wish to remove performance caps if the manager is able to sustain extremely high returns over a long period of time. Perhaps the manager will earn incentive fees on the first 30 percent of performance in any given year, and at the end of five years (or when the investor terminates the relationship), the manager earns incentive fees on all performance in excess of 30 percent per year, once the manager has proven that the performance is more likely attributed to skill rather than luck. This type of structure would dramatically reduce the incentive fees paid to "one-year wonders" such as Eifuku and encourage managers to build a long-term relationship with their investors.

Compute Incentive Fees Based on Risk-Adjusted Returns

Although investors desire to buy lower-risk funds, managers of lower-risk funds typically earn lower incentive fees than managers of more risky funds that earn higher returns. Structuring incentive fees based on low risk, rather than on high returns, will more fairly compensate managers who deliver the low-risk, low-correlation funds that are most appropriate for investors seeking risk reduction rather than return enhancement.

There are advantages to compensating managers for risk-adjusted performance, whether measured by the Sharpe ratio, Sortino ratio, or the M-squared measure. The most important advantage is that managers do not have a blind incentive to increase the volatility of the fund, but will choose to increase risk only when there is a clear increase in return. Also, many investors believe that they should not pay fees for returns that they could earn themselves. For example, investors may pay lower total fees if they add leverage to their fund returns in their own account, rather than allowing the hedge fund manager to add the leverage. The standard incentive fee structure gives hedge funds the incentive to add leverage, which certainly adds volatility that expands the range of returns. However, Coleman and Siegel (1999) show that the Sharpe ratio is unchanged when leverage is added at the risk-free rate, as excess returns and volatility increase at the same rate. Using risk-adjusted returns allows investors to separate investing skill from the ability to use leverage, making their fees more directly attributed to the skills of the manager than to the structure of the product.

As with any other compensation scheme, managers compensated by Sharpe ratios or any other type of risk-adjusted returns may have an incentive to misrepresent performance to increase the amount of their fees. Spurgin (2001) shows methods by which a fund can reduce the perceived volatility of its returns by smoothing returns. These methods often involve derivative securities, which may materially reduce fund volatility without affecting return. Managers may also have the temptation to delay price changes for illiquid securities, which would also reduce the volatility of the reported returns of the fund. Coleman and Siegel (1999) also suggest that some minimal level of volatility be used in the calculation of performance, which avoids the nasty issue of paying an infinite performance fee to a fund with risk that approaches zero.

Whether incentive fees are paid on Sharpe ratios or on absolute returns, investors must be careful to supervise their managers' performance reporting to ensure that they are being charged appropriate fees.

CONCLUSION

Some industry participants believe that the principal/agent problem in the standard hedge fund fee structure is not as perverse as these examples may illustrate. Many fund of funds managers, as well as academics such as Kouwenberg and Ziemba (2004), state that the principal/agent problem is largely resolved when the fund manager has a significant personal stake in the fund. They believe that if managers have at least 30 percent of their net worth in the fund, the incentive to take significant risks with investor money is largely reduced.

Black (2004) quotes a Van Hedge Fund Advisors study that states that 82 percent of hedge fund managers have at least $500,000 of personal capital invested in their fund. These managers may have the incentive to moderate volatility if the potential of increased fee income from risky trading strategies is smaller than the potential loss of personal capital from this increased risk.

Hedge fund managers who seek to maximize their current-year income by charging high fees and chasing volatile strategies may reach their goal of large short-term incomes, while destroying the long-term potential of their business. With the increasing consolidation of the hedge fund industry, managers can profit from growing a long-term business that can be sold to a major investment bank, which can provide a billion-dollar payday for the selling hedge fund managers. Managers who understand that investors need long-term sustainable returns with low volatility and low correlation to traditional investment returns can build a long-term relationship with their investors. Those managers with a shareholder orientation can likely gather large pools of assets under management, which can lead to long-term gains and fees that are far larger than could be attained using the myopic wealth maximization strategy, which is often practiced to the detriment of their investors. Should fees stay high and managers continue to act in a greedy manner, institutions will be justified should they decide to abandon hedge funds or internalize their management of alternative investment strategies, especially if the massive inflows into hedge funds continue to reduce the potential returns. Kurdas (2004) quotes Byron Wien on the future of the hedge fund industry, which he believes has already moved from focusing on performance to focusing on the gathering of assets. Wien suggests that the industry could be headed for a period of mediocre returns, which could reduce the fees that investors are willing to pay. If the senior investment strategist of Morgan Stanley believes in these trends, hedge funds managers ignore his view of the future at their own peril. Hedge funds with the first-mover advantage toward investor-friendly structure may be able to maintain this advantage when the industry turns from a seller's market to a buyer's market.

CHAPTER 10

Profiles of Hedge Fund Indexes against Conventional Asset Style Indexes

Barry Feldman

Global hedge fund, short selling, and managed futures indexes are profiled against conventional asset markets using daily and monthly data. High-frequency style tilts are observed in the daily data analysis of global indexes, along with strong international influence. Short-selling indexes appear to vary substantially in cap exposures and gearing. Managed futures indexes show a robust hedging relationship with the large-cap growth style. These results indicate the importance of monitoring the conventional asset profiles of hedge funds and further research into their determinants.

INTRODUCTION

It is now clear that hedge fund performance is significantly affected by simple exposures to conventional asset markets. Asness, Krail, and Liew (2001) first forcefully make this point by showing that lagged market betas may significantly increase measured market exposure. Fung and Hsieh (2004a) demonstrate that five simple conventional asset factors—without lags—are able to effectively explain approximately 84 percent of the monthly variation in the Hedge Fund Research (HFR) equally weighted composite index over the nine years from January 1994 to December 2002.

The principal goal of this chapter is to extend research into the relationship between hedge funds and conventional asset markets by addressing these questions:

- How variable is this profile over time? Fung and Hsieh (2004b) find that there has been structural change in hedge fund indexes over long intervals, but do not study the potential degree of short-term variation. Here daily hedge fund indexes and rolling window analysis is used to examine the variability of this profile over time.
- How variable is the profile of a strategy against conventional assets among different providers of similar indexes? There are significant differences in conventional asset benchmarks. Some of these differences are definitional: What is the line that divides "small cap" from "mid cap"? Others, particularly in fixed income indexes, are due to sampling and selection. Also important are construction rules such as equal versus cap weighting and how indexes are updated over time. All these differences are evident in hedge fund indexes as well.
- How complex are hedge fund style exposures? Most published analyses of hedge fund indexes use a basic set of conventional asset benchmarks and have a limited ability to identify style bets, such as going long small value and short small growth, perhaps while taking the opposite bet with large-cap equities. This study uses an extensive set of equity style benchmarks.
- How important will daily hedge fund indexes be in the quantitative analysis of hedge fund performance? There are now more than two years of daily hedge fund performance index data. Daily data on a menu of strategies are now available from at least three index providers.

Here are summary answers. First, not surprisingly, it appears that some elements of hedge fund profiles against conventional asset markets change quite quickly over time. Using daily data, it is easy to find large exposures that last two months or less and switching, where a long profile becomes short or vice versa. Second, while there appear to be reassuring commonalities in the profiles indexes from different providers, there are also important differences that are important to consider when deciding which index to use for a particular purpose. Third, it appears that hedge fund equity style exposures can be quite complex on the index level, for example, being short both large growth and small value. Finally, it appears that daily indexes will become increasingly important in hedge fund analysis. There are important potential biases in these indexes due to the quality of daily pricing of less-liquid securities and the self-selection of hedge funds willing to report on a daily basis.[1] However, the additional

---

[1] Daily reporting typically involves allowing the indexer to see actual fund positions. Many managers will be reluctant to provide this level of transparency

statistical resolving power—the ability to detect changes in exposures down to the scale of weeks and months—is very important. Daily hedge fund indexes have surprisingly high correlations with convention+al asset benchmarks. Some of the analyses presented here based on a 50-day rolling window have greater statistical precision than those based on three years of data.

It is not possible to present a complete analysis of index profiles in this chapter, particularly because some of the most interesting results come from rolling window analysis, which requires a lot of space. Accordingly, we make some general comments regarding results not presented here and refer the reader to an online appendix to this chapter.

Why is the profile of a hedge fund against conventional asset markets important? First and foremost because of the maturing of the hedge fund industry. Institutional investors are increasing their allocations to hedge funds, and more individuals are adding hedge funds to their portfolios. As a result, there is an increasing emphasis on the need to develop demonstrably prudent procedures for building hedge fund portfolios. The importance of understanding the relationship between hedge funds and conventional assets rises sharply with the percentage of a portfolio invested in hedge funds.

There are many ideas on how to integrate hedge funds into a total investor asset portfolio (see, e.g., Waring and Siegel 2003; Henriksson 2004; Till 2004b). However, there is no widely accepted framework. Most common are rules of thumb and stories. The foremost story up to now is that hedge funds generate alpha in the form of absolute returns by exploiting market inefficiencies and that they are uncorrelated with conventional markets. This story can no longer be considered a reliable guide for prudent investment decisions.

Two issues should concern investors. The first, and most elementary, is that investors may not want to pay hedge fund management fees to earn money through indirect exposures to conventional asset markets. However, even if the exposure to conventional betas is only incidental to the generation of real alpha (or exposure to "alternative asset betas"), investment management should be aware of and be ready to compensate for conventional asset exposures. To provide one example, the asset allocation policy may be to be equity style neutral, but a significant exposure to managed futures may generate a short large-cap growth tilt. It may be that the magnitude of the tilt may not be of practical concern in many cases. Still, it could become important under particular market circumstances, and it could be that a number of other hedge funds in the same portfolio had similar tilts. Prudent fund management requires awareness of these exposures at multiple levels of the investment management process.

There is no question that effects such as survivorship bias (Brown, Goetz-mann, and Ibbotson 1999; Amin and Kat 2003c), backfill bias (Posthuma and Van der Sluis 2004), reporting accuracy (Liang 2003a), and, recently, interesting work on the causes of hedge fund attrition (Malkiel and Saha 2004) could bias profiles against conventional asset markets. Due to the complexity of trying to control for these effects, such investigation will have to wait. Estimated alphas are reported for the record; however, we offer no opinion on the level of index construction bias impounded in these estimates.

METHODS

The basic method utilized here is the factor model. The returns of the hedge fund index under study are regressed on the set of conventional asset bench-marks. In addition to the basic factor model results, the factor model is used to generate a variance decomposition of hedge fund index returns. This decomposition attributes this variance to the conventional asset bench-marks in the factor model. Variance decomposition provides an estimate of the relative importance of factors from the point of view of their contribu-tion to the total explained variance of the model. Relative importance is dif-ficult to infer from factor betas, principally because betas do not reflect the variance of their factors. T-statistics are essentially marginal or conditional measures, like F-tests, that do not provide a consistent attribution of explained variance for these purposes because of vulnerability to factors such as multicolinearity. The variance decomposition method used is pro-portional marginal variance decomposition (PMVD) (Feldman 2004).

The factor model is estimated imposing the no-arbitrage constraint. Betas are required to sum to unity. The factor model betas are then arbi-trage price theory betas (Ross 1976) when the Treasury bill (T-bill) is included as a factor, and all factors represent pure long positions. This con-straint is implicitly imposed when an analysis is based on excess returns.

The no-arbitrage constraint improves the precision of factor betas and is valid for conventional investment instruments, but may be inappropriate when significant use is made of options, futures, and other derivatives. The reduction in R^2 when the constraint is imposed can be used to test the con-straint with an F-test. If the constraint is not rejected, the T-bill beta is valid estimator of the net position of the fund. Betas less than 0 indicate positive gearing. Betas between 0 and 100 percent indicate long bias. A beta of 100 percent implies net neutrality. Betas over 100 percent indicate a net short position, where 200 percent is equivalent to being 100 percent short.

Variance decomposition results are calculated based on the uncon-strained factor model. In this case, T-bill variance components should be small due to the low volatility of cash unless levered cash returns are obtained from T-bill futures (or spurious correlations with T-bill yields).

The PMVD method produces a weighted average of marginal contributions to explained variance, where the average is overall possible orders that factors might enter into the model. The PMVD method, however, weights each marginal contribution by the probability that a particular ordering is the correct ordering according to increasing relative importance. An ordering is more likely if it is better ordered according to increasing (intermediate) marginal contributions to explained variance. The weakest factor receives a variance share perhaps only slightly greater than its marginal contribution to the complete model. The strongest factor may receive a variance share only slightly smaller than the square of its correlation with the index. Variance shares are inherently positive, but they are signed by the sign of the associated factor beta to facilitate interpretation. The sum of the absolute value of reported variance shares is the R^2 of the unconstrained factor model.

In addition to simple single-period analyses, results are also presented using rolling window analysis. This method is used to examine changes in factor exposures over time. The window is a period of time that is shorter than the history being analyzed. For example, in the daily analysis presented later in the chapter, the window is 50 days. The analysis for a particular date is based on the data for that date and the trailing 49 days.

Rolling window results are based on exponentially weighted regressions, in which more recent data are given slightly more weight. The analyses presented here are based on a 1 percent decay rate. This is a modest decay rate that has a minimal effect on the statistical quality of results. Under 1 percent decay, observation 50 in the rolling window has only 61 percent of the weight of the first observation. The average day without weighting is 25.5, the middle of the observation window. Under 1 percent decay, the weighted average day is reduced to 18.5.

HEDGE FUND INDEXES

Today there are a large number of index suppliers (see *www. hedgefundmarketing.org/hedgefundindexes.htm* for a comprehensive list). Comparisons will be presented here between indexes constructed by Credit Suisse First Boston/Tremont (the HEDG indexes), Hedge Fund Research (HFR), the Hennessee Group, Standard and Poor's (S&P), Van Hedge, and Center for International Securities and Derivatives Markets/ Managed Account Reports (CISDM/MAR). These are among the oldest and most well-known indexes. Space limitations prohibit a more comprehensive presentation. Arguably the most important characteristic of these indexes is

TABLE 10.1   Descriptive Statistics for Daily Data Analysis, September 30, 2003, to November 30, 2004

Benchmark / Index	Symbol	Mean	Std	Skew	Excess Kurtosis
Daily Hedge Fund Indexes					
HFRXGL Global Hedge Fund		0.015%	0.16%	−0.82	1.15
S&P Hedge Fund Index		0.026%	0.13%	−0.10	1.48
Conventional Asset Benchmarks					
S&P BARRA Large-cap Growth	LCG	0.040%	0.74%	0.00	−0.01
S&P BARRA Large-cap Value	LCV	0.090%	0.74%	−0.25	0.26
S&P BARRA Mid-cap Growth	MCG	0.068%	0.88%	−0.16	−0.33
S&P BARRA Mid-cap Value	MCV	0.103%	0.84%	−0.18	−0.05
S&P BARRA Small-cap Growth	SCG	0.109%	1.06%	−0.12	−0.44
S&P BARRA Small-cap Value	SCV	0.126%	1.06%	−0.20	−0.29
MSCI EAFE	DM	0.108%	0.94%	−0.13	0.24
MSCI Emerging	EM	0.135%	1.24%	−0.32	1.11
LB High Yield	HY	0.024%	0.43%	−0.15	0.75
LB 20+	LB	0.029%	0.65%	0.04	0.90
LB AGG	MB	0.011%	0.29%	0.12	0.47
T-Bill Daily Yld	T-Bill	0.004%	0.00%	1.52	11.11
Trade Weighted Dollar	USDX	−0.026%	0.32%	0.36	0.15
Number of observations	~290				

their frequency. Monthly indexes have longer histories; HFR goes back to 1990. With the exception of managed futures, daily hedge fund indexes do not go back before 2002.

Using daily data, the HFR Global Hedge Fund Index will be compared with the S&P Hedge Fund Index. These indexes utilize different strategies to represent the performance of the hedge fund universe. The HFR index reweights the performance of the funds it tracks by the estimated dollars invested in the respective strategies. S&P equally weights each of its nine basic strategies. Table 10.1 presents descriptive statistics for daily indexes.

Monthly data will be used to compare short selling indexes provided by CSFB, Hennessee, HFR, and Van Hedge; and to compare Commodity Trading Advisor (CTA), global macro, and managed futures indexes from CISDM/MAR, CSFB, and Hennessee. Table 10.2 presents descriptive statistics for monthly indexes.

TABLE 10.2   Descriptive Statistics for Monthly Frequency Benchmarks and Indexes, Data January 1994 to October 2004[a]

Benchmark / Index	Symbol	Mean	Std	Skew	Excess Kurtosis
Short Selling Indexes					
HEDG Dedicated Short		–0.08%	5.08%	0.92	2.24
Hennessee Short Bias Index		–0.02%	5.89%	1.17	6.05
HFRI Short Selling Index		0.28%	6.46%	0.26	1.62
VAN Global Short Selling Index		–0.06%	6.71%	0.12	2.29
CTA/Macro/Managed Futures Indexes					
CISDM/MAR CTA INDEX— Cap Weighted		0.67%	2.51%	0.25	–0.04
CISDM/MAR CTA INDEX Equal Weighted		0.71%	2.53%	0.38	0.05
HEDG Managed Futures		0.58%	3.52%	0.04	0.47
HFRI Macro Index		0.84%	2.17%	0.06	0.82
Conventional Asset Benchmarks					
S&P/BARRA 500 Growth	LCG	0.93%	4.86%	–0.53	0.00
S&P/BARRA 500 Value	LCV	0.93%	4.46%	–0.63	1.11
S&P/BARRA Mid-cap 400 Growth	MCG	1.15%	6.02%	–0.13	1.45
S&P/BARRA Mid-cap 400 Value	MCV	1.22%	4.53%	–0.46	1.81
S&P/BARRA Small-cap 600 Growth	SCG	0.90%	5.97%	–0.26	1.36
S&P/BARRA Small-cap 600 Value	SCV	1.16%	4.94%	–0.91	2.36
MSCI EAFE Free	DM	0.51%	4.27%	–0.41	0.33
MSCI Emerging Mkts	EM	0.32%	6.68%	–0.80	2.15
LB Aggregate Bond	HY	0.56%	1.15%	–0.51	0.95
LB Hi-Yld	LB	0.60%	2.08%	–0.67	3.51
LB LT Gvt	MB	0.68%	2.56%	–0.53	1.31
U.S. 30 Day TBill	T-Bill	0.32%	0.15%	–0.57	–1.14
USDX return	USDX	0.20%	1.16%	0.13	1.13
Fama-French Factors					
Fama-French Market Factor	Market	0.60%	4.54%	–0.72	0.66
Fama-French Small Firm premium	SmB	0.27%	3.72%	0.40	1.47
Fama-French Value Premium	HmL	0.20%	4.49%	–0.74	5.29
Number of observations	130				

[a]Van Hedge short-selling index data runs from January 1995 to October 2004.

CONVENTIONAL ASSET BENCHMARKS

Monthly performance is based directly on index provider reports. Daily index performance is based on corresponding Exchange Traded Funds (ETFs) (except for the T-bill and U.S. dollar). The abbreviations used in the tables are presented here in parentheses.

S&P/Barra equity-style indexes are used to represent large-cap growth (LCG), large-cap value (LCV), mid-cap growth (MCG), mid-cap value (MCV), small-cap growth (SCG), and small-cap value (SCV) equity styles. The MSCI EAFE Free Float index is used to represent non-U.S. developed markets (DM). The MSCI Emerging Markets index is used to represent emerging markets (EM). The Lehman Brothers Long Term Government bond index is used to represent the long bond (LB). The Lehman Brothers Aggregate Bond index is used to represent medium-term bonds and other fixed income securities (MB). The Lehman Brothers High-Yield bond index is used to represent high-yield bonds (HY).[2] The T-bill daily yield is based on Federal Reserve 90-day constant maturity bills (T-bill). The U.S. dollar index is the Federal Reserve broad trade-weighted dollar index (USDX). Monthly T-bill returns use the Ibbotson U.S. 30-day T-bill Index.

The Fama-French (1993) market, size, and value premium factors are also used in the analysis of monthly data (available at *http://mba.tuck. dartmouth.edu/pages/faculty/ken.french/data_library.html*). These factors are based on market data from the Center for Research in Security Prices (CRSP) at the University of Chicago. The market factor is a broad measure of market performance based on the complete market covered by CRSP. SmB stands for "Small minus Big" and is the small-cap value premium. HmL stands for "High minus Low" and is the value premium as represented by the difference in performance between high book-to-market (value) firms and low book-to-market (growth). These premia are based on dollar-market neutral portfolios that are long small or value and short large or growth equities. Analysis using these benchmarks is done using excess returns, and the no-arbitrage constraint is not needed.

Descriptive statistics for daily frequency benchmarks is found in Table 10.1 and for monthly frequency benchmarks in Table 10.2.

---

[2]As there is currently no ETF for the Lehman Brothers High Yield index, the Goldman Sachs High Yield ETF (ticker LQD) is used instead. The correlation between this ETF and the daily Lehman High Yield index is over 78 percent based on 250 days of data; I have data for both.

HEDGE FUND PROFILES BASED ON DAILY DATA ANALYSIS

The stability of the profile of hedge fund indexes against conventional asset markets over time is not well understood. Most existing studies are based on monthly data. It takes at least three years of monthly data to obtain reasonably reliable multivariate statistical results using half a dozen benchmarks or more. Since statistical results are an average (or time-weighted average) over this period, it is difficult to observe shifts in factor exposures over much shorter time scales. It is true that the sensitivity of regression results to outliers sometimes allows regressions based on monthly data to quickly identify changes in factor exposures. But the use of daily data might be hoped to provide more reliable results.

Two daily hedge fund indexes are investigated, the HFR Global Hedge Fund Index and the S&P Hedge Fund Index. These are the daily indexes with the longest history, and, moreover, both are investable. Over the common return period from April 2003 to November 2004, the HFR index had an annualized daily return of 7.04 percent with an annualized standard deviation of 2.67 percent. The corresponding return of the S&P index was 6.79 percent with standard deviation 2.16 percent. (These are longer periods than reported in Table 10.1.)

Results are first presented based on factor model betas and T-statistics, and then using variance decompositions based on these models.

Factor Model Results

Tables 10.3 and 10.4 present all-history and rolling window factor models for the two indexes. The first rows present all-history results. These results are based on the time period from October 2003 to November 2004. The left set of columns present the factor betas. These are followed by the R^2 of the factor model and then by the T-statistics for each beta in the same order. Windows are formed at five-day intervals. Rolling window results are presented here only from April to November 2004 due to space limitations.

The R^2 summary statistics show that both indexes have substantial correlation with conventional markets. Remarkably for the use of daily data, the HFR index has an R^2 of 0.64 over this time period, indicating a multiple correlation coefficient of about 0.80. The R^2 for the S&P index is still relatively high at 0.40. The HFR R^2 is comparable to those reported by Fung and Hsieh (2004c) with monthly data. Note that rolling window R^2 values are considerably higher. It would not be surprising if daily correlations were much lower and that the higher monthly correlations were the result of an averaging process operating on longer timescales.

TABLE 10.3 Rolling Window Analysis of the HFRX Global Investable Hedge Fund Index, Daily Data September 30, 2003, to November 30, 2004 (Five-Day Sample Rate)

Date		LCG	LCV	MCG	MCV	SCG	SCV	EM	DM	LB	MB	T-Bill
ALL	88%	-9%	4%	4%	6%	4%	-5%	4%	4%	1%	-1%	88%
11/29/2004		1%	1%	2%	8%	-6%	2%	5%	2%	-5%	19%	71%
11/24/2004		2%	1%	3%	8%	-6%	2%	4%	1%	-3%	23%	65%
11/17/2004		3%	3%	2%	8%	-4%	0%	4%	0%	-1%	21%	65%
11/10/2004		-1%	6%	3%	5%	-3%	2%	1%	1%	-5%	21%	70%
11/3/2004		-2%	8%	3%	5%	-2%	1%	2%	0%	-1%	18%	68%
10/27/2004		-7%	11%	4%	1%	0%	1%	3%	-1%	-1%	14%	75%
10/20/2004		-11%	15%	-2%	0%	4%	1%	3%	-1%	-1%	15%	76%
10/13/2004		-13%	19%	-4%	-1%	8%	-2%	3%	1%	1%	9%	79%
10/6/2004		-12%	16%	0%	-2%	6%	0%	1%	1%	2%	7%	81%
9/29/2004		-6%	12%	-2%	-2%	8%	0%	2%	-2%	9%	0%	80%
9/22/2004		-7%	14%	-1%	-1%	8%	0%	2%	-3%	9%	0%	79%
9/15/2004		-9%	13%	-2%	-1%	10%	-2%	3%	0%	10%	-5%	83%
9/8/2004		-11%	13%	0%	-2%	10%	-3%	1%	2%	8%	-4%	85%
8/31/2004		-5%	6%	4%	-4%	7%	-1%	1%	2%	9%	-3%	83%
8/24/2004		-5%	6%	2%	-2%	7%	-2%	1%	1%	6%	-2%	87%
8/17/2004		-6%	8%	5%	-4%	9%	-5%	0%	3%	9%	-10%	91%
8/10/2004		-10%	7%	5%	0%	10%	-6%	0%	4%	8%	-11%	94%
8/3/2004		-6%	4%	8%	2%	6%	-6%	1%	2%	4%	-4%	89%
7/27/2004		-5%	-3%	8%	3%	4%	-4%	2%	3%	2%	-3%	92%
7/20/2004		-7%	4%	3%	4%	7%	-6%	3%	5%	0%	-7%	96%
7/13/2004		-7%	3%	2%	4%	7%	-5%	3%	6%	-1%	-7%	96%
7/6/2004		-9%	4%	6%	3%	4%	-7%	2%	8%	0%	-9%	98%
6/28/2004		-6%	2%	1%	7%	7%	-9%	2%	8%	-2%	-8%	97%

TABLE 10.3 *(continued)*

| Date | | | | | | Factor Model Betas | | | | | |
	LCG	LCV	MCG	MCV	SCG	SCV	EM	DM	LB	MB	T-Bill
6/14/2004	-8%	1%	4%	8%	6%	-9%	3%	7%	0%	-5%	94%
6/4/2004	-10%	3%	7%	8%	0%	-6%	3%	8%	-4%	0%	91%
5/27/2004	-11%	6%	8%	7%	-2%	-5%	3%	8%	-7%	4%	89%
5/20/2004	-12%	10%	7%	6%	-3%	-4%	3%	9%	-8%	0%	93%
5/13/2004	-9%	7%	6%	5%	-1%	-4%	4%	8%	-8%	6%	87%
5/6/2004	-13%	8%	16%	3%	-2%	-4%	5%	2%	-8%	15%	79%
4/29/2004	-16%	11%	19%	-2%	-7%	1%	5%	5%	-13%	22%	76%
4/22/2004	-13%	7%	15%	3%	-4%	-1%	7%	2%	-11%	20%	76%
4/15/2004	-8%	2%	10%	9%	-7%	3%	6%	2%	-8%	13%	77%
4/7/2004	-5%	-2%	11%	12%	-9%	4%	6%	0%	-6%	12%	76%
3/31/2004	-8%	-3%	12%	15%	-11%	4%	5%	3%	-6%	14%	75%
3/24/2004	-8%	1%	11%	15%	-10%	3%	4%	0%	1%	4%	79%
3/17/2004	-7%	0%	7%	11%	-1%	0%	5%	1%	2%	3%	79%
3/10/2004	-8%	2%	5%	13%	1%	-3%	4%	2%	-1%	8%	77%
3/3/2004	-10%	1%	5%	9%	3%	-2%	5%	2%	1%	6%	81%
2/25/2004	-12%	0%	7%	7%	8%	-6%	4%	5%	-3%	13%	77%
2/18/2004	-13%	1%	7%	5%	11%	-6%	5%	3%	0%	7%	81%
2/10/2004	-12%	0%	5%	7%	10%	-7%	4%	3%	0%	10%	80%
2/3/2004	-15%	1%	11%	6%	7%	-8%	3%	5%	-2%	7%	84%
1/27/2004	-8%	-5%	11%	6%	2%	-5%	0%	8%	-1%	-2%	94%
1/20/2004	-7%	-1%	7%	6%	6%	-8%	2%	7%	0%	-1%	89%
1/12/2004	-8%	1%	9%	7%	4%	-10%	2%	7%	1%	-4%	91%
1/5/2004	-7%	-2%	5%	14%	0%	-8%	3%	9%	0%	-2%	88%
12/26/2003	-7%	-2%	5%	13%	-3%	-7%	6%	7%	0%	-1%	88%
12/18/2003	-6%	-5%	1%	21%	-4%	-9%	5%	8%	2%	-4%	90%
12/11/2003	-8%	1%	3%	12%	-2%	-5%	5%	6%	3%	-8%	93%

TABLE 10.3 (continued)

Date	R^2	LCG	LCV	MCG	MCV	SCG	SCV	EM	DM	LB	MB
						Factor Model T-Statistics					
ALL	64%	-3.7	1.3	1.4	1.8	1.6	-1.9	4.3	2.2	0.4	-0.2
11/29/2004	73%	0.1	0.2	0.2	0.8	-0.9	0.2	1.6	0.4	-0.9	1.3
11/24/2004	75%	0.3	0.2	0.3	0.9	-0.8	0.2	1.0	0.1	-0.6	1.5
11/17/2004	75%	0.3	0.4	0.2	0.8	-0.4	0.1	1.0	-0.1	-0.2	1.4
11/10/2004	67%	-0.1	0.8	0.4	0.6	-0.4	0.3	0.4	0.2	-0.8	1.6
11/3/2004	70%	-0.3	1.1	0.4	0.6	-0.3	0.1	0.6	0.0	-0.2	1.3
10/27/2004	72%	-1.2	1.6	0.6	0.1	0.0	0.1	1.0	-0.2	-0.2	1.2
10/20/2004	76%	-1.8	2.0	-0.2	0.0	0.6	0.1	1.1	-0.2	-0.2	1.2
10/13/2004	72%	-2.1	2.0	-0.4	-0.2	1.0	-0.2	0.9	0.2	0.1	0.7
10/6/2004	68%	-1.9	1.9	0.1	-0.2	0.9	0.0	0.2	0.2	0.4	0.6
9/29/2004	74%	-0.8	1.4	-0.2	-0.2	1.1	0.1	0.6	-0.3	1.4	0.0
9/22/2004	73%	-0.9	1.4	-0.1	-0.1	1.1	0.0	0.5	-0.4	1.3	0.0
9/15/2004	69%	-1.1	1.5	-0.3	-0.1	1.3	-0.3	0.7	-0.1	1.5	-0.4
9/8/2004	68%	-1.5	1.4	0.0	-0.2	1.2	-0.4	0.4	0.4	1.3	-0.3
8/31/2004	64%	-0.7	0.7	0.5	-0.4	0.9	-0.2	0.4	0.3	1.6	-0.3
8/24/2004	55%	-0.8	0.8	0.4	-0.3	1.0	-0.3	0.3	0.4	1.1	-0.2
8/17/2004	64%	-0.8	0.8	0.6	-0.5	1.1	-0.6	0.1	0.6	1.6	-0.9
8/10/2004	63%	-1.3	0.8	0.6	0.0	1.2	-0.7	0.0	0.8	1.5	-1.0
8/3/2004	64%	-0.9	0.4	0.9	0.2	0.8	-0.7	0.2	0.4	0.8	-0.3
7/27/2004	66%	-0.6	-0.4	0.9	0.3	0.5	-0.4	0.9	0.7	0.4	-0.3
7/20/2004	71%	-0.9	0.4	0.2	0.4	0.7	-0.7	0.9	1.1	0.0	-0.5
7/13/2004	74%	-0.8	0.2	0.1	0.4	0.7	-0.6	0.9	1.2	-0.2	-0.5
7/6/2004	76%	-1.0	0.3	0.4	0.3	0.4	-0.7	0.8	1.5	0.0	-0.6
6/28/2004	75%	-0.7	0.2	0.1	0.6	0.6	-1.0	0.8	1.4	-0.2	-0.4
6/21/2004	78%	-1.1	0.3	0.2	0.5	0.5	-0.7	0.6	1.2	-0.4	-0.3

TABLE 10.3 *(continued)*

Date	R^2					Factor Model T-Statistics					
		LCG	LCV	MCG	MCV	SCG	SCV	EM	DM	LB	MB
6/14/2004	82%	-0.8	0.1	0.3	0.6	0.5	-0.8	0.7	1.0	0.0	-0.3
6/4/2004	84%	-1.1	0.3	0.5	0.6	0.0	-0.6	0.8	1.1	-0.4	0.0
5/27/2004	86%	-1.1	0.5	0.5	0.5	-0.1	-0.5	0.7	1.0	-0.7	0.2
5/20/2004	88%	-1.2	0.7	0.4	0.4	-0.2	-0.4	0.8	1.1	-0.7	0.0
5/13/2004	86%	-0.9	0.5	0.4	0.3	-0.1	-0.4	0.9	0.9	-0.7	0.3
5/6/2004	84%	-1.3	0.6	1.1	0.3	-0.2	-0.4	1.0	0.3	-0.9	0.7
4/29/2004	84%	-1.4	0.9	1.4	-0.1	-0.6	0.1	1.0	0.6	-1.3	1.0
4/22/2004	82%	-1.3	0.6	1.2	0.2	-0.4	-0.1	1.3	0.3	-1.2	1.0
4/15/2004	84%	-0.7	0.1	0.7	0.5	-0.5	0.2	1.0	0.3	-0.7	0.5
4/7/2004	83%	-0.4	-0.1	0.9	0.6	-0.7	0.3	1.0	0.1	-0.6	0.5
3/31/2004	80%	-0.7	-0.2	0.8	0.7	-0.8	0.3	0.8	0.4	-0.5	0.5
3/24/2004	77%	-0.8	0.1	0.9	0.9	-0.8	0.3	0.6	0.0	0.0	0.1
3/17/2004	76%	-0.7	0.0	0.5	0.6	-0.1	0.0	0.8	0.1	0.1	0.1
3/10/2004	74%	-0.9	0.1	0.4	0.9	0.1	-0.3	0.8	0.3	-0.1	0.3
3/3/2004	67%	-1.2	0.1	0.5	0.8	0.3	-0.3	1.1	0.4	0.1	0.3
2/25/2004	67%	-1.4	0.0	0.7	0.6	0.9	-0.8	1.0	1.0	-0.3	0.7
2/18/2004	68%	-1.5	0.1	0.7	0.4	1.4	-0.9	1.4	0.5	0.0	0.4
2/10/2004	63%	-1.4	0.0	0.5	0.7	1.4	-1.0	1.3	0.6	-0.1	0.6
2/3/2004	59%	-2.0	0.1	1.4	0.7	0.9	-1.3	1.0	1.0	-0.3	0.5
1/27/2004	58%	-1.4	-0.6	1.7	0.8	0.4	-1.1	0.1	1.9	-0.3	-0.2
1/20/2004	67%	-1.0	-0.1	0.9	0.8	0.9	-1.4	0.6	1.7	0.0	-0.1
1/12/2004	64%	-1.0	0.1	1.2	0.8	0.7	-1.7	0.8	1.8	0.2	-0.4
1/5/2004	64%	-0.9	-0.2	0.6	1.3	0.0	-1.2	0.9	1.7	0.0	-0.2
12/26/2003	62%	-0.9	-0.2	0.6	1.3	-0.3	-1.1	1.7	1.4	0.1	-0.1
12/18/2003	65%	-0.8	-0.5	0.2	1.7	-0.4	-1.3	1.5	1.6	0.3	-0.3
12/11/2003	59%	-1.3	0.1	0.3	1.0	-0.2	-0.7	1.6	1.4	0.6	-0.7

TABLE 10.4 Rolling Window Analysis of the S&P Hedge Fund Index, Daily Data September 30, 2003, to November 30, 2004 (Five–Day Sample Rate)

Date					Factor Model Betas						
	LCG	LCV	MCG	MCV	SCG	SCV	EM	DM	LB	MB	T-Bill
ALL	-8%	2%	-1%	6%	2%	-5%	3%	7%	1%	1%	92%
12/1/2004	-7%	-1%	-9%	22%	2%	-6%	1%	6%	0%	15%	77%
11/23/2004	-3%	0%	-8%	23%	-1%	-7%	2%	2%	0%	19%	72%
11/16/2004	-3%	1%	-9%	22%	0%	-5%	0%	2%	0%	20%	72%
11/9/2004	-4%	0%	-8%	22%	-1%	-4%	0%	3%	1%	17%	74%
11/2/2004	-6%	1%	-8%	20%	1%	-4%	0%	3%	2%	12%	79%
10/26/2004	-8%	-5%	-9%	20%	-1%	1%	-1%	6%	3%	6%	88%
10/19/2004	-5%	-4%	-6%	16%	-5%	3%	-1%	7%	1%	9%	86%
10/12/2004	-4%	-6%	-2%	12%	-4%	3%	-4%	8%	1%	10%	87%
10/5/2004	-5%	-6%	0%	10%	-4%	3%	-4%	7%	0%	10%	88%
9/28/2004	2%	-7%	2%	0%	0%	1%	1%	5%	9%	-6%	93%
9/21/2004	3%	-3%	2%	-2%	-1%	2%	0%	4%	8%	1%	87%
9/14/2004	1%	-2%	0%	-3%	2%	1%	-1%	7%	7%	2%	86%
9/7/2004	0%	0%	5%	-6%	2%	-2%	-2%	9%	7%	-3%	91%
8/30/2004	2%	-2%	2%	-5%	4%	-3%	-2%	7%	4%	0%	93%
8/23/2004	-1%	1%	3%	-6%	2%	-2%	-2%	8%	4%	-1%	95%
8/16/2004	0%	0%	3%	-6%	1%	-2%	-2%	8%	3%	-1%	96%
8/9/2004	-5%	1%	0%	-2%	6%	-5%	-2%	9%	3%	-6%	100%
8/2/2004	-5%	1%	0%	0%	9%	-7%	-2%	9%	1%	-5%	100%
7/26/2004	-8%	4%	2%	-1%	7%	-8%	0%	7%	-4%	-3%	102%
7/19/2004	-13%	9%	-1%	-2%	8%	-8%	2%	7%	-2%	-11%	112%
7/12/2004	-13%	8%	0%	-3%	7%	-8%	3%	7%	-2%	-11%	112%
7/2/2004	-13%	8%	7%	-5%	5%	-8%	2%	7%	-1%	-12%	111%
6/25/2004	-9%	6%	2%	-1%	3%	-7%	2%	7%	-3%	-7%	106%
6/18/2004	-8%	4%	3%	-1%	2%	-3%	3%	6%	-3%	-9%	107%

210

TABLE 10.4 *(continued)*

Date						Factor Model Betas					
	LCG	LCV	MCG	MCV	SCG	SCV	EM	DM	LB	MB	T-Bill
6/10/2004	-9%	5%	4%	0%	0%	-5%	4%	4%	1%	-8%	104%
6/3/2004	-10%	6%	5%	1%	-3%	-3%	4%	2%	-3%	-4%	103%
5/26/2004	-7%	9%	6%	0%	-6%	-4%	5%	3%	-1%	-4%	100%
5/19/2004	-8%	12%	4%	1%	-7%	-3%	5%	2%	-1%	-5%	101%
5/12/2004	-7%	9%	1%	-1%	-7%	0%	6%	4%	2%	-8%	101%
5/5/2004	-12%	12%	14%	-9%	-7%	2%	3%	2%	0%	6%	88%
4/28/2004	-16%	9%	16%	-9%	-9%	5%	5%	4%	-1%	7%	88%
4/21/2004	-17%	9%	13%	-14%	-7%	9%	8%	6%	2%	2%	91%
4/14/2004	-12%	2%	8%	-5%	-6%	9%	6%	6%	8%	-7%	92%
4/6/2004	-15%	4%	7%	-2%	-3%	4%	7%	4%	9%	-7%	91%
3/30/2004	-12%	-2%	3%	4%	-7%	9%	8%	6%	2%	9%	81%
3/23/2004	-7%	-7%	-1%	11%	-4%	3%	6%	7%	5%	6%	80%
3/16/2004	-5%	-12%	-3%	11%	3%	-1%	7%	10%	4%	7%	79%
3/9/2004	-4%	-13%	-3%	8%	5%	-2%	8%	10%	5%	9%	78%
3/2/2004	-4%	-14%	1%	6%	2%	0%	6%	11%	5%	11%	75%
2/24/2004	-8%	-12%	5%	5%	5%	-4%	6%	13%	2%	12%	76%
2/17/2004	-9%	-8%	6%	5%	3%	-4%	5%	13%	0%	13%	76%
2/9/2004	-8%	-7%	2%	4%	3%	-3%	5%	13%	-2%	23%	70%
2/2/2004	-7%	-10%	7%	4%	1%	-3%	4%	13%	-1%	18%	74%
1/26/2004	-4%	-7%	6%	8%	-6%	-3%	2%	13%	-3%	10%	84%
1/16/2004	0%	-3%	9%	1%	-5%	-4%	0%	13%	-2%	10%	82%
1/9/2004	-5%	0%	6%	2%	0%	-6%	-1%	12%	-4%	11%	84%
1/2/2004	-8%	2%	1%	7%	3%	-8%	-2%	13%	-3%	3%	93%
12/24/2003	-5%	-1%	0%	9%	2%	-8%	-2%	11%	-1%	0%	95%
12/17/2003	-9%	4%	-3%	8%	2%	-6%	1%	8%	-2%	3%	93%
12/10/2003	-10%	5%	-1%	8%	1%	-9%	2%	9%	-4%	6%	91%

TABLE 10.4 *(continued)*

| | | | | | | Factor Model T-Statistics | | | | | | |
Date	R^2	LCG	LCV	MCG	MCV	SCG	SCV	EM	DM	LB	MB	T-Bill
ALL	40%	-5.4	1.2	-0.3	2.8	1.3	-3.3	4.2	6.8	0.6	0.4	40.6
12/1/2004	70%	-1.3	-0.2	-1.1	2.7	0.3	-0.9	0.5	1.5	0.0	1.1	7.1
11/23/2004	71%	-0.4	0.0	-1.0	2.7	-0.1	-1.1	0.7	0.5	0.0	1.5	6.5
11/16/2004	68%	-0.5	0.1	-1.1	2.8	0.1	-0.8	0.1	0.3	-0.1	1.7	6.9
11/9/2004	61%	-0.7	0.0	-1.1	2.7	-0.1	-0.6	0.0	0.7	0.1	1.5	7.6
11/2/2004	50%	-1.1	0.1	-1.2	2.9	0.1	-0.8	0.0	0.9	0.4	1.1	8.3
10/26/2004	55%	-1.4	-0.8	-1.3	2.8	-0.2	0.2	-0.5	1.7	0.5	0.6	9.4
10/19/2004	46%	-1.1	-0.7	-1.0	2.4	-0.8	0.5	-0.5	2.0	0.3	1.0	10.3
10/12/2004	44%	-0.8	-1.0	-0.4	1.9	-0.8	0.5	-1.5	2.4	0.2	1.1	11.1
10/5/2004	35%	-1.1	-1.0	-0.1	2.0	-0.9	0.7	-1.5	2.0	0.1	1.5	13.3
9/28/2004	38%	0.5	-1.5	0.4	0.0	0.0	0.3	0.3	1.5	2.6	-0.8	15.4
9/21/2004	40%	0.6	-0.5	0.4	-0.4	-0.2	0.5	0.0	1.3	1.9	0.1	13.7
9/14/2004	41%	0.1	-0.3	0.0	-0.5	0.4	0.3	-0.4	1.9	1.7	0.2	13.3
9/7/2004	38%	0.1	0.0	0.9	-1.3	0.4	-0.5	-0.9	3.0	2.0	-0.4	16.8
8/30/2004	33%	0.6	-0.4	0.6	-1.4	1.0	-0.9	-1.2	3.0	1.6	0.1	22.4
8/23/2004	36%	-0.2	0.1	0.8	-1.6	0.5	-0.5	-1.5	3.5	1.4	-0.3	23.6
8/16/2004	40%	-0.1	0.0	0.8	-1.7	0.3	-0.6	-1.0	3.5	1.0	-0.2	22.4
8/9/2004	45%	-1.5	0.2	0.1	-0.5	1.7	-1.3	-1.2	4.1	1.1	-1.1	25.5
8/2/2004	47%	-1.3	0.1	0.0	-0.1	2.2	-1.8	-1.3	3.9	0.4	-0.9	24.7
7/26/2004	59%	-1.9	0.7	0.4	-0.2	1.5	-1.8	0.2	3.0	-1.2	-0.4	21.8
7/19/2004	65%	-2.6	1.5	-0.1	-0.4	1.2	-1.4	1.3	2.3	-0.4	-1.3	16.7
7/12/2004	66%	-2.4	1.2	-0.1	-0.4	1.2	-1.4	1.4	2.2	-0.4	-1.2	15.8
7/2/2004	64%	-2.4	1.2	0.8	-0.8	0.7	-1.4	1.0	2.1	-0.3	-1.2	15.4
6/25/2004	60%	-1.8	0.8	0.3	-0.1	0.5	-1.2	1.2	1.8	-0.6	-0.6	13.3
6/18/2004	60%	-1.4	0.5	0.3	-0.1	0.3	-0.5	1.2	1.3	-0.5	-0.8	13.1

TABLE 10.4 *(continued)*

Date	R^2	LCG	LCV	MCG	MCV	SCG	SCV	EM	DM	LB	MB	T-Bill
6/10/2004	54%	-1.6	0.8	0.5	0.0	-0.1	-0.8	1.8	1.0	0.1	-0.7	13.1
6/3/2004	52%	-2.0	1.0	0.7	0.2	-0.5	-0.6	2.0	0.6	-0.5	-0.3	12.9
5/26/2004	55%	-1.2	1.3	0.7	0.0	-0.8	-0.7	2.2	0.7	-0.1	-0.3	11.1
5/19/2004	57%	-1.4	1.6	0.4	0.1	-0.8	-0.5	2.2	0.5	-0.2	-0.4	10.6
5/12/2004	52%	-1.2	1.3	0.1	-0.1	-1.0	0.0	2.4	0.8	0.3	-0.6	10.3
5/5/2004	48%	-2.2	1.7	1.9	-1.3	-1.2	0.4	1.4	0.5	0.0	0.5	10.4
4/28/2004	50%	-2.6	1.3	2.1	-0.9	-1.4	0.7	1.6	1.0	-0.1	0.5	9.8
4/21/2004	60%	-2.5	1.0	1.5	-1.3	-1.0	1.1	1.9	1.2	0.3	0.1	7.9
4/14/2004	63%	-1.4	0.2	0.8	-0.4	-0.7	0.9	1.3	1.2	1.1	-0.4	7.0
4/6/2004	64%	-1.7	0.4	0.7	-0.1	-0.3	0.5	1.5	0.8	1.2	-0.4	6.6
3/30/2004	69%	-1.4	-0.2	0.2	0.3	-0.6	0.9	1.5	1.0	0.2	0.4	4.8
3/23/2004	74%	-0.7	-0.6	0.0	0.7	-0.3	0.3	1.2	1.2	0.5	0.2	4.2
3/16/2004	78%	-0.5	-0.8	-0.3	0.7	0.2	-0.1	1.3	1.5	0.3	0.3	4.1
3/9/2004	79%	-0.4	-1.0	-0.3	0.6	0.5	-0.2	1.6	1.6	0.4	0.4	4.6
3/2/2004	78%	-0.4	-1.0	0.1	0.5	0.2	0.0	1.3	1.9	0.4	0.5	4.4
2/24/2004	76%	-0.8	-0.9	0.4	0.4	0.6	-0.5	1.2	1.9	0.3	0.6	4.9
2/17/2004	74%	-1.0	-0.6	0.6	0.4	0.4	-0.6	1.3	1.9	0.0	0.7	5.7
2/9/2004	71%	-0.9	-0.5	0.3	0.4	0.4	-0.5	1.4	2.0	-0.3	1.4	5.5
2/2/2004	66%	-0.8	-0.8	0.8	0.4	0.1	-0.5	1.3	2.3	-0.2	1.2	6.2
1/26/2004	58%	-0.6	-0.7	0.8	1.0	-0.9	-0.5	0.7	2.8	-0.6	0.9	8.7
1/16/2004	56%	0.0	-0.3	1.2	0.1	-0.9	-0.9	0.1	3.4	-0.5	1.1	10.1
1/9/2004	50%	-0.8	0.1	1.1	0.3	0.0	-1.4	-0.4	3.8	-1.0	1.4	12.6
1/2/2004	46%	-1.7	0.3	0.1	1.0	0.5	-2.0	-1.0	4.1	-0.9	0.4	15.2
12/24/2003	36%	-1.4	-0.2	-0.1	1.5	0.5	-2.1	-0.8	4.0	-0.4	0.0	16.4
12/17/2003	33%	-2.5	0.8	-0.7	1.3	0.6	-1.8	0.5	3.3	-1.0	0.6	18.5
12/10/2003	38%	-2.5	1.0	-0.2	1.1	0.3	-1.8	0.9	3.5	-1.2	0.9	16.4

Turning to the all-history factor model results, it is apparent that the profiles of both indexes are quite similar. Both have similar betas against equity-style indexes, except that the signs of the mid-cap-growth betas disagree. Neither beta is statistically significant. The only difference appearing to be statistically significant is the beta for developed markets, which is 7 percent for the S&P index, but only 4 percent for the HFR index. The estimated alphas, not reported in the tables, are −1.28 percent per year (T-statistic: −0.68) for the HFR index and 1.43 percent (T-statistic: 1.16) for the S&P index.

Rolling window results, however, paint a different picture. Note first the large-cap growth betas for the October–November 2004 period. The HFR betas are decreasing sharply over this time period, while the S&P betas are relatively steady. Note, also, that HFR large-value betas are positive and also decreasing, indicating a large-value bet, while the S&P large-value betas are negative, indicating a short large-cap bet. The HFR large growth and values are both statistically significant for most of October. The S&P mid-cap value index is strongly and positive and statistically significant over this time period.

Two other notable differences in the profiles concern small growth and developed markets. The HFR index is long small growth over the September to October period while the S&P index is negative or weakly positive over this time. The S&P index has consistently high and statistically significant betas against developed markets over July and August 2004 while the HFR index betas are weakly positive or negative.

The T-bill betas indicate that that both funds have low net market exposure. The all-history T-bill beta of 88 percent for the HFR index compares with 92 percent for the S&P index. Both betas have very high precision, as indicated by the associated T-statistics. However, in both cases, the hypothesis that the summation constraint holds is statistically rejected ($p = 0.014$ for the HFR index and $p = .007$ for the S&P index). It must thus be concluded that these betas are significantly biased measures and should not be relied on for inferring net market position with additional investigation.

Variance Decomposition Results

Variance decomposition results for both indexes are presented in Table 10.5. The most striking aspect of these results is that for both indexes, the international indexes are attributed half or more of the explained variance of the all-history analysis and close to three-quarters for the S&P index. In the case of the HFR index, the variance components are 31 percent for emerging markets and 6 percent for developed markets out of the 65 percent explained variance. The factor betas on emerging and developed mar-

TABLE 10.5 Rolling Window Variance Decompositions of HFRXGL and SPHFI Indexes, Daily Data, September 30, 2003 to November 30, 2004 (Five–Day Sample Rate)

Date						HFR Global Hedge Fund Index						
	LCG	LCV	MCG	MCV	SCG	SCV	EM	DM	LB	MB	T-Bill	R^2
ALL	-3%	2%	8%	10%	3%	-2%	31%	6%	0%	0%	-1%	65%
12/1/2004	0%	0%	0%	23%	-3%	0%	36%	6%	-1%	3%	-3%	75%
11/23/2004	0%	0%	3%	40%	-3%	0%	21%	0%	-1%	6%	-2%	76%
11/16/2004	0%	14%	0%	31%	0%	0%	20%	0%	0%	8%	-1%	75%
11/9/2004	0%	26%	0%	30%	0%	0%	4%	0%	-1%	6%	0%	67%
11/2/2004	0%	32%	0%	25%	0%	0%	4%	0%	0%	8%	0%	70%
10/26/2004	-6%	44%	7%	0%	0%	0%	8%	0%	0%	6%	0%	71%
10/19/2004	-9%	46%	0%	0%	6%	0%	7%	0%	0%	7%	0%	75%
10/12/2004	-11%	40%	-2%	0%	7%	0%	7%	0%	0%	5%	0%	72%
10/5/2004	-11%	35%	0%	0%	15%	0%	0%	0%	2%	4%	0%	67%
9/28/2004	-5%	18%	0%	0%	36%	0%	1%	0%	13%	0%	0%	73%
9/21/2004	-6%	16%	0%	0%	38%	0%	0%	-1%	12%	0%	0%	73%
9/14/2004	-6%	20%	0%	0%	32%	0%	2%	0%	8%	0%	0%	68%
9/7/2004	-7%	23%	0%	0%	28%	0%	0%	1%	7%	0%	0%	67%
8/30/2004	-2%	7%	16%	0%	26%	0%	0%	0%	11%	0%	-4%	66%
8/23/2004	-2%	7%	0%	0%	34%	-4%	0%	0%	6%	0%	-5%	58%
8/16/2004	-2%	5%	18%	-3%	22%	-4%	0%	2%	7%	-1%	0%	64%
8/9/2004	-4%	3%	25%	0%	16%	-4%	0%	3%	6%	-1%	0%	63%
8/2/2004	-2%	2%	49%	0%	3%	-2%	0%	0%	4%	0%	0%	63%
7/26/2004	-3%	0%	34%	0%	0%	0%	25%	1%	0%	0%	-4%	67%
7/19/2004	-2%	0%	0%	7%	11%	-4%	35%	11%	0%	-1%	0%	70%
7/12/2004	-2%	0%	0%	4%	15%	-4%	26%	21%	0%	-1%	0%	74%
7/2/2004	-3%	3%	20%	0%	0%	-3%	17%	28%	0%	-1%	1%	77%
6/25/2004	-2%	0%	0%	4%	8%	-4%	34%	22%	0%	-1%	0%	74%
6/18/2004	-6%	2%	24%	0%	0%	-2%	0%	39%	-4%	0%	1%	78%

TABLE 10.5 *(continued)*

Date						HFR Global Hedge Fund Index						
	LCG	LCV	MCG	MCV	SCG	SCV	EM	DM	LB	MB	T-Bill	R^2
6/10/2004	-2%	0%	0%	10%	8%	-4%	44%	14%	0%	0%	0%	82%
6/3/2004	-3%	0%	11%	6%	0%	-2%	38%	22%	-1%	0%	0%	84%
5/26/2004	-3%	0%	9%	5%	0%	-2%	38%	27%	-1%	0%	0%	85%
5/19/2004	-3%	5%	0%	5%	0%	-2%	40%	31%	-2%	0%	0%	87%
5/12/2004	-3%	5%	8%	0%	0%	0%	41%	28%	-1%	1%	0%	86%
5/5/2004	-6%	4%	27%	0%	0%	-2%	42%	0%	-1%	2%	0%	84%
4/28/2004	-6%	5%	21%	0%	-4%	0%	40%	4%	-2%	2%	0%	84%
4/21/2004	-6%	4%	18%	0%	-2%	0%	48%	0%	-2%	1%	0%	82%
4/14/2004	-3%	0%	8%	39%	-3%	0%	30%	0%	-1%	1%	0%	84%
4/6/2004	-3%	0%	15%	35%	-4%	0%	24%	0%	0%	0%	0%	81%
3/30/2004	-5%	0%	16%	24%	-5%	0%	29%	0%	0%	0%	0%	79%
3/23/2004	-5%	0%	14%	36%	-5%	0%	16%	0%	0%	0%	-1%	77%
3/16/2004	-4%	0%	16%	29%	0%	0%	26%	0%	0%	2%	-2%	78%
3/9/2004	-4%	0%	0%	48%	0%	0%	19%	0%	0%	3%	-1%	75%
3/2/2004	-5%	0%	12%	23%	0%	0%	23%	2%	0%	3%	-2%	69%
2/24/2004	-5%	0%	16%	9%	5%	-2%	22%	4%	0%	4%	-3%	70%
2/17/2004	-7%	0%	21%	0%	11%	-3%	21%	4%	0%	3%	-3%	71%
2/9/2004	-7%	0%	18%	8%	9%	-4%	11%	5%	0%	2%	-8%	73%
2/2/2004	-9%	0%	24%	5%	3%	-3%	6%	6%	0%	0%	-8%	64%
1/26/2004	-6%	-2%	25%	3%	1%	-2%	0%	18%	-1%	0%	-1%	59%
1/16/2004	-4%	0%	19%	6%	6%	-5%	5%	21%	0%	0%	-1%	67%
1/9/2004	-4%	0%	21%	4%	3%	-6%	6%	21%	0%	0%	-1%	65%
1/2/2004	-3%	0%	3%	10%	0%	-4%	12%	32%	0%	0%	0%	64%
12/24/2003	-3%	0%	2%	7%	0%	-4%	30%	16%	0%	0%	0%	62%
12/17/2003	-3%	0%	0%	10%	0%	-5%	26%	18%	0%	0%	0%	63%
12/10/2003	-3%	0%	0%	6%	0%	-3%	25%	19%	1%	-1%	0%	59%

TABLE 10.5 *(continued)*

Date		LCG	LCV	MCG	MCV	SCG	SCV	EM	DM	LB	MB	T-Bill	R²
	S&P Hedge Fund Index												
ALL		-5%	1%	0%	2%	0%	-1%	9%	20%	1%	0%	-2%	42%
12/1/2004		-9%	0%	-5%	26%	0%	-4%	1%	9%	0%	16%	0%	70%
11/23/2004		0%	0%	-7%	25%	0%	-9%	3%	0%	0%	25%	0%	70%
11/16/2004		-1%	0%	-10%	28%	0%	-4%	0%	0%	0%	24%	0%	67%
11/9/2004		-4%	0%	-9%	22%	0%	-2%	0%	2%	0%	22%	-2%	62%
11/2/2004		-7%	0%	-7%	17%	0%	-2%	0%	2%	0%	15%	0%	50%
10/26/2004		-13%	-2%	-7%	17%	0%	0%	0%	7%	5%	3%	0%	54%
10/19/2004		-8%	-1%	-5%	10%	-3%	1%	-1%	11%	0%	7%	0%	47%
10/12/2004		-5%	-2%	0%	5%	-5%	1%	-5%	12%	0%	10%	1%	45%
10/5/2004		-6%	-1%	0%	5%	-2%	1%	-4%	9%	0%	7%	1%	36%
9/28/2004		0%	-3%	3%	0%	0%	0%	0%	15%	15%	-1%	0%	38%
9/21/2004		2%	-1%	0%	0%	0%	1%	0%	19%	17%	0%	0%	40%
9/14/2004		0%	0%	0%	-1%	3%	0%	0%	21%	15%	0%	0%	41%
9/7/2004		0%	0%	2%	-3%	0%	0%	-2%	20%	11%	0%	-1%	38%
8/30/2004		0%	0%	0%	-3%	3%	-2%	-2%	15%	7%	0%	-1%	33%
8/23/2004		0%	0%	2%	-6%	3%	0%	-3%	19%	5%	0%	-7%	43%
8/16/2004		0%	0%	2%	-8%	0%	-1%	-1%	24%	3%	0%	-3%	42%
8/9/2004		-5%	0%	0%	0%	3%	-3%	-4%	27%	2%	-1%	0%	44%
8/2/2004		-4%	0%	0%	0%	7%	-5%	-4%	27%	0%	-1%	0%	47%
7/26/2004		-6%	1%	0%	0%	5%	-4%	4%	28%	-9%	0%	-2%	59%
7/19/2004		-8%	5%	0%	-1%	4%	-4%	15%	19%	0%	-8%	0%	64%
7/12/2004		-8%	4%	0%	-2%	4%	-4%	17%	19%	0%	-7%	0%	66%
7/2/2004		-7%	3%	4%	-2%	3%	-4%	15%	18%	0%	-7%	-2%	65%
6/25/2004		-5%	2%	0%	0%	2%	-4%	26%	15%	-5%	-1%	-1%	61%
6/18/2004		-3%	1%	0%	0%	1%	-1%	39%	9%	-3%	-3%	0%	60%

TABLE 10.5 (continued)

Date		LCG	LCV	MCG	MCV	SCG	SCV	EM	DM	LB	MB	T-Bill	R^2
	S&P Hedge Fund Index												
6/10/2004		-3%	1%	1%	0%	0%	-2%	42%	3%	0%	-1%	0%	54%
6/3/2004		-4%	1%	1%	0%	0%	-1%	41%	1%	0%	-1%	-1%	52%
5/26/2004		-2%	2%	1%	0%	-2%	-2%	45%	0%	0%	0%	-2%	56%
5/19/2004		-2%	4%	0%	0%	-3%	0%	45%	0%	0%	-1%	-1%	57%
5/12/2004		-1%	3%	0%	0%	-4%	0%	41%	0%	0%	-1%	-3%	53%
5/5/2004		-5%	5%	6%	-2%	-3%	0%	22%	2%	0%	4%	0%	48%
4/28/2004		-7%	3%	6%	-1%	-3%	1%	20%	5%	0%	3%	0%	50%
4/21/2004		-8%	2%	3%	-2%	-2%	2%	31%	6%	5%	0%	0%	60%
4/14/2004		-5%	0%	4%	0%	-3%	6%	23%	9%	14%	0%	1%	63%
4/6/2004		-7%	2%	6%	0%	0%	0%	29%	4%	14%	-2%	0%	64%
3/30/2004		-9%	0%	1%	0%	-1%	4%	41%	8%	0%	4%	-1%	70%
3/23/2004		-6%	0%	0%	5%	0%	0%	39%	14%	8%	0%	-1%	73%
3/16/2004		-4%	-4%	0%	5%	0%	0%	36%	21%	8%	0%	-1%	79%
3/9/2004		0%	-5%	0%	4%	0%	0%	36%	20%	13%	0%	0%	78%
3/2/2004		0%	-5%	0%	3%	0%	0%	33%	23%	14%	0%	0%	77%
2/24/2004		-4%	-4%	4%	0%	2%	0%	29%	23%	0%	10%	0%	76%
2/17/2004		-5%	-2%	5%	0%	0%	0%	28%	23%	0%	9%	0%	73%
2/9/2004		-3%	-4%	3%	0%	0%	0%	26%	22%	0%	13%	-2%	73%
2/2/2004		-3%	-4%	4%	0%	0%	0%	23%	20%	0%	11%	0%	65%
1/26/2004		0%	-5%	1%	3%	-3%	0%	8%	34%	-1%	4%	5%	63%
1/16/2004		0%	-1%	4%	0%	-3%	-3%	0%	41%	-1%	3%	3%	59%
1/9/2004		-1%	0%	2%	0%	0%	-2%	-1%	34%	-1%	3%	11%	55%
1/2/2004		-3%	0%	0%	3%	1%	-4%	-2%	32%	-1%	0%	2%	47%
12/24/2003		-3%	0%	0%	3%	1%	-4%	-1%	25%	0%	0%	0%	36%
12/17/2003		-4%	1%	0%	3%	0%	-3%	0%	19%	-1%	1%	1%	33%
12/10/2003		-5%	3%	0%	2%	0%	-3%	1%	23%	-1%	1%	0%	39%

kets are both about 4 percent. The difference in variance shares is consistent with the T-statistics, EM 4.3 and DM 2.2. In the case of the S&P index, the variance components are EM 9 percent and DM 20 percent out of the total R^2 of 0.42. This is consistent with the betas and T-statistics.

In the time-series variance decomposition results, it is interesting to note that both indexes show high emerging-market variance shares over the April to July 2004 time period. The developed markets profile, however, shows the HFR index with a large exposure over the May to June 2004 period while the S&P index has its large exposure from July to September 2004.

Other notable features in the variance decomposition are the large LCV exposure in the HFR index over September through early November 2004 and the considerable short MCG/long MCV exposure evident over October and November 2004. These features were already noted in the factor model analysis.

Note also the low variance share associated with the T-bill. This is consistent with the implied T-bill leverage reported as the annualized standard deviation of daily T-bill yields is about 0.01 percent over the time period of the analysis.

Variance decomposition results are broadly consistent with conventional factor model results but put additional emphasis on the importance of international markets beyond that which is obvious from the factor model results. This is achieved by replacing T-statistics with a measure of relative importance that makes it easier to compare factors. However, it is not clear that international equity markets were actually as important as implied by these results for two reasons:

1. The variance decomposition procedure might not be reliable.
2. The EM and DM indexes might proxy for other economic factors.

Extended Analysis with Additional Factors

It appears that heavy loading on international markets could be a proxy for the U.S. dollar. Table 10.6 shows all-history analyses of the HFR Global Index and the S&P Hedge Fund Index with these factors added compared with the results in the previous tables, the addition of these factors leads to a modest increase in R^2 for the HFR index and large increase for the S&P index: from 40 to 52 percent. The addition of these factors also makes the statistical rejection of the no-arbitrage constraint considerably weaker ($p = .066$ for HFR and $p = .183$ for S&P).

The changes to the HFR all-history results are otherwise modest. In terms of variance shares, high-yield bonds (HY) receives 2 percent and USD receives −3 percent. In contrast, one variance component for the S&P index,

TABLE 10.6 All-History Results with U.S. Dollar Trade-Weighted Index Based on Monthly Data, January 1994 to October 2004

	HFRXGL			SPHFI		
Benchmark	Factor Model Constrained	T-Statistics Constrained	PMVD Unconstrained	Factor Model Constrained	T-Statistics Constrained	PMVD Unconstrained
LCG	–8%	–3.13	–2%	–6%	–3.17	–1%
LCV	4%	1.34	2%	2%	1.07	1%
MCG	4%	1.32	8%	–1%	–0.27	0%
MCV	5%	1.55	11%	5%	1.93	2%
SCG	5%	1.76	4%	3%	1.76	1%
SCV	–5%	–1.84	–2%	–5%	–2.71	–1%
EM	4%	3.83	31%	2%	2.81	10%
DM	2%	0.91	2%	3%	2.36	5%
HY	9%	2.41	2%	11%	4.02	5%
LB	0%	–0.03	0%	0%	–0.12	0%
MB	–5%	–0.95	0%	–5%	–1.37	–1%
T-Bill	91%	14.32	0%	105%	22.58	0%
USD	–7%	–2.08	–3%	–15%	–6.39	–25%
R^2	66.8%		67.2%	51.8%		52.1%
Alpha	–0.01%			0.00%		
S.E. Alpha	0.01%			0.01%		

developed markets, changes greatly: dropping from 20 to only 5 percent (Table 10.5). In contrast, the Federal Reserve broad trade-weighted dollar index (USDX) receives a –25 percent variance component, absorbing both this 15 percent drop and most of the 12 percent increase in total R^2. The variance share for LCG also goes from –5 to –1 percent, suggesting it is a much less important factor. These qualitative results are consistent with the factor model. The USDX beta is the largest and most statistically significant (besides that for the T-bill). It is followed by the HY beta. HY receives a 5 percent variance share, now larger than any U.S. equity factor.

Addition of these factors suggests that the S&P index's developed markets and large-cap growth exposures were partially driven by the dollar. In the case of developed markets, the huge change in the beta and statistical significance suggests that the beta was biased by the omission of the dollar exchange rate and acted as a proxy for it. In the case of large-cap growth, the change in beta and statistical significance is not as pronounced.

The considerable sensitivity of the S&P index to the dollar contrasts sharply with the muted sensitivity of the HFR index. However, the variance decomposition suggests that the S&P index was relatively insensitive to style factors in U.S. equity markets over the study period, but the HFR index was much more sensitive. These conclusions are supported by the time series results presented here and also by further rolling window analyses within the October 2003 to November 2004 time period of this study. Note that being short the dollar made good economic sense over the study time period, as the dollar declined at an annualized rate of over 6 percent. The 15 percent short beta against the dollar translates into about 1 percent annual return.

These differences may be partly explained by the differing index construction practices. The HFR index is cap weighted by the estimated total dollars invested in each hedge fund strategy. The S&P index is an equally weighted mix of its nine constituent strategies. Equity long/short is only one of these strategies, even though the majority of hedge dollars now invested in it. The S&P index also includes managed futures, which is not included in the HFR universe (see Table 10.2).

SHORT SELLING INDEXES

Short selling indexes provide another opportunity to compare index suppliers. Table 10.2 includes descriptive statistics for the CSFB/Tremont (HEDG), Hennessee, HFR, and Van Hedge Short Selling indexes. The period of analysis is from January 1994 to October 2004 except for the Van Hedge index, where coverage starts in January 1995 and ends in September 2004. Table 10.7 presents analytical results using conventional asset factors except the dollar exchange rate. The factor models employ the no-arbitrage constraint. Table 10.8 presents analytical results using the Fama-French market factors, described later.

The differences in R^2 shown in Table 10.7 between the constrained factor model and the unconstrained variance decompositions indicate that the constraint cannot be statistically rejected. The overall level of R^2 is quite high, running from 78 to 85 percent over approximately 10 years of history. The T-bill betas indicate that the funds are indeed short bias. The Hennessee index appears to be the least short biased: the T-bill beta of 153 percent suggests that the fund is about 50 percent net short by market betas. At the other extreme, the HFR index beta of 239 percent indicates it is about 140 percent net short. Note that the T-statistics indicate that these betas are not very accurately estimated.

TABLE 10.7 Short-Selling Indexes Profiled against Conventional Asset Markets, Monthly Data, January 1994 to October 2004[a]

Benchmark	HEDG Dedicated Short Bias Index			Hennessee Short Bias Index			HFRI Short Selling Index			VAN Global Short Selling Index		
	Factor Model	T-Statistics	PMVD	Factor Model	T-Statistics	PMVD	Factor Model	T-Statistics	PMVD	Factor Model	T-Statistics	PMVD
LCG	-40%	-2.06	-19%	-20%	-0.88	-6%	-39%	-1.57	-10%	-28%	-1.04	-4%
LCV	22%	0.73	0%	-22%	-0.67	-1%	29%	0.77	1%	24%	0.60	1%
MCG	-11%	-0.50	-17%	-34%	-1.35	-52%	-22%	-0.77	-11%	-43%	-1.43	-41%
MCV	-24%	-0.77	-1%	-3%	-0.08	0%	-15%	-0.36	0%	-14%	-0.32	0%
SCG	-38%	-1.68	-40%	-48%	-1.83	-14%	-75%	-2.56	-56%	-63%	-2.02	-33%
SCV	10%	0.35	0%	32%	0.99	1%	37%	1.02	4%	43%	1.10	4%
DM	7%	0.43	0%	17%	0.89	1%	-2%	-0.11	0%	-10%	-0.41	-1%
EM	-9%	-0.91	-3%	-14%	-1.25	-3%	-11%	-0.85	-2%	-11%	-0.75	-1%
HY	-16%	-0.13	0%	85%	0.59	0%	-73%	-0.45	0%	-19%	-0.11	0%
LB	-15%	-0.57	0%	-3%	-0.11	0%	4%	0.12	0%	12%	0.34	0%
MB	13%	0.24	0%	-43%	-0.68	0%	28%	0.39	0%	5%	0.07	0%
T-Bill	202%	2.84	1%	153%	1.88	0%	239%	2.59	0%	203%	1.91	0%
R^2	81%		81%	78%		78%	83%		83%	85%		85%
Alpha	0.17%			0.16%			0.52%			0.24%		
S.E. Alpha	0.43%			0.49%			0.56%			0.63%		

[a]Except for the Van Hedge index, which is January 1995 to September 2004.
R^2 values for constrained and unconstrained regressions indicate that the no-arbitrage constraint cannot be statistically rejected for any of these indexes.

TABLE 10.8 Short-Selling Indexes Profiled against the Fama-French Market Factors, Monthly Data, January 1994 to October 2004[a]

Factor	HEDG Dedicated Short Bias Index			Hennessee Short Bias Index			HFRI Short Selling Index			VAN Global Short Selling Index		
	Factor Model	T-Statistics	PMVD	Factor Model	T-Statistics	PMVD	Factor Model	T-Statistics	PMVD	Factor Model	T-Statistics	PMVD
Market	−84%	−9.27	−69%	−93%	−9.05	−63%	−93%	−7.63	−58%	−93%	−7.23	−58%
SmB	−33%	−2.90	−8%	−24%	−1.85	−3%	−53%	−3.36	−14%	−43%	−2.71	−10%
HmL	11%	1.13	1%	27%	2.43	7%	42%	3.19	14%	46%	3.37	18%
R^2	78%		78%	73%		73%	86%		86%	85%		85%
Alpha	0.17%			0.22%			0.57%			0.27%		
S.E. Alpha	0.40%			0.45%			0.53%			0.58%		

[a]Except for the Van Hedge index, which is January 1995 to September 2004.

Study of the factor betas and T-statistics in Table 10.7 suggest this pattern. The HEDG and HFRI indexes are short predominantly large and small growth. The Hennessee and Van indexes are mostly short small- and mid-cap growth. The PMVD variance shares are in general agreement with this pattern, except that mid-cap growth is approximately as strong as large growth for the HEDG and HFRI indexes and mid-cap growth dominates small growth for the Hennessee and HFRI indexes.

In general, mid-cap variance shares are larger than would be expected from the betas and T-statistics. In regard to the betas, this could be because of the higher standard deviation of mid-cap growth compared to the other benchmarks reported in Table 10.2. When converted to variances, mid-cap growth is at least 50 percent more volatile than either other index. This explanation, however, does not address the often significantly lower T-statistics for the mid-cap growth index.

The explanation for the difference between relative importance as implied by T-statistics and variance shares is in the weighting process used by the PMVD procedure to determine the probability associated with a particular marginal contribution. In spite of the mid-growth benchmark's weaker marginal contributions, the relative strength of the other benchmarks is not sufficient to offset the higher marginal contributions to explained variance obtained by the mid-cap growth benchmarks. For example, the correlations of small, mid-, and large growth with the Hennessee index are $-.75$, $-.85$ and $-.81$, respectively. These correspond to univariate R^2 values of 0.56, 0.73 and 0.66.

Variance decomposition results suggest that HEDG and HFRI index volatilities are predominantly driven by small growth, that the Hennessee index is driven by mid-cap growth, and that the Van Global index volatility is driven by both small and mid-cap growth.

A different perspective on these short selling indexes is provided by the use of the Fama-French (1993) three equity factor benchmarks. Results based on analysis with these benchmarks are provided in Table 10.8. The most important aspect of these results is the confirmation that the market is still the principal driving factor. Betas, T-statistics, and variance shares all suggest that the HEDG and Hennessee indexes are more similar in that the size and value premia are relatively less important, and that the HFRI and Van Global indexes are more similar in that these premia are more important. For the first group of funds, size and value premia variance shares total to 10 percent or less. For the second, they both total to 28 percent.

Note that being short Small minus big (SmB) is being short the small-cap premium, which is similar to favoring large cap. Hennessee has both the least negative SmB beta, implying it is the least short small cap, and is shown in Table 10.7 as having the least negative small-cap growth variance share. Being long high minus low is similar to being short growth. All measures in Table 10.8 suggest that HFRI and Van Global are shortest on growth. The results of Table 10.7 are not nearly so clear-cut because it is hard to disentangle growth and value factors.

The three-factor model is able to achieve comparable and even higher R^2 values than the large set of conventional asset benchmarks used here. The unimportance of the benchmarks other than equity style is not surprising, but the fact that an extensive model with six U.S. equity style benchmarks did not clearly outperform the three-factor model is notable.

MANAGED FUTURES AND RELATED STRATEGIES

Managed futures funds, commodity trading advisors (CTAs), and global macro funds primarily trade options and futures contracts. The focus of this section is on the relationship between these strategies and the large-cap growth style. In general, there is a consistent short profile between the performance of these strategies and large-growth performance. We do not offer an explanation for this relationship, but we do show that is most likely quite real. The robust nature of this relationship raises interesting questions and suggests portfolio strategies.

Analysis of Standard Indexes

The descriptive statistics for the four basic indexes to be profiled are presented in Table 10.2. It can be seen that these indexes have moderate volatility compared to short-selling indexes and equity indexes, moderate returns, and low levels of skew and excess kurtosis.

The static profiles against conventional asset markets are found in Table 10.9. The profiles of the CISDM indexes and the HEDG index are quite similar. The signs of betas correspond completely and they are of generally the same magnitude. The HFRI Macro Index disagrees in sign for small growth and high yield, but is otherwise remarkably similar to the other indexes, except for the importance of emerging markets. The fixed income exposures are about as might be expected.

One surprise, given the results from the analysis of daily indexes, is that the dollar exchange rate is not particularly important for any of these indexes. The explanation can be seen plainly in rolling window analysis. These strategies were generally long the dollar before 2001 and short the dollar after June 2002, and the net effect is quite small. Note, however, the strong negative dollar beta (−40 percent) for the HEDG index and the statistical significance implied by the T-statistic. The variance component suggests that being short the dollar explains about 10 percent of the volatility of this index.

TABLE 10.9 CTA, Macro, and Managed Futures Indexes Profiled against Conventional Asset Markets, Monthly Data, January 1994 to October 2004

Method	CISDM/MAR CTA CAP WTD			CISDM/MAR CTA INDEX EQUAL WTD			HEDG Managed Futures			HFRI Macro Index		
	Factor Model Constrained	T-Statistics Constrained	PMVD Unconstrained	Factor Model Constrained	T-Statistics Constrained	PMVD Unconstrained	Factor Model Constrained	T-Statistics Constrained	PMVD Unconstrained	Factor Model Constrained	T-Statistics Constrained	PMVD Unconstrained
LCG	-19%	-3.50	-2.1%	-26%	-4.50	-3.6%	-27%	-3.41	-3.9%	-13%	-1.97	-1.4%
LCV	20%	2.40	0.8%	29%	3.35	1.5%	16%	1.37	0.5%	20%	2.08	1.2%
MCG	8%	1.28	0.3%	11%	1.62	0.5%	3%	0.38	0.1%	3%	0.40	0.0%
MCV	-28%	-3.27	-0.8%	-37%	-3.96	-1.3%	-26%	-2.08	-0.7%	-24%	-2.35	-1.6%
SCG	-13%	-2.01	-0.5%	-13%	-1.98	-0.5%	-10%	-1.03	-0.3%	11%	1.45	10.3%
SCV	16%	2.02	0.4%	20%	2.43	0.7%	12%	1.02	0.2%	6%	0.62	0.0%
DM	6%	1.32	0.4%	4%	0.83	0.2%	22%	3.18	2.0%	1%	0.18	0.0%
EM	10%	3.58	1.8%	10%	3.29	1.8%	9%	2.24	0.9%	17%	5.15	17.9%
HY	-42%	-1.20	0.0%	-29%	-0.76	-0.6%	-25%	-0.48	0.0%	18%	0.42	0.0%
LB	-25%	-3.37	-1.6%	-34%	-4.27	-2.7%	-49%	-4.53	-4.4%	-11%	-1.25	-0.4%
MB	63%	4.10	15.3%	60%	3.60	14.7%	69%	3.02	12.3%	32%	1.77	13.8%
T–Bill	122%	5.20	0.4%	113%	4.51	0.3%	146%	4.22	0.0%	14%	0.51	0.7%
USDX	-17%	-1.59	-0.8%	-8%	-0.71	0.0%	-40%	-2.49	-2.3%	25%	1.99	1.2%
R^2	25%		25%	28%		28%	28%		28%	48%		49%
Alpha	0.38%			0.45%			0.35%			0.46%		
S.E. Alpha	0.12%			0.13%			0.18%			0.14%		

The large-growth beta is negative and statistically significant for every managed futures index, and quite strongly so for all except HFRI Macro. Macro strategies are much more likely to include directional bets, compared to the systematic and relatively nondiscretionary strategies of most CTAs and managed futures funds. This may provide one explanation for the differential large growth profiles of these strategies (see the next subsection). While large growth does not have the largest equity betas, large growth has the clearly the largest T-statistics and variance shares of all equity styles for all indexes except HFRI Macro.

Perhaps more important than the static all-history results is the picture that emerges from rolling window analysis. Table 10.10 presents partial results of the profile of the CISDM/MAR equally weighted CTA index against the conventional asset benchmarks utilized in Table 10.9. Due to space limitations, however, only total model R^2 and results for large-cap growth benchmark are presented here. It can be seen that the large-growth beta is consistently negative over time. There are only three months, September to November 2000, when the large-cap growth beta is positive, and the T-statistics and variance shares are very weak. Note the consistently large betas, T-statistics, and variance shares in the period following June 2000. It should be kept in mind, however, that the T-tests are based on overlapping data and are not independent. Large value has a similar general relationship, but with a weaker and long profile. The other equity style benchmarks do not show as strong or as stable a profile over time.

Following up on the time series observations, the profile of several of the CISDM/MAR subindexes against large-cap growth is examined over the 1994 to 2004 and the post-2000 periods separately. These results are presented in Table 10.11. Only model R^2 and coefficients for large-cap growth are provided.

Several patterns are clear. First, R^2 values tend to increase greatly over the much shorter periods of analysis. Betas and variance shares increase while T-statistics decrease. It is not surprising that T-statistics decrease with the much smaller number of observations. These results are all consistent with the pattern seen in Table 10.10.

What is most significant about these results, however, is that the short large-growth relationship is observed over all CISDM/MAR subindexes except, perhaps surprisingly, the stock subindex. For the stock trading index the relationship reverses. Variance shares, however, suggest a weak relationship in spite of the strong statistical significance over the period from 1994 to 2004. The systematic, trend-based, and diversified subindexes appear to show the strongest short large-growth profile. Over the complete history, the trend-based subindex has the highest variance share.

TABLE 10.10 Rolling Window R^2s and Performance Statistics for Large-cap Growth Benchmark in Profile of the CISDM/MAR CTA Equal Weighted Universe, Underlying Data, January 1994 to October 2004

Date	R^2	LCG beta	T-Stat	LCG PMVD Share	Date	R^2	LCG beta	T-Stat	LCG PMVD Share
Jan-97	44%	−10%	−0.31	0%	Dec-00	27%	−16%	−1.37	−10%
Feb-97	43%	−10%	−0.31	0%	Jan-01	28%	−18%	−1.53	−10%
Mar-97	47%	−6%	−0.18	0%	Feb-01	25%	−15%	−1.37	−8%
Apr-97	45%	−30%	−1.08	−2%	Mar-01	29%	−12%	−1.01	−10%
May-97	45%	−28%	−1.01	−2%	Apr-01	33%	−20%	−1.54	−14%
Jun-97	45%	−45%	−1.72	−3%	May-01	33%	−18%	−1.42	−14%
Jul-97	53%	−41%	−1.44	−4%	Jun-01	31%	−30%	−2.36	−14%
Aug-97	59%	−42%	−1.35	−5%	Jul-01	31%	−34%	−2.79	−14%
Sep-97	59%	−43%	−1.38	−5%	Aug-01	37%	−37%	−2.94	−15%
Oct-97	60%	−42%	−1.35	−5%	Sep-01	36%	−38%	−3.04	−18%
Nov-97	60%	−39%	−1.25	−5%	Oct-01	37%	−39%	−3.05	−16%
Dec-97	58%	−38%	−1.25	−5%	Nov-01	45%	−41%	−2.86	−19%
Jan-98	56%	−26%	−0.96	−3%	Dec-01	51%	−38%	−2.43	−20%
Feb-98	53%	−25%	−0.94	−2%	Jan-02	50%	−43%	−2.84	−20%
Mar-98	54%	−21%	−0.83	−1%	Feb-02	51%	−29%	−1.93	−14%
Apr-98	51%	−7%	−0.29	0%	Mar-02	47%	−30%	−2.07	−14%
May-98	56%	−25%	−0.92	−1%	Apr-02	39%	−29%	−2.07	−10%
Jun-98	56%	−13%	−0.59	0%	May-02	38%	−37%	−2.75	−12%
Jul-98	55%	−16%	−0.74	0%	Jun-02	47%	−42%	−2.53	−15%
Aug-98	55%	−12%	−0.49	0%	Jul-02	45%	−39%	−2.41	−15%
Sep-98	58%	−12%	−0.46	0%	Aug-02	45%	−39%	−2.42	−15%
Oct-98	58%	−11%	−0.43	0%	Sep-02	46%	−39%	−2.40	−15%
Nov-98	58%	−8%	−0.30	0%	Oct-02	47%	−44%	−2.59	−17%
Dec-98	57%	−7%	−0.28	0%	Nov-02	51%	−43%	−2.40	−18%
Jan-99	58%	−11%	−0.42	−1%	Dec-02	52%	−45%	−2.43	−20%
Feb-99	43%	−28%	−1.28	−2%	Jan-03	49%	−54%	−2.70	−20%
Mar-99	43%	−27%	−1.20	−2%	Feb-03	49%	−52%	−2.62	−18%
Apr-99	53%	−20%	−1.02	−3%	Mar-03	56%	−70%	−2.83	−17%
May-99	53%	−21%	−1.05	−3%	Apr-03	56%	−69%	−2.74	−17%
Jun-99	54%	−13%	−0.65	−2%	May-03	59%	−69%	−2.56	−12%
Jul-99	57%	−17%	−0.80	−2%	Jun-03	59%	−69%	−2.41	−10%
Aug-99	56%	−19%	−0.95	−2%	Jul-03	59%	−71%	−2.50	−13%
Sep-99	58%	−21%	−1.03	−3%	Aug-03	59%	−65%	−2.22	−15%
Oct-99	49%	−12%	−0.60	−1%	Sep-03	64%	−85%	−2.59	−22%
Nov-99	49%	−10%	−0.51	−1%	Oct-03	68%	−84%	−2.46	−23%
Dec-99	38%	−8%	−0.51	−1%	Nov-03	68%	−85%	−2.50	−23%
Jan-00	39%	−10%	−0.71	−2%	Dec-03	70%	−62%	−1.71	−16%
Feb-00	37%	−9%	−0.64	−2%	Jan-04	70%	−62%	−1.71	−16%
Mar-00	28%	−20%	−1.70	−6%	Feb-04	77%	−74%	−1.97	−21%
Apr-00	29%	−16%	−1.26	−4%	Mar-04	72%	−62%	−1.69	−16%
May-00	30%	−15%	−1.19	−4%	Apr-04	70%	−78%	−2.27	−13%
Jun-00	27%	−22%	−1.83	−5%	May-04	70%	−78%	−2.23	−13%
Jul-00	21%	−6%	−0.69	−2%	Jun-04	70%	−81%	−2.18	−13%
Aug-00	19%	−5%	−0.58	−1%	Jul-04	59%	−60%	−1.81	−7%
Sep-00	19%	7%	0.89	1%	Aug-04	54%	−66%	−2.06	−7%
Oct-00	21%	9%	1.07	1%	Sep-04	55%	−66%	−2.07	−7%
Nov-00	27%	6%	0.57	0%	Oct-04	56%	−70%	−2.14	−8%

TABLE 10.11 Model R^2 and Large-cap Growth Results for CTA, Macro, and Managed Futures Indexes, Profiles against Conventional Asset Markets, from Monthly Data, January 1994 to October 2004 and January 2000 to October 2004.

| | 1994–2004 | | | | 2000–2004 | | | |
Date	R^2	LCG beta	T-Stat	LCG PMVD Coeff	R^2	LCG beta	T-Stat	LCG PMVD Coeff
CISDM/MAR CTA INDEX CAP WTD	25%	−19%	−3.50	−2.1%	52%	−31%	−2.73	−9%
CISDM/MAR CTA INDEX EQUAL WTD	28%	−26%	−4.50	−3.6%	55%	−39%	−3.16	−12%
CISDM/MAR CURRENCY SUBINDEX	10%	−4%	−1.54	−0.2%	40%	−17%	−2.32	−4%
CISDM/MAR DISCRETIONARY SUBINDEX	22%	−7%	−2.35	−0.9%	49%	−14%	−2.87	−5%
CISDM/MAR DIVERSIFIED SUBINDEX	25%	−22%	−3.36	−2.5%	49%	−34%	−2.82	−9%
CISDM/MAR EUROPEAN CTA SUBINDEX	21%	−12%	−3.67	−2.4%	46%	−23%	−2.58	−7%
CISDM/MAR STOCK INDEX SUBINDEX	10%	18%	4.42	1.4%	25%	14%	1.75	1%
CISDM/MAR SYSTEMATIC SUBINDEX	25%	−17%	−2.86	−1.8%	53%	−30%	−2.81	−9%
CISDM/MAR TREND-BASED SUBINDEX	30%	−33%	−3.35	−4.1%	51%	−44%	−2.23	−8%
HEDG Managed Futures	28%	−27%	−3.41	−3.9%	52%	−32%	−1.84	−6%
HFRI Macro Index	48%	−13%	−1.97	−1.4%	59%	−19%	−2.27	−6%

Analysis of Calyon Simulated Trading Indexes

The implication of the pattern shown in the CISDM/MAR subindexes seems to be that nondiscretionary and diversified strategies have a stronger short large-growth profile. This implication can be studied further with the aid of a specialized set of indexes developed by Burghardt, Duncan, and Liu (2004) that cover 40 futures markets organized into commodity, equity, foreign currency, and interest rate sectors. These indexes utilize historical data to show the results of implementing completely nondiscretionary strategies in these futures markets. One nondiscretionary strategy, the 80-day range breakout, goes long if the price goes over the 80-day high and goes short if the price drops below the 80-day low. These are the only conditions allowing a change in position.

Table 10.12 shows partial results of factor model profiling of all Calyon 80-day range breakout indexes against conventional asset benchmarks.[3] Results are based on daily data over the period from January 2002 to August 2004. The model R^2 is shown, along with large growth betas, T-statistics, variance shares, and the percentage of variance explained defined as variance share divided by the model R^2. The table is ordered by sectors. Equity sector benchmarks come first, starting with the S&P 500 and ending with the Hang Seng Index. There are generally small betas and variance shares, and no apparent pattern. Next, the interest rate sector runs from the U.S. 30-year bond market to the Euro three-month note. Again, there is no apparent pattern. Currencies start with the sterling and end with the peso. Here, there is a clear short large-growth profile. A similar relationship is clearly visible with commodities from crude oil to copper. These results are summarized in the sector level and all-markets results shown in the bottom five rows of the table.

These results are not due to the specific trading strategy employed, as similar results are obtained using indexes reflecting returns from an 80-day moving average strategy. This strategy goes long when the price rises above the 80-day moving average and goes short when the price goes below the average. Neither do the results appear to be due to an inherent negative correlation between commodities and large growth equity. For example, the monthly correlation between the Goldman Sachs Commodity Index and the S&P/Barra 500 Growth Index is −.005 over the 1994 to 2004 period and falls only to −.029 over the 2000 to 2004 period. Instead, it seems that trend following itself has a negative association with large growth performance.

---

[3]The dollar exchange rate is not used in these models. Also, the Russell 2000 Growth and Value indexes are utilized in place of the S&P Barra Small Cap Growth and Value indexes.

TABLE 10.12 Summary R^2s and Performance Statistics for Large-cap Growth Benchmark in Profile of the Calyon 80-Day Range Breakout Simulated Futures Trading Indexes against Conventional Asset Markets, Based on Daily Data from January 2002 to August 2004

Futures Market	R^2	LCG beta	T-Stat	LCG PMVD Share	Pctg variance explained
S&P 500	51%	5%	2.72	3.3%	6%
CAC 40	45%	−2%	−1.05	−0.2%	0%
DAX 30	38%	6%	3.17	2.3%	6%
NIKKEI 225	5%	−1%	−1.20	0.0%	0%
AUSSIE SPX	4%	−5%	−10.11	−0.4%	9%
FTSE 250	40%	0%	0.00	0.0%	0%
SWEDISH OMX	6%	−3%	−4.87	−0.2%	3%
NASDAQ 100	18%	8%	9.37	2.0%	11%
DJ EURO STOXX	43%	3%	1.97	2.2%	5%
HANG SENG	6%	−2%	−4.59	−0.2%	4%
US 30 YEAR	12%	3%	2.16	0.8%	7%
US 10 YEAR	26%	0%	0.12	0.2%	1%
GERMAN BUND	16%	1%	0.94	0.0%	0%
GERMAN BOBL	15%	−3%	−2.08	−0.1%	1%
AUSSIE 10 YEAR	8%	−1%	−4.83	−0.8%	10%
UK 10 YEAR GILT	12%	3%	2.98	0.0%	0%
JAPAN 10 YEAR	2%	3%	7.87	0.1%	6%
JAPAN 3 MONTH	3%	−1%	−6.81	−0.2%	7%
US 3 MONTH	43%	0%	0.98	0.1%	0%
EUROPE 3 MONTH	11%	−4%	−5.31	−0.3%	3%
UK SHORT STERLING	5%	−5%	−8.89	−0.4%	8%
AUSSIE 3 MONTH	2%	0%	−9.10	−0.1%	7%
JAPANESE YEN	7%	−13%	−13.51	−1.0%	14%
EURO	18%	−18%	−7.70	−2.3%	13%
SWISS FRANC	11%	−10%	−6.25	−2.1%	18%
BRITISH POUND	18%	−19%	−9.10	−1.9%	10%
AUSTRALIAN DOLLAR	20%	−25%	−11.75	−3.2%	16%
CANADIAN DOLLAR	13%	−35%	−15.28	−2.9%	22%
MEXICAN PESO	5%	3%	4.58	0.3%	6%
CRUDE OIL	6%	−24%	−16.70	−1.3%	21%
NATURAL GAS	4%	−14%	−11.12	−0.5%	14%
SUGAR	2%	6%	10.96	0.2%	9%
HEATING OIL	7%	−21%	−13.23	−1.0%	14%
COTTON	1%	−2%	−3.18	−0.2%	13%
CORN	3%	−1%	−0.93	0.0%	0%
COFFEE	3%	−2%	−6.49	−0.2%	9%
SOYBEANS	2%	−4%	−4.54	−0.2%	9%
GOLD	10%	−26%	−12.83	−2.4%	23%
COPPER	5%	−6%	−7.04	−0.2%	5%
EQUITY SECTOR	41%	8%	0.79	1.1%	3%
INTEREST RATE SECTOR	23%	−4%	−0.51	0.0%	0%
FOREX SECTOR	22%	−116%	−11.33	−3.2%	15%
COMMODITY SECTOR	9%	−93%	−14.97	−2.0%	22%
PORTFOLIO	27%	−205%	−8.31	−4.0%	15%

An important fact that does not fit into the picture that has been developed here is that the profile of the Calyon simulated breakout indexes against large value yields substantially similar results. For example, the all-market beta is –201 percent versus –205 percent for large growth, the T-statistic for this beta is -8.00 versus –8.31 for large growth, and the variance share is -3.05 vs. –3.99 percent for large growth (with 0.27 R^2). This is problematic inasmuch as the standard indexes have a long profile against large value, as shown in Table 10.9.

One possible explanation would be that the relationship somehow reverses when aggregating to monthly sampling frequency. Analysis of daily CTA indexes provides mixed support for this idea. The S&P Managed Futures Index has a similar profile as the monthly indexes shown in Table 10.9. The Calyon-Barclay CTA Index, however, shows a strong short large-value profile.

CONCLUSION

This chapter has examined the profile hedge fund indexes and conventional asset markets in three cases: the daily performance of indexes representative of the universe of hedge fund strategies, the monthly performance of short sellers, and the monthly performance of traders that primarily utilize futures contracts. In each case, notable relationships with conventional asset markets are observed.

The daily data analysis demonstrates relatively high-frequency style tilts can be observed in aggregate indexes. These tilts could be deliberate timing of market exposures by hedge fund managers or incidental to other strategies. Regardless, from the perspective of institutional portfolio management, these exposures need to be monitored and, if necessary, corrected for through futures overlays or adjustment of the conventional asset portfolio.

The identification of high-frequency style tilts reinforces the perspective of Asness, Krail, and Liew (2001) in an unexpected way. Their central message is that hedge funds are more correlated with conventional asset markets than we think. The results developed here imply that a hedge fund could have a low profile based on monthly data and still have a very large market profile when analyzed with high-frequency data. This suggests the possibility that systemic market events could have unexpectedly large effects on funds with quickly changing market exposures. The daily data analysis also shows that index design decisions can have large effects on index market exposures.

The analysis of short-selling indexes demonstrates that indexes for the same strategy can have significantly different properties. The implied net position of these indexes ranges from 53 to 139 percent short. It also appears that there is considerable variation in style exposure, which should be taken into account when deciding which benchmark to use. Yet, there are significant commonalities in the indexes studied, such as the apparent tendency to be short growth as opposed to value stocks, to have high model R^2 values, and to have a very low profile against nonequity factors except for cash and international equity. Such commonalities should provide some confidence in index providers and the analytical methods used here.

The analysis of indexes of futures traders provides a new perspective on the widespread belief that managed futures provide a hedge for equity investments and of analyses such as Chance (2003) that focus on relationships with futures indexes as opposed to trading strategies. It is demonstrated that most of this hedge has been against the large-cap growth sector in recent years. This is a robust effect that appears strongest in indexes of nondiscretionary traders. Analysis of Calyon indexes that document the performance of simple trading rules appear to support the idea that trend following tends to generate a hedge against the large-growth sector. These results are, however, problematic in that they imply a similar short profile against large value when the opposite is observed in indexes of real traders. More research on this subject clearly appears warranted.

These results have implications for portfolio management, hedge fund performance evaluation, and our conception of hedge funds and their relationship to conventional investments. Most fundamentally, these results further reinforce the perspective that hedge funds are vehicles for concentrated active management rather than generators of absolute return uncorrelated with conventional markets. Rather than providing insulation from conventional markets, most hedge funds are intimately connected. Active management generates market exposures unless, and perhaps, even if care is taken to minimize them. Thus, an important current limit to the rate of growth of hedge fund investment is the degree to which the market exposures of a portfolio with a given percentage invested in hedge funds can be as prudently managed as a portfolio without hedge funds.

CHAPTER 11

Applying Securitization Technology to Hedge Funds

Paul U. Ali

Collateralized fund obligations (CFOs) represent the application to hedge funds of the Collateralized Debt Obligation (CDO) technology used by banks to securitize corporate loans. CFOs have been pioneered by the Man Group, the world's largest hedge fund company, and the Bahrain-based Investcorp Asset Management. For hedge fund managers, CFOs facilitate the taking of leveraged positions by enabling them to obtain low-cost funding from investors in the capital markets. For investors, CFOs offer similar diversification benefits to investments in hedge funds and funds of funds but in the form of credit-rated, debt securities. This chapter explains the legal structure of CFOs, considers the relevance of innovations in CDOs to hedge fund securitizations, and discusses the key legal issues arising out of the repackaging of hedge funds in this manner.

INTRODUCTION

One of the most exciting developments in the global investment markets has been the convergence of the hedge fund and securitization sectors. Over the last three years, the securitization technology routinely used by banks to remove loans from their balance sheets and finance fresh lending has been applied to hedge funds. This has led to the creation of a new class of securitizations known as collateralized fund obligations (CFOs), pioneered by the Man Group, the world's largest hedge fund company, and the Bahrain-based Investcorp Asset Management in 2002.

CFOs, like more conventional securitization transactions, permit the conversion or "securitization" of relatively illiquid assets (hedge fund investments that typically comprise unlisted equity interests in companies, trusts, and limited partnerships) into a form—debt securities—for which there is a significantly more liquid secondary market. This is a potential "win-win" situation for all parties. For hedge fund managers, CFOs offer the opportunity to broaden their investor base and also facilitate the taking of leveraged positions by enabling them to obtain low-cost debt funding from investors in the capital markets. For investors, CFOs offer analogous diversification benefits to equity investments in hedge funds but in the form of credit-rated debt securities that can be traded in the secondary market.

This chapter explains the legal structure of these securitized hedge funds and discusses the key issues for investors in CFOs.

GENERIC CFO STRUCTURE

Securitizing a Hedge Fund

CFOs are structured as market value cash securitizations. What this means is that a CFO has two key attributes: The investors in a CFO obtain actual or cash exposure to a pool of underlying hedge funds, and the claims held by the investors are serviced by the cash flow derived from actively managing the investments in the hedge funds, that is, from the appreciation of the capital or market value of those investments.

At the center of a CFO, as in all securitizations, is a special purpose vehicle (SPV). This SPV can take the form of a company, trust, or limited partnership, but, whatever type of entity that is chosen, that entity must be structured in such a way to ensure that its assets and liabilities will not be consolidated with the assets and liabilities of the party sponsoring the CFO, on the bankruptcy of the latter or for accounting purposes (Moody's Investors Service 2003). In other words, the SPV must be a bankruptcy-remote, off–balance sheet entity.

The SPV has two limited purposes:

1. To issue debt securities to investors in the capital markets
2. To invest the subscription proceeds of those debt securities either directly or indirectly in a pool of hedge funds

These proceeds are invested, typically by the sponsor of the CFO (which is itself a hedge fund manager), for the SPV in equity interests in a fund of hedge funds managed by the sponsor. The rationale for the use of a fund of hedge funds in a CFO and the investor issues arising out of that are discussed later in this chapter.

The exposure to hedge funds achieved by investing in a fund of hedge funds can be replicated through the entry by the SPV into a total return swap. Under the swap, the SPV would, in exchange for making certain fixed payments to a swap dealer, receive variable amounts linked to the performance of a notional pool of hedge funds. These total return swaps have been used in some private, unrated CFO structures but, by far, the more common means of securitizing hedge funds, particularly in rated CFO structures, is through the use of an intermediated fund of hedge funds.

The principal and interest payments on the debt securities are serviced mainly out of the cash flow generated by the secondary sale or, more commonly, the redemption of the equity interests held by the SPV in the fund of hedge funds—with such redemptions, in turn, being financed by the secondary sale or redemption of the equity interests in hedge funds held by the fund of hedge funds. The debt securities will, on maturity, be similarly redeemed for cash out of the proceeds of the sale or redemption of the SPV's equity interests in the fund of hedge funds. It is therefore essential that the fund of hedge funds is sufficiently liquid to permit the redemptions required to service the debt securities (Fitch Ratings 2003). The putative liquidity benefits of the fund of hedge funds structure is also discussed in the next section.

The debt securities issued in a CFO transaction are, in common with the debt securities issued in other securitizations, limited recourse securities. Accordingly, the claims of the investors against the SPV are limited to the amount generated from the sale or redemption of the equity interests held by the SPV, and the SPV is not liable to the investors for any shortfall on the principal amount of the debt securities following the distribution of the sale or redemption proceeds.

Investor Interests in Hedge Funds and CFOs

The key difference between a CFO and a hedge fund relates to the nature of the interests held by the investors. In the case of a hedge fund, the contributions of the investors to the capital of the fund are pooled and invested on their behalf by a third party (the manager of the hedge fund). In exchange for these contributions, the investors become members of the hedge fund; that is, they receive equity interests in the fund. The investors enjoy certain reserve powers, flowing from their membership of the fund, to intervene in the management of the fund (the key powers being the ability to remove the manager and terminate the fund). Moreover, the investors, through their equity interests, are fully exposed to the performance of the fund and the business and portfolio risks associated with the fund. They have a variable claim against the assets of the fund that is correlated to the capital value of the fund's assets. Accordingly, the investors fully participate in any over- or underperformance of the fund's portfolio, and, as members, their claims against the fund are subordinated to the claims of creditors.

In the case of a CFO, the contributions of investors are pooled by the securitization vehicle (the SPV) and invested on their behalf. However, the investors in a CFO do not obtain equity interests in the SPV. Instead, they receive debt instruments issued by the SPV and are thus creditors, not members, of the SPV. Accordingly, outside of a default by the SPV in the performance of its obligations to the investors, the investors have no right to intervene in the management of the SPV. In addition, the investors have, in general, only a fixed claim against the SPV, meaning that the quantum of their claims is not reduced by the underperformance of the SPV's portfolio of hedge fund investments (although the likelihood of the claims being met may be adversely affected). Nor does the overperformance of that portfolio result in an increase in the quantum of their claims. Further, as creditors, their claims against the SPV rank ahead of the claims of the members of the SPV.

In reality, the SPV in a CFO, in the same manner as the vehicles used in other securitizations, will usually only have nominal members. It is the creditors, not the members, that provide the capital utilized for investment by the SPV. The members are necessary only for the purposes of establishing the SPV as a bankruptcy-remote off–balance sheet entity, by providing the minimum capital required to incorporate a company, settle a trust or establish a partnership and a particular ownership structure for the entity.

Investor Protection: Credit-Tranched Securities

In common with other securitizations, the debt securities issued in a CFO are often credit-tranched. Credit-tranching is the division of the debt securities into differentially rated classes or tranches, with the higher-rated or more senior tranches of securities having a superior claim against the SPV. The lower-rated or more junior tranches of securities therefore insulate the more senior tranches against loss. Consequently, the coupon payable on a particular tranche differs in inverse proportion to the ranking of that tranche vis-à-vis other tranches.

Tranching is generally effected through the combination of a security interest and a priority agreement. The SPV grants a security interest over its assets to an independent security trustee for the benefit of the investors. However, the different tranches of debt securities do not share equally in the benefit of this security interest: The junior tranche's entitlement to principal and interest is limited to the residue remaining after principal and interest on the more senior tranches have been paid in full, and the mezzanine tranche's entitlement is likewise limited to the residue remaining after principal and interest on the senior-most tranche have been paid in full.

In a CFO, the junior tranche may be structured as a hybrid of debt and equity. Like the investors in the other tranches, the holders of the junior tranche of securities are normally creditors, not members of the SPV, in that the rights attached to the securities do not include rights to intervene in the management of the SPV. However, the coupon on the securities and the principal amount for which they will be redeemed on maturity may be more equitylike in character, with both the coupon and principal amount being linked to changes in the capital value of the SPV's assets.

Investor Protection: Principal-Protected Securities

The senior-most tranche of securities in a CFO may also be protected against the loss of principal on the maturity of the securities. This is usually achieved through the credit-wrapping of that tranche by a monoline insurer (Wachovia Securities 2003). Alternatively, principal protection can be achieved by allocating part of the subscription proceeds received by the SPV to either a static or dynamically managed portfolio of riskless assets (i.e., zero-coupon U.S. Treasury securities), to ensure the return of an amount sufficient on maturity to repay the principal amount of the principal-protected tranche in full (Wachovia Securities 2003). However, the utilization of the subscription proceeds to pay premiums to a monoline insurer or purchase riskless assets may depress the overall return of the SPV's assets, thus eroding the benefits of investing in CFO securities.

SECURITIZING A FUND OF HEDGE FUNDS

Although the performance of equity interests in hedge funds can be replicated through the use of hedge fund swaps, it is more common for CFOs to be structured around an actual, as opposed to a notional, portfolio of hedge fund investments. The debt securities issued by the SPV are therefore serviced by the cash proceeds from the realization or redemption of the underlying hedge fund investments, rather than by the cash flow generated by a collateralized hedge fund derivative.

The investment in the hedge funds is usually accomplished through the SPV utilizing the subscription proceeds to acquire equity interests in a fund of hedge funds. A fund of hedge funds is a pooled intermediation vehicle that, itself, invests in diversified pool of hedge funds.

The chief asset being securitized—namely, the fund of hedge funds—is no different in its legal structure from a mutual fund that invests in other mutual funds. Moreover, funds of hedge funds commonly adopt the same vehicles used by conventional funds of funds (unit trusts and limited liability companies), but, unlike the latter, these vehicles are usually incorporated in an offshore jurisdiction for the same reasons as hedge funds themselves make use of those jurisdictions. These reasons include maintaining confidentiality about the performance, asset allocation, and proprietary trading techniques of the hedge fund and also the investors in the hedge fund, as well as enabling the hedge fund to minimize the taxation impact of trades and investor redemptions (Ali, Stapledon, and Gold 2003). The most common offshore jurisdictions for funds of hedge funds are the Cayman Islands, the British Virgin Islands, Bermuda, and the Bahamas (Nicholas 2004).

The rationale for using an intermediated vehicle to obtain exposure to hedge funds rather than investing directly in hedge funds is examined next (Ali 2004).

Rationale for Funds of Hedge Funds

The key attraction of a fund of hedge funds is the access it offers to hedge funds. Hedge funds, in general, demand substantial minimum investments and, once they have reached what the fund manager considers to be an optimum size, will be closed to new investors.

The minimum investment requirement for an individual hedge fund is not a problem for the SPV, but it may well be an amount higher than what the SPV wishes to allocate to an individual hedge fund or a particular hedge fund strategy. The fund of hedge funds enables the SPV to obtain exposure to hedge funds without having to commit a substantial amount to an individual hedge fund (since the minimum investment requirements for funds of hedge funds are usually significantly lower than those for hedge funds), and the SPV's investment in a fund of hedge funds will be spread across a pool of hedge funds. In addition, the SPV can obtain exposure to hedge funds that are no longer accepting new investors by investing in a fund of hedge funds that is, itself, an existing investor in those closed hedge funds.

A further advantage offered by a fund of hedge funds to the SPV (and thus also the investors in the securities issued by the SPV) is increased liquidity. A fund of hedge funds can be viewed as a secondary market in the hedge funds in which it is invested. It therefore provides a means for the SPV to terminate its exposure to those hedge funds, through the redemption or buy-back of its equity interests in the fund of hedge funds.

Hedge funds are characterized by limited liquidity. They prescribe minimum holding or lockup periods for investments and will redeem the equity interests of investors only within specified exit windows and then only after lengthy advance notice. Funds of hedge funds, in contrast, permit more frequent investor exit and do not generally impose lockups. It is also more common for a fund of hedge funds to be listed on an official exchange than it is for a hedge fund. This secondary market provides an additional means of exit for the SPV, which can sell its equity interests in a listed fund of hedge funds on the exchange to incoming investors.

Yet another advantage of the fund of hedge funds structure for the SPV and its investors is that it introduces an independent third party (the fund manager) between the SPV and the underlying hedge funds. This fund manager is better placed than the SPV, due to expertise and resources and, in many instances, the relationship with the managers of the underlying hedge funds, to monitor the performance of those hedge funds. In particular, the fund manager is likely to be able to discern drawdowns, style drift, and the excessive use of leverage more readily than the SPV.

Investor Issues

The fund of hedge funds structure is, however, not without significant drawbacks (Ali 2004). It is essential that these are understood by the prospective investors in CFOs.

The first concern is a corollary of investing in a vehicle that, in turn, invests in a purportedly diversified pool of investments. The diversification benefits of investing in a fund of hedge funds are vulnerable to two factors. The fund of hedge funds may be overdiversified or spread across too many hedge funds or hedge fund strategies. This may result in a dilution of the contribution of the individual hedge funds to the overall return on the fund of hedge funds and will, in turn, undermine the diversification benefits to the SPV of investing in the fund of hedge funds (Lhabitant and De Piante Vicin 2004). In addition, there is a risk of multiple duplication of positions within the hedge funds invested in by the fund of hedge funds (Lhabitant 2004). Should that occur, the returns of the hedge funds will tend to be more strongly correlated to each other, undermining the diversification benefits accruing to the fund of hedge funds and, consequently, the SPV.

A second concern arises in respect of the putative liquidity benefits offered by funds of hedge funds. The increased liquidity of an investment in a fund of hedge funds over a direct investment in hedge funds carries with it an implicit cost. In order for a fund of hedge funds to offer greater liquidity (in essence, less stringent exit conditions) than the hedge funds in which it invests, the manager of the fund of hedge funds must maintain a cash buffer to finance the redemption of the equity interests of the SPV and other exiting investors. This cash buffer may seriously detract from the performance of the fund of hedge funds, by diluting the fund's investment returns. An alternative solution is for the fund of hedge funds to provide enhanced liquidity by investing hedge funds that themselves offer less stringent exit conditions. However, this may lead to the fund of hedge funds overselecting hedge funds that invest in liquid exchange-traded securities and futures contracts and underselecting hedge funds that invest in illiquid securities and futures contracts and in over-the-counter derivatives. This, again, may have serious adverse consequences for the performance of the fund of hedge funds (Ineichen 2003).

There is also the risk that the introduction of an intermediated vehicle between the SPV and the hedge funds to which the SPV is seeking exposure may, of itself, undermine the putative liquidity benefits of a fund of hedge funds. The presence of an intermediated vehicle may adversely affect the ability of the SPV to terminate its exposure to the underlying hedge funds in a situation of a sharp market downturn. This is because the SPV will, in essence, be seeking to redeem an interest in an interest—the former is the SPV's equity interest in the fund of hedge funds and the latter is the equity interest of the fund of hedge funds in the underlying hedge funds (Ali, Stapledon, and Gold 2003). Exiting the former interest depends on being able to exit the latter interest, and the exiting of that latter interest, in turn, depends on compliance with the exit requirements of the underlying hedge funds and those hedge funds, themselves, being able to exit their own investments in a falling market and thus finance the redemption of equity interests in the hedge funds. Financing redemption is accentuated by the fact that hedge funds are typically fully invested and thus do not maintain cash buffers.

A third concern with the fund of hedge funds structure relates to the cost to the ultimate investors: the investors in the securities issued by the SPV. The SPV, in common with all investors in a fund of hedge funds, will be paying two sets of fees (Brown, Goetzmann, and Liang 2004). The first set of fees are those paid directly by the SPV to the manager of the fund of hedge funds; the second set relates to the fees levied on the fund of hedge funds by the managers of the underlying hedge funds.

Finally, funds of hedge funds, like all pooled investment vehicles, expose the SPV and other investors to the decisions of their fellow investors. An investor exits a fund of hedge funds usually by redeeming its equity interests in the fund, and the redemption of those interests must be financed, as noted, out of either a cash buffer or by the redemption of the fund's investments in the underlying hedge funds. The latter incurs transaction costs and may also lead to the crystallization of a capital gain, both of which will be borne by the remaining investors in the fund of hedge funds, although some or all of the transaction costs may be recouped by the levying of an exit fee.

CONCLUSION

Collateralized fund obligations have the potential to deliver a mutually beneficial result for both hedge fund managers and investors. The application of tried-and-tested bank securitization technology to hedge funds enables fund managers to expand their institutional investor base and also obtain low-cost debt funding for their investment activities. For their part, institutional investors that face regulatory or constitutional limitations on investing in the unlisted equity interests in hedge funds can nonetheless obtain exposure to hedge funds by investing in the rated debt securities issued in a CFO transaction.

However, investors need to be aware that the upside potential on their CFO investments is limited relative to taking an equity position in a comparable hedge fund. Moreover, as CFOs normally create exposure to hedge funds through an intermediated fund of hedge funds, investors need also to be familiar with the advantages and disadvantages of the fund of hedge funds structure, especially in relation to the fee structure and the stated diversification and liquidity benefits of those funds.

CHAPTER 12

Maximum Drawdown Distributions with Volatility Persistence

Kathryn Wilkens, Carlos J. Morales, and Luis Roman

This chapter investigates the behavior of the volatility of various classes of fund returns and the corresponding distribution of drawdowns. Where volatility persistence is indicated, the distribution of maximum drawdowns implies a greater likelihood of larger losses. Monte Carlo simulations are used to hold the mean and standard deviation of hypothetical fund returns constant and verify the empirically observed impact of volatility persistence. The relationship between maximum drawdowns and volatility persistence and kurtosis is stronger for single-strategy funds and is not indicated for diversified funds.

INTRODUCTION

It is widely recognized that hedge funds and managed futures have unique characteristics that pose challenges to risk management. In particular, the highly

We wish to thank the Center for International Securities and Derivatives Markets for supplying the data used in this study and Galen Burghardt, director of research at Calyon Financial, for suggesting the topic.

active and complex nature of their investment process can result in returns with nonconstant volatility and nonnormal return distributions. Because the return distributions may not be symmetrical, hedge fund investors and risk managers are concerned with downside volatility. Drawdown statistics are also a practical measure of liquidity risk, consistent with the nature of investments that are marking to market and using stop orders to control risk.

We define drawdowns as the maximum percentage loss occurring between two high-water marks. A high-water mark is said to occur when the net asset value is higher than values preceding and following it.* In this chapter, we analyze distributions of maximum drawdowns with historical fund returns and Monte Carlo simulations. Our results replicate those of previous studies, showing that the maximum drawdown will be larger with a lower mean, higher standard deviation, and longer track record.

The focus of this study, however, is on the impact of volatility persistence, which provides a partial explanation for the observation of excess kurtosis (fat tails) in asset returns. Previous studies have shown that kurtosis in fund returns does not impact the distribution of maximum drawdowns. We present evidence that seems to indicate that kurtosis does impact maximum drawdown distributions, but recognize that persistence in volatility may provide a partial explanation. In particular, it is interesting to note that kurtosis influences maximum drawdowns for individual funds, but not for funds of funds. Funds of funds have an average kurtosis similar to individual funds, but are less likely to exhibit volatility persistence. We also present some evidence on which strategies are more likely to exhibit persistence in volatility than others.

PREVIOUS LITERATURE

There exists an extensive literature on the subject of drawdowns, ranging from the anecdotal to the rigorous, from the simple to the arcane. An important contribution in assessing the distribution of drawdowns is made by Burghardt, Duncan, and Liu (2003). In this work, the authors explore variables that are potential determinants of drawdown distributions. In particular, they find that length of track record, mean return, and the size of the volatility of a manager's returns account for differences in drawdown distributions. They also find that skewness and kurtosis in a return series do not affect the distribution. The expected size of a drawdown correlates

---

*The standard definition used with commodity trading advisors is from peak to trough. Our defintion is similar, and we concentrate on maximum drawdowns, making any difference in definitions inconsequential.

negatively with the mean return and positively with volatility. In addition, the authors observe that managers may deleverage when in a downturn, lowering their volatility. This suggests that the volatility in a manager's return might be changing over time. They pose as questions for further research how changes in a manager's volatility would affect the distribution of drawdowns and maximum drawdowns, and how accounting for serial correlation in a series might affect those distributions. In this work, we take on some of these issues by exploring the distribution of maximum drawdowns within a Generalized Autoregressive Conditional Heteroskedasticity (GARCH) framework, which accounts for time-varying volatility and is related to the presence of fat tails in returns.

In a recent contribution on the subject, Lopez de Prado and Peijan (2004) explore the effects of nonnormality as well as serial correlation assumptions in the return series to measures of risk based on drawdowns. They find via a simulation study that risk is usually underestimated (in the form of value at risk [VaR], or percentile estimates of drawdowns) when the distribution of returns is not normal (in particular, they assume that returns follow a mixture of normal distributions). Furthermore, if returns are assumed to follow an ARIMA(p,1,q) process, measures such as VaR do not fully capture all dimensions of risk in the market, so they suggest using measures based on drawdowns instead. While these authors explore both non-Gaussian and time dependence, they suggest that hedge fund returns exhibit, in addition, conditional volatility regimes. They claim that these different volatility regimes can be captured via their mixture model. In this chapter, in contrast, we explore directly the possibility that a hedge fund return's departure from Gaussian might be appropriately modeled by a GARCH process and investigate, under this paradigm, the distribution of drawdowns and maximum drawdowns.

On a more technical note, de Melo Mendes and Leal (2003) consider the distribution of maximum drawdowns under the assumption of an integrated GARCH model process for the returns series. They choose a parametric model for the distribution of maximum drawdowns based on extreme value theory. In particular, they assume that the distribution of maximum drawdowns follow a modified generalized Pareto distribution. Using simulated data from integrated GARCH, they estimate parameters for this distribution using maximum likelihood. Analyzing data from Nasdaq and the British Financial Times Stock Exchange (FTSE), they note that extreme maximum drawdowns tend to occur during periods of high volatility. They also point out, however, that uncharacteristic drawdowns are also possible in periods of relatively low volatility. In this chapter, while we consider the behavior of maximum drawdowns under a GARCH model for the returns, we do not assume a parametric form for the distribution of maximum drawdowns. Furthermore, we analyze fund returns rather than stock returns.

DATA AND METHODOLOGY

We use fund return series from the Center for International Securities and Derivatives Markets (CISDM) database that have track records with a minimum of two years and that start no later than January 1985. The data series ends in July 2004. These criteria yield a total of 2,071 individual funds and include several distinct hedge fund strategies, commodity trading advisors (CTAs), and funds of funds (FoFs). The summary statistics are presented in Table 12.1.

The maximum drawdowns, track records, and summary statistics are calculated for each fund. The entire sample is divided into two groups based on the Ljung-Box-Pierce Q-test (LBQ test) for a departure from randomness. We later use a dummy variable to distinguish between the group that fails to be rejected by the LBQ test and the group of funds that does not. Funds that are rejected by the test of randomness exhibit volatility persistence through the autocorrelation functions of the squared residuals from the mean. This is a common preestimation step for determining if autoregressive conditional heteroskedasticity (ARCH) effects exist in the data and provides results that are identical to Engle's ARCH test. We test several lags at 5 and 10 percent significance levels. We find that 21.6 percent of the funds in the sample have volatility persistence in their monthly returns at the 5 percent significance level, and volatility persistence is indicated in 30.7 percent of the funds at the 10 percent significance level. In the results presented here, we work with the larger sample. Although the results are similar, inferences made from working with the larger subsample of funds is actually more conservative than working with the smaller group at a more stringent LBQ test significance level because we are interested in comparing the two groups.

We graph the frequency distributions of the maximum drawdowns for various groups of funds. We form samples based on length of track record, presence of volatility persistence, and fund strategy classification. We also run simple regressions with maximum drawdown as the dependent variable and confirm previous findings relating to mean and standard deviation, and

TABLE 12.1 Overall Summary Statistics

Monthly Data	Track Record	Average Return	Standard Deviation	Kurtosis
Min	24	−2.302%	0.0063%	−1.2578
Max	235	6.224%	28.66%	83.983
Average	83.8	1.0247%	3.998%	3.6182

present new evidence on the impact of kurtosis on maximum drawdowns. In addition, we calculate the relative frequency of indications of volatility persistence among various fund strategies. Monte Carlo simulation results can be viewed as representing the theoretical maximum drawdown distribution for a single hedge fund obtained from multiple return histories calibrated with a mean and unconditional volatility representative of monthly hedge funds. These results are used to confirm the inferences drawn from the historical returns. This evidence, combined with the regression results on fund of funds, managed futures, and hedge fund strategies allow us to draw conclusions about the related impacts of kurtosis and volatility persistence on drawdown distributions.

RESULTS

Figure 12.1 illustrates the distribution of maximum drawdowns for all funds that do not exhibit volatility persistence as measured by the LBQ

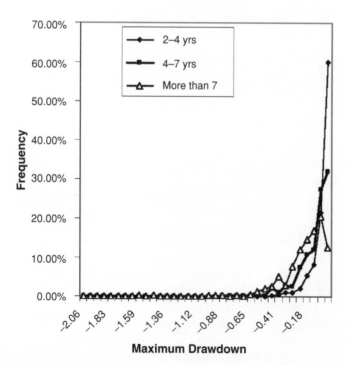

FIGURE 12.1 Frequency of Maximum Drawdowns: Track Records with No Volatility Persistence

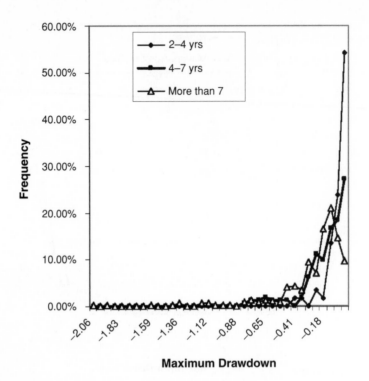

FIGURE 12.2 Frequency of Maximum Drawdowns: Track Records with Volatility Persistence

statistic. This group of funds is divided into three groups based on the length of the track record. Consistent with Burghardts, Duncan, and Liu (2003), the graph illustrates the tendency for funds with a longer track record to have a larger likelihood of experiencing larger drawdowns. Figure 12.2 shows that this intuitive result also holds for the group of funds that exhibits return volatility persistence.

Figure 12.3 indicates that funds that exhibit volatility persistence have a higher likelihood of experiencing a greater maximum drawdown. We find this interesting because previous studies have shown that kurtosis does not affect the distribution of theoretical maximum drawdowns, and volatility persistence is associated with fat tails. We are not aware of any other study that illustrates this empirical result. The analysis that follows focuses on investigating causes for this result.

In Table 12.2 we examine the relative frequency of funds that exhibit volatility persistence in various strategy classifications. The average frequency is 30.7 percent. Classifications that contain more than 30.7 percent

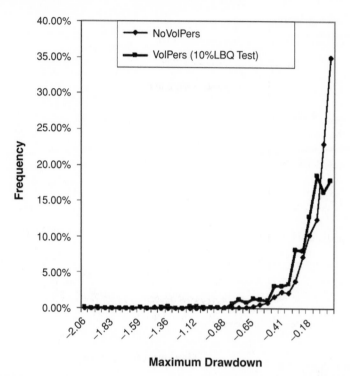

FIGURE 12.3 Frequency of Maximum Drawdowns: Track Records with and without Persistence

of the funds that exhibit volatility persistence include currency and financial CTAs and almost all of the hedge fund strategies, particularly short sellers. Hedge funds that do not exhibit a lot of volatility persistence include market-neutral and event-driven strategies. Volatility persistence also occurs with less frequency than average in fund of funds, diversified CTAs, and guaranteed products. One difficulty in this analysis is that while no fund is double-counted, the categories sometimes overlap. For example, an offshore fund may also be a currency CTA, but this classification system does not make the distinction. Nevertheless, we are able to draw the broad conclusion that volatility persistence seems more prevalent in less diversified funds.

In Figure 12.4 we graph simulation results to confirm the inference from the historical returns that volatility persistence impacts the distribution of maximum drawdowns. Two sets of 1,000 monthly returns representing an eight-year track record are simulated, each with a mean and unconditional volatility approximating the average of the entire sample (see Table 12.1).

TABLE 12.2 Frequency of Volatility Persistence by Hedge Fund Strategy

	w/VolPers	Total
FoF	132	454
Futures–CTA-Agricultural/Energy/Metals	2	15
Futures–CTA-Currency	17	33**
Futures–CTA-Diversified	40	138
Futures–CTA-Financial-Stock Index	25	68*
Futures–Public-Guaranteed U.S. & Non	2	7
Futures–Public-Offshore	24	104
Futures–Public–U.S. Closed & Open	20	46*
Futures–Private–U.S. Closed & Open	32	90*
Hedge Fund–Non & U.S.-Event Driven	37	153
Hedge Fund–Non & U.S.-Global Macro	15	45*
Hedge Fund–Non & U.S.-Global Emerging	32	101*
Hedge Fund–Non & U.S.-Global Established	95	281*
Hedge Fund–Non & U.S.-Global International	16	35**
Hedge Fund–Non & U.S.-Long Only	3	8*
Hedge Fund–Non & U.S.-Market Neutral	99	370
Hedge Fund–Non & U.S.-Sector	32	107
Hedge Fund–Non & U.S.-Short-Sales	13	16***
Total	636 (30.71%)	2071

*More likely to exhibit persistence in volatility of monthly returns.
**At a 5 percent level.
***At a 1 percent level.

The first set represents the case of no volatility persistence: $r_t = \mu_t + \sigma_t \varepsilon_t$, where $\sigma = .04$, $\mu = 0.01$, and $E[\varepsilon_t] = 0$ with a unit variance. The second set is simulated based on a return-generating model where the variance is described by a GARCH (1,1) process:

$$\sigma_t^2 = \kappa + G\sigma_{t-1}^2 + A\varepsilon_{t-1}^2 \qquad (12.1)$$

where $G = .3$
$A = .5$
$k = 0.00035$
μ in the return-generating process = 0.01.

While in both cases the theoretical mean and standard deviations are 0.01 and 0.04, the empirical mean and standard deviation for the first and second set of simulated returns are 0.010089 and 0.041992 and 0.01009 and 0.040036, respectively. The slightly lower standard deviation for the

Mean 1%, Standard Deviation 4%

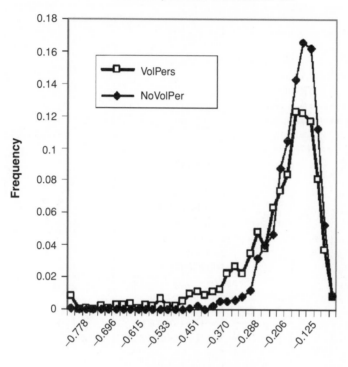

Maximum Drawdown

FIGURE 12.4 Simulation Results

second set of returns errs on the side of being conservative. The empirical excess kurtosis for the first set is close to zero at 0.1377, while the kurtosis for the second set is a much higher 1.996. The simulation results clearly illustrate that the returns with volatility persistence have a larger likelihood of a larger maximum drawdowns, confirming our results with historical returns. Because excess kurtosis is associated with the model's volatility persistence, we return to the historical returns to further investigate the relative impacts on maximum drawdowns.

In Table 12.3 we group the entire sample into three subsets: 454 fund of funds, 501 managed futures, and 1,116 hedge fund strategies. On average, each group exhibits kurtosis of 3.95, 2.35, and 4.05, respectively. Ordinary least squares (OLS) regression analyses are performed for each of the three groups where maximum drawdowns are the dependent variable. For

TABLE 12.3 Determinants of Maximum Drawdowns: Mean, Volatility, Kurtosis, Track Record, and Volatility Persistence

Fund of Funds, count = 454

MaxDrawdown	AveReturn	STDEV	KURT	TrackRecord	VPdummy
−0.0898					
Mean	0.0071	0.0188	3.9538	78.5815	0.2907
Coefficients	8.4094	−7.0320	−0.0004	−0.0005	0.0034
t Stat	9.7164	−30.1542	−0.9163	−6.8928	0.5134
P-value	0.0000	0.0000	0.3600	0.0000	0.6079

Futures/CTAs, count = 501

MaxDrawdown	AveReturn	STDEV	KURT	TrackRecord	VPdummy
−0.2171					
Mean	0.0107	0.0568	2.3540	105.8104	0.3234
Coefficients	6.4727	−5.1107	−0.0029	−0.0006	−0.0177
t Stat	9.9740	−34.7030	−3.5164	−7.4721	−2.1452
P-value	0.0000	0.0000	0.0005	0.0000	0.0324

Hedge Funds, count = 1116

MaxDrawdown	AveReturn	STDEV	KURT	TrackRecord	VPdummy
−0.1847					
Mean	0.0113	0.0411	4.0492	76.0197	0.3065
Coefficients	5.0935	−5.8702	−0.0014	−0.0008	−0.0205
t Stat	11.1920	−55.7695	−3.4337	−9.6741	−2.9800
P-value	0.0000	0.0000	0.0006	0.0000	0.0029

all three analyses, the independent variables discussed in Burghardt, Duncan, and Liu (2003) are significant: mean, standard deviation, and length of track record. Kurtosis and a dummy variable for volatility persistence are insignificant in the case of fund of funds, which is also consistent with those authors' results. However, both kurtosis and the dummy variable are significant for the second two groups.

CONCLUSION

We conclude that in less diversified strategies, there is more evidence of volatility persistence in fund returns and that this persistence increases the size of drawdowns. While volatility persistence and kurtosis are related and kurtosis remains present across all funds, they do not impact drawdowns in funds of funds. We attribute this discrepancy to a diversification affect. In summary, while we cannot make any definitive statements about the impact of kurtosis on drawdown distributions, we note that kurtosis and the presence of volatility persistence are positively related and that these effects do appear to impact the distribution of drawdowns in funds that are less diversified.

Three

Risk and Performance Measurement

Chapter 13 presents a literature review of current studies of hedge fund performance. It examines the biases found in hedge fund databases and explains how survivorship bias is usually calculated in academic studies. It also explains that performance persistence in hedge fund returns is usually short-lived and often due to the fact that losing managers continue to lose, rather than to winners repeating. Linear asset factor models, as applied to hedge funds, are examined and discussed. The chapter also explains why hedge funds have proven to be effective portfolio diversifiers. Finally, it ends with a discussion on the survival analysis of hedge fund lifetimes, an area of research that is only beginning to appear in the academic literature.

Chapter 14 looks at investors who make the decision to invest in hedge funds. They often look first to multimanager vehicles such as funds of hedge funds and, increasingly, index funds. Indeed, multimanager vehicles broaden the appeal of hedge funds to include both smaller investors (or allocations) and those with limited time and staff. This chapter examines the factors involved in choosing between single-manager hedge fund portfolios and prepackaged multimanager investments, as well as the specific benefits and drawbacks of each method of investing.

Chapter 15 provides a new look at the performance persistence of hedge fund managers. The existence of persistence among individual and hedge funds portfolios is mainly observed over one- to three- month horizons. This hot-hand effect vanishes as the horizon lengthens. The authors on previous research use an arbitrage pricing theory framework to adjust for risk, finding a slight overreaction pattern at long-term horizons, which is more pronounced among directional strategies.

Chapter 16 reexamines the performance of hedge funds over the period 1995 to 2003. The author assesses abnormal performance using a number of alternative benchmarks and an approach originally used in event studies. More specifically, the benchmarks employed allow for the standard capital asset pricing model, the GARCH extension, the Fama-French three-factor model, and the modified returns across time and securities (RATS) procedure. The author finds that hedge funds strategies outperform the market, while hedge funds managers prefer smaller stocks.

Chapter 17 discusses the characteristics of typical hedge funds and their attractiveness to investors as an asset class for investment. In particular, hedge funds promise absolute and positive returns while allowing an investor to diversify risks through uncorrelated returns. Consequently, hedge funds have become increasingly popular with high-net-worth individuals and institutional investors. The authors review various issues relating to the investment in hedge funds, as well as their empirical risk and return profiles. They further highlight the concerns regarding the empirical measurements and propose meaningful analytical methods to provide greater risk transparency in performance reporting. Finally, they also discuss the development and growth of the hedge fund industry in Asia.

Chapter 18 examines offshore and onshore funds of hedge funds using various data envelopment analysis (DEA) models. Using various inputs and outputs, the funds are ranked in order as a result of their efficiency scores. The authors suggest that DEA can be used as a complementary technique in selecting efficient hedge funds and funds of hedge funds.

Chapter 19 revisits the performance of hedge funds measured with simple asset pricing models in the presence of errors in variables. The authors introduce an estimator based on cross-sample moments of order three and four. This estimator sheds a new light on estimation of abnormal performance (α) by showing that significant alphas can be attributed to measurement errors at the level of explanatory variables.

Chapter 20 highlights the inadequacies of traditional RAPMs (risk-adjusted performance measures) and proposes AIRAP (alternative investments risk-adjusted performance), based on expected utility theory, as a RAPM better suited to Alternative Investments. AIRAP captures higher moment risks, penalizes for volatility and leverage, is customizable by risk aversion, dovetails with stressed scenarios, and can be expressed as a modified Sharpe ratio.

CHAPTER 13

A Literature Review of Hedge Fund Performance Studies

Fabrice Rouah

Investors are aware of the growing evidence that hedge funds can substantially reduce downside risk in their portfolios. Yet they are sometimes suspicious of the unregulated aspects of these funds and the long lockup period and infrequent redemption that these funds impose on their capital. Moreover, the varying results of studies dealing with survivorship bias, performance attribution, and hedge fund lifetimes suggest that academic studies on hedge funds are sometimes inaccurate and inconclusive. In this chapter we examine the studies most frequently encountered in the literature and attempt to reconcile their results in a clear and meaningful fashion.

INTRODUCTION

Much of the academic literature on hedge funds deals with performance issues, including performance persistence and the various biases inherent in hedge fund databases that can distort estimates of performance. Another strand of literature seeks to explain hedge fund returns using linear factor models and regression to explain risk-adjusted returns and volatility. Other authors have focused on the usefulness of hedge funds as portfolio diversifiers, either by demonstrating that hedge funds exhibit low or negative correlation coefficients with market indices, or by including hedge funds in portfolios comprised solely of stocks and bonds. Finally, one small group of studies deals with the survival of hedge funds, including the estimation of yearly hedge fund attrition rates from databases, estimates of their lifetimes, and multivariate analyses to show how these lifetimes are linked to a variety of hedge fund predictor variables.

BIASES IN HEDGE FUND DATABASES

Fung and Hsieh (2000) and Ackermann, McEnally, and Ravenscraft (1999) (AMR) discuss the major biases in hedge fund databases and research studies. Survivorship bias refers to the bias introduced when returns are calculated from databases that include only live funds. There are two general ways to estimate survivorship bias. The return on a portfolio of live funds is sometimes compared to the return of a portfolio of dead funds, but usually a portfolio of both live and dead funds is compared with a portfolio of live funds only. As explained by Brown, Goetzmann, and Ibbotson (1999) and Fung and Hsieh (2000), portfolios can be defined as including hedge funds alive during the entire study period (the complete portfolio), from a certain date until the end of the study period (the surviving portfolio), or at a particular date (the observed portfolio). Most studies estimate survivorship bias at 2 to 3 percent per year. Liquidation bias arises when returns of dead funds occur past the final monthly reported figure to the database vendor. When funds cease to operate, their assets are liquidated, but delays imply that redemption of funds to the investors will likely occur subsequent to the final reported performance figure. AMR find the average delay to be only 18 days, and the resulting liquidation bias on returns to be only 0.7 percent. Backfill bias, or instant history bias, occurs when database vendors backfill the returns and NAVs of newly added funds. Hedge funds typically begin reporting to database vendors only after running up a track record, thus entering the database with "instant histories." Backfill bias is usually estimated by eliminating the first one or two years of returns, since often the exact date of first reporting is not known. Thus, AMR eliminate returns during the first 24 months, but none of their estimates is statistically significant. Fung and Hsieh (2000) eliminate the first 12 months of returns from the TASS database and estimate the bias at 1.4 percent per year, but at only 0.7 percent per year for funds of funds, over the 1994 to 1998 period. Barry (2002) finds a backfill bias of 1.4 percent per year in the TASS database over the 1994 to 2001 period. Malkiel and Saha (2004) estimate yearly backfill bias at 5.84 percent for mean returns and 3.98 percent for median returns over the 1996 to 2003 period. These last estimates are likely quite accurate because they use the date of first reporting of hedge funds and eliminate all returns prior to this date. Multiperiod sampling bias arises because most studies of hedge fund performance require that each fund have a sufficiently long track recorded to be included in study samples, while funds with short track records are excluded. For example, AMR and Edwards and Caglayan (2001b) require at least 24 months, while Fung and Hsieh (1997a, 2000) require 36 months. Fung and Hsieh (2000) estimate this bias to be only 0.1 percent and 0.6 percent per year over 1989 to 1997, and 1994 to 1998, respectively. Overall, the effect of survivorship bias is the most studied and most important of the biases in hedge fund databases. Estimates of survivorship bias found in current studies of hedge funds are summarized in Table 13.1.

Fung and Hsieh (2000) point out that funds of funds (FoF, a basket of hedge funds) suffer less from biases than individual hedge funds. This is because part of the FoF manager's task is to provide investors with accurate return and net asset value (NAV) information on individual hedge funds that make up the FoF. These managers will often collect that data themselves, rather than relying on information supplied by database vendors. Because of the small number of funds that FoF managers track, and the high degree of due diligence they impose, this information will often be very accurate.

TABLE 13.1   Survivorship Bias in Current Studies of Hedge Fund Performance

Reference	Period	Bias/Year (%)	Database	Method
Ackermann et al. (1999)	88–95	0.16	HFR & MAR	Dead[a] vs. Live[b]
Amin & Kat (2003c)	94–01	1.89	TASS	Comp[c] vs. Surv[d]
Brown et al. (1999) (BGI)	89–95	0.75	Offshore Directory	Comp vs. Surv
Brown et al. (1999) (BGI)	89–95	2.75	Offshore Directory	Obs[e] vs. Surv
Fung & Hsieh (2000)	94–98	3.00	TASS	Obs vs. Surv
Liang (2000)	94–97	0.60	HFR	Obs vs. Surv
Liang (2000)	94–98	2.24	TASS	Obs vs. Surv
Liang (2001)	90–99	1.69	TASS	Obs vs. Surv
Liang (2001)	94–99	2.43	TASS	Obs vs. Surv
Barès et al. (2001)	96–99	1.30	FRM	Obs vs. Surv
Edwards & Caglayan (2001b)	90–98	1.85	MAR	Obs vs. Surv
Baquero et al. (2002)	94–00	2.10	TASS	Obs vs. Surv
Barry (2002)	94–01	3.80	TASS	Obs vs. Surv
Malkiel & Saha (2004)	96–03	3.75	TASS	Obs vs. Surv
Malkiel & Saha (2004)	96–03	7.40	TASS	Dead vs. Surv
Capocci & Hübner (2004)	84–00	4.45	MAR & TASS	Dead vs. Live
Capocci & Hübner (2004)	84–00	0.89	MAR & TASS	Obs vs. Surv

[a]Dead funds only   [b]Live funds only
[c]Complete portfolio   [d]Surviving portfolio
[e]Observed portfolio

PERFORMANCE PERSISTENCE

It is important to evaluate whether some hedge funds are able to produce superior returns relative to their peers on a continuing basis. Performance persistence in hedge fund returns is usually measured by contingency tables representing two time periods. Unfortunately, most of the persistence found in the literature is due to losers continuing to lose, rather than winners continuing to win. Brown, Goetzmann, and Park (2001) (BGP) define contingency tables as winners and losers in the first six months of a given year, and high and low variance in the second six months. They find strong evidence that poorly performing funds increase volatility during the 1989 to 1998 period, but only when winners and losers were defined as funds having returns above and below the median return of all funds, respectively. They find no such pattern when winners and losers were defined as funds having returns above and below their high-water marks. This motivates BGP to suggest that managers will benchmark themselves relative to other managers, but not necessarily to their high-water marks.

Agarwal and Naik (2000b) conduct contingency table tests using two measures of performance, alpha (defined as the return of a fund minus the average return of all funds in the same strategy) and the appraisal ratio (defined as alpha divided by the residual standard deviation from a regression of that fund's returns on the returns of all funds in the same strategy). Winners and losers are funds with alphas (appraisal ratio) above and below the median alpha (appraisal ratio) of all funds, respectively. Their results show that persistence is strongest when quarterly returns are used and that persistence does not depend on investment style. Agarwal and Naik (2000b) examine multiperiod persistence to investigate this claim more closely. Their results point to persistence among losers, and mostly when quarterly returns are used. Again, their results do not depend on hedge fund style, nor on whether prefee returns or returns net of all fees are employed. Using contingency tables, Agarwal and Naik (2000c) find persistence in roughly one-half of the quarters under consideration, but no persistence in the other quarters. Finally, Edwards and Caglayan (2001b) define winners and losers to be funds above and below the median alpha of all funds following the same strategy, where alpha is obtained from a six-factor linear model. Their contingency table analysis shows yearly persistence over the 1991 to 1998 period, but again, this was due more to losers rather than winners.

The other way in which persistence has been measured is through a cross-sectional simple linear regression of current returns on past returns, as done by Brown, Goetzmann, and Ibbotson (1999) (BGI). A positive and significant beta coefficient implies performance persistence in the sense that winners repeat from one period to the next. Their results show no consistent patterns of persistence, since winners repeat in one-half of the years under consideration, but winners lose in the other years. BGI repeat their analysis by grouping funds according to size, and according to fees, but again no consistent pattern is found. Agarwal and Naik (2000c) regress alphas (appraisal ratios) in one quarter on alphas (appraisal ratios) from the previous quarter and find that losers tend to be more persistent than winners. In their regression of yearly alphas from a six-factor linear model, Edwards and Caglayan (2001b), however, find more evidence of persistence than BGI or Agarwal and Naik (2000c). A positive and significant beta coefficient was found for all hedge fund strategies grouped together. When persistence was examined for each fund strategy separately, however, the results were inconclusive.

Harri and Brorsen (2002) use three regression-based methods to model persistence within each hedge fund strategy in the Managed Accounts Reports (MAR) database. The regressions of Sharpe ratios on a single lagged value show more persistence than do the same regression on returns. Autoregression of mean returns on 20 lagged values also pointed to persistence, but only in the short term since for most of the strategies the largest coefficient was associated with the first lagged value. Rejection of the null hypothesis that the intercepts (alpha) from style regressions are the same across each fund within a particular strategy indicates persistence. Using this method, persistence was found in 6 out of 10 hedge fund strategies, consistent with the finding of BGI that persistence exists for only half of managers. Finally, Spearman correlations using 36-month rolling periods on mean returns, on Sharpe ratios, and on alpha pointed to some persistence, however, this was heavily dependent on which performance measure was used in the correlation.

Overall, these studies point to some persistence in the performance of hedge fund returns. However, persistence is short-lived and dependent on the method used to measure it and on the time frame under consideration, and is often most evident for losing managers continuing to be losers. Unfortunately, there is little evidence to suggest that investors choosing winning hedge funds will continue to hold winners in the long term.

LINEAR MODELING

Motivated by the literature on mutual funds, several groups of authors have applied linear factor models in an attempt to measure the performance of hedge funds relative to financial assets such as equity and bond indices, commodities, or currencies. This has proven to be challenging because hedge funds employ dynamic trading strategies and there are no indices that are universally accepted as benchmarks for hedge fund performance. Linear factor models may erroneously point to net zero exposure of hedge funds to a particular asset class (Fung and Hsieh 1997a). For example, a manager who shorts the Standard & Poor's (S&P) 500 index during the first six months of the year, and then goes long on the same index during the last six months, will exhibit a net factor loading of zero with the index over the year. For comparative purposes, some of the studies that apply a linear factor model to hedge funds also apply the same model to mutual funds. For example, Liang (1999) uses an eight-factor linear model on hedge funds for each of the 16 investment styles in the Hedge Fund Research (HFR) database. His results show a wide range of different factor loadings for the different styles of hedge funds and that no single factor dominated the sixteen styles. Liang (1999) runs the same model on 19 mutual fund styles and finds the R^2 to be higher than for hedge funds. Furthermore, he finds several asset classes to exhibit consistently significant loadings on the 19 styles of mutual funds.

Fung and Hsieh (1997a) show that mutual funds obtain a much higher R^2 in a linear factor model than do hedge funds and commodity trading advisors (CTAs). They find 47 percent of mutual funds to exhibit R^2 higher than 0.75, but 48 percent of hedge funds to exhibit R^2 lower than 0.25. This despite the fact that most hedge funds have exposures to the same asset classes as mutual funds. Using factor analysis, they extract five principal components explaining 43 percent of return variance of hedge funds, define five quantitative styles based on these principal components, and apply a linear factor model to these five styles. The R^2 from those analyses are much higher than when hedge funds alone are used in the factor model. Still, a substantial amount of return variance (over half) is not accounted for in their model.

Agarwal and Naik (2000a, 2000c) adapt William Sharpe's style analysis in three ways.

1. They allow for negative coefficients (style weights), which captures short selling by hedge funds.
2. They assess the statistical significance of the weights through a two-step procedure.
3. They do not impose the restriction that the style weights add to 100 percent, which allows for hedge funds holding a portion of their assets in cash.

Like Fung and Hsieh (1997a), they find much variability in the exposure of directional and nondirectional funds to the different asset classes in their model. Their style analysis, with weights constrained to add to 100 percent, shows that nondirectional hedge funds have significant exposures to bond indices (corporate, government, and high-yield), suggesting that nondirectional hedge funds borrow from the domestic market and invest in distressed securities around the world. For directional funds, none of the bond indices (expect for one style) showed significant factor loadings.

Instead, these funds had significant exposures to domestic Standard & Poor's (S&P) 500 and international (MSCI) indices. Agarwal and Naik (2002a) repeat their analysis, without the constraint that the factor loadings add to 100 percent. Their results show that the increase in R^2 is greatest for directional strategies. In particular, the short sellers experience an increase from 0.01 with the constraint to 0.40 without, reflecting the fact hedge funds will put up cash as collateral for their short positions. In summary, style analysis can help explain hedge fund returns, but the constraints underlying such an analysis must be relaxed.

Fung and Hsieh (2002a) apply a linear factor model to two hedge fund indices (and their underlying subindices), the Hedge Fund Research (HFR) Composite index and the Credit Suisse First Boston (CSFB)/Tremont Hedge Fund index (CTI). These exhibit an R^2 of 0.876 and 0.414 respectively. However, only 6 of 16 HFR subindices have R^2 above 0.75, and 4 of 9 CTI subindices have R^2 above 0.50. In each subindex analysis, indices reflecting directional strategies were found to have the highest R^2. Just as in the previously reported studies, no single factor was consistently significant across all sub-indices.

Agarwal and Naik (2004) apply linear factor models to the HFR and CSFB/Tremont hedge fund subindices, using market factors and Fama and French factors, but also using at-the-money (ATM) and out-of-the-money (OTM) call and put options on the S&P 500. The factor loading on the OTM put option is negative for the event arbitrage, restructuring, event driven, and relative value arbitrage subindices. This is consistent with the notion that these strategies make money when events such as restructuring or takeovers are successful, which usually happens when markets are up. The R^2 from their models are high compared to those from other studies, ranging from 0.41 to 0.92, and five (out of eight) are above 0.60. Moreover, these high values are achieved with a minimum of factors in the model, usually four or five.

Finally, Capocci and Hübner (2004) apply a series of linear models to HFR and MAR data for each hedge fund strategy. Their results indicate that using a multi-factor model leads to better values of R^2 (average value of 0.66) than a four-factor model with Fame-French and momentum factors (average R^2 of 0.60), and especially a single-factor CAPM (average R^2 of 0.44). However the R^2 from the multi-factor model vary substantially across strategies. For example, the U.S. Opportunity strategy displays a very good fit (R^2 of 0.92), but the market timing is not as good (R^2 of 0.25).

Table 13.2 presents the equity, bond, commodity, and currency classes that were used as factors in some of the studies reviewed in this chapter, along with the range of R^2 produced by the models employed.

A few authors have applied regression using hedge fund characteristics to predict performance and volatility. Ackermann, McEnally, and Ravenscraft (1999) (AMR) find incentive fees to have a positive and significant

TABLE 13.2 Asset Classes Used as Factors in Linear Modeling and Style Analysis of Hedge Fund Returns

Reference	U.S. Equities	International Equities	Emerging Markets Equities	U.S. Debt	International Debt	Currencies	Commodities	Cash	R^2
Liang (1999)	S&P 500	MSCI-W	MSCI-EM	SBG	SBW	U.S. Fed TW	Gold	Euro$ Dep	0.20 to 0.70
Fung & Hsieh (1997)	MSCI	MSCI-W	—	JPM US	JPM NonUS	U.S. Fed TW	Gold	Euro$ Dep	48% below 0.25
Agarwal & Naik (2000a, 2000c)	S&P 500	MSCI-W	MSCI-EM	LEH-HY	SBW	U.S. Fed TW	Gold	—	0.10 to 0.84
Agarwal & Naik (2004)	RUS3000, FF, ATM and OTM calls & puts on S&P 500	MSCI-W	MSCI-EM	SBG, LEH-HY, Change in DEFS	SBW	U.S. Fed CW	GSCI	—	0.33 to 0.92
Edwards & Caglayan (2001b)	S&P 500, FF, WML	—	—	TERM, DEF	—	—	—	—	—
Fung & Hsieh (2002a)	WIL1750	—	IFC	CSFB-HY	—	—	—	—	0.134 to 0.890

S&P500: S&P 500 composite index
MSCI-EM: Morgan Stanley Capital emerging markets index
U.S. Fed TW: U.S. Federal Reserve trade-weighted dollar index
U.S. Fed CW: U.S. Federal Reserve competitiveness-weighted dollar index
JPM US/NonUS: JP Morgan US/NonUS government bond index
GSCI: Goldman Sachs commodity index
DEFS: Default spread (BAA corporate bonds minus 10-year Treasury bonds)
WIL1750: Wilshire 1750 small-cap index
CSFB-HY: CSFB high-yield bond index
Euro$ Dep: One-month Eurodollar deposit rate
FF: Size (SMB), book-to-market (HML), and momentum (MOM) factors
WML: Return on stock portfolio of past winners minus return on stock portfolio of past losers
TERM: Return on long-term US government bond portfolio minus one-month-lagged 30-day T-bill return
DEF: Return on long-term US corporate bond portfolio minus return on long-term government bond portfolio

MSCI-W: Morgan Stanley Capital world equity index
MSCI: Morgan Stanley Capital Index (US)
SBW: Salomon Brothers world government bond index
SBG: Salomon Brothers government & corporate bond index
LEH-HY: Lehman high-yield composite index
IFC: International Finance Corporation composite index
RUS3000: Russell 3000 index
ATM: At-the-money; OTM: Out-of-the-money
Gold: Price of gold

effect on Sharpe ratios, but not on volatility. This suggests that managers with high incentive fees produce superior risk-adjusted returns, but not at the expense of increased volatility. Furthermore, FoF and market-neutral funds were found to have the lowest volatility in all time periods. Unfortunately, the R^2 from the regressions ranged from only 0.177 to 0.373 for risk-adjusted returns and from only 0.234 to 0.310 for volatility, despite the high number of observations employed (from 547 funds over two years to 79 funds over eight years). Like AMR, Liang (1999) finds that funds with high incentive fees tend to produce superior returns, as do funds with a long lockup period and large assets under management. This is consistent with the notion that lockup periods prevent early redemption and reduce cash holdings.

Liang (1999) finds age to be negatively associated with returns, however, suggesting that managers of young funds tend to work hard to build their reputation and increase their client base. Boyson (2002) also finds manager age to be negatively related to returns, but manager education tends to be positively related to returns. Like Liang (1999) and AMR, a positive effect of incentive fee on returns was found, but this variable was not significant in any of the regressions. The R^2 from the regressions are low, ranging from 0.028 to 0.223, but those from the regressions of volatility range from 0.037 to 0.527. Like AMR, no effect of incentive fee on volatility was found, but manager education and tenure were negatively related to volatility, suggesting that older and more experienced managers take on less risk. Finally, Edwards and Caglayan (2001b) also find incentive fees and size to be positively associated with returns (using alpha from a six-factor linear model as dependent variable), but the R^2 from their regressions are low as well, ranging from 0.094 to 0.319.

The results of these studies demonstrate that linear factor modeling of hedge funds is problematic, because the dynamic trading employed by hedge fund managers yields nonlinear payoffs with the asset classes used as factors. Moreover, in these studies, no single factor dominates each hedge fund strategy, reflecting the wide range of trading practices inherent across strategies. In order to achieve high explanatory power from these models, it is necessary to use factors that exhibit nonlinear payoffs or use factors that proxy dynamic trading. Also, there is some evidence that the performance of hedge funds can be attributed to the characteristics of hedge funds and of their managers, but unfortunately the explanatory power of the models employed is generally low.

DIVERSIFICATION THROUGH HEDGE FUNDS

Hedge funds are attractive diversifiers because the dynamic trading strategies they employ and their use of options, leverage, and short selling allows them to generate absolute returns that are not linear with returns of other financial assets. Indeed, all studies that obtain the correlation of hedge fund returns with those of financial assets find these to be low or negative, irrespective of the database or time period used. Thus, Fung and Hsieh (1999b) find a correlation of 0.37 of hedge funds in the TASS database with the S&P 500 index. Agarwal and Naik (2004) find only 27 significant correlations (out of a possible 96) of eight HFR indices with 12 asset classes representing small-cap equities, bonds, emerging markets, commodities, and Fama and French factors, and only 5 of 27 to be larger than 0.60 in absolute value. The correlations of the 12 asset classes with the four CSFB/Tremont index were more significant: 19 out of a possible 48 were significantly different from zero, and 11 of those were greater than 0.60 (in absolute value). Brown, Goeztmann, and Ibbotson (1999) show that the correlation of offshore hedge funds with equity and bond indices tend to be low or negative, but the lack of statistical significance (no p-value reported) makes assessment of these correlations difficult. Still, only 31 of 140 correlations were above 0.60 in absolute value. Schneeweis and Martin (2001) find the correlation of the Evaluation Associates Capital Management index (EACM 100) with the S&P 500 to be 0.37, the same that Fung and Hsieh (1999a) found with the TASS database, and the correlation of the EACM 100 with the Lehman Bond index to be only 0.19. Moreover, the correlation of the EACM subindices with the S&P 500 all ranged between −0.11 and 0.63 (except short sellers, with a correlation of −0.74), and only two of seventeen were above 0.60. With the Lehman Bond index, the EACM subindex correlations were even more modest, ranging from −0.16 to 0.25.

If hedge funds are useful portfolio diversifiers, they ought to perform better than equities when returns on equities are low or negative, but not necessarily as well when returns are positive and large. This stress testing of hedge funds has brought encouraging results for diversification. Fung and Hsieh (2002a) analyze the performance of two trend-following hedge fund indices, the Zurich Capital Markets Trend-Follower Index and an asset-based trend-following index constructed by the authors. Both indices show positive returns during the worst declines of the S&P 500 over the 1983 to 2001 period. Agarwal and Naik (2000c) show that nondirectional strategies show less variability than directional strategies during large up and down moves of the S&P 500. During August 1998, for example, the S&P 500 returned −10.52 percent, while hedge fund returns ranged from −8.87 to −1.18 percent for nondirectional strategies and from −20.98 to −3.94 percent for directional strategies (but 19.53 for short sellers). During November 1996, the S&P 500 returned 7.68 percent, while nondirectional hedge funds returned between 0.37 and 2.03 percent and directional hedge funds returned between 2.96 and 4.72 percent (but −2.95 percent for short sellers). Schneeweis and Martin (2001) show that during August 1990, the

S&P 500 returned −9.1 percent, but the EACM subindices returned between −3.6 and 10.0 percent.

Gregoriou and Rouah (2001) argue that in addition to exhibiting low correlation to market indices, nondirectional hedge funds should not be cointegrated with any index. Indeed, if a hedge fund is moving in tandem with an index so that the spread between them is constant, then the fund manager is likely adopting a buy-and-hold strategy to most of the stocks that comprise the index, bringing little value to the investor seeking absolute returns. Using NAVs of the 10 largest hedge funds in the Zurich Capital Markets database, they find evidence of only two cointegrating relationships, one with the Morgan Stanley Capital International (MSCI) World index, and the other with the Nasdaq index.

Fung and Hsieh (1997a) show how hedge funds can produce optionlike returns. They rank the returns of each asset class under consideration into five quintiles, or "states," from best to worst performance. The idea is that a buy-and-hold trading strategy ought to generate returns that are linear across the five states, while a dynamic trading strategy will produce non-linear returns. They demonstrate that three of the five styles, as extracted by principal components, produce payoffs that are similar to calls, puts, and straddles on equities, bonds, commodities, and currencies.

Fung and Hsieh (1999b) apply a similar methodology to individual hedge fund styles. They show that the global/macro style has a payoff that varies linearly with U.S. equities, and that this strategy performs better than equities during low and medium states but worse than equities during high states. The fixed income arbitrage style produces constant return across all states of U.S. equities, with very little volatility, while the short sellers style produces a linear payoff with U.S. equities, with high payoffs in low states and low payoffs in high states. Anson and Ho (2004) show that managed futures hedge funds commodity trading advisors (CTAs) provide an exposure whose payoff is similar to a long put option.

Some authors have demonstrated that adding hedge funds to a "traditional" portfolio comprised solely of equities and bonds can improve the risk-return profile of the portfolio. Schneeweis and Martin (2001) show that adding a 20 percent exposure to the EACM 100 index in a portfolio of domestic equities and bonds increases the mean return and reduces the standard deviation of the portfolio over the 1990 to 2000 period. The Sharpe ratio of the portfolio increases from 0.90 to 1.15, and the maximum drawdown drops from −7.16 percent to −6.31 percent. When an alternate world equities and bonds portfolio is constructed, the results are similar. The Sharpe ratio increases from 0.46 to 0.72, and the maximum drawdown drops from −10.15 percent to −7.37 percent. Capocci (2003) shows how adding convertible arbitrage hedge funds in increments of 5 percent achieves the same improvements. His simulations suggest that the optimal allocation of convertible arbitrage funds to the portfolio is between 5 to 15 percent.

The results of these studies suggest that the correlation of hedge funds and CTAs with asset classes is low or negative, due in part to the nonlinear, optionlike payoffs that they produce. It is difficult to ignore the benefits of including hedge funds in portfolios comprised solely of stocks and bonds. The optimal allocation of hedge funds to portfolios seems to be on the order of 5 to 20 percent. In 2003, for example, American university endowments with over U.S.$1 billion in assets had, on average, nearly 20 percent of their portfolios allocated to hedge funds (NACUBO 2003).

SURVIVAL ANALYSIS OF HEDGE FUNDS

The objective of many early studies of hedge fund and CTA survival was to investigate factors driving hedge fund mortality, to help identify factors driving survivorship bias. Hence, many of these studies focused on the yearly attrition rate of hedge funds, estimated as the number of hedge funds dying during a given year divided by the number of funds alive at the beginning of the year. Next, researchers began to apply methods of survival analysis to hedge fund lifetimes, by using probit regression on hedge fund status (dead versus live) or estimating 50 percent survival times using the Kaplan-Meier estimator. Finally, more sophisticated multivariate analyses, linking survival to a variety of hedge fund predictor variables, began to appear in the literature.

Estimates of the attrition rates of hedge funds are inconsistent. Amin and Kat (2003c) found the yearly attrition rate to be only 2.20 percent during 1994–1995, but that attrition increased steadily throughout the 1990s, to arrive at 12.30 percent during 2000–2001. Liang (2001) finds a similar pattern: attrition was estimated at 4.13 percent during 1994 and rose steadily to 13.00 percent during 1998. Amin and Kat (2003) find that small funds, funds with low performance, and funds employing the global/macro strategy tend to experience higher attrition rates. Brown, Goetzmann, and Ibbotson (1999) estimated yearly attrition at roughly 20 percent over the 1988 to 1995 period. Brown, Goetzmann, and Park (2001) find a yearly attrition rate of roughly 15 percent over the 1977 to 1998 period, and 20 percent for CTAs. Barry (2002) estimates yearly attrition at 8 to 10 percent, while Barès, Gibson, and Gyger (2001) at only 5 percent up to 1999. Barry (2002) finds the technical/trend-following strategy to experience higher attrition than the other strategies, but finds no difference in attrition between funds that employ leverage and those that do not. Baquero, ter Horst, and Verbeek (2002) found a yearly attrition rate of 8.6 percent over the 1994 to 2000 period, very close to the estimate of 8.3 percent found by

Liang (2000) over the 1994 to 1998 period in the same database (TASS). However, Liang (2000) finds a yearly attrition rate of only 2.72 percent in the HFR database over the 1994 to 1997 period. While estimates of hedge fund attrition are quite varied, these studies point to one consistent pattern. The attrition rate of hedge funds was high during 1998, following the Asian crisis of 1997 and the near collapse of Long-Term Capital Management in September 1998. Many hedge funds died during that period, and few were born.

Subsequent to these findings, and to examine factors driving survivorship bias, some authors began applying probit regression to hedge fund survival status (live versus dead). Liang (2000) finds that funds with poor performance, low assets, low incentive fees, high leverage, young age, and low manager personal investment are at increased risk of death. This is consistent with the finding of Brown, Goetzmann, and Park (2001) that funds with negative returns over a holding period one and two years prior to the last month of reporting are at increased risk of death, as are young funds and those with low excess returns. Malkiel and Saha (2004) also find high volatility to be a strong predictor of death.

Estimating the lifetimes of hedge funds is important, since the infrequent redemption and long lockup period on capital imposed by hedge funds implies that investors need to be assured that the funds they choose will not die prematurely. Because many hedge fund deaths correspond to fund liquidation, investors need to predict if and when a fund is likely to liquidate, since liquidation is often associated with large capital losses. Brown, Goeztmann, and Park (2001) (BGP) were the first to apply rigorous methods of survival analysis to the lifetimes of hedge funds. They found a 50 percent survival time of only 2.5 years for hedge funds in the TASS database. Amin and Kat (2003c) obtained a 50 percent survival time of roughly 5.0 years from the same database (TASS), Gregoriou (2002) and the Securities and Exchange Commission (2003c) each obtained 5.5 years, while Gregoriou, Hübner, Papageorgiou, and Rouah (2005) obtained 4.42 years for CTAs. Barès, Gibson, and Gyger (2001), however, obtained roughly 10 years, much higher than that found in the other studies.

Multivariate analyses of hedge fund lifetimes were more consistent and pointed to a number of predictor variables related to survival. BGP (2001), Gregoriou (2002), and Boyson (2002) all apply the Cox proportional hazards model to hedge fund lifetimes. BGP (2001) find that funds with low returns, and young funds, are at increased risk of failure. Gregoriou (2002) finds that funds with low returns, low assets under management, and low minimum purchase are at increased risk of failure. Boyson (2002) finds that funds with young and uneducated managers are at risk of failure, even after adjusting for returns and volatility. Gregoriou, Hübner, Papageorgiou, and Rouah (2005) find CTAs with high returns and high assets to survive longer, and those with high volatility and high management fees to be at increased risk of failure. Finally, Malkiel and Saha (2004) find that large hedge funds and funds with low volatility survive longer.

Current studies of hedge fund lifetimes have aggregated all funds exiting the database as terminated (liquidated), when, in fact, many funds exit because they have reached their target size and are closed to new investors, or because they no longer wish to report performance figures to database vendors. Aggregating exit types introduces a bias when estimating hedge fund lifetimes, because some funds counted as "dead" may actually be alive and well (Fung and Hsieh 2000). In their estimates of survivorship bias, Ackermann, McEnally, and Ravenscraft (1999) distinguish between funds that terminate and those that stop reporting (self-select). They argue that the low returns of funds that terminate and the high returns of funds that self-select can cancel each other out, to yield a small net estimate of survivorship bias.

Estimates of the attrition rates of hedge funds over the 1990 to 2003 period are heavily dependent on the database used, and vary from roughly 5 to 20 percent per year. However, most studies point to a 50 percent survival time of roughly five years. The results of multivariate analyses are also more consistent and indicate that hedge funds with low returns, low size, and high volatility are at increased risk of failure, whether survival is modeled through a probit model or the Cox proportional hazards model.

CONCLUSION

In this chapter, we have reviewed many of the important studies on hedge fund performance that have appeared in the literature. Investors must be aware that substantial biases exist in hedge fund databases, which can sometimes severely distort estimates of hedge fund performance. Moreover, these biases tend to be heavily dependent on the database employed and the time period under consideration. Unfortunately, there is little evidence of performance persistence in the returns produced by hedge fund managers, regardless of how persistence is measured. Moreover, explaining those returns using linear factor models is problematic, since hedge funds display nonlinear payoffs with asset classes used to explain mutual funds—equities, bond, commodities, and currencies. The evidence in favor of hedge funds as portfolio diversifiers, however, is overwhelming, since all studies point to low or negative correlations with these asset classes. There is also some recent evidence to suggest that hedge funds are not as short-lived as previously thought. Investors need to be cautioned, however, that the lifetimes of hedge funds are dependent on a variety of predictor variables, such as returns, volatility, and size.

CHAPTER 14

Investing in Hedge Funds through Multimanager Vehicles

Meredith A. Jones

Funds of hedge funds and hedge fund index products are often viewed as entry-level investments and have thus become a popular method for investors making a first foray into alternative investments. This chapter examines suitability issues for investors attempting to choose between single-manager hedge fund portfolios and multimanager vehicles, as well as the universes of available funds of hedge funds, single managers, and index funds. Performance, fees, liquidity, structure, and drawbacks of each invest-ment type also are examined to present a balanced view of the hedge fund investment vehicle options available to investors.

INTRODUCTION

Uncertain stock markets and lackluster traditional investment returns have driven an increasing number of individual and institutional investors into hedge funds during the past several years. After making the decision to invest in alternatives, one of the first decisions that these new investors face is whether to invest directly in single-manager hedge funds or to invest through a multimanager vehicle. Indeed, funds of hedge funds and hedge fund index funds offer a less complicated way for entry-level investors to access a diversified hedge fund portfolio. It enables them to avoid having to engage in the lengthy screening, due diligence, and ongoing monitoring process on a number of single-manager funds. Although the benefits of the various hedge fund products are generally easy to identify, investing through single managers, fund of hedge funds, and indexes all have drawbacks that should be explored prior to making an investment decision.

BUILD VERSUS BUY

There are a number of issues to consider when deciding between a direct investment with single-manager funds and buying a ready-made multimanager product, such as a fund of hedge funds or index product. There are certainly some advantages to building a diversified portfolio of single-manager hedge funds. For example, those opting to go the single-manager route have more control over their investments. They can decide when to hire and fire a manager; when to increase, change, or reduce allocations within the portfolio; and what level of due diligence and ongoing monitoring to impose. Investors in single-manager portfolios also can develop customized portfolios that meet their specific investment needs and mandate. If, for example, an investor has a significant allocation to a certain asset class or strategy in the long-only portfolio, he or she can balance and adjust that exposure with the hedge fund portfolio. Finally, direct investments in hedge funds have, in almost all cases, lower fees than do multimanager hedge fund products, which add a layer of fees to cover the cost of manager screening, due diligence, and monitoring.

As investors weigh the option of a single-manager portfolio against a prepackaged, multimanager portfolio, they must ask themselves: How much money do we want to allocate to hedge funds? Will that amount be sufficient to buy a diversified single-manager portfolio when each manager has minimum investments generally ranging from $100,000 to $1 million and more? What resources do we have for manager screening, due diligence, and ongoing monitoring? Are those resources enough to support a diversified single-manager portfolio of hedge funds? If not, are we willing to invest the necessary capital to secure those resources?

The question of diversification is really the overriding issue in the hedge fund investing equation. With several well-publicized blowups and frauds, including Long-Term Capital Management, the Manhattan Fund, Maricopa, Integral, Beacon Hill, and others, it is vital that investors protect themselves from catastrophic return scenarios by investing in a diversified portfolio of noncorrelated managers. Even without fraud or cataclysmic structural, market, or strategy-related events, hedge fund returns can be volatile. Figure 14.1 shows the percentile breakdowns of performance for more than 3,000 funds over the past 12 months, ending October 31, 2004. The histogram shown below displays returns between the 5th and 95th percentiles for various periods.

Although returns for the 95th percentile do not generally exceed −10 percent, it is important to note that the outliers can produce losses exceeding −50 percent. If an investor allocated to a fund that suddenly exhibited this kind of return profile, the portfolio would ideally need to be structured to

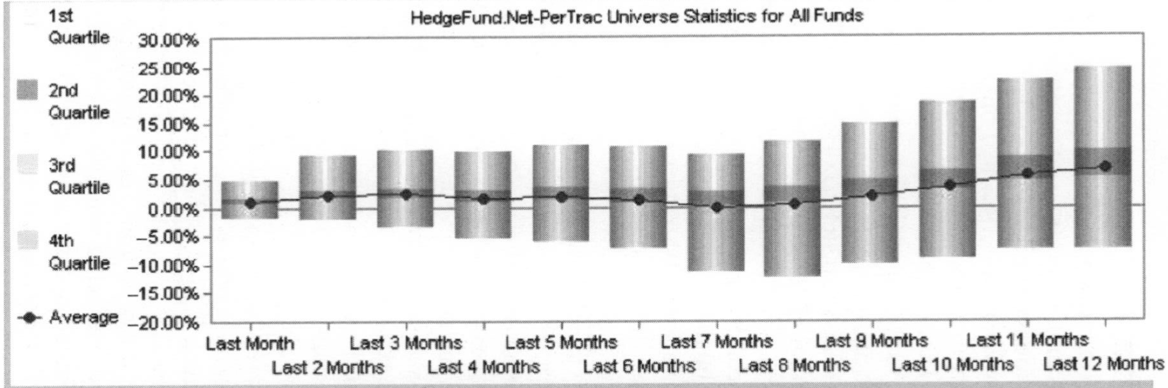

HedgeFund.Net-PerTrac Universe Statistics for All Funds

Last 12 Months	Last Month	Last 2 Months	Last 3 Months	Last 4 Months	Last 5 Months	Last 6 Months	Last 7 Months	Last 8 Months	Last 9 Months	Last 10 Months	Last 11 Months	Last 12 Months
Funds In Universe	3,611	3,606	3,584	3,563	3,510	3,460	3,433	3,377	3,350	3,299	3,199	3,162
Mean	0.97%	2.30%	2.31%	1.62%	1.91%	1.33%	-0.03%	0.47%	1.89%	3.63%	5.58%	6.58%
Median	0.67%	1.45%	1.56%	1.08%	1.43%	0.85%	0.20%	0.63%	1.54%	2.98%	4.44%	5.05%
Standard Deviation	2.86%	5.62%	6.69%	7.26%	7.91%	8.07%	8.65%	9.41%	9.83%	10.26%	11.73%	13.16%
Maximum	71.00%	207.46%	239.74%	243.48%	260.65%	239.73%	234.30%	240.98%	216.09%	155.13%	219.41%	237.81%
Minimum	–47.69%	–48.84%	–46.25%	–55.49%	–58.09%	–58.16%	–56.48%	–55.10%	–59.02%	–50.35%	–53.25%	–53.06%

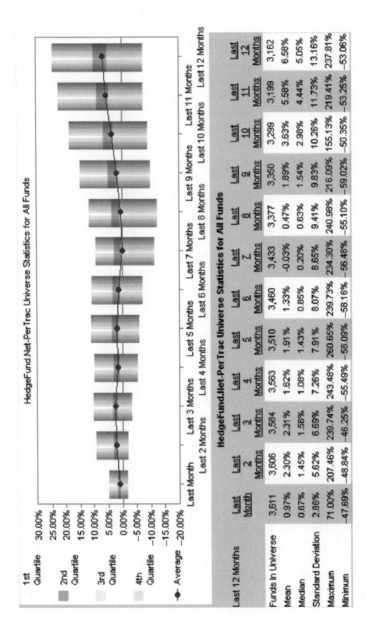

FIGURE 14.1 Hedge Fund Performance
Source: HedgeFund.Net—PerTrac Online Universes.

absorb the blow without a significant loss. A well-diversified hedge fund portfolio should consider the number of funds within the portfolio, their correlations to one another, their correlations to the market, and the degree to which they pursue a more aggressive or conservative investment strategy.

The subject of how many single-manager funds constitute a diversified portfolio is an issue of much debate within the hedge fund industry. While there is no universally agreed on number of funds, and while issues such as correlation among managers certainly play a role, it is possible to get some guidance by looking at other investors in the space. For example, in a 2004 Investor Sentiment Survey compiled by Infovest21, 74 investors were asked a variety of questions about their particular investing goals and habits. The investors polled were diverse: 49 percent of the respondents were funds of funds, while another 20 percent were consultants, 14 percent were family offices/high-net-worth investors, 8 percent were endowments/foundations, and another 7 percent were pension funds. When asked about the number of managers to whom they allocate, 19 percent responded that they allocate to between 1 and 10 managers. Another 18 percent allocate to between 31 and 40 managers, while 11 percent allocate to between 21 and 30 managers and another 9 percent allocate to between 11 and 20 managers.

Of course, this diversification does not come without a price. The most obvious dilemma is meeting the minimum investment required for investing in a large portfolio of single-manager hedge fund investments. A search of the HedgeFund.net database, which contains information on more than 4,000 hedge funds, reveals only 32 U.S.-domiciled, single-manager hedge funds with minimums less than $100,000, and only 131 U.S.-domiciled, single-manager funds with minimum investment requirements of less than $250,000. Therefore, individual investors or smaller institutional investors, or even large institutions that want to allocate only a small percentage of their assets to alternative investments, may, by default, have to consider only multimanager investments. If investors do have the means to invest in a diversified, single-manager hedge fund portfolio, they still may not have the staff to execute this strategy. Deutsche Bank's Equity Prime Services Group 2004 Institutional Alternative Investment Survey (conducted in the fourth quarter of 2003) of 323 institutions including funds of funds, family offices, banks, endowments, consultants, insurance companies and others, shows how time- and labor-intensive investing in hedge funds can be. Deutsche Bank's survey found that investors interview a large number of managers prior to making a single allocation. For example, pension plans evaluate 40 managers on average to make only one to three allocations per year, while endowments research 90 managers for four to six placements and funds of funds typically conduct over 450 meetings with managers to make a mere 15 allocations. It is almost a universally acknowledged fact that the qualitative and quantitative screening processes for making hedge fund investments can be time-consuming, labor intensive, and expensive, and these costs multiply based on the number of funds that an investor evaluates.

The process for hedge fund screening and due diligence is complex because it entails a number of steps that all serious investors must follow. First, an investor must gather hedge fund information. Although this process has become far easier in recent years due to the proliferation of high-quality hedge fund databases, amassing hedge fund information is still not as simple as collecting information on traditional investments. Even if an investor purchases a hedge fund database, the costs of which range between U.S.$1,750 and U.S.$7,000, they still will not have a complete sample of hedge fund data. Ideally, they should purchase two or more databases and/or supplement their data collection through interactions with marketers and prime brokers, as well as through publications, conferences and word of mouth.

To illustrate this point, one can look to the 2004 Strategic Financial Solutions, LLC Database Study. The study examined the hedge fund listings from 12 of the major hedge fund databases, including Alternative Asset Center, Altvest from InvestorForce, Barclay's Global HedgeSource, CISDM, Cogenthedge, Eurekahedge Asian Hedge Fund Database, Eurekahedge European Hedge Fund Database, Eurekahedge Fund of Hedge Funds Database, HedgeFund.net, Hedge Fund Research, Morgan Stanley Capital International (MSCI) Hedge Fund Classification Standard indices and database, and Tremont TASS (Europe) Ltd. After combining these databases, the resulting 24,627 funds were analyzed. Duplicate funds, funds of funds, and "clone" funds were tagged using analytical methods, and the data were manipulated in a number of ways to yield aggregate information on the hedge fund universe.

The study identified approximately 8,100 distinct hedge funds and funds of hedge funds in the various hedge fund databases once duplicate funds were removed. Approximately 5,500 single-manager hedge funds were identified, as well as approximately 2,600 funds of hedge funds. Nearly 3,200 hedge fund managers (general partners) were counted.

Although significant overlap was noted between the various databases, Figure 14.2 shows that very few hedge funds and fund of hedge funds report to more than 2 or 3 databases, and no fund reports to all 12 databases. In fact, nearly 3,800 of the hedge funds and fund of hedge funds in the 12-database sample appeared only in a single database. General databases in the study, which cover all geographic areas and all strategies, average more than 400 exclusive funds each when all 12 databases are combined. Specialty databases, which cover only funds of hedge funds, Asian, or European hedge funds, each contain an average of nearly 150 exclusive funds when all 12 databases are combined. Obviously, the number of unique funds in each database rose as the number of databases compared

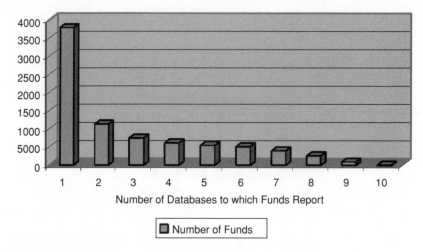

FIGURE 14.2   How Many Databases Do Hedge Funds and FoFs Report to?
Source: 2004 SFS Hedge Fund Database Study.

decreased. Since investors cannot rely on a single data source, the simple act of collecting hedge fund data can be a time-consuming process.

Once data have been gathered, the investor still needs to develop an investment mandate, select screening statistics and criteria, conduct peer group analysis, and then embark on the full due diligence process. The process is generally lengthy. According to the Deutsche Bank Study, only 38 percent of survey participants have allocated to a hedge fund within the first month of due diligence; 60 percent take three months to complete due diligence; and 20 percent take at least six months or more to complete the due diligence process.

Not only does the hedge fund screening and investment process entail a significant time commitment, but it also can necessitate a considerable investment in staff. Table 14.1 shows what funds of hedge funds pay the staff that covers alternative investments. Institutions adding experienced staff to screen, qualify, and monitor their hedge fund investments can expect to pay similar salaries, depending on location.

Investing in a diversified portfolio of single-manager hedge funds may be considered by some to be optimal. For some investors it is not and cannot be practical. Those investors are effectively forced into prepackaged, multimanager vehicles, and must decide whether a fund of hedge funds or an index fund best fits their particular needs. Both offer diversification for a single investment minimum, but each also offers specific benefits and drawbacks that should be considered before choosing between them.

TABLE 14.1 Salary Requirements of Alternative Investment Staff

	Investment Analysis	Quantitative/ Risk Analysis	Operations/ Fund Administration	Compliance	Information Technology
1–5 years of industry experience	40K–100K base plus bonus, which can be a percentage of base	50K–140K base plus bonus, which can be a percentage of base	40K–80K base plus bonus, which can be a percentage of base	40K–80K base plus bonus, which can be a percentage of base	40K–100K base plus bonus, which can be a percentage of base
6–10 years of industry experience	100K–150K base plus bonus, which can reach a multiple of base	140K–175K base plus bonus, which can reach a multiple of base	80K–150K base plus bonus, which can reach a multiple of base	80K–125K base plus bonus, which can reach a multiple of base	100K–125K base plus bonus, which can reach a multiple of base
10+ years of industry experience	150K+ base plus bonus/equity	175K+ base plus bonus/equity	150K+ base plus bonus/equity	125K+ base plus bonus/equity	125K+ base plus bonus/equity

Source: Jonathon Stadin, "Paying Now vs. Paying Later: A Financial Recruiter's Perspective on Compensation Packages," *PerTrac Solutions newsletter,* Vol. 2, Issue 4 (2003):1–5.

Investing in Funds of Hedge Funds

A fund of hedge funds is, by definition, a hedge fund that invests in other hedge funds. According to the 2004 SFS Hedge Fund Database Study, there are approximately 2,600 funds of hedge funds (FoFs) that report to hedge fund databases, encompassing approximately 600 onshore FoFs and 2,000 offshore FoFs. Approximately 900 of these are "clone" FoFs, meaning that the portfolio of one fund is substantially similar to an existing fund of hedge funds portfolio managed by the same general partner. There appears to be approximately $415 billion invested in hedge funds through fund of hedge fund vehicles, although the majority of FoFs manage less than $50 million. This is illustrated in Figure 14.3.

A Look at Fund of Hedge Funds Performance

Like single-manager funds, funds of hedge funds offer a wide range of performance profiles. However, the returns of FoFs tend to be less volatile than those of single managers. One could argue this is due to diversification and superior manager selection. Notice that, unlike the single-manager returns in Figure 14.1, even the worst multistrategy FoFs in Figure 14.4 keep losses to single or low double digits.

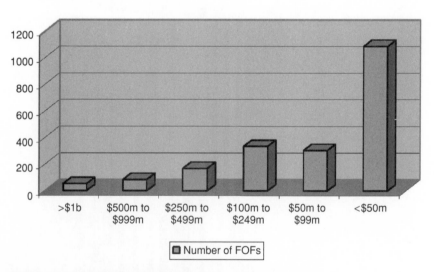

FIGURE 14.3 Breakdown of FoFs by Assets under Management
Source: 2004 SFS Hedge Fund Database Study.

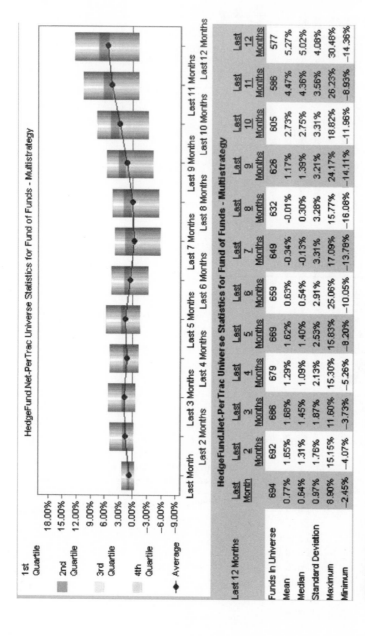

HedgeFund.Net-PerTrac Universe Statistics for Fund of Funds - Multistrategy											
	Last Month	Last 2 Months	Last 3 Months	Last 4 Months	Last 5 Months	Last 6 Months	Last 7 Months	Last 8 Months	Last 9 Months	Last 10 Months	Last 11 Months	Last 12 Months
Funds In Universe	694	692	686	679	669	659	649	632	626	605	586	577
Mean	0.77%	1.65%	1.68%	1.29%	1.62%	0.63%	-0.34%	-0.01%	1.17%	2.73%	4.47%	5.27%
Median	0.64%	1.31%	1.45%	1.09%	1.40%	0.54%	-0.13%	0.30%	1.39%	2.75%	4.36%	5.02%
Standard Deviation	0.97%	1.76%	1.87%	2.13%	2.53%	2.91%	3.31%	3.28%	3.21%	3.31%	3.56%	4.08%
Maximum	8.90%	15.15%	11.60%	15.30%	15.83%	25.06%	17.09%	15.77%	24.17%	18.82%	26.23%	30.48%
Minimum	-2.45%	-4.07%	-3.73%	-5.26%	-8.20%	-10.05%	-13.76%	-16.08%	-14.11%	-11.96%	-8.93%	-14.36%

FIGURE 14.4 Performance of Funds of Hedge Funds
Source: HedgeFund.Net—PerTrac Universes.

TABLE 14.2 Percentile Rankings of Top FoFs Performers, 2000 to Present

	2000 Percentile Rank	2001 Percentile Rank	2002 Percentile Rank	2003 Percentile Rank	2004 YTD Percentile Rank
Fund A	1	4	4	49	31
Fund B	2	12	4	13	97
Fund C	2	7	8	83	8
Fund D	2	99	13	12	18
Fund E	3	6	4	6	21
Fund F	3	57	28	81	41
Fund G	4	5	3	7	56
Fund H	4	53	9	100	92
Fund I	4	8	14	6	38
Fund J	5	3	1	100	59
Fund K	5	33	2	49	1
Fund L	6	35	91	66	47

Superior manager selection, along with diversification, is one of the key arguments for investing in a fund of hedge funds. In theory, a skilled FoF manager should be able to produce alpha over the average fund or a hedge fund index. Some argue, however, that selecting a manager with historically

TABLE 14.3 Cumulative Performance of Top FoFs Performers over/under the Mean

	Cumulative Performance +/– Mean
Fund A	174.6%
Fund B	91.1%
Fund C	97.5%
Fund D	61.0%
Fund E	139.6%
Fund F	39.4%
Fund G	109.7%
Fund H	29.4%
Fund I	94.0%
Fund J	48.4%
Fund K	77.4%
Fund L	5.9%

TABLE 14.4 Percentile Rankings of Bottom FoFs Performers, 2000 to Present

	2000 Percentile Rank	2001 Percentile Rank	2002 Percentile Rank	2003 Percentile Rank	2004 YTD Percentile Rank
Fund P	90	98	100	2	12
Fund Q	91	89	87	15	73
Fund R	91	95	98	14	94
Fund S	92	91	52	35	67
Fund T	92	2	5	9	100
Fund U	93	87	99	7	85
Fund V	92	89	24	38	2
Fund W	93	99	99	14	33
Fund X	94	39	34	45	28
Fund Y	94	64	66	22	16
Fund Z	95	74	16	68	98

high returns does not necessarily guarantee high returns in the future. To further examine whether past FoFs performance has an impact on future results, we looked at the top 12 multistrategy funds of hedge funds performers in the HedgeFund.Net database in 2000 and tracked them through the next four years. Results of this analysis appear in Table 14.2. It is true that appearing in the top 10 percent based on performance in 2000 did not assure a place in the top decile or even the top half of the group on a year-to-year basis. However, as indicated in Table 14.3, all of the funds in the group did outperform the average multimanager FoFs over the 2000 to October 2004 period. Likewise, the bottom 12 funds of hedge funds performed better in some years than in others, with a couple of funds even reaching as high as the 2nd percentile, but only one FoFs from this group managed to outperform the index on a cumulative basis for the period. This pattern is evident from Tables 14.4 and 14.5. One can only assume that screening on more than performance alone could enhance an investor's ability to identify top-performing fund of funds managers who can generate hedge fund alpha over time.

Fund of Hedge Funds Fees

The ability of some FoFs managers to generate consistent alpha over the average FoFs may help ease some investors through the issue of FoF fees. Indeed, fee compounding seems to be a significant issue for a number of

TABLE 14.5 Cumulative Performance of Bottom FoFs Performers over/under the Mean

	+/– Mean
Fund P	–31.9%
Fund Q	–29.2%
Fund R	–42.9%
Fund S	–29.1%
Fund T	25.5%
Fund U	–36.0%
Fund V	–16.0%
Fund W	–45.1%
Fund X	–19.4%
Fund Y	–21.9%
Fund Z	–33.9%

investors who are considering an FoFs investment. However, it is important for investors to remember what they are paying for. First, these fees compensate the manager for their fund selection expertise. Second, they compensate the manager and his or her staff, who must gather hedge fund information, screen investments, monitor those investments on an ongoing basis, make allocation and reallocation decisions, generate monthly statements, and more. Before investors argue about additional fees, they should consider what it would cost them to replicate those efforts (see Table 14.1).

In addition, a study of 813 funds of hedge funds in the Eurekahedge database shows that FoFs fees appear to be slowly falling. Looking at funds of hedge funds by year of inception reveals that, while management fees have remained fairly steady over the past 13 years (Table 14.6), incentive fees appear to have peaked in 2000 and have retreated some since then (Table 14.7). This is likely due to the rapid increase in the number of funds of hedge funds starting in 1998–1999 (Figure 14.5), which increased competition and put downward pressure on fees. It also is likely that, in the future, fund of hedge fund fees will continue to decrease due to index fund competition as well.

Additional Considerations When Evaluating Fund of Hedge Funds Investments

It is important to remember that funds of hedge funds, while listed as a hedge fund strategy by most of the major index providers, are not technically an investment strategy. The decision to invest in an FoFs should not be the end result of developing an investment mandate. A fund of hedge

TABLE 14.6 Average FoFs Management Fees by Inception Year

Inception Year	Fee (%)
1990	1.16
1991	1.50
1992	1.48
1993	1.30
1994	1.58
1995	1.50
1996	1.53
1997	1.39
1998	1.51
1999	1.31
2000	1.43
2001	1.31
2002	1.35
2003	1.42

funds is a vehicle or a means by which to make a hedge fund investment, but it is not a fully formed investment strategy. Funds of funds can be single or multistrategy, market neutral or aggressive, and exhibit various return, reward, and risk profiles. For example, Figures 14.6 and 14.7 show the mean, median, standard deviation, and maximum and minimum returns

TABLE 14.7 Average FoFs Incentive Fees by Inception Year

Inception Year	Fee (%)
1990	5.88
1991	1.00
1992	4.72
1993	7.73
1994	9.58
1995	7.28
1996	7.64
1997	5.48
1998	9.08
1999	9.77
2000	10.30
2001	8.04
2002	9.61
2003	9.03

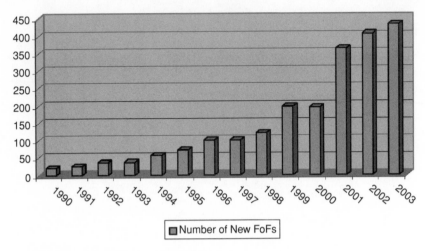

Figure 14.5   Growth of the Funds of Hedge Funds Universe
Source: 2004 SFS Hedge Fund Database Study.

of the HedgeFund.net-PerTrac Universes for market-neutral and single-strategy funds of hedge funds. Note that the return profile for market-neutral FoFs and single-strategy FoFs are quite different. Single-strategy funds offer higher upside return potential on average (44.9 percent) than do market-neutral FoFs (28.8 percent). However, those potential returns do not come without some prospective pitfalls. The average minimum return for the single-strategy funds of hedge funds trails that of market-neutral funds of hedge funds by more than 17 percentage points. The standard deviation for the single-manager funds of hedge funds universe is also nearly double that of market-neutral funds of hedge funds.

Additionally, making an investment in a fund of funds, and indeed any actively or passively managed, prepackaged portfolio, does entail giving up a significant amount of control over issues like due diligence, transparency, and investment structure. For example, a fund of hedge funds manager may do more or less due diligence or ongoing monitoring than an investor would ideally desire. In addition, an investor generally cannot pressure an FoF manager into investing in or withdrawing from an underlying fund. Therefore, it is important for investors to understand the degree of control they surrender when investing in a fund of hedge funds.

In addition, like single-manager funds, funds of hedge funds have varying levels of transparency. Some may provide full details, due diligence, and

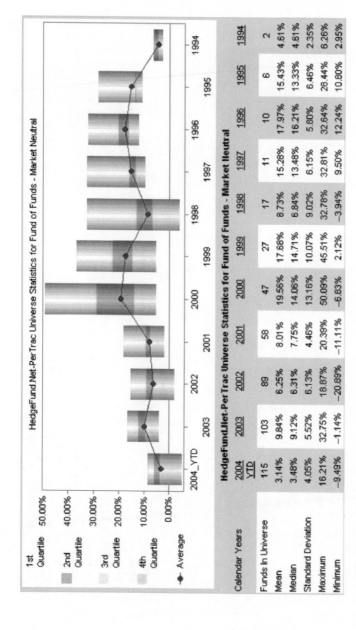

HedgeFund.Net-PerTrac Universe Statistics for Fund of Funds - Market Neutral

Calendar Years	2004 YTD	2003	2002	2001	2000	1999	1998	1997	1996	1995	1994
Funds In Universe	115	103	89	58	47	27	17	11	10	6	2
Mean	3.14%	9.84%	6.25%	8.01%	19.56%	17.68%	8.73%	15.28%	17.97%	15.43%	4.61%
Median	3.48%	9.12%	6.31%	7.75%	14.06%	14.71%	6.84%	13.48%	16.21%	13.33%	4.61%
Standard Deviation	4.05%	5.52%	6.13%	4.46%	13.16%	10.07%	9.02%	6.15%	5.80%	6.46%	2.35%
Maximum	16.21%	32.75%	18.87%	20.39%	50.09%	45.51%	32.78%	32.81%	32.64%	28.44%	6.26%
Minimum	-9.49%	-1.14%	-20.89%	-11.11%	-6.83%	2.12%	-3.94%	9.50%	12.24%	10.80%	2.95%

FIGURE 14.6 Performance of Market-Neutral Funds of Hedge Funds
Source: HedgeFund.Net—PerTrac Universes.

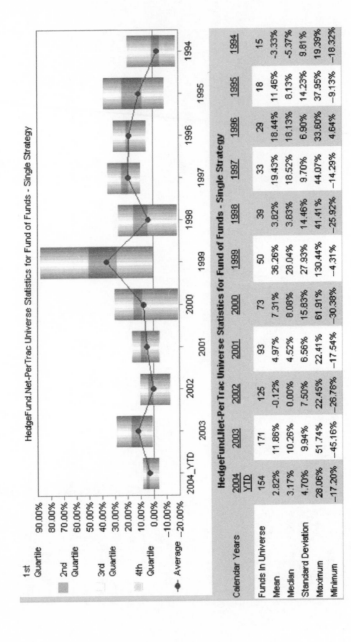

FIGURE 14.7 Performance of Single-Strategy Funds of Hedge Funds
Source: HedgeFund.Net—PerTrac Universes.

ongoing monitoring information on the underlying fund managers, while others may provide only performance and strategy information and even go as far as to obscure the names of underlying funds. Still others may resist sharing details of their proprietary manager selection and risk-monitoring systems. It is therefore important to fully consider what level of transparency and due diligence will be provided prior to making an investment, and whether the investor is comfortable with the amount of information provided.

Finally, funds of hedge funds generally invest directly into single-manager hedge funds through a limited partnership vehicle. This means that the fund of hedge funds is subject to the redemption policies of the limited partnership, including any lockups, notice periods, and early redemption penalties. Additionally, a fund of hedge funds can experience significant problems if the fund is structured to offer more liquidity than the underlying funds. A liquidity mismatch can result in the suspension of redemptions, either in whole or in part, for the investors in the fund of hedge funds. Some FoFs bypass this problem either by negotiating with the underlying funds for better liquidity terms or by securing a line of credit to provide for normal redemptions in between liquidity events in the underlying funds. However, it is important for investors to consider these possibilities when selecting an FoF investment.

Because FoFs exhibit such diversity of strategy, risk/reward profiles, and structure, it is just as important that investors spend time developing an investment mandate when selecting a fund of funds as when selecting single-manager investments. It is important to ask some tough but important questions about a potential fund of hedge funds investment: What does risk mean to you? Is it the risk of losing money? The risk of not achieving a certain return? The risk of not having money available when you need it? If a fund delivers high returns, are you willing to accept large drawdowns (losses)? Similarly, if an FoF delivers high returns, are you willing to sacrifice the amount of transparency you receive, and if so, how much? What is the minimum an investment has to return to be meaningful to your portfolio? Are there asset classes, such as small caps, commodities, or tech stocks, that you are predisposed against? What are your liquidity requirements? Only after such questions are answered will investors know what types of FoFs, what underlying strategies, and what transparency and return profiles to target in investment screening and analysis.

Investing in Hedge Fund Indexes

For those seeking the diversification offered by a ready-made multimanager portfolio, there is an alternative to FoFs. Passively managed index funds offer a multimanager approach that attempts to provide investors with a diversified index of funds designed to replicate the average performance for a given hedge fund universe or a particular strategy subset. Generally offering lower fees, daily net asset values, and more transparency than FoFs, index products are now being offered by a variety of providers, including Dow Jones, Van Hedge Fund Advisors, Standard & Poor's (S&P), Hedge Fund Research (HFR), Credit Suisse First Boston/Tremont (CSFB), Morgan Stanley Capital International, and Talenthedge.

ISSUES IN INDEX CONSTRUCTION

While index funds certainly offer many benefits to investors, there are some inherent difficulties in hedge fund index construction that raise important questions. For example, hedge fund indexes must be based on available hedge fund information. As mentioned earlier, the 2004 SFS Hedge Fund Database Study reveals the difficulty in gathering a complete sample of the hedge fund universe. When the 12 hedge fund databases that participated in the study were combined, approximately 8,100 distinct hedge funds and funds of hedge funds and approximately 5,500 single-manager hedge funds were identified. Although this is certainly an impressive number of hedge funds and funds of hedge funds covered by the various data vendors, it would be foolhardy to assume that this tally encompasses the entire hedge fund universe. A comparison of the 100 largest hedge fund firms in the world (as compiled by Institutional Investor, May 2004) to the master list of funds bears this out. As it turns out, just over two-thirds of the firms on the Institutional Investor list had funds that reported to one or more databases.

However, we do not believe this indicates that 33 percent of hedge funds do not report to a data source. In the case of hedge funds, it is often the large funds that are most reluctant to report to a database. Therefore, a more accurate estimate might be that the databases cover approximately 75 to 85 percent of commercial hedge funds. Without a central repository of all hedge fund information, it is inconceivable that a single index could capture the entire universe of hedge fund investments. Therefore, the indexes cannot be representative of the hedge fund universe, and will not be so until all hedge funds are forced to report to one or more data collectors.

Further complicating index construction is the fact that there is no regulatory requirement for hedge funds to report to any of the indexes. A fund that begins reporting to an index may stop providing performance numbers for any number of reasons. Much attention has been paid to the phenomenon of survivorship bias, but perhaps a more insidious foe to index construction is participation bias, which comes into play when a manager simply opts to stop reporting to an index provider. Unlike survivorship bias, one cannot simply assume that performance is skewed to the upside by participation bias. A fund may elect to stop reporting because performance is poor, but it is equally likely to stop because of strong performance that results in the fund closing to new investment. This means that index returns may be suboptimized from the start, based on past performance assumptions that fail to consider a significant amount of upside or downside performance.

Strategy definitions are another difficult aspect of index construction, particularly when an index fund offers a strategy subcategory to investors. An index must have enough strategy categories to capture the primary nuances in hedge fund investing, but not so many that each category is composed of only one or two funds. These strategy categories are individually determined by each of the major index providers and vary from index to index. As such, a fund that traditionally goes long a merger acquisition target and short the acquirer in a merger may be listed as merger arbitrage in one index, as event driven in another, as relative value or arbitrage in another, or even as long/short in yet another. Further complicating the matter, hedge funds are generally not limited to any one strategy by their offering documents. Consider again the example of a merger specialist. As merger deal flow dried up in 2001 and 2002, this manager might have decided to try a hand at other types of strategies, finally settling on distressed investing, where deal flow is at an all-time peak. Now, where does that fund end up in our index? Distressed securities? Opportunistic? Unfortunately, investors who rely on preconstructed indexes have no choice but to submit to the definitions and classifications assigned by the index providers.

To deal with these issues, many of the index providers have developed rigorous standards to determine strategy classification, attempt to find only style-pure managers, and have made allowances for reclassification or removal for strategy drift. However, these measures may remove one of the key advantages of hedge funds, namely adaptability.

All of these factors combine to create indexes where the performance of a fund in the same index category may or may not be correlated to other funds in that same strategy category. Table 14.8 shows the correlations of 10 constituent funds from a convertible arbitrage index. Notice the low correlations between funds, with many below even 0.5. A closer look at these funds shows that some use higher leverage than others, some utilize a convertible arbitrage strategy with only public converts, while others also invest in private converts (Reg D investments). Some of the managers use other forms of arbitrage in their funds, including merger arbitrage and sta-

TABLE 14.8 Correlations of Convertible Arbitrage Managers

	Fund 1	Fund 2	Fund 3	Fund 4	Fund 5	Fund 6	Fund 7	Fund 8	Fund 9	Fund 10
Fund 1	1.0									
Fund 2	0.4	1.0								
Fund 3	0.4	0.2	1.0							
Fund 4	0.3	0.0	0.6	1.0						
Fund 5	0.3	0.2	0.7	0.6	1.0					
Fund 6	0.3	0.1	0.8	0.7	0.7	1.0				
Fund 7	0.2	0.2	0.7	0.7	0.7	0.7	1.0			
Fund 8	0.0	0.1	0.4	0.2	0.3	0.2	0.4	1.0		
Fund 9	0.3	0.2	0.6	0.7	0.5	0.7	0.5	0.1	1.0	
Fund 10	0.4	0.4	0.5	0.6	0.6	0.6	0.6	0.2	0.6	1.0

tistical arbitrage, but because the main strategy is convertible arbitrage, they are assigned to a convertible arbitrage index.

Not only are these managers not correlated to one another, they also are not particularly correlated to their index. In one SFS study, more than two-thirds of the funds in the convertible arbitrage universe had a correlation of less than 0.6 to the noninvestable CSFB and HFR convertible arbitrage indexes. A correlation of 0.5 is the statistical equivalent of flipping a coin. Low correlation to an index, by itself, is not a problem. After all, stocks in the S&P 500 often have low correlations to one another and to that index. However, it becomes problematic when investors rely on an index to replicate the performance of the asset class, and there is no good definition of what constitutes that asset class.

Adding to the construction issues faced by hedge fund index funds is the question of whether the index should be asset weighted or equal weighted, with valid points being made in favor of both types of weightings. Those index providers that advocate asset weighting believe it is more indicative of the hedge fund universe as a whole, much like a market cap weighted stock index. Others believe that equal weighting is preferable since it tends to avoid some of the herding bias, which can create inconsistencies in the index as investing trends change.

PERFORMANCE OF HEDGE FUND INDEXES

Because of the inherent difficulties in constructing a hedge fund index, the index providers have been left to make their own arbitrary decisions about the number of funds they include, fund weightings, and strategy classifications. It is therefore not surprising that there is a fair amount of variation in terms of construction and performance of these indexes. Table 14.9 illustrates some key construction factors and performance variations in three of

TABLE 14.9 Variations in Investable Hedge Fund Index Construction

	Number of Constituent Funds	Weighting	Strategy Diversification	2004 YTD Performance (October)
CSFB/Tremont	387 Funds	Asset Weighted	10 Strategies	5.12%
MSCI Hedge Invest	110 Funds	Asset Weighted	31 Strategies	3.42%
S&P Hedge Fund Index	40 Funds	Equal Weighted	9 Strategies	1.15%

the major investable hedge fund indexes. Note that the performance through October 2004 varies for each index.

BENEFITS OF HEDGE FUND INDEX INVESTING

Despite problems involved with constructing a hedge fund index, they do offer unique features in hedge fund investing that attracts investors. Two of the major benefits in hedge fund index investing are liquidity and transparency. Many of the indexes have been constructed to invest in separately managed accounts (SMAs) rather than in the underlying fund's limited partnership vehicles. Because SMAs usually offer superior liquidity, daily or weekly in many cases, the index provider has greater flexibility than a fund of hedge funds manager might enjoy when rebalancing or redeeming from a manager. In addition, SMAs often offer greater transparency than do fund vehicles. An index provider can request daily positions directly from the manager's prime broker and, in turn, use these to carefully monitor the underlying investments. However, this does not mean that the end investor receives this additional, position-level data from the index provider, but investors will usually get daily or weekly net asset values and can benefit from transparency at the index level and the maneuverability that increased liquidity affords the index.

Another potential benefit to investing in a hedge fund index is that, while there is still an added layer of fees above the underlying fund's management and incentive fees, these fees are generally lower than those of an FoF. For example, rather than charging both a management and performance fee, the S&P Hedge Fund Index charges between a 1 percent and 5 percent up-front fee and a flat 2 percent annual service fee. The CSFB Hedge Fund Certificate charges an annual 1.16 percent replication fee, 0.36 percent for currency hedging for the Euro and Swiss franc tranches, and a one-time sales load of up to 3 percent. For many investors, these fees may seem more palatable when compared to the management and incentive fees typically charged by the average fund of hedge funds.

Additional Considerations When Evaluating Hedge Fund Index Investments

One important thing to consider when evaluating a hedge fund index is that these investments are designed to give the investor the performance of the average hedge fund. For many investors, particularly hedge fund investors, enduring average returns is unacceptable, particularly since the hedge fund industry is founded on the principles of absolute and above average returns.

Index investors essentially end up buying hedge fund beta or the hedge fund market. Some investors take a chance that through superior manager selection (either single managers or funds of funds), careful due diligence, and ongoing monitoring, they can consistently outperform the average fund, thus generating alpha over the indexes.

However, given the redemption policy of the average hedge fund and fund of hedge funds, it can be difficult to actively manage a hedge fund portfolio. Even if investors decide to redeem from a fund or rebalance a portfolio, they may have to wait months, a year, or more for their redemption date. It could therefore be difficult for the average hedge fund investor to consistently outperform an index, particularly if that index has greater flexibility in its underlying investments. In addition, for those used to traditional investments, the concept of matching index performance can be key, and hedge fund index fund investing could be particularly attractive to an institutional investor.

CONCLUSION

There is no one-size-fits-all solution in hedge fund investing. Funds of hedge funds, hedge fund index funds, and single-manager portfolios all have benefits for investors. It is up to the individual or institution to decide which approach is best, given time, money, and staff considerations, as well as performance and portfolio goals.

CHAPTER 15

Performance in the Hedge Fund Industry

An Analysis of Short- and Long-term Persistence

Sébastien Gyger, P.-A. Bares, and R. Gibson

In this chapter we analyze the performance persistence of hedge funds over short- and long-term horizons. Using a nonparametric test, we first observe that the relative value and the specialist credit strategies contain the highest proportion of outperforming managers. We next analyze the performance persistence of portfolios ranked according to their average past returns. Persistence is mainly observed over one- to three-month holding periods but rapidly vanishes as the formation or the holding period is lengthened. We examine the long-term risk-adjusted returns' persistence of hedge fund portfolios within an arbitrage pricing theory (APT) framework. This leads us to detect a slight overreaction pattern that is more pronounced among the strategies of directional hedge funds.

This chapter originally appeared in the *Journal of Alternative Investments*, Vol. 6, No. 3 (Winter 2003). This article is reprinted with permission from Institutional Investor, Inc.

Financial support by the National Centre of Competence in Research "Financial Valuation and Risk Management," a Swiss research program managed by the University of Zurich, the Institute of Theoretical Physics of the Swiss Federal Institute (Lausanne), and Olivier d'Auriol Asset Management SA (Pully, Switzerland) is gratefully acknowledged. We also thank Financial Risk Management (FRM) for providing part of their hedge fund database and J. Brandon for valuable comments and suggestions.

INTRODUCTION

The main objective of this chapter is to analyze the performance persistence of hedge funds over short- and long-term investment horizons. For that purpose, we rely on a unique proprietary database maintained by Financial Risk Management (FRM) that contains approximately 5,000 hedge funds. More precisely, we aim at answering three questions:

1. Do some hedge funds systematically outperform their investment category peers?
2. Do hedge funds portfolios formed on the basis of hedge funds' past average return rankings display short- and long-term performance persistence?
3. Do hedge funds display long-term risk-adjusted persistence in performance?

Within a specific investment category, relative performance can play an important role in consolidating reputation and for the purpose of attracting new funds under management. Our methodology differs from the one proposed by Brown, Goetzmann, and Ibbotson (1999) and Agarwal and Naik (2000c), who compare the number of winners and losers that follow winners or losers and test the significance of the difference from one year (or quarter in the case of Agarwal and Naik 2000c) to the next. Here we rely on a nonparametric test to analyze the relative performance persistence of the funds included in the FRM database over the period that extends from January 1992 to December 2000. Managers are considered to be persistent when they compare favorably or unfavorably to their median a number of times that is significantly different from half the number of return observations. The analysis is performed for distinct investment strategies and is based on four different time horizons. While Brown, Goetzmann, and Ibbotson (1999) find no evidence of performance persistence in raw returns, we document that specialist credit and relative value dominate the other investment strategies in terms of the proportion of managers who consistently outperform their median peers. Besides, there is no evidence that managers performing above the median are more risky than their peers.

Understanding the duration and the patterns in hedge funds portfolios' persistence can offer valuable insights regarding the type of strategies, in particular, momentum and/or contrarian, that are better suited for hedge fund investors. Several studies have examined the issue of momentum and reversal in the stock markets to determine whether trading strategies that select stocks based on their past returns might be profitable or not (Jegadeesh and Titman 1993, 2001; Rouwenhorst 1998). We follow a comparable path and aim at examining the duration of hedge funds portfolios' performance persistence. For that purpose, we rank managers according to their average returns over 1-month to 36-month formation periods. We then form five portfolios that contain the top-performing funds and five others that contain the worst performers. Portfolios are held during periods that extend from 1 to 36 months. We find evidence of short-term—mostly over a one-month holding period—persistence, which rapidly vanishes as the formation and holding periods lengthen. This phenomenon is commonly referred to as a hot-hand effect in the mutual fund literature (Hendricks, Patel, and Zeckhauser 1993). We note that the average monthly return of the best and worst portfolios tends to level out when the holding period and the formation period extend beyond 12 months. This observation points toward a half performance reversal while a significant reordering of the average returns of the portfolios is never observed. This is documented in DeBondt and Thaler (1985) for U.S. stocks.

It is useful to know whether some managers can consistently generate superior performance after accounting for their systematic risk exposures and whether risk-adjusted performance reversals can be observed for some hedge funds categories over long-term horizons. In order to address these issues, we rely on the arbitrage pricing theory (APT) framework developed by Ross (1976) to estimate hedge fund portfolio alphas over two independent holding periods. Three observations are worth reporting:

1. The existence of a slight reversal in the portfolio alphas is confirmed over a 36-month holding period.
2. The directional trading, traditional, and stock selection strategies, which are the most directional in nature, exhibit the greatest tendency to overreact.
3. Hedge fund portfolio alphas are very unstable over time.

Overall, our empirical results indicate that investors need to be very cautious when relying on past raw and/or risk-adjusted performance measures to select hedge fund portfolios for long-term investment horizons.

DATA DESCRIPTION

We rely on Financial Risk Management's hedge fund database, which at the end of December 2000 contained data on 4,934 funds. FRM is an independent research-based investment services company, specializing in constructing portfolios of hedge funds to achieve absolute return investment objectives. Morgan Stanley Capital International, in collaboration with FRM, has developed a Strategy Classification System that classifies hedge funds according to three characteristics, namely the investment process, the asset class, and the geographical region. This structured framework allows one to group similar funds or funds sharing common characteristics together and to build hedge fund indices. The style (or the investment process) is the core characteristic of hedge fund strategies and describes the methodology that managers follow when creating and managing their portfolios. The investment strategy is subdivided into a two-level hierarchy. The upper level identifies six broad groups of similar strategies, while the lower level is more specific. FRM uses six distinct upper-level designations:

1. Directional trading (abbreviated DT)
2. Traditional (T)
3. Stock selection (SS)
4. Specialist credit (SC)
5. Relative value (RV)
6. Multistrategy (MS)

The asset class describes the type of securities in which managers invest (typically equities, fixed income, or convertibles) and geographical region is the location where the investments originate (countries and/or regions). The methodology aims at supporting fund managers' decisions when classifying their funds within the system. The upper-level investment strategies and their lower-level subdivisions are fully described in Appendix 15.1. The FRM database contains information on both live and defunct funds.

Managers report their monthly performance on a fund-by-fund basis in a net return form. The net return of a fund over a period is defined as the change in the fund's net asset value over that period, as a percentage of the starting value of the fund. This return is adjusted for subscriptions and redemptions, after periodic fees have been charged. Hedge funds usually charge two kinds of fees, a management fee and an incentive fee. The management fee is based on a percentage of the size of assets under management. The mean, the median, and the standard deviation of the annual management fee are respectively equal to 1.3, 1.0, and 0.4 percent (computed over 4,382 reporting funds). The incentive fee gives the hedge fund manager a percentage of the profits earned by the fund. The mean, the median, and the standard deviation of the annual incentive fee are respectively equal to 18.8, 20.0, and 2.9 percent (computed over 4,325 reporting funds). In addition, many funds use a high-water mark, which requires a manager to recover previous losses before incentive fees can be charged.

We consider managers rather than funds as the standard entity of interest, because managers may have been hired based on their potential skills, and because they may have managed several funds during the course of their careers. Consequently, funds managed by the same manager with the same strategy are linked together from the outset to the end of the sample period, in order to allow monitoring of performance track record over a longer time horizon for statistical accuracy.

In this study, we define three time periods. The first one extends from January 1992 to December 2000. This choice is dictated by the availability of a sufficient number of funds with an adequate number of return observations. The remaining two periods extend from January 1995 to December 1997 and from January 1998 to December 2000, respectively. In the first one, the hedge fund industry has benefited from a bull market, while it has suffered from the Asian and the Russian crises and the turmoil in the new economy during the second subperiod.

As can be seen from Appendix 15.1 and as mentioned, each upper-level investment strategy involves significantly different techniques, financial instruments, and manager skills to generate returns. In order to characterize each of the different investment strategies, we first build six equally weighted indices, rebalanced every month, to compare the hedge funds' monthly returns statistics within each style or investment strategy. The statistics are free of the survivorship bias associated with the database since the indices include those funds that have ceased to report performance prior to the end of the sample. We compute the average monthly return, the standard deviation, and the Sharpe ratio (assuming a risk-free rate of 5 percent per annum) for each index portfolio. We calculate the downside risk deviation and the skewness and excess kurtosis of the empirical return distributions to evaluate their departure from the normal. The downside deviation measures the quadratic deviation of the returns below a specific target return, in order not to penalize the realizations above the target. We compute the downside deviation as

$$\sqrt{(1/n) \times \sum_{i=1}^{n} (r(i) - r_f)^2 \cdot 1_{(r(i) < r_f)}} \tag{15.1}$$

where $r(i)$ = net return during month i
r_f = risk free rate, assuming a risk free rate of 5 percent per annum
$1_{(r(i) < r_f)}$ = the indicator function taking on the value one when $r(i) < r_f$
n = number of observations

Finally, for the sake of completeness, the minimal, maximal return observations and the linear correlation coefficient with a broad market index (Standard & Poor's [S&P] 500) are also displayed. Table 15.1 reports these monthly summary statistics for the six indices and the number of funds alive at the beginning and at the end of each period.

The stock selection style, followed by directional trading, dominates the other investment strategies in terms of their monthly average return in each period. In addition, the low and high standard deviations of, respectively, relative value and traditional drive their Sharpe ratios to the extreme ends of the spectrum. The values of skewness and excess kurtosis suggest that the return distributions of certain indices, traditional and relative value, for example, can deviate substantially from the normal distribution. Comparison of the two nonoverlapping periods shows that the hedge funds industry performed poorly during the period that extends from January 1998 to December 2000. The highest decrease in the net monthly average return when moving from the 1995 to 1997 to the 1998 to 2000 period corresponds to 75 and 108 basis points for directional trading and traditional, respectively. This supports the view that traditional investment strategies are the most sensitive to adverse market movements. In comparison, investment strategies oriented toward market neutrality, such as stock selection and relative value, experience a smaller decrease (28 and 55 basis points, respectively). The last column of Table 15.1 indicates that, as expected, the traditional and stock selection strategies display a higher linear correlation with the market proxy index S&P 500. The style that exhibits the lowest correlation with the market is directional trading. Finally, the maximal loss for all the investment strategies except directional trading occurred during the month of August 1998, following the Asian and the Russian crises.

To conclude this section, we estimate the survivorship bias for each of the six investment strategies. For that purpose, we build equally weighted indices of the hedge funds that survived during the entire subperiods described earlier. During the most turbulent period, extending from January 1998 to December 2000, the annualized difference between the indices that contain all the funds reporting and the indices that contain the surviving funds, namely the surviving portfolios, is equal to 1.92, 1.92, 1.44, 0.60, 0.84, and 0.7 percent respectively for the investment strategies mentioned. This pattern reverses when we consider the subperiod extending from January 1995 to December 1997. In that case, the surviving portfolios are underperforming the observable portfolios by values ranging from 0.05 percent (directional trading and relative value) to 0.14 percent (multistrategy). As mentioned by Ackermann, McEnally, and Ravenscraft (1999), managers who voluntarily stop reporting are responsible for this pattern.

These figures show that the survivorship bias associated with the FRM database is smaller than the one generally found in the hedge funds literature (Brown, Goetzmann, and Ibbotson 1999; Fung and Hsieh 2000). There are two possible explanations for this difference:

1. Our database does not distinguish between funds that stop reporting due to self-selection or termination (Ackermann, McEnally, and Ravenscraft 1999).
2. We compute the survivorship bias over different time periods from those in previous studies.

TABLE 15.1 Net Monthly Return Statistics for the FRM Data

Style	#Funds start	#Funds end	Period start	Period end	Monthly Statistics mean	st dev	Sharpe	downdev	skewness	kurtosis	min	max	corr
DT	122	230	31/01/1992	31/12/2000	1.36	2.27	0.43	0.94	0.47	0.10	-4.43	7.62	0.13
DT	248	343	31/01/1995	31/12/1997	1.67	2.48	0.51	0.97	0.24	-0.60	-2.84	7.62	0.50
DT	349	230	31/01/1998	31/12/2000	0.92	1.75	0.29	0.79	0.75	0.67	-1.87	6.27	-0.04
T	57	163	31/01/1992	31/12/2000	1.23	3.56	0.23	2.39	-1.07	4.28	-16.26	11.39	0.68
T	156	253	31/01/1995	31/12/1997	1.62	2.58	0.47	1.45	-0.70	-0.42	-4.7	5.37	0.61
T	253	163	31/01/1998	31/12/2000	0.54	5.08	0.03	3.72	-0.70	1.54	-16.26	11.39	0.73
SS	111	488	31/01/1992	31/12/2000	1.69	2.58	0.50	1.21	0.13	2.41	-7.84	10.69	0.6
SS	302	487	31/01/1995	31/12/1997	1.96	1.87	0.83	0.70	-0.41	-0.43	-2.64	4.96	0.57
SS	499	488	31/01/1998	31/12/2000	1.68	3.79	0.34	1.90	0.18	0.28	-7.84	10.69	0.61
SC	23	62	31/01/1992	31/12/2000	1.27	1.56	0.56	0.82	-0.68	2.8	-5.5	6.03	0.36
SC	35	70	31/01/1995	31/12/1997	1.60	0.92	1.31	0.17	-0.45	-0.72	-0.19	3.16	0.32
SC	72	62	31/01/1998	31/12/2000	0.70	1.96	0.15	1.36	-0.79	1.09	-5.50	4.53	0.45
RV	63	246	31/01/1992	31/12/2000	1.16	0.71	1.08	0.37	-2.08	7.78	-2.62	2.32	0.35
RV	163	267	31/01/1995	31/12/1997	1.41	0.38	2.67	0.00	-0.19	-0.58	0.57	2.2	0.49
RV	274	246	31/01/1998	31/12/2000	0.86	0.91	0.50	0.64	-2.09	4.86	-2.62	1.99	0.3
MS	51	148	31/01/1992	31/12/2000	1.03	1.94	0.33	1.11	-0.41	1.92	-7.09	6.10	0.49
MS	136	203	31/01/1995	31/12/1997	1.36	1.64	0.58	0.68	0.03	-0.3	-1.92	5.36	0.48
MS	208	148	31/01/1998	31/12/2000	0.71	2.42	0.13	1.57	-0.41	1.48	-7.09	6.1	0.54

RELATIVE PERFORMANCE PERSISTENCE OF NONPARAMETRIC INDIVIDUAL HEDGE FUNDS

The first objective of this study is to examine the relative performance persistence of individual hedge fund managers over different time periods. We distinguish between the six investment strategies mentioned earlier and split the entire period, which extends from January 1992 to December 2000, into nonoverlapping subperiods, or time horizons, of either 1, 3, 6, or 12 months. Managers overperform when they compare favorably to the median performance level of their peers. The converse is true for underperforming managers. In this section, the performance of a manager is defined as his or her total return. Only two outcomes are possible during each subperiod: The manager is either performing above the median or below. A manager shows significant performance persistence if we cannot accept the null hypothesis that the manager performance is equally distributed, with probability ½, on each side of the median over time, using a one-sided binomial test. The analysis is conditioned on those managers who report performance during at least five consecutive subperiods. Although it might introduce a survivorship bias, this is the minimal number of observations that allows us to test the null hypothesis at a 5 percent significance level.

Compared to the methodologies employed in Brown, Goetzmann, and Ibbotson (1999) and Agarwal and Naik (2000c) where persistence is examined over a single horizon, the present technique tests for the existence of persistence throughout managers' entire performance history over several time horizons. Our analysis is similar in spirit to that of Agarwal and Naik (2000b).

We compute the number of managers who have a significant tendency to perform above or under the median benchmark (denoted ↑ or ↓), for each strategy and over each time horizon. The empirical results are displayed in Table 15.2.

As the horizon lengthens, the percentage of managers who show relative persistence decreases. This observation supports the view that high (and poor) returns exhibit more relative persistence over the short term (1 month) than over longer horizons (12 months). The smallest decrease, when moving from the 1-month to the 12-month time scale, occurs for the stock selection managers who are mostly targeting market neutrality. The results displayed in different rows are not independent from each other, since a manager who shows persistence over a short time period is more likely to be persistent over a longer one. We find that two investment strategies consistently beat the others in terms of the proportion of managers that are consistently performing above their median. Over the shortest horizon (one month), these are specialist credit with 22.0 percent and relative value

TABLE 15.2 Individual Performance Persistence of the Hedge Fund Managers, January 1992 to December 2000

Time Horizon	Funds Selection	Investment Strategies					
		DT	T	SS	SC	RV	MS
1 month	Total	473	300	768	91	404	250
	signif. ↑ or →	97 (20.5%)	61 (20.3%)	141 (18.4%)	38 (41.8%)	156 (38.6%)	80 (32.0%)
	signif. ↑	52 (11.0%)	28 (9.3%)	76 (9.9%)	20 (22.0%)	78 (19.3%)	41 (16.4%)
	signif. →	45 (9.5%)	33 (11.0%)	65 (8.5%)	18 (19.8%)	78 (19.3%)	39 (15.6%)
3 months	Total	441	284	667	85	374	237
	signif. ↑ or →	68 (15.4%)	36 (12.7%)	101 (15.1%)	28 (32.9%)	115 (30.7%)	52 (21.9%)
	signif. ↑	40 (9.1%)	15 (5.3%)	52 (7.8%)	18 (21.2%)	60 (16.0%)	27 (11.4%)
	signif. →	28 (6.3%)	21 (7.4%)	49 (7.3%)	10 (11.8%)	55 (14.7%)	25 (10.5%)
6 months	Total	383	244	533	72	289	208
	signif. ↑ or →	49 (12.8%)	23 (9.4%)	76 (14.3%)	24 (33.3%)	80 (27.7%)	29 (13.9%)
	signif. ↑	25 (6.5%)	11 (4.5%)	28 (5.3%)	13 (18.1%)	41 (14.2%)	16 (7.7%)
	signif. →	24 (6.3%)	12 (4.9%)	48 (9.0%)	11 (15.3%)	39 (13.5%)	13 (6.3%)
12 months	Total	242	148	291	43	165	139
	signif. ↑ or →	22 (9.1%)	9 (6.1%)	33 (11.3%)	5 (11.6%)	32 (19.4%)	17 (12.2%)
	signif. ↑	11 (4.5%)	5 (3.4%)	13 (4.5%)	4 (9.3%)	17 (10.3%)	9 (6.5%)
	signif. →	11 (4.5%)	4 (2.7%)	20 (6.9%)	1 (2.3%)	15 (9.1%)	8 (5.8%)

with 19.3 percent. Over longer horizons (six months), the proportion reduces to 18.1 and 14.2 percent, respectively. A similar conclusion is reached with regard to the proportion of managers consistently underperforming their peers. Further, we see that in most cases, the proportion of managers who outperformed their median is similar to the proportion who underperformed. The only obvious exception concerns the specialist credit case over a three-month horizon, where 18 out of 85 managers are performing above the median, but 10 out of 85 managers are performing below the median. Focusing on the 12-month horizon, relative value managers exhibit the greatest propensity to regularly perform above and below their peers. When looking at persistence from a relative performance angle, this analysis suggests that specialist credit and relative value dominate the other strategies. Finally, multistrategy comes in third position when ranking strategies according to their relative performance over 1-month to 12-month horizons, which seems to indicate that only a few of these managers can meaningfully exploit the flexibility to invest in different styles and benefit from their ability to time the market.

We complete this section by assessing whether relative persistence is driven by relative return volatility. Schneeweis (1998) shows that forecasts of future returns are more consistent with prior volatility than with prior return levels. We are aware of the limitation of volatility as a meaningful measure of risk in the context of nonnormally distributed returns. We thus investigate whether relative persistence might be linked to relative skewness as well. We build a contingency table with those managers who exhibit one-month rolling performance persistence with higher or lower volatility and/or skewness levels compared to the median volatility and skewness of the managers following a similar investment strategy. For the sake of brevity, we do not display this table, and discuss only those results significant at the 5 percent level. Negatively persistent specialist credit (18 managers) display in general low volatility (13 managers) and low skewness (14), while positively persistent ones display high skewness (15 out of 20 managers). Negatively persistent relative value exhibits low volatility (59 managers out of 78). In addition, we find that positively persistent directional trading shows low volatility and low skewness. Finally, positively persistent stock selection display high skewness.

In conclusion, we have shown that two investment strategies, namely specialist credit and relative value, dominate the others in terms of the fraction of managers who are consistently performing above their median style cohort. In addition, it appears that performance persistence is not a consequence of increased return volatility. The main lesson to be learned from these empirical results is that with the exception of specialist credit and relative value managers, less than 10 percent of the managers are able to beat their peers consistently over investment horizons that extend beyond six months. This short-term feature of performance persistence may lead to career concerns and to high volatility in the level of assets under management if indeed money is chasing short-term past relative performance.

THE DURATION OF PERFORMANCE PERSISTENCE OF HEDGE FUND PORTFOLIOS

The second objective of this chapter is to examine the duration of the performance persistence of hedge fund portfolios. As a corollary, we wish to examine if their positive short-term performance persistence is followed by reversals over longer investment horizons.

We use 1-, 3-, 6-, 12-, 18-, and 36-month formation and holding periods. Based on their total returns during the formation period, we rank managers from best to the poorest performing. Managers must have reported during the entire formation period to be ranked. We form and hold 10 equally weighted portfolios, attributing to Portfolio 1 the 20 managers who have performed the best during the formation subperiod, to Portfolio 2 the managers ranked from positions 21 to 40, and to Portfolio 5 the managers ranked from positions 81 to 100. At the opposite, portfolios labeled 6 to 10 contain the 100 worst-performing managers. Portfolios are rebalanced each month and remain equally weighted during the entire period that extends from January 1992 to December 2000. To ensure that each month enters the analysis only once, holding periods are chosen to be nonoverlapping, and their length must be greater than or equal to one of the formation periods. In the case when a selected manager stops reporting performance, the portfolio is rebalanced between the remaining funds. Our methodology is designed to limit the potential impact of survivorship bias. It does not, however, prohibit managers from disappearing from the portfolios during the holding periods.

Our portfolio construction method differs slightly from the one traditionally used when examining mutual fund performance persistence (Hendricks, Patel, and Zeckhauser 1993; Elton, Gruber, and Blake 1996) or when analyzing stock momentum strategies (Jegadeesh and Titman 1993; Chan, Jegadeesh, and Lakonishok 1996). Instead of building decile portfolios and using all the funds in the sample, we restrict the analysis to the managers who are ranked in the upper five and lower five extreme portfolios. Two reasons motivate this choice.

1. This ensures that a different number of managers will not enter the analysis over time, which would otherwise be the case given the growing number of managers reporting their performance in the database, from 427 in January 1992 to 1,377 in December 2000, with a peak of 1,677 in July 1998, and might render forthcoming results more difficult to interpret.

2. Our portfolio construction methodology is aimed at replicating—as much as possible—actual investment strategies. Indeed, practitioners might be interested in implementing strategies limited to a reasonable number of hedge funds. Constructing decile portfolios does not provide a relevant answer to this particular issue, since the size of our hedge fund universe is rather large (up to 1,677 managers).

We do not consider the impact of lockup, redemption, and withdrawal notice periods in our analysis.

Table 15.3 reports the monthly mean returns and standard deviations of ranked hedge funds portfolios computed over the period that extends from January 1992 to December 2000. The mean and standard deviation of each portfolio are separated by a slash. The portfolios are labeled from 1st to 10th for the best to the worst performer, respectively. We do not distinguish between the different investment strategies to ensure that a sufficient number of managers qualify for the analysis. The table provides clear indication of short-term persistence. To check the existence of performance persistence, we use a two-sample t-statistic at a 5 percent level without assuming equal standard deviations to compare the average monthly return of the portfolios numbered 1st to 5th with the average return of the portfolios labeled 6th to 9th. This requires 20 comparisons in total for each set of formation and holding periods. In the case where we consider a formation and a holding subperiod equal to 1–1 month and 1–3 months, we find that all 20 comparisons are favorable to the portfolios numbered 1st to 5th.

Indeed, the latter significantly outperform the portfolios numbered 6th to 9th. However, one can also check that this difference loses statistical significance as the formation or holding horizon lengthens (except in a few marginal cases). In comparison, Agarwal and Naik (2000b) find a reasonable degree of persistence in hedge fund performance over quarterly horizons. The average returns of the best portfolios (1st to 5th) exhibit a downward tendency as the length of the holding horizon increases. At the opposite, the mean returns of the worst portfolios (5th to 10th) present an upward tendency, which is particularly pronounced when the length of the formation period is short (from one to three months). Therefore, the hedge fund performance persistence observed is comparable to the hot-hands effect documented in Hendricks, Patel, and Zeckhauser (1993) for mutual funds, since it fades away as the formation or holding period lengthens. Moreover, without achieving a complete reordering of the portfolio average returns, a half reversal is discernible over longer formation and holding periods (one year and longer). Indeed, the portfolios' average returns tend to level to similar values. The overreaction pattern is not symmetric since it is more patent for winners than for losers. A full reversal like the one reported by Lakonishok, Shleifer, and Vishny (1994) is only observed for an

TABLE 15.3 Monthly Mean Return and Standard Deviation of 10 Ranked Hedge Fund Portfolios, January 1992 to December 2000

Formation and Holding Periods	Monthly Mean Returns / Standard Deviation of Ranked Hedge Funds Portfolios									
	1st	2nd	3rd	4th	5th	6th	7th	8th	9th	10th
1-1	4.24/6.60	2.76/4.98	2.92/4.23	2.60/4.19	2.53/4.01	0.29/3.73	0.43/3.78	0.47/4.20	0.40/4.56	1.41/8.34
1-3	3.07/6.86	2.57/4.74	2.61/4.96	2.02/4.14	2.11/3.66	0.85/4.11	1.00/3.79	0.80/4.32	0.74/4.75	1.38/7.21
1-6	2.34/8.05	1.90/5.69	1.82/5.21	1.50/4.51	1.70/4.97	1.36/3.27	1.34/3.20	1.08/3.60	1.19/4.19	1.67/5.40
1-12	2.26/7.19	2.03/5.49	1.59/4.86	1.70/4.04	1.61/4.30	1.28/2.77	1.26/3.26	1.38/3.18	1.34/4.28	1.80/4.88
1-18	2.19/5.86	1.84/4.10	1.33/3.60	1.59/3.58	1.65/4.42	1.35/3.11	1.34/4.12	1.11/3.11	0.75/3.90	1.38/5.26
1-36	1.90/5.00	1.57/3.31	1.25/3.34	1.32/3.66	1.38/2.95	1.44/3.59	1.45/5.26	1.37/4.05	1.02/4.49	1.62/5.32
3-3	2.75/6.31	1.98/4.69	2.05/3.60	1.65/3.62	1.82/3.67	0.94/3.56	0.91/4.90	0.83/3.35	0.90/4.31	0.81/7.35
3-6	2.77/7.11	1.99/5.11	2.04/4.14	1.84/4.29	1.99/4.08	0.62/3.70	0.62/4.84	0.48/3.49	1.09/4.50	1.15/6.27
3-12	2.21/7.75	2.03/6.08	2.01/4.64	1.62/4.93	1.79/4.11	0.64/3.75	1.06/3.82	0.80/3.70	0.69/4.31	1.04/4.52
3-18	2.19/6.15	1.58/3.93	1.82/3.69	1.48/3.69	1.47/3.69	0.94/3.88	0.83/4.00	0.77/3.78	0.99/4.45	1.86/4.44
3-36	1.49/3.92	1.35/3.38	1.70/2.01	1.09/2.45	1.48/2.00	0.98/4.84	1.24/5.71	0.72/4.93	0.97/5.69	1.55/5.24
6-6	2.69/7.76	1.62/4.88	2.07/4.27	1.55/4.38	1.94/4.13	0.96/3.06	0.63/3.25	0.83/3.61	0.87/4.09	1.14/6.67
6-12	2.04/7.51	1.46/5.15	1.77/4.16	1.27/4.34	1.43/4.05	1.06/3.72	0.81/3.22	1.01/3.85	1.10/3.87	1.76/5.70
6-18	2.25/5.60	1.79/3.92	2.09/3.67	1.30/3.58	1.56/4.40	0.70/3.01	0.68/2.98	1.08/4.23	0.97/4.11	1.44/5.63
6-36	1.88/3.60	1.59/3.44	1.52/2.70	1.45/3.35	1.45/2.95	0.86/3.53	0.63/3.50	1.12/4.63	1.15/4.84	1.27/5.20
12-12	1.93/7.38	1.44/4.56	1.47/4.13	1.58/3.30	1.34/4.21	1.20/2.81	0.95/2.73	1.30/3.20	1.02/3.29	1.95/5.76
12-18	1.79/5.46	1.37/3.49	1.56/3.97	1.71/4.26	1.17/2.74	1.10/3.48	1.15/3.22	1.16/2.74	1.20/4.33	1.77/4.89
12-36	1.55/4.77	1.01/3.46	1.24/2.90	1.26/2.36	1.24/2.42	1.09/2.99	1.12/3.59	1.23/3.52	1.05/3.55	1.13/5.27
18-18	1.21/5.02	1.84/4.04	1.70/3.13	1.11/3.41	1.67/3.62	1.20/2.38	0.99/2.99	1.15/3.51	1.04/3.57	2.07/5.97
18-36	1.13/4.14	1.23/2.57	1.22/2.84	0.96/2.66	1.33/2.09	1.21/2.19	0.98/2.75	1.03/2.75	1.08/3.73	1.35/5.27
36-36	1.03/3.89	1.19/3.16	1.25/2.89	0.95/2.65	0.99/3.37	0.92/2.12	0.87/2.42	0.80/2.87	0.92/2.26	0.98/3.76

18-month formation period, but is never statistically significant when using a two-sample *t*-statistic.

We observe that the average return does not decrease (or increase) with the rank of the portfolio as smoothly as is generally the case for the momentum (or reversal) studies carried out in the stock market or when analyzing the persistence of mutual fund performance. One should therefore be cautious when discussing the existence of under- and overreaction effects in our hedge fund sample.

It is interesting that the average monthly return of the worst portfolio (labeled 10th) is larger than the one of the penultimate portfolio (9th) in 20 cases out of 21. The difference between their average return, however, is never significant at the 5 percent level. This might be explained by the fact that the 10th portfolio is riskier than the 9th, in terms of a higher standard deviation.

An investment strategy based on short-term persistence is trading intensive and requires frequent rebalancing of the portfolio positions. To exploit the potential benefits documented in this section, one-month holding period hedge fund strategies should be adopted. Lockup periods and transaction and redemption fees may significantly reduce or even wipe out gains when setting up such strategies in the case of hedge funds. Furthermore, due to their smoothing, the significance of monthly hedge fund returns is questionable (Getmansky, Lo, and Makarov 2003).

This section provides evidence on the profitability of short-term trend-following strategies on an average return basis. We now examine the persistence of the risk-adjusted performance of hedge fund portfolios. As advocated by Elton, Gruber, and Blake (1996), it is necessary to adjust for systematic risk when measuring performance. It is instructive to observe in Table 15.3 that the extreme portfolios, those labeled 1st and 10th, exhibit in most cases the highest standard deviations.

RISK-ADJUSTED PERFORMANCE PERSISTENCE OF HEDGE FUND PORTFOLIOS IN AN APT FRAMEWORK

This section examines the long-term performance persistence of hedge fund portfolios ranked on a risk-adjusted basis. A risk-adjusted framework is desirable because hedge funds are marketed as being oriented toward absolute return performance and because the spectrum of their investment philosophies requires an adjustment for risks to detect superior managerial skills across the sample. First we describe the methodology we apply to compute the abnormal return of a hedge fund and to rank the managers accordingly. Then we present the empirical results obtained with the entire sample of hedge funds and those obtained for each investment strategy.

Description of the Methodology

We rely on principal component analysis (PCA) to extract the factors driving the hedge fund economy. Our motivation differs from that stated in Fung and Hsieh (1997a) since we do not intend to provide an economic interpretation of statistical factors. Although statistical factors lack the intuitive appeal of macroeconomic factors, they do not suffer the problem associated with an ad hoc choice of the factors. As mentioned in Elton and Gruber (1995), if a method other than principal component or factor analysis is used to obtain the factors for testing the APT, one is conducting a joint test of the APT and of the relevance of the factors that have been hypothesized as determining the securities returns.

The general procedure used to estimate the hedge funds' risk-adjusted performance is described in Appendix 15.2. When a risk factor is not priced by the market—that is, when its premium is not significantly different from zero—it is not incorporated into equation 15.4 when estimating abnormal performance. In addition, since hedge fund managers may be running dynamic trading strategies (Fung and Hsieh 1997a), the factors, the risk premia, the factor sensitivities, and the abnormal performances may not be constant over long time periods. We therefore divide the sample period under analysis that extends from January 1992 to December 2000 into three subperiods of equal length. Two nonoverlapping holding periods are investigated. The first extends from January 1995 to December 1997 and the second from January 1998 to December 2000. The managers are first ranked according to their abnormal performance computed over a formation period that extends from January 1992 to December 1994 and from January 1995 to December 1997, respectively. Note that managers have to report during an entire subperiod to be eligible to belong to a random portfolio and thus to enter the principal component analysis. Unfortunately, since managers must report during at least 36 months to be allowed to form the statistical factors, a selection bias as well as a survivorship bias might be introduced at this stage.

Different approaches have been proposed for selecting the appropriate number of factors. Here, we choose $k = 8$ factors for two reasons. It is a reasonable statistical compromise between explaining as much as possible of the individual hedge fund cross-sectional return variations and using a limited number of factors. In our case, shifting from five to eight factors increases the model explanatory power from 44 to 54 percent, from 43 to 52 percent, and from 51 to 60 percent for individual hedge fund managers selected during, the first, second, and third subperiods, respectively. Also, it is motivated by Brown and Goetzmann (2003), who suggest that eight distinct factors is sufficient to describe the wide spectrum of hedge fund manager strategies. For purposes of homogeneity, we select the same number of factors during each subperiod. The number of priced factors is equal to six, seven, and seven (out of eight) for the 36-month subsample periods. The role of those excluded factors, however, is marginal in explaining the variations in returns of hedge funds. The proportion of variance explained by the factors excluded from the APT is equal to 4, 2, and 1 percent for the 36-month periods ending December 1994, December 1997, and December 2000, respectively.

For illustrative purposes, Table 15.4 displays summary statistics of the parameters estimated in the return-generating process and in the APT pricing equations for each subsample period. In panel A, we use the set of 1,000 randomly drawn portfolios; in panel B, the set of individual managers. Panels A and B reveal that the factors computed with the principal component procedure have a high explanatory power since the mean of the goodness-of-fit measure R^2 lies between 0.79 and 0.90 for the portfolios and between 0.52 and 0.60 for the individual hedge fund managers. Because portfolios are formed randomly so that each fund enters approximately the same number of different portfolios, values of μ are not different depending on whether one considers the random portfolios or the individual funds. In addition, since we deal with a large number of portfolios, the average value of α is similar in panels A and B. The average factor loadings β are much smaller for the portfolios, due in part to the benefits of diversification. Results are displayed in panels C and D for the sets of individual managers exhibiting, respectively, positive and negative abnormal performance. The results indicate that the fraction of managers with a negative abnormal performance is chronologically equal to 14.1 percent (58 of 412), 12.6 percent (118 of 935), and 23.0 percent (219 of 954) and that, on average, they have a higher risk exposure than those with a positive abnormal performance. Overall, shifting from the second to the most recent period shows that the average abnormal performance decreases while the average factor sensitivities increase. There is strong evidence that hedge fund managers have experienced large factor risk exposures over the period that extends from January 1998 to December 2000, a period of abrupt events and high market volatility.

We next follow a comparable methodology to the one described in the previous section to form the five best and the five worst portfolios, except that the managers are now ranked according to their abnormal risk-adjusted performance.

Empirical Results

In the first step, the analysis is conducted for all the different investment strategies taken together by forming the five best and the five worst alpha-ranked portfolios, respectively. Each portfolio contains 20 funds at the beginning of the holding period and is rebalanced every month. If a hedge fund return is missing in a subsequent month, then from that moment on,

TABLE 15.4 Summary Statistics of Parameters Appearing in the Return-Generating Process, Equation 15.2, and in the APT Pricing Model, Equations 15.3 and 15.4

Panel A: 1,000 Random Portfolios of 20 Hedge Funds Each

Period start	end	# portfolios	average(μ)	average(R^2)	average(α)	median(α)	average(β)
01/92	12/94	1000	1.29	0.79	0.78	0.79	1.39
01/95	12/97	1000	1.56	0.85	0.90	0.90	1.73
01/98	12/00	1000	1.15	0.90	0.60	0.60	2.61

Panel B: All Individual Managers

Period start	end	# managers	average(μ)	average(R^2)	average(α)	median(α)	average(β)
01/92	12/94	412	1.30	0.54	0.79	0.68	3.12
01/95	12/97	935	1.57	0.52	0.89	0.82	3.10
01/98	12/00	954	1.15	0.60	0.60	0.54	4.34

Panel C: Individual Hedge Fund Managers Whose α Is Positive

Period start	end	# managers	average(μ)	average(R^2)	average(α)	median(α)	average(β)
01/92	12/94	354	1.46	0.53	0.98	0.81	3.04
01/95	12/97	817	1.77	0.52	1.09	0.89	2.94
01/98	12/00	735	1.52	0.61	0.98	0.78	4.19

Panel D: Individual Hedge Fund Managers Whose α Is Negative

Period start	end	# managers	average(μ)	average(R^2)	average(α)	median(α)	average(β)
01/92	12/94	58	0.30	0.59	−0.39	−0.30	3.63
01/95	12/97	118	0.13	0.55	−0.51	−0.35	4.22
01/98	12/00	219	−0.07	0.58	−0.66	−0.46	4.90

the fund is permanently withdrawn from the portfolio and the allocated capital redistributed among the surviving funds. Results are displayed in Table 15.5. We report the monthly abnormal return and the average geometric sensitivity $\beta = (\sum_{j=1}^{8} \beta_j^2)^{1/2}$ computed during the formation period. We also report the average monthly return μ after 6, 12, 24, and 36 months, the monthly abnormal return α, and the average geometric sensitivity β estimated during the holding period.

TABLE 15.5 Monthly Summary Statistics of the Five Upper and Five Lower Extreme Hedge Fund Portfolios

Panel A: Formation Period from January 1992 to December 1994 and Holding Period from January 1995 to December 1997								

Portfolio Number	Formation						Holding	
	α	β	μ_6	μ_{12}	μ_{24}	μ_{36}	α	β
1	3.46	0.85	1.78	1.47	1.86	1.86	1.23	2.77
2	2.77	0.90	2.52	2.17	1.79	1.84	0.86	2.65
3	1.78	0.87	1.84	1.44	1.50	1.07	0.59	2.38
4	1.71	0.78	2.18	2.02	1.59	1.45	0.87	1.34
5	1.35	0.62	1.60	1.31	1.29	1.24	0.56	1.53
6	0.34	0.64	1.68	1.68	1.47	1.38	0.69	1.14
7	0.32	0.82	1.95	1.53	1.46	1.47	0.83	1.87
8	0.37	0.80	1.59	1.66	1.55	1.40	0.66	1.91
9	0.22	0.92	1.15	1.61	1.40	1.38	0.73	1.94
10	−0.28	1.17	0.82	1.82	1.68	1.36	0.64	2.20

Panel B: Formation Period from January 1995 to December 1997 and Holding Period from January 1998 to December 2000								

Portfolio Number	Formation						Holding	
	α	β	μ_6	μ_{12}	μ_{24}	μ_{36}	α	β
1	3.88	2.14	0.58	−0.06	0.37	0.25	−0.35	2.76
2	2.87	2.37	0.37	0.09	0.82	0.72	0.04	2.41
3	2.49	1.91	0.35	0.10	0.94	1.26	0.83	2.04
4	2.23	2.55	−0.53	−0.23	1.34	1.00	0.56	4.47
5	2.04	2.42	−0.05	−0.54	1.18	1.47	0.95	4.62
6	−0.12	1.67	−0.29	−0.82	0.67	0.33	0.10	2.29
7	−0.26	2.64	−0.15	0.66	0.88	0.60	−0.04	2.73
8	−0.43	2.72	0.41	0.77	1.18	0.76	0.14	2.47
9	−0.66	2.28	−0.34	−0.50	2.07	1.12	0.17	6.08
10	−1.53	3.66	−1.68	0.42	2.63	0.79	0.22	5.91

Results in panels A and B indicate the existence of a slight reversal pattern in the performance persistence of the hedge funds industry. Both panels indicate that the abnormal performance of the five upper portfolios decreases from the formation to the holding period, while the converse holds for the five lower portfolios. The reversal pattern varies over time and is highly asymmetric, since it is much larger for winners than for losers. This finding differs from that of DeBondt and Thaler (1985), who found that the overreaction effect in the stock market is dominated by securities that have performed poorly over a prolonged past formation period. Similarly to the previous section, the results do not reveal a monotonic relation between ex-post performance (the monthly abnormal performance) and portfolio ranks. Hence, hedge funds do not exhibit reversal patterns that are comparable in magnitude to those reported for example by DeBondt and Thaler (1985) and Lakonishok, Shleifer, and Vishny (1994). Panel A indicates that the best portfolio, that with abnormal performance of 1.23 percent per month, clearly outperforms the other nine portfolios by about 0.52 percent per month, or 6.19 percent per year. Panel B indicates that this feature does not repeat during the 1998 to 2000 period, since Portfolio 1 then displays the worst ex-post abnormal performance. This result suggests that the benefit of forming portfolios of winning managers selected on a risk-adjusted basis is period specific and thus unstable. In terms of the average monthly return computed over the first 6, 12, 24, and 36 months, the overreaction pattern reaches a peak 24 months after the starting month during the second holding period: The mean across the respective average monthly returns of the five upper and five lower portfolios is equal to 0.93 percent and 1.48 percent in that case. There is some evidence that the highest overreaction is reached 12 months after the starting month for the first holding period. Regarding the sensitivities, the average betas are somewhat larger for winners in panel A, while they are much larger for losers in panel B. In order for the betas to be meaningful, and to be able to compare them from one period to the other, we standardize all statistical factors to have a unit variance (see Appendix 15.2).

Finally, one sees that the sensitivities computed either during the formation or the holding periods increase from the first to the second subsample periods. Hence, our empirical results point to a slight overreaction in hedge fund portfolios' returns that seems to be more pronounced in simple than in risk-adjusted returns and that is more pronounced under extreme market conditions.

In the second step, we conduct the risk-adjusted performance analyses while differentiating among the six investment strategies. The analyses are carried out following the same methodology, the only differences being that the number of funds incorporated at the beginning of each holding period in the extreme portfolios is equal to 5 for the specialist credit strategy and is equal to 10 for the five remaining strategies, and that we only construct and display results for the two upper and the two lower portfolios. These choices are dictated by the small size of the sample of available managers by strategy. Results are reported in Table 15.6. We report only the monthly abnormal performance. The sequence of alphas does not possess similar characteristics across the different strategies, and the alphas are not homogenous over time. The directional trading, traditional, and stock selection

TABLE 15.6 Monthly Abnormal Performance by Investment Style of the Two Upper and Two Lower Extreme Hedge Fund Portfolios

Panel A: Formation Period from January 1992 to December 1994 and Holding Period from January 1995 to December 1997

Portfolio Number	Formation						Holding					
	DT	T	SS	SC	RV	MS	DT	T	SS	SC	RV	MS
1	3.59	2.02	2.27	1.45	1.97	1.41	1.03	0.80	0.53	1.30	1.06	0.84
2	2.18	1.11	1.52	1.23	1.06	0.58	0.89	0.38	0.96	0.57	0.63	0.66
3	-0.20	0.43	-0.07	0.95	0.21	0.03	1.32	0.99	0.73	0.70	0.53	0.43
4	-0.79	-0.03	-0.58	0.39	-0.13	-0.23	0.64	0.93	0.37	0.82	0.73	0.35

Panel B: Formation Period from January 1995 to December 1997 and Holding Period from January 1998 to December 2000

Portfolio Number	Formation						Holding					
	DT	T	SS	SC	RV	MS	DT	T	SS	SC	RV	MS
1	3.63	3.09	3.59	2.41	2.61	1.50	-0.14	0.26	-0.46	0.46	0.19	0.43
2	2.46	2.24	2.78	1.17	1.76	1.06	1.05	-0.58	0.53	-1.10	0.87	0.13
3	-0.37	-0.35	-0.47	0.61	0.30	-0.01	-0.02	-0.25	0.65	-0.19	0.38	-0.31
4	-0.70	-1.44	-1.28	0.03	-0.32	-0.51	0.05	-0.11	0.77	-0.26	-0.19	-0.11

strategies reveal an instructive result. Panels A and B suggest that these styles possess the most pronounced overreaction patterns. One potential explanation is that directional hedge fund strategies (especially stock selection) may be related to the well-documented presence of a reversal effect in the stock market. A different type of alpha sequence is proper to the multistrategy, which clearly displays the strongest continuity of risk-adjusted performance. This feature strongly supports the view that long-term noncontrarian investors may benefit from the diversification potential of this strategy on a risk-adjusted basis.

In the specialist credit strategy, the winner portfolio shows the largest abnormal performance among all strategies over the two holding periods. Due to the limited number of funds included in this category (62 at the end of 2000), this observation should be taken with caution.

It is worthwhile to mention that the APT analysis should ideally be performed using all assets in the economy, whereas our universe is limited to hedge funds. The impact of this restrictive assumption is somewhat mitigated given that hedge fund managers are known to invest in a wide spectrum of asset classes and in different markets. Furthermore, the APT might not be the most appropriate model to capture the nonlinearities characterizing hedge fund returns. Yet we find that the null hypothesis of normally distributed hedge fund managers' returns cannot be accepted in 92 cases out of 412 for the first subperiod (using a one-sample Kolmogorov-Smirnov test at a 5 percent significance level), but that this number drops to 32 when we test for the normality of the return residuals. For the second subperiod, the number of cases diminishes from 208 to 94 (out of 935), and of the third subperiod it diminishes from 338 to 125 (out of 954). Furthermore, this potential drawback is mitigated by the use of statistical factors, which already capture the individual hedge funds' nonlinear exposures.

To conclude this section, it is worth recalling that the alphas of hedge funds, as obtained by the APT, do not account for transaction costs that follow from implementing strategies intended to benefit from reversal patterns, nor for the lock-in over prescribed time periods. Transaction costs play an important role in explaining the apparent excess returns of hedge funds, as suggested for risk-arbitrage strategies by Mitchell and Pulvino (2001). Finally, our results may suffer from a selection bias inherent in the construction of our portfolios during the formation period.

CONCLUSION

In this chapter, we investigate an important issue in the hedge fund industry, namely the performance persistence of hedge funds. We used a binomial representation to examine the existence of relative performance persistence among individual hedge funds. The methodology differs from the one presented in past hedge fund studies, in that managers are considered to be persistent when their total return compares favorably or unfavorably to their median style cohort a number of times that is significantly different from half the number of return observations. The analysis was performed for distinct investment strategies and was based on different holding periods ranging from one month to one year. We found the specialist credit and relative value investment strategies to contain the highest proportion of managers who are continuously outperforming their peers and that persistence vanished rapidly as the time horizon lengthened. The analysis displayed no evidence that persistence is driven by return volatility, except in the case of relative value hedge funds.

We analyzed the duration of the performance persistence in more detail by examining under- and overreaction patterns in hedge fund portfolio performance. We ranked managers according to their past realized returns over 1-month to 36-month formation periods. We then formed five portfolios that contained the top-performing funds and five others that contained the worst performers. Portfolios were held during periods extending from 1 to 36 months. Even though the results did not reveal a monotonic relationship between ex-post performance and portfolio ranks, we observed significant short-term (one to three months) persistence. This hot-hand effect, as it is usually referred to in the mutual fund literature, vanished rapidly as the formation or holding period was lengthened. A complete reversal of the portfolios' average return only occurred (but was not statistically significant) for an 18-month formation period and a holding period equal to 18 or 36 months.

Finally, we used the APT model as a performance-ranking criterion. When we ranked the managers according to their abnormal performance computed over a 36-month formation period, we detected a slight overreaction pattern at long-term horizons when the analysis was conducted for all the different investment strategies taken together. When we distinguished between the different investment strategies, we noticed that directional trading, traditional, and stock selection strategies exhibited the highest propensity to reproduce the overreaction patterns revealed in previous stock market studies. Overall, these results confirm previous empirical evidence regarding the short-term persistence of hedge fund portfolios, but they also shed new light on their performance tendency to revert over long-term horizons. The latter finding should be a matter of concern to long-term investors who decide to stay committed to hedge funds with good historical track records. The latter observation should also have direct implications for studying the career concerns and the volatility of funds' flows within the hedge fund industry.

APPENDIX 15.1 DESCRIPTION OF FRM MAIN INVESTMENT STRATEGIES

Here we briefly describe the six distinct investment strategies considered by Financial Risk Management and Morgan Stanley Capital International when developing the MSCI hedge fund indices. The following description is based heavily on FRM documents.

Directional trading strategies are based on speculating on the direction of market prices of currencies, commodities, equities, and bonds, in the futures and cash markets. The key to this investment strategy is the fact that managers can quickly reverse their positions to take advantage of market opportunities. Strategic allocation (often referred to as global macro) managers are typically opportunistic and move between markets and instruments based on their forecasts of changes in interest and exchange rates. They are long term in nature and establish market positions to take advantage of broad macroeconomic trends. Discretionary traders use fundamental analysis to identify profitable trades. The trades are usually based upon participation in market-driven price actions. The portfolio turnover is often very high since the positions are held for short time periods. The key difference between discretionary and systematic traders is that the former make the final investment decision, while the latter rely on computer trading models based decisions implemented in a systematic fashion.

Traditional is a long-only investment strategy, which includes growth, value, and tactical allocation substrategies. The growth managers attempt to find shares of companies that are growing and will continue to grow rapidly, while the value managers aim to find companies whose shares are undervalued compared to similar companies. The objective of tactical allocation managers is to obtain returns above benchmarks with lower volatility by forecasting the returns of several asset classes and varying exposure accordingly.

Stock selection managers combine long positions and short sales with the aim of benefiting from their superior ability to select stocks while offsetting systematic market risks. Market exposure can vary substantially, leading to a wide range of risk and return profiles. Managers attempt to find opportunities that they consider to be under/overvalued and then buy and sell positions accordingly, before the market reacts. Managers may attempt to remove all market exposure by balancing long positions and short sales to achieve beta neutrality, or to maintain market exposure to desired levels. They are classified under the following substrategy designations: long, short, no, or variable bias.

Specialist credit managers lend to credit-sensitive issuers. Their ability to perform a high level of due diligence, to precisely time the investments, and to properly manage credit risk governs the success of their investments.

Distressed securities managers invest in the securities of firms in or near bankruptcy and negotiate the terms of the restructuring. Positive-carry managers participate in large portfolios of credit-sensitive securities, with a view to making a positive carry over their funding rate. Private placement managers make short- to medium-term privately placed investments issued by companies that are in need of rapidly available capital. The deals typically involve investments in debt instruments with free options to buy the company's stock at a low price.

Relative value managers attempt to hedge out most market risk by taking offsetting positions, often in different securities issued by the same issuer. The opportunities being exploited have low risk and low returns. Therefore, many managers use leverage to amplify the returns to attractive levels. Managers aim for market neutrality and actively hedge systematic risks using a variety of instruments. Convergence arbitrage focuses on capturing anomalies in the price spreads between related or similar instruments. The assets most frequently traded include convertibles, equities, fixed income, and mortgages. Merger arbitrage seeks to capture the price spread between current market prices of securities and their value on successful completion of a takeover, a merger, or a restructuring. Statistical arbitrage is a model-based investment strategy that aims to build long and short portfolios whose relative value is currently different from a theoretically or quantitatively predicted value. The portfolios generate profits as future security prices converge to some equilibrium-model prices.

Finally, multistrategy managers employ two or more of the preceding investment strategies to a significant extent.

APPENDIX 15.2 THE APT MODEL

The APT approach (Ross 1976) is based on the assumption that security returns can be described by a small number k of factors, which translates into this linear return-generating process

$$r_{it} = \mu_i + \sum_{j=1}^{k} \beta_{ij} \tilde{f}_{jt} + \varepsilon_{it} \tag{15.2}$$

where r_{it} = return of security i at time t
μ_i = expected return
$\tilde{f}_{jt}$ = jth standardized factor, with zero mean and unit variance
β_{ij} = sensitivity (factor loading) of security i on factor j
ε_{it} = error term

Each factor is common to all securities, but what distinguishes one security from another is its loading on the factors and also its residual risk. The APT pricing equation that arises from the return-generating process and from the no-arbitrage assumption (equation 15.3) can be written as

$$\mu_i \cong \lambda_0 + \sum_{j=1}^{k} \lambda_j \beta_{ij} \qquad (15.3)$$

where λ_j = unitary risk premium for the jth factor
λ_0 = risk-free rate, or zero beta

The coefficient λ_j represents the expected return of a basis portfolio that is only subject to a unit risk on factor j, while λ_0 can be interpreted as the risk-free rate (or zero beta). The abnormal performance of security i, denoted α_i, is written

$$\alpha_i = \mu_i - \lambda_0 - \sum_{j=1}^{k} \lambda_j \beta_{ij} \qquad (15.4)$$

If a security's average return conforms to the APT, then α_i as defined by (15.4) should be zero.

The last step before computing the abnormal performance of each manager is to estimate the common systematic factor risk premia. This stage is performed using equation 15.3. A single least-squares regression of the mean returns vector $\vec{\mu}$ on the k sensitivity predictors $\vec{\beta}_1, \ldots, \vec{\beta}_k$ produces the factor premia and their standard deviations. We do not expect each factor to be associated with a risk premium that is significantly different from zero. If the null hypothesis that a specific risk premium is equal to zero is accepted, this corresponds to not paying an extra return for bearing the risk associated with the related factor, since it can be diversified away. Such a non-priced factor does not contribute to expected returns, even though it helps to explain the variability of manager returns. Finally, the abnormal performance α_i is estimated by substituting μ_i, λ_j, and the β_{ij} into Equation 15.4. Note that only those values of β_{ij} that are significantly different from zero are used for the calculation (the others are set to zero).

CHAPTER 16

Further Evidence on Hedge Fund Performance

A Calendar-Time Approach

Maher Kooli

Previous work has suggested that hedge funds can outperform a market index, and the purpose of this chapter is to examine the robustness of this finding. We reexamine the evidence on the long-term returns of hedge funds using a calendar-time approach with a set of hedge funds indices over the period 1995 to 2003. We also compare abnormal performance based on a number of alternative methods including the capital asset pricing model, the General Autoregressive Conditional Heteroskedastic (GARCH) estimation, the Fama and French (1993) three-factor model, and the Ibbotson (1975) returns across time and securities (RATS) technique. We find that hedge funds as a whole deliver significant excess returns and managers seem to prefer smaller stocks.

INTRODUCTION

The early 1990s saw the explosive development of hedge funds. Even though the attraction of these funds was tempered by many huge losses suffered in 1994 and 1998, the hedge fund industry continued to prosper. According to Van Hedge Fund Advisors International, http://www.vanhedge.com, the hedge fund industry has been growing at an average yearly rate of over 17 percent over the last decade, and significant growth is expected to continue. For instance, Van Hedge reports a total of 8,100 global hedge funds managing around $820 billion in capital for the year 2003. These funds are gaining in popularity and performance, attracting new investors around the world. They are like mutual funds in that a fund manger invests a pool of money obtained from investors. However, unlike mutual funds, hedge funds are not required to register with the Securities and Exchange Commission (SEC), are generally free to pursue almost any investment style they wish, are not required to maintain any particular degree of diversification or liquidity, and are limited to financially sophisticated investors.

The importance of the hedge fund industry justifies the growing body of research that attempts to evaluate the performance levels and persistence of these funds. However, results of previous studies are controversial. Agarwal and Naik (2000b) find that persistence in hedge funds performance exists. Brown, Goetzmann, and Ibbotson (1999) find that offshore hedge funds display positive returns adjusted for risk, but they attribute this performance to style effect. Ackermann, McEnally, and Ravenscraft (1999) and Liang (1999), who compare the performance of hedge funds to mutual funds and several indices, find that hedge funds constantly obtain better performance than mutual funds, although lower than the market indices considered. Fung and Hsieh (1997a) and Schneeweis and Spurgin (1997) show that including hedge funds in a portfolio can significantly improve its risk/return profile, due to their weak correlation with other financial securities. Amin and Kat (2003a) find that stand-alone investment hedge funds do not offer a superior risk/return profile, but when hedge funds are mixed with the Standard & Poor's (S&P) 500, they do. These divergent results can partly be explained by the limited access to individual fund data and the private characteristics of each hedge fund.

The work in this study is closely related to that of Capocci and Hübner (2004) but differs through the use of a different approach to measure hedge fund performance, never previously used in this context, as well as different statistical tests.

DATA AND METHODOLOGY

Hedge Fund Data

As stressed by Ackermann, McEnally and Ravenscraft (1999), Brown, Goetzmann, and Ibbotson (1999), Fung and Hsieh (2000), and Brown, Goetzmann, and Park (2001), among others, performance data from hedge funds databases and indexes suffer from serious biases. These biases can make historical return hedge funds performance difficult to interpret and may severely hinder statistical inference (Hendricks, Patel, and Zeckhauser 1993; Carhart, Carpenter, Lynch, and Mosto 2000). In this study, to minimize such issues, we use hedge fund indices rather than individual funds. Van Hedge Fund Indices are the industry's first performance benchmarks and are based on a large and representative sample of hedge funds. Initially compiled in 1994 and published in 1995, the Van Hedge Fund Indices reflect the average performance of hedge funds back to 1988. The indices are currently produced on a monthly basis in three primary forms. The Van Global Hedge Funds Index represents the average performance of hedge funds around the world and therefore tracks the performance of the overall hedge fund universe. The Van U.S. Hedge Funds Index represents the average performance of hedge funds domiciled in the United States only. The Van Offshore Hedge Funds Index represents the average performance of hedge funds domiciled outside the United States. For each of these indices, average returns are published for the overall group and for various categories within the overall group as defined by investment strategy. Funds of funds are not included in the Van indices. All index returns are based on hedge funds returns that are net of fees, and are simple non–dollar-weighted averages. Index returns for different time periods may be based on different funds, depending on the hedge funds reporting to Van at the time. In this chapter, we consider only Van U.S. Hedge Funds U.S. indices, representing those funds that must register with the SEC and are subject to the modest regulations imposed by the National Securities Markets Improvement Act (NSMIA) of 1996. Almost all U.S. hedge funds have their main offices in the United States.

For this study, we retain 18 Van U.S. Hedge Funds indices with available data for the 1995 to 2003 period.

Market Proxy and Risk-Free Return

Following Fama and French (1993) and Capocci and Hübner (2004), we choose the value-weighted portfolio of all New York State Stock Exchange, Amex, and Nasdaq stocks as a market index. Agarwal and Naik (2004) use the Russel 3000 instead. The comparison of descriptive statistics of the two proxies suggests that they are very similar. The results of this study should not be influenced by the choice of market proxy. We use the one-month T-bill from Ibbotson Associates as the risk-free rate.

Methodology

In the hedge fund literature, different models have been used in performance evaluation. Capocci and Hübner (2004) note that it is necessary to realize performance studies based on multifactor models, rather than simply use the capital asset pricing model (CAPM), but there exists no unanimously accepted model. In line with these researchers, we use five specifications to compare the results obtained.

Market Model   We use the CAPM, developed by Sharpe (1964) and Lintner (1965), as the Market Model and assume that hedge fund returns follow the CAPM (equation 16.1):

$$R_{jt} = \alpha_j + \beta_j R_{Mt} + \varepsilon_{jt} \tag{16.1}$$

where R_{jt} = rate of return of the hedge fund j at month i
        R_{Mt} = rate of return of a market index at month t
        β_j = parameter that measures the sensitivity of R_{jt} to the market index
        ε_{jt} = error term with an expected value of zero and that is uncorrelated with R_{Mt} uncorrelated R_{kt} with for $k \neq j$, not autocorrelated, and homoskedastic

Define the out- or underperformance relative to the market proxy (equation 16.2) used (the abnormal return) for the fund on month t as

$$A_{jt} = R_{jt} - (\hat{\alpha}_j + \hat{\beta}_j R_{Mt}) \tag{16.2}$$

where $\hat{\alpha}_j$ and $\hat{\beta}_j$ = the ordinary least squares estimates of α_j and β_j.
The average abnormal return AAR_t is the sample mean (equation 16.3):

$$AAR_t = \frac{\sum_{j=1}^{N} A_{jt}}{N} \tag{16.3}$$

where t is defined in trading days relative to the event date. For example, $t = 60$ means two trading months after the event.

Over an interval of two or more trading months beginning with month T_1, and ending with T_2, the cumulative average abnormal return (equation 16.4) is:

$$CARR_{T_1, T_2} = \frac{1}{N} \sum_{j=1}^{N} \sum_{T_1}^{T_2} A_{jt} \tag{16.4}$$

Market Model with GARCH Estimation   The performance of the hedge fund is measured using a single-actor market model with GARCH(1,1) errors as in equation 16.5:

$$R_{jt} - R_{ft} = \alpha_j + \beta_j(R_{Mt} - R_{ft}) + \varepsilon_{jt} \quad \text{for } t = 1,2,\ldots,T \qquad (16.5)$$

where R_{jt} = return of fund j in month t
           R_{ft} = risk-free return in month t
           R_{mt} = return of the market portfolio in month t
           ε_{jt} = error term in month for fund j in month t
           α_j, β_j = intercept and slope of the regression, respectively

In this model, conditional on ψ_{t-1}, the information set at time t–1, the errors are distributed with mean zero and conditional variance h_{jt} given by the GARCH(1,1) process (equation 16.6):

$$h_{jt} = \omega_j + \delta_j h_{j,t-1} + \gamma_j \varepsilon_{j,t-1}^2 \qquad (16.6)$$

with $\omega_j > 0$, $\delta_j > 0$, $\gamma_j > 0$, and $\delta_j + \gamma_j < 1$. We estimate the parameters by maximum likelihood.

Fama-French Calendar Time Portfolio Regressions   The Fama and French (1993) three-factor model is estimated from an expected form of the capital asset pricing model developed by Sharpe (1964) and Lintner (1965) regression. It takes the size and the book-to-market ratio of the firms into account. It is estimated from this following extension of the CAPM regression (equation 16.7)

$$R_{jt} - R_{ft} = \alpha_j + \beta_j(R_{Mt} - R_{ft}) + \gamma_t SMB_t + \lambda_t HML_t + \varepsilon_{jt} \quad \text{for } t = 1,2,\ldots,T$$
$$(16.7)$$

where SMB_t = factor-mimicking portfolio for size (small minus big)
        HML_t = factor-mimicking portfolio for book-to-market equity
                 (high minus low)
        γ_t = regression coefficient for SMB
        λ_t = regression coefficient for HML

A portfolio is formed monthly in calendar time. Portfolios are equally weighted. The regression is estimated on portfolio returns. The estimate of the average abnormal return is $\alpha_j = 0$. We use ordinary least squares to estimate the model and test the null hypothesis $\alpha_j = 0$.

Ibbotson's Returns Across Time and Securities Model   The returns across time and securities, or RATS (Ibbotson 1975), procedure requires that the first-period returns from all funds be regressed on the concurrent market returns to produce a single beta estimate for all funds during the first period. This procedure is repeated for each subsequent time period to produce a time series of cross-sectional beta estimates. This procedure allows the estimate of beta to vary during the returns window. The betas of each fund should vary over time as new information about the fund is available. The RATS model is equation 16.8:

$$R_{jt} - R_{ft} = \alpha_j + \beta_{jt}(R_{Mt} - R_{ft}) + \varepsilon_{jt} \quad \text{for } t = 1, 2, \ldots, T \qquad (16.8)$$

where R_{jt} = return of fund j in month t
R_{ft} = risk free return in month t
R_{mt} = return of the market portfolio in month t
ε_{jt} = error term in month t
α_j, β_j = intercept and the slope of the of the regression, respectively

Unlike the conventional market model, the RATS regression is estimated for each month. The estimate of the out- or underperformance relative to the market proxy used (abnormal return) is α_j. We use ordinary least squares to estimate the model and test the null hypothesis that $\alpha_j = 0$.

Fama-French Factors with Ibbotson's RATS Model   The modified version of the RATS model incorporates Fama-French (1993) factors, as in equation 16.9:

$$R_{jt} - R_{ft} = \alpha_j + \beta_{jt}(R_{Mt} - R_{ft}) + \gamma_t SMB_t + \lambda_t HML_t + \varepsilon_{jt} \quad \text{for } t = 1, 2, \ldots, T$$
$$(16.9)$$

where SMB_t = factor-mimicking portfolio for size (small minus big)
HML_t = factor-mimicking portfolio for book-to-market equity (high minus low)

The regression is estimated for each month. The estimate of the abnormal return is α_j. We use ordinary least squares to estimate the model and test the null hypothesis $\alpha_j = 0$.

Calendar-Time Approach and Portfolio Formation

In this chapter, we employ the calendar-time method developed by Jaffe (1974) and Mandelker (1974), also adopted by Loughran and Ritter (1995), and, more recently, by Brav and Gompers (1997) to measure the long-run performance of initial public offerings. Loughran and Ritter (1995) point out that in the presence of cross-correlation in contemporaneous returns, *t*-statistics assessing the significance of abnormal returns are likely to be overstated since the test assumes that the observations are independent. The calendar-time approach controls for cross-correlation, and Lyon, Brad, and Tsai (1999) show that it yields well-specified test statistics. This approach involves calculating average returns of rolling, calendar-time portfolios of event stocks or funds. Specifically, for each calendar month, we form an equally weighted τ-month portfolio set up to include any hedge funds index that has a return during the previous τ-months, for $\tau = 12$, 24, 36, 48, 60, 72, 84, and 96 months. This calendar-time approach has the added advantage in that it provides a direct measure of the opportunities available to investors attempting to exploit any abnormal performance.

Statistical Tests

Here we describe the statistical tests of hedge fund abnormal returns. To test the null hypothesis that the mean abnormal return is equal to zero for a sample of n funds, we first employ a cross-sectional *t*-statistic. The standard error for this test for each month is computed across securities, not across time.

Neyman and Pearson (1928) and Pearson (1929) indicate that skewness has a greater effect on the distribution of the *t*-statistic than does kurtosis and that positive skewness in the distribution from which observations arise results in the sampling distribution of *t* being negatively skewed. This leads to an inflated significance level for lower-tailed tests, so that reported *p*-values will be smaller than they should be, and a loss of power for upper-tailed tests, so that *p*-values will be too large. To eliminate the skewness bias when long-run abnormal returns are calculated, we use the bootstrapped skewness-adjusted *t*-statistic.

HEDGE FUND PERFORMANCE

Basic Performance

Panel A of Table 16.1 contains descriptive statistics of the hedge funds indices considered in this study. We compare hedge funds data against descriptive statistics of the market proxy, the Morgan Stanley Capital International (MSCI) World excluding the United States, Fama and French (1993) small minus large (SML) and high minus low (HML) factors, Lehman U.S. Aggregate Bond Index, Lehman BAA Corporate Bond Index (default spread), and panel B of Table 16.1. Panel A shows that the highest mean return was achieved by the U.S. Opportunistic Index (20.62 percent) followed by the

TABLE 16.1 Descriptive Statistics of Hedge Funds and Passive Indices, 1990 to 2003

Panel A: Van U.S. Hedge Fund Indices	Geometric Mean (%)	t-statistic	Arithmetic Mean (%)	Standard Deviation (%)	Median (%)	Skewness	Kurtosis	Highest Return (%)	Lowest Return (%)	Sharpe Ratio
Market Neutral Group Index	15.34	8.45	15.49	5.87	16.77	0.18	3.09	6.90	-4.50	1.87
Distressed Securities Index	15.15	6.86	15.36	7.18	15.39	1.02	4.82	9.30	-3.50	1.51
Market Neutral Arbitrage Index	14.71	11.48	14.78	4.11	13.35	0.38	0.16	4.10	-1.20	2.49
Special Situations Index	16.40	5.53	16.80	9.79	16.08	0.44	4.32	11.70	-8.00	1.25
Long/Short Equity Group Index	19.02	4.78	19.76	13.48	21.70	0.52	2.50	14.50	-7.80	1.13
Aggressive Growth Index	17.45	3.04	19.14	20.56	18.16	0.65	1.94	20.10	-11.40	0.71
Market Neutral Securities Hedging	16.25	8.94	16.39	5.90	15.39	1.62	6.27	8.10	-2.50	2.01
Opportunistic Index	20.62	4.77	21.47	14.78	21.70	1.82	9.78	21.20	-7.90	1.15
Value Index	20.47	4.94	21.29	14.15	25.34	-0.34	0.52	9.90	-9.10	1.19
Directional Trading Group Index	13.50	4.26	13.97	10.44	10.03	0.28	-0.15	7.50	-6.20	0.90
Macro Index	6.32	1.46	7.47	15.87	10.03	0.18	1.20	15.00	-9.90	0.19
Market Timing Index	14.96	4.15	15.57	12.04	10.69	0.90	1.78	12.70	-5.60	0.92
Futures Index	14.32	3.09	15.40	16.03	9.38	0.36	0.06	11.90	-7.40	0.68
Specialty Strategies Group Index	9.75	5.32	9.90	5.83	12.01	-1.06	2.04	4.40	-4.50	0.92
Emerging Markets Index	10.45	2.01	12.06	19.07	19.56	-0.60	3.03	16.20	-18.90	0.40
Income Index	10.01	5.62	10.16	5.66	11.35	-1.35	7.01	4.30	-7.00	1.00
Multistrategy Index	14.63	4.12	15.24	11.85	18.86	-0.33	1.59	8.80	-9.60	0.90
Short Selling Index	-4.40	-0.15	-1.29	25.50	-5.84	0.34	2.25	29.10	-21.30	-0.23

TABLE 16.1 *(continued)*

Panel B: Passive Indices	Geometric Mean (%)	t-statistic	Arithmetic Mean (%)	Standard Deviation (%)	Median (%)	Skewness	Kurtosis	Highest Return (%)	Lowest Return (%)	Sharpe Ratio
S&P 500	12.20	2.37	13.69	18.47	20.91	-0.64	0.26	9.78	-14.44	0.50
Russell 3000	12.02	2.34	13.51	18.45	23.22	-0.75	0.50	8.17	-15.32	0.49
Market Proxy	11.78	2.25	13.36	18.94	24.97	-0.79	0.49	8.42	-15.77	0.47
Fama & French SMB factor	2.71	0.78	3.68	14.36	-1.49	0.37	1.04	14.62	-11.60	-0.06
Fama & French HML factor	0.40	0.33	1.86	17.27	0.84	-0.68	4.23	14.92	-20.79	-0.15
Lehman Bros Govt	7.91	5.16	8.01	4.82	7.70	-0.50	1.11	4.03	-4.13	0.72
Lehman Bros Corp BAA	8.80	4.76	8.95	5.86	9.90	-0.13	0.56	4.80	-4.49	0.76
Lehman Bros Aggregate	8.10	6.19	8.18	4.11	8.99	-0.41	1.14	3.87	-3.36	0.89
MSCI World excluding U.S.	4.77	1.13	6.04	16.49	8.05	-0.45	0.22	10.44	-12.75	0.09
Goldman Sachs Commodity	8.23	1.48	10.37	22.15	8.91	0.16	0.22	16.88	-14.41	0.26

Value Index (20.47 percent) and by the Long/Short Equity Group Index (19.02 percent). Indices that offer the lowest mean return are Short Selling Index Foreign Exchange (−4.40 percent), Macro Index (6.32 percent), and Specialty Strategies Group Index (9.75 percent). The geometric mean return of the 18 indices is 13.61 percent. When standard deviation is taken into account through the Sharpe ratio, the results change somewhat. Indices offering the best Sharpe ratio are the U.S. Market Neutral Arbitrage Index, with a Sharpe ratio of 2.49, followed by the Market Neutral Securities Hedging (2.01) and the Market Neutral Group Index (1.87). The worst Sharpe ratio is obtained by the Short Selling Index (−0.23), which is also in the worst-performing indices when risk is not taken into account.

Panel B of Table 16.1 shows that the mean return of the Market Proxy is 11.78 percent and that this mean return is statistically significant. This large value indicates that the period under study is bullish. The mean excess premium of the MSCI World excluding the United States is an insignificant 0.43 percent per month. The average SMB and HML returns are insignificant, unlike the results obtained by Fama and French (1993). The highest mean return was obtained by the S&P 500 for equity and by the Lehman BAA Corporate Bond Index for the bond. On average, the Sharpe ratio obtained by the 18 hedge funds indices (1.06) is higher than the one for the Market Proxy (0.47).

Correlation

Table 16.2 reports correlation coefficients among and between hedge funds indices and passive strategies. Panel A reports correlations among hedge funds indices. There is a high variability between different indices, ranging from 0.96 (between Long/Short Equity Group Index and Aggressive Growth Index) to −0.86 (between Long/Short Equity Group Index and Short Selling Index). Twenty-six correlation coefficients (17 percent of them) are greater than 0.70, and 25 (16.34 percent) are negative. In particular, Short Selling Index is negatively correlated with all the other hedge fund indices except with the Futures Index and the Specialty Strategies Group Index.

Panel B reports correlation coefficients between hedge funds indices and equity, bond and commodity indices. Correlation coefficients between hedge funds indices and the Market Proxy are, in 11 cases, greater or equal to than 0.5. They are always smaller than 0.3 with the Goldman Sachs commodity index and than 0.5 with bond indices. Amin and Kat (2003a), among others, report a weak correlation between hedge funds and other securities. Hence, the addition of hedge funds to a traditional portfolio should improve its risk/return trade-off.

TABLE 16.2 Correlation between Van U.S. Hedge Funds Indices and Passive Strategies, 1995 to 2003

Panel A: Correlation between Van Hedge Fund Indices

	MNGI	DSI	MNAI	SSI	LSEGI	AGI	MNSH	OI	VI	DTGI	MI	MTI	FI	SSGI	EMI	II	MSI	SHSI
MNGI	1																	
DSI	0.70	1																
MNAI	0.81	0.50	1															
SSI	0.95	0.60	0.63	1														
LSEGI	0.85	0.57	0.64	0.87	1													
AGI	0.79	0.46	0.60	0.83	0.96	1												
MNSH	0.64	0.38	0.53	0.62	0.59	0.56	1											
OI	0.83	0.57	0.58	0.87	0.95	0.90	0.62	1										
VI	0.80	0.58	0.63	0.81	0.95	0.87	0.46	0.84	1									
DTGI	0.36	0.13	0.51	0.26	0.31	0.32	0.34	0.33	0.24	1								
MI	0.51	0.33	0.55	0.44	0.49	0.45	0.37	0.48	0.46	0.61	1							
MTI	0.63	0.32	0.54	0.64	0.77	0.79	0.52	0.76	0.68	0.55	0.42	1						
FI	−0.03	−0.11	0.19	−0.13	−0.15	−0.13	0.04	−0.12	−0.18	0.83	0.20	0.09	1					
SSGI	0.23	0.26	0.23	0.16	0.12	0.00	0.10	0.11	0.23	0.05	0.22	0.01	−0.03	1				
EMI	0.68	0.59	0.56	0.64	0.69	0.60	0.42	0.68	0.71	0.27	0.49	0.51	−0.08	0.58	1			
II	0.58	0.41	0.46	0.54	0.46	0.40	0.35	0.40	0.51	0.21	0.20	0.33	0.05	0.46	0.51	1		
MSI	0.68	0.41	0.49	0.74	0.82	0.79	0.38	0.73	0.82	0.13	0.37	0.58	−0.24	0.30	0.59	0.43	1	
SHSI	−0.71	−0.45	−0.50	−0.76	−0.86	−0.88	−0.42	−0.78	−0.82	−0.19	−0.31	−0.68	0.19	0.06	−0.64	−0.44	−0.7405	1

MNGI: Market Neutral Group Index
DSI: Distressed Securities Index
MNAI: Market Neutral Arbitrage Index
SSI: Special Situations Index
LSEGI: Long/Short Equity Group Index
AGI: Aggressive Growth Index
MNSH: Market Neutral Securities Hedging
OI: Opportunistic Index
VI: Value Index
DTGI: Directional Trading Group Index

MI: Macro Index
MTI: Market Timing Index
FI: Futures Index
SSGI: Specialty Strategies Group Index
EMI: Emerging Markets Index
II: Income Index
MSI: Multistrategy Index
SHSI: Short Selling Index

TABLE 16.2 *(continued)*

Panel B: Correlation Between Van U.S. Hedge Fund Indices and Passive Strategies

	S&P 500	Russell 3000	Market Proxy	SMB	HML	MSCI World excluding U.S.	Goldman Sachs Commodity	Lehman Bros Govt	Lehman Bros Corp BAA	Lehman Bros Aggregate
Market Neutral Group Index	0.51	0.58	0.64	0.54	-0.46	0.56	0.18	-0.10	0.22	-0.02
Distressed Securities Index	0.33	0.38	0.43	0.50	-0.14	0.34	0.05	-0.11	0.24	-0.02
Market Neutral Arbitrage Index	0.44	0.47	0.50	0.32	-0.33	0.46	0.13	0.01	0.25	0.07
Special Situations Index	0.54	0.62	0.67	0.55	-0.48	0.58	0.17	-0.15	0.17	-0.07
Long/Short Equity Group Index	0.68	0.75	0.81	0.59	-0.55	0.66	0.22	-0.16	0.14	-0.09
Aggressive Growth Index	0.65	0.72	0.78	0.54	-0.66	0.64	0.22	-0.16	0.11	-0.10
Market Neutral Sec. Hedging	0.16	0.22	0.28	0.37	-0.48	0.26	0.19	0.02	0.10	0.05
Opportunistic Index	0.54	0.62	0.68	0.58	-0.58	0.58	0.19	-0.13	0.12	-0.07
Value Index	0.73	0.80	0.84	0.57	-0.38	0.67	0.19	-0.18	0.18	-0.09
Directional Trading Group Index	0.16	0.17	0.20	0.12	-0.26	0.23	0.29	0.36	0.34	0.36
Macro Index	0.32	0.34	0.38	0.29	-0.28	0.37	0.24	0.04	0.21	0.08
Market Timing Index	0.56	0.60	0.65	0.32	-0.57	0.55	0.15	0.07	0.19	0.10
Futures Index	-0.17	-0.18	-0.18	-0.12	0.04	-0.10	0.22	0.45	0.30	0.41
Specialty Strategies Group Index	0.19	0.18	0.17	0.03	0.28	0.21	0.05	-0.08	0.13	-0.01
Emerging Markets Index	0.52	0.56	0.61	0.48	-0.29	0.58	0.09	-0.20	0.12	-0.11
Income Index	0.37	0.41	0.44	0.30	-0.16	0.43	0.14	0.14	0.39	0.22
Multi Strategy Index	0.73	0.78	0.80	0.37	-0.31	0.67	0.16	-0.27	0.11	-0.17
Short Selling Index	-0.69	-0.76	-0.80	-0.49	0.61	-0.67	-0.16	0.19	-0.07	0.13

TABLE 16.2 *(continued)*

Panel C: Correlation Between Passive Strategies

	S&P 500	Russell 3000	Market Proxy	SMB	HML	MSCI World excluding U.S.	Goldman Sachs Commodity	Lehman Bros Govt	Lehman Bros Corp BAA	Lehman Bros Aggregate
S&P 500	1	0.99	0.97	0.02	-0.18	0.79	0.03	-0.14	0.19	-0.03
Russell 3000	0.99	1	0.99	0.12	-0.23	0.80	0.06	-0.17	0.19	-0.06
Market Proxy	0.97	0.99	1	0.21	-0.31	0.81	0.08	-0.17	0.20	-0.06
Small Minus Big	0.02	0.12	0.21	1	-0.38	0.21	0.16	-0.21	0.01	-0.18
High Minus Low	-0.18	-0.23	-0.31	-0.38	1	-0.25	-0.18	0.02	0.03	0.03
MSCI World excluding U.S.	0.79	0.80	0.81	0.21	-0.25	1	0.12	-0.22	0.11	-0.14
Goldman Sachs Commodity	0.03	0.06	0.08	0.16	-0.18	0.12	1	0.08	0.09	0.06
Lehman Bros Government	-0.14	-0.17	-0.17	-0.21	0.02	-0.22	0.08	1	0.78	0.98
Lehman Bros Corp BAA	0.19	0.19	0.20	0.01	0.03	0.11	0.09	0.78	1	0.86
Lehman Bros Aggregate	-0.03	-0.06	-0.06	-0.18	0.03	-0.14	0.06	0.98	0.86	1

Panel C displays correlations among passive strategies. All coefficients between equity market indices are higher than 0.75. Thus, the choice of a market index should not alter the results of this study.

Hedge Fund Performance

Here we attempt to determine whether hedge funds outperformed the market during the 1995 to 2003 period.

Performance Measurement Using the CAPM   The first performance model used is the CAPM-based single index model. Table 16.3 reports the results for the whole sample for the 1994 to 2003 period. We estimate each fund index individually using the calendar-time approach. Thus, funds are formed into portfolios by event date. A portfolio standard deviation is estimated from the time series of portfolio abnormal returns in the estimation period and used to standardize the portfolio return.

Starting from 1994, all hedge fund indices outperform the market. In all cases, the alphas are significant. Moreover, only two funds have negative five years of the portfolio's construction. After 96 months, the cumulative abnormal return for the sample is 61.17 percent, with a bootstrapped skewness-corrected t-statistic of 4.58, which corresponds to an abnormal return of 0.63 percent per month.

For a robustness check, we use the CAPM with Ibbotson's (1975) RATS procedure that allows the estimate of beta to vary during the returns window (panel B of Table 16.3). For each calendar month in the period 1995 to 2003, we confirm the outperformance of hedge funds portfolio. For example, after 12 and 96 months of VAN portfolio's formation, the cumulative abnormal performance is 18.61 percent, with a t-statistic of 9.50, and 106.58 percent, with a t-statistic of 13.99, respectively. These translate to abnormal returns of 1.55 and 1.11 percent per month, respectively.

For the robustness of the results, we also perform an additional test in the context of the calendar-time approach. We estimate abnormal performance using the GARCH extension. Panel C of Table 16.3 reports the result with the CAPM using GARCH extension. It shows that the long-run performance of the hedge funds portfolio is again significantly positive. For a period of 96 months, the cumulative abnormal return for the sample is 60.64 percent with a bootstrapped skewness-corrected t-statistic of 4.47, which corresponds to an abnormal return of 0.63 percent per month.

Performance Using the Fama and French Three-Factor Model   In panel A of Table 16.4, we report the results for Fama and French (1993) three-factor model applied to hedge funds indices. The table reveals the premium on the

TABLE 16.3 Performance Measurement Using the CAPM on Van U.S. Hedge Fund Indices, 1995 to 2003

	Panel A: Performance Measurement Using the CAPM			
Calendar Month	Mean Abnormal Return (%)	Positive: Negative	Cross-sectional *t*-statistic	Bootstrapped Skewness Corrected *t*-statistic
12	5.69	13:5	2.40	2.42
24	12.92	15:3	3.29	3.55
36	16.96	14:4	2.81	2.51
48	14.83	13:5	1.55	1.33
60	31.75	14:4	3.22	2.48
72	43.79	16:2	3.83	2.88
84	52.05	16:2	4.35	3.58
96	61.17	16:2	4.46	4.58

	Panel B: Performance Measurement Using the CAPM with Ibbotson (1975) RATS Procedure			
Calendar Month	Mean Abnormal Return (%)	Positive: Negative	Cross-sectional *t*-statistic	Bootstrapped Skewness Corrected *t*-statistic
12	18.61	13:5	9.50	—
24	35.52	15:3	11.60	—
36	49.39	14:4	13.74	—
48	58.19	13:5	11.25	—
60	82.71	14:4	14.19	—
72	96.47	16:2	13.74	—
84	102.22	16:2	13.90	—
96	106.58	16:2	13.99	

	Panel C: Performance Measurement Using the CAPM with GARCH Estimation			
Calendar Month	Mean Abnormal Return (%)	Positive: Negative	Cross-sectional *t*-statistic	Bootstrapped Skewness Corrected *t*-statistic
12	5.62	13:5	2.37	2.37
24	12.80	15:3	3.25	3.47
36	16.77	14:4	2.77	2.44
48	14.58	13:5	1.52	1.29
60	31.44	14:4	3.17	2.42
72	43.41	16:2	3.78	2.82
84	51.59	16:2	4.28	3.47
96	60.64	16:2	4.39	4.47

SMB factor is significantly positive. It seems that all hedge funds managers prefer smaller stock. However, the HML factor does not prove to be a strong indicator of hedge fund behavior. On average, we find an alpha of 0.61 percent per month, which is statistically significant at the 1 percent level. Again, we confirm that the hedge funds strategies can outperform the market.

Panel B of Table 16.4 reports the result of Fama and French (1993) three-factor model applied to hedge funds indices using RATS procedure. Results confirm that hedge funds indices can outperform the market. For example, after 96 months of Van Hedge portfolio formation, the cumulative abnormal performance is 60.64 percent, with a t-statistic of 13.99. This translates to an abnormal return of 0.63 percent per month, a result that matches that obtained using the calendar-time approach with the Fama and

TABLE 16.4 Performance Measurement Using the Fama and French (1993) Three-Factor Model on Van U.S. Hedge Fund Indices, 1995 to 2003

Panel A: Fama and French (1993) Three-Factor Model (Period of estimation: 96 months)			
	Coefficient	t-statistic	Heteroskedasticity consistent t-statistic
Intercept (abnormal Return)	0.0061	5.85	6.11
$R_{Mt} - R_{ft}$	0.2208	8.49	9.08
SMB	0.1728	6.62	7.30
HML	0.0353	1.03	1.12
R^2	0.66		

Panel B: Fama and French (1993) Three-Factor Model with Ibbotson (1975) RATS Procedure			
Calendar Month	Mean Abnormal Return (%)	Positive: Negative	t-statistic
12	13.14	13:5	6.70
24	24.95	15:3	8.15
36	33.71	14:4	9.37
48	37.84	13:5	7.32
60	57.71	14:4	9.90
72	65.61	16:2	9.34
84	67.97	16:2	9.24
96	70.75	16:2	9.29

French three-factor model. Overall, even if other factors are needed, it seems that the Fama and French model does a good job in describing hedge fund behavior, as evidenced by the R^2 of 0.66. Our results are in line with those of Capocci and Hübner (2004). Using hedge funds rather than hedge fund indices, they find that the increase in terms of R^2_{adj} from the CAPM to the four-factor model of Carhart (1997), an extension of the Fama and French factor model with the momentum effect, is 10 percent, and from Carhart's model to a combined model, an extension of Carhart's four-factor model, of the international model of Fama and French (1998), and of the model used by Agarwal and Naik (2004), is another 7 percent. This extended model contains the zero-investment strategies representing size and value, international value, a momentum factor, a default factor, a factor for non-U.S. equities investing funds, three factors to account for hedge funds investing in U.S. and foreign bond indices, and, finally, a commodity factor.

Comparison with Other Studies Brown, Goetzmann, and Ibbotson (1999) analyze the performance of 399 offshore hedge funds for the period 1989 to 1995. They conclude that hedge funds for this period have been able to outperform the S&P 500 index in terms of higher Sharpe ratios and positive alphas. Edwards and Caglayan (2001b) estimate a multifactor model for eight different strategy classifications for a total sample of 836 hedge funds for the period 1990 to 1998. They find that 25 percent of the funds have yielded significantly positive alphas. A similar conclusion is reached by Capocci and Hübner (2004) in their analysis of the performance of 2,796 hedge funds. Using a combined multifactor model comprising 11 different factors, they find that approximately 25 percent of the funds have obtained significantly positive alphas for the 1994 to 2000 period.

CONCLUSION

In this chapter we reexamined the performance of hedge funds over the 1995 to 2003 period. We assessed abnormal performance using a number of alternative benchmarks and an approach originally used in event studies. More specifically, the benchmarks employed allowed for the standard CAPM, the GARCH extension, the Fama-French three-factor model, and the modified Returns across Time and Securities procedure. In addition, we used the calendar-time approach as developed by Jaffe (1974) and Mandelker (1974). This approach has the added advantage that it provides a direct measure of the opportunities available to investors attempting to exploit any abnormal performance. We find that, in line with Capocci and Hübner (2004), hedge fund strategies can outperform the market. We also find that hedge fund managers seem to prefer smaller stocks.

As noted by several academics, research into hedge funds is in its infancy. Hedge funds address new challenges to financial theory, and much remains to be done to identify hedge fund performance drivers. For example, it would be interesting to reexamine the issue of performance in a calendar-time framework using hedge funds across different strategies rather than hedge fund indices.

CHAPTER 17

Investing in Hedge Funds

Risks, Returns, and Performance Measurement

Francis C. C. Koh, Winston T. H. Koh, David K. C. Lee, and Kok Fai Phoon

Hedge funds are collective investment vehicles that are often established with a special legal status that allows their investment managers a free hand to use derivatives, short sell, and exploit leverage to raise returns and cushion risk. We review various issues relating to the investment in hedge funds, which have become popular with high-net-worth individuals and institutional investors, and discuss their empirical risk and return profiles. Concerns regarding the empirical measurements are highlighted, and meaningful analytical methods to provide greater risk transparency in performance reporting are proposed. We also discuss the development of the hedge fund industry in Asia.

INTRODUCTION

In 1990 the entire hedge fund industry was estimated at about U.S. $20 billion. As of 2004, there are close to 7,000 hedge funds worldwide, managing more than $830 billion. Additionally, about $200 to $300 billion is estimated to be held in privately managed accounts. While high-net-worth individuals remain the main source of capital, hedge funds are becoming more popular among institutional and retail investors. Funds of hedge funds and other hedge fund–linked products are increasingly being marketed to the retail market.

While hedge funds are well established in the United States and Europe, they have only begun to grow aggressively in Asia. According to *AsiaHedge* magazine, there are more than 300 hedge funds operating in Asia (including those in Japan and Australia), of which 30 were established during 2000 and 20 during 2001. In 2003, 90 new hedge funds were started in Asia, compared with 66 in 2002, according to an estimate by the Bank of Bermuda. Currently estimated at more than $15 billion, hedge fund investments in Asia are expected to grow rapidly. Several factors support this view. Asian hedge funds currently account for a tiny slice of the global hedge fund pie and a mere trickle of the total financial wealth of high-net-worth individuals in Asia.

Hedge funds have posted attractive returns. From 1987 to 2001 the Hennessee Hedge Fund Index posted annualized returns of 18 percent, higher than the Standard & Poor's 13.5 percent. Hedge funds are seen as a natural hedge for controlling downside risk because they employ exotic investment strategies that generate returns uncorrelated to traditional asset classes. Hedge funds vary in their strategies. Macro funds, such as the Quantum Fund, generally take a directional view by betting on a particular bond market, say, or a currency movement. Other funds specialize in corporate events, such as mergers or bankruptcies, or identify pricing anomalies in stock markets. Hedge funds vary widely in both their investment strategies and the amount of financial leverage.

There are a number of factors behind the meteoric rise in demand for hedge funds. The unprecedented bull run in the U.S. equity markets during the 1990s expanded investment portfolios. This led to an increased awareness on the need for diversification. The bursting of the technology and Internet bubbles, the string of corporate scandals that hit corporate America, and the uncertainties in the U.S. economy have led to a general decline in stock markets worldwide. This in turn provided fresh impetus for hedge funds from investors searching for absolute returns.

Since the early 1990s, there has been a growing interest in the use of hedge funds among both institutional and high-net-worth individuals. Due to their private nature, it is difficult to obtain adequate information about the operations of individual hedge funds and reliable summary statistics about the industry as a whole.

Hedge funds are known to be growing in size and diversity. At the end of 1997, the Managed Account Reports (MAR)/Hedge database recorded more than 700 hedge fund managing assets of $90 billion (see Table 17.1).

This is only a partial picture of the industry, as many funds are not listed with MAR/Hedge. In practical terms, it is not easy to estimate the current size of the hedge fund industry unless all funds are regulated or obligated to register their operations with a common authority. Brooks and Kat (2002) estimated that, as of April 2001, there were approximately 6,000 hedge funds in existence, with an estimated $400 billion in capital under management and $1 trillion in total assets.

Three interesting features differentiate hedge funds from other forms of managed funds. Most hedge funds are small and organized around a few experienced investment professionals. In fact, more than half of U.S hedge funds manage amounts of less than $25 million. Further, most hedge funds are leveraged. It is estimated that 70 percent of hedge funds use leverage and about 18 percent borrowed more than one dollar for every dollar of capital (Eichengreen and Mathieson 1998). Another peculiar feature is the short life span of hedge funds. Hedge funds have an average life span of about 3.5 years (Lavinio 2000). Very few have a track record of more than 10 years. These features lead many to view hedge funds as risky and opportunistic.

TABLE 17.1 Descriptive Statistics of Hedge Fund Returns, by MAR Classification, 1990 to 1997

			1990–1997		
Category	Number	Assets (U.S.$ billion)	Mean Return (%)	Standard Deviation (%)	Risk-adjusted Returns
Event-driven	120	8.6	18.9	5.9	3.2
Global	334	30.9	17.7	9.4	1.9
Global Macro	61	29.8	28.1	16.3	1.7
Market Neutral	201	18.0	8.6	2.1	4.1
Sector	40	1.8	29.6	15.9	1.9
Short Sellers	12	0.5	7.0	15.2	0.5
Long Only	15	0.4	27.3	15.4	1.8

Source: Eichengreen and Mathieson (1998, p. 37).
The mean returns are annually compounded returns over the period 1990 to 1997, except for the long-only funds, which were computed from 1994 to 1997. The annualized standard deviations were computed from the standard deviation of monthly returns for each investment style.

WHAT ARE HEDGE FUNDS?

Hedge funds are innovative investment structures that were first created more than 50 years ago by Alfred Winslow Jones. Jones:

- Created hedges by investing in securities that he determined to be undervalued and funding these positions partly by taking short positions in overvalued securities, creating a market neutral position.
- Designed an incentive-fee compensation arrangement in which he was paid a percentage of the profits realized from his clients' assets.
- Invested his own capital in the fund, ensuring that his incentives and those of his investors were aligned and forming an investment partnership.

Most modern hedge funds possess these features, and are set up as limited partnerships with a lucrative incentive-fee structure. In most hedge funds, managers also often have a significant portion of their own capital invested in the partnerships. The term "hedge fund" has been generalized to describe investment strategies that range from the original market-neutral style of Jones to many other strategies and opportunistic situations, including global/macro investing.

Due to the large variety of hedge fund investing strategies, there is no standard method to classify hedge funds. There are at least eight major databases set up by data vendors and fund advisors. We follow the classification used by Eichengreen and Mathieson (1998), which relied on the MAR/Hedge database. Under this classification, there are eight categories of hedge funds with seven differentiated styles and a fund-of-funds category:

1. **Event-driven funds.** These funds take positions on corporate events, such as taking an arbitraged position when companies are undergoing restructuring or mergers. For example, hedge funds would purchase bank debt or high-yield corporate bonds of companies undergoing reorganization (often referred to as distressed securities). Another event-driven strategy is merger arbitrage. These funds seize the opportunity to invest just after a takeover has been announced. They purchase the shares of the target companies and short the shares of the acquiring companies.
2. **Global funds.** This is a catch-all category of funds that invest in non-U.S. stocks and bonds with no specific strategy reference. This category has the largest number of hedge funds. It includes funds that specialize in emerging markets.
3. **Global/macro funds.** These funds rely on macroeconomic analysis to take bets on major risk factors, such as currencies, interest rates, stock indices, and commodities.

4. **Market-neutral funds.** Such funds bet on relative price movements by utilizing strategies such as long-short equity, stock index arbitrage, convertible bond arbitrage, and fixed income arbitrage. Long-short equity funds use the strategy of Jones by taking long positions in selected stocks and going short on other stocks to limit their exposure to the stock market. Stock index arbitrage funds trade on the spread between index futures contracts and the underlying basket of equities. Convertible bond arbitrage funds typically capitalize on the embedded option in these bonds by purchasing them and shorting the equities. Fixed income arbitrage funds bet on the convergence of prices of bonds from the same issuer but with different maturities over time. Market-neutral is the second largest grouping of hedge funds after the global category.
5. **Sector funds.** These funds concentrate on selective sectors of the economy. For example, they may focus on technology stocks and rotate across to other sectors if stocks are overpriced.
6. **Short sellers.** These funds focus on engineering short positions in stocks with or without matching long positions. They play on markets that have risen too fast and on mean reversion strategies.
7. **Long-only funds.** Such funds take long equity positions typically with leverage. Emerging market funds that do not have short-selling opportunities also fall under this category.
8. **Funds of funds.** This term refers to funds that invest in a pool of hedge funds. They specialize in identifying fund managers with good performance and rely on their business relationship in the industry relationships to gain entry into hedge funds with good track records.

Table 17.1 presents statistics on the various categories of hedge funds in the MAR database over the 1990 to 1997 period. The sectoral hedge funds provided the best mean return over the period studied, while the market-neutral funds had the lowest standard deviation of returns. On a risk-adjusted basis (dividing the mean return by the standard deviation), the category of fund that ranks highest is the market-neutral funds followed by event-driven funds.

Unlike registered investment companies, hedge funds are not required to publicly disclose performance and holdings information that might be construed as solicitation materials. This makes it more difficult for investors to evaluate hedge fund managers.

Funds of Hedge Funds

Fund of hedge fund managers are hedge funds established to hold shares in other investment companies and charge a fee for doing so. Like hedge funds, funds of hedge funds are limited partnerships, and are restricted to at most

99 investors with at least 49 accredited investors. Funds of hedge funds do not make direct investments but allocate their capital to individual hedge funds.

A hedge fund charges a management fee and incentive fee; a fund of hedge funds not only charges fees at the fund-of-fund (FoF) level, but also passes on individual hedge fund fees in the form of after-fee returns to the FoF investors. In fact, underlying hedge fund fees will be transferred to the FoF investors regardless of whether the FoF makes a profit. As a result, total fees from an FoF can exceed the total realized return on the fund.

Fund of hedge funds have grown in popularity over the last decade because of their specialized investment strategies and objectives. At present, fund of hedge funds managed around 20 to 25 percent of this amount. At March 2000, the Trading Advisors Selection System (TASS)/Tremont hedge fund database contained 2,104 hedge funds, including 1,330 survived funds and 774 dissolved funds. The total assets under management totaled about $198 billion. According to TASS, 328 funds are classified as fund of hedge funds, compared with 1,442 regular hedge funds. According to the Zurich Capital Markets database, funds of hedge funds represent 23 percent (in terms of assets) of the hedge fund universe as of December 31, 2001. Between January 1990 and October 2003, the data set provided by TASS consisted of 4,241 funds that reported monthly return information, of which 2,796 were regular hedge funds (1,621 live funds and 1,175 dead funds), 838 were funds of hedge funds, and 484 were managed futures funds. Acito and Fisher (2002) estimated that funds of hedge funds managed in excess of $100 billion to $120 billion in capital worldwide.

INVESTING IN HEDGE FUNDS

It is commonly believed that hedge funds have superior returns. There are many anecdotal stories about the stunning success of hedge fund managers and their skills. George Soros's Quantum Fund was reported to have obtained returns in excess of 30 percent per annum over a long period. From Table 17.1, there is also evidence that hedge funds, as a group, have returns that are impressive. For example, over the period 1990 to 1997, all the hedge funds had positive absolute returns. Global macro funds obtained mean returns of 28.1 percent per annum with a standard deviation that is comparable to equity funds.

Traditional asset allocation optimizes the use of equities, bonds, real estate, and private equity to invest in a portfolio that maximizes returns and minimizes the portfolio risk. Thus, hedge funds become a natural candidate for enhancing returns in an investment portfolio. Moreover, in a bear market, many investment managers are not satisfied with merely beating the market index, which may have negative returns. They generally prefer to go

TABLE 17.2 Performance Measures for Hedge Fund Indices (from January 1990 to April 2000)

	Annualized Return (%)	Annualized Standard Deviation (%)	Correlation with S&P 500	Correlation with Lehman Brothers Government Corporate Bond Index
EACM 1001[a]	15.2	4.4	0.37	0.19
Equity-Market Neutral	9.1	3.2	−0.11	0.15
Equity Hedged	20.6	10.3	0.20	0.00
Event Driven	13.7	5.4	0.48	0.09
Global International	20.8	11.5	0.61	0.15

Source: Lehman Brothers (2000).
[a]The EACM 100 is an index of hedge funds representing a wide range of strategies.

short (or avoid long positions) to have positive returns. Investing in appropriately chosen hedge funds may provide the possibility of obtaining positive absolute returns.

It is also generally believed that hedge funds have returns that are generally uncorrelated with traditional asset classes. In fact, hedge funds may even have a lower risk profile. For example, Anjilvel, Boudreau, Johmann, Peskin, and Urias (2001) reported that hedge funds exhibit a low correlation with traditional asset classes. They suggest that hedge funds should play an important role in strategic asset allocation.

Table 17.2 shows a common presentation of the underlying relationships between hedge funds and the other assets.

Why Invest in a Fund of Hedge Funds?

Using the TASS database, Brown, Goetzmann, and Liang (2004) found that a fund of hedge funds reduces the standard deviation of monthly hedge fund returns by one-third and significantly reduce the value at risk (VaR) of hedge fund investment. Hence, funds of hedge funds can also provide significant diversification potential. A well-diversified fund of hedge funds manager can therefore take advantage of market-specific risks while maintaining low correlations to stock, bond, and currency markets. As a result, the manager can theoretically provide superior returns and generate alpha (reflecting managerial skills). More generally, since funds of hedge funds deliver more consistent returns with lower volatility than individual hedge funds, they are considered to be ideal for diversifying traditional portfolios.

During the 1993 to 2001 period, fund of hedge funds outperformed the S&P 500 index on a risk-adjusted basis (Gregoriou 2003c).

More generally, fund of hedge funds managers are able to add value through manager selection, portfolio construction, and regular monitoring of the portfolio. They provide professional management services and access to information that would be difficult or expensive to obtain on a fund-by-fund basis by the investor. These managers often employ multiple investment strategies and styles through a diversified portfolio of individual fund managers.

Investing in fund of hedge funds is not cheap. The cost of investing in a well-known and established fund of hedge funds can be higher than the cost of building, monitoring, and maintaining a proprietary portfolio of hedge funds. Thus, while it is true that the fund of hedge funds structure allows for diversification and hence reduction of risk at the fund level, this comes at a cost, since the more diversified the fund is, the greater the likelihood that the investor will incur an incentive fee on one or more of the constituent managers, regardless the overall performance of the fund of hedge funds. In fact, sometimes the incentive fee for a fund of hedge fund is so large that it absorbs all of the annual fund return.

COMMERCIAL DATABASES AND STATISTICAL INFERENCES

There are very persuasive reasons for hedge funds to be considered as alternative investments. However, statistics compiled from public databases are fraught with data biases. Uninformed investors may be misled into common misperceptions about the return and risk of hedge funds. Here we discuss some of the issues that must be dealt with when analyzing hedge funds. There are three main issues: data collation, selection bias, and survivorship bias.

Data Collation Issues

Hedge funds do not generally disclose their investment activities to the public, since they are organized as private limited partnerships and often as offshore investment vehicles. This has resulted in frequent complaints about the lack of transparency in the industry. Fortunately, to attract new investors, many funds release selective information to publicize themselves and their performance. Hedge fund data are collected by a small number of data vendors and fund advisors. A few large advisors and vendors are currently publishing performance data and indices that correspond to the various investment strategies employed by hedge funds. A listing of hedge funds databases and descriptive details is provided in Appendix 17.1.

Voluntary participation in performance reporting, however, leads to incompleteness of information regarding the hedge fund universe as a whole. Thus, sampling biases are present whenever an investor analyses a hedge fund database on a stand-alone basis. Some of theses biases are briefly discussed next.

Selection Bias

Database vendors impose their own criteria before a hedge fund may enter their databases. The criteria include the type of fund involved, its track record, and assets under management. Databases may also exclude hedge funds whose trading activities or instruments do not meet their criteria. Again, the result is a likely upward bias in the database. Park (1995) analyzes a subset of selection bias termed "instant history bias." This bias arises because when a new fund is first included, database managers often "back-fill" its performance history. Up to one year or more of data may be added to the database.

Survivorship Bias

Funds that perform poorly often choose not to submit their performance. Thus, poorly performing funds are likely to be missing from a database. Therefore, a survivorship bias arises when a database includes only the performance of funds that are alive and present at the end of the sample period. A subset of survivorship bias, called liquidation bias, occurs when disappearing funds may not report final periods leading up to and including their liquidation. If funds cease operation due to poor performance, the historical returns of surviving funds in the database is biased upward with risk biased downward relative to the population of hedge funds.

Database vendors often delist funds that do not provide reliable information. Hedge funds may also exit a database for other reasons than poor performance. Some popular funds also stop reporting their performance when they have reached a desired size and do not need to further solicit new money. Omissions of these funds also introduces a bias.

Brooks and Kat (2002) find that around 30 percent of newly established funds do not survive the first three years, primarily due to poor performance. Thus, not including defunct funds is likely to lead to overestimation of returns. Fung and Hsieh (2001) found that estimates of survivorship biases differed across two commonly used databases, Hedge Fund Research (HFR) and TASS. The survivorship bias (and attrition rate) was much higher in TASS than that in HFR. They estimated that survivorship bias would over-report hedge fund mean returns by about 1.5 to to 3 percent per annum.

Collation and statistical biases not only present problems in the measurement of returns and risk across different categories of hedge funds.

These biases also affect the computation of hedge fund indices. Brooks and Kat (2002) showed that different databases have different sample statistics for similar categories of funds. Table 17.3 shows that the mean return for macro hedge funds computed by the various databases ranges from 10.2 to 17.2 percent. Yet this is a statistic for a common class of hedge funds over

TABLE 17.3 Hedge Fund Indices from Different Databases Mean and Standard Deviation of Returns from January 1995 to April 2001

Category/Database	Mean (%)	Standard Deviation (%)
Risk Arbitrage	**14.1**	
Zurich	13.2	12.8
Hennesse	13.0	11.8
Tuna	14.9	12.4
Altvest	15.6	13.4
HFR	13.6	12.7
Macro	**13.3**	
Zurich	10.2	19.3
Hennesse	10.4	30.6
HFR	13.2	28.1
CSFB/Tremont	17.2	50.2
Tuna	15.6	33.8
Altvest	17.0	32.6
Van	9.4	41.8
Equity-Market Neutral	**12.8**	
Zurich	11.9	6.5
Hennesse	8.5	10.4
HFR	10.9	13.3
CSFB/Tremont	13.7	10.8
Tuna	15.2	19.2
HFR	16.8	17.2
Market Indices		
S&P 500	18.6	54.4
DJIA	18.1	54.7
Russell 2000	13.7	69.1
Nasdaq	21.6	106.9
Lehman Government Bond	7.4	10.3

Source: Brooks and Kat (2002).
The major databases are explained in Appendix 17.1. Zurich Capital Markets computes the indices using the MAR/Hedge database that it acquired in March 2001. Simple average of returns estimated using the different databases.

the same time period. More interestingly, the standard deviation ranges from 19.3 to 50.2 percent. This is compelling evidence for investors to be wary about obtaining statistics from hedge fund databases.

PERFORMANCE MEASUREMENTS OF HEDGE FUNDS

Most mutual funds are generally engaged in buy-and-hold activities—acquiring and holding stocks and bonds over a longer period of time. Although some mutual funds engage in activities such as leverage or short sell, most do not. The organization structure of hedge funds, their investment objectives, trading strategies, and managerial compensation differentiate them significantly from mutual funds.

Mean, Variance, Skewness, and Kurtosis

There is strong evidence that hedge fund returns and hedge fund indices returns are not normally distributed due to the type of strategies employed by hedge fund managers. Typically, hedge fund investments are based on absolute return strategies. They are expected to deliver good performance regardless of market conditions. Hedge fund managers use two main approaches to achieve absolute return targets, directional (or market timing), and nondirectional approaches.

The directional approach bets on the expected directions of markets. Funds will invest long or sell short securities to capture gains from their advance and decline. In contrast, the nondirectional approach attempts to extract value from a set of embedded arbitrage opportunities within and across securities. The nondirectional approach typically exploits structural anomalies in the financial market.

Mean-variance analysis is appropriate when returns are normally distributed or investors' preferences are quadratic. The reliability of mean-variance analysis therefore depends on the degree of nonnormality of the returns data and the nature of the (nonquadratic) utility function. While the utility function may not be a serious problem, the nonnormal distribution of returns presents an issue.

Fung and Hsieh (1999a) state that when returns are not normally distributed the mean and standard deviation are not sufficient to properly describe the returns distribution. They found that hedge fund returns are leptokurtic or fat-tailed. One likely explanation is that net returns include spreads that are distributed with fat tails.

Many hedge fund indices exhibit relatively low skewness and high kurtosis, especially in the case of funds investing in convertible arbitrage, risk arbitrage, and distressed securities. Brooks and Kat (2002) found that hedge fund index returns are not normally distributed. They argued that while hedge funds may offer relatively high means and low variances, these funds give investors third- and fourth-moment attributes that are exactly the opposite of those that are desirable. Investors obtain a higher mean and a lower variance at the expense of more negative skewness and higher kurtosis.

In sum, the dynamic trading strategies of hedge funds render traditional mean-variance measures meaningless. While some hedge funds may have a low standard deviation, this does not mean they are relatively riskless. They may in fact harbor skewness and kurtosis, which make them risky.

Correlations of Returns

Fung and Hsieh (1997a) examined the returns of hedge funds and commodity trading advisors (CTAs). They found that hedge fund managers and CTAs generate returns that have low correlations to the returns of mutual funds and standard asset classes. This is the benefit often cited by portfolio managers in their choice of hedge funds as an alternative investment. Having an additional asset with a low or negative correlation permits the diversification of risk in a means-variance environment. However, complications arise in the case of hedge funds where correlation-based diversification may not be valid.

Fung and Hsieh (2001) argue that risk management in the presence of dynamic trading strategies is also more complex. Hedge fund managers have a great deal of freedom to generate returns that are uncorrelated with those of other asset classes. But this freedom comes at a price. Dynamic trading strategies predispose hedge funds to extreme or tail events. Thus, low correlations may come at a cost. They caution that hedge fund portfolios can become overly concentrated in a small number of markets so that market exposures can converge. This would lead to an implosion due to lack of diversification.

Lavinio (2000) argues that many hedge funds are not consistently and continuously negatively or poorly correlated with other asset classes over time. Hedge funds also may not have meaningful standard deviations. In fact, many hedge funds have distributions with fat tails, so that normality assumptions on the distribution of hedge fund returns are generally not correct. This means it is not appropriate to use correlation as a gauge with which to diversify portfolios.

Lo (2001) reinforces this view, explaining that many investors participate in hedge funds to diversify their returns, as hedge fund returns seem uncorrelated with market indexes, such as the S&P 500. However, uncorrelated events can become synchronized in a crisis, with correlation changing from 0 to 1 overnight. These situations are examples of "phase-locking" behavior often encountered in the physical and natural sciences.

OTHER PERFORMANCE MEASURES FOR HEGDE FUNDS

The preceding discussion argues that the means and standard deviations used to report the returns and risks of hedge funds are not entirely adequate. Providing skewness and kurtosis statistics is helpful. Relying on simple correlation measures to diversify portfolio risks is not appropriate when deciding to add hedge funds to a portfolio of other assets.

Sortino and Price (1994) have proposed evaluating downside risk rather than total risk. They define a new measure, the Sortino ratio. This ratio differentiates between deviations on the upside and on the downside and is more consistent with investor concern about risk of losses in investments. The Sortino ratio is similar to the Sharpe ratio, except that it uses downside deviation instead of standard deviation in the denominator. The Sortino ratio also allows for the setting of a user-defined benchmark return. The numerator is the difference between the return on the portfolio and the minimum acceptable return (MAR). The MAR is usually the risk-free rate, zero, or specified by the analyst (e.g., 5 percent).

Earlier we highlighted that the high skewness of hedge fund returns may be connected to the hedge fund manager's selection of high reward and low variance opportunities. Lavinio (2000) has defined another measure to capture this (equation 17.1):

$$d\text{-ratio} = \text{Abs}\,(d/U) \tag{17.1}$$

where d = number of returns less than zero times their value
U = number of returns greater than zero times their value
Abs = absolute value

The d-ratio compares the value and frequency of a manager's winners to losers to capture the skewness in returns. This statistic, which does not require any assumption on the underlying distribution, may be used as a proxy for a fund's risk, with $d = 0$ representing a distribution with no downside and $d = $ infinity representing one in which the manager does not make any positive returns.

In analyzing the performance of hedge funds, we also need to gain insights into the permanence of a manager's skill. One way to examine if good performance is merely transitory is to see if it is mean-reverting (whether the performance will reverse and converge toward some predictable long-term value). We can capture this with the Hurst ratio,[1] which is defined as (equation 17.2):

$$\text{Hurst ratio} = \log M / (\log N - \log a) \tag{17.2}$$

where $M(t) = (\text{Max}(t) - \text{Min}(t)) / S(t)$
N = length of shorter subperiods into which a manager's return record has been subdivided
t = number of subperiods into which a manager's return record has been subdivided
$S(t)$ = standard deviation of data over subperiod t
a = constant term that is negligible if track record is five years or less

A Hurst ratio between 0 and 0.5 means that a manager's return will tend to fluctuate randomly, but converge to a stable value over time. With a Hurst ratio of about 0.5, a hedge fund manager's track performance will be regarded as random, so that returns in one period will not be affected by returns in another period. Such hedge funds are deemed to be risky because any stellar short-term gains may be accompanied by substantial losses in another time period.

A Hurst ratio between 0.5 and 1 describes returns that are persistent. These fund managers have "hot" hands. However, such a finding should be interpreted with care. The same managers should be able to maintain their Hurst ratio in future time periods that are beyond the chosen sampling periods. More rigorous testing is required with out-of-sample data to provide meaningful conclusions.

Although the Sortino and Hurst ratios could provide additional insights into the performance and risk of hedge fund investing, further work is needed before these analytical methods can be used to report on the risk and return performance of hedge funds.

PRACTICAL ISSUES IN PERFORMANCE MEASUREMENT

Hedge fund performance measures are beset by many practical business issues, which make it extremely difficult to have a simple measure to fully

---

[1]Lo (1991) applied the Hurst ratio to stock returns and found that short-range dependence adequately captured the time series behavior of stock returns.

describe risk and return. In the last section we discussed various data issues and how these may create problems for the comparison of hedge fund performance. However, even if one possesses a set of reliable data, it is unlikely that there exists a satisfactory measure of risk-adjusted return that would satisfy a sophisticated investor.

Specifically, hedge funds face many practical issues that increase their riskiness. We have identified at least six types of practical issues that confound risk and return measurements:

1. Style purity
2. Consistency
3. Fund size
4. Use of leverage
5. Liquidity
6. Asset concentration

Many hedge funds are assumed to have a pure and consistent style. This is rarely the case, however. Many funds may be opportunistic and operate with more than one style. Thus, many hedge funds do not always function exactly as their self-reported classifications indicate. From the outside looking in, it is almost impossible to classify hedge funds accurately.

A hedge fund's style purity over time is definitely less consistent when compared to unit trusts (and mutual funds), which by nature are buy-and-hold accounts. Fung and Hsieh (2002a) and others have suggested using factor analysis to discern the underlying dimensions or factors that drive the returns of hedge funds. This could possibly determine unique hedge fund strategies that differentiate one fund from another. This might enable an investor to detect style purity, style consistency, and, most important, style deviations.

Till (2001a,b) suggested that a number of hedge fund strategies might appear to earn their returns from assuming risk positions in a risk-averse financial world, and not from inefficiencies in the marketplace. In this sense, returns are made from a risk transfer and not due to managerial abilities. If this is indeed the case, then the skill of selecting the appropriate hedge fund styles and the type of managers who can execute the styles consistently, and of allocating funds across these managers, become important to achieve superior returns. Viewed from this standpoint, style purity and consistency are important attributes to measure exposure to hedge fund risks. These may be more appropriate measures than statistical measures such as variance and skewness.

A hedge fund's assets under management (AUM) growth may be internally generated through performance, externally induced because of inflows, or magnified through use of leverage. Hedge fund size has significant implications for risk and return. A hedge fund's risks increases proportionately with its AUM. This is because the use of specialized strategies naturally limits a hedge fund to some optimal size beyond which it becomes increasingly difficult to keep the same strategy or have the opportunities for execution (often with leverage). Because they understand the trade-offs between size and performance, hedge fund managers are inclined to close their funds for further investments as soon as a target size is reached.

Hedge fund managers are drawn to the use of leverage to magnify potential returns from small arbitrage opportunities. They are also inclined to concentrate their investible funds in a small subset of potentially rich opportunities. Weisman and Abernathy (2000) demonstrate the importance of guarding against excessive leverage, which is compounded by a lack of liquidity when a disastrous event strikes. They point out that if one were to construct a nondiversified, illiquid, and/or leveraged portfolio and let it grow over time, it would eventually lead to bankruptcy of the fund, if a misfortune strikes.

The potential risk in employing these strategies is very high since a well-constructed downside-oriented measure using past data may not reveal the potential risks from the occurrence of a future disastrous event. This is because a catastrophic event has not yet struck. These potential risks, which are usually unforeseen, are large and threaten the eventual survival of the fund.

ACCOUNTING FOR VARIOUS SOURCES OF RISK

The next example should help illustrate how hedge funds should be compared. Suppose there are two hedge funds with similar statistical attributes: the same average holding period returns adjusted by its standard deviation. We want to know which fund has a better risk-adjusted return. Let us further assume that the first fund is less leveraged than the second, invests in more liquid assets, is less concentrated and more diversified, and is more disciplined in its application of investment styles. We are most likely inclined to prefer the first fund over the second. That is because the second fund, although it has the same average return adjusted by its standard deviation, has taken extraneous risk to achieve the same results. This is more obvious if analyzed in the context of possible disastrous events. Depending on the strategy employed, it is generally correct to conclude that a nonleveraged, more liquid, more diversified, and more disciplined fund has a better chance of survival in the long term.

Perhaps the crucial issue has now become more obvious: How should risk-adjusted returns be modified to account for the many other forms of risk not captured statistically? We define risk-adjusted return as equation 17.3:

$$\frac{(\text{Observed Returns} - \text{Benchmark Returns})}{\text{Indicated Risk Measure}} \tag{17.3}$$

This measure assumes that all the named variables are observable, measurable, and reliable. The benchmark return may be a stock index, a peer measure, or the interest rate of the 90-day Treasury bill. The risk measure may be the tracking error, standard deviation, or some other measure. While this risk-adjusted measure allows us to measure the risk of hedge funds, another metric that can be used to account for the numerous risks faced by a hedge fund investor. We define in equation 17.4:

$$\text{Risk-Adjusted Return} = \frac{(\text{Observed Returns} - \text{Benchmark Returns})}{\text{Indicated Risk Measure}}$$
$$\times \text{Penalty Function} \tag{17.4}$$

We postulate that the penalty function is a discount factor that takes into account various dimensions, such as hedge fund style (purity and consistency), size, leverage, liquidity, and asset concentration. These dimensions penalize the statistically measured risk-adjusted returns of hedge funds. Table 17.4 itemizes the risk dimensions and suggests avenues to discount them in the penalty function.

Using a penalty function would provide a method to scale the observed return for the many practical risks assumed by the hedge fund manager. A properly constructed risk-adjusted return with penalty that has accounted for practical business risks is more meaningful to an investor than a return measure that is merely adjusted by the standard deviation. This latter measure cannot alert an investor to risks such as leverage or liquidity.

The data requirements are higher, however, since the leverage, liquidity, and concentration measures necessitate the supply of additional data by hedge fund managers. In turn, this calls for more disclosure and transparency from the managers.

ASIAN HEDGE FUNDS

The Asian hedge fund industry has been expanding rapidly. Being a relatively young market, fewer than 100 hedge funds have been in existence for more than two years. In fact, according to one estimate (Douglas 2004), only about 60 funds have been around for more than five years. Based on

TABLE 17.4 Discount to Risk-Adjusted Returns to Account for Various Types of Practical Risk

Sources of Risks	To Penalize for	Suggested Measurement Method	Predicted Discount to Returns
Style purity	Deviation from self-reported investment style	Deviation from style benchmark	The higher the style impurity, the higher the discount
Style consistency	Style inconsistency	Deviation from factors models	The higher the style inconsistency, the higher the discount
Asset growth	Unexpected increases in fund size (and assets under management)	Change in fund size	The higher the increase in fund size in the period under review, the higher the discount
Leverage	Excessive leverage	(a) Average gross exposure (b) Active use of leverage (computed from a comparison of returns with and without the use of leverage following the standards recommended by the Association for Investment Management and Research)	The higher the use of leverage, the higher the discount
Liquidity	Low asset liquidity	(a) Average days to complete sales (b) Ratio of position to trading volume	The higher the threat of illiquidity, the higher the discount
Asset concentration	(a) Single security exposure (b) Erratic returns	(a) Average percentage of 10 largest holding over reporting period (b) Fractal dimension or inverse of Hurst ratio	The higher the asset concentration, the higher the discount

data from two Asian fund databases, AsiaHedge and EurekaHedge, the number of funds that invest predominantly in Asia has risen dramatically, from approximately 75 in January of 1999 to approximately 290 in June 2003. This represents a 276 percent increase over roughly four years. Liang (2000), Agarwal and Naik (2000b), and Brown and Goetzmann (2003) have improved our understanding of the survivorship bias, persistence, and style issues with hedge funds in general. There are, however, other areas where our understanding of hedge fund performance can be further deepened. Table 17.5 presents the breakdown of Asian hedge funds by size of funds under management.

Almost 80 percent of Asian hedge funds employ either Goldman Sachs or Morgan Stanley as their prime broker. In all, 58 percent charge management fees of 1 to 1.5 percent and performance fees of 20 percent. Approximately 14 percent have a hurdle rate, but all face a high-water mark. Almost 70 percent are opened on a monthly basis for subscriptions and redemptions, and 28 percent require minimum investment of $1 million or higher.

Of the hedge funds included in the Asia Hedge Fund Directory or Eureka Hedge, 57 percent are domiciled in Cayman Islands; 15 percent are situated in the British Virgin Islands. The estimated geographical distribution of the Asia-Pacific hedge funds is shown in Table 17.6. Most of the decision makers of the funds are located in a number of Asian cities, with Australia, Singapore, and increasingly China being the preferred locations. Depending on their investment strategies, hedge fund managers may concentrate on one financial market or on the most liquid markets.

TABLE 17.5 Distribution of Asian-based Hedge Funds by Assets under Management

Asset Size (U.S.$m)	Number of Funds
Less than 10	70
10–50	112
50–100	43
100–200	51
200–500	40
500–1000	8
More than 1000	4
Total Number	328

Source: EurekaHedge, April 2003,
http://www.eurekahedge.com/news/archive_
2003.asp.

TABLE 17.6 Estimated Geographical Distribution of Asia-Pacific Hedge Fund Managers

Country	Distribution (%)
Australia	14
Hong Kong	19
Japan	9
Korea	1
Malaysia	2
Singapore	14
Thailand	1
United Kingdom	20
United States	20

Previous studies have tended to pool hedge funds with fund of hedge funds (Ackermann, McEnally, and Ravenscraft 1999; Liang 1999). Koh, Koh, and Teo (2003) analyzed the performance of Asian hedge funds from three angles:

1. The relationship between fund characteristics and fund returns
2. The drivers of the various Asian hedge funds investment styles
3. The persistence of hedge fund return over various time horizons

Koh, Koh, and Teo (2003) find that hedge funds managed by larger holding companies attain greater returns on average than funds managed by smaller holding companies. An increase in the size of the fund holding company to the next size category results in an economically significant 17 basis point increase in monthly returns (2 percent per annum) for the funds it manages. The use of both holding company size and fund size in regressions enables a separation of the effects of economies of scale from that of a diminishing investment opportunity set (Goetzmann, Ingersoll, and Ross 2003). This is because controlling for hedge fund size, an increase in holding company size does not require a fund to scale up its investment strategy. Hence, our finding that a fund benefits by belonging to a larger holding company is consistent with the view that economies of scale exist in the hedge fund industry.

Koh, Koh, and Teo (2003) also found no evidence to suggest that funds with higher management and performance fees reap greater postfee returns.

TABLE 17.7 Performance of Asian Hedge Funds

Strategy	Average Annualized Return (%)	Average Annualized Return (%)	Average Maximum Drawdown (%)
Convertible arbitrage	−0.23	4.57	−5.03
CTA	15.61	13.06	−6.46
Distressed debt	26.53	9.80	−2.00
Fixed income	13.82	2.65	−0.55
Long/short equities	3.40	9.65	−8.30
Macro	15.36	16.18	−10.37
Multistrategy	2.71	8.37	−8.12
Relative value	12.84	11.66	−4.93

Source: Asia and Japan Hedge Fund Directory, 2003, Eureka Hedge Pte Ltd.

This is consistent with results from the mutual fund literature that mutual funds on average do not make up for their expenses, and investors are better off investing in mutual funds with lower fees.

Hedge funds with longer redemption and lockup periods tend to perform better than hedge funds with shorter periods. An increase in redemption period of 10 days is associated with an 11 basis point increase in fund monthly postfee return (1.3 percent per annum). The reason for the differential performance is that longer redemption periods allow funds to close out of their positions in a more timely fashion and incur less transactions costs while doing so.

Koh, Koh, and Teo (2003) also found that Asian hedge fund returns persist at various horizons. This persistence is strongest at one-month to two-month horizons but dies off beyond the six-month to nine-month horizons. This short-term return persistence is due neither to the persistence or imputation of expenses nor to style. Table 17.7 provides an overview of the performance of Asian hedge funds.

CONCLUSION

This chapter presents an overview of hedge funds, describing their development and characteristics. We also discuss the various issues related to the measurement of hedge fund performance, and we examine alternative performance measures. We end this chapter with several remarks on the development of the hedge fund industry in Asia.

Investor demand for Asian hedge funds is likely to increase as investors in the region build up a better understanding of this new asset class. From an investment perspective, the volatility in the Asian markets in recent years has allowed long-short and other strategic plays to outperform regional indices. The relative inefficiency of the regional markets also presents arbitrage opportunities.

The Asian financial crisis has put the spotlight on hedge funds and their impact on the stability of developing economies. There have been calls among Asian governments to regulate hedge funds. It is unlikely that direct regulation of hedge funds will work. There is the practical problem of regulatory arbitrage—hedge funds can easily relocate if regulation is forced on them. In deciding whether to restrict the activities of hedge funds, there are three sets of considerations to bear in mind.

1. Hedge funds typically invest on behalf of wealthy individuals and institutional investors who do not need consumer protection. Hedge funds are thus private businesses and need not be subject to the same strict regulations and disclosure demands as financial institutions that collect money from the general public.
2. Financial institutions that lend to hedge funds should be sufficiently prudent in provisioning enough capital for relation lending. Hedge funds are not rated by commercial rating agencies, since their portfolios and strategies are not disclosed publicly.
3. Due to their sheer size and leverage, hedge funds can have a significant impact on the stability of financial markets.

Of course, many other institutions engage in investment activities similar to those of hedge funds. The contrarian and arbitrage investment strategies of hedge funds can help to stabilize and even enhance the efficiency of financial markets.

APPENDIX 17.1 LIST OF COMMERCIAL HEDGE FUND DATABASES

Name	Description	Features of Indices
HFR (www.hfr.com)	Hedge Fund Research (HFR) is a hedge fund research and consulting firm that has collected data on around different 4,000 hedge funds.	Around 1,500 funds are used to calculate 33 indices that reflect the monthly net of fee returns on equally weighted baskets of funds.
Zurich Capital Markets (www.marhedge.com)	Originally developed by Managed Accounts Reports (MAR) but sold to Zurich Capital Markets in March 2001.	Database contains 1,500 hedge funds, which are used to calculate 19 indices that reflect median monthly net of fee returns.
CSFB/Tremont (www.hedgeindex.com)	The TASS database tracks around 2,600 funds. There are strict rules for fund selection. The universe consists only of funds with a minimum of U.S.$10 million under management and a current audited financial statement. Funds are re-selected quarterly as necessary.	Using a subset of around 650 funds, CSFB/Tremont calculates 10 indices that the monthly net of fee returns on an asset-weighted basket of funds. Large fund have a larger influence in these indices.
Hennesse (www.henessegroup.com)	The Hennesse Group is a hedge fund advisory firm that maintains a database of around 3,000 funds	Based on subset of about 500 funds, Hennessee calculates 23 indices that reflect the monthly net of fee returns on equally weighted basket of funds.
Van (www.vanhedge.com)	Van Hedge Fund Advisors is a hedge fund advisory firm with a database of about 3,400 funds.	Using a subset of around 500 funds, Van calculates 15 indices that reflect the monthly net of fees returns on equally weighted baskets of funds.

APPENDIX 17.1 (*continued*)

Name	Description	Features of Indices
Altvest (www.altvest.com)	Altvest is hedge fund Web site that provides information on alternative investments. The Altvest database contains information on around 2,000 hedge funds.	Altvest calculates 14 equally weighted indices from the monthly net of fee returns of the funds in its database.
Tuna (www.hedgefund.net)	Hedgefund.net is a Web site providing free hedge fund information and performance data. Its database covers 1,800 hedge funds.	Hedgefund.net calculates 35 equally weighted indices from the monthly net of fee returns of the funds in its database. In Tuna's case, if a fund shuts completely removed from the indices.
AsiaHedge (www.hedgefundintelligence.com)	AsiaHedge is a subscription database that provides information Pacific Region. Publishes a league table of 156 funds.	AsiaHedge establish the Bank of Bermuda AsiaHedge indices. There are 4 indices to measure the performance of hedge funds in 4 geographies based on the median net of fee returns of funds in its league table.

Source: Brooks and Kat (2002).

CHAPTER 18

Efficiency of Funds of Hedge Funds

A Data Envelopment Analysis Approach

Greg N. Gregoriou and Kevin McCarthy

This chapter investigates the efficiency of the funds of hedge funds classification using various data envelopment analysis models. Our objective is to examine which funds are the most efficient in producing the highest returns with the least amount of volatility. From a practitioner's point of view, selecting funds of hedge funds can be an arduous process because of the traditional static market benchmarks used to compare their performance. We circumvent the benchmark problem using data envelopment analysis.

INTRODUCTION

The bursting of the technology stocks juggernaut during the spring of 2000 prompted investors to take a second and closer look at hedge funds to diversify their traditional stock and bond portfolios. Known as absolute return vehicles, hedge funds aim to attain profits in all types of market environments. Funds of hedge funds (FoFs) have become an increasingly fashionable tool for diversifying portfolios among institutional investors, pension funds managers, and high-net-worth individuals, since a great majority of institutional investors do not have the proficiency to objectively invest in individual hedge funds (Ineichen 2002b).

Since hedge fund managers are not legally obliged to divulge information to their investors or to the public, gathering enough information to logically choose good-performing FoFs is extremely difficult and expensive. FoFs can be considered as value adders to a diversified portfolio by providing access to a diversified group of hedge funds, while circumventing the large minimum investments required and providing access to closed hedge funds.

Appropriately measuring and appraising FoF performance remains a dilemma. Since hedge funds utilize dynamic trading strategies, using standard market indices as a comparison can be fundamentally incorrect (Brealey and Kaplanis 2001). Utilizing FoF indices as benchmarks may also be inherently flawed. Indices are passive, whereas FoFs use active management to alter the allocation of hedge fund strategies in their portfolio depending on market conditions. We propose to eliminate the weakness of traditional evaluation techniques by using various data envelopment analysis (DEA) models to rank and evaluate the efficiency of FoFs in a risk-return framework.

Many investors naively compare hedge fund performance to traditional benchmarks such as the Standard & Poor's (S&P) 500 and the Morgan Stanley Capital International (MSCI) World index. This comparison proves more suitable for mutual funds that primarily exhibit long-only passive strategies than hedge funds and FoFs. DEA avoids the problem associated with these traditional long-only indices using linear optimization and results in a single measure of performance to estimate a FoF's efficiency. The power of DEA lies in its ability to deal with a number of inputs and outputs. This is extremely useful with FoFs because the funds themselves are used as benchmarks of ranking hedge funds. This is achieved by both self-appraisal and peer group appraisal, thus allowing investors to identify the reasons behind a FoF's poor performance.

LITERATURE REVIEW

FoFs are becoming the predominant avenue for investors who do not have the resources or experience to invest in hedge funds (Brown, Goetzmann, and Liang 2004). Prior research has proven that FoFs can be useful portfolio diversifiers because of low correlation displayed between fund managers (Schneeweis and Spurgin 2000a,b). In addition, the primary benefit of investing in FoFs is the ability for the manager to add value through manager selection, portfolio construction, and regular monitoring of managers. The FoF manager controls the combination of underlying hedge funds (Ineichen 2000, 2002b). Moreover, Ineichen (2002a) points out that FoFs operate in an environment where experienced and talented FoF managers have an informational advantage.

A well-diversified portfolio of hedge funds is usually the best way to invest in the industry (Fothergill and Coke 2001). Ghaleb-Harter and

McFall-Lamm Jr (2000) suggests that a diversified portfolio of hedge funds can produce double-digit net returns with volatility similar to that of bonds. Furthermore, diversifying risk among managers and hedge fund styles will reduce individual fund and manager risk (Fothergill and Coke 2001). Many investors are interested in allocating a portion of their portfolios to FoFs for capital preservation, since FoFs display lower volatility than other hedge fund strategies (Gregoriou and Rouah 2002). Hedge funds are attractive portfolio diversifiers because they are not correlated to traditional markets (Schneeweis and Spurgin 2000a).

Offshore FoFs have lower tax restrictions and are subject to less supervision and regulation than their onshore counterparts (Kim and Wei 2001). Since offshore funds are located in tax havens, such as the Cayman Islands, the Bahamas, Jersey, Guernsey, Luxembourg, and Switzerland, Kim affirms that offshore funds trade more frequently and more aggressively than their onshore counterparts. This is partly due to the zero or lower capital gains tax, which can reduce the compulsory anticipated gains for hedge funds to trade.

On October 26, 2004, the U.S. Securities Exchange Commission (SEC) adopted a law that will oblige hedge fund advisors to register for the first time and will require them to submit to SEC examinations. This new regulation will take effect in February 2006 and will certainly cause many onshore funds to relocate to offshore jurisdictions due to the stricter regulations in the United States.

Ineichen (2002b) concludes that funds of funds primarily add value by manager selection. When selecting hedge funds for inclusion in an FoF, the FoF manager must understand how the combination of investment strategies is expected to perform in different market environments, while minimizing volatility and providing diversification (Sharpe 1999). Baquero, ter Horst, and Verbeek (2002) find that large hedge funds survive longer than small ones. Gregoriou (2003a) confirms that large FoFs survive longer than small ones and further observes that FoFs, in general, have the longest median survival time (7.45 years) along with the smallest survivorship bias.

The use of traditional measures of performance using standard benchmarks, such as the MSCI World, Lehman Brothers Bond, and the S&P 500, are not suitable because hedge funds and FoFs have low correlations to traditional assets. Finding a benchmark that reflects the overall performance characteristics of the hedge fund industry is difficult (Fung and Hsieh 2002b). In addition, passive hedge fund indices do not capture the diversity of dynamic risk and return characteristics of hedge funds and FoFs.

We look to mitigate the benchmarking problem in the hedge fund industry by applying data envelopment analysis. DEA will enable us to rank and evaluate performance and efficiency of offshore and onshore FoF in a risk-return framework as previously examined in Gregoriou (2003b) and Gregoriou, Sedzro, and Zhu (2005). Gregoriou (2003a) explains that DEA allows the funds themselves to be benchmarks. This is done by finding the most efficient funds and without using erroneous indices. We propose that DEA be used as a complementary technique to other qualitative and quantitative analysis for selecting hedge funds and funds of hedge funds.

DATA

We use FoF data from the Center for International Securities and Derivatives Market (CISDM) database and examine the largest 25 onshore and offshore FoFs (in terms of ending assets under management) during the January 1994 to June 2004 time period. We use this time frame because it encapsulates all the extreme market events (tequila crisis of 1994, Asian currency crisis of 1997, Russian ruble crisis of 1998, and the September 11, 2001, attacks) that have occurred since 1994. Data prior to 1994 are not used because they are subject to backfill bias and are generally deemed unreliable (Fung and Hsieh 2002c). This data set was also chosen because pension funds generally select large FoFs with an operating history of at least five years.

Our data set includes monthly net returns, with management and performance fees deducted. We use only live funds in our examination because dead funds are considered inefficient and are not part of our data set. One onshore FoF had to be removed from the sample because of incomplete data.

METHODOLOGY

Data envelopment analysis was first developed by Charnes, Cooper, and Rhodes (1978) to measure the efficiency of individual decision-making units (DMUs). Using DEA avoids the problems traditionally associated with regression-based models that require arbitrary assumptions about the precise relationships between inputs and outputs (Darling, Mukherjee, and Wilkens 2004). In DEA, performance measures are grouped into inputs, where smaller values are preferred, and outputs where larger values are preferred.

DEA calculates an efficiency score for each FoF and generates a best practices frontier. The most efficient FoFs are the ones that use the least amount of inputs to attain the greatest amount of output. FoFs achieving an efficiency score of 1.0 are deemed efficient and are located on the efficient (for best-practices) frontier. The inputs and outputs chosen for analysis are important and must be chosen carefully because they are the foundation for the analysis. As noted in Gregoriou and Zhu (2005), using other inputs and outputs for DEA models is not incorrect but must be justified.

To appraise and rank onshore and offshore FoFs, we use three DEA models. To maintain consistency in each of the models we use the same inputs and outputs. First we use an input-oriented variable returns to scale (VRS) Banker, Charnes, and Cooper (BCC) model, then we apply a cross-efficiency model, and finally an input-oriented variable returns to scale (RTS) model is employed. We use two inputs and three outputs for the analysis since the rule of thumb is that the sample size should be approximately twice the number of inputs plus outputs.

The average standard deviation and downside deviation statistics are generated by the LaPorte Asset Allocation software (*www.laportesoft.com*) and are used as inputs (risks) for our models. These inputs are justified because FoFs try to minimize volatility and are mainly concerned with downside volatility.

For outputs we use monthly percent profitable, annualized monthly compounded return, and maximum consecutive gain generated by the Pertrac software (*www.pertrac.com*). The outputs will identify how efficiently an FoF can produce the largest outputs (compound return) and the greatest number of consistent positive months. The resulting efficiency score will indicate how FoFs rank with respect to their peers.

BCC Model

Banker, Charnes, and Cooper (1984) modified the DEA model of Charnes, Cooper, and Rhodes (1978) to use variable returns to scale. In this model an increase in inputs will not produce a proportional increase in outputs. The use of a variable returns-to-scale model is justified because FoFs and their underlying hedge fund managers make use of leverage to amplify their returns.

We adapt the notation from Zhu (2003) for BCC efficiency and reproduce this methodology section for simple (BCC) and cross-efficiency from Gregoriou (2003b). For BCC DEA, we maximize the ratio of outputs divided by inputs in equation 18.1, which forms the objective function for the particular FoF $h_0{}^*$. We denote FoFs by $j = \{1,2,\ldots,n\}$, which uses quantities of i inputs with $i = \{1,2,\ldots,m\}$ to produce quantities of r outputs with $r = \{1,2,\ldots,s\}$. W define x_{ij} to be the quantity of input i for j used to produce the quantity y_{rj} of output r. Each FoF uses a variable quantity of m different inputs $\{i = 1,2,\ldots,m\}$ to generate s different outputs $\{r = 1,2,\ldots,s\}$. In particular, FoF j uses amount x_{ij} of output i and generates y_{rj} of output r. We then presume that $x_{ij} \geq 0, y_{rj} \geq 0$, and that each FoF has at least one positive input value and one positive output value. DEA optimization handles the observed vectors of x_j and y_j as given and selects values of output and input weights for a particular FoF. In equation 18.1 a free variable, denoted by u_0, is added in the Banker, Charnes, and Cooper (1984) BCC model to allow for variable returns to scale.[1] Therefore, in an input-oriented BCC model, the formulation minimizes the inputs given the outputs. We obtain the optimization in equation 18.1:

$$h_0^* = \max \frac{\displaystyle\sum_{r=1}^{s} u_r y_{r0} + u_0}{\displaystyle\sum_{i=1}^{m} v_i x_{i0}} \qquad (18.1)$$

subject to equation 18.2:

$$\frac{\displaystyle\sum_{r=1}^{s} u_r y_{r0} + u_0}{\displaystyle\sum_{i=1}^{m} v_i x_{ij}} \leq 1, j = 1, 2, \ldots, n \qquad (18.2)$$

where
s = number of outputs
m = number of inputs
u_r = weight of output r
v_i = weight of input i
x_{ij} = amount of i used by FoF
y_{rj} = amount of r used by FoF
u_0 = free variable

Equation 18.2 is the constraint that imposes that the equivalent weights, when implemented to all funds, do not allow any FoF to have an efficiency score greater than 1.0. If the efficiency score is less than unity, a fund is regarded as inefficient.

---

[1] If an increase in a hedge fund's inputs does not produce a proportional change in its outputs, then the fund exhibits variable returns to scale. Therefore, as the fund alters its scale of operations, its efficiency will increase or decrease.

Cross-Efficiency Model

Cross-efficiency provides a peer appraisal score (average score) whereby each FoF evaluates all others in terms of all inputs and outputs. The cross-efficiency model was first developed in Sexton, Silkman, and Hogan (1986) and later appeared in Doyle and Green (1994) and Anderson, Hollingsworth, and Inman (2002). Cross-efficiency establishes a ranking procedure and computes the efficiency score of each FoF n times using optimal weights obtained via DEA models. The count n represents the number of times the problem needs to be generated to distinguish the efficiency scores. Cross-efficiency provides additional perspectives into the efficiency and performance of each FoF and establishes whether the FoFs perform well in all areas according to inputs and outputs used in the analysis. In other words, cross-efficiency allows for all FoFs to vote on the relative efficiency of the other funds in the sample. A cross-efficiency matrix consists of rows and columns whereby each is equal to the number of FoFs in the sample. The efficiency of FoF j is calculated with the optimal weights by the DEA software for FoF k. By calculating the average score of each column, the peer-appraisal efficiency score of each FoF will be displayed. The cross-efficiency model is reproduced from Adler, Friedman and Sinuany-Stern (2002) and is represented by equation 18.3:

$$h_{kj} = \frac{\sum_{r=1}^{s} y_{rj} u_{rk}}{\sum_{i=1}^{m} x_{ij} v_{ik}}, \ k = 1, 2, \ldots, n, \quad j = 1, 2, \ldots, n \qquad (18.3)$$

where the problem is generated n times and h_{kj} is the score of the FoF j cross-evaluated by the weight of FoF k. In the cross-efficiency matrix, all FoFs are bounded by $0 < h_{kj} \leq 1$, and the components in the leading diagonal, h_{kk}, represent the simple DEA efficiency score, so that $h_{kk} = 1$ for efficient FoFs and $h_{kk} < 1$ for inefficient FoFs.

Returns-to-Scale Model

Wilkens and Zhu (2003) show how a returns-to-scale (RTS) DEA model can be used to classify hedge funds. If FoF managers produce greater returns in proportion to their inputs (because of leverage), then they are operating under increasing returns to scale (Gregoriou and Zhu 2005). However, if a FoF is operating under decreasing returns to scale, then an increase in the FoF inputs would yield in a somewhat smaller than proportionate increase in the FoF outputs. We demonstrate how DEA can be used to classify the performance of onshore and offshore FoFs using RTS.

A FoF manager under constant returns to scale can scale inputs and outputs in a linear fashion without increasing or decreasing efficiency. Under this scenario, the FoF can attain a proportional output with a proportional amount of input. As mentioned, RTS can be increasing, decreasing, or constant. In essence, the efficiency scores from the inputs and outputs will be identical. However, when variable returns to scale are present, inputs and outputs are not the same. Therefore, when inputs are increased, outputs can either change (either increase or decrease).

Returns to scale is primordial for the selection of FoF since it is based on increasing or decreasing efficiency as well as on assets under management of the FoF. Constant RTS indicates that doubling the inputs will proportionally double the outputs, decreasing RTS implies that doubling the inputs will less than double the outputs, and increasing RTS means that doubling the inputs will more than double the outputs.

The RTS regions in Zhu (2003) obtained by DEA can be compared to the factor analysis technique used by Fung and Hsieh (1997a), and the general style classification (GSC) used by Brown and Goetzmann (2003), which generates five to eight distinct fund groups. Hedge fund and CTA classifications used by database vendors are not very accurate and not properly defined because the styles coded in the databases are provided by the hedge fund managers themselves. Brown and Goetzmann (2003) suggest that this may result in incorrect self-classification.

Hedge fund strategies are highly correlated to the self-reported style information and qualitative groupings of hedge fund managers and commodity trading advisors. RTS can play an important role in manager selection by grouping the individual funds into the appropriate RTS regions.

Empirical Results

Tables 18.1 and 18.2 display the BCC efficiency scores of the offshore and onshore FoFs respectively. In Table 18.1, of 25 funds examined, only 5 are efficient with a score of 1.0. Table 18.2 displays four efficient onshore funds. Funds with an efficiency score of 1.0 lie on the best-practices frontier. Efficient FoFs are regarded as the best in transforming its inputs into outputs. An FoF that is inefficient (score less than 1.0), such as Key Global (Table 18.1) with a score of 0.72091, is only 72.09 percent as efficient as the most efficient FoFs in the analysis. However, funds with a score of 1.0 do not provide the same return during the examination period, only that the return is at the maximum of the incurred risk. The efficiency score is not absolute. An FoF with an efficiency score of 1.0 returning 20 percent is considered more risky than a fund with a score of 1.0

TABLE 18.1   Offshore Funds of Hedge Funds BCC Input
Oriented Varying Returns-to-Scale Model

FoF	Efficiency Score	Sharpe Ratio
Asian Capital Holdings Fund	1.00000	0.10
GAM Trading Fund	1.00000	1.28
La Fayette Holdings	1.00000	0.54
GAM Trading Fund (euro)	1.00000	0.77
Arden Intl Capital	1.00000	1.64
Saranac Investors Ltd	0.96475	0.28
Key Hedge Fund	0.89825	0.65
Optima Fund Ltd	0.87774	0.76
GAM Multi-Europe Fund (euro)	0.80324	0.58
Green Way Investments (euro)	0.73151	0.33
Key Global	0.72091	0.12
GAM Multi-Europe Fund	0.71305	0.49
GAM Diversity Fund	0.68695	0.61
Olympia Global Hedge Trust	0.63707	0.61
Ocean Strategies	0.59402	0.30
Gems Low Volatility Fund	0.59333	0.49
Global Hedge Fund (CHF)	0.57051	0.01
Haussman Holdings NV	0.51539	0.41
Prima Capital Fund	0.50229	0.27
Permal Investment Holdings NV (A)	0.49542	0.40
Sperry Complete Manager Fund (A)	0.47282	0.32
Permal Emerging Mkts Holdings (A)	0.41789	0.17
Leveraged Capital Holdings	0.41070	0.41
Eagle Capital International Fund	0.41068	0.39
GAM Emerging Markets Multi-Fund	0.37179	0.14

Spearman: 0.482** significant at the 0.01 level.

returning 15 percent, even if both have scores of 1.0. When the efficiency scores are compared against the Sharpe ratio using the Spearman's Rank correlation coefficient, a strong link is present and is indicated as a footnote in Tables 18.1 to 18.4. Furthermore, the relationship of the cross-efficiency scores against the Sharpe ratio is stronger when using the cross-efficiency model.

Tables 18.3 and 18.4 display the cross-efficiency scores for offshore and onshore FoFs, respectively. Table 18.3 indicates that of the five efficient offshore FoFs in Table 18.1, all are in the top six funds that have attained the highest cross-efficiency scores. Of the four efficient onshore funds in Table 18.2, only two have attained the highest cross-efficiency scores in Table 18.4 This suggests that Univest (B) and Arden Advisers in Table 18.4 can be regarded as all-around efficient funds with the highest average efficiency scores from peer-group analysis.

TABLE 18.2 Onshore Funds of Hedge Funds BCC Input Oriented Varying Returns-to-Scale Model

FoF	Efficiency Score	Sharpe Ratio
Univest (B)	1.00000	2.14
Blue Rock Capital Fund	1.00000	0.29
Arden Advisers	1.00000	2.01
P&A Diversified Managers Fund	1.00000	0.84
Mesirow Arbitrage Trust	0.92583	1.43
Rosewood Associates (D)	0.85527	0.76
Pleiades Partners	0.74935	1.01
Upstream Capital Fund	0.72735	1.01
Pointer (Qp)	0.70619	1.12
Regency Fund	0.62201	0.62
Aurora	0.59355	1.14
Paradigm Master Fund	0.54463	0.75
Access Fund	0.54289	0.71
Oxbridge Associates	0.46787	0.81
Austin Capital All Seasons	0.45124	0.76
Summit Private Investments	0.41356	0.76
Acorn Partners	0.37859	0.35
Preferred Investors	0.36290	0.66
Birchwood Associates	0.33852	0.45
Millburn MCO Partners	0.33442	0.60
Optima Fund	0.32827	0.70
CAM	0.30768	0.57
Long Point Investors	0.30697	0.69
Praesideo ULQ Intl Investors	0.24835	0.44
Torrey Global Fund	0.22349	0.41

Spearman: 0.645^{**} significant at the 0.01 level.

TABLE 18.3 Offshore Funds of Hedge Funds
Cross-Efficiency Model

FoF	Efficiency Score	Sharpe Ratio
Arden Intl Capital	99.65	1.64
GAM Trading Fund	83.24	1.28
GAM Trading Fund (euro)	76.97	0.77
Optima Fund Ltd	67.56	0.76
La Fayette Holdings	61.91	0.54
Asian Capital Holdings Fund	60.13	0.10
GAM Diversity Fund	55.53	0.61
Key Hedge Fund	55.07	0.65
Saranac Investors Ltd	54.19	0.28
GAM Multi-Europe Fund (euro)	53.14	0.58
GAM Multi-Europe Fund	51.30	0.49
GEMS Low Volatility Fund	46.52	0.49
Key Global	45.71	0.12
Green Way Investments (euro)	45.62	0.33
Olympia Global Hedge Trust	44.63	0.61
Permal Investment Holdings Nv (A)	41.55	0.40
Haussman Holdings NV	41.47	0.41
Ocean Strategies	41.12	0.30
Permal Emerging Mkts Holdings (A)	32.23	0.17
Leveraged Capital Holdings	31.54	0.41
Sperry Complete Manager Fund (A)	31.23	0.32
Prima Capital Fund	30.97	0.27
Eagle Capital International Fund	30.09	0.39
GAM Emerging Markets Multi-Fund	27.86	0.14
Global Hedge Fund (CHF)	23.83	0.01

Spearman: 0.690** significant at the 0.01 level.

Table 18.5 displays the six RTS regions as described in Zhu (2003), who states that "some IRS, CRS and DRS regions are uniquely determined no matter which VRS model is employed (they are Region I, II, and III)." Table 18.6 displays the RTS methodology with four different groups of offshore FoFs (Region I, Region II, Region III, and Region VI). The only FoF that falls into Region I is Saranac Investors Ltd. This fund produces increasing returns to scale (IRS) according to the selected inputs and out-

TABLE 18.4 Onshore Funds of Hedge Funds
Cross-Efficiency Model

Fof	Efficiency Score	Sharpe Ratio
Univest (B)	99.09	2.14
Arden Advisers	92.36	2.01
Mesirow Arbitrage Trust	71.34	1.43
Rosewood Associates (D)	54.85	0.76
Pleiades Partners	51.88	1.01
Pointer (QP)	50.91	1.12
Aurora	50.03	1.14
Regency Fund	43.64	0.62
Upstream Capital Fund	42.53	1.01
P&A Diversified Managers Fund	36.24	0.84
Oxbridge Associates	33.49	0.81
Austin Capital All Seasons	30.51	0.76
Summit Private Investments	30.11	0.76
Optima Fund	26.92	0.70
Long Point Investors	26.70	0.69
Access Fund	25.15	0.71
Preferred Investors	24.62	0.66
Paradigm Master Fund	24.60	0.75
Millburn MCO Partners	23.10	0.60
CAM	21.96	0.57
Birchwood Associates	21.00	0.45
Blue Rock Capital Fund	17.76	0.29
Acorn Partners	13.41	0.35
Praesideo ULQ Intl Investors	13.41	0.44
Torrey Global Fund	12.97	0.41

Spearman: 0.913** significant at the 0.01 level.

TABLE 18.5 Six Returns-to-Scale Regions

Region I	Increasing Returns to Scale (IRS)
Region II	Constant Returns to Scale (CRS)
Region III	Decreasing Returns to Scale (DRS)
Region IV	IRS (input-oriented) and CRS (output-oriented)
Region V	CRS (input-oriented) and DRS (output-oriented)
Region VI	IRS (input-oriented) and DRS (output-oriented)

Source: Zhu (2003).

TABLE 18.6 Offshore Funds of Hedge Funds Returns-to-Scale Model

DMU Name	RTS Region	Input-oriented VRS	Input-oriented RTS	Ending Millions Managed
GAM Diversity Fund	Region III	0.68695	Decreasing	$2,963,150,000
Permal Investment Holdings NV (A)	Region III	0.49542	Decreasing	$2,900,000,000
Haussman Holdings NV	Region VI	0.51539	Increasing	$2,700,000,000
Leveraged Capital Holdings	Region VI	0.41070	Increasing	$1,079,000,000
Asian Capital Holdings Fund	Region II	1.00000	Constant	$722,235,000
GAM Trading Fund	Region II	1.00000	Constant	$568,080,000
GEMS Low Volatility Fund	Region VI	0.59333	Increasing	$427,270,000
La Fayette Holdings	Region III	1.00000	Decreasing	$416,223,000
Global Hedge Fund (CHF)	Region VI	0.57051	Increasing	$403,266,000
GAM Emerging Markets Multi-Fund	Region VI	0.37179	Increasing	$396,650,000
GAM Multi-Europe Fund	Region III	0.71305	Decreasing	$315,470,000
Green Way Investments (euro)	Region VI	0.73151	Increasing	$260,000,000
Permal Emerging Mkts Holdings (A)	Region VI	0.41789	Increasing	$256,000,000
Prima Capital Fund	Region VI	0.50229	Increasing	$245,000,000
Key Hedge Fund	Region VI	0.89825	Increasing	$224,567,000
Saranac Investors Ltd	Region I	0.96475	Increasing	$221,200,000
GAM Multi-Europe Fund (euro)	Region III	0.80324	Decreasing	$210,940,000
Olympia Global Hedge Trust	Region VI	0.63707	Increasing	$198,000,000
GAM Trading Fund (euro)	Region III	1.00000	Decreasing	$165,700,000
Optima Fund Ltd	Region III	0.87774	Decreasing	$163,700,000
Sperry Complete Manager Fund (A)	Region VI	0.47282	Increasing	$161,000,000
Ocean Strategies	Region VI	0.59402	Increasing	$67,700,000
Arden Intl Capital	Region II	1.00000	Constant	$46,460,000
Eagle Capital International Fund	Region VI	0.41068	Increasing	$38,643,000
Key Global	Region VI	0.72091	Increasing	$36,986,000

puts. In Region II, three FOFs experience achieved constant returns-to-scale, according to which a proportionate amount of inputs resulted in a proportionate amount of outputs. In Region III, seven funds attained decreasing returns-to-scale and finally, in Region VI, the majority (14) of FoFs experience IRS (input-oriented).

TABLE 18.7 Onshore Funds of Hedge Funds Returns-to-Scale Model

DMU Name	RTS Region	Input-oriented VRS Efficiency Score	Input-oriented RTS	Ending Millions Managed
Aurora	Region VI	0.59355	Increasing	$1,404,000,000
Pointer (QP)	Region III	0.70619	Decreasing	$584,000,000
Univest (B)	Region II	1.00000	Constant	$439,810,000
Austin Capital All Seasons	Region VI	0.45124	Increasing	$298,000,000
Blue Rock Capital Fund	Region II	1.00000	Constant	$224,422,000
Optima Fund	Region VI	0.32827	Increasing	$203,400,000
Arden Advisers	Region II	1.00000	Constant	$150,000,000
Paradigm Master Fund	Region VI	0.54463	Increasing	$124,298,000
Summit Private Investments	Region VI	0.41356	Increasing	$118,084,000
Acorn Partners	Region VI	0.37859	Increasing	$110,000,000
P&A Diversified Managers Fund	Region III	1.00000	Decreasing	$101,300,000
Torrey Global Fund	Region VI	0.22349	Increasing	$100,423,000
Rosewood Associates (D)	Region III	0.85527	Decreasing	$100,400,000
Millburn MCO Partners	Region VI	0.33442	Increasing	$97,878,000
Preferred Investors	Region VI	0.36290	Increasing	$95,400,000
Upstream Capital Fund	Region VI	0.72735	Increasing	$86,900,000
Oxbridge Associates	Region VI	0.46787	Increasing	$85,000,000
Long Point Investors	Region VI	0.30697	Increasing	$72,300,000
Mesirow Arbitrage Trust	Region III	0.92583	Decreasing	$63,400,000
Regency Fund	Region III	0.62201	Decreasing	$61,200,000
Access Fund	Region VI	0.54289	Increasing	$61,000,000
Pleiades Partners	Region VI	0.74935	Increasing	$57,000,000
Praesideo ULQ Intl Investors	Region VI	0.24835	Increasing	$51,700,000
Birchwood Associates	Region VI	0.33852	Increasing	$50,400,000
CAM	Region VI	0.30768	Increasing	$48,700,000

Table 18.7 displays the RTS methodology for three different groups of onshore FOFs (Region II, Region III, and Region VI). Region II has three funds producing constant returns to scale, while Region III has five funds producing DRS. Region VI has the greatest number of funds (17), and all experience IRS (input-oriented). In addition, the majority of funds as identified in Table 18.6 and 18.7 experience IRS. This could suggest that FoFs tend to increase inputs to attain larger proportional increases in outputs.

CONCLUSION

When selecting FoFs, prudent investors must use more than one method to examine returns, volatility, and other statistical properties of each fund. Using BCC and cross-efficiency models allows investors to obtain further insight into what drives FoFs performance and how each fund scores in terms of its relative efficiency ranking. Furthermore, DEA groups funds into specific regions, such as increasing, decreasing, or constant returns to scale, just as factor analysis and Generalized Style Classification (GSC) are frequently used to group hedge funds and FoFs. Last, an FoF manager may use DEA as a complementary technique in evaluating the performance of hedge fund and FoF managers.

CHAPTER 19

The Performance of Hedge Funds in the Presence of Errors in Variables

Alain Coën, Aurélie Desfleurs, Georges Hübner, and François-Éric Racicot

I n this chapter we revisit the performance of hedge funds in presence of errors in variables. We investigate hedge fund performance using various simple asset pricing models. To reduce the bias induced by measurement and specification error, we introduce an estimator based on cross-sample moments of order three and four. Our results show that our technique has great and significant consequences on the measure of factor loadings. Our estimator sheds a new light on performance attribution and estimation of abnormal performance alpha by showing that significant alphas can be attributed to measurement errors at the level of explanatory variables.

INTRODUCTION

Since the exploratory studies of Liang (1999) and Ackermann, McEnally, and Ravenscraft (1999) showing that hedge funds tend to outperform mutual funds, the performance of hedge fund strategies has become a blossoming and almost inexhaustible subject of research.

These studies advocated the use of the Sharpe ratios as a metric for performance measurement. It would be justified because of the relatively poor fit of classical asset pricing models used in the mutual funds literature, as in Fama and French (1993) and Carhart (1997), to the time series of hedge fund returns.

Nevertheless, many subsequent studies have been aimed at adjusting pricing models that would account for a significant fraction of the variability of hedge fund returns and, with these specifications, at applying Jensen's alpha as the risk-adjusted performance measure. Fung and Hsieh (1997a) were the first to propose the use of the Sharpe (1992) asset class model. With the nine-factor model they proposed, they reported adjusted R^2 for style- and location-based portfolios of hedge funds that ranged from 17 to 70 percent, much less than the significance levels achieved by mutual funds but still quite promising.

A stream of subsequent research has focused on the identification of relevant risk premiums (Schneeweis and Spurgin 1998b; Liang 1999, 2004; Amenc, Martellini, and Vaissié 2003; Agarwal and Naik 2004; Capocci and Hübner 2004; Capocci, Corhay, and Hübner 2005) in order to refine the measurement of performance by Jensen's alpha, as well as to assess the persistence of hedge funds' abnormal performance.

Results have been quite promising so far. Most studies conclude that, for the period subsequent to 1994,[1] the average alpha of hedge fund returns tends to be significant for most strategies (Agarwal and Naik 2004; Capocci and Hübner 2004), but with differences depending on the period studied, as the period of bearish market after March 2000 drove down abnormal performance (Capocci, Corhay, and Hübner 2005). Yet some strategies, such as event driven (Edwards and Caglayan 2001a; Mitchell and Pulvino 2001), global macro (Edwards and Caglayan 2001a; Capocci and Hübner 2004), and, most consistently across all studies, the market-neutral strategy (Edwards and Caglayan 2001a; Amenc, Martellini, and Vaissié 2002[2]; Capocci, Corhay, and Hübner 2005), appear to achieve significant and even, to some extent, persistent abnormal performance.

Amin and Kat (2003a) and Agarwal and Naik (2004), however, provide a very serious warning. Because the market timing behavior of hedge fund managers induces returns to exhibit a significant tendency to load on option-based strategies, as shown by Fung and Hsieh (2001, 2002b) and by Agarwal and Naik (2004), neither the Sharpe ratio nor Jensen's alpha is likely to adequately measure abnormal performance with ordinary least squares (OLS). Any properly designed performance measure has to account for the significant skewness and kurtosis displayed by hedge fund returns. In particular, a highly nonnormal behavior of returns is likely to bias sta-

---

[1]Capocci and Hübner (2004) find that data prior to 1994 may not be reliable due to the presence of significant survivorship bias.
[2]Amenc, Martellini, and Vaissié (2003) distinguish between long/short and equity-market-neutral strategies.

tistical inference if there is evidence of measurement errors in the explanatory variables, as they are very likely to influence the point estimators for the risk factor loadings.

In this chapter, we address this issue by applying an econometric technique developed by Dagenais and Dagenais (1997) to measure betas in similar problems. The goal of our study is to determine whether an asset pricing model that would not incorporate these optional effects in the risk factors, thus leaving residual skewness and kurtosis in the returns, would yield reliable performance measures. In order to ensure that we restrict ourselves to this measurement issue, we do not focus on the development of a comprehensive asset class model. We opt for a very classical asset pricing specification and study the effects of removing a significant risk factor on one side and of adding another superfluous risk factor on the other side.

ECONOMETRIC METHOD

It is well known in the economic literature that errors in explanatory variables tend to lead to inconsistent OLS estimators in linear regression models. As underlined by Dagenais and Dagenais (1997), they lead to more perverse effects related to the confidence intervals of the regression parameters and the increase of the sizes of the type I errors. Many studies (Aigner, Hsiao, Kapteyn, and Wansbeek 1984; Bowden, 1984; Fuller 1987) have suggested the use of instrumental variables to obtain consistent estimators, when information on the variances of these errors is not available. Despite these suggestions, instrumental variables techniques are often neglected (Pal 1980; Klepper and Leamer 1984).

Consider this regression model (equation 19.1):

$$Y = ai_N + \tilde{X}\beta + u \qquad (19.1)$$

where $\quad \tilde{X} =$ a $N \times K$ matrix that contains stochastic exogenous variables measured without error;

$\lim_{N\to\infty} \dfrac{\tilde{X}'\tilde{X}}{N} = Q$ where Q is a finite nonsingular matrix;

$Y =$ a $N \times 1$ vector of observations of the dependent variable;

$u =$ a $N \times 1$ vector of normal residual errors with $E(u) = 0$, $E(uu') = \sigma^2_u I_N$;

$\beta =$ a $K \times 1$ vector to estimate;

$\alpha =$ the constant;

$i =$ a $N \times 1$ unit vector.

The fact that $var(u) = \sigma_u^2 I_N$ implies that errors are uncorrelated and that the variance is homoskedastic.

We assume that $\tilde{X}$ is unobservable and that the matrix X is observed instead in equation 19.2, where:

$$X = \tilde{X} + v \qquad (19.2)$$

where v = an $N \times K$ matrix of normally distributed errors in the variables.

This matrix v is assumed to be uncorrelated with u (equation 19.3) and

$$var[vech(v)] = \Sigma \otimes I_N \qquad (19.3)$$

where $var[.]$ = the covariance matrix;
$\qquad I_N$ = the identity matrix of dimension N;
and Σ = a $K \times K$ symmetric positive definite matrix (equation 19.4).

$$\Sigma = \begin{pmatrix} \sigma_{11} & \cdot & \cdot & \sigma_{1K} \\ \sigma_{21} & \sigma_{22} & \cdot & \sigma_{2K} \\ \cdot & \cdot & \cdot & \cdot \\ \cdot & \cdot & \cdot & \cdot \\ \sigma_{K1} & \cdot & \cdot & \sigma_{KK} \end{pmatrix} \text{ and } var\big[vech(v)\big] = \begin{pmatrix} \sigma_{11}I_N & \cdot & \cdot & \sigma_{1K}I_N \\ \sigma_{21}I_N & \sigma_{22}I_N & \cdot & \sigma_{2K}I_N \\ \cdot & \cdot & \cdot & \cdot \\ \cdot & \cdot & \cdot & \cdot \\ \sigma_{K1}I_N & \cdot & \cdot & \sigma_{KK}I_N \end{pmatrix} \qquad (19.4)$$

The hypotheses on measurement errors of explanatory variables imply that errors are independent across observations, so that $cov(v_{ij}, v_{i+k,j'}) = 0$; $i = 1,\ldots, N$; $j, j' = 1,\ldots, K$; $k \neq 0$. But they are dependent between variables for the same observation, so that $cov(v_i, v_j) \neq 0$, $i \neq j$. In this case, the variance of errors is homoscedastic.

The estimator β_D suggested by Durbin (1954) is given by equation 19.5:

$$\beta_D = (z_1' x)^{-1} z_1' y \text{ where } z_1 = \begin{pmatrix} x_{11}^2 & \cdot & \cdot & x_{1K}^2 \\ x_{21}^2 & x_{22}^2 & \cdot & x_{2K}^2 \\ \cdot & \cdot & \cdot & \cdot \\ \cdot & \cdot & \cdot & \cdot \\ x_{N1}^2 & \cdot & \cdot & x_{NK}^2 \end{pmatrix} \qquad (19.5)$$

The x_{ij} are the elements of $x = AX$, where $A = I_N - ii'/N$. The matrix x stands for the matrix X calculated in mean deviation. We use the same notation for y, so that $y = AY$.

The univariate version of Durbin's estimator is given by $\beta_D = \dfrac{\Sigma x_i^2 y_i}{\Sigma x_i^3}$

where $x_i = X_i - \bar{X}$;
$\quad\quad y_i = Y_i - \bar{Y}$.

Similarly, Pal's (1980) estimator, β_P, is given by equation 19.6:

$$\beta_P = (z_2'x)^{-1} z_2' y \quad \text{where} \quad z_2' = z_3' - 3D(x'x/N)x' \quad \text{and}$$

$$z_3 = \begin{pmatrix} x_{11}^3 & \cdot & \cdot & x_{1K}^3 \\ x_{21}^3 & x_{22}^3 & \cdot & x_{2K}^3 \\ \cdot & \cdot & \cdot & \cdot \\ \cdot & \cdot & \cdot & \cdot \\ x_{N1}^3 & \cdot & \cdot & x_{NK}^3 \end{pmatrix} \quad\quad (19.6)$$

where x and y are, as before, expressed in mean deviation;
$\quad D(x'x/N) = $ a $K \times K$ matrix of the diagonal elements of $x'x/N$.

The univariate version of Pal's estimator is given by:

$$\beta_P = \frac{\Sigma x_i^3 y_i - 3(\Sigma x_i^2 / N)\Sigma x_i y_i}{\Sigma x_i^4 - 3(\Sigma x_i^2 / N)\Sigma x_i^2}$$

Under the null hypothesis of no measurement error in variables (H_0), these two estimators are unbiased. As demonstrated by Kendall and Stuart (1963) and Malinvaud (1978), however, higher-moments estimators are more erratic than the corresponding least squares estimators.

Dagenais and Dagenais (1997) introduce new unbiased higher-moment estimators for linear regressions showing considerably smaller standard errors. They propose an estimator, β_H, which is a linear matrix combination of the generalized version of β_D and β_P. This estimator is given by equation 19.7:

$$\beta_H = W \begin{pmatrix} \beta_D \\ \beta_P \end{pmatrix} \quad \text{with} \quad W = (C'S^{-1}C)^{-1} C'S^{-1}, \, C = \begin{pmatrix} I_K \\ I_K \end{pmatrix} \quad\quad (19.7)$$

where $S = $ the covariance matrix for $\begin{pmatrix} \beta_D \\ \beta_P \end{pmatrix}$ under H_0.

Now we apply the generalized least square (GLS) method (equation 19.8):

$$\begin{pmatrix} \beta_D \\ \beta_P \end{pmatrix} = C\beta + \begin{pmatrix} u_D \\ u_P \end{pmatrix} \tag{19.8}$$

where $\quad C = \begin{pmatrix} I_K \\ I_K \end{pmatrix}$;

$u_D = (z_1'x)^{-1}z_1'\, Au;$
$u_P = (z_2'x)^{-1}z_2'\, Au.$

Thus, we get equation 19.9:

$$\beta_H = (C'S^{-1}C)^{-1}C'S^{-1}\begin{pmatrix} \beta_D \\ \beta_P \end{pmatrix}. \tag{19.9}$$

The estimator β_H is unbiased[3] because β_D and β_P are unbiased under H_0. This application of GLS gives us an estimator that is an optimal linear matrix combination of β_D and β_P. Using the theorem of Theil and Goldberger (1961), it is easy to show that the variance of this estimator will be smaller than or equal to the smallest variance of the both estimators β_D and β_P.[4]

We intend to underline their main results by applying this higher-moment estimator to our financial series related to hedge funds, to avoid the problem of misspecification very often neglected in the literature.[5]

Therefore, we use this new estimator based on cross-sample moments of order three and four in presence of errors in variables. Thanks to the consistency of this estimator, the bias should asymptotically disappear while it

---

[3]The detailed proof is available in Dagenais and Racicot (1993).

[4]We can easily demonstrate that β_H converges in probability when there are errors in the explanatory variables. Another approach would be to use the artificial regressions method developed by MacKinnon (1992). For an illustration of this approach, see Davidson and MacKinnon (1993). The detailed proof is available from the authors on request. An application of this new econometric estimator β_H to financial time series used for asset pricing models can be found in Coën and Racicot (2004).

[5]It would be possible to develop an alternative estimator (β_E), which would be a linear matrix combination asymptotically optimal for β_D and β_P under the hypothesis H_1 (presence of measurement errors in explanatory variables).

is inherent to the OLS estimator. This econometric improvement justifies its use in this study.

For the estimator β_H, we use the regression in equation 19.10:

$$Y = \alpha_{H,i} + \sum_{j=1}^{K} \beta_{H,j,i} V_{j,i} + \beta_{\hat{w},j,n} \hat{w}_{j,n} + e_n \qquad (19.10)$$

where V = the vector of explanatory variables;
             Y = the dependent variable;
             n = the number of observations;
     $\hat{w}_{k,n}$ = a vector obtained using the artificial regression technique;
     $\beta_{w,j,n}$ (j = 1 to K, the number of explanatory variables) = a combination of a matrix with instrumental variables uncorrelated with the errors e.

This specification ensures the consistency of our estimator despite the presence of errors in variables.

METHODOLOGY AND DATA

Pricing Models

Given the fact that the purpose of this chapter is to assess the impact of regression methodologies to evaluate portfolio performance, we rely on a classical family of asset pricing models, whose roots can be found in the empirical version of the capital asset pricing model (CAPM) developed by Fama and French (1993).

According to the three-factor asset pricing model proposed by Fama and French (1993), and assuming that the dependent variables are measured without errors and that the pricing errors are homoskedastic and normally distributed, the next market model is estimated with OLS (equation 19.11):

$$r_t = a + \beta_1 Mkt_t + \beta_2 SMB_t + \beta_3 HML_t + \varepsilon_t \qquad (19.11)$$

where r_t = the hedge fund return in excess of the 13-week Treasury-bill rate;
     Mkt_t = the excess return on the market index proposed by Fama and French (1993);
     SMB_t = the factor-mimicking portfolio for size (*small minus big*);
     HML_t = the factor-mimicking portfolio for the book-to-market effect (*high minus low*).

Factors are extracted from French's Web site (*http://mba.tuck.dartmouth. edu/pages/faculty/ken.french/data_library.html*).

We then implement the four-factor model proposed by Carhart (1997), supposedly achieving better significance levels than the Fama and French (1993) specification for hedge fund returns (see Agarwal and Naik 2004; Capocci and Hübner 2004). This market model is taken as the benchmark of a correctly specified model (equation 19.12):

$$r_t = a + \beta_1 Mkt_t + \beta_2 SMB_t + \beta_3 HML_t + \beta_4 UMD_t + \varepsilon_t \qquad (19.12)$$

where UMD_t = the factor-mimicking portfolio for the momentum effect (up minus down).

Finally, we add a fifth factor related to the risk premium associated with high-yield dividend-paying stocks. The choice of this additional candidate factor, called HDMZD (high dividend minus zero dividend), is motivated by the hypothesized positive relationship set forth by Litzenberger and Ramaswamy (1979, 1982), theoretically explained by tax differential arguments. Christie (1990) finds that this hypothesis of a significant dividend risk premium was reinforced for zero-dividend stocks. However, more recent findings have cast doubt on the role of dividend yields to explain stock returns. Christie and Huang (1994) do not support a linear relationship between returns and dividend yields, while Goyal and Welch (2003) deny any stock returns forecasting ability of dividends for periods less than five years. Hübner (2004) finds that this factor can complement Carhart's (1997) model for mutual funds. Due to its controversial and at best weak contribution to explaining equity returns, this source of risk is an ideal candidate for playing the role of a "supernumerary" factor to test the effect of measurement error in the presence of an over-specified model. This results in the next model (equation 19.13):

$$r_t = a + \beta_1 Mkt_t + \beta_2 SMB_t + \beta_3 HML_t + \beta_4 UMD_t + \beta_5 HDMZD_t + \varepsilon_t \quad (19.13)$$

where $HDMZD_t$ = the factor-mimicking portfolio for the dividend effect.

For each of the three specifications, we then implement the regression presented in equation (19.10). This yields equation 19.14:

$$
\begin{aligned}
r_t = \alpha^H &+ \beta_1^H Mkt_t + \beta_2^H SMB_t + \beta_3^H HML_t + \beta_4^H UMD_t + \beta_5^H HDMZD_t \\
&+ \beta_{1w}^H \hat{w}_{Mkt,t} + \beta_{2w}^H \hat{w}_{SMB,t} + \beta_{3w}^H \hat{w}_{HML,t} + \beta_{4w}^H \hat{w}_{UMD,t} \qquad (19.14) \\
&+ \beta_{5w}^H \hat{w}_{HDMZD,t} + \varepsilon_t
\end{aligned}
$$

where β_k^H and β_{kiv}^H ($k = 1,...,5$) = a combination of a matrix with instrumental variables, whose variables are highly correlated with the variables included in the risk factors, but uncorrelated with the errors ε.

Data

We use the Barclay Group database with monthly net returns on 2,617 funds belonging to 11 strategies (event driven, funds of funds, global macro, global, global emerging markets, global regional established, short selling, sector, global international markets, market neutral, long-only leveraged) for the period January 1994 to December 2002. Out of these funds, 1,589 were still alive at the end of the period and 1,028 funds have ceased reporting. Funds that reported less than one consecutive year of returns have been removed from the database.[6] Data from the same period were used by Capocci, Corhay, and Hübner (2005) with the managed account reports (MAR) database, and have been found to be relatively reliable in terms of survivorship and instant return history biases.

The series of dependent variables in our regression are built by computing the equally weighted average monthly returns of all funds, living or dead, that follow a particular strategy during a given month.

The descriptive statistics of our sample is given in Table 19.1. Our database includes a substantially higher number of dead funds (+446) than in the MAR database used by Capocci, Corhay, and Hübner (2005), especially for the global established (+97 dead funds), funds of funds (+77), and market-neutral (+72) strategies.

Consistent with previous studies, some strategies appear to achieve extremely favorable performance for all measures. Sector, global established, global emerging, and market-neutral strategies exhibit average monthly returns greater than 1 percent. The Sharpe ratio of Market Neutral funds is up to eight times greater than that of the market proxy. Event-driven, sector, global established, macro and funds of funds strategies also obtain Sharpe ratios more than twice higher than the market proxy. Thus, a classical model-free performance measure suggests that there might be significant abnormal performance present in hedge fund returns.

The correlation between and among hedge funds and among risk factors is reported in Table 19.2. The correlations between the regressors and

---

[6]This treatment explains why we have a lower number of funds remaining than Capocci, Corhay, and Hübner (2005).

TABLE 19.1 Descriptive Statistics of Hedge Fund Strategies and Risk Premiums, January 1994 to December 2002

	# funds	Living	Dead	Mean	Std Dev.	t(mean)	Median	Min	Max	M. exc.	t(m. exc.)	Sharpe
EVT	226	154	72	0.95	1.90	5.23	1.12	-8.45	4.96	0.58	3.24	0.308
FoF	599	410	189	0.71	1.76	4.21	0.68	-6.71	6.45	0.34	2.05	0.195
MAC	129	52	77	0.81	2.20	3.86	0.56	-4.06	7.05	0.44	2.13	0.202
GLB	156	1	155	0.45	3.97	1.18	0.54	-28.39	13.90	0.08	0.21	0.021
GEM	147	100	47	1.19	5.04	2.44	1.80	-21.85	14.35	0.82	1.69	0.162
GES	467	306	161	1.27	3.24	4.09	1.10	-9.96	12.24	0.90	2.92	0.279
SHS	34	21	13	0.89	4.52	2.05	0.67	-13.63	13.24	0.52	1.20	0.115
SEC	182	111	71	1.66	4.43	3.89	2.07	-13.11	19.90	1.29	3.04	0.291
GIN	71	50	21	0.88	2.43	3.78	0.93	-6.80	8.92	-0.02	-0.11	-0.008
MKN	574	365	209	1.19	1.15	10.73	1.17	-3.49	3.86	0.82	7.59	0.712
LOL	32	19	13	0.91	5.85	1.61	1.50	-17.44	13.28	0.54	0.96	0.092
MKT				0.78	4.76	1.70	1.58	-15.69	8.33	0.41	0.90	0.086
SMB				0.02	4.47	0.04	-0.36	-16.26	21.38	-0.35	-0.82	-0.079
HML				0.60	4.16	1.50	0.68	-8.91	13.67	0.23	0.58	0.055
UMD				1.14	5.71	2.08	1.27	-25.13	18.21	0.77	1.39	0.135
HDMLD				0.39	7.42	0.54	0.29	-23.90	20.55	0.01	0.02	0.002

This table shows the mean returns, t-stats for mean = 0, standard deviations, medians, minima maxima, mean excess returns, t-stats for mean excess return = 0, Sharpe ratios for the individual hedge funds in our database following 11 active strategies and for 5 passive investment strategies.

funds represent the number of funds following a particular strategy, living funds and dead funds represent the number of surviving and dead funds (in December 2002, without considering the new funds established in 12/2002). We calculate the mean excess return and the Sharpe ratio considering Ibbotson Associates one-month T-bills. Numbers in the table are in percentages. EVT = Event Driven, FoF = Funds of Funds, MAC = Global Macro, GLB = Global, GEM = Global Emerging Markets, GES = Global Regional Established, SHS = Short Selling, SEC = Sector, GIN = Global International Markets, MKN = Market Neutral, LOL = Long Only Leveraged, MKT = Market Proxy.

TABLE 19.2 Correlations among and between Hedge Funds and Risk Premiums, January 1995 to December 2002

	EVT	FoF	MAC	GLB	GEM	GES	SHS	SEC	GIN	MKN	LOL	MKT	SMB	HML	UMD	HDMZD
FoF	0.85	1.00														
MAC	0.73	0.88	1.00													
GLB	0.71	0.67	0.51	1.00												
GEM	0.71	0.80	0.62	0.76	1.00											
GES	0.87	0.87	0.84	0.62	0.69	1.00										
SHS	-0.69	-0.64	-0.67	-0.52	-0.56	-0.84	1.00									
SEC	0.81	0.82	0.79	0.56	0.61	0.94	-0.84	1.00								
GIN	0.78	0.88	0.81	0.61	0.76	0.83	-0.61	0.75	1.00							
MKN	0.80	0.81	0.70	0.58	0.62	0.72	-0.50	0.66	0.73	1.00						
LOL	0.83	0.80	0.78	0.60	0.66	0.91	-0.82	0.87	0.72	0.66	1.00					
MKT	0.72	0.65	0.68	0.57	0.59	0.85	-0.78	0.79	0.68	0.57	0.86	1.00				
SMB	0.51	0.48	0.41	0.31	0.34	0.48	-0.51	0.58	0.36	0.37	0.42	0.15	1.00			
HML	-0.34	-0.32	-0.37	-0.32	-0.31	-0.51	0.57	-0.52	-0.32	-0.18	-0.55	-0.56	-0.26	1.00		
UMD	-0.06	0.16	0.21	-0.06	-0.04	0.02	-0.03	0.12	0.04	0.03	-0.09	-0.20	0.18	0.10	1.00	
HDMZD	0.00	-0.06	-0.10	0.04	-0.01	-0.06	0.09	-0.08	-0.09	0.09	-0.03	-0.03	-0.01	0.21	-0.14	1.00
RF	0.14	0.17	0.15	-0.12	-0.04	0.18	0.03	0.17	0.12	0.26	0.13	0.14	-0.11	0.08	-0.06	0.05

EVT = Event Driven, FoF = Funds of Funds, MAC = Global Macro, GLB = Global, GEM = Global Emerging Markets, GES = Global Regional Established, SHS = Short Selling, SEC = Sector, GIN = Global International Markets, MKN = Market Neutral, LOL = Long Only Leveraged, MKT = Market Proxy.

the hedge fund returns do not exceed 0.80, except long-only leveraged and global established, which display high correlations with the market proxy. The correlation among the regressors is very low, thereby raising no serious concern about multicolinearity.

RESULTS

The OLS Regression

The estimations of the OLS betas for the 11 hedge fund strategies are given in Table 19.3. The asset pricing models perform surprisingly well in explaining returns of our hedge fund indexes. The lowest adjusted R^2 is achieved by the global strategy, but this can be understood by the fact that this strategy has gradually faded away and its funds have been reshuffled to other categories, making its recent history very dubious. Otherwise, the percentage of returns variance explained by the regression ranges between 39 percent and as much as 87 percent. Even the market-neutral index obtains a coefficient of determination that is close to 45 percent. In general, though, these coefficients are extremely close to the ones reported in Capocci, Corhay, and Hübner (2005) with the Carhart (1997) model, except for the market-neutral strategy (their adjusted R^2 is 10 percent higher) and the event driven (their adjusted R^2 is 3 to 10 percent lower depending on the subcategory). This is due to different classification schemes from one database to another.

In general, the best fit is obtained with the four-factor model, except for the event driven, global emerging, long-only leveraged, and global strategies, where the Fama and French (1993) specification is better. The dividend-related factor only contributes to the regression significance for the global international strategy. Otherwise, it is redundant and uninformative, thereby playing its role of supernumerary factor.

Reported alphas are significantly positive for six strategies (Table 19.3, panel A). They range from a yearly compounded performance of 12.6 percent (sector) to a barely significant 3.5 percent (macro). Among them, the passage to the four-factor model sharply decreases the alpha except for the event-driven strategy for which the momentum factor is redundant and the short-selling strategy for which the effect is opposite. With the exception of this latter (which is a market contrarian) strategy, the alpha seems to be lower when the model is better specified.

Table 19.3, panel B, shows a similar pattern. All alphas decrease as the up minus down (UMD) factor is added. Only the global strategy obtains a negative, but insignificant abnormal performance.

TABLE 19.3 OLS Regressions on Hedge Fund Strategies

			Panel A: Strategies with Significant Abnormal Performance					
				Coefficients				
	R^2 adj	F-Test	α	Mkt	SMB	HML	UMD	HDMZD
MKN	0.448	29.94	0.710	0.158	0.092	0.076		
			(8.54)	(7.65)	(4.88)	(3.15)		
	0.450	22.87	0.689	0.162	0.087	0.076	0.017	
			(8.12)	(7.75)	(4.52)	(3.12)	(1.17)	
	0.449	18.43	0.686	0.161	0.085	0.070	0.020	0.010
			(8.08)	(7.65)	(4.41)	(2.80)	(1.31)	(0.91)
SEC	0.838	185.46	0.992	0.674	0.472	0.020		
			(5.63)	(15.40)	(11.81)	(0.39)		
	0.872	182.85	0.812	0.712	0.430	0.013	0.148	
			(5.07)	(17.98)	(11.80)	(0.28)	(5.33)	
	0.872	146.44	0.818	0.715	0.433	0.025	0.143	−0.021
			(5.10)	(18.00)	(11.84)	(0.52)	(5.08)	(−0.99)
GES	0.859	218.88	0.645	0.558	0.274	0.041		
			(5.39)	(18.75)	(10.09)	(1.18)		
	0.872	182.55	0.564	0.575	0.255	0.038	0.067	
			(4.82)	(19.89)	(9.59)	(1.14)	(3.30)	
	0.871	145.25	0.567	0.576	0.256	0.043	0.065	−0.010
			(4.83)	(19.82)	(9.58)	(1.25)	(3.14)	(−0.62)
EVT	0.709	87.98	0.400	0.302	0.194	0.095		
			(3.98)	(12.10)	(8.53)	(3.24)		
	0.706	65.37	0.403	0.301	0.195	0.095	−0.003	
			(3.90)	(11.82)	(8.32)	(3.23)	(−0.16)	
	0.704	51.87	0.405	0.302	0.196	0.098	−0.004	−0.005
			(3.91)	(11.76)	(8.28)	(3.20)	(−0.22)	(−035)
SHS	0.773	122.30	0.742	−0.648	−0.390	0.086		
			(3.48)	(−12.21)	(−8.06)	(1.38)		
	0.782	96.66	0.844	−0.669	−0.366	0.090	−0.084	
			(3.94)	(−12.65)	(−7.53)	(1.47)	(−2.27)	
	0.780	76.90	0.840	−0.671	−0.369	0.081	−0.080	0.017
			(3.91)	(−12.62)	(−7.53)	(1.27)	(−2.12)	(0.59)
MAC	0.551	44.80	0.284	0.311	0.164	0.050		
			(1.97)	(8.65)	(4.99)	(1.18)		
	0.633	47.18	0.146	0.340	0.131	0.044	0.114	
			(1.09)	(10.30)	(4.32)	(1.16)	(4.92)	
	0.632	37.82	0.150	0.342	0.134	0.053	0.111	−0.016
			(1.12)	(10.32)	(4.37)	(1.34)	(4.69)	(−0.88)

Strategies are ranked from the highest to the lowest 3-factor alpha. Panel A displays the six strategies with significant alphas (*t*-test > 1.96). Panel B displays the remaining strategies.

TABLE 19.3   *(continued)*

			Panel B: Strategies without Significant Abnormal Performance				

				Coefficients			
	R^2 adj	F-Test	α	Mkt	SMB	HML	UMD	HDMZD
GIN	0.530	41.17	0.304	0.366	0.164	0.096		
			(1.85)	(8.95)	(4.39)	(2.00)		
	0.541	32.50	0.238	0.379	0.149	0.093	0.054	
			(1.43)	(9.25)	(3.93)	(1.97)	(1.87)	
	0.544	26.57	0.246	0.384	0.153	0.110	0.047	−0.030
			(1.49)	(9.36)	(4.06)	(2.25)	(1.63)	(−1.35)
FoF	0.583	50.79	0.195	0.249	0.168	0.072		
			(1.75)	(8.97)	(6.63)	(2.21)		
	0.626	45.79	0.113	0.266	0.148	0.069	0.068	
			(1.05)	(9.97)	(6.05)	(2.23)	(3.62)	
	0.625	36.61	0.116	0.267	0.150	0.075	0.065	−0.011
			(1.07)	(9.98)	(6.08)	(2.35)	(3.42)	(−0.78)
GEM	0.399	24.65	0.476	0.635	0.313	0.122		
			(1.23)	(6.60)	(3.56)	(1.08)		
	0.393	18.35	0.452	0.640	0.307	0.121	0.020	
			(1.14)	(6.52)	(3.40)	(1.07)	(0.30)	
	0.388	14.54	0.453	0.641	0.308	0.125	0.019	−0.007
			(1.13)	(6.48)	(3.38)	(1.06)	(0.27)	(−0.13)
LOL	0.818	161.44	0.145	0.977	0.390	−0.028		
			(0.59)	(15.97)	(6.99)	(−0.38)		
	0.817	120.29	0.117	0.983	0.384	−0.029	0.023	
			(0.46)	(15.75)	(6.68)	(−0.40)	(0.52)	
	0.815	95.30	0.117	0.983	0.384	−0.029	0.023	0.001
			(0.46)	(15.63)	(6.62)	(−0.39)	(0.52)	(0.02)
GLB	0.354	20.55	−0.155	0.473	0.213	0.065		
			(−0.50)	6.01	(2.96)	(0.70)		
	0.350	15.26	−0.158	0.473	0.212	0.065	0.002	
			(−0.48)	(5.89)	(2.87)	(0.70)	(0.03)	
	0.344	12.20	−0.164	0.470	0.208	0.051	0.008	0.026
			(−0.50)	(5.81)	(2.79)	(0.53)	(0.13)	(0.59)

MKN = Market Neutral, SEC = Sector, GES = Global Regional Established, EVT = Event Driven, SHS = Short Selling, MAC = Global Macro, GIN = Global International Markets, FoF = Funds of Funds, GEM = Global Emerging Markets, LOL = Long Only Leveraged, GLB = Global. Student *t*-stats are exhibited in parentheses.

The Higher-Moment Estimators Regression

We now turn to the estimation of the extended model when measurement errors in the dependent variables are treated by the methodology developed earlier. For each risk premium, we now construct the instrumental variables $\hat{w}_{j,t}$ and perform the regression proposed in equation 19.14. The betas are obtained by applying the weighting method proposed by Dagenais and Dagenais (1997) on the Durbin and Pal estimators (see equation 19.9). Thus, we now obtain two coefficients for each risk premium. The significance level of each $\beta_{k\hat{w}}^{H}$ indicates whether there is suspicion of measurement error in the corresponding risk premium that would affect the contributive level of this variable in the estimated market model.

The results of this procedure are reported in Table 19.4, which can be interpreted as the core of this chapter. Quite unexpectedly, the results are very sharp. Alphas are no longer significant, and there is significant indication of measurement error when alphas were significant.

The comparison between the OLS alphas and the higher-moment estimators (HME) alphas reveals a very pronounced tendency to fall around zero, both in absolute and in standardized values, as indicated in Table 19.4, panels A and B. The t-stats never exceed 1 in absolute value and very often switch to a negative sign.

Only the alphas of the market-neutral, event driven, short sellers, and global international remain consistently positive across all specifications. Their economic significance is very low, however. The highest alpha, recorded for the short-sellers strategy, barely corresponds to a yearly 2.2 percent. Event-driven and market-neutral funds peak to a yearly 1.3 percent and 0.7 percent, respectively.

These results can be considered seriously only provided that the evidence of significant measurement error effects is documented. In this respect, the contrast between Table 19.4, panels A and B, is remarkable. In panel A, there appears to be at least one source of measurement error that is adequately tracked by the HME method. The adjusted R^2 for the four-factor model increases by 3.89 percent for market-neutral, 1.4 percent for sector, 0.2 percent for global established, 2.3 percent for event driven, 0.9 percent for short-sellers, and 0.6 percent for macro. All these improvements are recorded despite the fact that we have doubled the number of independent variables and that at most two variables exhibit a significant impact of measurement error per regression, leaving at least two superfluous new variables. In panel B, improvement can be observed for the global strategy only, driving the negative values of alpha toward zero.

The measurement error does not seem to affect the market risk premium. The UMD factor coefficient measured with OLS appears to be

TABLE 19.4 Higher Moment Estimators Regressions on Hedge Fund Strategies

Panel A: Strategies with OLS Significant Abnormal Performance

	R^2_{adj} OLS	R^2_{adj} HME	α OLS	α HME	Mkt β	Mkt β_w	SMB β	SMB β_w	HML β	HML β_w	UMD β	UMD β_w	HDMZD β	HDMZD β_w
								Coefficients						
MKN	0.448	0.448	0.710 (8.54)	0.059 (0.61)	0.232 (4.67)	−0.090 (−1.57)	0.045 (1.14)	0.056 (1.22)	0.135 (1.84)	−0.061 (−0.77)				
	0.450	0.489	0.689 (0.43)	0.040 (4.30)	0.194 (−0.60)	−0.032 (2.37)	0.084 (0.22)	0.009 (2.21)	0.150 (−0.78)	−0.057 (−1.78)	−0.054 (3.04)	0.106		
	0.449	0.474	0.686 (8.08)	0.031 (0.34)	0.171 (3.98)	−0.009 (−0.16)	0.101 (2.75)	−0.008 (−0.16)	0.104 (1.30)	−0.110 (−0.13)	−0.045 (−1.12)	0.098 (2.24)	−0.001 (−0.03)	0.006 (0.18)
SEC	0.838	0.863	0.992 (5.63)	−0.137 (−0.73)	0.700 (7.22)	−0.075 (−0.67)	0.616 (8.07)	−0.278 (−3.09)	0.271 (1.89)	0.271 (−2.47)				
	0.872	0.884	0.812 (5.07)	−0.167 (−0.97)	0.732 (8.72)	−0.048 (−0.47)	0.509 (7.67)	−0.146 (−1.82)	0.298 (2.35)	−0.383 (−2.80)	0.109 (1.95)	−0.005 (−0.08)		
	0.872	0.885	0.818 (5.10)	−0.142 (−0.84)	0.717 (9.11)	−0.030 (−0.31)	0.603 (9.02)	−0.261 (−3.20)	0.357 (2.42)	−0.422 (−2.69)	0.036 (0.50)	0.067 (0.83)	−0.121 (−2.20)	0.106 (1.77)
GES	0.859	0.859	0.645 (5.39)	0.026 (0.18)	0.657 (9.16)	−0.123 (−1.48)	0.226 (4.00)	0.039 (0.59)	0.193 (1.82)	−0.176 (−1.55)				
	0.872	0.874	0.564 (4.82)	−0.018 (−0.13)	0.626 (9.82)	−0.043 (−0.56)	0.222 (4.41)	0.053 (0.87)	0.211 (2.20)	−0.168 (−1.62)	−0.005 (−0.12)	0.092 (1.87)		
	0.871	0.868	0.567 (4.83)	−0.024 (−0.18)	0.572 (9.31)	0.014 (0.19)	0.263 (5.04)	0.006 (0.09)	0.095 (0.83)	−0.040 (−0.33)	0.016 (0.28)	0.070 (1.12)	−0.006 (−0.13)	−0.014 (−0.29)

MKN = Market Neutral, SEC = Sector, GES = Global Regional Established. Student t-stats are exhibited in parentheses.

TABLE 19.4 (continued)

Panel A: Strategies with OLS Significant Abnormal Performance (continued)

	R^2_{adj}		α		Mkt		SMB		HML		UMD		HDMZD	
	OLS	HME	OLS	HME	β	β_w	β	β_w	β	β_w	β	β_w	β	β_w
EVT	0.709	0.722	0.400	0.107	0.400	−0.111	0.101	0.131	0.131	−0.016				
			(3.98)	(0.94)	(6.81)	(−1.64)	(2.18)	(2.40)	(1.51)	(−0.17)				
	0.706	0.729	0.403	0.088	0.364	−0.062	0.145	0.082	0.155	−0.026	−0.063	0.100		
			(3.90)	(0.79)	(6.67)	(−0.95)	(3.36)	(1.54)	(1.89)	(−0.29)	(−1.73)	(2.37)		
	0.704	0.721	0.405	0.069	0.334	−0.029	0.181	0.042	0.116	0.020	−0.065	0.103	−0.020	0.014
			(3.91)	(0.61)	(6.40)	(−0.45)	(4.09)	(0.78)	(1.19)	(0.19)	(−1.35)	(1.94)	(−0.56)	(0.35)
SHS	0.773	0.789	0.742	0.179	−0.811	0.188	−0.292	−0.050	−0.455	0.633				
			(3.48)	(0.75)	(−6.59)	(1.32)	(−3.01)	(−0.44)	(−2.50)	(3.24)				
	0.782	0.791	0.844	0.052	−0.834	0.204	−0.345	0.006	−0.384	0.552	0.029	−0.107		
			(3.94)	(0.22)	(−7.22)	(1.47)	(−3.78)	(0.05)	(−2.21)	(2.94)	(0.38)	(−1.19)		
	0.780	0.789	0.840	0.076	−0.792	0.162	−0.403	0.053	−0.340	0.500	0.040	−0.115	0.040	0.006
			(3.91)	(0.32)	(−7.27)	(1.21)	(−4.35)	(0.47)	(−1.67)	(2.30)	(0.40)	(−1.04)	(0.53)	(0.08)
MAC	0.551	0.550	0.284	−0.032	0.250	0.056	0.257	−0.132	−0.013	0.040				
			(1.97)	(−0.19)	(2.88)	(0.56)	(3.76)	(−1.64)	(−0.10)	(0.29)				
	0.633	0.639	0.146	−0.086	0.235	0.141	0.206	−0.077	0.011	0.061	0.046	0.099		
			(1.09)	(−0.58)	(3.22)	(1.60)	(3.56)	(−1.10)	(0.10)	(0.51)	(0.95)	(1.76)		
	0.632	0.642	0.150	−0.073	0.223	0.155	0.212	−0.094	−0.027	0.117	0.053	0.091	−0.001	−0.022
			(1.12)	(−0.49)	(3.26)	(1.85)	(3.64)	(−1.33)	(−0.21)	(0.86)	(0.84)	(1.30)	(−0.02)	(−0.43)

EVT = Event Driven, SHS = Short Selling, MAC = Global Macro. Student t-stats are exhibited in parentheses.

TABLE 19.4 (continued)

Panel B: Strategies without OLS Significant Abnormal Performance

	R^2_{adj}		α		Mkt		SMB		HML		UMD		HDMZD	
	OLS	HME	OLS	HME	β	β_w	β	β_w	β	β_w	β	β_w	β	β_w
GIN	0.530	0.519	0.304	0.049	0.433	-0.080	0.117	0.058	0.155	-0.059				
			(1.85)	(0.25)	(4.35)	(-0.69)	(1.49)	(0.62)	(1.05)	(-0.38)				
	0.541	0.532	0.238	0.054	0.458	-0.080	0.065	0.120	0.168	-0.063	0.052	0.006		
			(1.43)	(0.28)	(4.96)	(-0.72)	(0.88)	(1.35)	(1.21)	(-0.42)	(0.85)	(0.08)		
	0.544	0.524	0.246	0.052	0.404	-0.022	0.121	0.049	0.070	0.057	0.057	0.000	-0.001	-0.022
			(1.49)	(0.28)	(4.61)	(-0.20)	(1.63)	(0.54)	(0.43)	(0.33)	(0.70)	(0.00)	(-0.02)	(-0.43)
FoF	0.583	0.571	0.195	0.012	0.256	-0.015	0.256	-0.023	0.072	-0.086				
			(1.75)	(0.09)	(3.78)	(-0.19)	(3.78)	(-0.37)	(0.72)	(-0.08)				
	0.626	0.624	0.113	-0.022	0.249	0.037	0.153	0.009	0.103	-0.012	0.017	0.075		
			(1.05)	(-0.18)	(4.17)	(0.51)	(3.26)	(0.16)	(1.14)	(-0.13)	(0.41)	(1.63)		
	0.625	0.621	0.116	-0.022	0.228	0.060	0.186	-0.031	0.080	0.023	0.006	0.086	-0.029	0.018
			(1.07)	(-0.18)	(4.06)	(0.87)	(3.90)	(-0.53)	(0.76)	(0.20)	(0.12)	(1.50)	(-0.74)	(0.42)
GEM	0.399	0.394	0.476	0.079	0.0786	-0.141	0.090	0.315	0.278	-0.105				
			(1.23)	(0.18)	(3.37)	(-0.52)	(0.49)	(1.46)	(0.81)	(-0.28)				
	0.393	0.396	0.452	-0.036	0.691	0.028	0.178	0.244	0.357	-0.145	-0.137	0.231		
			(1.14)	(-0.08)	(3.16)	(0.11)	(1.03)	(1.17)	(1.08)	(-0.41)	(-0.94)	(1.37)		
	0.388	0.380	0.453	-0.085	0.590	0.133	0.227	0.200	0.131	0.088	-0.073	1.065	0.034	-0.063
			(1.13)	(-0.19)	(2.83)	(0.52)	(1.28)	(0.92)	(0.33)	(0.21)	(-0.38)	(0.78)	(0.24)	(-0.40)
	0.871	0.868	0.567	-0.024	0.572	0.014	0.263	0.006	0.095	-0.040	0.016	0.070	-0.006	-0.014
			(4.83)	(-0.18)	(9.31)	(0.19)	(5.04)	(0.09)	(0.83)	(-0.33)	(0.28)	(1.12)	(-0.13)	(-0.29)

GIN = Global International Markets, FoF = Funds of Funds, GEM = Global Emerging Markets. Student t-stats are exhibited in parentheses.

TABLE 19.4 (continued)

Panel B: Strategies without OLS Significant Abnormal Performance (continued)

	Coefficients													
	R^2_{adj}		α		Mkt		SMB		HML		UMD		HDMZD	
	OLS	HME	OLS	HME	β	β_w	β	β_w	β	β_w	β	β_w	β	β_w
LOL	0.818	0.814	0.145	0.059	1.084	−0.133	1.084	0.048	0.093	−0.139				
			(0.59)	(0.21)	(7.26)	(−0.77)	(7.26)	(0.35)	(0.42)	(−0.59)				
	0.817	0.816	0.117	−0.091	0.941	0.078	0.435	−0.043	0.127	−0.130	−0.125	0.201		
			(0.46)	(−0.32)	(6.74)	(0.47)	(3.94)	(−0.32)	(0.60)	(−0.57)	(−1.34)	(1.86)		
	0.815	0.813	0.117	−0.087	0.855	0.164	0.460	−0.092	−0.111	0.119	−0.046	0.116	0.055	−0.078
			(0.46)	(−0.30)	(6.45)	(1.02)	(4.08)	(−0.67)	(−0.45)	(0.45)	(−0.38)	(0.86)	(0.59)	(−0.78)
GLB	0.356	0.354	−0.155	−0.011	0.639	−0.156	−0.021	0.309	0.368	−0.279				
			(−0.50)	(−0.03)	(3.37)	(−0.71)	(−0.14)	(1.76)	(1.31)	(−0.93)				
	0.350	0.394	−0.158	−0.066	0.505	0.031	0.209	0.061	0.453	−0.315	−0.305	0.431		
			(−0.48)	(−0.19)	(2.92)	(0.15)	(1.53)	(0.37)	(1.74)	(−1.12)	(−2.65)	(3.23)		
	0.344	0.382	−0.164	−0.132	0.461	0.082	0.313	−0.029	0.483	−0.346	−0.362	0.492	−0.099	0.111
			(−0.50)	(−0.37)	(2.80)	(0.41)	(2.24)	(−0.17)	(1.57)	(−1.06)	(−2.38)	(2.95)	(−0.86)	(0.89)

LOL = Long Only Leveraged, GLB = Global. Student t-stats are exhibited in parentheses.

overestimated for four strategies (market-neutral, global established, event driven and macro), as the corresponding value of β_{4w}^{H} is significantly positive at the 10 percent level. This is likely to shed new light on the momentum effect. It appears to be much less pronounced for hedge fund strategies that record positive alphas, as the UMD variable can substantially corrupt the estimates of all regression coefficients, including Jensen's alpha.

Evidence is less pronounced for the book-to-market and size effects, as the sign of the measurement error coefficient is either positive or negative when it is significant. The coefficients β_{3w}^{H} for the HML factor are significant for three strategies (positive for short sellers, negative for sectors and global established), and the coefficients for SMB are negative for sectors and positive for event driven.

The significance levels of these instrumental variables tend to decrease as the fourth factor is introduced in the regression. This effect is still present, but less pronounced when a fifth, redundant factor is included, as the opposite can be found for the macro (market factor) and sectors (SMB factor).

Overall, it seems that measurement error problems become more pronounced as the explanatory power of the risk premiums decrease. Measurement problems are almost absent for the market risk premium, slightly present for the size risk premium, more pronounced for the book-to-market premium, and pervasive for the momentum effect.

In fact, our regressions suggest that the introduction of a fourth variable (UMD) makes sense only if its measurement error is simultaneously taken into account. In the OLS regression, the variation of adjusted R^2 induced by adding this variable spans from −0.2 percent to 8.2 percent. After accounting for measurement errors, the span only ranges from 1.5 percent to 8.8 percent.

Finally, we note that the sum of each pair of coefficients is very close to the original OLS beta reported in Table 19.3. Thus, the HME method mostly reshuffles the original coefficient between the economic and the instrumental variable. Unfortunately for performance measures, the resulting total risk premium tends to increase, thereby reducing the value of alpha and removing all evidence of abnormal performance.

From this exploratory discussion, we can conjecture that most attributed hedge fund performance, as measured by alpha, may instead indicate an additional source of risk corresponding to the measurement error in risk premiums. The lower the explanatory power of the risk premium, the higher is the source of measurement risk. But when a risk premium is redundant, it remains superfluous after accounting for measurement error. This risk appears to be priced in our framework.

CONCLUSION

This chapter seems to bring bad news for hedge fund managers. It indicates that the positive abnormal returns reported by several hedge fund strategies over the 1994 to 2002 period may be due to the spurious effects of measurement errors that would have not been taken into account adequately in the OLS regression.

We believe, however, that this is not a problematic issue. This chapter justifies the use of a powerful econometric technique for a problem that is prone to these issues. Blind application of this technique to hedge fund returns seems to remove all performance, irrespective of whether the higher-moment estimator specification is relevant or not. Furthermore, we deliberately chose an incomplete returns-generating model, leaving aside some risk premiums that have proven to be very useful for the understanding of the source of risks taken by hedge fund managers. In particular, their well-documented use of optionlike strategies is likely to account better for skewness and kurtosis in portfolio returns than the traditional Fama and French (1993) and Carhart (1997) factors. Further research is therefore needed in this area.

Furthermore, analyzing alpha may not be the proper way to address this issue. From our approach, we document that alpha could account for a new type risk corresponding to measurement error. But if risk and returns are measured relative to a benchmark portfolio, this benchmark must also be exposed to the same sources of risk. It may not be sensible to conclude, via Table 19.3, that the 574 market-neutral funds (among which 209 have ceased reporting probably due to bad performance) have beaten the market by, on average, 8.5 percent per year during nine years. Even for researchers or professionals who do not blindly follow the efficient market hypothesis, this seems very hard to swallow. Our research definitely calls for a more detailed analysis, at the level of individual funds.

One solution to performance measurement in this context could be the generalized Treynor ratio proposed by Hübner (2004), which introduces the notion of risk per unit of benchmark-corrected systematic risk, in the spirit of the classical Treynor ratio, in a multi-index framework. Eventually, our main conclusion is that alpha is not a proper measure of performance for hedge fund returns.

CHAPTER 20

Alternative RAPMs for Alternative Investments

Milind Sharma

This chapter highlights the inadequacies of traditional RAPMs (risk-adjusted performance measures) and proposes AIRAP (alternative investments risk-adjusted performance), based on expected utility theory, as a RAPM better suited to alternative investments. AIRAP is the implied certain return that a risk-averse investor would trade off for holding risky assets. AIRAP captures the full distribution, penalizes for volatility and leverage, is customizable by risk aversion, works with negative mean returns, eschews moment estimation or convergence requirements, and can dovetail with stressed scenarios or regime-switching models. A modified Sharpe ratio is proposed. The results are contrasted with Sharpe, Treynor, and Jensen rankings to show significant divergence. Evidence of nonnormality and the trade-off between mean-variance merits vis-à-vis higher moment risks is also noted. The dependence of optimal leverage on risk aversion and track record is noted. The results have implications for manager selection and fund of hedge funds portfolio construction.

INTRODUCTION

The heterogeneity of hedge fund strategies, their idiosyncratic bets, the complexity inherent in their dynamic trading, and the extra degrees of freedom they possess (given the absence of leverage or shorting constraints) makes the task of judging managerial skill and performance particularly daunting. An increasingly popular alternative is to invest indirectly through funds of hedge funds (FoHFs). Liew (2003) suggests that FoHFs with "good discernment," can outperform their passively indexed counterparts. However, good discernment presupposes the existence of good RAPMs.

A flurry of recent papers, such as those by Goetzmann, Ingersoll, Spiegel, and Welch (2002), Spurgin (2001), and Bernardo and Ledoit (2000), have highlighted the inadequacies of traditional RAPMs such as the Sharpe ratio. Alternatives and modifications to the Sharpe ratio have been proposed, such as Madan and McPhail (2000), Shadwick and Keating (2002), Kazemi, Mahdavi, and Schneeweis (2003), while Leland (1999) proposes modifying the capital asset pricing model (CAPM) beta. In that vein, this chapter introduces the proposed RAPM, AIRAP, as the certainty equivalent. We follow the CRRA (constant relative risk aversion) framework of Osband (2002) but take the distribution-free route along the lines of CARA (constant absolute risk aversion) solutions by Davis (2001). This is the first work to investigate the utility of certainty equivalence as a RAPM for hedge funds and to contrast the significantly different rankings obtained vis-à-vis the Sharpe ratio and Jensen's alpha. Sharma (2004) applies the AIRAP framework to revisit empirical tests as well as to contrast hedge fund strategies at the index and fund levels.

SURVEY OF RAPMS

While there exists no consensus on how to measure risk or risk-adjusted performance for hedge funds, the menagerie of RAPMs in circulation that could be applied includes the Sharpe ratio, Jensen's alpha, Modigliani-Squared (M^2), M^2-alpha, M^3, SHARAD,[1] the Treynor ratio, the Information ratio, the Sortino ratio, Calmar, Sterling, gain/loss, and so on. Related performance statistics include maximum drawdown, number of months to recovery, peak-trough, value added monthly index (VAMI), up/down market returns, and upside/downside capture. Finally, the associated risk metrics are beta, active risk, total risk, variance, semivariance (upside/downside and capture), mean absolute deviation (MAD), value at risk (VaR), VarDelta, marginal VaR, CVaR (conditional VaR or expected shortfall), and CDaR (conditional drawdown at risk).

Absolute RAPMs consider portfolio returns in excess of the risk-free rate (viz., Sharpe and Treynor ratios) or zero (Calmar and Sterling). Rela-

---

[1]The SHARAD (skill, history, and risk-adjusted) RAPM has been proposed by Muralidhar (2001) as an extension of M^3 (Muralidhar 2000), since it explicity adjusts for disparate performance history.

tive risk adjustment performance measures (RAPMs), on the other hand, consider portfolio returns in excess of benchmark (Information ratio), beta-adjusted benchmark (Jensen's alpha), or some threshold of minimum acceptable return (MAR). The Sharpe and Information ratios both use the standard deviation of differential returns in the denominator to risk adjust, the Treynor ratio uses beta, the Sortino ratio uses downside deviation (DD), Calmar uses maximum drawdown over three years, and Sterling uses the average maximum drawdown over each of the past three years. Benchmark risk-equivalent RAPMs such as M^2, M^2-alpha, M^3, and SHARAD lever or delever portfolio performance in order to risk-equalize with the benchmark volatility, while borrowing at the risk-free rate. Since M^2 is an affine transform of the Sharpe ratio, it always produces the same rankings. Further, M^2-alpha is a close cousin of the Treynor ratio and produces identical rankings. Hence, we do not dwell on either M-squared measures separately. M^3 was proposed by Muralidhar (2000) to augment M^2 by explicitly adjusting for benchmark correlation while SHARAD goes further by adjusting for disparate performance history (length of manager track records). Both M^3 and SHARAD differ from the Sharpe ratio and are particularly germane to institutional benchmark relative performance measurement and risk-budgeting considerations. Despite the progressive institutionalization of hedge funds, correlation adjustment and tracking-error budgeting do not now appear central to a class of investments still largely perceived as an absolute return class.

The applicability and appropriateness of these RAPMs to hedge funds depends on the efficacy of their associated risk measure in capturing hedge fund risk. To the extent that standard deviation, beta, downside deviation and maximum drawdown are not sufficient risk statistics under non-normality, none of the corresponding RAPMs should suffice for hedge funds. That said, each of these has its attractions worth highlighting. Calmar and Sterling are well suited for presenting the worst-case scenario since they take into account maximum drawdown (the worst losing streak). The Sortino ratio only adjusts by downside deviation. The benefit is that downside deviation does not penalize for upside variability but only for underperformance vis-à-vis some threshold of minimum acceptable return. For predictably asymmetric returns, Sortino can be a better ex-post RAPM than the Sharpe ratio, since downside deviation will case pick up on the realized skew and produce better portfolio rankings. Indeed, generalizing to the notion of lower partial moments (LPM) can yield a host of new risk and corresponding risk-adjusted measures. The zero LPM is shortfall risk or the frequency of underperformance vis-à-vis some minimum acceptable return. The first LPM is just the mean underperformance, while the second LPM turns out to be downside variance.

Risk of RAPM Shortfall

Recent literature highlights the vulnerability of traditional RAPMs given the vagaries of leverage, nonnormality, and derivatives usage—issues that typify hedge fund returns. In the domain of risk measures, even the most popular candidates, such as value at risk, fall short in that they cannot handle liquidity, credit, or tail risk that are often characteristic of hedge funds. Further, VaR is not a coherent risk measure under nonnormality (Artzner, Delbaen, Eber, and Heath 1999), a deficiency that has led to the growing preference for expected shortfall as a quantifier of tail risk, coupled with coherent scenario testing.

Among absolute RAPMs, we first consider the Treynor ratio, which can be magnified without bound, via beta in the denominator. As a market-neutral hedge fund approaches beta neutrality, the Treynor ratio approaches infinity. This is an issue for nondirectional strategies in general. The Treynor ratio is unsatisfactory for ranking and comparing hedge funds.

The Sortino ratio performs a valuable function in adjusting by downside deviation but can look deceptively high (on trend reversal) if the ex-post estimation is based on a period of upwardly trending returns, since downside deviation underestimates the two-sided risk if the estimation period is not long enough to include loss periods. In this case, the Sharpe ratio would perform better since the standard deviation is not as vulnerable to a skewed sample when the underlying population is symmetrical.

Jensen's alpha is not leverage invariant. Instead it scales in direct proportion with leverage, thereby providing the perverse incentive to increase leverage without bound. In fact, hedge fund strategies, particularly relative-value strategies such as fixed income or statistical arbitrage, are known to employ significant leverage in order to scale up their alpha. Leland (1999) shows that alpha can be systematically misguided because the CAPM beta ignores higher moments. Even if the single-index CAPM were appropriate, Roll (1978) shows the arbitrariness of alpha rankings. If the benchmark used is mean-variance efficient, the securities market line is unable to discern outperformance. If not, then there exists some other nonefficient index, which can reverse the ranking obtained.

Perhaps the most commonly used and widely respected RAPM in industry circulation is the Sharpe ratio. It has many desirable properties, such as proportionality to the t-statistic (for returns in excess of zero) and the centrality of its squared value to optimal portfolio allocation.

The Sharpe ratio, however, is leverage invariant, and it is not as intuitive as M^2, M^3, and SHARAD, which measure performance in basis point terms. It does not incorporate correlations, nor can it handle iceberg risks lurking in the higher moments. It is plagued by another deficiency that limits its usefulness during bear markets. Table 20.1 uses the Evaluation Asso-

TABLE 20.1   Sharpe Ratios of Negative Returns, 1997 to 2001

EACM Index	Bond Hedge	Fixed Income Hedge Fund
Annual volatility	6.02%	12.04%
Annual % excess returns	–4.50%	–4.50%
Annual Sharpe ratio	–0.75	–0.37

ciates Capital Markets (EACM) Bond Hedge index over the 1997 to 2001 period to show that a fund with the same excess return (–4.5 percent) but twice the risk (12 percent) has a Sharpe ratio twice as good instead of twice as worse. This happens because –0.37 is larger than –0.74 even though smaller in absolute magnitude.

Further, by manipulating the returns profile, the Sharpe ratio can be substantially modified. Spurgin (2001) shows how this can be achieved by truncating the right tail. Similarly, Goetzmann, Ingersoll, Spiegel, and Welch (2002) derive the optimal static strategy via short out-of-the-money (OTM) puts and calls, which maximizes the Sharpe ratio. This corresponds to a distribution with a truncated right tail (smooth monthly returns) but with a fat tail representing periodic crashes. They remark that the peso problem may be ubiquitous in any investment management industry that rewards high Sharpe ratio managers. Bernardo and Ledoit (2000) specifically demonstrate the limitations of the Sharpe ratio under nonnormality. They show that outside the realm of normality, attractive investments (i.e., arbitrage opportunities) can have arbitrarily low Sharpe ratios while poor investments may have high Sharpe ratios. Given normality, the Sharpe ratio suffices in completely characterizing investment desirability. Without normality, however, it is impossible to make general statements that are preference-free other than no-arbitrage (Bernardo and Ledoit 2000).

A number of cases manager hubris based on short but impressive track records (possibly attributable to short option profiles) have been documented. Jorion (2000) points this out for the risk signature of Long-Term Capital Management (LTCM). Similarly, the well-respected Neiderhoffer became victim to short OTM puts as a result of a sudden 7 percent market drop on October 27, 1997. More recently, Agarwal and Naik (2004) find the majority of hedge fund strategies to be characterized by short option profiles. They extend the findings of Mitchell and Pulvino (2001) for merger arbitrage. While there are isolated cases that put manager integrity into question, the broader issue remains one of investor suitability and whether that necessitates regulating access to hedge fund investments.

To assess suitability we must ask whether hedge fund investors are, in effect, unwittingly underwriting disaster insurance. The operative principle in insurance is that risk transfer should result in the concentration of risk with the less risk-averse party. Arguably, the existing requirement of investor accreditation (which limits the audience to the less risk-averse) should assuage suitability concerns, although the emergence of vehicles that lower those requirements may not. The issue is germane to hedge funds not only because of their extensive use of derivatives and the optionlike characteristics of their incentive fees, but also because they are often marketed on the basis of RAPMs such as the Sharpe ratio. To the extent that financial intermediaries, such as registered brokers, are sufficiently trained to assess suitability and investors sufficiently aware of risks when viewed as stand-alone investments, then the focus can shift to the potential portfolio level benefits of adding hedge funds based on marginal risk-return characteristics.

Bookstaber and Clarke (1981) show that options can skew portfolio returns distribution, rendering the mean-variance framework inadequate. While market participants may be aware that the October 1987 crash was an abnormal extreme event, they may perceive the relevance of higher moments as merely an esoteric concern. Table 20.2 shows negative skew and excess positive kurtosis for the Standard & Poor's (S&P) 500 over each of the trailing 10-, 20-, 30- and 40-year periods[2] running from February 1962 to January 2002.

Goodness of fit tests for the past 40 years confirms our suspicion. Table 20.3 shows rejections of normality by the Bera-Jarque test at the 99 percent level and by the Lilliefors test at the 95 percent level.

TABLE 20.2 Skewness and Excess Kurtosis of the S&P 500 Index, February 1962 to January 2002

S&P 500 Returns	Excess Kurtosis	Skewness	Volatility	Average Monthly Return
40 yrs (2/62–1/02)	1.91	(0.32)	4.33	0.97
30 yrs (2/72–1/02)	2.20	(0.36)	4.49	1.06
20 yrs (2/82–1/02)	2.96	(0.67)	4.43	1.29
10 yrs (2/92–1/02)	1.10	(0.66)	4.04	1.10

[2]The effect would be more pronounced with daily instead of monthly data.

TABLE 20.3 Goodness of Fit Tests on the S&P 500
Index, February 1962 to January 2002

Test	*p*-value	Test stat	95% Critical Value	99% Critical Value
Lilliefors	0.0486	0.0408[a]	0.0404	0.0503
Bera-Jarque	—	77.2904[b]	5.9915	9.2103

[a]Significant at the 5 percent level.
[b]Significant at the 1 percent level.

Figure 20.1 and Table 20.4 show that for hedge funds, the mean, median and mode of skewness are all negative as is the skew of skewness.

Figure 20.2 and Table 20.4 show that the mean, median, and mode of kurtosis (in excess of normality) are significantly positive with positive skew and kurtosis of kurtosis.

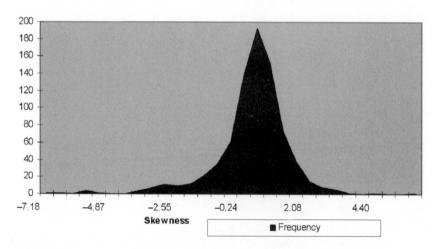

FIGURE 20.1 Distribution of Skewness
The distribution of HF skewness shows mild negative skew of −1.24 apparently due to the counterbalancing effect of including CTAs. Still the left tail is longer given min of −7.18 vs. max of 5.78 while mean, median & mode are all negative.
Source for 787 HFs used: Hedge Fund Research, Inc., © HFR, Inc.,
www.hedgefundresearch.com.

TABLE 20.4 RAPM Statistics for the HFR Universe, 1997 to 2001

Spearman Correlations	ExTR	Volatility	Monthly Skewness	Monthly Excess Kurtosis	Treynor	Jensen	Beta	Sharpe	AIRAP	MSR
ExTR	1.00	0.06	0.26	0.02	0.41	0.90	0.08	0.73	0.76	0.49
Vol	0.06	1.00	0.22	(0.13)	(0.32)	0.11	0.55	(0.50)	(0.47)	(0.73)
Skew mo	0.26	0.22	1.00	(0.18)	0.11	0.32	(0.03)	0.07	0.14	(0.02)
Excess Kurt mo	0.02	(0.13)	(0.18)	1.00	0.10	0.04	(0.05)	0.12	0.08	0.14
Treynor	0.41	(0.32)	0.11	0.10	1.00	0.34	0.04	0.60	0.50	0.57
Jensen	0.90	0.11	0.32	0.04	0.34	1.00	(0.16)	0.66	0.66	0.43
Beta	0.08	0.55	(0.03)	(0.05)	0.04	(0.16)	1.00	(0.23)	(0.24)	(0.37)
Sharpe	0.73	(0.50)	0.07	0.12	0.60	0.66	(0.23)	1.00	0.86	0.92
AIRAP	0.76	(0.47)	0.14	0.08	0.50	0.66	(0.24)	0.86	1.00	0.80
MSR	0.49	(0.73)	(0.02)	0.14	0.57	0.43	(0.37)	0.92	0.80	1.00

Significance	ExTR	Volatility	Monthly Skewness	Monthly Excess Kurtosis	Treynor	Jensen	Beta	Sharpe	AIRAP	MSR
ExTR	—	0.11	0.00	0.57	—	—	0.03	—	—	—
Vol	0.11	—	0.00	0.00	0.00	0.00	—	—	—	—
Skew mo	0.00	0.00	—	0.00	0.00	—	0.44	0.05	0.00	0.53
Excess Kurt mo	0.57	0.00	0.00	—	0.01	0.29	0.17	0.00	0.02	0.00
Treynor	—	—	0.00	0.01	—	—	0.23	—	—	—
Jensen	—	0.00	—	0.29	—	—	0.00	—	—	—
Beta	0.03	—	0.44	0.17	0.23	0.00	—	0.00	0.00	—
Sharpe	—	—	0.05	0.00	—	—	0.00	—	—	—
AIRAP	—	—	0.00	0.02	—	—	0.00	—	—	—
MSR	—	—	0.53	0.00	—	—	—	—	—	—

TABLE 20.4 *(continued)*

Stats/RAPMs	Mean ExTR	Median ExTR	Volatility	Monthly Skewness	Monthly Excess Kurtosis	SR	Treynor
Pearson Correl (AIRAP)	0.22	0.12	(0.74)	0.06	(0.09)	0.46	(0.01)
Mean	0.69%	0.58%	16.55%	(0.14)	3.02	0.75	0.05
Standard Error	0.02%	0.03%	0.46%	0.04	0.19	0.03	0.16
Median	0.59%	0.53%	13.83%	(0.01)	1.28	0.57	0.19
Mode	0.78%	0.75%	46.06%	(0.37)	4.00	0.09	(0.03)
Standard Deviation	0.66%	0.73%	12.87%	1.23	5.39	0.82	4.43
Sample Variance	0.00%	0.01%	1.66%	1.50	29.08	0.67	19.60
Kurtosis	4.87	3.77	4.98	5.89	28.46	14.57	103.59
Skewness	1.20	(0.03)	1.78	(1.24)	4.54	2.68	(6.82)
Minimum	-1.54%	(0.03)	0.00	(7.18)	(0.86)	(1.72)	(60.66)
Maximum	5.25%	0.04	1.00	5.78	51.41	7.54	38.93

Stats/RAPMs	Jensen	Beta (S&P)	ExTR	AIRAP	Risk Prem	MSR
Pearson Correl (AIRAP)	0.37	(0.38)	0.62	1.00	(0.82)	0.06
Mean	6.22%	0.29	6.53%	-0.02%	6.55%	13.65
Standard Error	0.28%	0.02	0.28%	0.49%	0.39%	3.05
Median	5.64%	0.20	6.01%	2.99%	2.97%	2.13
Mode	14.36%	(1.45)	-7.19%	-46.41%	39.22%	(0.18)
Standard Deviation	7.93%	0.46	7.92%	13.78%	10.82%	85.69
Sample Variance	0.63%	0.21	0.63%	1.90%	1.17%	7,341.92
Kurtosis	5.71	2.26	2.19	10.70	22.44	235.44
Skewness	0.84	0.32	0.23	(2.73)	4.12	14.70
Minimum	-24.36%	(1.75)	(0.25)	(0.93)	0.00	(74.00)
Maximum	66.53%	2.12	0.45	0.26	0.89	1,600.14

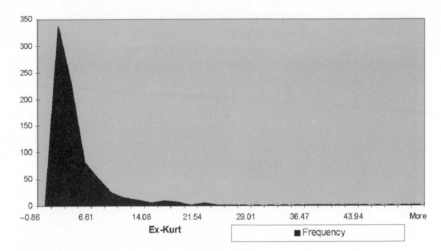

FIGURE 20.2   Distribution of Excess Kurtosis
The distribution of excess kurtosis for hedge funds during the 5 years (01/97–12/01)
is clearly right skewed (+4.54) with a long tail (max of 51.4 but min of –.86).
Average Ex-Kurt of 3.0 is significantly non-Gaussian with 87.4% of all funds with
excess kurtosis.
Source for 787 HFs used: Hedge Fund Research, Inc., © HFR, Inc.,
www.hedgefundresearch.com.

Sharpe (1994) points out that comparisons based on the first two
moments of a distribution do not consider possible differences in higher
moments among portfolios. Nor do they consider differences in distributions of outcomes that may be associated with different levels of investor
utility. What is needed is a measure that incorporates investor preferences
via risk aversion and that adjusts for iceberg risks lurking in the higher
moments.

EXPECTED UTILITY THEORY AND AIRAP

Expected utility theory is central to the foundations of modern economics
and dates back to the axioms of Von Neumann–Morgenstern. Under tran-
sitivity, completeness, independence, and the Archimedean axioms, investor
preferences have an expected utility representation (which is unique up to
affine transforms). The expected utility property allows for the expression
of the Von Neumann–Morgenstern utility u of a lottery with payoffs $z1$ and

$z2$ and probabilities p and $(1-p)$ as $[pu(z1) + (1 - p)u(z2)]$. Here u is the real-valued Bernoulli utility, which is a function of payoffs. Allowing a lottery to be represented by a real-valued random variable enables lotteries to be equivalently stated in terms of preferences over cumulative distributions F as shown by this expression:

$$\text{For lotteries } w \And w' : F_w \geq F_{w'} \equiv U(F_w) \geq U(F_{w'})$$

where $U(F_w) = \int_R u(x)dF_w(x)$

For RAPMs to be useful, they should incorporate risk aversion since the investor expects to be paid a risk premium for owning risky assets. In this case risk aversion is embodied by the concavity of u.

Given the concavity of u and Jensen's inequality, we obtain equation 20.1:

$$u(E(z)) = u(pz_1 + (1 - p)z_2) > pu(z_1) + (1 - p)u(z_2) = E(u(z)) \quad (20.1)$$

Risk aversion is captured by $u(E(z)) > E(u(z))$, since the utility of the mean payoff $E(z)$ exceeds the utility of the uncertain lottery (with payoffs $z1$ and $z2$). The certainty equivalent lottery can thus be defined as that lottery that pays $CE(z)$ and has the same utility as the uncertain lottery $u(CE(z)) = E(u(z))$, as shown in Figure 20.3. Risk-aversion qua concavity entails that the payoff

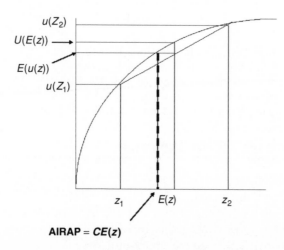

AIRAP = CE(z)

FIGURE 20.3 AIRAP (Certainty Equivalent for CRRA = 4) under Risk Aversion

be such that $CE(z) < E(z)$. Hence, the risk-premium (RP) in equation 20.2 is defined as

$$RP(z) = (E(z) - CE(z)), RP(z) \geq 0 \qquad (20.2)$$

In the RAPM world, $CE(z)$ is the implied equivalent return that the risk-averse investor desires with certainty in exchange for the uncertain return from holding risky assets. Consequently, $RP(z) \geq 0$ (under risk-aversion) is the price paid for trading off the risky asset with $CE(z)$. Hence, certainty equivalence provides an intuitive risk adjustment for our definition of AIRAP. By stripping out varying risk premia earned, it facilitates a fair comparison of hedge fund performance. Further, strict monotonicity and continuity of the chosen utility function ensure invertibility, resulting in $CE(z)$ rankings that are identical to maximizing $E(u)$, since by definition, $CE(z) = u^{-1}(E(u))$. See Huang and Litzenberger (1988) for a discussion of utility theory in financial economics.

We now proceed with choosing the appropriate form of utility. The standard mean-variance framework is justified either on the basis of quadratic utility (for arbitrary distributions) or multivariate normality (for arbitrary preferences). However, neither assumption is satisfactory. Quadratic utility displays satiation and IARA (increasing absolute risk aversion), since it views risky assets as inferior goods, while normality is a poor assumption for hedge fund data. In fact, hedge fund data do not even usually satisfy the premises of the central limit theorem (Getmansky, Lo, and Makarov 2003).

A CRRA formulation has the benefit of being impartial to wealth level, which is to be expected of asset managers from a fiduciary perspective, excluding negative wealth, which is consistent with hedge fund losses under limited liability being bounded below by the principal invested, and scale invariance. For instance, a high-net-worth family in the top 39.1 percent tax bracket will be relatively indifferent to a $10,000 loss, which represents less than 3.4 percent of income, compared to a family at the poverty line (annual income less than $18,000) for whom the same loss amounts to 55.3 percent of income. See Osband (2002) for an exposition of utility functions and the relative merits of CARA versus CRRA utility.

The best-known measure of risk aversion is the Arrow-Pratt measure. Assuming concavity, monotonically increasing, and twice-differentiable utility, CRRA is tantamount to requiring that the Arrow-Pratt RRA coefficient is a constant c in equation 20.3:

$$-\frac{u''(w)}{u'(w)} w = c \qquad (20.3)$$

We assume the NAV (net asset value) process represents hedge fund total returns in equation 20.4:

$$\%TR_t = \frac{(NAV_t - NAV_{t-1})}{NAV_{t-1}} \tag{20.4}$$

CRRA utility corresponds to the family of power utility functions defined for terminal wealth W_T as:

$$U(W_T) \equiv \frac{W_T^{(1-c)} - 1}{(1-c)}, c \neq 1, c \geq 0. \tag{20.5}$$

Equation 20.5 reduces to when $U(W_T) = \ln(W_T)$ when $c = 1$. Given that terminal wealth is just the initial wealth W_0 compounded at rate TR, we obtain equation 20.6:

$$W_T = W_0(1 + TR) \tag{20.6}$$

Since CRRA rankings are scale invariant, then $U(W_T)$ rankings are the same as $U(1+ TR)$, so we obtain equation 20.7:

$$U(1+TR) \equiv \frac{(1+TR)^{(1-c)} - 1}{(1-c)}, c \neq 1, c \geq 0 \tag{20.7}$$

which reduces to $U(1 + TR) = \ln(1 + TR)$ when $c = 1$. For a finite discrete distribution, we can now solve directly for CRRA certainty equivalence, albeit not explicitly parsed in terms of higher moments. Let p_i represent the probability of the ith return of N observed rates TR_i for $i = 1, \dots, N$ such that:

$$EU \equiv \sum_i \left[\frac{(1+TR_i)^{(1-c)} - 1}{(1-c)} \right] . p_i = U \Leftrightarrow \left[\sum_i p_i . (1+TR_i)^{(1-c)} - \sum_i p_i \right] = (1+CE)^{(1-c)} - 1$$

$$\Leftrightarrow \left[\sum_i p_i . (1+TR_i)^{(1-c)} \right] = (1+CE)^{(1-c)} \Leftrightarrow$$

$$AIRAP = CE = \left[\sum_i p_i . (1+TR_i)^{(1-c)} \right]^{1/(1-c)} - 1 \tag{20.8}$$

where $c \geq 0$ but $c \neq 1$

To avoid restrictive distributional assumptions, we can proceed with any one of many available nonparametric estimation techniques. We emphasize the generality of this result, since the choice of nonparametric method is a matter of taste, and the resulting AIRAP estimate need not be tied to it. Still, it is worth highlighting a particularly simple solution that results from fitting a histogram where p_i denotes the frequency of observations in the ith bin, $i = 1, \ldots, M$. Since an arbitrary choice of bin size results in an arbitary number M of bins and arbitrary precision of the AIRAP estimate, we set the bin width ε as in equation 20.9:

$$\varepsilon = \frac{1}{2} \times \text{Min} \left| TR_i - TR_j \right| \qquad (20.9)$$

for every $i \neq j$. Starting with the leftmost observation, the ε-bins are centered on each TR_i such that all distinct TR_i fall in exactly one bin. Thus, for all nonempty bins, we obtain $p_i = 1/N$. Substituting $1/N$ for p_i in AIRAP yields a convenient closed form simplification. When $c = 1$, we proceed in a similar manner to solve for AIRAP under log utility (equation 20.10):

$$\Leftrightarrow \ln \left\{ \prod_i (1 + TR_i)^{p_i} \right\} = \ln(1 + CE)$$

$$EU \equiv \sum_i \ln(1 + TR_i).p_i = U \equiv \ln(1 + CE)$$

$$\Leftrightarrow AIRAP = CE = \left[\prod_i (1 + TR_i)^{p_i} \right] - 1, \quad c = 1 \qquad (20.10)$$

Again setting $p_i = 1/N$ provides a closed form solution that has a straight-forward spreadsheet implementation. In general, any nonparametric estimate as just outlined has the dual benefit of being distribution free and of capturing all observed moments. Note that an analogous derivation is obtainable under exponential utility (CARA), which would be a special case of the closed form solution in Davis (2001) for histograms. Hence, AIRAP could be formulated for CARA with ease. For comparison, we note that Madan and McPhail (2000) as well as Davis (2001) use exponential utility while Osband (2002) and Leland (1999) use power utility.

Recommended Arrow-Pratt Coefficient

For power utility, $c > 0$ represents risk-aversion. When $c = 0$, $U(TR)$ is linear in TR and AIRAP is simply the arithmetic mean or in the annualized case it is the geometrically compounded monthly arithmetic mean excess return. For $c = 1$, logarithmic utility results in AIRAP as the geometric mean of monthly excess returns. Since $0 < c < 1$ implausibly allows rational investors to entertain bets potentially resulting in insolvency, we restrict our attention to $c \geq 1$. In the latter case, the pain of insolvency is unbounded, precluding bets that could risk total ruin.

The plausible range for c is from 1 to 10. Osband (2002) suggests using c from 2 to 4. Ait-Sahalia, Parker, and Yogo (2001) propose a resolution to the equity premium puzzle by examining data on the consumption of luxury goods by the very rich, who also constitute the majority of equity ownership. Their point estimate of $c = 3.2$ for ultra-high-net-worth individuals seems most pertinent to hedge fund investors. To be quite conservative, we assume $c = 4$, in which case the CRRA agent is willing risk no more than a fifth of her wealth for even odds of doubling.

The dependence of this approach on parameter c may be viewed as undesirable from a practical standpoint, given the ongoing academic debate over the true value of c and its implications for the equity risk premium puzzle. However, for RAPM purposes, this is not an impediment. As long as we can target a plausible but fixed c, the ranking of all funds under AIRAP will be comparable and consistent. There is a possible significant benefit to the flexibility of being able to tweak risk aversion. Technology can enable financial advisors and investment managers to query data on investor risk preferences and map them to an individualized c, thereby generating customized AIRAP rankings.

DATA AND ANALYSIS

We use monthly data from January 1997 to December 2001, from the Evaluation Associates Capital Markets (EACM) indices for our index-level analysis, since these indices are recognized for their style-pure categorization. The EACM100 is an equally weighted, annually rebalanced composite of 100 funds rigorously screened to represent 5 strategies (13 style subindices). It has adequate data history (extending to 1996) and does not allow closed funds. At the individual fund level, where EACM does not disclose constituents, we resort to Hedge Fund Research (HFR) data because of its wide usage and lower survivorship bias. Of the 2,445 entries in HFR as of June 2003, only 887 hedge funds existed for the entire five-year period. One hundred time series corresponding to HFR indices were excluded. The final 787 hedge funds include onshore and offshore funds, FoHFs, managed futures, as well as sector hedge funds. Table 20.5 provides descriptive statistics on the EACM sub-indices.

TABLE 20.5 Descriptive Statistics of the EACM Subindices, 1997 to 2001

	Relative Value				Event Driven		
	Long/Short Equity	Convertible Hedge	Bond Hedge	Multi-Strategy	Risk Arbitrage	Bankruptcy Distressed	Multi-Strategy
Mean ExTR monthly	0.00%	0.32%	-0.37%	0.73%	0.35%	0.29%	0.73%
Median ExTR monthly	0.09%	0.50%	0.15%	0.97%	0.49%	0.51%	0.86%
Vol ExTR annual	2.98%	5.99%	6.02%	8.44%	4.87%	6.22%	6.18%
Skew ExTR monthly	(0.56)	(2.11)	(2.12)	(4.61)	(2.49)	(1.87)	(2.31)
Excess Kurt ExTR monthly	1.65	6.28	5.76	24.70	9.06	8.32	11.49
Ann Sharpe	0.02	0.65	(0.73)	1.04	0.86	0.56	1.41
Ann Treynor	(0.10)	0.60	(1.24)	2.20	0.31	0.22	0.57
Ann Jensen's Alpha	0.09%	3.40%	-4.67%	8.51%	3.24%	2.34%	7.64%
CAPM Beta	(0.01)	0.06	0.04	0.04	0.13	0.16	0.15

	Equity Hedge Funds			Global AA			
	Domestic Long Bias	Domestic Opportunistic	Global/ International	Discretionary	Systematic	Short Sellers	S&P 500 Index
Mean ExTR monthly	0.66%	1.06%	0.58%	0.19%	0.19%	0.25%	0.59%
Median ExTR monthly	0.35%	0.85%	0.66%	0.03%	-0.16%	-0.46%	0.71%
Vol ExTR annual	21.93%	12.91%	13.05%	10.19%	12.06%	22.78%	17.91%
Skew ExTR monthly	(0.06)	1.03	0.22	(2.60)	0.62	0.72	(0.54)
Excess Kurt ExTR monthly	0.23	2.14	0.89	14.90	1.15	0.47	
Ann Sharpe	0.36	0.99	0.54	0.22	0.19	0.13	0.39
Ann Treynor	0.10	0.62	0.16	0.07	(0.44)	(0.03)	0.07
Ann Jensen's Alpha	2.04%	11.28%	3.92%	-0.01%	2.65%	10.55%	0.00%
CAPM Beta	0.83	0.20	0.44	0.32	(0.05)	(1.08)	1.00

TABLE 20.5 (continued)

	Relative Value				Event Driven		
	Long/Short Equity	Convertible Hedge	Bond Hedge	Multi-Strategy	Risk Arbitrage	Bankruptcy Distressed	Multi-Strategy
Corr to S&P500	(0.03)	0.19	0.10	0.08	0.49	0.46	0.45
Lilliefors GoF test*	0	1	1	1	1	1	1
Bera-Jarque GoF test*	1	1	1	1	1	1	1
P value Lilliefors*	0.10	NaN	NaN	NaN	NaN	0.04	NaN
P value Bera-Jarque*	0.05	—	—	—	—	—	—
Ann ExTR	0.01%	3.75%	-4.50%	8.75%	4.14%	3.32%	8.89%
Ann AIRAP [CRR = 4]	-0.13%	3.16%	-5.06%	7.32%	3.75%	2.69%	8.23%
Ann Risk Prem [CRR = 4]	0.13%	0.59%	0.55%	1.43%	0.39%	0.63%	0.66%
Modified SR	0.05	6.38	(8.12)	6.12	10.66	5.27	13.46

	Equity Hedge Funds			Global AA		Short Sellers	S&P 500 Index
	Domestic Long Bias	Domestic Opportunistic	Global/ International	Discretionary	Systematic		
Corr to S&P500	0.68	0.28	0.60	0.56	(0.08)	(0.84)	1.00
Lilliefors GoF test*	0	0	0	1	0	0	
Bera-Jarque GoF test*	0	1	0	1	1	0	
P value Lilliefors*	NaN	NaN	NaN	NaN	0.11	NaN	
P value Bera-Jarque*	0.97	0.00	0.37	—	0.04	0.07	
Ann ExTR	5.66%	12.60%	6.37%	1.72%	1.59%	0.46%	5.61%
Ann AIRAP [CRR = 4]	-1.71%	10.08%	3.77%	v0.14%	-0.49%	-6.42%	0.45%
Ann Risk Prem [CRR = 4]	7.37%	2.52%	2.59%	1.86%	2.08%	6.88%	5.16%
Modified SR	0.77	5.01	2.45	0.93	0.76	0.07	1.09

*2-sided, 95%

TABLE 20.5 *(continued)*

Spearman Correlations	ExTR	Volatility	Monthly Skewness	Monthly Excess Kurtosis	Treynor	Jensen	Beta	Sharpe	AIRAP	MSR
ExTR	1.00	0.23	(0.05)	0.24	0.85	0.65	0.60	0.90	0.84	0.74
Volatility	0.23	1.00	0.57	(0.53)	(0.06)	0.37	0.27	(0.07)	(0.20)	(0.25)
Monthly Skewness	(0.05)	0.57	1.00	(0.85)	(0.25)	0.31	(0.07)	(0.30)	(0.19)	(0.43)
Monthly Excess Kurtosis	0.24	(0.53)	(0.85)	1.00	0.49	(0.01)	0.05	0.54	0.48	0.60
Treynor	0.85	(0.06)	(0.25)	0.49	1.00	0.66	0.37	0.94	0.84	0.86
Jensen	0.65	0.37	0.31	(0.01)	0.66	1.00	(0.06)	0.63	0.57	0.47
Beta	0.60	0.27	(0.07)	0.05	0.37	(0.06)	1.00	0.39	0.37	0.35
Sharpe	0.90	(0.07)	(0.30)	0.54	0.94	0.63	0.39	1.00	0.87	0.93
AIRAP	0.84	(0.20)	(0.19)	0.48	0.84	0.57	0.37	0.87	1.00	0.77
MSR	0.74	(0.25)	(0.43)	0.60	0.86	0.47	0.35	0.93	0.77	1.00

2-Sided Correlation p-values	ExTR	Volatility	Monthly Skewness	Monthly Excess Kurtosis	Treynor	Jensen	Beta	Sharpe	AIRAP	MSR
ExTR	—	0.45	0.87	0.43	0.00	0.02	0.03	0.00	0.00	0.00
Volatility	0.45	—	0.04	0.06	0.84	0.21	0.36	0.82	0.51	0.42
Monthly Skewness	0.87	0.04	—	0.00	0.40	0.31	0.82	0.32	0.54	0.14
Monthly Excess Kurtosis	0.43	0.06	0.00	—	0.09	0.97	0.87	0.06	0.09	0.03
Treynor	0.00	0.84	0.40	0.09	—	0.01	0.22	0.00	0.00	0.00

TABLE 20.5 *(continued)*

				Monthly Excess						
Jensen	0.02	0.21	0.31	0.97	0.01	—	0.84	0.02	0.04	0.10
Beta	0.03	0.36	0.82	0.87	0.22	0.84	—	0.19	0.22	0.24
Sharpe	0.00	0.82	0.32	0.06	0.00	0.02	0.19	—	0.00	0.00
AIRAP	0.00	0.51	0.54	0.09	0.00	0.04	0.22	0.00	—	0.00
MSR	0.00	0.42	0.14	0.03	0.00	0.10	0.24	0.00	0.00	—

Ascending ranks by RAPM	ExTR	Volatility	Monthly Skewness	Monthly Excess Kurtosis	Treynor	Jensen	Beta	Sharpe	AIRAP	MSR
L/S Eq	2	1	8	5	3	3	3	2	6	2
Converts	7	3	6	8	11	8	6	9	8	11
Bond Hedge	1	4	5	7	1	1	4	1	2	1
RV Multi-Strategy	11	7	1	13	13	11	5	12	11	10
Risk Arbitrage	8	2	3	10	9	7	7	10	9	12
Bankruptcy/D	6	6	7	9	8	5	9	8	7	9
ED Multi-Strategy	12	5	4	11	10	10	8	13	12	13
Domestic Long Domestic	9	12	9	1	6	4	13	6	3	5
Opportunistic	13	10	13	6	12	13	10	11	13	8
Global International	10	11	10	3	7	9	12	7	10	7
GAA Discretionary	5	8	2	12	5	2	11	5	5	6
GAA Systematic	4	9	11	4	2	6	2	4	4	4
Shorts Sellers	3	13	12	2	4	12	1	3	1	3

Our data set is long enough to be meaningfully subject to analysis, without being too long to be affected by survivorship bias. Furthermore, the choice of this period was motivated by the desire to include the Asian crisis (1997), the Russian crisis, and LTCM debacle (1998), the bubble era (through 1999), and the subsequent Nasdaq collapse. We do not explicitly adjust for survivorship, instant history, selection, and other well-known biases, since our objective is to study relative rankings. Table 20.4 shows the aggregate statistics for the first four moments and various RAPMs for the HFR universe. This in conjunction with Figure 20.2 shows the distribution of excess kurtosis to be right skewed (+4.54) with a long right tail, as evidenced by a maximum of 51.4. The average excess kurtosis of 3 indicates nonnormality. Indeed, over 87 percent of funds show positive excess kurtosis. The mean skewness is –0.14, while the skewness of skewness is also negative (–1.24). This could have been worse at the composite level if not for the counterbalancing effect of managed futures and macro funds in the sample (Table 20.5).

Rank discrepancies at the intrastrategy level are likely to be fewer if HFR strategies are sufficiently style pure to reduce heterogeneity. While the 90 percent average reversal rate from intrastrategy rankings in Table 20.6 is somewhat lower, it is well known that the self-proclaimed style of managers in databases such as HFR need not be a reliable indicator of the factors they load on. The magnitude of intrastrategy rank discrepancies and how that relates to the aggregate level across databases is further documented in Sharma (2004). Table 20.7 summarizes RAPM statistics for the HFR universe.

Scatter plots of RAPM rankings (Figure 20.4) and the abundance of off-diagonal funds visually confirm the noted lack of correlation. The picture is essentially the same for CRRA in the 2 to 4 range. The Treynor ratio, with the lowest AIRAP correlation of 0.49, erroneously penalizes funds with slight negative beta exposures or negative means, resulting in the clus-

TABLE 20.6 Percentage Rejections of Normality versus Percentage Rank Reversals, 1997 to 2001

HFR Intra-Style	Number of Rejections	Percentage of Rejections	Number of of Funds	Number of Reversals	Percentage of Reversals
Short Sellers	4	36%	11	9	82%
Equity Nonhedged	22	37%	60	53	88%
Convertible Arbitrage	20	51%	39	34	87%
Merger Arbitrage	19	66%	29	29	100%
Event Driven	35	80%	44	41	93%
Full HFR universe	418	53%	788	787	100%

TABLE 20.7 RAPM Measures on 787 Funds from the HFR Universe, 1997 to 2001

	Average	Median	Minimum	Maximum
ExTR	6.53%	6.01%	−25.10%	44.76%
Vol	16.55%	13.83%	0.12%	100.07%
Skewness	−0.14	−0.01	−7.18	5.78
Excess kurtosis	3.02	1.28	−0.86	51.41
Treynor ratio	0.05	0.19	−60.66	38.93
Alpha	6.20%	5.60%	−24.40%	66.50%
Beta	0.29	0.2	−1.75	2.12
Sharpe ratio	0.75	0.57	−1.72	7.54
AIRAP	−0.02%	2.99%	−93.25%	25.63%
MSR	13.65	2.13	−74	1,600.14

ter to the southeast corner. Alpha, on the other hand (+.66 correlation), creates a cluster to the northwest composed of funds that are in most cases either negative beta or where the CAPM beta fails to capture risk. Short sellers are grossly misrepresented due to their negative betas, resulting in

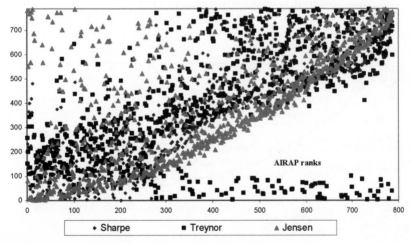

FIGURE 20.4 Comparative RAPM Rankings (HFR Universe)
All RAPM ranks are in ascending order with higher ranks being more desirable. AIRAP (CRRA = 4) rankings are shown on the *x*-axis. The abundance of off-diagonal data shows the extent of divergence between the 3 RAPMS vis-à-vis AIRAP. The cluster of pyramids in the top left represents high JA funds demoted by AIRAP. The cluster of squares at the bottom right represents high AIRAP funds demoted by Treynor.
Source for 787 HFs used: Hedge Fund Research, Inc., © HFR, Inc., *www.hedgefundresearch.com*.

Jensen's alpha being artificially boosted and the Treynor ratio being inappropriately depressed.

We display rank correlations and reversals between the Sharpe ratio, Jensen's alpha, and power utility (AIRAP) for the full HFR universe of 787 funds, as a function of the parameter c (between 0.1 and 30), in Table 20.8 and Figure 20.5. RAPM ranks and correlations for the 13 EACM style subindices appear in Table 20.5.

The Sharpe ratio rank correlations (Table 20.8) are similar to those of Fung and Hsieh (1999a) except that their study used 233 funds, they define the Sharpe ratio in terms of total and not excess returns, and they did not look across style categories and databases. More important, their objective was to check for the near sufficiency of mean-variance in portfolio construction as opposed to the suitability of RAPMs for hedge funds.

The performance of the Sharpe ratio in ranking hedge funds is significantly misleading with respect to the investor's true utility rankings as per both ranks reversals and correlations (Table 20.8). Pearson correlations (Table 20.4) are even weaker at 0.46, 0.37 and −0.01 for the Sharpe ratio, Jensen's alpha, and the Treynor ratio, respectively. Our correlations

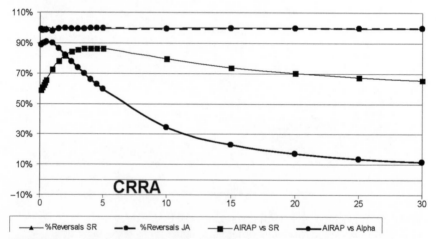

FIGURE 20.5 Percentage Reversals and Rank Correlations by Risk Aversion AIRAP vs. Sharpe & Jensen represent Spearman rank correlations. Correlations with Jensen tapers off rapidly. %Reversals SR show nearly 100% rank reversals between Sharpe & AIRAP. %Reversals JA show nearly 100% rank reversals between Jensen & AIRAP. Data: 787 funds in HFR for the period 1997 to 2001. *Source*: Hedge Fund Research, Inc., © HFR, Inc., *www.hedgefundresearch.com*.

TABLE 20.8 AIRAP, Sharpe Ratio and Jensen's Alpha Rank Correlations as a Function of Risk Aversion, 1997 to 2001

c parameter	#Reversals Sharpe ratio	#Reversals Jensen's alpha	%Reversals Sharpe ratio	%Reversals Jensen's alpha	AIRAP vs. Sharpe ratio	AIRAP vs. Jensen's Alpha	Fung and Hsieh (1999) Correlations
0.1	781	779	99%	99%	0.59	0.89	0.49
0.2	780	775	99%	98%	0.61	0.89	0.50
0.3	784	777	99%	99%	0.63	0.90	0.52
0.4	783	776	99%	98%	0.64	0.90	0.53
0.5	786	776	100%	98%	0.66	0.91	0.55
1	783	772	99%	98%	0.73	0.90	0.52
1.5	784	783	99%	99%	0.78	0.86	0.68
2	787	785	100%	100%	0.82	0.82	0.73
2.5	785	784	100%	99%	0.84	0.78	0.77
3	785	784	100%	99%	0.86	0.74	0.81
3.5	786	783	100%	99%	0.86	0.70	0.84
4	787	786	100%	100%	0.86	0.66	0.85
4.5	786	786	100%	100%	0.87	0.63	0.87
5	783	787	99%	100%	0.87	0.60	0.89
10	785	784	100%	99%	0.80	0.34	0.89
15	788	786	100%	100%	0.74	0.23	0.87
20	788	786	100%	100%	0.70	0.17	0.85
25	784	787	99%	100%	0.68	0.14	0.83
30	786	787	100%	100%	0.66	0.11	0.81

Source: Hedge Fund Research, Inc. (*www.hedgefundresearch.com*)

(Table 20.8) are similar to those of Fung and Hsieh (1999a) for CRRA in the range [3, 5], but theirs drop off much faster for lower values of CRRA while ours decline faster for higher levels of risk aversion. Further correlations of AIRAP with alpha decrease dramatically with increasing risk aversion. This may be explicable since AIRAP imposes a steeper risk penalty, as an increasing but nonlinear function of risk aversion, while alpha is invariant with regard to risk aversion.

Table 20.9 shows that fund 512 has the worst AIRAP rank (#1) even though the Sharpe ratio ranks it as #133 (out of 787), because not only are returns low (10) and volatility very high extreme (#786 rank) but iceberg risks are high. Excess kurtosis (ExKurt) is ranked #682 while skewness is ranked #58. Fund 235 has the worst Sharpe ratio (#1) due to negative mean. AIRAP correctly handles the negative mean and boosts the rank by 201 notches since the higher moments are tame and volatility is exceptionally low. Fund 229 has the highest Jensen's alpha (ranked #787 due to negative beta), moderate Sharpe ratio (ranked #482), but AIRAP is 775 notches lower because of the penalty for high volatility (83.2 percent). For EACM subindices, AIRAP penalizes on average 2 percent more than does Jensen's alpha. It is systematically lower than Jensen's alpha for all but event-driven subindices. In the case of multistrategy Relative Value, the penalty is 1.2 percent, largely due to the −4.6 skewness and excess kurtosis of nearly 25.

To show that AIRAP conveys new information not already captured by traditional RAPMs, we show Spearman rank and Pearson correlations in Table 20.4. For the HFR universe, AIRAP is positively correlated with ExTR, skewness, the Treynor ratio, Jensen's alpha, and the Sharpe ratio, but negatively correlated with volatility and beta, as expected. To the extent that a large dispersion in mean-variance profiles has been documented across strategies and these effects often dominate higher order effects, one should expect drastic rank reversals for the full HFR universe that aggregates across strategies. We find that rank reversals are in excess of 99 percent across the board. At the universe level, there is almost no agreement between AIRAP and Sharpe ratio or Jensen's alpha rankings. This observation needs to be tempered by the realization that for a given rank order <1,2,...,787>, the trivial permutation <2,3,...,787,1> results in 100 percent reversals despite near-perfect correlation. The key is that the magnitude of some of these reversals (in addition to their prevalence) can be substantial as indicated by Figure 20.4, anecdotal evidence, and the rank correlations previously noted.

Strategies with higher iceberg risks, such as HFR Merger Arbitrage and Event Driven, seem to have higher reversal rates (Table 20.6) than more liquid strategies like short sellers (82 percent). Short sellers display a much

TABLE 20.9 Representative Fund RAOM Comparisons

Panel A: Rankings

Fund ID	AIRAP	Sharpe	Treynor	Jensen	Beta	ExTR	Vol	Skew	ExKurt
229	13	482	62	788	25	787	787	719	590
230	11	362	302	753	786	679	781	398	507
231	10	420	351	777	783	747	780	373	550
235	202	1	48	65	176	69	8	423	74
272	2	234	256	781	655	223	788	788	786
512	1	133	151	81	771	10	776	58	682
636	788	699	599	776	635	784	545	667	361
762	373	788	784	221	143	201	2	485	174

Panel B : Values

Fund ID	AIRAP	Sharpe	Treynor	Jensen	Beta	ExTR	Vol	Skew	ExKurt
229	−48.57%	0.76	(1.27)	66.53%	(0.50)	37.92%	83.16%	1.13	3.23
230	−51.15%	0.53	0.19	20.27%	1.75	14.09%	61.08%	0.01	2.27
231	−51.64%	0.62	0.23	25.93%	1.64	20.12%	60.23%	(0.05)	2.68
235	−2.76%	−1.72	(1.40)	−2.88%	0.02	−2.72%	1.60%	0.07	(0.10)
272	−86.14%	0.34	0.49	29.23%	0.69	3.03%	100.07%	5.78	41.15
512	−93.25%	0.15	0.06	−2.09%	1.45	−13.39%	56.17%	(1.82)	6.00
636	25.63%	1.54	0.48	25.40%	0.62	31.96%	19.32%	0.80	1.13
762	2.41%	7.54	9.38	2.37%	0.00	2.41%	0.32%	0.22	0.34

lower incidence of non-Gaussian profile (36 percent) as compared to event driven (80 percent). Indeed, our results for EACM subindices (Table 20.5) show event driven as well as relative value and event driven multi-strategy being demoted a notch under AIRAP. Liquid equity strategies with controlled volatility, such as domestic opportunistic, global and long/short move up two to four notches. It would therefore appear that style categories exhibiting greater departures from normality (higher-moment risks) also exhibit greater rank discrepancies between the Sharpe ratio and AIRAP. However, the picture is muddled by the complex interaction of volatility with higher moments (since manifestation of higher kurtosis can percolate into volatility and skewness and vice-versa) and the fact that the higher magnitude volatility penalty often dominates. High volatility results in AIRAP severely penalizing long biased (RP = 7.37 percent) and short EACM subindices (RP = 6.9 percent). This interaction is often easier to disentangle at the individual fund level than at the aggregate category level.

The related claim that high Sharpe ratios in hedge funds may represent a trade-off for higher-moment risk is investigated in Sharma (2004). Here we simply note the positive and statistically significant rank correlation of the Sharpe ratio with excess kurtosis for both EACM and HFR data (Tables 20.4 and 20.5). To the extent that some hedge fund strategies pay for a better mean-variance profile by assuming iceberg risks, it seems less plausible that they are better exploiting inefficiencies or expanding the investment opportunity set. At least part of their mean-variance attraction may stem from the pre-meditated but potentially suicidal (short volatility) act of scooping up pennies before the onslaught of the steamroller.

Scott and Horvath (1980) show that risk-averse investors prefer positive odd central moments such as skewness and dislike even central moments such as kurtosis. Unlike traditional RAPMs, which are largely oblivious to the impact of higher moments, AIRAP critically penalizes for negative skewness and positive kurtosis.

IMPACT OF LEVERAGE

Traditionally, the leverage invariance of the Sharpe ratio has been considered desirable. This makes sense for traditional investments since leverage is neither central to the investment strategy nor usually permissible under existing regulation. If used at all, leverage is usually employed by means external to the core investment vehicle, perhaps at the allocation level or through structured products.

Leverage to the hedge fund manager is a critical extra degree of freedom, especially for relative value/arbitrage strategies. The decision whether to use leverage and to what extent is integral to the hedge fund investment process. The impact of leverage on the realized distribution should not be ignored. For ranking and comparison purposes, we must either use unlevered returns or account for leverage directly. Given the lack of transparency of hedge funds, computing unlevered returns may be impractical. Moreover, investor utility is a function of the realized total return achieved, not some hypothetical unlevered return that may have been achieved had the manager used leverage. Hence, appropriately accounting for leverage requires accommodating preferences. In other words, a good hedge fund RAPM should encapsulate aversion to excessive leverage under risk aversion.

To understand how AIRAP incorporates leverage, we consider only financing leverage, that is, the impact of levered exposure to the same risky fund enabled through borrowing. This suffices since AIRAP already adjusts for the market risk of the underlying fund based on returns data. Table 20.10 shows the impact of leverage on the EACM100 index. We assume that n-times leverage corresponds to the excess return scaled up by n, since the differential return is a self-financed portfolio. Hence, the mean monthly excess return of 0.40 percent doubles to 0.80 percent for 2× and rises to 6 percent for 15× leverage. Volatility, beta and Jensen's alpha also rise linearly by exactly the leverage factor n. Since Jensen's alpha rises in proportion to leverage, it is inappropriate for hedge funds as it indiscriminately rewards higher leverage without bound. The proportional rise in beta does not sufficiently penalize for the rise in volatility under risk aversion, even though skewness and excess kurtosis are unchanged. The Sharpe ratio and Treynor ratio, however, are both leverage invariant. To ensure that leverage invariance holds, we assume that the numerators in these ratios are annualized. They are oblivious to the impact of leverage since the first and second moments rise in tandem and cancel out in equation 20.11:

$$Sharpe_{P,Levered} = \frac{\mu_{P,Levered}}{\sigma_{P,Levered}} = \frac{n \times \mu_P}{n \times \sigma_P} = Sharpe_P$$

$$Treynor_{P,Levered} = \frac{\mu_{P,Levered}}{\beta_{P,Levered}} = \frac{n \times \mu_P}{n \times \beta_P} = Treynor_P$$

$$\beta_{P,Levered} = \rho \times \frac{\sigma_{P,Levered}}{\sigma_B} = \rho \times \left(\frac{n \times \sigma_P}{\sigma_B}\right) = n \times \beta_P, \quad \text{since} \quad \sigma_{P,Levered} = n \times \sigma_P$$

$$\alpha_{P,Levered} = R_{P,Levered} - \beta \times R_B = n \times (R_P - \beta \times R_B) = n \times \alpha_P \quad (20.11)$$

AIRAP penalizes for increased leverage as a function of risk aversion. The impact of leverage on the returns distribution is captured via credit for the higher mean and penalty for the higher volatility as a function of the CRR parameter. As an example, in going from 5× to 10× leverage, R_p jumps by 46.4 percent, from 12.3 to 58.7 percent (CRR = 4), turning AIRAP negative (−18.9 percent despite +39.8 percent excess TR). This is illustrated in Table 20.10.

The alpha of 37.3 percent and static value of 0.90 for the Sharpe ratio would be misleading. Assuming lower risk aversion, with $c = 2$, AIRAP only turns negative in going from 10× to 15× leverage, as shown in Figure 20.6. Hence, AIRAP provides risk-adjustment for leverage customized to the investor's risk aversion. An AIRAP based on the Sharpe ratio, defined as a function of CRR, would also respond to leverage because the denominator incorporates risk aversion, though not identically. This is shown with equation 20.12:

$$MSR - AIRAP = \left(\frac{ExcessTR}{RP4}\right) \qquad (20.12)$$

The difference is attributable to penalizing for risk-premium multiplicatively (in MSR-AIRAP) vis-à-vis additively (in AIRAP).

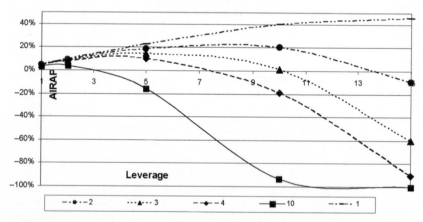

CRRA/ Leverage	1	2	5	10	15
1.00	4.77%	9.44%	22.63%	39.85%	45.23%
2.00	4.62%	8.84%	18.48%	20.32%	−9.44%
3.00	4.48%	8.24%	14.39%	0.86%	−60.10%
4.00	4.33%	7.64%	10.30%	−18.89%	−90.27%
10.00	3.47%	4.07%	−15.83%	−93.48%	−100.00%

FIGURE 20.6 AIRAP across CRRA and Leverage for EACM 100®

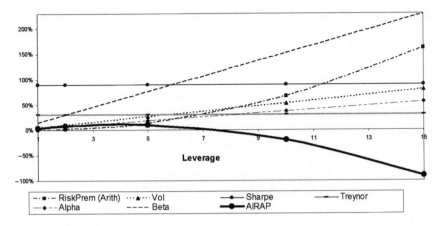

FIGURE 20.7 RAPM versus Leverage (CRR = 4)

Finally, the dependence of AIRAP on leverage, as shown by Figures 20.6 and 20.7 and Table 20.10, tells both the hedge fund manager and the institutional investor what degree of leverage is optimal for a given track record. Standard optimization techniques that use first- and second-order conditions in terms of the partial derivative of AIRAP on leverage can provide the optimal leverage, which maximizes AIRAP. Figure 20.6 shows the AIRAP profile across varying leverage for a range of CRRA. For the growth-optimal case, the Kelly criterion (Kelly 1956) provides the answer.

TABLE 20.10 Change in RAPMs with Change in Leverage

Leverage factor	2	5	10	15	Variable Response
Leverage increase	2.00	2.50	2.00	1.50	
ExTR	2.00	2.50	2.00	1.50	Linear
Volatility	2.00	2.50	2.00	1.50	Linear
Skewness	1.00	1.00	1.00	1.00	Invariant
Excess kurtosis	1.00	1.00	1.00	1.00	Invariant
Sharpe ratio	1.00	1.00	1.00	1.00	Invariant
Treynor ratio	1.00	1.00	1.00	1.00	Invariant
Jensen's alpha	2.00	2.50	2.00	1.50	Linear
Beta	2.00	2.50	2.00	1.50	Linear
AIRAP	1.76	1.35	−1.83	4.78	Nonlinear
ExTR geom	1.98	2.40	1.76	1.14	Nonlinear
Risk premium	4.15	6.98	4.88	2.43	Nonlinear

HEDGE FUND PEER PERCENTILE RANKINGS

Realized hedge fund peer rankings within categories can be based on realized AIRAP. However, for a prospective measure that may better handle iceberg risks without the complications of a regime-switching implementation, we propose for future implementation a composite percentile ranking framework based on a weighted average of the funds style category percentile and stressed scenario percentile. The weights w_1 and w_2 should be fixed from intrastyle category testing such that:

$$\text{Composite AIRAP Percentile} = w_1 \times \text{AIRAP Style Percentile} \\ + w_2 \times \text{AIRAP Stress Percentile}$$

and

$$\text{AIRAP Style Percentile} = 5\text{-year AIRAP Percentile Ranking} \\ \text{within Style Category}$$

Given that most hedge funds have a far shorter history than their traditional counterparts, this may appear to be impractical. However, a number of simulation and optimization techniques have emerged for backfilling history, which can remedy the paucity of available data. Attractive candidates include fitting optimal factor or style exposures to fund profiles based on available history. This will allow one to extend the style signature back in time via factor or style exposures that have adequate history. A plethora of multifactor models have been proposed for hedge funds (Fung and Hsieh 1997a, Schneeweis and Spurgin 1998b). Further, one can use style analysis, originally proposed by Sharpe (1992) for mutual funds, and applied to hedge funds by Agarwal and Naik (2000c), among others. Indices better known for their style pure classification (i.e., Standard & Poor's, EACM, or Zurich) should be used to extend backward the earliest known weighted-average style signature (assuming no style drift) to facilitate calculation of AIRAP style percentile.

The inclusion of AIRAP stress percentile is warranted due to dormant dangers that may be lurking in the higher moments but not manifest in the five-year trailing period. Industry consensus is required for establishing representative, preset crash test scenarios encompassing credit, interest rate, volatility and equity events. Obvious candidates for equity include 1987 and 2000, 1994 for fixed income, while 1997 and 1998 may suffice for credit and default scenarios. Incorporating historical crises is critical to capturing higher-moment risks, hence potential rank reversals. The volatility spike that resulted from the Russian default dealt swift justice to short volatility players, whose previously pristine track records abruptly realized the dormant dangers of their risk profile. In fact, using only the three-year period from December 1999 to November 2002, which omits these credit and volatility spikes, shows rather different results, with nondirectional strategies displaying dramatically lower kurtosis (even less than directional strategies during this period) and more favorable skewness.

CONCLUSION

AIRAP presents a radical departure from preference-free RAPMs currently in use. At the same time, it benefits from the familiar and established lineage of expected utility theory. Salient features of AIRAP, which enhance its suitability as a RAPM for hedge funds in a distribution-free framework, include their ability to appropriately treat the leverage employed by hedge funds and incorporation of investor preferences via power utility, which, given CRRA, is more realistic than the quadratic utility assumed by mean-variance analysis. Moreover, AIRAP is scale invariant and can better handle nonnormality since it utilizes the full empirical distribution. Unlike higher-order approximations, such as the modified Sharpe ratio based on a Cornish-Fisher modified VaR, there is no sacrifice in accuracy due to the truncation of higher-order terms. It produces consistent rankings even when mean excess returns are negative and can be intuitively expressed in familiar units of performance.

AIRAP maximization is equivalent to maximizing expected utility. Hence, it can be utilized for portfolio optimization as in the case of FoHFs. ARAP can better handle nondirectional/market-neutral strategies, and it can be expressed as a modified Sharpe ratio to preserve the reward-risk format. Furthermore, when using this measure, no complications regarding the estimation of higher moments, comoments, or convergence of Taylor series arise. AIRAP can dovetail with regime-switching models or be combined with scenario stresses, for handling iceberg risks. While regime-switching models provide a systematization of the ad hoc scenario analysis prevalent in practice, they do require regime identification and technical complexities that may present barriers to practicability. It is also possible to use closed-form solutions that are easily implemented on a spreadsheet.

Traditional portfolio construction of FoHFs based on Sharpe ratio maximization can result in a bias toward illiquidity and short volatility. Measures such as AIRAP that mitigate the vulnerabilities of the Sharpe ratio can help circumnavigate the dangers lurking in higher moments. As FoHF portfolio construction usually entails a two-step top-down procedure where the optimal style weights are determined before individual manager weights, refining the first optimization by transcending the mean-variance framework should help in avoiding the pitfalls of improperly weighting styles. Properly identifying allocation implies that the FoHF manager can focus more on the selection challenge of picking the right managers and performing the necessary due diligence to avoid operational risk or fraud. We have demonstrated the relevance of AIRAP to the selection challenge via better rankings. AIRAP as presented in this chapter maximizes ease of practical use at the stand-alone fund level. We leave the application of expected utility theory toward FoHF portfolio construction using marginal considerations and correlations with other investments as fodder for future research.

Effects such as putatively managed or stale pricing may also be masking the true statistical properties (Asness, Krail, and Liew 2001). Lo (2002) and Getmansky, Lo, and Marakov (2003) have documented the extent of serial correlation observed in hedge fund returns and its upward bias on RAPMs such as the Sharpe ratio. It would be interesting to apply AIRAP to unsmoothed returns since it would adjust for illiquidity/stale pricing in addition to higher-moment risks. To the extent that survivorship would likely bias mean and skewness upward while depressing volatility and kurtosis, even if survivorship were adjusted for, the divergence between AIRAP and the Sharpe ratio or Jensen's alpha reported in this chapter would only be exacerbated. Although the Sharpe ratio would also drop given the mean-variance impact, it may not be impacted as much as AIRAP upon incorporation of higher moments.

The debate on the adequacy of the Sharpe ratio and the mean-variance framework continues. We believe that RAPMs such as AIRAP should also be considered, since these measures are likely more appropriate under stressed scenarios.

Four

Statistical Properties of Hedge Funds

Chapter 21 examines how volatility affects all asset prices, including the net asset value of hedge funds. The authors explore the impact of stock market volatility on hedge fund returns. Specifically, they determine whether it is the level of volatility or the change in volatility that effects the return to hedge funds. They analyze several different hedge fund strategies to determine whether volatility has a positive or negative impact on hedge fund returns. They also examine how hedge fund returns are impacted by different volatility regimes: high, low, and mid volatility, as well as whether lagged volatility has an impact on hedge fund returns. The authors find that almost all hedge fund investment styles are impacted negatively by the current level of stock market volatility and not the change in volatility, with high and low levels of volatility having the greatest impact on hedge fund returns. They also find only limited evidence of any lagged impact from volatility on hedge fund returns.

Chapter 22 examines historical hedge fund time series is used to compute the fund of hedge fund weights using the modified value at risk and the conditional value at risk optimizations with different confidence levels, and measure the effects on the optimal fund of hedge fund weights. The results show that extreme risks affect fund of funds composition.

Chapter 23 relies on leading edge academic and practitioner research to explain managed futures strategies to hedge fund investors. The chapter emphasizes the unique diversification benefits of futures strategies, which are becoming more important to hedge fund investors as they attempt to construct "all-weather" portfolios during an era of subdued investment returns.

Chapter 24 analyses the risk when combining hedge funds, stocks, and bonds. The risk of portfolios is quantified by the value at risk and the expected shortfall derived from extreme value theory. This approach considers the impact of higher moments. The authors show that the risk of a traditional investment portfolio is reduced by the inclusion of hedge funds.

Chapter 25 demonstrates that most asset classes are not Gaussian (bell-shaped) normal curves, but are asymmetrical return distributions causing the employment of higher statistical moments such as skewness and kurtosis. Utilizing higher moments in conjunction with volatility parsed between upside and downside returns, the authors demonstrate the use of alternative investments within a traditional asset portfolio.

Chapter 26 investigates if all investable equity long/short hedge fund indices created equal? The author examines the behavior (both constant and variable) of the betas of various investable equity long/short indices and finds that the variability of these betas over time is modest and is different from each other for some investable equity long/short indices.

Chapter 27 looks at why the current performance measures, such as the Sharpe ratio, are prone to manipulation with option-based techniques. Using multimoment risk measures, however, it is possible to create performance ratios more robust to option-based gambling. In addition, higher-moment-based, so-called variance-equivalent risk measures may provide a useful tool in separating "optimized" option strategies from superior skill-based performance in the hedge fund world.

CHAPTER 21

Volatility Regimes and Hedge Fund Management

Mark Anson, Ho Ho, and Kurt W. Silberstein

This chapter examines different stock market volatility regimes (high, low, and moderate) and determines which hedge fund strategies work best during each period of volatility. We first identify a systematic exposure to volatility (beta) using the Chicago Board Options Exchange (CBOE) volatility index. We also explore whether there is price smoothing by hedge fund managers with respect to a volatility event by examining lagged betas to determine the true exposure of a hedge fund manager to volatility. We next ascertain whether this beta is constant or varies across different volatility regimes. Last, we examine the impact of volatility on hedge fund returns in a stepwise regression with other independent variables added to determine whether volatility might be a proxy for other economic drivers of hedge fund returns.

INTRODUCTION

There is a difference between an investment manager who can generate alpha through an informational advantage—a demonstration of manager skill—compared to a manager who claims to generate alpha by assuming certain risks and earning a corresponding risk premium; this is really beta exposure. As noted by Jaeger (2002), the search for alpha begins with an understanding of beta. That is, hedge fund managers can earn significant returns simply by accepting risks for which a risk premium must be earned to compensate for the risk taken.

In this chapter we examine the extent to which hedge fund managers earn risk premiums from their exposure to volatility. There are different beliefs on how volatility affects hedge fund returns. For instance, Wood (2004) states that hedge funds have a difficult time making money in trend-less markets. Conversely, Anson (2002b) notes that certain hedge fund managers such as merger arbitrage and event driven perform poorly when stock market volatility is high. Yet Jaeger (2002) notes that other strategies, such as convertible arbitrage, can perform well when volatility increases.

The reason for such differing conclusions results from hedge fund managers having different beta exposure to stock market volatility. For example, merger arbitrage, event driven, and fixed income arbitrage strategies are effectively selling financial market insurance against volatility events in the financial markets. Should a merger event break off, the merger arbitrage manager is on the hook for the lost value. Similarly, if credit spreads widen dramatically, a fixed income arbitrage manager—who is betting that credit spreads will decline—will be on the short end of the stick when this financial market crisis unfolds. Conversely, merger arbitrage managers and fixed income arbitrage managers should perform well when financial market volatility is low to moderate. During periods of relative market calm, these types of hedge fund managers collect "insurance premiums" for their arbitrage strategy.

Consequently, there is no clear guidance regarding how hedge fund managers should perform during different periods of stock market volatility. In our next section we apply basic regression techniques to determine the impact of stock market volatility on hedge fund returns.

INITIAL STATISTICAL ANALYSIS

To resolve the issue of when and where hedge fund managers perform during different periods of volatility, we regress hedge fund returns against the VIX index. The VIX is the Chicago Board Options Exchange SPX volatility index and reflects a market estimate of the future volatility of the Standard & Poor's (S&P) 500 based on the weighted average of implied volatilities for a number of put and call options on the S&P 500 stock market index. For hedge fund data, we use the Hedge Fund Research Inc. (HFRI) databases over the January 1990 through September 2004 period.[1]

---

[1]We acknowledge that there are many issues with hedge fund databases that provide an upward bias to hedge fund returns. The purpose of our research is not to determine the absolute size of hedge fund returns, but rather to observe how hedge fund returns react to stock market volatility. For a full discussion on hedge fund data biases, see Fung and Hsieh (2002b).

We acknowledge that the VIX is just one measure of financial market volatility. However, we believe that it is an appropriate proxy for three reasons.

1. Many hedge fund strategies involve the purchase and sale of equity securities, and the VIX measures directly the volatility of the equity markets.
2. The predominate, if not overwhelming, risk in most institutional and high-net-worth portfolios is equity risk.
3. Volatility tends to wash over markets at the same time. For instance, a volatility event in the bond markets or currency markets will tend to flow into the equity markets as well (witness the Russian bond default in July of 1998 and its impact on stock markets around the world, or the Asian contagion of autumn 1997 and its similar, negative, impact on stock markets).

Our idea is simple: We attempt to estimate the beta of hedge fund manager returns with respect to stock market volatility. In other words, we document whether there is a systematic exposure among hedge fund managers to the amount of volatility experienced in the financial markets. Our goal is to observe to what extent volatility can have an impact on a hedge fund manager's return.

Our initial results are presented in Table 21.1. As shown, most hedge fund styles react negatively to financial market volatility. Starting with the HFRI Composite of all hedge fund styles, we see both an economically and statistically significant impact of volatility on hedge fund returns. The beta of −0.125 indicates that hedge returns are impacted negatively by increasing financial market volatility. In addition, the t statistic of −5.70 for the Hedge Fund Composite is statistically significant, and the R^2 of 0.152 indicates a significant amount of variation in hedge fund returns is explained by financial market volatility.

When we break down the hedge fund composite returns into individual strategies, we observe in almost every case that financial market volatility has a statistically significant, negative impact on hedge fund returns. Certain hedge fund strategies such as event driven and distressed debt seem to be particularly adversely affected by financial market volatility.

Only two hedge fund strategies demonstrated an ability to perform well under increasing volatility. In particular, short-selling hedge funds were the only group to demonstrate a positive beta associated with financial market volatility. Further, this beta was statistically significant. Evidently, short sellers use stock market volatility to their economic advantage. In addition, although market-neutral hedge funds had a beta of −0.028, this figure was neither economically nor statistically significant.

TABLE 21.1 Hedge Fund Returns and Volatility for Full Sample and High, Mid, and Low Volatility

	Intercept Coefficients	t Statistic	Volatility Coefficients	t Statistic	Adj R^2
HRFRI-Comp					
Full Data	3.63261	7.90713	−0.12497	−5.69746	0.15165
High Vol	8.21626	4.58474	−0.28674	−4.40781	0.24112
Mid Vol	5.96283	2.63592	−0.23200	−1.97807	0.04705
Low Vol	6.10688	4.18393	−0.34503	−3.18883	0.13856
ConvArb					
Full Data	1.45355	6.06600	−0.02913	−2.54612	0.03021
High Vol	3.53037	4.18846	−0.10080	−3.29435	0.14521
Mid Vol	2.33400	2.24122	−0.07337	−1.35890	0.01415
Low Vol	3.32804	2.84496	−0.18114	−2.08890	0.05572
DisDebt					
Full Data	3.75117	9.55007	−0.12724	−6.78508	0.20375
High Vol	7.71227	5.87365	−0.27147	−5.69559	0.35152
Mid Vol	5.40997	2.54630	−0.18705	−1.69802	0.03093
Low Vol	5.54167	4.02054	−0.30340	−2.96944	0.12061
Eq–Hedge					
Full Data	3.61995	5.83844	−0.11188	−3.77939	0.07018
High Vol	8.32177	3.38317	−0.27748	−3.10763	0.12988
Mid Vol	7.13151	2.33555	−0.27859	−1.75975	0.03432
Low Vol	6.81233	3.26029	−0.38929	−2.51333	0.08532
MktNeutral					
Full Data	1.12569	4.93403	−0.01865	−1.71180	0.01085
High Vol	1.67706	1.94784	−0.03840	−1.22853	0.00870
Mid Vol	0.76950	0.71843	0.00294	0.05300	−0.01719
Low Vol	2.40673	2.30555	−0.11978	−1.54789	0.02391
Event					
Full Data	3.72153	8.65027	−0.12804	−6.23366	0.17703
High Vol	7.98564	4.65949	−0.27992	−4.49935	0.24913
Mid Vol	5.46380	2.82969	−0.19971	−1.99484	0.04807
Low Vol	7.26639	5.30166	−0.43110	−4.24314	0.22977
FI–Arb					
Full Data	1.81542	6.04440	−0.05635	−3.92968	0.07584
High Vol	3.67830	3.35062	−0.12450	−3.12434	0.13124
Mid Vol	2.55072	1.71795	−0.08299	−1.07811	0.00274
Low Vol	1.24390	0.96019	−0.03187	−0.33192	−0.01586

TABLE 21.1 *(continued)*

	Intercept Coefficients	*t* Statistic	Volatility Coefficients	*t* Statistic	Adj R^2
Macro					
Full Data	3.49376	5.97758	−0.11030	−3.95276	0.07672
High Vol	4.03715	2.42115	−0.12647	−2.08946	0.05485
Mid Vol	2.78527	0.84594	−0.07609	−0.44571	−0.01377
Low Vol	9.38986	3.08216	−0.55381	−2.45230	0.08085
MergerArb					
Full Data	2.05107	6.98968	−0.06123	−4.37048	0.09326
High Vol	4.70753	3.73436	−0.15520	−3.39163	0.15332
Mid Vol	1.67948	1.48174	−0.03417	−0.58141	−0.01135
Low Vol	4.52544	4.68807	−0.26500	−3.70337	0.18239
Rel–Value					
Full Data	2.04722	8.26356	−0.05337	−4.51184	0.09908
High Vol	4.13793	5.50590	−0.12703	−4.65637	0.26285
Mid Vol	0.86653	0.59432	0.01272	0.16833	−0.01674
Low Vol	4.69708	4.59369	−0.26453	−3.49002	0.16398
ShortSell					
Full Data	−3.91523	−2.57959	0.21309	2.94067	0.04164
High Vol	−13.39840	−2.29391	0.53933	2.54373	0.08619
Mid Vol	−20.51154	−2.70886	1.05212	2.67994	0.09484
Low Vol	−13.60019	−2.50106	1.01991	2.53022	0.08657
FoF					
Full Data	2.30672	5.94872	−0.07540	−4.07251	0.08135
High Vol	6.96529	4.95416	−0.23866	−4.67632	0.26459
Mid Vol	2.34702	1.23450	−0.07070	−0.71724	−0.00830
Low Vol	4.74234	3.23972	−0.28401	−2.61740	0.09309

In sum, most hedge fund strategies react negatively to financial market volatility. Perhaps the question raised by Asness, Krail, and Liew (2001) is appropriate: Do hedge funds really hedge? Our results suggest that, with respect to financial market volatility, the answer is no.

We also considered whether hedge fund returns are affected not only by the absolute level of financial market volatility, but also by changes in volatility. To examine this question, we regress hedge fund returns on the month to month changes in the VIX index. Our results are presented in Table 21.2.

TABLE 21.2   Change in Volatility and Hedge Fund Returns

Strategy	Intercept	t Statistic	Beta	t Statistic	R^2
Composite Index	1.14	7.59	−0.094	−2.31	0.03
Convertible Arbitrage	0.88	12.04	−0.042	−2.107	0.025
Distressed Debt	1.21	9.21	−0.096	−2.69	0.04
Equity Hedge	1.39	7.12	−0.095	−1.8	0.018
Market Neutral	0.754	10.75	−0.016	−0.84	0.004
Event Driven	1.167	8.13	−0.077	−1.97	0.02
Fixed Income Arbitrage	0.69	7.31	−0.136	−1.377	0.011
Global Macro	1.3	7.03	−0.076	−1.52	0.013
Merger Arbitrage	0.83	8.86	−0.003	−0.12	0.001
Relative Value	0.99	12.41	−0.018	−0.86	0.004
Short Selling	0.34	0.73	0.14	1.09	0.007
Fund of Funds	0.81	6.67	−0.093	−2.83	0.044

In general, hedge fund returns are impacted much more by the current level of financial market volatility rather than changes in volatility. Although the betas remain negative, consistent with Table 21.1, they are generally less significant, both economically and statistically. Consequently, we conclude that hedge fund returns are impacted to a greater extent by the current level of financial market volatility than by changes in the level of that volatility.

We performed one more test of the sensitivity of hedge fund returns to market volatility. Asness, Krail, and Liew (2001), Anson (2002b), and Weisman and Abernathy (2000) document that the returns to alternative assets often lag the returns of the financial markets. Part of this effect may be the lack of liquidity of certain alternative strategies that have less frequent mark-to-market points than the daily stock or bond markets. Also, it is possible that hedge fund managers smooth their asset returns by marking their positions up or down gradually to account for sudden increases in financial market volatility.

To test this theory, we regress hedge fund returns on the returns to current and past monthly stock market volatility. Specifically, we determine the beta coefficient of hedge fund returns to the current level of stock market volatility as well as the volatility for each of the three prior months. This provides us with a multiple regression model where we have four beta measures, one with respect to current volatility as well as the prior three months. The results are presented in Table 21.3.

In Table 21.3, VIX measures the impact of current market volatility on hedge fund returns, while VIX $(t − 1)$, VIX $(t − 2)$, and VIX $(t − 3)$ measure,

TABLE 21.3 Lagged Volatility and Hedge Fund Returns

	Intercept	VIX	VIX $(t-1)$	VIX $(t-2)$	VIX $(t-3)$	Adj R^2
HFRI-Comp	2.4433	−0.3092	0.1440	0.0720	0.0272	0.3183
	5.3183	−8.6839	3.1347	1.5667	0.7637	
ConvArb	0.9414	−0.0530	−0.0311	0.0310	0.0503	0.1250
	3.7686	−2.7359	−1.2444	1.2396	2.6003	
DisDebt	2.5908	−0.2350	0.0149	0.0589	0.0906	0.3545
	6.5451	−7.6603	0.3753	1.4878	2.9547	
Eq–Hedge	2.3592	−0.3221	0.1960	0.0462	0.0300	0.1875
	3.6772	−6.4777	3.0550	0.7196	0.6049	
MktNeutral	1.0838	−0.0182	0.0283	−0.0870	0.0599	0.0692
	4.3500	−0.9441	1.1375	−3.4931	3.1066	
Event	2.4238	−0.2894	0.0878	0.1033	0.0351	0.3806
	6.0550	−9.3287	2.1926	2.5803	1.1333	
FI–Arb	1.7920	−0.0215	−0.0628	−0.0174	0.0457	0.1051
	5.4289	−0.8389	−1.9018	−0.5284	1.7870	
Macro	3.0268	−0.1751	0.0476	0.0281	0.0124	0.0746
	4.6140	−3.4447	0.7251	0.4280	0.2447	
MergerArb	1.4146	−0.1294	0.0357	0.0462	0.0189	0.2021
	5.1413	−6.0674	1.2988	1.6801	0.8866	
Rel–Value	1.6039	−0.1163	0.0437	0.0196	0.0211	0.1659
	5.9881	−5.6021	1.6321	0.7305	1.0156	
ShortSell	−0.6169	0.8642	−0.6043	−0.2876	0.0741	0.2448
	−0.4085	7.3851	−4.0017	−1.9045	0.6337	
FoF	1.7431	−0.1541	0.0634	0.0044	0.0384	0.1173
	4.0780	−4.6510	1.4825	0.1026	1.1590	

respectively, the impact on the prior month's, two months' prior, and three months' prior volatility on hedge fund returns. The table demonstrates that there is, in some cases, a lagged impact with respect to volatility. For example, examining the returns for the HFRI composite index of all hedge funds, we see that VIX and VIX $(t-1)$ are both economically and statistically significant. Interestingly, the sign on VIX $(t-1)$ is positive, indicating a positive relation between prior volatility and composite hedge fund returns, while the sign on VIX remains negative.

We can only speculate as to why this might be. It is possible that hedge funds get "whipsawed" by volatility; therefore, correctly predicting volatility in one month may be short-lived by the following month.

Overall, the impact of lagged volatility on hedge fund returns is sporadic. For instance, VIX $(t-3)$ is significantly positive for convertible arbitrage, distressed debt, and equity-market neutral, but no other strategy. Similarly, the lagged variable VIX $(t - 2)$ is significantly negative for market neutral hedge funds and significantly positive for event-driven hedge funds, but has no impact on any other hedge fund strategy. Unlike the clearly documented negative impact that current volatility has on hedge fund returns as demonstrated in Table 21.1, we cannot discern any consistent pattern in the lagged volatility terms and hedge fund returns.

We also note the R^2 measure in Table 21.3 increases for every hedge fund style compared to Table 21.1. However, this is not surprising given that more economic variables are added in attempt to explain more of the variation in hedge fund returns. Consequently, we would expect the R^2 measure to improve. In most cases, the increase in R^2 is significant, suggesting that lagged exposure to stock market volatility has more than an insignificant impact on hedge fund returns. The one exception is global macro hedge funds, where the R^2 remained virtually unchanged when adding the lagged variables.

To conclude, from Table 21.3, we observe only sporadic instances where lagged volatility had an impact on hedge fund returns. In addition, these instances did not follow any consistent pattern. These findings tend to refute the suggestion that hedge fund managers might smooth the impact of a sudden increase in volatility as well as illiquid hedge fund strategies reacting slowly to financial market volatility. It is clear that current financial market volatility has significant explanatory power with respect to hedge fund returns, but prior financial market volatility has only a limited impact on hedge fund returns.

VOLATILITY REGIMES AND HEDGE FUND RESULTS

We next consider whether hedge fund returns are affected by different volatility regimes. To examine this issue, we divide our VIX data into terciles of volatility: high volatility, mid-volatility, and low volatility, each with an equal number of observations. We match up the returns of each hedge fund strategy with its corresponding volatility tercile and determine whether periods of high, low, or mid-volatility have a greater or less impact on hedge fund returns.

The results of the tercile regressions are also presented in Table 21.1 so that we can compare the different volatility regimes to the full sample of data. Starting with the HFRI composite index, we see that volatility has a significant negative impact across a wide range of hedge fund styles during high-, mid-, and low-volatility regimes, although the mid-volatility range shows the least impact, economically and statistically, on hedge fund returns.

These results are consistent across the individual hedge fund styles. In almost every hedge fund style, the high-volatility and low-volatility regimes have the most negative impact on hedge fund returns with the mid-volatility regime having the least and, in some cases, insignificant impact on hedge fund returns. For example, with distressed debt hedge funds, the beta for high-volatility regime is −0.27 with a t statistic of −5.70, the beta for low-volatility regime is −0.30 with a t statistic of −2.97, and the beta for mid-volatility regime is −0.187 but with a t statistic of only −1.69.

We also find that in most cases, the R^2 measure is greater when we divide the data into high- and low-volatility regimes compared to the full sample of data. It is evident that the relationship between hedge fund returns and volatility is weakest as measured by the R^2 in the mid-volatility range. This indicates that hedge fund returns are affected more by extreme volatility levels, both high and low, than by mid-volatility levels. This is consistent with the statement of Wood (2004), cited earlier.

There are two exceptions. The first is short-selling hedge funds where volatility has a consistent positive impact on returns across the high, low and mid ranges. In fact, the R^2 measure with respect to short-selling hedge funds is amazingly consistent across the high-, low-, and mid-volatility levels. Second, market-neutral hedge funds show no significant impact from volatility in any regime. This is consistent with their strategy to minimize exposure to the equity markets and any volatility that accrues to the equity market.

VOLATILITY AND THE ECONOMIC DRIVERS OF HEDGE FUND RETURNS

In our final analysis, we follow the factor analysis of Agarwal and Naik (2004) for examining hedge fund returns. They perform a stepwise regression across a number of economic variables, including option strategies, to determine the source of hedge fund returns. We repeat their analysis, but instead of option-based strategies, we use the VIX to capture the impact of volatility on hedge fund returns in conjunction with other potential drivers of hedge fund value.

Again, our idea is simple. We wish to determine whether volatility has consistent explanatory power with respect to hedge fund returns when other potential explanatory variables are added to our analysis. If volatility fails to remain a significant explanatory variable in our hedge fund analysis, it could be that volatility is acting as a proxy for other economic variables with which it might be related.

Agarwal and Naik (2004) use a multivariate model (equation 21.1) stated as:

$$R_{i,t} = \alpha_i + \sum_{k=1}^{K} \beta_{i,k} F_{k,t} + u_{i,t} \tag{21.1}$$

where $R_{i,t}$ = net of fees excess return (in excess of the risk-free rate) on
hedge fund index i at month t

α_i = intercept for hedge fund index i over the regression period

$B_{i,k}$ = regression estimate of the factor loading of hedge fund i on
factor k

$F_{k,t}$ = excess return (in excess of the risk-free rate) on the kth factor
during month t

$u_{i,t}$ = regression residual term

The factors we include in the regression follow from Agarwal and Naik
(2004):

RUS is the monthly excess return on the Russell 3000 (small-cap) stock
index.

MXUS is the monthly excess return on MSCI world stock index ex-U.S.
stocks.

MEM is the monthly excess return of the MSCI emerging markets stock
index.

SMB (small minus big) is the monthly excess return premium to small capitalized stocks over large capitalized stocks.

HML (high minus low) is the monthly excess return to high book-to-market stocks minus low book-to-market stocks.

SBG is the monthly excess return to the Salomon Brothers government and
corporate bond index.

SBW is the Salomon Brothers excess return on the world government bond
index.

LHY is the monthly excess return for the Lehman Brothers high yield bond
index.

FRBI is the monthly excess return of the Federal Reserve Bank trade-
weighted dollar index.

GSCI is the monthly excess return of the Goldman Sachs Commodity Index.

DEFSPR is the month change in the default spread (BAA corporate bonds
minus the 10-year Treasury bond yield).

VIX is the monthly stock market volatility index.

Our final results are presented in Table 21.4. In a stepwise regression,
only those variables that have a statistically significant impact in explaining
the variation of hedge fund returns are included in the final equation. Independent economic variables that might have explanatory power with
respect to hedge fund returns are added one by one, and the final regression

TABLE 21.4 Volatility and Other Economic Factor Analysis of Hedge Fund Returns

	Intercept	RUS	MXUS	MEM	SMB	HML	SBG	SBW	LHY	FRBI	GSCI	DEFSPR	VIX	Adj R^2
HFRI-Comp														
Full Data	1.2263	0.2185		0.0826	0.1913	-0.0645		0.1136			0.0283		-0.0354	0.8552
	5.8252	*12.2937*		*7.0163*	*10.2024*	*-4.1470*		*3.5605*			*2.6701*		*-3.6029*	
High Vol	2.1856	0.2128		0.0793	0.1914	-0.0927							-0.0679	0.8667
	2.5447	*6.3215*		*2.9617*	*6.0790*	*-3.8265*							*-2.1539*	
Mid Vol	0.4139	0.3272	-0.1300	0.0641	0.1957			0.1883		-0.1737	0.0369			0.8685
	4.4187	*10.2546*	*-4.2634*	*4.0226*	*7.1354*			*3.5315*		*-2.8237*	*2.2329*			
Low Vol	0.7287	0.2144		0.1018	0.2269				0.2212					0.7519
	7.1106	*5.0808*		*5.9880*	*5.5885*				*2.8697*					
ConvArb														
Full Data	0.5264	0.0453			0.0483				0.0732					0.1788
	7.7471	*2.6467*			*2.3758*				*3.0306*					
High Vol	0.6245					-0.0663			0.2074					0.2929
	4.5068					*-2.2768*			*5.0023*					
Mid Vol	0.4832	0.0669												0.1094
	5.0492	*2.8716*												
Low Vol	0.5531					-0.1250			0.4606					0.3063
	5.3264					*-2.6313*			*4.9387*					
DisDebt														
Full Data	2.3352			0.0676	0.1423		0.0643		0.1723				-0.0776	0.5632
	7.2268			*4.3299*	*5.0490*		*2.0356*		*5.4703*				*-5.1434*	
High Vol	5.4256								0.3845				-0.1878	0.6479
	5.3609								*7.2341*				*-5.0472*	
Mid Vol	1.0916			0.0684	0.1271		0.1001		0.0931			-3.0263		0.4788
	6.6042			*2.6159*	*2.2835*		*2.0573*		*2.4180*			*-2.4010*		
Low Vol	0.9488		0.0756	0.0554	0.1483				0.5146					0.5678
	7.6058		*2.2599*	*2.5045*	*2.9331*				*5.4716*					

TABLE 21.4 (continued)

	Intercept	RUS	MXUS	MEM	SMB	HML	SBG	SBW	LHY	FRBI	GSCI	DEFSPR	VIX	Adj R²
Eq–Hedge														
Full Data	0.7672	0.3268		0.0440	0.2376	−0.1347		0.1211			0.0656			0.7530
	7.5381	*11.0958*		*2.2848*	*7.5740*	*−5.1884*		*2.2707*			*3.7034*			
High Vol	0.8578	0.2790	0.1316		0.2350	−0.1379					0.0921			0.7833
	4.0855	*4.8459*	*2.3552*		*4.8736*	*−3.4687*					*3.1199*			
Mid Vol	0.6409	0.5501	−0.1521		0.2646									0.7650
	4.1219	*10.8725*	*−3.4276*		*5.9070*									
Low Vol	1.0684	0.4161			0.4730									0.6485
	7.2384	*6.4688*			*7.3505*									
MktNeutral														
Full Data	0.9138					−0.0528						1.5825	−0.0261	0.1437
	4.4160					*−3.4825*						*3.9499*	*−2.6426*	
High Vol	0.2630					−0.0530								0.0655
	1.9727					*−2.2510*								
Mid Vol	0.4750					−0.0630						1.4450		0.2342
	5.5119					*−2.6492*						*2.2705*		
Low Vol	0.3147	0.1065					0.0579				0.0607	2.6893		0.1936
	2.9384	*2.2923*					*2.2400*				*2.1859*	*2.6671*		
Event														
Full Data	1.9208	0.2609			0.2509	0.0650	0.0637						−0.0599	0.7012
	6.9502	*12.7940*			*10.3301*	*3.0686*	*2.2998*						*−4.5552*	
High Vol	3.0409	0.2148			0.1753				0.2054				−0.0948	0.7690
	2.9200	*6.2530*			*4.3619*				*3.2182*				*−2.4738*	
Mid Vol	0.8406	0.2202			0.1902							−2.5235		0.6462
	6.8159	*7.3203*			*4.7871*							*−2.5726*		
Low Vol	3.6693	0.2013		0.0692					0.2358				−0.2156	0.5134
	3.0114	*3.2920*		*2.9880*					*2.1859*				*−2.4371*	

TABLE 21.4 (continued)

	Intercept	RUS	MXUS	MEM	SMB	HML	SBG	SBW	LHY	FRBI	GSCI	DEFSPR	VIX	Adj R^2
FI-Arb														
Full Data	**1.1185**	**-0.1074**		**0.0680**								**-2.1622**	**-0.0429**	0.2719
	3.7757	*-4.4324*		*4.1213*								*-3.8780*	*-3.0900*	
High Vol	**4.2468**	**-0.1566**							**0.1847**				**-0.1575**	0.3523
	4.1378	*-4.6149*							*3.2549*				*-4.1640*	
Mid Vol	**0.3878**	**-0.0872**		**0.1291**										0.4004
	3.2572	*-2.7148*		*6.4159*										
Low Vol	**0.3433**			**0.0557**								**-5.9517**		0.4026
	2.6950			*2.6842*								*-5.3070*		
Macro														
Full Data	**0.6934**		**0.1465**	**0.1178**	**0.1540**		**0.2593**					**4.2615**		0.4190
	4.6173		*3.8204*	*4.0025*	*3.3960*		*5.0218*					*4.2337*		
High Vol	**0.4558**		**0.1334**		**0.1737**	**-0.0933**								0.4310
	2.0356		*3.4460*		*3.3813*	*-2.2298*								
Mid Vol	**0.2436**	**0.2480**		**0.1044**				**0.3828**						0.5161
	1.0270	*3.8359*		*2.5983*				*3.4089*						
Low Vol	**0.7703**		**0.2672**	**0.1175**				**0.5050**				**7.2141**		0.4402
	2.5963		*3.2367*	*2.1197*				*3.7050*				*2.7588*		
MergerArb														
Full Data	**1.1061**	**0.1170**			**0.0721**								**-0.0336**	0.3005
	4.1101	*6.0679*			*3.1934*								*-2.6239*	
High Vol	**0.3036**	**0.1624**			**0.0862**									0.3442
	1.6157	*4.8536*			*2.0882*									
Mid Vol	**0.5738**	**0.0560**		**0.0619**	**0.0608**									0.1307
	5.8335	*2.3324*		*3.6839*	*2.0869*									
Low Vol	**2.9943**											**3.1310**	**-0.1924**	0.4136
	3.5465											*3.6020*	*-3.1315*	

TABLE 21.4 *(continued)*

	Intercept	RUS	MXUS	MEM	SMB	HML	SBG	SBW	LHY	FRBI	GSCI	DEFSPR	VIX	Adj R^2
Rel–Value														
Full Data	1.1436			0.0453	0.0494				0.0626				-0.0286	0.2996
	4.8045			*3.9419*	*2.3865*				*2.7252*				*-2.5713*	
High Vol	2.9473								0.1462				-0.0915	0.3809
	4.1593								*3.9276*				*-3.5122*	
Mid Vol	0.5967				0.1112			0.1639				-1.8991		0.3340
	5.2955				*2.9700*			*3.0300*				*-2.0919*		
Low Vol	3.7914		0.0770										-0.2275	0.2265
	3.6830		*2.4602*										*-2.9966*	
ShortSell														
Full Data	0.3667	-0.9378			-0.6100	0.4335								0.8243
	1.8519	*-19.5405*			*-10.1145*	*8.2607*								
High Vol	0.0053	-0.8565			-0.5791	0.4880								0.8842
	0.0152	*-13.5537*			*-7.1080*	*7.3728*								
Mid Vol	-9.1930	-0.8958	-0.2046		-0.5340	0.2685							0.5192	0.8375
	-2.6960	*-7.4084*	*-2.0681*		*-5.3028*	*2.8045*							*2.9757*	
Low Vol	0.5198	-1.2828			-0.8265	0.4478								0.7424
	1.5627	*-8.5594*			*-5.0003*	*2.7244*								
FoF														
Full Data	0.2243		0.0565	0.0950	0.0666	-0.0931	0.1212				0.0534			0.5009
	2.4221		*2.3803*	*5.3834*	*2.3819*	*-4.0835*	*3.8313*				*3.3631*			
High Vol	4.0122			0.0861	0.0917	-0.1214					0.0597		-0.1423	0.6212
	3.5190			*3.3230*	*2.2222*	*-3.7972*					*2.5232*		*-3.4079*	
Mid Vol	0.1510		-0.1057	0.0755				0.2276						0.4670
	1.0187		*-2.5930*	*3.1137*				*4.0435*						
Low Vol	0.1197		0.1053	0.0959	0.1069							3.1273		0.6010
	0.9509		*3.0971*	*4.0858*	*2.0900*							*2.9013*		

450

equation includes only those variables that have explanatory power. Some economic variables might fall out of the equation as others variables are added so that the resulting regression reflects only the most significant drivers of hedge fund returns.

In Table 21.4 we conduct our stepwise regression analysis for the full sample of hedge fund data as well as the high-, mid-, and low-volatility regimes. Estimated coefficients appear in boldface, and corresponding *t* statistics are in italics. The results indicate that volatility is still a significant explanatory variable for several hedge fund styles when other economic variables are added, but it does not have the same impact as indicated in Table 21.1.

For example, for the HFRI composite index, volatility (VIX) still has a significant negative impact on hedge fund returns for the full sample of data as well as for the high-volatility regime. However, for the mid- and low-volatility regime, volatility does not have a significant impact on the composite index of hedge fund returns. Other variables have a more consistent impact on the HFRI composite hedge fund returns than volatility, including the returns to small-cap stocks (RUS), emerging markets (MEM), and the premium for small-cap stocks over large-cap stocks (SML).

Similarly, for the equity hedge fund returns, volatility (VIX) drops out as an explanatory variable when other stock market variables are added, specifically, the return to small-cap stocks (RUS) and the spread of small-cap stocks over large-cap stocks (SML). It seems that volatility can be a consistent proxy for small-cap stock market returns with respect to explaining the variation of equity hedge funds.

We also observe that with respect to the returns to convertible arbitrage, volatility has no impact in explaining the variation of returns to hedge funds in this strategy when other independent economic variables are added to the regression equation. Of these other variables, the Lehman Brothers High Yield Bond Index has the most consistent impact. In fact, based on these observations, we might conclude that volatility is a proxy for the returns to high yield bonds when it is the only variable in the regression as in Table 21.1.

For most hedge fund strategies, volatility still has explanatory power for hedge fund returns and cannot be discounted completely. Its impact might not be as consistent as Table 21.1 when other economic variables are added, but it cannot be ignored entirely, either.

CONCLUSION

Our initial results demonstrate that volatility has a significant and negative impact on hedge fund returns. In addition, we found the current level of volatility to have a greater explanatory impact on hedge fund returns than the change in volatility. We also found some evidence that lagged volatility has an impact on hedge fund returns, but this impact was sporadic and followed no consistent pattern across hedge fund styles. Furthermore, we found that high- and low-volatility regimes have a much greater (negative) impact on explaining hedge fund returns than mid-volatility ranges. We conclude that significant shifts in volatility away from its midrange have a detrimental impact on hedge fund returns.

We examined the impact of volatility in conjunction with other potential economic drivers of hedge fund returns. We conducted a stepwise regression and found evidence that volatility can be a proxy for other economic drivers of hedge fund returns. For instance, with respect to convertible arbitrage, the returns to high-yield bonds have a greater impact in explaining the returns to this hedge fund strategy than volatility. Similarly, with respect to equity-hedged strategies, we found the returns to small-cap stocks and the premium earned by small-cap stocks over large-cap stocks to be better explanatory variables than volatility. Nonetheless, volatility continued to have a significant impact on hedge fund returns across a wide variety of hedge fund styles. Volatility clearly retains significant independent explanatory power over hedge fund returns.

CHAPTER 22

Does Extreme Risk Affect the Fund of Hedge Funds Composition?

Laurent Favre

The suspiciously low volatility of hedge fund historical time returns has led researchers to investigate other models in search of an explanation: a correction model for higher moments, a volatility correction model for autocorrelation, a return correction model for illiquidity, a survivorship bias return correction model, and a credit risk model. In this chapter, we use the historical hedge fund time series, apply a correction for extreme returns, and measure the effects on the optimal fund of hedge fund weights. The results show that extreme risks affect fund of funds composition. After deleting the 1998 extreme negative returns, the optimal fund of hedge fund weights are independent of value at risk confidence level optimizations.

INTRODUCTION

The Barclay Group estimates that the hedge fund industry, as of March 2005, has assets under management of $1,035 billion. This amount, however, is not as impressive if we consider that the mutual fund industry worldwide is estimated to have $14.460 trillion under management, according to the Investment Company Institute. The current fashionable nature of hedge funds is reflected not only in their low return volatility or impressive consecutive positive returns, but also in financial publications and newspapers that have devoted a great deal of copy to this investment category in 2003 and 2004.

This chapter addresses the issue of whether extreme risk affects the optimal fund of hedge fund weights. By extreme risk, we mean returns that depart from a normal distribution. These returns can be extremely positive or extremely negative. We distinguish between traditional risks, such as those in equity markets, interest rates, and credit ratings, and nontraditional risks, such as liquidity risk, spreads, commodities, currencies, value versus growth, momentum, small versus large caps, legal risk, operational risk, model risk, and risks due to economic stagnation. We assume that traditional risks lead to normally distributed returns, but this is not the case for certain nontraditional risks. Strategies based on liquidity risk, for example, collect a premium when liquidity is high. When liquidity dries up, the fund incurs a large loss, which is counted as an extreme loss. If risk is not managed correctly, losses that are not included in a normal return distribution will occur. For example, correct risk management might be to close 50 percent of positions if the fund has lost –3 percent, to close 75 percent of positions if the fund has lost –5 percent and to close 100 percent of positions if the fund has lost –7 percent till the beginning of the next month. Incorrect risk management neglect to test a model under all market conditions.

Arbitrage strategies (spreads, value versus growth, small versus large caps) generate small and constantly positive premiums, but extreme losses appear when the arbitrages fail to converge due to what is sometimes referred to as irrational exuberance. Legal, operational, and model risks can affect fund returns in the form of extraordinary events that produce sudden large losses. These nontraditional risks affect the fund of funds position through extreme returns, but we need to determine how they affect the weights.

Mean-variance optimization accounts only for mean and volatility. Mean-modified value at risk (MVaR) and mean-conditional VaR (CVaR) account for mean, volatility, and higher moments. The extreme return effects are captured by these two measures of value at risk. To determine the impact of extreme returns on fund of hedge fund optimal weights, we compare the results from the mean-variance optimization with those from the mean VaR optimizations under different confidence levels.

EXTREME RISKS

Extreme risk is defined as a crystallizing event. Observers around the world focus on crystallizing events because they have obvious directional implications for the market. Millions of decisions that drive the market are no longer randomly independent. Normal distribution is temporarily broken, and we see a sudden extreme observation.

Extreme value theory (EVT) uses two approaches to treat extreme risks. The first approach is the block maxima, where the maximum loss of a certain time period (e.g., two years) is recorded during several years (Embrechts, Klüppelberg, and Mikosch 1997). All the maximum losses represent the extreme returns of each time period. The second approach is the peak over threshold (POT), which says that all returns over a certain threshold are considered extreme events (e.g., all returns below −5 percent per month). We use the POT approach, the most common among researchers.

OPTIMIZATION MODELS

The allocation techniques used to construct funds of hedge funds are currently biased toward a qualitative approach among many European multimanagers. However, we believe a shift toward quantitative techniques is approaching in the near future, since nearly one third of European multimanagers use optimization techniques to construct their funds of funds.

To construct funds of hedge funds quantitatively, we use three techniques, the mean-variance optimization from Markowitz (1952), the MVaR from Favre and Galeano (2002), and the CVaR from Rockafellar and Uryasev (2002). All three models have pitfalls. The mean-variance approach does not account for nonnormal distributions; the MVaR does not provide reliable results for highly skewed assets; and the CVaR requires a long time history in order to have enough data points below the VaR threshold. The MVaR combined with the CVaR allows us to test the robustness of our conclusions about the impact of extreme risks on fund of fund weights.

Mean-Variance Optimization

Using mean-variance optimization, we compute the portfolio with the lowest volatility for a selected portfolio return. The optimization appears in equation 22.1:

$$
\min_{w_i} w^T \Omega w
$$
$$
\text{such that} \sum_{i=1}^{N} w_i = 1 \text{ and } w_i \geq 0 \tag{22.1}
$$

where w_i = asset weight included in the fund of hedge funds, $i = 1, 2, \ldots, n$
Ω = variance-covariance matrix between the asset's historical time series

MVaR Optimization

By using the modified value-at-risk optimization, we can include mean and variance in the objective function, as well as portfolio skewness and excess kurtosis (kurtosis minus 3). The optimization function to compute the asset weights is presented in equation 22.2:

$$\underset{w_i}{Min}\, M\,VaR\left(z_c\right)$$

where

$$MVaR\left(z_c\right)=w^T R-\left(z_c+\frac{1}{6}(z_c^2-1)S+\frac{1}{24}(z_c^3-3z_c)K-\frac{1}{36}(2z_c^3-5z_c)S^2\right)\sigma \quad (22.2)$$

$$\text{such as } \sum_{i=1}^{N} w_i =1 \text{ and } w_i \geq 0$$

where $\displaystyle S=\frac{1}{T}\sum_{t=1}^{T}\left(\frac{R_{t-1,t}-\bar{R}}{\sigma}\right)^3$ is the portfolio skewness

$$K=\frac{1}{T}\sum_{t=1}^{T}\left(\frac{R_{t-1,t}-\bar{R}}{\sigma}\right)^4 -3 \text{ is the portfolio excess kurtosis}$$

$$\sigma=\sqrt{\frac{1}{T-1}(R_{t-1,t}-\bar{R})^2} \text{ is the portfolio volatility}$$

$z_c = N^{-1}(0,1,p)$ is the critical value for a normal distribution for probability p

$\bar{R}$ = average return on the portfolio

The parentheses in equation 22.2 show that when the portfolio skewness and excess kurtosis are zero, the formula is reduced to the normal VaR in equation 22.3:

$$MVaR(z_c) = w^T R - (z_c)\sigma \quad (22.3)$$

This optimization allows selection of assets with positive (co)skewness, small (co)kurtosis, and low (covariance) volatility for a given return. In this chapter, systematic skewness is the coskewness divided by the skewness, coskewness is the covariance between the asset return and the squared portfolio returns, systematic kurtosis of an asset is the cokurtosis divided by the kurtosis, and cokurtosis is the covariance between the asset return and the cubed portfolio returns.

CVaR Optimization

Using the conditional VaR optimization allows us to include all distribution moments below the given threshold T in the objective function. The threshold T is the VaR at a certain confidence level. The CVaR optimization function is equation 22.4:

$$CVaR = \lambda VaR_\alpha + (1-\lambda)CVaR_\alpha^+$$
where
$$\lambda = \frac{\alpha - P[R \leq VaR_\alpha]}{\alpha}$$

(22.4)

where VaR_α = portfolio value at risk at the a probability for a discontinuous distribution

$CVaR_\alpha^+$ = conditional VaR at the a probability for a discontinuous distribution

λ = a constant to adjust for discontinuous distribution

$P[R < VaR_\alpha]$ = probability that a return is below the threshold VaR_α

This optimization favors assets with low historical probabilities of returns below VaR_α (i.e., a low probability of extreme negative historical portfolio returns). It also favors assets with positive (co)skewness, small (co)kurtosis, and low volatility (covariance) for a given return.

EMPIRICAL RESULTS

We use data from the Hedge Fund Research (HFR) indices from January 1997 to July 2004. To test the robustness of our results, we also use the Edhec indices from the same time period. The Edhec indices are computed by using principal component analysis and several public hedge fund indices (Hedge Fund Research (HFR), Credit Suisse First Boston (CSFB), Evaluation Associates Capital Markets (EACM) Advisors, Zurich, Altvest, Hennessee, Van Hedge, Managed Account Reports (MAR), Hedge Fund Net (HF Net), and Barclay for Commodity Trading Advisors (CTAs)). The optimization results done with the Edhec indices are provided in Appendix 22.1. We construct the minimum risk portfolio for each of the three optimizations, which eliminates the need to use historical index returns or to estimate future index returns.

Thirty-six-month past returns are used to compute the first optimization. The full window is then rolled forward one month, and a new optimization is completed. From January 1997 through July 2004, 56 optimizations are performed. To examine the effects of using extreme returns in the optimization, we use VaR confidence levels between 85 and 99 percent. The closer we move to the 99 percent optimization confidence level, the more weight is given to the extreme returns. By using these 15 VaR confidence levels, the number of optimizations increases by 15 times to 840 optimizations. The maximum weight for each index in the fund of funds is set at 40 percent, and the minimum weight is zero.

TABLE 22.1 HFR Index Performance, January 1997 to July 2004

	Annualized Return (%)	Annualized Volatility (%)	Monthly Skewness	Monthly Excess Kurtosis	Monthly 99% MVaR (%)	Monthly Maximum Loss (%)	Maximum Drawdown (%)	Time Under the Water (months)
Barclays CTA	6.08	8.18	0.3	0.0	-4.5	-4.5	-6.8	17
Convertible Arbitrage	10.90	3.37	-0.9	2.8	-2.4	-3.2	-4.7	4
Distressed	11.32	6.17	-1.6	7.8	-6.9	-8.5	-12.8	11
Emerging Markets	9.71	16.60	-0.9	4.1	-16.8	-21.0	-43.4	31
Equity Hedge	14.09	10.22	0.4	1.5	-5.8	-7.7	-10.3	34
Equity-Market Neutral	7.21	3.44	0.5	0.6	-1.5	-1.7	-2.7	9
Event Driven	11.81	7.17	-1.3	4.9	-6.9	-8.9	-10.8	12
Fixed Income Arbitrage	4.62	4.40	-3.2	15.4	-5.3	-6.5	-14.4	33
Macro	10.82	7.01	0.5	0.7	-3.3	-3.7	-7.3	19
Merger Arbitrage	8.45	4.08	-2.1	8.9	-4.4	-5.7	-6.3	13
Relative Value	9.69	3.43	-3.1	20.7	-5.0	-5.8	-6.6	9

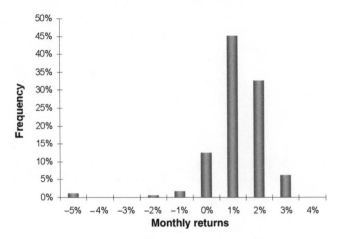

FIGURE 22.1 Historical Monthly Returns

As Table 22.1 shows, most of the HFR indices exhibit negative skewness historically, meaning they have at least one return far to the left of the mean. Historically, the most risky has been emerging market, and the least risky has been equity-market neutral. HFR relative value has the most negative skewness. This is due to only one extreme negative return, as Figure 22.1 shows. If we optimize without accounting for this extreme negative return (e.g., by using conditional VaR at 90 percent), the allocation to relative value will be higher than if we optimized with it, by using conditional VaR at 99 percent, e.g.). In this chapter, risk refers to mean modified value at risk, not volatility. We see that MVaR is consistent with maximum loss, as equity-market neutral has the highest MVaR and the highest maximum loss, but not the lowest volatility, due to its position skewness.

The next section shows the effects of these extreme returns on the fund of hedge fund weights.

Optimization versus Confidence Level

Figure 22.2 shows the optimized index weights for different confidence levels using VaR. The closer we move to the right, the more the extreme negative index returns impact the allocation. The graph does not contain any returns, because the minimum MVaR portfolio is computed for each confidence level.

Figure 22.2 shows that the more investors are aware of extreme portfolio negative returns, the more they are likely to invest in the CTA index. For an optimization at the 90 percent confidence level, the weight in CTA is zero. For an optimization at the 99 percent confidence level, the weight in CTA is 18 percent. This means that CTA adds positive skewness and/or

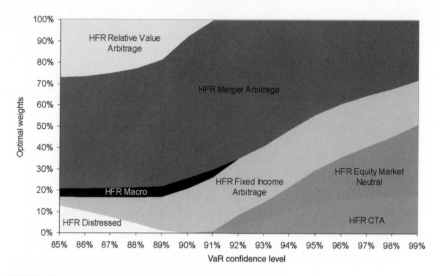

FIGURE 22.2   MVaR Confidence Level

negative kurtosis to the portfolio, thereby decreasing the portfolio extreme risks. Equity-market neutral has the same characteristics.

However, relative value, macro, and distressed all add negative skewness or positive kurtosis because they are in the portfolio for optimizations at 88 percent VaR, but not at 99 percent. In other words, they increase the portfolio extreme risks. Each of these indices had some extreme negative returns between January 1997 and July 2004. In August 1998, relative value had one 6.55 standard deviation event, something that should occur only once every 432 million years under a normal distribution assumption. Macro had three extreme events: in August 1998, corresponding to a 2.25 standard deviation event or once every 2.6 years; in April 2000, corresponding to a 2.24 standard deviation event; and in April 2004, corresponding to a 1.80 standard deviation event. For distressed, the extreme event occurred in August 1998, a 5.27 standard deviation event or once every 233,000 years.

These three indices show that only some unlikely and very extreme returns will impact the fund of funds allocation. But if we believe these extreme events will recur in the future, we should account for them now by using an extreme risk optimization model. Alternatively, we could delete them from the historical data.

Fixed income arbitrage has no impact on portfolio extreme risks, as its weights are almost constant for every VaR confidence level. It therefore has no systematic skewness and no systematic kurtosis versus the portfolio.

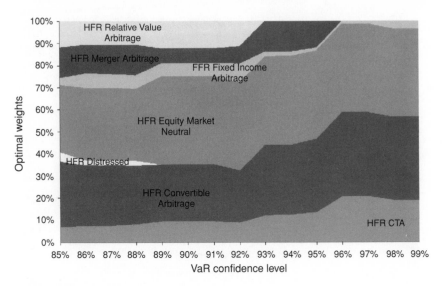

FIGURE 22.3   CVaR Confidence Level

As Figure 22.3 shows, CVaR optimization exhibits the same features as MVaR optimization. As the VaR confidence level increases so that extreme negative returns increasingly impact the portfolio allocation, the relative value and distressed weights decrease, and convertible arbitrage replaces merger arbitrage. CVaR optimization prefers convertible arbitrage because its maximum loss (−3.2 percent in August 1998) is better than the maximum loss of merger arbitrage (−5.69 percent in August 1998) and CVaR is highly influenced by maximum loss when the time series is short.

In order to visualize the effect of extreme risks on fund of fund weights, we perform a mean variance optimization for all confidence levels (see Figure 22.4). The weights are constant independent of the VaR confidence levels. This is normal, because mean variance uses volatility only as a risk measure, and has no higher moments. The weights in Figure 22.4 are almost the same as a CVaR 92 percent confidence level optimization, and are slightly comparable to an MVaR 95 percent optimization. Note that extreme risks eliminate relative value, merger arbitrage plus distressed, and increase equity-market neutral plus CTA.

Optimization versus Confidence Level and Time Window

Because extreme negative returns affect fund of hedge fund weights as VaR confidence levels increase, it is important to understand the impact of the

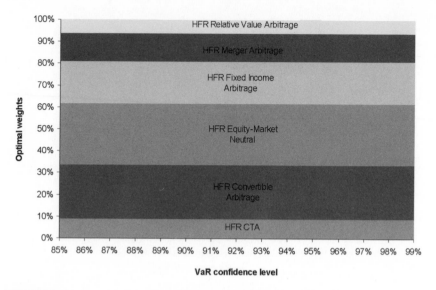

FIGURE 22.4 Minimum Risk Fund of Funds Weights with Mean Variance Optimization: 85% to 99% Confidence Levels, January 1997–July 1997

historical time window used for the optimization. There are two ways to test this impact, by using a rolling time window in the optimization and by deleting or altering the extreme negative returns with robust optimization.

We choose the first technique because the results are easier to explain and interpret. We use a 36-month rolling window, and perform an optimization for every confidence level. We then move the time window by one month, and continue the process through the last window (from August 2001 to July 2004). In total, 840 optimizations are performed.

The results are shown in Figure 22.5, a three-dimensional graph. The dates are on the x-axis, the confidence levels are on the y-axis, and the asset weights are on the z-axis. For visibility reasons, it is possible to exhibit only one asset per graph.

Our aim is to determine the impact, if any, of having the extreme negative returns in the fund of funds time series. We focus on the indices already discussed, CTA and equity market-neutral, which hedge against extreme risks, and distressed and relative value, which do not. To verify whether these hedging features are time-independent, we use optimizations with rolling windows.

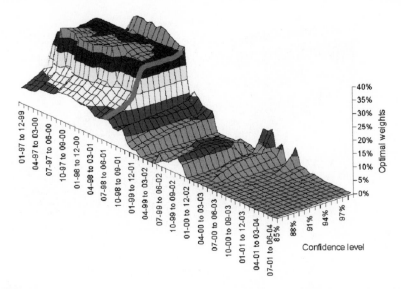

FIGURE 22.5 CTA Weights in a Minimum Risk Fund of Fund Weights with MVaR Optimization: 85% to 99% Confidence Levels, 36-Month Rolling Window

Figure 22.5 shows the CTA weights in a fund of funds where the MVaR has been maximized for confidence levels between 85 and 99 percent. When the returns of the 1998 crisis are included, around the highest peaks of the graph, the CTA weight increases to 23 percent, for the 92 to 99 percent confidence levels. When those returns are excluded, the CTA weight decreases to almost zero.

The CTA weight can only increase to 10 percent with a confidence level above 92 percent for some time window between 1999 and 2002. But this fact can be easily explained. The CTA return in August 1998 was 5.72 percent, during which time all other HFR indices had large negative returns. The extreme risk optimization perceives this good CTA performance as an implicit hedge. The lesson is important. If we expect CTA to perform positively during the next crisis, we should allocate approximately 20 percent CTA weight in the fund of funds. If not, we should eliminate this strategy. If a CTA manager proves his or her strategy can react faster in crisis situations, we should invest in this manager. Otherwise, it is better to invest in other hedge fund strategies with higher potential returns.

Figure 22.6 for equity-market neutral has the same characteristics. As its name suggests, this index is neutral to equity movements. The figure shows that as the confidence level increases on the y-axis, that is, as more

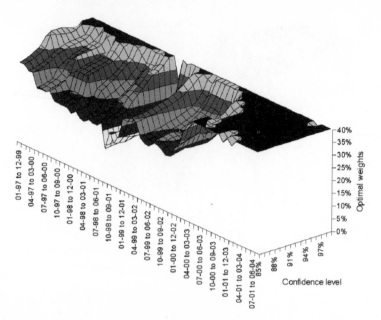

FIGURE 22.6 Equity-Market Neutral Weights in a Minimum Risk Fund of Fund Weights with MVaR Optimization: 85% to 99% Confidence Levels, 36-Month Rolling Window

extreme risk is taken into account in the optimization, the equity-market neutral weight increases on the z-axis. The weights are independent of the time windows.

In contrast, Figure 22.7 shows exactly the opposite feature, but for the distressed index. When the returns of the 1998 crisis are included, the distressed weight is zero. When the data from the 1998 crisis are excluded, the distressed weight is approximately 20 percent for 85 to 95 percent confidence levels and around 10 percent for 96 to 99 percent confidence levels. Note that even when the extreme risks are taken into account, the distressed weights are at least 10 percent for time windows from 1999 until year-end 2002. Since 2003, distressed is no longer considered a risk reducer in funds of funds, which explains why its weight is approximately zero.

Figure 22.8 shows the same characteristics as Figure 22.7. When the 1998 crisis is excluded from the optimization, the relative value weights increase to almost the maximum of 40 percent since the end of 1999. This means that several managers in the HFR relative value index, since the end of 1999, have changed their strategies and are currently adding fund of funds risk reduction (volatility risk and extreme risks).

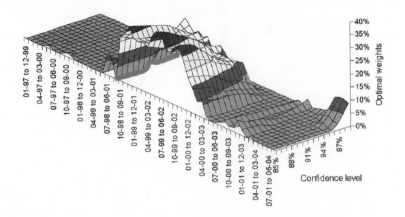

FIGURE 22.7 Distressed Weights in a Minimum Risk Fund of Fund Weights with MVaR Optimization: 85% to 99% Confidence Levels, 36-Month Rolling Window

The risk characteristics of each index are summarized in Table 22.A1 in Appendix 22.1. The second column, volatility reducer, determines whether the index adds diversification power in a fund of funds context, that is, whether it decreases the fund of fund volatility. The third column, extreme risk reducer, determines whether the index adds volatility, skew-

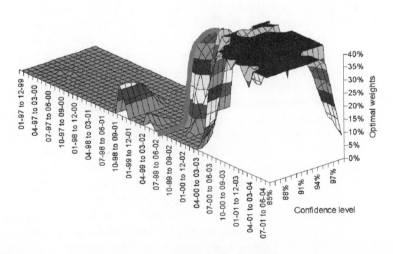

FIGURE 22.8 Relative Value Weights in a Minimum Risk Fund of Fund Weights with MVaR Optimization: 85% to 99% Confidence Levels, 36-Month Rolling Window

ness, and kurtosis to the fund of funds. The fourth and fifth columns show which fund of fund weights are optimal if there are no future extreme negative events (column 4), and if there are such events (column 5). The time windows including the 1998 crisis are considered with extreme risks, and those without it are considered without extreme risks (i.e., the most recent 36-month time windows). To compute the weights in column 4, we take the average of the weights from 1997 to 1999 for confidence levels between 96 and 99 percent, in the three-dimensional graph, computed with the MVaR optimization. The weights in column 5 are the average of all the weights from 2000 to 2004 for all confidence levels.

Investors should not necessarily rule out any of the indices we have not discussed until now: emerging markets, equity hedge, event driven, macro. If reliable index forecasts predict higher returns for these indices, their weights should be higher than zero. For example, the distressed recommended weight for a minimum risk fund of funds is 1 percent. Historically, the distressed annual return is 11.32 percent, which is much higher than that of equity-market neutral at 7.21 percent. Investors wishing to increase expected fund of funds returns and who have reliable index return forecasts may wish to invest in distressed instead of equity-market neutral.

Accordingly, note that five indices are considered volatility reducers: convertible arbitrage, equity-market neutral, fixed income arbitrage, merger arbitrage, and relative value. To be a volatility reducer in Figures 22.2 and 22.3, the index weights for the 85 to 95 percent confidence levels should be equal to or higher than those for the 96 to 99 percent confidence levels, and also be present for the 85 to 95 confidence levels. The five indices represent arbitrage strategies and, among them, only equity-market neutral reduces the fund of funds extreme risks. This means that by investing in equity-market neutral, fund of funds volatility and extreme risks both decrease. Naturally, this has a cost, namely a low historical return. The CTA index is also capable of diversifying away the fund of funds extreme risks, but its own volatility is high, so it is not considered a volatility reducer.

Two indices are therefore extreme risk reducers: equity-market neutral and CTA. To be an extreme risk reducer, the index weights for the 96 to 99 percent confidence levels should equal or be higher than those for the 85 to 95 percent confidence levels and also be present for the 96 to 99 percent confidence levels. Columns 4 and 5 in Table 22.2 show which weights protect against extreme risks and which do not.

The most extreme change in weights, when considering extreme risks or not, is for relative value. Considering possible extreme risks in the future decreases the relative value weight from 35 percent to zero. The relative value strategies are dividend arbitrage, pairs trading, options arbitrage, and

TABLE 22.2　Risk Characteristics of the Hedge Fund Indices in a Fund of Funds

	Volatility Reducer	Extreme Risk Reducer	Weights If Extreme Risks Do Not Occur in the Future	Weights If Extreme Risks Occur in the Future	Weights Without August 1998 Return
Barclays CTA	No	Yes	1%	23%	8%
Convertible Arbitrage	Yes	No	13%	33%	18%
Distressed	No	No	1%	1%	11%
Emerging Markets	No	No	0%	0%	0%
Equity Hedge	No	No	0%	0%	0%
Equity-Market Neutral	Yes	Yes	39%	38%	13%
Event-Driven	No	No	0%	0%	0%
Fixed-Income Arbitrage	Yes	No	8%	1%	0%
Macro	No	No	1%	0%	0%
Merger Arbitrage	Yes	No	1%	3%	14%
Relative Value	Yes	No	35%	0%	36%
Total			100%	100%	100%

yield curve trading. Each strategy works well with normal price volatility, but not with price disruptions such as occurred in August 1998.

Relative value has a low historical annual volatility of 3.43 percent, at the same level as convertible arbitrage and equity-market neutral. Price disruptions can impact the optimal weight of a low-volatility strategy like relative value, which explains why it decreases from 35 percent to zero if the extreme August 1998 return is included in the optimization. The August 1998 return is −5.68 percent, a 6.55 standard deviation event.

To verify the results in Figure 22.2 and the weights in Table 22.2, column 4, we perform an optimization without August 1998. The results are not surprising given the illustration in Figure 22.9. The weights are independent of the confidence levels. Even the relative value weight, which was zero when the August 1998 data were included, is now 40 percent, the maximum. This confirms our assertion for fund of funds allocation that it is important to determine whether an extreme risk is likely to appear in the future. If the answer is positive, the fund of funds weights must be adjusted as in Table 22.2, column 5. Although the weight of 33 percent for convertible arbitrage in Table 22.2, column 3 is higher than the weight if extreme

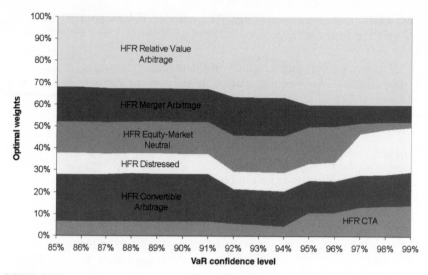

FIGURE 22.9 VaR Confidence Level, Minimum Risk Fund of Funds Weights with MVaR optimization excluding the August 1998 return: 85% to 99%

risks do not occur, convertible arbitrage is not an extreme risk reducer. This is due to the fact that since 2000, this index has lost a great deal of its diversification power, in terms of volatility. Before 2000, the optimal index weight was 40 percent, but it reduces to 13 percent if only volatility is considered, as exhibited in Tabel 22.2, column 4.

CONCLUSION

In hedge fund indices, extreme risks, in terms of returns more than 1.75 standard deviations away from the historical mean or 96 percent probability on one side, affect the fund of fund weights. We use mean modified value at risk and conditional value at risk optimizations to determine the effects of these extreme risks. Relative value, macro, and distressed weights are negatively affected by extreme risks. CTA, equity-market neutral, and convertible arbitrage weights are not, or are positively affected by extreme risks. This means that extreme risk management must be done on relative value managers, who engage in dividend arbitrage, pairs trading, options arbitrage, and yield curve trading; on macro managers, who trade in equity markets, interest rates, foreign exchange; and commodities; and on distressed managers, who are active in reorganizations, bankruptcies, distressed sales, and corporate restructurings. The extreme risk management can be performed in four different ways:

1. By using classical due diligence on the manager strategies
2. By using a tactical style allocation model with predictive power on the strategy future returns
3. By increasing the fund of funds' expected return to lower the impact of extreme negative returns on the strategies' annual returns
4. By using structured products on the strategies

We compute the minimum fund of fund risks, which does not require any strategy return forecasts. As Amenc and Martellini (2002) mention, the ex-post volatility of minimum variance portfolios generated using implicit factor-based estimation techniques is between 1.5 and 6 times lower than that of a value-weighted benchmark. This strongly suggests that optimal inclusion of hedge funds in an investor portfolio can generate a potentially dramatic volatility decrease on an out-of-sample basis. Differences in mean returns, between the minimum variance portfolios and the equally weighted portfolios, are not statistically significant, suggesting that the improvement in terms of risk control does not necessarily come at the cost of lower expected returns.

APPENDIX 22.1

TABLE 22.A1   Edhec Index Performance, January 1997 to July 2004

	Annualized Return (%)	Annualized Volatility (%)	Monthly Skewness	Monthly Excess Kurtosis
Convertible Arbitrage	11.54	3.87	−1.0	2.0
Distressed Securities	12.25	5.86	−1.8	9.3
Emerging Markets	10.91	14.19	−1.2	5.8
Equity-Market Neutral	10.08	2.28	0.3	0.6
Event-Driven	11.44	6.03	−2.1	10.4
Fixed-Income Arbitrage	6.55	4.15	−4.7	30.3
Global Macro	11.43	6.57	0.9	1.6
Long/Short Equity	12.24	7.88	0.0	0.7
Merger Arbitrage	9.68	3.96	−2.2	9.6
Relative Value	10.39	3.54	−1.3	3.4
Convertible Arbitrage	11.54	3.87	−1.0	2.0

TABLE 22.A1 *(continued)*

	Monthly 99% MVaR	Monthly Maximum Loss (%)	Maximum Drawdown (%)	Time Under the Water (months)
Convertible Arbitrage	−2.6%	−3.2	−7.1	7
Distressed Securities	−6.9%	−8.4	−11.6	12
Emerging Markets	−15.7%	−19.2	−35.5	28
Equity-Market Neutral	−0.6%	−1.1	−1.1	2
Event-Driven	−7.2%	−8.9	−10.9	11
Fixed-Income Arbitrage	−5.0%	−8.0	−12.6	16
Global Macro	−2.3%	−3.0	−5.4	9
Long/Short Equity	−4.7%	−5.5	−12.6	30
Merger Arbitrage	−4.2%	−5.4	−5.4	20
Relative Value	−2.7%	−3.4	−4.7	7
Convertible Arbitrage	−2.6%	−3.2	−7.1	7

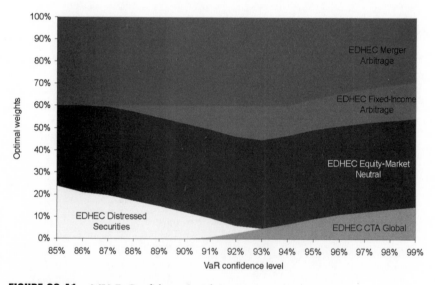

FIGURE 22.A1 MVaR Confidence Level-1

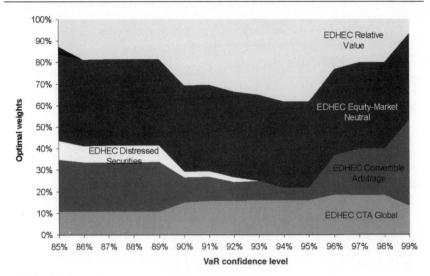

FIGURE 22.A2 MVaR Confidence Level-2

CHAPTER 23

A Hedge Fund Investor's Guide to Understanding Managed Futures

Hilary F. Till and Joseph Eagleeye

Managed futures are a niche within a niche in the global capital markets. So why should hedge fund investors become knowledgeable about this investment category? This chapter answers this question by discussing how futures strategies provide unique diversification properties for investments, including hedge funds. The chapter also discusses the main characteristics of futures strategies as well as alternative statistical measures that are appropriate for evaluating managed futures investments.

INTRODUCTION

The current size of the global capital markets is estimated to be about $55 trillion, according to Anjilvel, Boudreau, Johmann, Peskin, and Urias (2001). Investments in mutual funds make up about 18 percent of this total; investments in hedge funds amount to almost 1 percent of this amount, according to estimates by the above-mentioned authors, as shown in Figure 23.1. Jaeger (2002) estimates that managed futures strategies make up about 5 percent of the hedge fund universe, as shown in Figure 23.2.

Managed futures strategies are a niche within a niche in capital markets. Despite this niche status, managed futures have become of particular interest to hedge fund investors. By focusing on this strategy's unique diversification properties, this chapter discusses why this has become the case. We also briefly cover the main characteristics of this investment category, its underlying sources of return, and alternative statistical measures that are appropriate for comparing managed futures investments with hedge fund investments. We will rely on leading edge academic and practitioner research in covering each of these topics.

PERFORMANCE DURING EQUITY DECLINES

When one examines all the declines in the Standard & Poor's (S&P) 500 that were greater than 6 percent since 1980, one finds that managed futures programs have outperformed the S&P 500 by 17 percent on average during each time of major equity loss. According to Horwitz (2002), during each period of equity loss, the average S&P 500 decline was about −12 percent with the average managed futures return increasing by +5 percent. This comparative performance history is shown in Table 23.1. The table also shows that since 1990, hedge funds have generally declined during major equity losses.

The returns of 2002 are a striking illustration of managed futures programs outperforming during large equity declines. This is illustrated in

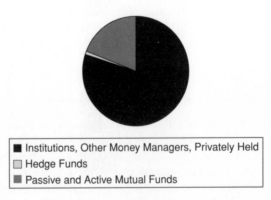

- ■ Institutions, Other Money Managers, Privately Held
- ☐ Hedge Funds
- ■ Passive and Active Mutual Funds

FIGURE 23.1   Breakdown of Global Capital Markets by Type of Investment Manager
Does not include cash equivalents and short-duration fixed income. Estimates for year-end 2000, based on ICI, MSCI, MAR, FRM, (and) Morgan Stanley estimates.
Source: Anjilvel, Boudreau, Johmann, Peskin, and Urias (2001), *Exhibit 1.*

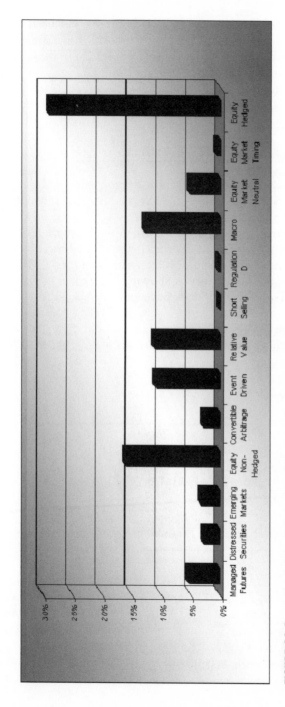

FIGURE 23.2 Breakdown of Hedge Fund Universe by Strategy Sector
Author's Data Source: Hedge Fund Research.
Source: Jaeger (2002), *Figure 2.2.*

TABLE 23.1 Declines in the S&P 500 of Greater than 6% since 1980 and Corresponding Performance of Hedge Fund Indices

		S&P 500	Managed Futures[a]	Hedge Funds[b]
1	September–November 1987	–30%	8.5%	
2	April–July 2002	–20%	10.6%	–4.4%
3	June–September 2001	–17%	1.9%	–3.8%
4	July–August 1998	–15%	5.8%	–9.4%
5	February–March 2001	–15%	4.0%	–3.8%
6	June–October 1990	–15%	19.4%	–1.9%
7	September–November 2000	–13%	2.7%	–6.4%
8	September 2002	–11%	1.9%	–1.5%
9	December 2002 to February 2003	–10%	12.1%	0.5%
10	August–September 1981	–10%	0.1%	
11	February–March 1980	–10%	10.3%	
12	December 1981–March 1982	–10%	7.9%	
13	September 1986	–8%	–4.2%	
14	December 1980–January 1981	–7%	9.5%	
15	February–March 1994	–7%	0.3%	–2.1%
16	January–February 2000	–7%	0.9%	6.8%
17	January 1990	–7%	3.2%	–2.1%
18	May–July 1982	–7%	1.4%	
19	July–September 1999	–6%	–0.5%	0.7%
	Average	–12%	5%	–2%

Source: Horwitz (2002), slide 8.
[a]CISDM (Center for International Securities and Derivatives Markets) Trading Advisor Qualified Index.
[b]HFR (Hedge Fund Research) Fund Weighted Composite Index.

Table 23.2. Collectively, managed futures programs produced amongst the highest returns of any investment strategy in the face of a –23.4 percent drop in the S&P 500 during 2002.

Managed futures programs are also referred to as commodity trading advisors (CTAs). The 2000–2003 equity bear market coincided with such good performance on the part of CTAs that over the time period December 1989 through June 2004, CTAs outperformed equities. This is illustrated in Figure 23.3. The CTA proxy index shown in this figure is based on an index of trend followers, which, as is discussed later, is the dominant investment style of CTAs.

TABLE 23.2   Index Returns During 2002

Long-Only Indices	Return
S&P 500	−23.37%
Nasdaq Composite	−31.53%
MSCI EAFE	−17.06%

Hedge Fund Indices	Return
Hennessee Hedge Fund	−3.43%
CSFB Tremont	3.04%
MSCI Hedge Fund Composite	3.90%

Managed Futures Indices	Return
Barclays CTA Index	11.81%
Carr CTA Index	13.28%

Source: Phillips (2003), p. 45.

Net Asset Value Chart
End-December 1989 through End-June 2004

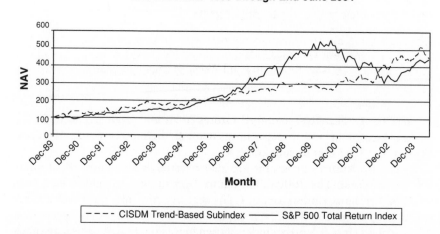

FIGURE 23.3   Net Asset Value Chart, December 1989 through June 2004
CISDM: Center for International Securities and Derivatives Markets.

CHARACTERISTICS OF
MANAGED FUTURES PARTICIPANTS

Low Barriers to Entry, But Assets Are Concentrated in the Hands of the Few

The managed futures landscape is notable for the large number of managers within it, and yet the vast majority of assets are managed by a select few. Aleks Kins of Access Asset Management notes in Collins (2003) that CTAs with less than $50 million under management account for 75 percent of the CTA universe. According to Phillips (2003), 90 percent of the assets are concentrated in the hands of a few large players who have been in the market for 20 years or more.

The large number of small CTA's is likely due to the low cost of entry. According to McGuinness (2003), a start-up hedge fund generally requires at least $20 million in trading capital to effectively cover operating costs. In contrast, CTAs trade in exchange-traded options and futures with relatively low margin requirements. It is not unusual for a start-up CTA to trade an account as small as $250,000, which would only require about $25,000 in margin. A start-up securities hedge fund, however, requires lines of credit with prime brokers and all manner of over-the-counter derivatives documentation. McGuinness (2003) notes that the start-up costs of a securities hedge fund are about $275,000. In contrast, judging by our personal experience, the start-up costs of a managed futures business are a small fraction of this figure.

Trend-Following Is the Predominant Style

Although there are two basic types of CTAs, discretionary and trend following, the investment category is dominated by trend followers. Trend followers are also known as systematic traders. The operative word here is systematic. Automated programs screen the markets using various technical factors to determine the beginning or end of a trend across different time frames. Lungarella (2002, p. 10) states that "the trading is based on the systematic application of quantitative models that use moving averages, break-outs of price ranges, or other technical rules to generate the 'buy' and 'sell' signals for a set of markets." In this investment process, automation is key, and discretionary overrides of the investment process tend to be taboo.

Discretionary traders occupy the other end of this bifurcated CTA spectrum. As Lungarella (2002, p. 9) explains, for discretionary traders: "Personal experience and judgment are the basis of trading decisions. They tend to trade more concentrated portfolios and use fundamental data to assess the markets, and also technical analysis to improve the timing."

While it is easier to make generalizations regarding trend followers, discretionary traders are not readily compartmentalized. Their trading styles run the gamut from opportunistic niche strategies to thematic, global macro trading opportunities.

Schneeweis and Spurgin (1998b) confirm that systematic trend following is the dominant style among CTAs. The authors draw their conclusion from the fact that the correlations between a general CTA index and systematic CTA subindices are about 90 percent while the correlations between a general CTA index and discretionary CTA indices are approximately 50 percent. Citing some of their previous research, Fung and Hsieh (2001) note that when they apply principal component analysis on CTA funds, they find a single dominant style, which they interpret as the trend-following style.

Schneeweis and Spurgin (1998b, p. 9) further clarify that: "CTAs who follow discretionary (e.g., mixed markets and strategies) or unique markets (e.g., energy, currency, and agriculture) [may require] separate explanatory return variables [from the ones used for systematic traders.]" That is, there are different drivers behind systematic trend-following strategies and discretionary trading strategies. As the managed futures investment category is dominated by trend followers and because academic research correspondingly centers around them, the focus of this chapter is on trend following.

TREND-FOLLOWING APPROACH

Description

The basic idea underlying trend-following strategies is that all markets trend at one time or another. Rulle (2003, p. 5) notes that "a trend-following program may trade as many as 80 different markets globally on a 24-hour basis. Trend-followers try to capture long-term trends, typically between 1 and 6 months in duration when they occur." Trend followers will scan the markets with quantitative screens designed to detect a trend. Once the model signals a trend, a trade will be implemented. A successful trend follower will curb losses on losing trades and let the winners ride. That is, false trends are quickly exited and real trends are levered into. In a sense this is the distinguishing feature among trend-following CTAs. Good managers will quickly cut losses and increase their exposure to winning trades. In a sense, the alpha may come from this dynamic leverage. As Fung and Hsieh (2003, p.78) note:

> *trend-following alpha will reflect the skill in leveraging the right bets and deleveraging the bad ones as well as using superior entry/exit*

strategies. Negative alphas will be accorded to those managers that failed to lever the right bets and showed no ability in avoiding losing bets irrespective of the level of overall portfolio return—luck should not be rewarded.

Optionlike Payoff Profile

A trend-following strategy aims for a payout profile similar to a long option strategy, as indicated in Figure 23.4. The figure also shows that CTA returns are positively skewed. Lungarella (2002, p. 11) notes that:

> *Almost like a call option, the downside risk is to a certain extent limited, and the upside potential rather open.... [This is because the dominant strategy, trend following,] will generate strong returns in times when the markets are trending, and during sideways markets the risk management guidelines will try to limit the losses.*

Because of this call-option–like return profile, trend followers are sometimes classified as a long option strategy. This is in contrast to short option strategies, where one earns steady, small returns but is exposed to infre-

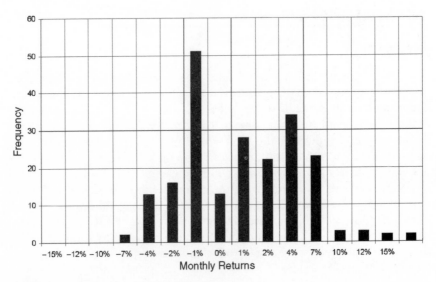

FIGURE 23.4 History of Monthly Returns of the Barclay CTA Index, January 1985 to August 2002
Author's Data Source: Barclay Trading Ltd.
Source: Lungarella (2002), *Figure 1.*

quent, but large, drawdowns. Some hedge fund arbitrage strategies appear to provide the latter type of return profile. The portfolio implications of these observations are later in this chapter.

While there seems to be little dissension on categorizing trend following as a long option strategy, it is somewhat controversial to refer to trend following as a long volatility strategy. Schneeweis and Spurgin (1998b) note that the returns of CTAs are not exclusively related to volatile markets, but instead are due to markets that show trends or large intramonth moves. In explaining the returns of CTAs, the authors further clarify that standard deviation is often less significant in the presence of intramonth drawdowns or drawups.

Fung and Hsieh (1997b) highlight another optionlike aspect of trend-following returns. Figure 23.5 shows the returns of the six largest trend-following funds across five different world equity market environments. State 1 maps into the average returns of world equities and CTAs during the worst equity months while State 5 consists of the average returns of world equities and CTAs during the best equity months. The authors note that trend-following CTA returns are similar to the payoff profile of call and put options (or a straddle) on equities.

Table 23.1 and Figure 23.5 suggest that trend followers may have a negative beta with equities when the equity market is doing poorly. Rulle

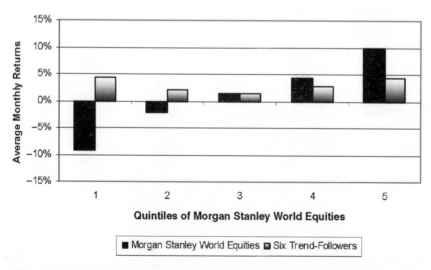

FIGURE 23.5   Average Monthly Returns of Six Large Trend-Following Funds in Five Different Morgan Stanley World Equity Market States, April 1983 to March 1997
Source: Fung and Hsieh (1997b), *Exhibit 2.*

(2003, p.30) provides an intuitive rationale for why this has been the case historically:

> [Trend-following] has a high negative correlation to equity markets during periods of perceived crisis in those markets. We believe this occurs because a global consensus emerges about macroeconomic conditions, which causes various markets, particularly currencies, interest rates and equities to move in tandem. When this consensus is further confronted by an "event," such as a major country default, the "event" will reinforce the crisis mentality already in place and drive those trends toward their final conclusion.

Another way of characterizing Rulle's argument is that CTAs have historically benefited from event risk.

Return Replication of Trend-Following Systems

There have been at least two attempts at modeling the returns of trend-following CTAs. Spurgin, Schneeweis, and Georgiev (2001) create a benchmarking algorithm centered around a set of mechanical momentum strategies. In contrast, Fung and Hsieh (2001) replicate the returns of trend followers with a basket of straddles on interest rates, currencies, and physical commodities.

A Combination of Momentum Strategies

Spurgin, Schneeweis, and Georgiev (2001) create a passive benchmark that tracks trend following returns with a tracking error similar to what is encountered between a typical equity mutual fund and the S&P 500 index.

The authors create passive momentum strategies based on three different crossover points, 15, 27, and 55 days. That is, if a futures price is greater than its price t days ago, where $t = 15, 25$, and 55 days, a long position in a particular market is adopted. Otherwise, a short position is adopted. This process is done for futures contracts in the currencies, interest rates, physical commodities, and equity indices futures markets. These momentum strategies are the building blocks for their passive CTA style benchmarks.

The passive CTA style benchmarks are created by obtaining the combined weightings of the passive momentum strategies that would best fit various Managed Account Reports (MAR)[1] indices. The MAR indices represent the performance of CTAs who categorize themselves as belonging in

---

[1]The MAR indices are now the Center for International Securities and Derivatives Markets (CISDM) indices.

TABLE 23.3 Composition of Passive CTA Style Benchmarks

MAR Index	Average Annual Subindex Weights (%) of Style Benchmarks				Average Annual Results	
	Interest Rates	Currencies	Physical Commodities	Equities	In-Sample R^2	Implied Leverage
Dollar Weight	99.6	100.6	48.5	1.6	0.68	2.5
Equal Weight	82.5	104.4	42.0	11.6	0.71	2.4
Currency	60.3	146.8	—	—	0.64	1.6
Discretionary	36.8	30.4	24.2	—	0.17	0.9
Diversified	107.3	93.0	60.8	13.4	0.60	2.7
Financial	142.2	120.6	45.6	—	0.66	3.1
Systematic	128.8	109.3	68.9	13.8	0.61	3.2
Trend-following	154.3	167.5	77.7	19.2	0.72	4.2

Source: Spurgin, Schneeweis, and Georgiev (2001), *Exhibit 2.*

one or more of the currency, discretionary, diversified, financial, systematic, and trend-following categories.

The authors use data over the January 1988 through December 2000 period. Their procedure uses four years of monthly data to calculate the weightings on the passive strategies. For example, they use 1988 to 1992 data to model the 1993 out-of-sample performance of MAR indices. To the extent that the returns of the in-sample models are systematically under or over the actual returns, an adjustment is made to the next period's out-of-sample prediction. Table 23.3 shows the average composition of the style benchmarks versus the MAR indices from 1993 to 1999.

Columns 1 through 4 of the table show the average weight for each of the momentum strategies (or subindices). The interest rates and currency subindices receive the largest weightings.

Table 23.4 compares the average R^2 of the in-sample models with the average R^2 of out-of-sample models, whereas Table 23.5 compares the average out-of-sample difference between each MAR index and its corresponding passive style benchmark. A positive entry means the passive style benchmark underperformed the corresponding MAR index.

Tables 23.3, 23.4, and 23.5 indicate that the momentum subindices explain very little of the discretionary CTAs returns. Only 17 percent of the price variation is explained with the momentum subindices. Out-of-sample the R^2 drops down to 4 percent. This is additional evidence that there are different fundamental factors driving trend-following versus discretionary strategies. As would be expected, the predictive power of the passive benchmarks drops somewhat when using out-of-sample data. With the exception

TABLE 23.4 In-Sample Versus Out-of-Sample Performance of Passive CTA Style Benchmarks

| | Average Annual Results | |
| | In-Sample | Out-of-Sample |
MAR Index	R-squared	R-squared
Dollar Weight	0.68	0.54
Equal Weight	0.71	0.60
Currency	0.64	0.62
Discretionary	0.17	0.04
Diversified	0.60	0.50
Financial	0.66	0.62
Systematic	0.61	0.58
Trend-following	0.72	0.62

Source: Spurgin, Schneeweis, and Georgiev (2001), *Exhibit 2.*

of the discretionary MAR index, the passive benchmarks underestimate the returns. This is most notable with the MAR trend-following index. The passive benchmark underestimates the MAR trend-following index by about 44 basis points per month. This finding is consistent with the idea that the core strength of a good trend follower is the ability to lever up a winning trade. This is not a criticism of the authors' benchmarking approach, how-

TABLE 23.5 Average Monthly Out-of-Sample Difference between MAR Index and Passive Style Benchmarks

| | Average Monthly Difference |
MAR Index	in Basis Points
Dollar Weight	14
Equal Weight	37
Currency	23
Discretionary	−13
Diversified	60
Financial	30
Systematic	14
Trend-following	44

Source: Spurgin, Schneeweis, and Georgiev (2001), *Exhibit 2.*

ever, since one would hope that active managers could indeed outperform passive style benchmarks.

Lookback Straddles

Fung and Hsieh (2001) formalize the notion of trend followers as being long options by likening the strategy to a portfolio of lookback straddles. Under a straddle strategy, a put and a call are held together. Under an option strategy with a lookback feature, the owner is allowed to exercise the option at the underlying asset's extreme price over the life of the option. The owner of a lookback put would have the benefit of selling the underlying asset at highest price over the option's horizon while the owner of the lookback call would have the benefit of buying at the lowest price. The owner of a lookback straddle would have the benefit of the difference of the maximum and minimum price of the underlying asset over the straddle's time horizon.

When only examining times of extreme equity moves, Fung and Hsieh are able to explain about 61 percent of the variation in trend-following returns. The time period of this study runs from January 1989 through December 1997. The key variables in explaining trend-following returns are lookback straddles on U.S. bonds, dollar/mark exchange, wheat, and silver. Lookback straddles on short rates (eurodollar and short sterling) and dollar/yen exchange are also noted as contributing factors. On a stand-alone basis, lookback straddles on currencies have the highest explanatory power, followed by commodities, short-rates and bonds.

When one performs this same set of regressions over the full sample, rather than just during extreme equity moves, CTA returns are linked once again to lookback straddles on commodities, currencies, and bonds; these variables, however, now only explain about 47 percent of the variation in trend-following returns.

Fung and Hsieh (2003) provide out-of-sample results of their model. Their model accurately predicts that trend followers would do well during three of the four large equity declines since the beginning of 1998. But like the momentum indices approach, the lookback straddle methodology cannot capture the magnitude of returns (again likely due to the dynamic nature of leverage used by trend followers).

APPROPRIATE METRICS FOR COMPARING MANAGED FUTURES STRATEGIES WITH HEDGE FUND INVESTMENTS

As noted earlier, successful trend followers tend to do well in the face of extreme equity market returns and generally have a low correlation to the equity market. As such, one might expect trend followers to compete with other hedge fund strategies as a diversifying investment in a traditional stock/bond portfolio. Yet, as noted before, CTAs represent only about 5 percent of the overall hedge fund market. One may wonder why this number is so low.

A key metric for comparing strategies is the Sharpe ratio, the excess return divided by the standard deviation. And on this risk-adjusted return metric, trend followers are not as attractive as other hedge fund strategies. However, it is useful to examine two frameworks that are more favorable to trend followers.

Portfolio Skewness

This section briefly explains how taking into consideration the higher moments of an investment's return distribution will put CTAs in a more favorable light. But before doing so, we build an economic argument that explains why the higher moments of an investment's return distribution matter.

The first thing to understand is how a strategy earns its returns. As noted in Till (2001b), multiple sources of risk besides the market risk factor can produce high average returns. If an investor passively bears any of these risks, the investor will earn a return that is not conditioned upon superior information. There may be large losses from bearing one of these risk factors, resulting in a short option–like return distribution, but the returns over time are sufficient to make the activity profitable. These returns are called risk premia.

A number of hedge fund strategies appear to be earning risk premia. In other words, they earn returns because they are performing an economic function, which involves some form of risk transfer. For example, one could argue that a relative-value bond fund earns its returns by taking on the illiquid assets that international banks wish to get rid of when banks reduce risk. The fund hedges this risk by shorting liquid assets. A relative-value bond fund thereby provides reinsurance for financial institutions, but it also exposures the fund to liquidity crises. An examination of empirical data shows that relative-value bond funds have short option–like returns. An investor in such funds assumes the risk of systemic financial distress and provides other investors with the flexibility of being able to readily liquidate their investments. A relative-value bond fund is in essence providing real options to other investors.

One issue with the Sharpe ratio is that it can inadvertently favor short option strategies. One may be earning premia in compensation for taking on the risk of rare events. In other words, by undertaking a maximum

Sharpe ratio strategy, an investor may be accepting negatively skewed returns in exchange for improving the mean or variance of the investment.

To the extent that a portfolio of hedge funds contains strategies that have short-option-like profiles, allocations to CTAs with their long-option-like profiles may provide helpful diversification benefits. This suggestion particularly comes to mind when viewing panels A and B of Figure 23.6.

Framing the matter in a concise statistical fashion, the issue for hedge fund investors, as noted by Feldman (2002), is that most hedge fund styles achieve high Sharpe ratios at the expense of high levels of kurtosis and negative skew. Skewness and kurtosis are the higher moments of a statistical distribution. The mean is the first moment of a distribution, standard deviation the second, and skewness and kurtosis the third and fourth respectively.

Bacmann and Scholz (2003) explain that skewness describes the asymmetry of a distribution. Positive skewness indicates that more observations are found to the right tail of the distribution. The authors further explain that kurtosis depends on the existence of extreme returns. The higher the kurtosis, the more likely extreme observations. For given levels of mean returns and variance, risk averse investors prefer positive skewness but dislike high kurtosis.

Panels A and B of Figure 23.6 indicate that the arbitrage strategy has negative skewness while the CTA strategy has positive skewness.

Amin and Kat (2003b) find evidence that when mean-variance optimization is used to construct portfolios that include a sufficiently large number of hedge funds, those portfolios have lower skewness as well as higher kurtosis. They find a trade-off between improving a portfolio's mean-variance characteristics and taking on more risk of rare, but large losses.

Could the addition of CTAs with their positive skewness help in portfolio optimization? Kat (2004b, p. 10) formally examines the role of CTAs within both a traditional stock and bond portfolio, which may also include hedge funds. He pays particular attention to the impact that hedge funds and CTAs have on a portfolio's higher moments. He finds that:

> *Adding managed futures to a portfolio of stocks and bonds will reduce that portfolio's standard deviation more and quicker than hedge funds will, and without the undesirable side-effects on skewness and kurtosis. Overall portfolio standard deviation can be reduced further by combining both hedge funds and managed futures with stocks and bonds.*

It appears that in order to view CTAs in a more favorable light, their diversifying properties during infrequent, crisis events may need to be valued more than has been the case so far.

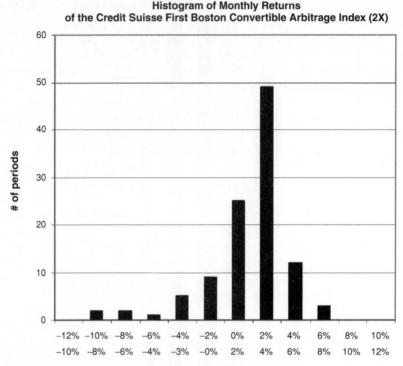

FIGURE 23.6   Stop Losses and Returns Distributions, Panel A

Arbitrage strategies exhibit return distributions with left tails. Arbitrage strategies have frequent small gains (capturing the arbitrage spread) and rare but sometimes sizable losing trades.

⇒SHORT OPTION DISTRIBUTION TYPE, 2X: two times leveraged.

Source: Molinero (2003), *Slide 10.*

Beta-Adjusted Return Metric

Besides understanding the tail risk of strategies, another key attribute to understanding and evaluating strategies is the quality of the data used to make decisions.

As noted in Till (2004b), the principals of AQR Capital Management have built a convincing argument in Asness, Krail and Liew (2001) that the lack of relationship of hedge fund indices to the S&P 500 is largely due to the reporting of stale prices for hedge fund positions. The researchers use the Credit Suisse First Boston (CSFB)/Tremont hedge fund indices in their study.

When the CSFB/Tremont Aggregate Hedge Fund Index's returns are regressed on lagged returns of the equity market, they find a strong rela-

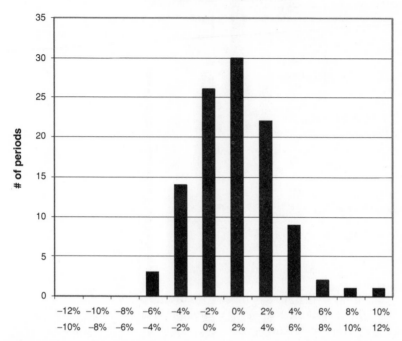

**Histogram of Monthly Returns
of the Carr Barclay CTA Index**

FIGURE 23.6 *(continued)* Panel B
CTAs exhibit return distributions with right tails. Although CTAs incur more frequent small losses (due to stops), winning trades tend to be significant.
⇒LONG OPTION DISTRIBUTION TYPE
Source: Molinero (2003), *Slide 10.*

tionship between the hedge fund index and the S&P 500 during the January 1994 to September 2000 period. They compare the hedge fund index's returns to dated returns in the stock market and infer that hedge funds making up the index may have been using stale pricing to evaluate their holdings.

Investors might consider hedge funds for their portfolios because they would like to diversify away some of their equity market exposure. Given that investment rationale, the AQR researchers recalculate the Sharpe ratio of a number of hedge fund styles if one hedged out their true equity-market exposure, taking into consideration the stale-pricing effect.

Table 23.6 shows the results of Asness, Krail, and Liew (2001). In this table, Monthly Unhedged Sharpe Ratio is the unadjusted Sharpe ratio of the hedge fund style, Monthly Beta Hedged Sharpe Ratio is the Sharpe ratio of

TABLE 23.6   Annual Sharpe Ratios of Unhedged and Hedged Hedge Fund Returns, January 1984 to September 2000

Portfolio	Monthly Unhedged Sharpe Ratio	Monthly Beta Hedged Sharpe Ratio	Summed Beta Hedged Sharpe Ratio
Aggregate Hedge Fund Index	0.8	0.31	−0.4
Convertible Arbitrage	1.07	0.95	−0.11
Event Driven	1.05	0.55	−0.27
Equity Market Neutral	1.85	1.55	1.06
Fixed Income Arbitrage	0.35	0.28	−0.56
Long/Short Equity	0.94	0.39	−0.23
Emerging Markets	0.11	−0.47	−0.82
Global Macro	0.54	0.18	−0.4
Managed Futures	−0.1	−0.12	0.14
Dedicated Short Bias	−0.38	0.61	0.89

Source: Asness, Krail, and Liew (2001)

the hedge fund style if it were hedged according to its relationship with the stock market based on regressing contemporaneous returns, and Summed Beta Hedged Sharpe Ratio is the Sharpe ratio of the hedge fund style if it were hedged according to its relationship with the stock market, which includes the stale-pricing effect.

Table 23.6 shows that the ranking of managed futures goes from second from the bottom using the unadjusted Sharpe ratio, to third from the top once one takes into consideration stale pricing and the actual equity beta of a strategy. Thus, once one adjusts for the actual relationship of hedge fund strategies with the equity market, CTAs are once again painted in a much more favorable light.

CONCLUSION

Despite the small size of managed futures relative to other alternative investment strategies, this investment strategy has risen in prominence mainly because of its positive performance during the March 2000 to March 2003 equity market decline. Even with an improving equity market, investments in managed futures can be expected to grow as hedge fund investors' understanding of this strategy's unique diversification benefits becomes more widespread.

CHAPTER 24

Fat-Tail Risk in Portfolios of Hedge Funds and Traditional Investments

Jean-François Bacmann and Gregor Gawron

In this chapter we analyze the risk of portfolios mixing hedge funds, stocks, and bonds. The risk of the portfolios is quantified by value at risk and the expected shortfall derived from extreme value theory. This approach enables us to take the impact of higher moments into account. We show that the risk of a traditional portfolio is reduced when hedge funds are added. An optimal weight of 50 percent hedge funds is found when the traditional portfolio is mostly composed of bonds. In equity-dominated portfolios, investors should incorporate as much hedge funds as possible. Furthermore, we examine the extreme dependence between funds of hedge funds and stocks or bonds using multivariate extreme value theory. We do not find any significant extreme dependence between hedge funds and bonds. The evidence is more mixed between stocks and funds of hedge funds. Funds of hedge funds without a significant investment in managed futures exhibit significant dependence in the extreme with the stock market. The August 1998 event linked to the Russian crisis and the failure of Long-Term Capital Management is the cause of this dependence.

INTRODUCTION

Over the last decade, hedge funds have been the fastest growing asset class of the financial sector. According to TASS Research, the total net assets in single manager hedge funds are estimated to be approximately U.S.$800 billion at the third quarter of 2003, including assets run by hedge fund managers in privately managed accounts. The attractiveness of hedge funds may be explained by their good performance associated with low volatility and low correlation to traditional investments. Indeed, hedge funds are known in the financial community to present bondlike volatility. According to McFall-Lamm Jr (1999), hedge funds should even replace bonds in investors' portfolios.

However, recent evidence cast doubts on the validity of volatility as the risk measure for hedge funds (Brooks and Kat 2002; Schmidhuber and Moix 2001). Indeed, the returns of hedge fund indices are not normally distributed and exhibit unusual levels of skewness and kurtosis. These characteristics are consistent with the complex trading strategies used by hedge funds, which often present option-like payoffs. As a consequence, the analysis of hedge funds based solely on mean and variance may be leading to wrong conclusions and decisions. This is discussed by Bacmann and Scholz (2003) in the context of performance measurement, and by Bacmann and Pache (2004) in the context of portfolio optimization. In a recent paper, Amin and Kat (2003b) show that while hedge funds combine well with stocks and bonds in the mean variance framework, this is no longer the case when skewness is considered.

The preferences of risk averse investors to the different moments of the return distribution imply a trade-off between these moments (Scott and Horvath 1980; Pratt and Zeckhauser 1987). Risk-averse investors tend to like positive skewness but dislike high levels of kurtosis. In other words, an investor may accept more negative skewness if the variance is reduced at the same time. Thus, the preferences of investors have strong implications for the analysis of risk in the hedge fund world. In particular, analyzing individually the different moments, as in Amin and Kat (2003b), impedes on measuring the substitution effects between the moments and their implications on the portfolio allocation decision.

Here we advocate the use of extreme value theory (EVT) to investigate the behavior of extreme events. This area of statistics enables the estimation of value at risk and the expected shortfall under fairly general types of distributions. Value at risk and expected shortfall estimated via EVT do not require the analyst to explicitly describe the substitution between the different moments. These measures rely on the standard deviation of the distribution as well as on a shape parameter describing the left tail of the distribution. The substitution effects are treated as endogenous.

This chapter contributes to the growing literature on the risk associated to hedge funds in two main directions. First, it carefully examines the risk of portfolios built with stocks, bonds, and hedge funds using EVT. Several studies have used value at risk derived from EVT in the context of single funds or hedge fund indices (Blum, Dacorogna, and Jaeger 2003; Gupta and Liang 2003; Lhabitant 2003). However, none has explored the risk properties of portfolios including stocks, bonds, and hedge funds. Second, we measure the dependence between hedge funds and traditional investments in periods of crisis. For that purpose, we test explicitly the existence of asymptotic dependence between hedge funds and traditional investments, namely stocks or bonds.

MEASURING THE RISK OF HEDGE FUNDS

How to Measure Risk

The definition of risk is a particularly difficult since no commonly accepted definition of risk exists. In the financial community, risk is usually related to the uncertainty of the future outcome of a decision made today. The different possible outcomes are linked to specific probabilities. Analyzing the entire range of probabilities, the probability distribution, is not tractable in practice. This is why simple statistical measures are used to assess the magnitude of risk. The standard deviation, also known as volatility, is the most widely used measure of risk. However, this measure relies on the assumption that the return distribution is symmetric around its mean and implies that the sensitivity of the investor is the same on the upside as on the downside. This very strong assumption has been challenged by the emergence of prospect theory (Kahneman and Tversky 1979). In this framework, the investor is more affected by a drop in wealth than by an increase.

In order to take the asymmetry of the return distribution as well as of the investor preferences into account, the use of downside deviation as risk measure has been frequently advocated (Sortino and Price 1994; Bacmann and Pache 2004). However, even though this measure is sensitive to extreme events of the return distribution, it does not provide a full characterization of these extreme events as defined by the extreme percentiles of the distribution. In such a context, value at risk (VaR), designed to capture the maximum loss over a target time horizon with a given degree of confidence, is far better suited. Value at risk has been gaining a very wide acceptance throughout the financial community as it translates a complex risk notion into a simple and synthetic monetary amount. Moreover, VaR serves as the basis for regulatory requirements in terms of capital adequacy in banks and financial institutions. In the context of hedge funds, Gupta and Liang (2003) report that most hedge funds are well funded according to VaR and to the guidelines from the Basel Committee on Banking Supervision.

The major drawback of VaR is that it considers only one particular point of the distribution. Indeed, no information is given when the loss exceeds the VaR level. As pointed out by Artzner, Delbaen, Eber, and Heath (1999), VaR is not a coherent risk measure because under certain circumstances, it neglects diversification effects. Another measure, known as conditional VaR or expected shortfall, has been designed to address this issue. It measures the expected loss given that the loss will be exceeding the VaR level. Contrary to VaR, the expected shortfall qualifies as a coherent risk measure.

The estimation of VaR and of the expected shortfall relies on three different variables: the target horizon, the confidence level, and the estimation model. Following Gupta and Liang (2003), we set the target horizon to one month. The choice of the estimation model for VaR and the expected shortfall is critical in the hedge fund context. The estimation of VaR based on the log normality assumption of prices following the delta approximation is not applicable for hedge funds that exhibit fat-tailed and asymmetric returns. In order to capture the extreme tail better than the standard VaR calculation, Li (1999) proposes to estimate VaR based on volatility, skewness, and kurtosis. Signer and Favre (2002) and Favre and Galeano (2002) introduce a similar concept, with the modified VaR based on a Cornish-Fisher expansion. However, this kind of approach suffers from an important drawback in that it assumes that the first four moments exist. As pointed out by Dacorogna, Müller, Pictet and De Vries (2001), the convergence of the fourth moment is not guaranteed for financial data. In other words, these quantities can always be computed but cannot be used to obtain a reliable estimate of value at risk. Moreover, the expected shortfall cannot be derived within the Cornish-Fisher expansion framework. As a consequence, value at risk and expected shortfall should be estimated via a more reliable theory, namely extreme value theory.

EXTREME VALUE THEORY

Extreme value theory provides a very powerful tool for analyzing risk in the extremes. In this section, we briefly review the main aspects of EVT. A more detailed and comprehensive description of this theory can be found in Embrechts, Klüppelberg, and Mikosch (1997), Focardi and Fabozzi (2003), and Focardi and Fabozzi (2004).

Two different approaches have been employed in the EVT framework, the block maxima method and the peak-over-threshold method. In practice, the block maxima method suffers from an important drawback. It requires very large dataset as it considers nonoverlapping blocks (or subperiods) of a given size n. Rather than dividing the data set into subperiods and selecting the maximum value in each subsample, the peak-over-threshold method offers a more efficient use of the data set, where all values exceeding a (high) prespecified threshold are considered. The theoretical background of this methodology is derived by Pickands (1975). Conditional on the event that the random variable X is larger than the threshold u and denoting these exceedances by Y, we can define the distribution function (equation 24.1) F_u called the conditional excess distribution function as

$$F_u(y) = P(X - u \le y \mid X > u), \quad 0 \le y \le x_F - u \tag{24.1}$$

where $x_F \le \infty$ = right endpoint of F

Pickands (1975) shows that the generalized Pareto distribution (GPD) is the limiting distribution for the distribution of the excesses, $F_u(y) \approx GPD_{\xi,\sigma}(y)$, for $u \to \infty$. The GPD is defined in equation 24.2 as

$$GPD_{\xi,\sigma}(y) = \begin{cases} 1 - \left(1 + \dfrac{\xi}{\sigma} y\right)^{-1/\xi} \\ 1 - e^{-y/\sigma} \end{cases} \text{ if } \begin{cases} \xi \ne 0 \\ \xi = 0 \end{cases} \tag{24.2}$$

where σ = scale parameter
      ξ = shape parameter

The mean of this distribution exists if $\xi < 0$ and the variance exist if $\xi < 1/2$. More generally, the kth moment exists if $\xi < 1/k$. Redefining the generalized Pareto distribution as a function of x with $x = u + y$, that is, $GPD_{\xi,\sigma}(x)$, the model in equation 24.3 can be derived to build a tail estimate of $F(x)$:

$$\hat{F}(x) = (1 - F(u))GPD_{\xi,u,\sigma}(x) + F(u) \tag{24.3}$$

In equation 24.3, F_u is replaced by the GPD, and $F(u)$ can be estimated by $(n - n_u)/n$, where n is the total number of observations and n_u the number of observations exceeding the threshold u in equation 24.4. This translates into the next expression for $\hat{F}(x)$:

$$\hat{F}(x) = 1 - \frac{n_u}{n}\left(1 + \hat{\xi}\frac{x - u}{\hat{\sigma}}\right)^{-1/\hat{\xi}} \tag{24.4}$$

Value at risk is obtained by inverting for a given probability α, resulting in equation 24.5:

$$\hat{VaR}_{1-\alpha} = u + \frac{\hat{\sigma}}{\hat{\xi}}\left(\left(\frac{n}{n_u}(1-\alpha)\right)^{-\hat{\xi}} - 1\right) \tag{24.5}$$

The derivation of the expected shortfall ES_{1-a} is straightforward. It is given by $ES_{1-a} = VaR_{1-a} + E[X - VaR_{1-a} \mid X > VaR_{1-a}]$. It can be shown in equation 24.6 that an estimator for the expected shortfall is

$$\hat{ES}_{1-\alpha} = \frac{\hat{VaR}_{1-\alpha}}{1-\hat{\xi}} + \frac{\hat{\sigma} - \hat{\xi}u}{1-\hat{\xi}} \tag{24.6}$$

Extreme Dependences

Measuring the risk of individual asset classes is usually not sufficient. More insight can be gained by analyzing the dependences between the different classes. However, measures such as correlation are not applicable when returns are not normally distributed (Kat 2003c). Here we measure extreme dependences between asset classes. To our knowledge, only one paper (Blum, Dacorogna, and Jaeger 2003) measures dependences between hedge funds and traditional assets. However, that paper assumes that the bivariate distributions are well described by elliptical distributions. We believe that this assumption is too strong since the distributions of hedge fund returns are usually asymmetric. As a consequence, we apply the concept of asymptotical dependence (Ledford and Tawn 1996, 1997). More specifically, we test the existence of asymptotical dependences between the different asset classes, as suggested by Poon, Rockinger, and Tawn (2004).

Following Poon, Rockinger, and Tawn (2004), we transform the bivariate returns (X,Y) to unit Fréchet marginals (S,T). This transformation removes the influence of the marginal aspects of the initial random variables while keeping the differences due to dependences aspects. More specifically, the transformation can be expressed as

$$S = -1/\log \hat{F}_X(X) \text{ and } T = -1/\log \hat{F}_Y(Y) \tag{24.7}$$

where $\hat{F}_X, \hat{F}_Y$ = empirical marginal distribution functions of X and Y, respectively

Two different types of bivariate distributions can be identified, depending on the value of the coefficient of dependence. This coefficient is defined as

$$\chi = \lim_{s \to \infty} \Pr(T > s \mid S > s) \qquad (24.8)$$

In this expression, we have $0 \le \chi \le 1$, provided the limit exists. The extreme dependence coefficient χ represents the conditional probability of an extreme event occurring in one variable given that an extreme event occurs in the other. In other words, χ measures the degree of dependence that is persistent into the limit. The random variables are said to be asymptotically dependent if $\chi > 0$ and asymptotically independent if $\chi = 0$.

When the two variables are asymptotically independent such that $\chi = 0$, the coefficient χ is not sufficient to describe the dependence of the two variables. Thus, Coles, Heffernan, and Tawn (1999) advocate the use of $\bar{\chi}$, defined in equation 24.9:

$$\bar{\chi} = \lim_{s \to \infty} \frac{2 \log \Pr(S > s)}{\log \Pr(S > s, T > s)} - 1 \qquad (24.9)$$

In this expression we have $-1 < \bar{\chi} \le 1$. This quantity measures the rate at which the conditional probability $\Pr(T > s \mid S > s)$ tends to zero, and is useful for assessing the degrees of dependence at finite levels of s. In the context of the bivariate normal distribution, $\bar{\chi}$ is equal to the correlation coefficient.

In practice, the hypothesis $\bar{\chi} = 1$ should be tested first. If the hypothesis is rejected, $\bar{\chi}$ serves as a measure of dependence. If the hypothesis cannot be rejected, χ is computed and serves as the measure for the extreme dependence. In this chapter, our primary goal is to determine if hedge funds and traditional assets are asymptotically dependent or if their dependences drop to zero at a certain rate.

Under weak conditions, it can be shown that the estimator for $\bar{\chi}$ can be expressed as

$$\hat{\bar{\chi}} = \frac{2}{n_u} \left(\sum_{j=1}^{n_u} \log\left(\frac{z_{(j)}}{u} \right) \right) - 1 \qquad (24.10)$$

This estimator has variance $Var(\hat{\bar{\chi}}) = (\hat{\bar{\chi}} + 1)^2 / n_u$, where $Z = \min(T, S)$. The estimator $\hat{\bar{\chi}}$ is the Hill (1975) estimator of $\bar{\chi}$. Moreover, $\hat{\bar{\chi}}$ is asymptotically normally distributed. The Hill estimator can easily be used in this context, as the variables have been transformed to a Fréchet distribution.

Finally, when the hypothesis $\overline{\chi} = 1$ cannot be rejected, the measure of dependence, χ, is estimated by equation 24.11:

$$\hat{\chi} = \frac{un_u}{n} \qquad (24.11)$$

This estimator has variance $Var(\hat{\chi}) = \frac{u^2 n_u (n - n_u)}{n^3}$.

EXTREME RISK IN INDIVIDUAL ASSET CLASSES

Here we present the data used in our analysis and estimate the value at risk and the expected shortfall of stocks, bonds, and hedge funds.

Data

We use several indices as proxies of asset classes. We use the Morgan Stanley Capital International (MSCI) World (total return) for stocks, the Citigroup Global Government Index for bonds, and the Hedge Fund Research Inc. (HFRI) fund of funds composite index for hedge funds. There are at least four reasons to choose a fund of funds (FoF) index as representative for the hedge fund universe:

1. As mentioned by Fung and Hsieh (2002b), an FoF index is less subject to the various biases in hedge fund databases, such as survivorship bias, selection bias, and backfill bias.
2. Funds of funds invest in funds that are not necessarily listed in any database and thus provide a better and larger coverage of the whole sector.
3. Funds of funds constitute well-diversified portfolios. This implies that an FoF index is less sensitive to operational risk.
4. More and more institutional investors choose FoFs as investments.

We consider additional fund of funds indices because the number of FoFs being offered has grown over the last few years. Hedge Fund Research (HFR) provides a classification of FoF into four different categories. We investigate whether the choice of the fund of funds index has an impact on the risk behavior of the portfolios built out of stocks, bonds, and hedge funds.

1. Funds of funds classified as conservative by HFR seek consistent returns by primarily investing in funds that generally engage in more

conservative strategies, such as equity market neutral, fixed income arbitrage, and convertible arbitrage.

2. Those classified as diversified invest in a variety of strategies among multiple managers.
3. Market defensive funds of funds invest in funds that generally engage in short-biased strategies, such as short selling and managed futures.
4. Funds of funds classified as strategic seek superior returns by primarily investing in funds that generally engage in more opportunistic strategies, such as emerging markets, sector specific, and equity hedge.

As the number of data points is critical to our analysis, we use the maximum available time period, that ranging from January 1990 to August 2003. For each time series, we have 164 monthly returns. This number is small compared to other applications of EVT that use daily or weekly financial market data. Consequently, we expect to obtain large confidence intervals for our estimates.

Table 24.1 reports standard statistics on the various indices. The hedge fund indices show the best mean return and usually smaller volatility than bonds. Moreover, the classification of hedge fund indices is reflected in the different statistics. The strategic FoF index shows the best returns and the highest volatility whereas the conservative index exhibits the smallest standard deviation. All the FoF indices exhibit nonnormal distributions, according to the Jarque Bera statistics. The normality cannot be rejected for the two

TABLE 24.1 Statistics for Indices Representing Funds of Funds, Equities, and Bonds, January 1990 to August 2003

	Stocks	Bonds	Composite	Conservative	Diversified	Defensive	Strategic
Mean (%)	0.55	0.62	0.82	0.72	0.76	0.84	1.10
Volatility (%)	4.33	1.86	1.68	0.97	1.80	1.75	2.72
Skewness	−0.40	0.26	−0.27	−0.52	−0.10	0.19	−0.39
Excess Kurtosis	0.27	0.10	4.06	3.57	3.96	1.35	3.30
JB Statistic[a]	4.82	1.93	114.73	94.35	107.50	13.37	78.59
Min (%)	−13.32	−3.63	−7.47	−3.88	−7.75	−5.42	−12.11
Max (%)	10.55	5.94	6.85	3.96	7.73	7.38	9.47
Correlation lag 1	−0.01	**0.24**[b]	**0.31**	**0.31**	**0.32**	0.10	**0.29**
Correlation lag 2	−0.07	−0.02	0.12	0.21	0.10	0.01	0.10
Correlation lag 3	0.01	0.01	0.01	0.05	−0.03	0.05	0.05

[a]Jarque-Bera statistic.
[b]Values in bold are significant at the 1 percent level.

traditional indices at the 1 percent confidence level. Significant autocorrelation at lag one is found in the hedge fund indices except the diversified index, as well as for the bond index. At lag two we find evidence for autocorrelation only in the conservative fund of funds index. This is consistent with the fact that market neutral hedge funds present longer autocorrelation (Lo 2002).

Risk of the Asset Classes

We analyse the risk of the different indices by computing their VaR and their expected shortfall (ES) at several confidence levels. We compare the VaR obtained from EVT with the VaR obtained assuming normality and the modified VaR derived using the Cornish-Fisher expansion. The EVT VaR and the EVT ES are computed by estimating the shape parameter of the gross domestic product (GDP) distribution via maximum likelihood. We first center the returns by the median of their distribution. In order to avoid overfitting bias, we define the threshold u as the product of the percentile p and the empirical standard deviation of the returns. The percentile p is determined by evaluating the mean excess function as suggested by Davison and Smith (1990). We find that the 81st percentile is a good definition of the threshold for the different time series analyzed as it usually gives stable results. On average, we obtain 30 exceedance points, usually ranging between 25 and 40.

Table 24.2 displays the results for the different methods for estimating VaR and expected shortfall. All numbers are percentages, except those for the shape parameter. We also report several confidence levels for the VaR and expected shortfall estimates, as well as the 95 confidence intervals. Several observations are striking. First, the VaR derived assuming normality always underestimates that estimated using EVT. The normal VaR is outside the boundaries of the 95 percent EVT confidence interval in 12 out of 14 cases. The same is true to a lesser extent for the modified VaR. The estimates lie outside the previous boundaries in 9 out of 14 cases. In other words, the normal VaR and the modified VaR provide results that are statistically different from the EVT VaR. For the MSCI world index, the modified VaR is always below the one derived assuming normality. Given that the MSCI world shows negative skewness and slight excess kurtosis, this is surprising. Second, all hedge fund indices except the strategic index present lower 95 percent VaR than the bond index. For the 99 percent VaR, the picture is reversed, except for the conservative index. This is a direct consequence of the fat-tail behavior of the FoF indices. In addition, the expected shortfall shows a more robust behavior than VaR. Indeed, the expected shortfall of the bond index is smaller than those of the hedge fund indices

TABLE 24.2 Value at Risk and Expected Shortfall for the Raw Returns of Indices Representing Funds of Funds, Equities, and Bonds, January 1990 to August 2003

	Stocks	Bonds	Composite	Conservative	Diversified	Defensive	Strategic
Shape ξ	−0.18	−0.58	0.16	−0.03	0.21	0.06	0.12
			Confidence level: 95%				
VaR EVT	8.04	3.00	2.46	1.73	2.56	2.50	4.38
VaR EVT CI[a]	[7.11; 9.52]	[2.90; 3.32]	[2.09; 3.11]	[1.46; 2.18]	[2.16; 3.27]	[2.16; 3.07]	[3.74; 5.43]
VaR Normal	6.58	2.43	1.94	0.87	2.20	2.04	3.37
VaR Modified	6.06	2.56	1.67	0.65	2.01	2.08	2.88
ES EVT	10.24	3.51	3.74	2.49	4.02	3.51	6.32
ES EVT CI[a]	[8.84; 12.47]	[3.37; 3.94]	[2.91; 5.17]	[1.99; 3.31]	[3.08; 5.67]	[2.85; 4.60]	[5.05; 8.40]
			Confidence level: 99%				
VaR EVT	11.67	3.85	4.42	2.96	4.76	4.10	7.41
VaR EVT CI[a]	[9.97; 14.38]	[3.68; 4.35]	[3.36; 6.29]	[2.33; 4.01]	[3.55; 6.89]	[3.25; 5.50]	[5.79; 10.06]
VaR Normal	9.54	3.70	3.08	1.52	3.43	3.23	5.23
VaR Modified	8.28	4.05	4.30	1.86	4.97	4.00	6.39
ES EVT	13.32	4.05	6.08	3.68	6.80	5.20	9.78
ES EVT CI[a]	[11.27; 16.58]	[3.87; 4.60]	[4.42; 8.96]	[2.84; 5.10]	[4.83; 10.25]	[4.01; 7.18]	[7.40; 13.68]

[a]95 percent confidence interval.

for all confidence levels. The only exception is the conservative index at the 95 percent confidence level.

Serial independence and identical distribution of returns is a key assumption of peak over threshold method. As seen in Table 24.1, the hedge fund and bond returns are autocorrelated at lag one (lag two for the conservative index). We also checked for auto-regressive conditional heteroskedasticity (ARCH) effects, but did not find any. As suggested by Kat and Lu (2002) and Okunev and White (2004), we unsmooth the returns using the formula in equation 24.11:

$$R_t = \frac{R_t^* - \hat{\rho} R_{t-1}^*}{1 - \hat{\rho}} \qquad (24.11)$$

where R_t = unsmoothed return
  R_t^* = return computed from the index
  $\hat{\rho}$ = coefficient of autocorrelation at lag one

After adjusting the returns for first order autocorrelation, we check for additional autocorrelation at longer horizons but do not find any evidence even in the case of the conservative index. Consequently, we do not apply any additional adjustments. Table 24.3 reports the results of the VaR and the expected shortfall computed using the unsmoothed time series. As expected, the VaR and expected shortfall both increase for the autocorrelated indices. The increase of VaR is not only due to an increase in the underlying variance but also to a modification of the shape parameter. The 95 percent confidence intervals of the different estimates are wider than those computed with raw returns. Finally, the order of VaR and of the expected shortfall is not modified, and the difference between the VaR of the MSCI World index and the other indices are still significantly reduced.

EXTREME RISK IN PORTFOLIOS OF HEDGE FUNDS, STOCKS, AND BONDS

Portfolio Risk

In order to analyze how hedge funds, stocks, and bonds fit together, we start by building portfolios out of the different asset classes. Contrary to Amin and Kat (2003b), we do not run optimizations for at least three reasons.

1. Any optimization framework relies on the definition of expected returns, which are particularly prone to errors. Consequently, the choice of

TABLE 24.3 Value at Risk and Expected Shortfall for the Unsmoothed Returns of Indices Representing Funds of Funds, Equities, and Bonds, January 1990 to August 2003

	Stocks	Bonds	Composite	Conservative	Diversified	Defensive	Strategic
Shape ξ	−0.20	−0.67	0.26	0.08	0.31	−0.01	0.18
				Confidence level : 95%			
VaR EVT	7.98	3.82	3.09	2.32	3.25	4.09	5.3
VaR EVT CI[a]	[7.08; 9.45]	[3.75; 4.21]	[2.65; 3.87]	[1.95; 2.92]	[2.78; 4.14]	[3.54; 5.01]	[4.60; 6.66]
VaR Normal	6.67	3.27	2.97	1.47	3.37	3.40	4.92
VaR Modified	6.14	3.38	2.59	1.14	3.06	3.23	4.35
ES EVT	10.15	4.60	4.79	3.37	5.36	5.62	7.89
ES EVT CI[a]	[8.80; 12.34]	[4.50; 5.16]	[3.70; 6.73]	[2.68; 4.50]	[4.01; 7.90]	[4.62; 7.27]	[6.26; 10.60]
				Confidence level : 99%			
VaR EVT	11.56	5.11	5.61	3.99	6.56	6.28	9.23
VaR EVT CI[a]	[9.92; 14.22]	[4.98; 5.77]	[4.21; 8.11]	[3.11; 5.42]	[5.29; 8.66]	[4.55; 9.55]	[7.15; 12.70]
VaR Normal	9.59	4.88	4.54	2.37	5.08	5.15	7.42
VaR Modified	8.33	5.23	6.02	2.77	6.87	5.36	8.97
ES EVT	13.13	5.38	8.19	5.19	8.06	9.77	12.59
ES EVT CI[a]	[11.17; 16.32]	[5.25; 6.10]	[5.80; 12.45]	[3.94; 7.22]	[6.35; 10.87]	[6.58; 15.76]	[9.37; 17.97]

[a]95 percent confidence interval.

expected returns coming from a model or from a historical perspective influences the optimal weights of hedge funds, stocks, and bonds in the portfolio.

2. Optimization methods are very sensitive to errors in the different estimates and tend to exacerbate the impact of the errors on the optimal weights (Michaud 1998).

3. The behavior of institutional investors is not well captured by an optimization framework. Indeed, institutional investors tend to favor limited investment (between 1 and 5 percent) when considering the inclusion of a new asset class in their portfolio.

We build different sets of portfolios by choosing the initial composition between stocks and bonds. Eleven sets are defined, where the allocation to stocks (bonds) ranges from 0 percent (100 percent) to 100 percent (0 percent) in increments of 10 percent. In each of the sets, we add different levels of hedge funds (0, 1, 5, 10, 15, and 20 percent, up to 100 percent, in increments of 5 percent). When hedge funds are added to the portfolio, the proportion of stocks (or bonds) is kept constant in the traditional part of the portfolio. In total, we analyze 242 portfolios for a given FoF index, which corresponds to 1,210 portfolios for the five fund of funds indices. This method provides more information than a standard optimization would.

The unsmoothed return series of the different portfolios are constructed using the individual unsmoothed return series of each index. In this context, each portfolio is constructed using the same underlying returns. However, this implies that we do not consider any possible cross-autocorrelation between the return series that might induce autocorrelation at the portfolio level. Consequently, we also calculate the linear autocorrelation for each portfolio; no significant autocorrelation has been found at the portfolio level. The results are not reported in this chapter, but are available upon request.

Panels A, B, and C of Figure 24.1 illustrate the different behavior, depending on the composition of five selected traditional portfolios. The introduction of hedge funds in a traditional portfolio reduces the risk, as measured by VaR and ES, for all the considered cases. The optimal level depends strongly on the initial traditional portfolio composition and on the type of fund of funds added. For example, when the traditional portfolios contain mostly stocks, the VaR and the ES are strictly decreasing to the VaR and the ES of the individual FoF. In other words, these portfolios should contain as many hedge funds as possible. On the other side, when the traditional portfolio contains mostly bonds, diversification effects can be

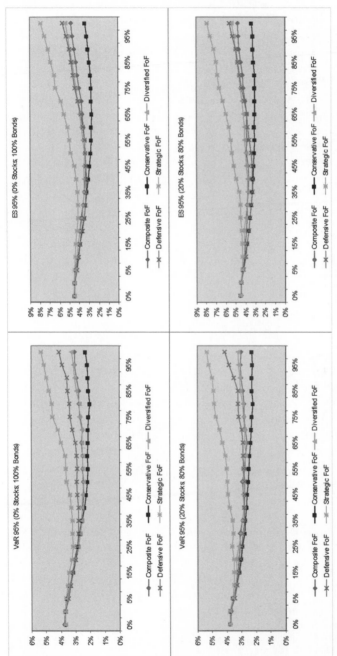

FIGURE 24.1 Evolution of the Value at Risk and the Expected Shortfall with Respect to the Investment in Hedge Funds (Unsmoothed Returns), Panel A

Note: Schematic illustrations. Each line represents the impact of the addition of a particular fund of funds index. The x-line depicts the weights of hedge funds.

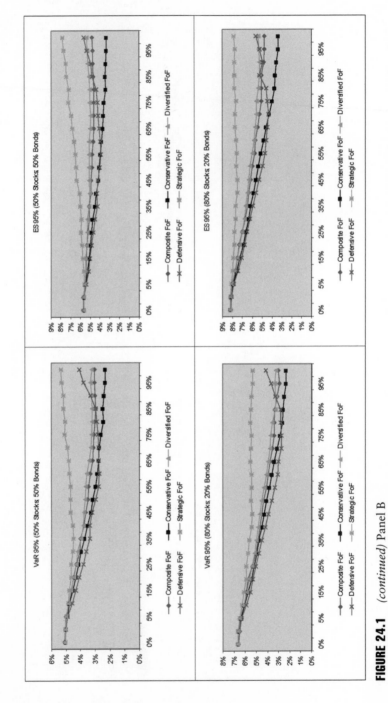

FIGURE 24.1 *(continued)* Panel B

Note: Schematic illustrations. Each line represents the impact of the addition of a particular fund of funds index. The x-line depicts the weights of hedge funds.

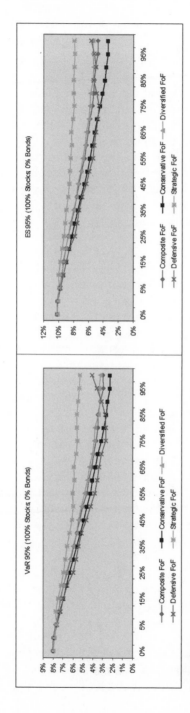

FIGURE 24.1 *(continued)* Panel C

Note: Schematic illustrations. Each line represents the impact of the addition of a particular fund of funds index. The *x*-line depicts the weights of hedge funds.

achieved. In the overall portfolio we find an optimal allocation of between 50 and 60 percent for hedge funds and between 40 and 50 percent for bonds. Moreover, the reduction of VaR and ES is significant at the 5 percent confidence level. For example, the VaR and ES of a bond only portfolio are 3.79 and 4.57 percent, respectively. When 50 percent composite FoF are added to this portfolio, the VaR and ES drop to 2.48 and 3.39 percent, respectively. The upper limit of the confidence intervals for VaR and ES become 3.01 and 4.39 percent, respectively.

The characteristics of the FoF index added to the traditional portfolio have a strong impact on the risk profile of the blended portfolio. The lowest risk reduction is achieved with the strategic index, likely due to the high risk behavior of the index. The most important reduction of risk is obtained with the conservative index when the traditional portfolio contains mostly bonds. In the case of the addition of market defensive fund of funds to the traditional portfolio, we find an optimal allocation of hedge funds for each traditional portfolio. The level of hedge funds to be added is a function of the composition of the traditional benchmark. In other words, the market-defensive category provides a different risk profile and brings diversification regardless of the initial traditional portfolio. Market defensive funds of funds are overweighed toward managed futures and short sellers. Our findings are consistent with those of Kat (2004b) that managed futures substantially reduce the risk of traditional portfolios. From a risk perspective, a hedge fund portfolio should contain managed futures in order to diversify the extreme risk in the traditional portfolio part.

As the choice of the threshold is critical in the EVT framework, we explore the impact of this choice. As already mentioned, we use a parametric definition of the threshold corresponding to the product of the percentile p of the standard normal distribution and the empirical standard deviation of the return time series. We consider three different percentiles, the 75th, 81st (the usual one), and 85th. Figure 24.2 summarizes the results for selected portfolios. We do not find significant differences between the results of the various thresholds.

Extreme Dependences

So far, we have shown that hedge funds fit well in a traditional portfolio. Indeed, they are able to reduce the risk of the different traditional portfolios. However, when building portfolios, the dependence between hedge funds and the other asset classes is treated as endogenous. In this section, we explicitly evaluate the extreme dependence between the different assets as defined in the context of multivariate EVT.

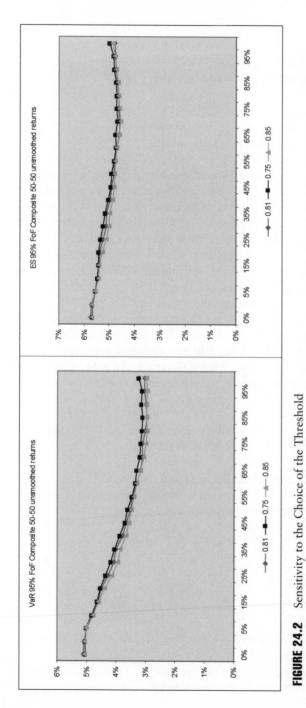

FIGURE 24.2 Sensitivity to the Choice of the Threshold

The figure displays the change in the value at risk and in the expected shortfall according to the choice of the threshold for a traditional portfolio (50% bonds, 50% stocks). The x-line depicts the weights of hedge funds. The values reported at the bottom of the graphs correspond to a percentile (81st, 75th, 85th). We define the threshold as the x-th percentile of a normal distribution whose variance is given by the empirical distribution of the returns.

We start by estimating the parameter $\bar{\chi}$ for each pair of assets without boundaries. We perform the next test of the null hypothesis H_0 versus the one-sided alternative H_1 on this parameter:

$$H_0 : \bar{\chi} = 1$$
$$H_1 : \bar{\chi} < 1$$

(24.12)

If the parameter $\bar{\chi}$ is not significantly less than unity, we cannot rule out the possibility of asymptotic dependence. In this case, it is conservative to examine the tail dependence coefficient χ under the assumption that $\bar{\chi} = 1$.

Tables 24.4 to 24.6 report the different values for the extreme dependence coefficients and their associated standard errors in parentheses. A bold value indicates that the estimates are smaller than one, using the one-sided test in equation 24.12 at the 5 percent level. The parameters $\bar{\chi}$ displayed in Table 24.4 are of the same magnitude or even smaller than the ones reported by Poon, Rockinger, and Tawn (2004) for different stock markets. In particular, none of the parameters is above one even though they were not constrained. However, the standard errors in our study are larger since our sample size is small. Despite this, several conclusions can be drawn. First, we do not find any evidence of asymptotic dependence between hedge funds and bonds. The market-defensive fund of funds index is even negatively related to the bond index. These findings may be related to the reduc-

TABLE 24.4   Estimates of the $\bar{\chi}$ Parameters on Indices Representing Funds of Funds, Equities, and Bonds, January 1990 to August 2003

	Stocks	Bonds	Composite	Conservative	Diversified	Defensive	Strategic
Stocks	**0.19**	0.53	0.51	**0.46**	**0.18**	0.68
	(0.23)	(0.31)	(0.30)	(0.29)	(0.24)	(0.34)
Bonds		**0.12**	**0.22**	**0.24**	**−0.10**	**0.29**
		(0.22)	(0.25)	(0.25)	(0.18)	(0.26)
Composite			0.80	0.73	0.41	0.70
			(0.36)	(0.35)	(0.28)	(0.34)
Conservative				0.90	0.35	0.67
				(0.38)	(0.27)	(0.33)
Diversified					0.36	0.77
					(0.27)	(0.35)
Defensive						**0.25**
						(0.25)
Strategic						

Note: Values in bold indicate an estimate smaller than 1 at the 5 percent level.

TABLE 24.5   Estimates of the $\bar{\chi}$ Parameters on Indices Representing Funds of Funds, Equities, and Bonds, January 1990 to August 2003

	Stocks	Bonds	Composite	Conservative	Diversified	Defensive	Strategic
Stocks			**0.45** (0.08)	**0.45** (0.08)			**0.43** (0.08)
Bonds							
Composite				**0.58** (0.11)	**0.82** (0.15)		**0.71** (0.13)
Conservative					**0.49** (0.09)		**0.50** (0.09)
Diversified							**0.64** (0.12)
Defensive							
Strategic							

Note: Values in bold indicate an estimate smaller than 1 at the 5 percent level.

tion of value at risk and expected shortfall in portfolios dominated by bonds and hedge funds. The optimal composition found previously is a direct consequence of the absence of extreme dependence between hedge funds and bonds.

Second, the stock market index and several fund of funds indices, namely the composite, conservative, and strategic indices, are asymptoti-

TABLE 24.6   Estimates of the $\bar{\chi}$ Parameters on Indices Representing Funds of Funds, Equities, and Bonds, January 1990 to August 2003, with August 1998 Removed

	Stocks	Bonds	Composite	Conservative	Diversified	Defensive	Strategic
Stocks		0.20 (0.24)	0.31 (0.26)	0.45 (0.29)	0.29 (0.26)	−0.15 (0.17)	0.45 (0.29)
Bonds			0.18 (0.24)	0.28 (0.26)	0.30 (0.26)	−0.11 (0.18)	0.38 (0.29)
Composite				0.66 (0.33)	0.69 (0.34)	0.22 (0.24)	0.55 (0.31)
Conservative					0.72 (0.34)	0.17 (0.23)	0.42 (0.29)
Diversified						0.15 (0.23)	0.74 (0.35)
Defensive							0.03 (0.21)
Strategi							

Note: Values in bold indicate an estimate smaller than 1 at the 5 percent level.

cally related. The diversified and market-defensive indices do not exhibit extreme dependence with the stock market. For the diversified index, its constituents are well diversified across the strategies covered by hedge funds. This implies that this type of fund of funds is exposed to a wide range of sources of risk, which reduces the link to the stock market. The results obtained with the market defensive index are consistent with previous findings showing that managed futures provide some downside protection to equity markets (Kat 2004b). Again, this is consistent with the strong reduction of value at risk and expected shortfall when the market-defensive index is added to portfolios containing mostly equities. Moreover, the market-defensive index exhibits a different behavior from the other fund of funds indices. Indeed, all the hedge fund indices, except the market defensive, present asymptotic tail dependence.

Table 24.5 displays the estimated asymptotic dependence coefficient χ for the pairs displaying a parameter $\bar{\chi}$ not statistically different from one. The link between hedge fund indices is stronger than that between hedge fund indices and the stock market index. In Table 24.6, we attempt to determine the cause of the dependence in the tails between the different indices. We eliminate the observation for August 1998, which corresponds to the Russian crisis. This crisis reflects a global liquidity crisis that affected primarily relative value arbitrage hedge funds, such as Long-Term Capital Management, as well as equity markets. All the tail dependence coefficients $\bar{\chi}$ are reduced and the extreme dependence between hedge fund indices and the stock market is no longer significant. However, most of the hedge fund indices are remaining dependent in the extreme. We conjecture that hedge funds are able to control their market risk but may be strongly impacted by extremely bad liquidity conditions.

CONCLUSION

In this chapter we analyze the behavior in the extreme left tail of funds of hedge funds, stock, and bond indices. Unlike Amin and Kat (2003b), we do not analyze individually the first three moments of the distribution without measuring substitution effects. Instead we use extreme value theory to estimate value at risk and expected shortfall. This enables us to evaluate and to compare the risk of the different asset classes, taking higher moments into account.

We find that the benefits of the inclusion of hedge funds in a traditional portfolio depend on the initial composition of the portfolio and on the type of hedge fund added to the portfolio. When the initial portfolio is dominated with stocks, inclusion of every type of fund of funds reduces the risk, as measured by value at risk and expected shortfall. If the added funds of hedge funds are mostly managed futures, the risk reduction of an equity-dominated portfolio is bigger. An optimal level for minimizing risk is obtained with approximately 80 percent invested in funds of hedge funds. When the initial portfolio is composed mostly of bonds, the optimal composition corresponds to approximately 50 percent invested in funds of hedge funds.

We also examine the asymptotic dependence between hedge funds and traditional investments using two nonparametric measures. We do not find any statistical evidence of dependence between hedge funds and bonds. Some fund of funds indices and stock markets present statistically significant asymptotic dependence. This is not the case for funds of hedge funds consisting mostly of managed futures. This finding is consistent with the diversification effects brought on by mixing equities and market-defensive funds of funds. Furthermore, we find that the asymptotic dependence between hedge funds and stocks is a consequence of the events of August 1998. Consequently, it would be interesting to investigate whether liquidity is responsible for the extreme link between equity indices and hedge funds. This is left for future research.

CHAPTER 25

Skewing Your Diversification

Mark S. Shore

This chapter reviews the performance metrics and use of alternative asset allocations within a traditional asset portfolio. We that show that the returns of most asset classes are not normally distributed, as modern portfolio theory assumes. Instead, the returns are asymmetrical to the right or left, which justifies the use of higher statistical moments such as skewness and kurtosis in describing returns distribution. Indeed, the first and second statistical moments (mean and variance) are not sufficient alone to determine risk-adjusted returns of a portfolio. Utilizing higher moments in conjunction with volatility parsed between upside and downside returns, we demonstrate how managed futures and hedge funds perform individually and simultaneously as diversifiers in a traditional portfolio.

INTRODUCTION

As the realization of asset allocation has found itself in the vocabulary of many investors in recent years, it is interesting to view the upside return/downside return volatility (the standard deviation ratio or S-ratio), skewness, correlations, and returns in traditional portfolios when managed futures and hedge funds are introduced into the portfolio.

For years, investors would diversify their portfolios with the use of stocks, bonds, and cash. Harry Markowitz's (1952) mean-variance work

The author would like to thank the following for their support: Rudi Schadt, Robert Kieman III, Hilary Till, Maureen Kaelin, and Patrick Egan. *The views in this article represent those of the author and do not necessarily represent the views of Morgan Stanley Investment Management and VK Capital Inc.*

assisted the advancement of portfolio diversification. Darst (2003) points out during the 1930s, asset allocation was defined as 60 percent bonds and 40 percent equity. By the 1960s, the U.S. economy was growing and the asset allocation model shifted to 60 percent domestic equity, 30 percent bonds, and 10 percent cash. By the 1990s, sophisticated investors were integrating absolute-return strategies such as hedge funds and managed futures into their portfolios.

The objective of this chapter is to understand how managed futures and hedge funds affect a traditional portfolio when allocated individually and simultaneously. Schneeweis and Spurgin (2000b) stress the benefits of including alternative investments in traditional portfolios. The issue of independent returns of these investments is not as important as how they may benefit the overall portfolio. We discuss this point later in the chapter.

The first and second statistical moments, better known as mean and variance, are conventional tools that determine the risk and return of an investment. The third and fourth moments, skewness and kurtosis, have been receiving greater attention in recent years by academics and practitioners. Skewness relates to the symmetrical characteristics of the return distribution. Returns shifted toward the right (left) create positive (negative) skewness and cause asymmetrical returns distributions. When considering components of a portfolio, one must consider the coskewness of each component and how portfolio skewness is affected when a new asset is introduced. Harvey and Siddique (2000) define coskewness as the component of an asset's skewness related to the market portfolio's skewness. Coskewness may be utilized to reduce volatility shocks to the portfolio. Kurtosis describes the fatness of the tail by the peak or flatness of the distribution. The higher the excess kurtosis of the return distribution, the lower is its peak. Bacmann and Scholz (2003) describe a higher kurtosis as a greater probability for extreme returns.

Positive skewness of returns reflects the potential for greater variance of positive returns than negative returns. This is a desirable property for most investors. Kraus and Litzenberger (1976) support rational investor preference for positive skewness and reduced volatility. As Till (2002) writes, the use of the mean-variance metric is most appropriate when an investment's return distribution is symmetrically distributed. If this risk measure is used for asymmetrically distributed investments, it implies that investors are indifferent between upside risk and downside risk. To assume investors are indifferent between gains and losses contradicts the behavioral finance work of Kahneman and Tversky (1979) on prospect theory of loss aversion, according to which an investor's preference of losses carries more weight than similar gains on a utility curve. This preference justifies investigating the downside risk of a portfolio. By avoiding the third and fourth moments, investors may overlook how the components of a portfolio compliment or decay the long-run effects of a portfolio.

If a return distribution is asymmetrical, an investor must consider if the investment is prone to greater variance of positive or negative returns. One could argue positive (negative) skewness is similar to long (short) option position because the payoff structure is similar to buying (writing) options. Agarwal and Naik (2004) find many hedge fund strategies have negative skewness. This is due to dynamic trading strategies that create payoff structures similar to writing puts, which induces greater left tail risk. Managed futures are more prone to long optionality observed in the positive skewness and therefore less left-tail risk. This is due in part to the tendency for commodity trading advisors (CTAs) to be trend followers.

According to Sharpe (1994), the mean and variance are adequate for characterizing normally distributed returns. Analyzing nonnormal return distributions using only the mean and variance is not recommended. Most asset classes are not normally distributed. Some of the assumptions of the Sharpe ratio are that historic returns have some predictive ability, that the mean and variance are sufficient for evaluating the portfolio risk/return profile, that investments should have similar correlations (an investment with a smaller correlation to a portfolio, such as alternative investments, may add greater value with a smaller Sharpe ratio), and finally, that the distribution is symmetric.

Kat (2004b) found that hedge funds and managed futures may complement each other in a portfolio, but only when managed futures receive at least 45 to 50 percent of the alternative allocation. Kat (2004b) used the Standard & Poor's (S&P) 500 index, the 10-year Salomon Brothers Government Bond index, a median equally weighted portfolio of 20 hedge funds, and the Stark 300 index to benchmark managed futures. His test period ran from June 1994 to May 2001.

To test for benchmark robustness we use the S&P 500, the Citigroup Corporate Bond index (formerly Salomon Corporate Bond index), the Hedge Fund Research (HFR) Fund of Fund index, and the Center for International Securities and Derivatives Markets (CISDM) Public Fund index (formerly Zurich Public Fund index). Descriptive statistics on these indices appear in Table 25.1.

We form five portfolios with these allocations:

1. 100 percent stocks
2. 60 percent stocks and 40 percent bonds
3. 60 percent stocks, 30 percent bonds, and 10 percent hedge funds
4. 60 percent stocks, 30 bonds, and 10 percent managed futures
5. 60 percent stocks, 30 percent bonds, and 5 percent each of hedge funds and managed futures

TABLE 25.1 Descriptive Statistics of Each Index, January 1990 to December 2003

	S&P 500	Citigroup	DJ	Nasdaq	HRF	CISDM	Barclay	EAFE
Monthly Avg Return	0.97%	0.70%	0.89%	1.25%	0.84%	0.59%	0.61%	0.40%
Monthly StdDev	4.35%	1.36%	4.38%	7.58%	1.66%	3.68%	2.67%	4.95%
Annual Return	11.60%	8.44%	10.73%	14.97%	10.06%	7.11%	7.36%	4.85%
Annual StdDev	15.07%	4.71%	15.18%	26.27%	5.74%	12.75%	9.25%	17.14%
Total Returns	329.86%	219.60%	279.87%	394.93%	297.57%	141.54%	163.41%	60.56%
Skewness	-0.46	-0.30	-0.55	-0.41	-0.29	0.51	0.38	-0.15
Kurtosis	0.50	0.85	0.89	0.81	4.25	1.25	0.36	0.30
Monthly Max	11.40%	4.70%	10.60%	22.00%	6.85%	15.72%	10.03%	15.60%
Monthly Min	-14.50%	-4.42%	-15.13%	-22.80%	-7.47%	-9.60%	-5.49%	-13.90%
Info Ratio	0.77	1.79	0.71	0.57	1.75	0.56	0.80	0.28
Sharpe Ratio[a]	0.44	0.73	0.38	0.38	0.88	0.17	0.25	-0.01
Avg of + Months	3.63%	1.35%	3.49%	5.78%	1.51%	3.14%	2.47%	3.74%
Avg of − Months	-3.53%	-1.01%	-3.54%	-6.11%	-1.07%	-2.50%	-1.69%	-4.22%
StdDev + Months	2.50%	0.91%	2.53%	4.59%	1.20%	2.73%	1.92%	2.97%
StdDev − Months	2.91%	0.85%	3.15%	5.39%	1.26%	1.87%	1.33%	3.10%
S-Ratio	0.86	1.07	0.80	0.85	0.96	1.46	1.44	0.96

[a]The Sharpe ratio is calculated using a risk-free rate of 5 percent.
Note: The Dow Jones Industrial Index, NASDAQ Composite Index, Barclay CTA Index and MSCI EAFE are listed above for comparison purposes.

The statistical results of hedge funds and managed futures are based on industry representative indices. Results may vary with individual funds and/or trading strategies.

Source: CISDM Public Fund Index (Formerly Zurich and Mar Public Fund Index) Managed Accounts Reports, LLC, New York, NY. S&P 500 Index, Citigroup Corporate Bond Index (formerly, Salomon Corporate Bond Index), NASDAQ Composite Index, Dow Jones Industrial Average Index and MSCI EAFE Index are provided by Strategic Financial Solutions, LLC, Memphis, TN. Barclay CTA Index provided by Barclay Trading Group, Fairfield, IA. HFR Fund of Fund Index provided by HFR Asset Management, Chicago, IL.

The 10 percent allocation to alternative assets in the last three portfolios allows for more potential of noncorrelation among the portfolio components. We tested each portfolio, not so much for their returns, but to examine how volatility and skewness are affected when hedge funds and managed futures are introduced. Portfolios 3 and 4 also test for efficiency of allocation, where efficiency is defined as improved portfolio skewness and reduced downside risk. The results are presented in Table 25.1 and indicate that managed futures are more allocation efficient than hedge funds.

Brooks and Kat (2002) test various hedge funds indices and found the return distributions to be asymmetrical or nonnormal because of negative skewness and positive excess kurtosis, causing an overstatement of risk-adjusted returns when based on the Sharpe ratio. Their study found hedge fund indices to be highly correlated to the stock market.

The indices used in this chapter cover domestic and international equities, bonds, hedge funds, and managed futures. Only the CISDM Public Fund index and the Barclay CTA index, both representing the managed futures industry, show positive skewness. The Barclay CTA index, the CISDM Public Fund index, and the HFR Fund of Fund index are calculated net of expenses. The annualized standard deviation of the alternative asset indices is lower than that of the equity indices. The S-ratio better indicates whether volatility originates more from positive or negative monthly returns. An S-ratio above one implies positive months result in greater volatility than negative months. If an investment has greater dispersion of positive returns than of negative returns, the resulting positive skewness should add value to the portfolio. In fact, the results of Table 25.2 support this contention. On a risk-adjusted basis determined by the S-ratio, the indices are ranked as CISDM, Barclay, Citigroup, HFR, EAFE, S&P 500, Nasdaq, and Dow Jones.

The average monthly returns and total returns are similar across the four combined portfolios. When 40 percent of assets in Portfolio 1 are allocated to bonds, the annual standard deviation and returns are reduced by 36 and 11 percent, respectively (Portfolio 2). Skewness and kurtosis also show improvement. The reduction of volatility is seen in the reduced dispersion between the monthly maximum and minimum returns, the average positive and negative months, standard deviation of the positive and negative months, and the S-ratio. Although the S-ratio is still below one, it did improve. The S-ratio improved with skewness, reflecting a positive relationship between skewness and the S-ratio. Indeed, both metrics measure the variance of positive and negative monthly returns.

The skewness of the HFR index (−0.29) is an improvement over the skewness of Portfolio 2 of −0.39. Allocating 10 percent to hedge funds

TABLE 25.2 Descriptive Statistics of the Five Portfolios, January 1990 to December 2003

	Portfolio (1)	Portfolio (2)	Portfolio (3)	Portfolio (4)	Portfolio (5)
Monthly Average Return	0.97%	0.86%	0.87%	0.85%	0.86%
Monthly Standard Deviation	4.35%	2.80%	2.82%	2.73%	2.77%
Annual Return	11.60%	10.33%	10.50%	10.20%	10.35%
Annual Standard Deviation	15.07%	9.70%	9.77%	9.47%	9.59%
Total Returns	329.86%	295.76%	304.39%	289.81%	297.15%
Skewness	−0.46	−0.39	−0.47	−0.24	−0.36
Kurtosis	0.50	0.26	0.49	0.26	0.34
Monthly Maximum	11.40%	8.08%	8.22%	9.34%	8.78%
Monthly Minimum	−14.50%	−8.62%	−9.39%	−7.86%	−8.62%
Information Ratio	0.77	1.07	1.07	1.08	1.08
Sharpe Ratio[a]	0.44	0.55	0.56	0.55	0.56
Average of + Months	3.63%	2.48%	2.48%	2.36%	2.44%
Average of − Months	−3.53%	−2.21%	−2.25%	−2.25%	−2.20%
Standard Deviation + Months	2.50%	1.65%	1.65%	1.70%	1.66%
Standard Deviation − Months	2.91%	1.77%	1.84%	1.61%	1.73%
S-Ratio	0.86	0.93	0.90	1.06	0.96

[a]The Sharpe ratio is calculated using a risk-free rate of 5 percent.

diminishes the skewness of Portfolio 3, to −0.47. This reduction of skewness is coupled with high excess kurtosis of hedge funds (4.25) and causes the kurtosis of Portfolio 3 to increase from 0.26 to 0.49. A portfolio of decaying skewness and higher kurtosis is not an investor's ideal scenario, as it may increase tail risk. The standard deviation marginally increases from 9.7 to 9.77 percent. The S-ratio finds the negative returns increase volatility while the volatility of positive returns remains stable from Portfolio 2 to Portfolio 3. This is supported by the slight decay of the average down month in Portfolio 3 from Portfolio 2, while the average up month remained constant.

On the flip side, the CISDM index has a skewness of 0.51 and a kurtosis of 1.25. When 10 percent is allocated to the CISDM index, the skewness of Portfolio 4 improves from −0.47 to −0.24. The S-ratio increases above one as the positive volatility increases and the negative volatility decreases. The monthly maximum return increases from 8.22 to 9.34 percent and the monthly minimum return increases from −9.39 to −7.86 percent. The CISDM index has a relatively low Sharpe ratio, yet it improves the portfolio's risk-adjusted returns. As pointed out by Sharpe (1994), an investment with a low Sharpe ratio and low correlation to the portfolio may be a good diversifier for the portfolio. The improvement of the risk/return profile demonstrates the addition of noncorrelated assets to a highly concentrated portfolio has the potential to reduce downside volatility more than it reduces returns.

We find hedge funds exhibit asymmetrical distributions with negative skewness and high excess kurtosis, a high correlation of hedge funds to equity indices, and a noncorrelation of managed futures to equities (see Table 25.3) confirming the finding of Brooks and Kat (2002). This is not surprising in light of Till's (2003b) finding that 60 percent of hedge funds in the HFR universe are equity-based strategies.

Table 25.3 presents the correlations of alternative investments to traditional investments. For example, the HFR Fund of Funds index shows a correlation of 0.42, 0.38, 0.53, and 0.36 to the S&P 500, DJ, Nasdaq and MSCI EAFE indices, respectively. The correlations of the CISDM index to the benchmarks are −0.14, −0.15, −0.22, and −0.11, respectively. These results point to a stronger positive correlation of hedge funds to equities than managed futures. From January 1990 to December 1999, the correlation of the HFR index to the S&P 500 remained at 0.42, while that of the S&P 500 to the CISDM index was 0.01. This suggests that, since 2000, managed futures have become more negatively correlated to the S&P 500 index.

TABLE 25.3 Correlations of Each Benchmark, January 1990 to December 2003

	S&P 500	Citigroup	DJ	Nasdaq	HFR	CISDM	Barclay	EAFE
S&P 500	1.00	0.26	0.93	0.80	0.42	−0.14	−0.17	0.64
Citigroup		1.00	0.19	0.14	0.19	0.26	0.17	0.15
DJ			1.00	0.67	0.38	−0.15	−0.19	0.64
Nasdaq				1.00	0.53	−0.22	−0.22	0.54
HFR					1.00	0.15	0.21	0.36
CISDM						1.00	0.93	−0.11
Barclay							1.00	−0.14
MSCI EAFE								1.00

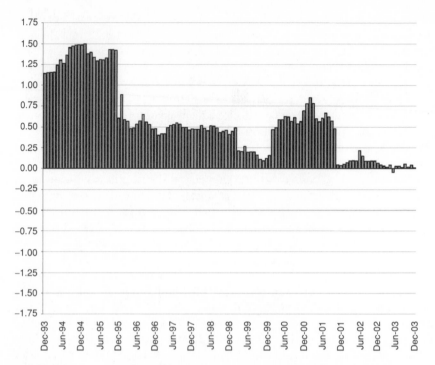

FIGURE 25.1   Four-Year Rolling Skewness of the CISDM Public Fund Index, January 1990 to December 2003

Identifying assets to include in a portfolio based on correlations is best done in conjunction with metrics that use higher moments. On a four-year rolling basis, the skewness of each index has varied, but the S&P 500 and HFR indices both exhibited negative skewness during much of the 14-year observation period running from January 1990 to December 2003. The negative skewness of the HFR index and the S&P 500 index occurs at similar instances, as illustrated in Figures 25.1 and 25.2, panels A and B. The CISDM index also exhibited varying skewness, but became negative only once during the observation period. This suggests that managed futures are more efficient diversifiers.

Figure 25.3 supports the argument of adding positively skewed investments to a naturally negatively skewed portfolio. The benchmarks and portfolios are clustered in the northwest corner of the chart, with the exception of the CISDM benchmark. There is modest dispersion of returns among the portfolios. As noted earlier, Portfolio 3 introduces hedge funds to a stock and bond portfolio and creates greater negative skewness and

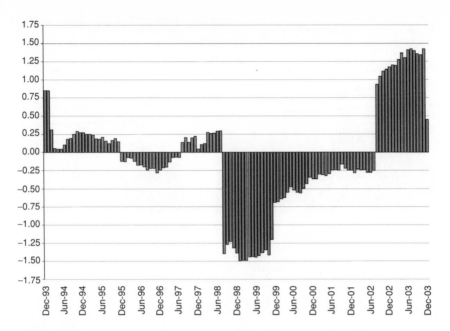

FIGURE 25.2 Four-Year Rolling Skewness, from January 1990 to December 2003, Panel A: HFR Fund of Fund Index

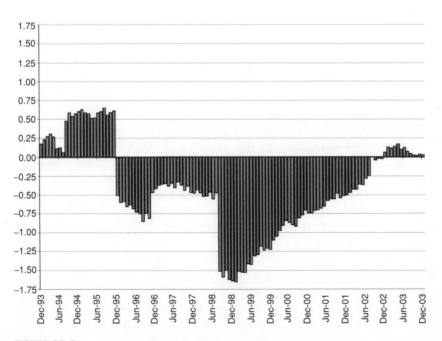

FIGURE 25.2 *(continued)* Panel B: S&P 500 Index

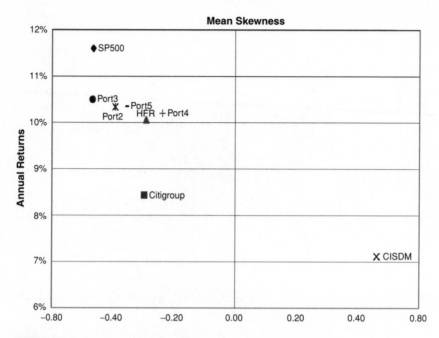

FIGURE 25.3 Mean Annual Return to Skewness of Benchmarks and Portfolios, January 1990 to December 2003

increased volatility. Portfolio 4 introduces managed futures into a stock and bond portfolio and improves both skewness and volatility. Note the location of Portfolio 2, a stock and bond portfolio, in Figure 25.3. Allocating either managed futures (Portfolio 4) or an equal allocation of managed futures and hedge funds (Portfolio 5) improves the skewness.

Figure 25.4 illustrates the annual average returns versus the negative standard deviation for each benchmark and portfolio. The conclusion is the same as for Figure 25.3. The allocation to managed futures or managed futures with hedge funds improves the risk-adjusted returns (Portfolios 4 and 5) relative to stocks and bonds only (Portfolios 1 and 2). The portfolio returns are once again clustered, and Portfolio 4 shows less downside risk.

CONCLUSION

The Sharpe ratio may overestimate the risk-adjusted returns by deemphasizing the downside volatility of investments containing negative skewness.

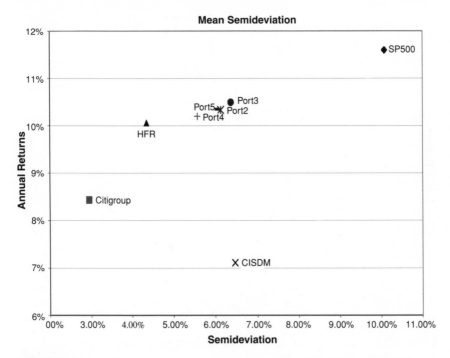

FIGURE 25.4 Mean Annual Return to Semideviation Frontier, January 1990 to December 2003

The Sharpe ratio may also understate the risk-adjusted returns of investments containing positive skewness by penalizing positive volatility. To understand risk-adjusted returns, it is necessary to know from where the volatility originates. Managed futures have a reputation for high volatility. When positive and negative returns are parsed, however, more volatility is found among the positive returns than the negative returns, which leads to positive skewness. This lends support to managed futures as an efficient allocation that adds value to a traditional portfolio by reducing downside risk. The S-ratio is an appropriate metric for this analysis. If the correlations of investments are low and the monthly returns are asymmetrical, higher statistical moments must be used to measure the coskewness and downside risk effect to the portfolio. Even though managed futures demonstrate greater efficiency than hedge funds, both may play a pivotal role in a traditional portfolio. Hedge funds show greater S-ratio volatility and negative skewness, but may enhance the returns of a traditional portfolio when allocated properly with managed futures.

CHAPTER 26

Investable Equity Long/Short Hedge Funds: Properties and Behavior

Edward Leung and Jacqueline Meziani

Are all investable equity long/short hedge fund indices created equal? In this chapter we examine constant and variable behavior of the betas of several investable equity long/short indices, such as the S&P equity long/short Index (SPELSI), using rolling regressions. We find that on average, equity long/short hedge fund returns are driven by returns of the global equity market, size premium, and the value premium. But when we examine different subperiods, the impact of value premium becomes less robust. The variability of these betas over time is modest, and this variability is different among the investable equity long/short indices.

INTRODUCTION

Equity long/short represents the largest classification in the hedge fund universe. According to Ineichen (2003), the assets under management held by this classification went from $39 billion (6 percent) in 1990 to $537 billion (42.5 percent) at the end of 2001. It is therefore very important to gain a deeper understanding of the equity long/short class of hedge funds.

The class of equity long/short hedge funds is both broad and varied. Managers have at their disposal a wide range of securities from multiple geographies, sectors, and capitalization sizes. Equity options and futures, equity index options and futures, exchange-traded funds, contracts for difference, and swaps may be deployed in addition to equity (Leung, Roffman, and Meziani 2004; Jacobs, Levy, and Starer 1998, 1999; Lhabitant 2003; Ineichen 2003). The manager may attempt to profit from a double-alpha strategy, that is, may try to generate alpha from both long and short stock positions independently. The short position serves to generate alpha, hedge market risk, and earn interest on the short position while collecting the short rebate.

Managers may also occasionally invest in a small number of relative value trades that attempt to profit from the price movement of an equity, relative to the price movement of another. Generally speaking, the net exposures of equity long/short managers to long positions minus short positions tend to have a positive bias. There is great variation in the net exposure between long/short managers.

High-beta funds generally have high net market exposure and are often concentrated, while moderate-beta funds are likely to hold proportionally more short positions that would lower net market exposure. Measuring the equity long/short universe via fund betas allows an a priori (without access to the fund details) selection of a variety of investment styles in the space and more precise peer groups against which to measure style conformity.

Low-beta funds have insignificant net market exposure or high-beta variability and deserve more analysis to ensure that they are not better classified as equity-market-neutral funds. It is important to stress that equity long/short funds will encompass elements also found in equity-market neutral, merger arbitrage, or even special situations strategies. It is a matter of degree that ultimately determines classification. Last, negative beta funds employ investment methodologies and strategies that can result in a return stream that runs counter to traditional equity market indices.

Another element that is critical to understanding equity long/short funds is the degree to which betas vary over time and over different market conditions. High-beta variability may indicate that the manager consistently includes securities different from those in the benchmark index, that a market-timing fund manager is deliberately controlling beta based on a market view (Fung and Hsieh 2001), or even that a stock-picking fund manager is concerned primarily with the fundamental characteristics of the stocks in the portfolio and does not manage beta.

This chapter focuses on discovering factors that influence returns of classic equity long/short hedge funds and how fund exposures change in response to changing market conditions.

TABLE 26.1 Return and Risk Summary for S&P Equity Long/Short Pro Forma Indices, January 2000 to March 2004

Performance (%)	2000	2001	2002	2003	2004[a]	Average Annual Return	Annual Standard Deviation	Sharpe Ratio
SPELSI	12.31%	6.71%	-5.13%	17.41%	0.07%	6.64%	6.32%	0.56
SPELSI US	9.26%	5.77%	-3.14%	11.28%	-0.25%	4.94%	6.03%	0.31
SPELSI Global Ex-US	14.72%	7.42%	-7.15%	23.70%	0.41%	8.13%	7.69%	0.66
CSFB	4.84%	-6.50%	-8.65%	17.59%	0.62%	1.29%	11.49%	-0.16
FTSE	9.38%	9.60%	1.01%	15.32%	3.75%	8.59%	5.39%	1.02
Edhec	12.01%	-1.20%	-6.38%	19.31%	1.53%	5.18%	6.95%	0.30
S&P Global 1200 TR	-10.79%	-15.01%	-19.55%	32.93%	1.65%	-4.21%	16.39%	-0.44
Size Premium	21.32%	20.69%	8.30%	8.20%	2.77%	13.43%	14.91%	0.69
Value Premium	29.13%	-1.09%	2.70%	4.60%	0.57%	7.42%	13.10%	0.33
Lehman 3 Months Treasury	6.20%	4.44%	1.78%	1.15%	0.39%	3.08%	0.63%	0.00
Lehman Global Aggregate	3.18%	1.57%	16.52%	12.48%	-1.24%	7.01%	6.21%	0.63

[a]Partial year.

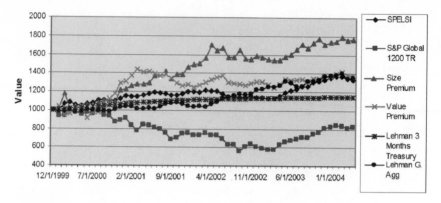

FIGURE 26.1   SPELSI versus Other Major Asset Classes

DESCRIPTIVE STATISTICS

Table 26.1 and Figure 26.1 present the performance of various investable equity long/short indices and other asset classes from January 2000 to May 2004. The figures show that the SPELSI outperformed the S&P Global 1200 by a huge margin and with much less volatility. The SPELSI historical return is constructed using net of fees returns from constituents. The size premium is the difference between the S&P SmallCap 600 and the S&P 500, while the value premium is the difference between the S&P 500/Barra Value and S&P 500/Barra Growth. The Sharpe ratio is calculated using the annualized return of Lehman Brothers' three-month Treasury rate.

While the equity market suffered a downturn after the end of the tech boom, equity long/short hedge funds did not. It is therefore important to understand how equity long/short hedge funds react to this downturn in the equity market so as to avoid losses. Did they change the exposure? If yes, by how much? Were there other factors that impact the profitability of equity long/short hedge funds other than movements in equity markets? We are interested in answering these questions.

Various index providers maintain investable hedge fund indices for the equity long/short classifications. Figure 26.2 and Table 26.2 indicate that the S&P equity long/short index provides an excellent representation of the equity long/short class compare to other investable equity long/short indices. Edhec's equity long/short index, which is a weighted average of all equity long/short indices regardless of investability, is also included. Other

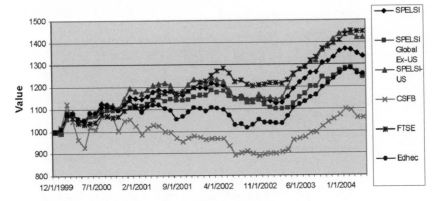

FIGURE 26.2 Investable Equity Long/Short Indices

investable equity long/short index providers such as Hedge Fund Research (HFR) and Dow Jones are not included because their return histories are too short.

MODEL-CONSTANT BETAS

Using data from January 2000 to May 2004, we apply stepwise factor regression to decompose the returns of investable equity long/short indices. For each equity long/short hedge fund index, we regress returns of monthly

TABLE 26.2 Correlation of Various Equity Long/Short Hedge Fund Indices, January 2000 to March 2004

Correlation	SPELSI	SPELSI Global Ex-US	SPELSI US	CSFB	FTSE	Edhec
SPELSI	1.00					
SPELSI Global Ex-US	0.88	1.00				
SPELSI US	0.94	0.67	1.00			
CSFB	0.74	0.64	0.70	1.00		
FTSE	0.81	0.78	0.71	0.73	1.00	
Edhec	0.91	0.73	0.92	0.80	0.77	1.00

indices against a set of risk factors that capture hedge fund returns (equation 26.1):

$$R_t = \alpha + \sum_{j=1}^{n} \beta_j F_{j,t} + \varepsilon_t \qquad (26.1)$$

where R_t = equity long/short index's return at time t
         β_j = jth factor loadings (weights)
         $F_{j,t}$ = factor j at time t
         ε_t = error at time t

For example, factor 1 can be a factor that measures broad movement of the global equity market such as the S&P Global 1200. Factor 2 can be a factor that measures broad movement of the bond market, such as the Lehman Global Aggregate. Factor regressions decompose the returns of each equity long/short hedge fund index into different factor exposures so each factor loading is an approximation of the fund's underlying investments.

Table 26.3 presents the set of 15 factors we use on our analysis that impact hedge fund returns.

Given the set of independent variables, we expect a classic equity long/short hedge fund to have a statistically significant relationship with equity,

TABLE 26.3   Risk Factors/Independent Variables of Factor Regression

Risk Factors	Proxy
Global Equity	S&P Global 1200
Size Premium	S&P Small Cap 600 minus S&P 500
Value Premium	S&P/Barra Value minus S&P/Barra Growth
Volatility	VIX
Volatility Lagged	VIX (lagged 1 period)
Commodity	Goldman Sachs Commodity Index
Currency	Federal Reserve Bank of New York Major Currency Index (real)
Cash	Lehman 3-month Treasury
Bond	Lehman Global Aggregate
Mortgage Backed	Lehman Mortgage Backed security Index
High Yield	Lehman Global High Yield
Yield Curve	Merrill 7-10 year treasury minus Merrill 3 month treasury
Yield Curve (lagged 1 period)	
Credit Spread	Lehman Int AAA minus Lehman Int BAA
UpMarket	Max(Returns,0) so as to capture market timing and option-like behavior

size, or value premium and have no significant relationship with other asset classes such as currency, commodity, or mortgage-backed securities (Amenc, El Bied, and Martellini 2002). The upmarket variable is added to see if equity long/short hedge funds can perfectly time the market. If market return is less than zero, then its value is zero. Otherwise, its value is the market return (Leung, Roffman, and Meziani 2004; Agarwal and Naik 2004).

Table 26.4 presents the regression results. Regression coefficients that are statistically significant are in bold, and their corresponding *p*-values are in parentheses. Independent variables that fail to reach statistical significance are excluded by the stepwise regression.

As expected, Table 26.4 shows that returns of the major investable equity long/short hedge fund indices in the market place have a significant positive relationship with global equity market return and size premium. This finding supports the conventional wisdom that equity long/short funds have a net long bias. They usually long small-capitalization stocks and short large-capitalization stocks, and their managers want more liquidity on the short side. Furthermore, they have a significant positive relationship with cash, possibly due to interest earned from short positions. These indices also have a significant negative relationship with the value premium. This suggests that these managers are taking long position with growth stocks and short position with value stocks. All the regressions show decent fit, as evidenced by the R^2 values, which range from 0.42 to 0.84. We conclude that risk factors such as equity, size premium, and value premium do a descent job in explaining the returns of long/short equity indices.

Given the similarity of the regression results, and the results of Table 26.2 and Figure 26.2, we conclude that the S&P equity long/short index is as representative as the other providers. Note that the investable equity long/short index of Credit Suisse First Boston (CFSB) behaves differently from the rest because the betas (in absolute value) for size premium and value premium are substantially larger. The beta of yield curve is also statistically significant.

Yield curve, high yield, and credit spread also affect some of the indices, but they are not as significant compared to equity, size premium, and cash. For example, yield curve is a driver of the investable equity long/short returns of CSFB, but not of the others. These secondary variables may therefore indicate differences in constituents among the equity long/short indices. Given that no macroeconomic variables are included, however, it is possible that factors like yield curve and credit spread become proxies for economic/business cycles. Indeed, credit spread widening is often associated with economic downturns, as is an inverted yield curve.

We focus on the three main independent variables that characterize the equity long/short returns: equity, size premium, and value premium.

TABLE 26.4 Stepwise Factor Regression Results on Equity Long/Short Hedge Fund Indices, January 2000 to March 2004

	SPELSI	SPELSI US	SPELSI Global Ex-US	CSFB	FTSE	Edhec
Intercept	−0.15 (0.56)	−0.28 (0.31)	−0.13 (0.71)	−0.49 (0.13)	0.47 (0.002)**	−0.11 (0.59)
Global Equity	0.24 (0.0000)**	0.33 (0.0000)**	0.15 (0.0008)**	0.19 (0.05)*	0.15 (0.0000)**	0.3 (0.0000)**
Size Premium	0.18 (0.0000)**	0.19 (0.0000)**	0.19 (0.0001)**	0.41 (0.0000)**	0.24 (0.0000)**	0.21 (0.0000)**
Value Premium	−0.1 (0.02)*	−0.08 (0.06)	−0.12 (0.02)*	−0.22 (0.005)**		−0.09 (0.006)**
Volatility				−0.04 (0.13)		
Lagged Volatility						
Commodity				0.08 (0.07)		
Currency						
Cash	2.48 (0.006)**	3.46 (0.0004)**	1.76 (0.12)			1.44 (0.04)*
Bond						
Mortgage Backed						
High Yield						0.11 (0.04)*
Yield Curve				1.79 (0.02)*		
Lagged Yield Curve						
Credit Spread	−0.34 (0.1)	−0.56 (0.009)**		−0.7 (0.08)		
UpMarkets						
R-Square	0.69	0.8	0.42	0.69	0.59	0.84

*significant at the 5 percent level.
**significant at the 1 percent level.

THE MODEL-VARIABLE BETAS

Our regression model for time variable betas is given in Equation 26.2.

$$R_t = \alpha_t + \beta_{1t}market + \beta_{2t}size + \beta_{3t}value + \varepsilon_t \qquad (26.2)$$

where, at time t:

R_t = return of Long/Short
α_t = value of the intercept (alpha)
$\beta_{1t}, \beta_{2t}, \beta_{3t}$ = value of coefficients for Market, Size, and Value premium
ε_t = error term

Note that the alpha and betas depend on time. A common approach to model variable alpha and betas are rolling regressions. The advantage of rolling regression is its simplicity, but its limitation is the dependence on the size of the rolling window (Leung, Roffman, and Meziani 2004). In addition, rolling regressions can indicate whether the results of Figure 26.4 (later, this chapter) are robust over different time periods.

Rolling Regression: 24-Month Rolling Window

Figure 26.3 illustrates the results of the rolling alphas. The standard errors of all the rolling regressions are adjusted for serial correlation using the Newey-West heteroskedasticity and autocorrelation consistent (HAC) covariance matrix estimation (Zivot and Wang 2002). We denote the 95 percent confidence intervals as "CI".

ROLLING ALPHAS

Figure 26.3, panels A to F, shows that the alphas are statistically insignificant because zero lies within the 95 percent confidence interval most of the time. We therefore cannot reject the null hypothesis that alpha is different from zero. This suggests that returns of equity long/short funds can be explained by equity, size, and value premium. Similar to other research on hedge funds, there is no evidence to support the claim that managerial skill is persistent. Recall that the returns of SPELSI are net of fees, so they do not have enough value added to offset these fees. The alphas across all equity long/short indices decrease and stabilize around the beginning of 2003. The rolling alphas of CSFB are mostly negative.

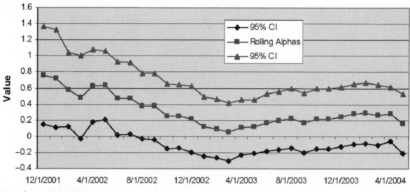

Panel A: SPELSI

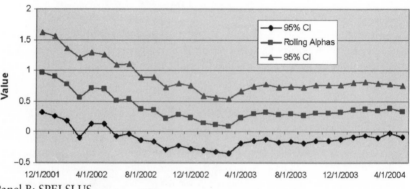

Panel B: SPELSI US

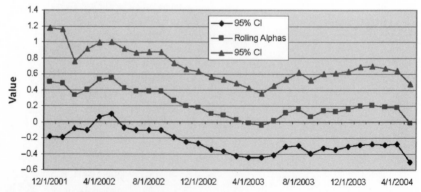

Panel C: SPELSI Global Ex-US

FIGURE 26.3   Statistical Insignificance of Alphas

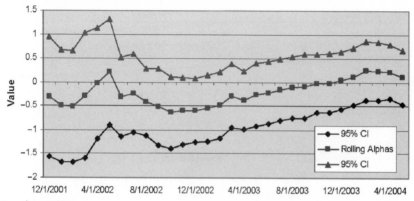

Panel D: CSFB

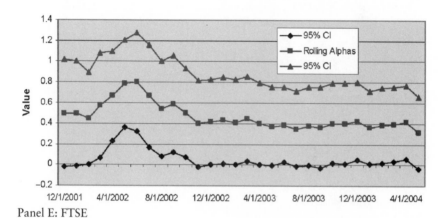

Panel E: FTSE

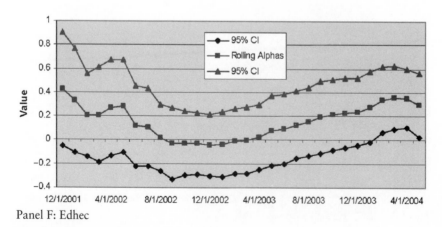

Panel F: Edhec

FIGURE 26.3 *(continued)*

ROLLING BETAS OF GLOBAL EQUITY

Figure 26.4, panels A to F, shows that the beta for the global equity market is statistically significant for most of the time period. For the SPELSI in the United States, it fluctuates between 0.3 and 0.4, so it is fairly stable. For the SPELSI Global Ex-US, it increases over time from virtually zero to 0.25. For SPELSI, the result is a mixture of the two subindices. Its rolling betas also have an upward trend but less steep compared to SPELSI Global Ex-US: its betas range from 0.2 to 0.33. For CSFB, the pattern is slightly different from S&P, Financial Times Stock Exchange (FTSE), and Executive Development Hautes Études Commerciales (Edhec). The betas range from 0.1 to 0.4. It

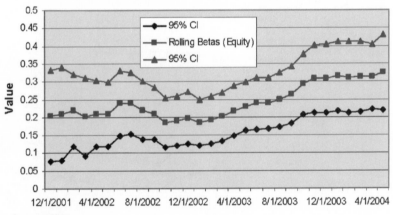

Panel A: SPELSI

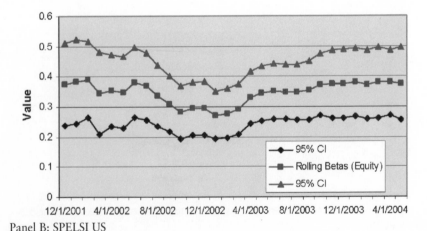

Panel B: SPELSI US

FIGURE 26.4 Statistical Significance of Beta

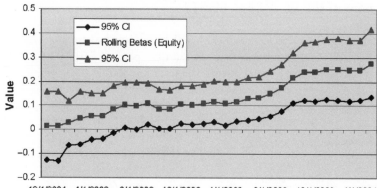

Panel C: SPELSI Global Ex-US

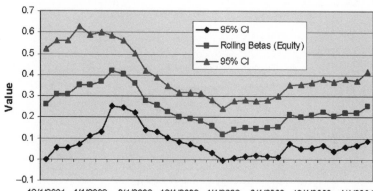

Panel D: CSFB

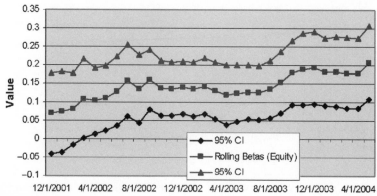

Panel E: FTSE

FIGURE 26.4 *(continued)*

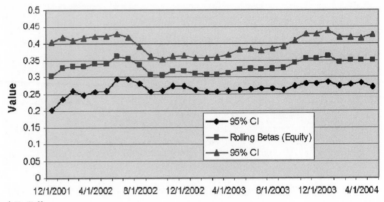

Panel F: Edhec

FIGURE 26.4 *(continued)*

first increases from 0.25 to 0.4 then decreases to 0.1 and finally increases back to 0.2. For FTSE, the pattern is similar to SPELSI Global ex-US. It shows an increasing trend, and the betas range from 0.05 to 0.2. Finally, for Edhec, the pattern is similar to SPELSI and the beta ranges from 0.3 to 0.35.

ROLLING BETAS OF SIZE PREMIUM

Figure 26.5, panels A to F, indicate that the rolling beta for size premium is statistically significant most of the time. The only exception is SPELSI

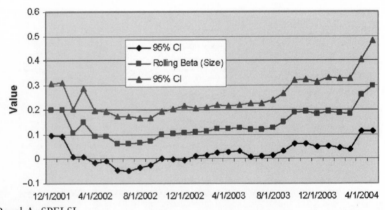

Panel A: SPELSI

FIGURE 26.5 Statistical Significance of Rolling Beta for Size Premium

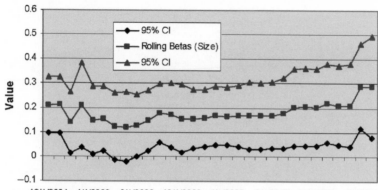

Panel B: SPELSI US

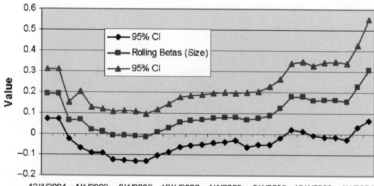

Panel C: SPELSI Global Ex-US

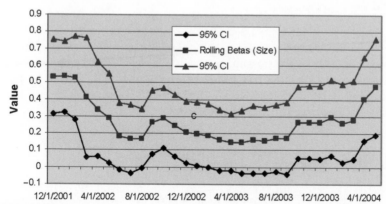

Panel D: CSFB

FIGURE 26.5 *(continued)*

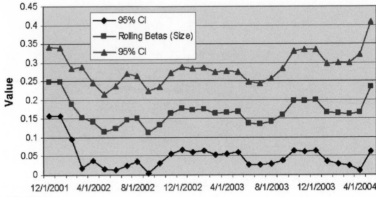

Panel E: FTSE

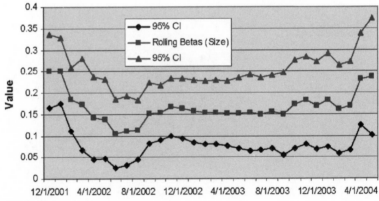

Panel F: Edhec

FIGURE 26.5 *(continued)*

Global Ex-US (zero lies within the 95 percent confidence interval for most of the time) due to the possibility of S&P Global 1200 being an inappropriate benchmark of the Asia and European market. The general pattern of the rolling betas is U-shaped. The betas of CSFB range from 0.1 to 0.5, which is wider than for the other indices.

ROLLING BETAS OF VALUE PREMIUM

Compared to the results of the regressions with constant beta, Figure 26.6, panels A to F, indicates that the beta associated with the value premium is statistically insignificant most of the time. The results of both the constant and variable betas imply that the robustness of the beta for value premium

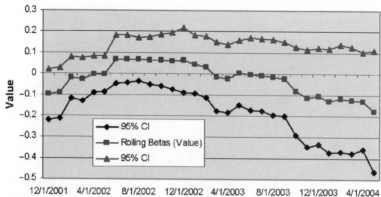

Panel A: SPELSI

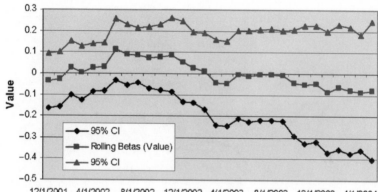

Panel B: SPELSI US

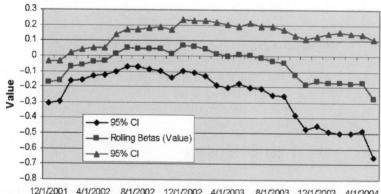

Panel C: SPELSI Global Ex-US

FIGURE 26.6   Statistical Insignificance of Beta Associated with the Value Premium

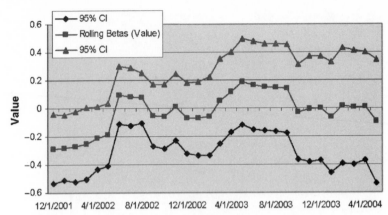

Panel D: CSFB

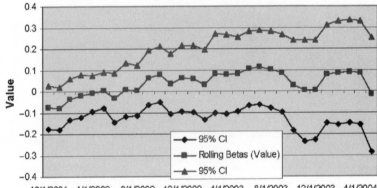

Panel E: FTSE

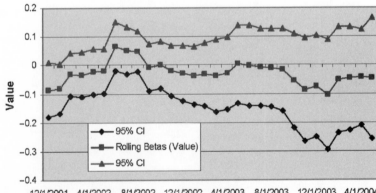

Panel F: Edhec

FIGURE 26.6 *(continued)*

is sensitive to the period being chosen or to the number of observation being used. In our regression with constant betas, 54 observations are used relative to 24 observations in the rolling regressions. So drivers such as global equity and size premium are much more robust than value premium. For the SPELSI, the pattern of the rolling betas for value premium shows an inverted U-shape. It takes on negative values most of the time. Equity long/ short funds are therefore taking long position on growth stocks and short position on value stocks. The patterns of CSFB and Edhec are similar. Both show a sharp increase around June 2002 and are mostly negative, whereas FTSE has a weak increasing trend that lies mostly in positive territory.

In general, the results of the rolling regressions indicate that the betas of equity and size premium are robust, and that their statistical significance is insensitive to the number of observations or time period being chosen. The statistical significance of the beta for the value premium is less reliable. Consistent with Fung and Hsieh (2004b), we conclude that equity and size premium are the more reliable drivers of equity long/short returns.

CONCLUSION

Are all investable equity long/short hedge fund indices created equal? Using rolling regressions, we examine both constant and variable behavior of the betas of various investable equity long/short indices. We find that on average, equity long/short hedge fund returns are driven by returns of the global equity market, the size premium, and the value premium. But when we examine different subperiods over time, the impact of value premium becomes less robust. The variability of these betas over time is modest, and this variability is different among the different investable equity long/short indices.

Future research could focus on applying this methodology to individual equity long/short hedge funds. This could provide more insights into understanding of the equity long/short class of hedge funds.

CHAPTER 27

Hedge Funds and Portfolio Optimization: A Game of Its Own?

Zsolt Berenyi

Hedge funds and alternative investments make use of alternative sources of return—this is a common belief. However, in some cases, superior knowledge or strategy may be replaced by certain optimized portfolio composition strategies that do not depend on superior skills. The reason is that industry-standard performance ratios may be subject to gambling. By using options, it is easy to defeat most performance measures of optimized portfolio strategies. It is often possible to modify the Sharpe ratio by using option strategies, namely by selling out-of-the-money calls. This has been noted in several studies.

One way to get rid of this exposure is to examine higher statistical moments of the underlying return distribution. In this chapter we examine those optimized option strategies that offer the most attractive returns in terms of different performance measures. Special emphasis is placed on multimoment, variance-equivalent performance measures. The return profiles of the optimized portfolio will be compared to those hedge funds. We present useful results on optimized option strategies and how they can be used to evaluate hedge fund performance.

INTRODUCTION

The most important question faced by investors has been which hedge fund to select, in terms of superior performance. It is now known that options or optionlike performance strategies, often used by hedge fund managers, may be used to enhance artificially performance. The Sharpe ratio and other common risk-value performance measures are, as evidence shows, sensitive to option strategies. It is possible to manipulate them with plain options (Dert and Oldenkamp 2000). This kind of manipulation is possible since risk and reward artificially reduce the return distribution to a single number, thereby neglecting many characteristics of the underlying returns. A growing number of studies focus on this particular issue and attempt to identify how performance can be enhanced without superior skills and how these manipulative strategies can be eliminated.

Using a higher-moment framework could be useful since the risk measure is designed to account for nonnormality in returns caused by optionlike strategies (Dert and Oldenkamp 2000). In the four-moment case, for example, the risk measure contains the mean, variance, skewness, and kurtosis to capture any nonnormality present in return series.

In this chapter we investigate option-based strategies with conventional (mean-variance) as well as higher-moment (mean-variance-skewness, mean-variance-skewness-kurtosis) measures of performance to determine optimal portfolios for each risk/reward measure. A simple methodology is used to construct optimized portfolios. We calculate a set of hypothetical call options with a maturity of one year and combine them with the underlying and the risk-free asset. We attempt to answer these questions:

- By using options, how can superior performance be achieved?
- How robust are the performance measures used?
- How many options are required to significantly enhance performance?
- How close are the obtained option portfolios to real hedge funds?
- Can certain funds employ such option-based strategies in order to enhance performance?

We expect fund managers to be discouraged from gambling behavior when higher-moment methods are used to measure performance. The results of this chapter can provide a tool for identifying funds that employ option-based performance enhancement strategies.

PERFORMANCE EVALUATION FRAMEWORK

Sharpe Ratio

The most common industry standard performance measure, the Sharpe ratio, is defined by equation 27.1 (Sharpe 1994):

$$SR(r_p) = \frac{E(r_p) - r_F}{\sigma(r_p)} \qquad (27.1)$$

where r_F = the return on the risk-free asset
           r_p = the return on portfolio p
           $\sigma(r_p)$ = the standard deviation of the return on portfolio p

Variance-Equivalent Risk Measures

In this chapter, higher-moment-based variance-equivalent (VeR) risk measures are used to evaluate the inherent risk of an arbitrary return distribution (Berényi 2003). These risk measures are termed as variance-equivalent since they build on market prices between expected return, variance, and higher moments—here skewness and kurtosis only—to compute a single variance-equivalent number. This number is a preference-neutral, market-based evaluation of virtually any return distribution. The derivation of the variance-equivalent measures is based on the fact that investors can trade moments of return distributions. Note that the easiest way to obtain market prices is through options markets.

A higher value of the risk measure indicates higher dispersion of the possible returns around the expected return. In addition, these measures penalize higher variance, kurtosis, and negative skewness. Since positive skewness is attractive for the investor, it is risk decreasing. If investors do not attach value to higher moments, the risk measure collapses back to variance. Similarly to the variance, the VeR measures can be used for performance assessment purposes in a manner completely analogous to the conventional two-dimensional risk and reward approach.

DEFINING VARIANCE-EQUIVALENT CLASS PERFORMANCE MEASURES: THE VeR RATIO

The most straightforward way to define distributional performance measures is to use the generalized Sharpe ratio principle. The composite performance ratio is defined by substituting the variance of the Sharpe ratio with a more general measure, in this case with the variance-skewness, or variance-skewness-kurtosis VeR measures (Dowd 1998).

VeR-Skewness Ratio

The variance-skewness VeR ratio uses the three-moment risk setting, in which the denominator is a risk measure containing the variance and skewness. This measure takes the form of equation 27.2, which is a reduced form of the four-moment case

$$VeR(\sigma,s)\,Ratio\,(r_p) = \frac{E(r_p)-r_F}{\sigma(r_p)+\dfrac{\kappa}{\tau}s(r_p)} \qquad (27.2)$$

where $s(r_p)$ = raw skewness of the return on asset p

$\dfrac{\kappa}{\tau}$ = market price parameters

As described in Berényi (2003), the four-moment replicating market pricing formula is

$$\frac{\kappa}{\tau} = \frac{2}{3}\frac{\sigma(r_M)}{s(r_M)}\frac{\left(E(r_s)-r_F\right)}{\left[\left(E(r_M)-r_F\right)-\left(E(r_s)-r_F\right)-\left(E(r_k)-r_F\right)\right]} \qquad (27.3)$$

where $\qquad E(r_M)$ = expected return on the market

$E(r_s), E(r_k)$ = expected return on the skewness and kurtosis factor portfolios, respectively, each constructed by nonlinear optimization that combines the underlying with options and the riskless asset

$\sigma(r_M), s(r_M), k(r_M)$ = standard deviation, skewness, and kurtosis of the underlying market portfolio, respectively

VeR–Kurtosis Ratio

The four-moment VeR-ratio contains, in addition to the skewness, the kurtosis of the underlying return distribution. This risk measure can be described by equation 27.4:

$$VeR(\sigma,s,k)\,Ratio\,(r_p) = \frac{E(r_p)-r_F}{\sigma(r_p)+\dfrac{\kappa}{\tau}s(r_p)+\dfrac{\delta}{\tau}k(r_p)} \qquad (27.4)$$

where $k(r_p)$ = kurtosis of the returns on asset p

The parameters δ / τ can be calculated as in equation 27.5:

$$\frac{\delta}{\tau} = \frac{1}{2} \times \frac{\sigma(r_M)}{k(r_M)} \frac{\left(E(r_k) - r_F\right)}{\left[\left(E(r_M) - r_F\right) - \left(E(r_s) - r_F\right) - \left(E(r_k) - r_F\right)\right]} \quad (27.5)$$

In equations 27.4 and 27.5, the similarity of the variance-equivalent measures to the Sharpe ratio makes explaining these performance measures relatively straightforward. The economic interpretation of the VeR ratios is intuitive. The expected excess return is compared to the risk-free rate per unit of risk (standard deviation or VeR measures) chosen. Higher ratios indicate portfolios with higher efficiency.

TESTING FRAMEWORK

Options and Underlying Market

For the risk-free asset, we use the annualized average yield of the one-month Treasury-bills. For the underlying index we choose monthly returns from the Standard & Poor's (S&P) 500 index over the January 1991 to December 1999 (for the same period as the hedge funds). Amin and Kat (2003a) also use the S&P 500 index with dynamic strategies to analyze hedge fund performance. For options we use a set of hypothetical calls with exercise prices spread around the current level of the S&P 500 index as underlying. This current level is then scaled down to 100 for the sake of simplicity. The exercise prices and additional information appear in Table 27.1. A total of eleven call options are used. We opt for using call options only, since selling the underlying and buying a call replicates a put option.

TABLE 27.1 Information on the Applied Call Options

	Option					
	1	2	3	4	5	6
Exercise price	80	84	88	92	96	100
Price	24.22	20.53	16.97	13.62	10.58	7.93

	Option				
	7	8	9	10	11
Exercise price	104	108	112	116	120
Price	5.73	3.99	2.67	1.72	1.07

Option prices are calculated using the Black-Scholes option-pricing formula, using the annual average volatility of the S&P 500 based on bootstrapped data, and assuming a maturity of one year.

Hedge Fund Data

For testing and analyzing the performance-ranking characteristics of different measures, we use 54 hedge funds from the TASS database, with a history of 108 months ranging from January 1991 to December 1999. We generate bootstrapped annual returns by drawing 12 samples with replacement from the set of monthly data and using 1,000 repetitions for each fund.

RESULTS

Optimized Portfolios with One Option

In the first step, we analyze the properties of optimized portfolios when only one option and the underlying index are used. The objective is to assess whether a significant performance increase can be achieved with one option only. Neglecting the riskless asset is legitimate since the addition of the riskless asset should not greatly affect performance. Only one option at a time is used for the portfolio optimizations. No further restrictions are applied.

Sharpe Optimized Portfolios

Significant performance improvement is always possible when using the Sharpe ratio to measure performance. No superior knowledge is required to enhance performance. It is sufficient to sell call options on the underlying. This can be seen from the first row of Table 27.2. It shows that buying or selling one option enhances the observed performance in practically every case. The improvement in the Sharpe ratio is between 21 and 84 percent compared to the Sharpe ratio of the underlying index. This is a significant increase.

The optimal strategy is usually to sell call options or, analogously, buy puts and sell the index, either in-the-money or out-of-the-money, so as to sell a part of the possible returns. Consequently, the price of this increase in performance lies in selling the upside potential of the underlying return distribution. That is, fund managers sell low-probability–high-impact scenarios for a fee to enhance the expected return. This, however, should not be the optimal strategy to be followed by a fund manager. The portfolio value distribution for the end-of-holding period (one year) and for an initial investment appears in Figure 27.1.

TABLE 27.2 Results of the Underlying Index Plus One Option Optimization for the Sharpe Ratio

	S&P 500 only	Opt 1	Opt 2	Opt 3	Opt 4	Opt 5	Opt 6	Opt 7	Opt 8	Opt 9	Opt 10	Opt 11
Sharpe Ratio	0.928	1.703	1.397	1.310	1.286	1.277	1.266	1.247	1.221	1.192	1.159	1.127
VeR-Skew	1.619	0.567	0.557	0.583	0.611	0.636	0.655	0.667	0.675	0.679	0.681	0.683
VeR-Kurt	0.716	0.250	0.275	0.313	0.348	0.379	0.404	0.424	0.440	0.451	0.460	0.466
Asset weights:												
Riskless	0.00	0.00	0.00	0.00	0.00	0.00	0.00	0.00	0.00	0.00	0.00	0.00
S&P500		1.32	1.25	1.20	1.15	1.11	1.08	1.06	1.04	1.03	1.02	1.01
Opt 1		−0.32	0.00	0.00	0.00	0.00	0.00	0.00	0.00	0.00	0.00	0.00
Opt 2		0.00	−0.25	0.00	0.00	0.00	0.00	0.00	0.00	0.00	0.00	0.00
Opt 3		0.00	0.00	−0.20	0.00	0.00	0.00	0.00	0.00	0.00	0.00	0.00
Opt 4		0.00	0.00	0.00	−0.15	0.00	0.00	0.00	0.00	0.00	0.00	0.00
Opt 5		0.00	0.00	0.00	0.00	−0.11	0.00	0.00	0.00	0.00	0.00	0.00
Opt 6		0.00	0.00	0.00	0.00	0.00	−0.08	0.00	0.00	0.00	0.00	0.00
Opt 7		0.00	0.00	0.00	0.00	0.00	0.00	−0.06	0.00	0.00	0.00	0.00
Opt 8		0.00	0.00	0.00	0.00	0.00	0.00	0.00	−0.04	0.00	0.00	0.00
Opt 9		0.00	0.00	0.00	0.00	0.00	0.00	0.00	0.00	−0.03	0.00	0.00
Opt 10		0.00	0.00	0.00	0.00	0.00	0.00	0.00	0.00	0.00	−0.02	0.00
Opt 11		0.00	0.00	0.00	0.00	0.00	0.00	0.00	0.00	0.00	0.00	−0.01

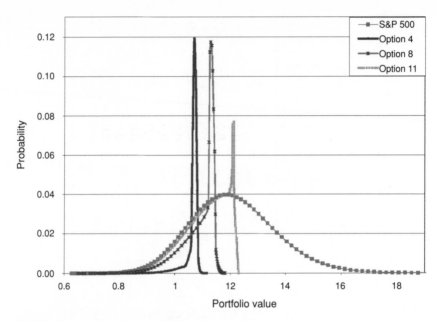

FIGURE 27.1 Portfolio Value Distributions of the Underlying Index Plus One Option, Sharpe Ratio Optimization

These examples demonstrate that an optimal strategy based on the Sharpe ratio leads to significant distortions of the original return distribution. That is, in order to enhance the Sharpe ratio, it is sufficient to reduce the overall dispersion and throw the upside part of the value distribution away as observed for the Sharpe optimized portfolios that appear in Table 27.2. These are by no means optimal, neither in terms of the VeR-skew ratio, nor in terms of the VeR-kurtosis ratio. On the contrary, in terms of the respective performance measures, they are all worse than the market portfolio. Therefore, optimal portfolios based on the Sharpe ratio may be suboptimal in terms of the other performance measures and also according to common intuition, which would actually preclude such strategies as using the Sharpe ratio.

VeR–Skewness Optimized Portfolios

We next examine optimized portfolios constructed with the underlying index and one option each, with no riskless asset included at this stage, according to the VeR-skew optimality rule. No additional restrictions are imposed on the optimization setting. The results are summarized in Table 27.3.

TABLE 27.3 Results of the Underlying Index Plus One Option Optimization for the VeR-Skew Ratio

	S&P 500 only	Opt 1	Opt 2	Opt 3	Opt 4	Opt 5	Opt 6	Opt 7	Opt 8	Opt 9	Opt 10	Opt 11
Sharpe Ratio	0.928	0.998	0.959	0.935	0.911	0.887	0.860	0.830	0.798	0.762	0.721	0.670
VeR-Skew	1.619	1.671	1.632	1.619	1.622	1.639	1.669	1.716	1.779	1.863	1.979	2.143
VeR-Kurt	0.716	0.746	0.728	0.719	0.711	0.704	0.696	0.687	0.674	0.654	0.626	0.585
Asset weights:												
Riskless	0.00	0.00	0.00	0.00	0.00	0.00	0.00	0.00	0.00	0.00	0.00	0.00
S&P500	1.00	1.27	1.16	1.03	0.93	0.89	0.90	0.92	0.94	0.95	0.96	0.97
Opt 1	0.00	−0.27	0.00	0.00	0.00	0.00	0.00	0.00	0.00	0.00	0.00	0.00
Opt 2	0.00	0.00	−0.16	0.00	0.00	0.00	0.00	0.00	0.00	0.00	0.00	0.00
Opt 3	0.00	0.00	0.00	−0.03	0.00	0.00	0.00	0.00	0.00	0.00	0.00	0.00
Opt 4	0.00	0.00	0.00	0.00	0.07	0.00	0.00	0.00	0.00	0.00	0.00	0.00
Opt 5	0.00	0.00	0.00	0.00	0.00	0.11	0.00	0.00	0.00	0.00	0.00	0.00
Opt 6	0.00	0.00	0.00	0.00	0.00	0.00	0.10	0.00	0.00	0.00	0.00	0.00
Opt 7	0.00	0.00	0.00	0.00	0.00	0.00	0.00	0.08	0.00	0.00	0.00	0.00
Opt 8	0.00	0.00	0.00	0.00	0.00	0.00	0.00	0.00	0.06	0.00	0.00	0.00
Opt 9	0.00	0.00	0.00	0.00	0.00	0.00	0.00	0.00	0.00	0.05	0.00	0.00
Opt 10	0.00	0.00	0.00	0.00	0.00	0.00	0.00	0.00	0.00	0.00	0.04	0.00
Opt 11	0.00	0.00	0.00	0.00	0.00	0.00	0.00	0.00	0.00	0.00	0.00	0.03

The most striking result is that the optimal strategy suggests buying far-out-of-the-money call options. It is remarkable that a small amount invested in out-of-the-money calls can significantly improve performance. This is in accordance with the skewness preference noted by a series of scholars (Scott and Horvath 1980) and very much in line with the expectations that in the real world, investors prefer bets with low probability but high positive possible outcomes. The second result is that for in-the-money options, the optimal strategy may be not to buy but to *sell* call options. In this view the results are similar to the Sharpe ratio optimized portfolios, but with less share in options in each case. However, this increase in the skewness-based performance is not significant.

With increasing exercise prices, the optimal strategy regarding call options changes from sell to buy. This increase in performance lies between 10 and 30 percent, which could be seen as significant if investors use the VeR-skew ratio as a measure. The resulting portfolio value distributions for the VeR-skewness optimization are illustrated in Figure 27.2.

The positive skewness of the optimized portfolios, except for the portfolios with deep-in-the-money calls, is again remarkable. The higher the option exercise price, the higher the skewness and the related performance ratio.

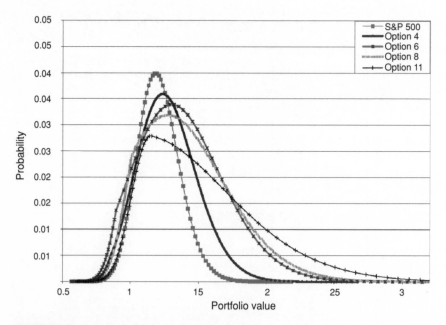

FIGURE 27.2 Portfolio Value Distributions of the Underlying Index Plus One Option, VeR-Skew Ratio Optimization

Finally, for the Sharpe ratio and the VeR-kurtosis ratio optimizations, the resulting portfolio value distributions are monotonically increasing like their parent index distribution (the S&P 500); the VeR-skewness–based optimal portfolios show a buckle in the payoff distribution, but not in the value distribution. That is, they do not necessarily increase as the underlying value distribution of the market portfolio increases.

VeR–Kurtosis Optimized Portfolios

In the third step, we examine VeR-kurtosis optimized portfolios generated using the underlying index and one call option each. The results are presented in Table 27.4.

For the optimal portfolio, the sign of the investments in different options is similar to the skewness case, because, for out-of-the-money options, it is positive (optimal is buying the given call option), and, for in-the-money options, negative (selling the calls). Selling in-the-money calls may improve this type of variance-equivalent performance measure as well, but not significantly. This slight increase can be attributed to the fact that the Black-Scholes pricing formula does not always correctly reflect true option prices (as evidenced by volatility smiles), but it is still an accepted estimate. Figure 27.3 illustrates the portfolio value distributions resulting from this phase of optimization.

These distributions are much like the underlying distributions, with no extreme deviation from normality in any direction. This means the optimized portfolios do not differ much from the market portfolio. Put differently, the performance increase induced from using the VeR-kurtosis ratio is not significant. It is not possible to substantially improve hedge fund performance by using a single option only. This has an important implication. Since it is not possible to increase performance through portfolio redesign with options, this performance ratio could be a useful tool to filter out option-based (or dynamic) manipulation techniques. This performance measure proves to be robust to such option strategies.

OPTIMAL PORTFOLIO WITH MORE OPTIONS

In the next phase, we apply two optimization scenarios, with different constraints on optimal solutions. First, we relaxed the constraint on the number of options in the portfolio optimization at the same time. During the optimization, we impose no restrictions regarding which options to hold, only restrict the amount to be invested in a particular option. In the two optimization scenarios, we restrict the maximum amount of each option to 5 percent (Scenario 1) and 20 percent (Scenario 2) of the fund's

TABLE 27.4 Results of the Underlying Index Plus One Option Optimization for the VeR-Kurtosis Ratio

	S&P 500 only	Opt 1	Opt 2	Opt 3	Opt 4	Opt 5	Opt 6	Opt 7	Opt 8	Opt 9	Opt 10	Opt 11
Sharpe Ratio	0.928	1.007	0.978	0.964	0.953	0.942	0.932	0.923	0.915	0.910	0.906	0.905
VeR-Skew	1.619	1.670	1.625	1.605	1.598	1.600	1.612	1.630	1.652	1.677	1.701	1.722
VeR-Kurt	0.716	0.747	0.731	0.724	0.719	0.717	0.716	0.716	0.717	0.718	0.719	0.720
Asset weights:												
Riskless		0.00	0.00	0.00	0.00	0.00	0.00	0.00	0.00	0.00	0.00	0.00
S&P500		1.27	1.18	1.11	1.05	1.02	1.003	0.998	0.997	0.997	0.998	0.999
Opt 1		-0.27	0.00	0.00	0.00	0.00	0.00	0.00	0.00	0.00	0.00	0.00
Opt 2		0.00	-0.18	0.00	0.00	0.00	0.00	0.00	0.00	0.00	0.00	0.00
Opt 3		0.00	0.00	-0.11	0.00	0.00	0.00	0.00	0.00	0.00	0.00	0.00
Opt 4		0.00	0.00	0.00	-0.05	0.00	0.00	0.00	0.00	0.00	0.00	0.00
Opt 5		0.00	0.00	0.00	0.00	-0.02	0.00	0.00	0.00	0.00	0.00	0.00
Opt 6		0.00	0.00	0.00	0.00	0.00	-0.003	0.00	0.00	0.00	0.00	0.00
Opt 7		0.00	0.00	0.00	0.00	0.00	0.00	0.002	0.00	0.00	0.00	0.00
Opt 8		0.00	0.00	0.00	0.00	0.00	0.00	0.00	0.003	0.00	0.00	0.00
Opt 9		0.00	0.00	0.00	0.00	0.00	0.00	0.00	0.00	0.003	0.00	0.00
Opt 10		0.00	0.00	0.00	0.00	0.00	0.00	0.00	0.00	0.00	0.002	0.00
Opt 11		0.00	0.00	0.00	0.00	0.00	0.00	0.00	0.00	0.00	0.00	0.001

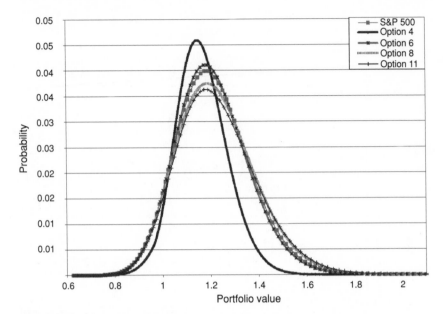

FIGURE 27.3   Portfolio Value Distributions of the Underlying Index Plus One Option, VeR-Kurt Ratio Optimization

total volume. Then we restricted the amount invested in the riskless asset as well as the underlying index to ± 100 percent (Scenario 1) and 120 percent (Scenario 2) of the fund's total volume. Under both scenarios, the optimized portfolios should have a variance greater than or equal to the variance of the underlying S&P 500. With this restriction, we focus on portfolios with risk levels comparable to the market index and eliminate portfolios that make use of pricing discrepancies with very low dispersion (near arbitrage).

The optimization scenarios were computed by nonlinear programming using General Algebraic Modeling System (GAMS). An overview of the two optimized portfolios and the related performance ratios is given in Table 27.5 for Scenario 1, and in Table 27.6 for Scenario 2.

The portfolio value distributions for the one-year holding period are contained in Figure 27.4 for Scenario 1 and Figure 27.5 for Scenario 2. An overview of the results in the particular optimization scenarios and performance ratios is given in the next three sections.

TABLE 27.5 Results of the Unconstrained Optimization, Scenario 1

	Sharpe Optimal Portfolio	VeR-Skewness Optimal Portfolio	VeR-Kurtosis Optimal Portfolio
Sharpe Ratio	**1.156**	0.675	0.921
VeR-Skew Ratio	0.673	**2.553**	1.843
VeR-Kurt Ratio	0.453	0.575	**0.728**
Expected return	1.228	1.155	1.193
Risk measure	0.151	0.040	0.191
Standard deviation	0.151	0.151	0.151
Skewness	−0.184	0.189	0.129
Kurtosis	0.235	0.255	0.215
Riskless	−0.189	0.001	−0.053
S&P index	1.000	1.000	1.000
Option 1	0.050	0.050	0.050
Option 2	0.050	0.050	0.050
Option 3	0.050	0.025	0.050
Option 4	0.050	−0.050	−0.046
Option 5	0.050	−0.050	−0.030
Option 6	0.050	−0.014	−0.016
Option 7	−0.043	−0.008	−0.003
Option 8	−0.050	0.003	−0.001
Option 9	−0.016	−0.001	−0.004
Option 10	0.006	−0.050	−0.003
Option 11	−0.009	0.045	0.007

Sharpe Optimized Portfolio

We find the optimal Sharpe ratio strategy to be similar under both scenarios. This strategy is analogous to the optimal Sharpe ratio strategy with one option described earlier: hold a long position in the index, buy in-the-money call options, sell out-of-the-money calls, and short the riskless asset. We find higher negative skewness and higher kurtosis under Scenario 2. This is not surprising and can be attributed to the higher share in options.

VeR–Skewness Optimized Portfolio

The optimal strategy for this portfolio can be described as holding long the underlying index and holding long in-the-money options. The direction and amount to be invested in at-the-money as well as out of-the-money options, however, is not obvious. This likely requires a case-by-case individual optimization.

TABLE 27.6   Results of the Unconstrained Optimization, Scenario 2

	Sharpe Optimal Portfolio	Skewness Optimal Portfolio	Kurtosis Optimal Portfolio
Sharpe Ratio	**1.220**	0.676	0.925
VeR-Skew Ratio	0.667	**2.564**	1.853
VeR-Kurt Ratio	0.430	0.575	**0.729**
Expected return	1.238	1.156	1.193
Risk measure	0.151	0.040	0.192
Standard deviation	0.151	0.151	0.151
Skewness	−0.213	0.189	0.129
Kurtosis	0.283	0.256	0.216
Riskless	−0.417	−0.040	−0.094
S&P index	1.000	1.000	1.000
Option 1	0.200	0.200	0.200
Option 2	0.200	0.122	0.126
Option 3	0.200	−0.200	−0.200
Option 4	0.200	−0.027	0.013
Option 5	−0.156	−0.024	−0.024
Option 6	−0.189	−0.021	−0.018
Option 7	−0.008	−0.001	−0.003
Option 8	−0.014	−0.014	−0.001
Option 9	−0.013	0.025	−0.003
Option 10	0.005	−0.070	−0.004
Option 11	−0.008	0.050	0.007

VeR–Kurtosis Optimized Portfolio

We find several notable differences between the VeR-skewness and VeR-kurtosis optimization cases. However, they are similar in going long the underlying index and in-the-money call options. Furthermore, in these cases, individual optimization is needed. Looking at the two portfolio value distributions for Scenarios 1 and 2 in Figures 27.4 and 27.5, we find that they have a very similar value distribution sequence. This indicates some persistence in the strategy to be followed in the VeR-kurtosis case as well.

Variance-skewness-kurtosis optimal portfolios are very close to the market index, both in shape and performance. This can probably be traced back to the robustness and insensitivity of this particular performance ratio to manipulation techniques that use options. In this case, insensitivity means that it is not possible to achieve a higher performance than the market portfolio by using portfolio construction methods only.

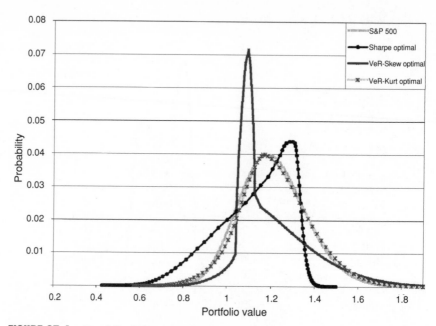

FIGURE 27.4   Portfolio Value Distributions, Scenario 1

Robustness of the Performance Measures

Higher-moment performance measures, which account for return nonnormality induced by options, may be indeed suitable for performance measurement. It is conceivable that option manipulation techniques that aim to enhance performance artificially can be identified. Four-moment measures seem to be robust enough to make gambling unprofitable. Further testing will still be needed, but the beginning is promising.

CLOSENESS OF THE HEDGE FUNDS AND OPTIMIZED PORTFOLIOS

The last issue addressed in this chapter deals with whether real hedge funds employ such option-based performance enhancement strategies. We conduct a plain test to confirm whether hedge funds resemble optimized portfolios. First, we obtain correlation coefficients between portfolio value distributions. Then, to identify cases in which the performance ratio show specific patterns that could be attributed to option manipulation, we com-

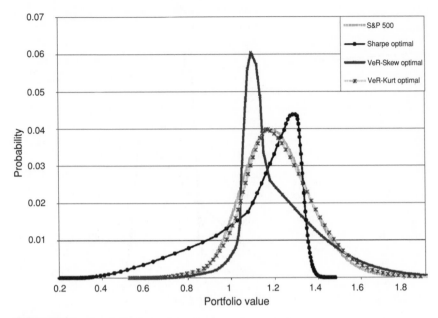

FIGURE 27.5 Portfolio Value Distributions, Scenario 2

pare performance measures for hedge funds with the optimized portfolios as well as the market portfolio.

Correlation Test

The correlation coefficient can be used to compare the distributions of two portfolios. We calculate correlation by using the 100-pin-setting value distribution of the underlying index (S&P 500) as well as the 100-pin-setting value distribution from the three optimized portfolios obtained from Scenario 1. To match these pins, we calculate 100-pin-value probability distributions (but not the probability density function) of portfolio values for each of the hedge funds by bootstrapping. Correlation coefficients can then be readily calculated.

Findings

The majority of the hedge funds show a strong and significant positive correlation with the market index. Somewhat surprisingly, the correlation coefficients are lower for the three optimized portfolios. They are, however, still very high. We identify only five funds where the correlation between the fund and the VeR-kurtosis optimized portfolio was lower than the same ratio calculated using the Sharpe optimized portfolio. Looking at the performance measures of those portfolios, we find evidence to suggest that they could indeed be using such techniques. The overall result, however, points to no stable pattern, which could denote the presence of Sharpe ratio–enhancing option-based strategies over the long time period under investigation. The picture could certainly be different when examining shorter time periods. This area still needs further investigation.

Searching for Performance Patterns

We examine the relationship between the different performance ratios calculated for all hedge funds, since we find a pattern that suggests performance ratio switching. By switching we mean a fund with a Sharpe ratio higher than that of the optimized portfolio, but with VeR performance ratios lower than those of the underlying index. Switching could also indicate the use of Sharpe ratio–enhancing methodologies.

Findings

Among 54 hedge funds, we identify 30 with a Sharpe ratio higher, but with VeR-skew or VeR-kurt ratio lower, than that of the market portfolio. This may indicate the presence of some Sharpe ratio enhancement methodology since such strategies cannot enhance all higher-moment-based ratios at the same time. Furthermore, 19 of the 54 hedge funds had a Sharpe ratio higher, but a VeR-skew or VeR-kurt ratio lower, than that of the Sharpe optimized portfolio. These funds are not superior to the Sharpe optimized portfolio, because, under certain conditions, this kind of performance can be replicated by using options.

CONCLUSION

We show how optimized portfolios can be built using an underlying index and call options for different performance measures. The optimal strategies that use one call option, as well as several options, are presented and illustrated for each performance measure under investigation: the Sharpe ratio, the VeR-skewness ratio, and the VeR-kurtosis ratio. In addition, we examine the robustness of the performance measures to option-based gambling strategies.

We find that the performance measure based on variance-skewness-kurtosis (variance-equivalent) is not sensitive to option strategies in that the performance cannot be artificially enhanced by using only options. Hedge funds can be analyzed by using higher-moment performance ratios, and these ratios can help distinguish between superior performance and performance achieved by option-based manipulation only. While higher-moment-based VeR ratios can be useful in identifying truly superior performance, we find only weak evidence for the use of performance enhancing option-based strategies. This can be attributable to the fact that option strategies may change over time. This issue therefore needs to be examined in the short term.

Our evidence suggests that some funds may have superior performance in terms of the Sharpe ratio, but this superior performance can be traced back in part to the presence of option-based strategies only. Thus, in terms of higher-moment VeR performance ratios, these hedge funds do not benefit from superior performance.

Special Classes of Hedge Funds

Chapter 28 examines principal protected notes (PPNs) and how the main variants of PPNs work to protect the investor's principal. The author analyzes how PPNs perform with respect to prevailing market conditions either with or without leverage exposure to the underlying fund of funds. He demonstrates an analytical approach to evaluating PPN variants based on outcomes and argues that such an approach is required to evaluate PPNs in relation to the investor's risk appetite and ultimate investment aims.

Chapter 29 examines the issue of stale pricing. The authors suggest the advantages and disadvantages investors may face if hedge funds and funds of hedge funds maintain illiquid securities in their portfolio. As a result of these illiquid securities, monthly returns of hedge funds that trade these type of securities may not be accurate.

CHAPTER 28

Structured Products on Fund of Fund Underlyings

Jens Johansen

Structured products on fund of fund underlyings, and in particular principal protected notes (PPNs), have proliferated in recent years and have become a key source of assets for funds of funds. A number of different structures can be used to achieve principal protection. In this chapter we describe how the main PPN variants work. These include simple as well as path-dependent option structures and PPNs that employ the constant proportion portfolio technique (CPPT) method of dynamic hedging. These achieve the goal of protecting the investor's principal, but do so using very different mechanics. Using simulation on a sample of real hedge fund returns, we examine the relative merits of each type of PPN, both with and without leverage. We use this analysis to show how PPNs perform depending on prevailing market conditions and also with or without leveraged exposure to the underlying fund of funds. We conclude that underlying conditions as well as terms of the PPN do make a difference as to which variants are more effective. Moreover, we show that an investor's risk appetite should matter in deciding on one PPN variant over another, even though all PPNs provide protection of principal. We advocate an analytical approach based on an understanding of PPN mechanics and risk appetite in choosing the most suitable PPN for an investor's needs.

This chapter draws on material from UBS (2004). The views and opinions expressed in this chapter are those of the author and are not necessarily those of UBS. UBS accepts no liability over the content of the chapter. It is published solely for informational purposes and is not to be construed as a solicitation or an offer to buy or sell any securities or related financial instruments.

INTRODUCTION

Some of the people I know lost millions. I was luckier. All I lost was two hundred and forty thousand dollars. I would have lost more, but that was all the money I had.

—Groucho Marx on the 1929 crash (Marx and Thurber, 1994, p. 152)

Review of the Fund of Funds Industry

In 2001 UBS pointed out that all hedge funds are not created equal (UBS September, 2001). In our experience, hedge funds make every effort to create asymmetrical returns (UBS 2002a). They use risk management techniques to limit losses at the minimum possible expense to upside returns. Generally speaking, hedge funds have been fairly successful at this in the past, as Figure 28.1 shows.

The dark bars in Figure 28.1 represent the average fund of hedge funds net of two layers of fees. The light bars show the performance of long-only equity investments represented by total returns of the Morgan Stanley Capital International (MSCI) World index. However, it says nothing about the dispersion of returns. The dispersion of returns are relevant to anyone

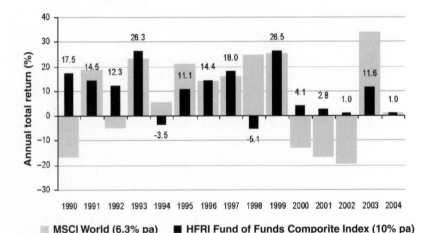

FIGURE 28.1 MSCI World and HFRI Fund of Funds Composite Index
Source: UBS (using Hedge Fund Research, Thomson Financial Datastream data). Both indices are total returns in U.S. dollars, August 2004 inclusive.

selecting a fund of funds (FoF) from the roughly 1,500 available to choose from' today.

The growth in FoF assets under management has also been spectacular, particularly in recent years. In 2002 assets under single-style hedge fund management grew by 16 percent, while assets under FoF management grew by more than 30 percent. In 2003 FoF assets under management grew by around 46 percent while assets under management in the hedge funds in which fund of funds invest grew by just over 31 percent. Growth in the first half of 2004 was even more phenomenal: The billion-dollar club (FoF with U.S.$1 billion or more under management) managed assets worth $438 billion. Meanwhile, the first half of 2004 proved a difficult one for underlying hedge funds. Growth in assets under management for the industry as a whole has not kept pace with fund of funds growth.

Funds of funds are taking an increasing share of the capacity supplied by hedge fund managers. Approximately 50 to 70 percent of new money going into hedge funds comes from fund of funds, compared with less than half in 2000. As a natural consequence, this will increase the pressure on some FoF managers to invest with hedge funds of poorer average quality than they might have done in the past.

There are three main reasons for this growth.

1. Well-established funds of hedge fund managers have forged lasting relationships in the hedge fund community. They understand the business models and investment approaches of hedge funds, their associated risks, and how to manage them. They therefore have a competitive advantage over the average beginner in constructing successful portfolios of hedge funds.

2. They can provide access to a diversified portfolio of hedge funds (attractive to institutional money) with much less capital than would otherwise be required (attractive to retail money). Many hedge funds will not accept investments under $500,000, and some require more. To build a portfolio of 20 hedge funds requires investment capital amounting to roughly $10 million to $20 million. Funds of funds also have a minimum required investment, but this is typically in the region of $250,000. So they can provide access to hedge funds with diversification, but for one-fortieth of the capital. Moreover, the proliferation of structures in recent years has made it possible to invest in a fund of funds for as little as $10,000.

3. The regulatory environment in many jurisdictions is in the process of easing, allowing greater access to hedge funds through fund of funds. The most notable example is Germany, where the Investment Modernization Act and tax code revision have considerably liberalized access to hedge funds.

Growing Pains?

Figure 28.2 shows how the number of funds of funds available has increased dramatically since the late 1980s. As the number of funds has grown, so has the dispersion of quarterly returns. In the figure, each vertical line represents the range of quarterly returns produced, and each marker on a line represents the quarterly return of one fund of funds.

Figure 28.2 shows that the dispersion has not only increased over the period, but the proportion of funds producing negative quarterly returns in any one quarter has gone up. There are a number of possible reasons for this. One possibility is that the growth of assets seeking hedge fund management has attracted more new managers to the field and shifted assets from talented to less talented managers. The recent growth of FoF assets under management may exacerbate this source of poor performance.

Another possible source of underperformance is that FoF managers may have been long particular segments of the market that have suffered losses during market shocks, such as the Russian debt default in third quarter 1998 or the bursting of the technology bubble in second quarter of 2000. Evidence of this can be seen in Figure 28.3.

Figure 28.3 shows the proportion of funds that have made large and very large losses in each quarter. Here "large" means posting a quarterly loss of more than 5 percent, and "very large" means posting a quarterly loss of more than 15 percent. In this figure, the effect of the Russian debt default on

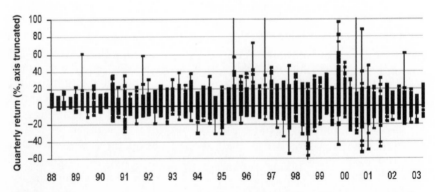

FIGURE 28.2   Dispersion of Fund of Funds Returns, 1988 to Q2 2003 (quarterly returns)
Source: UBS (using Van Hedge Fund Advisers data).
Note: Data include funds that are know to have wound up and liquidated and funds that have ceased to report returns. The fund of funds in the database vary in terms of both size and risk appetite.

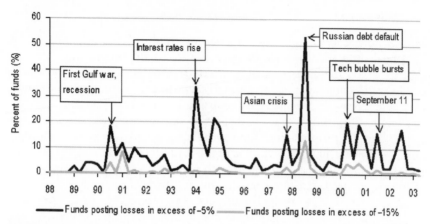

FIGURE 28.3   Percentage of FoFs Making Large Losses, 1988 to Q2 (quarterly returns)
Source: UBS (using Van Hedge Fund Advisers data).
Note: Data include funds that are know to have wound up and liquidated and funds that have ceased to report returns. The fund of funds in the database vary in terms of both size and risk appetite.

fund of funds is clearly visible. Other events also become visible: the first Gulf War, the surprise interest rate hike in 1994, the Asian crisis in 1997, the bursting of the technology bubble in 2000, and the September 11, 2001, terrorist attacks. The other peaks in the chart that do not coincide with specific events in markets are potentially due to deterioration in manager skill, as the FoF industry began to grow more rapidly during the equity bear market.

Figure 28.3 also shows that loss events affect a wide range of fund of funds when two circumstances coincide: there is a high degree of leverage among hedge funds and there is a shock in borrowing costs or liquidity. Such shocks cause problems not only because they tend to increase the cost of borrowing money,[1] but because they tend to increase the cost of borrowing anything. So any type of hedge fund with a short side to its portfolio will have experienced some level of difficulty during these periods. According to Figure 28.3, hedge funds, despite their focus on managing downside risk while taking advantage of upside opportunities, are not immune to market shock events.

---

[1]This is true unless you happened to be the U.S. government in 1988. In 1988, the increase in the cost of borrowing was mainly due to widening credit spreads, not a spike in government bond rates, which actually fell as the Federal Reserve eased and the market saw a flight to quality.

In the current economic environment, interest rates are currently near a multigenerational low, and household borrowing is very high. Anecdotal evidence points to an increased appetite from fund of funds for more leveraged hedge fund opportunities. Moreover, it is likely that funds of funds have been relaxing their standards in terms of a reduction in the length of live track record they are willing to accept from early-stage managers. New hedge fund styles (i.e., credit arbitrage, capital structure arbitrage, reinsurance catastrophe bonds, and synthetic banking products) are also increasingly popular as funds of funds seek to squeeze performance out of dull underlying capital markets and achieve better portfolio diversification. The trade-off, however, is that the market as a whole has relatively little experience of how these styles will perform or feed back on capital markets in times of market shocks[2] such as that related to the near collapse of Long-Term Capital Management (LTCM). Moreover, underlying funds in the new styles tend to have longer liquidity terms, which in turn will likely be passed on to fund of funds and ultimately to investors in funds of funds—including issuers of principal-protected notes on fund of funds.

Protecting Principal

The bear side doesn't appeal to me any more than the bull side or vice versa. My one steadfast prejudice is against being wrong.

—Lefèvre 1994, p. 6

The current environment is one of increased risk appetite by FoF managers against a backdrop of arguably more risky capital markets. Consequently, an increasing number of investors, on both the institutional and the retail side, have sought protection in addition to the asymmetry of returns offered by a fund of funds. Principal protection has typically been achieved through structures offered by an intermediary, usually an investment bank. This has proved to be convenient for funds of funds as well as investors, as these structures provide funds of funds with a relatively sticky source of assets. Moreover, the source of assets is more predictably tied to the FoF performance, since early

---

[2]The very worst thing about shocks, in our view, is that they are certain to happen sooner or later. With reference to LTCM, we are often asked how likely we think it is that another failure event could happen that threatens to bring down the whole finance system. We invariably answer that far-from-equilibrium events are almost certain to happen again, but we do not know when. Shifts happen. The important question is: How well prepared are we and our investment portfolios for such events?

redemption of structures by end investors is usually penalized in some way, and the algorithm behind the structure is often well defined and predictable.

There are two basic ways to structure principal protected notes. The first, and simplest, way is to buy a zero-coupon bond (ZCB) paying out the value of the principal at maturity. The other is by using dynamic hedging, which we describe later. A wide variety of other structures exists to achieve exposure with different features, some of which have conservative properties but do not necessarily remove all risk to the investor's principal.

In a bond-plus-call PPN, the ZCB is purchased at a discount, so the amount left over can be used to purchase a call option on a fund of funds struck at the fund's current net asset value (NAV) expiring at ZCB maturity. Since the call option pays out nothing at maturity if the NAV of the fund of funds' falls below the strike value at maturity, the least amount of money the end investor will have at maturity is the amount initially invested (the ZCB payout). The investor would only forgo the opportunity to invest the principal elsewhere, and the interest that could have been earned. On the other hand, if the NAV of the fund of funds rises, the end investor participates in that upside. We will refer to these structures as option-based or bond-plus-call structures. The payoff is shown in Figure 28.4.

Participation will generally not be 100 percent. Much depends on the prevailing interest rate and time to maturity, which determines the discount of the zero-coupon bond, which in turn determines how much is left to spend on call options. The fewer calls the investor owns, the lower the participation. This is shown in Figure 28.4. Note that the structure pays out slightly less than the underlying above 100. Figure 28.5 shows how participation varies with interest rate for a seven-year bond-plus-call structure. The figure shows that a bond-plus-call structure on a fund of funds with 18 percent volatility in an environment where five-year zero-coupon rates are at 5 percent gives the investor just under 85 percent participation.

Notice how rapidly participation drops off for zero-coupon interest rates below 5 percent in the case of options with implied volatility of 18 percent or below. Note also how the more expensive option (i.e., the one with the highest volatility) requires a much higher interest rate (a much more deeply discounted bond) to achieve high participation.

Figure 28.6 shows how participation varies with volatility. Once again it shows that for a fund of funds with implied volatility of 18 percent, participation in a 5 percent zero-coupon interest-rate environment is just under 85 percent. Like Figure 28.5, Figure 28.6 also shows the sensitivity of participation rates to the prevailing interest rates at any given time. Finally, it shows that in low-interest-rate environments, participation rates are extremely sensitive to volatility, particularly for low-volatility underlyings.

Time is also a factor in determining participation. Figures 28.7 and 28.8 show how participation varies with maturity for different implied

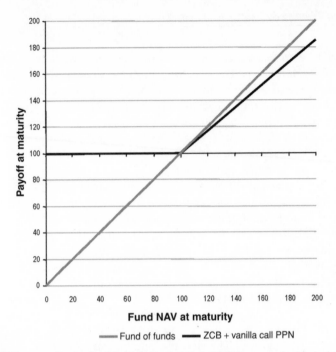

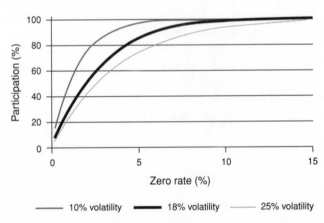

FIGURE 28.4 Payoff of a Vanilla Call Option Based PPN versus the Underlying FoF
Source: UBS (illustrative only, participation of real products may differ from what is shown).

FIGURE 28.5 Participation at Different Interest Rates (Theoretical)
Source: UBS.
Note: This example values a seven-year bond-plus-call structure under the following assumptions: implied volatility of call options is fixed; the underlying fund of funds pays no dividends or other distributions during the life of the option; call options are European-style options. This is illustrative only. Actual pricing depends on the characteristics of the underlying fund of funds and may deviate from this illustration.

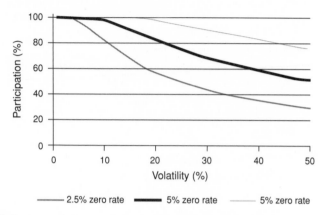

FIGURE 28.6   Participation at Different Volatilities (Theoretical)
Source: UBS.
Note: This example values a seven-year bond-plus-call structure under the following assumptions: zero-coupons rates are fixed; the underlying fund of funds pays no dividends or other distributions during the life of the option; call options are European-style options. This is illustrative only. Actual pricing depends on the characteristics of the underlying fund of funds and may deviate from this illustration.

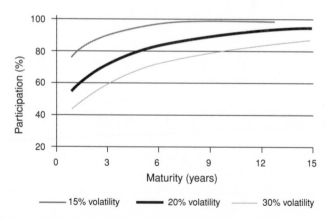

FIGURE 28.7   Participation at Different Maturities (Theoretical)-1
Source: UBS.
Note: This example values a bond-plus-call structure under the following assumptions: zero-coupons rates are fixed at 3.97 percent; the underlying fund of funds pays no dividends or other distributions during the life of the option; call options are European-style. This is illustrative only. Actual pricing depends on the characteristics of the underlying fund of funds and may deviate from this illustration.

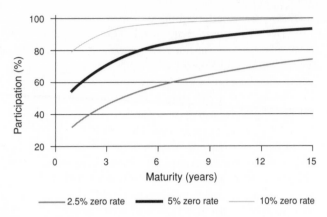

FIGURE 28.8 Participation at Different Maturities (Theoretical)-2
Source: UBS.
Note: This example values a bond-plus-call structure under the following assumptions: implied volatility of call options are fixed at 18 percent; the underlying fund of funds pays no dividends or other distributions during the life of the option; call options are European-style options. This is illustrative only. Actual pricing depends on the characteristics of the underlying fund of funds and may deviate from this illustration.

volatilities and zero rates. These figures show that, in general, participation increases with maturity. As expected, the longer the term of the structure, the more sensitive participation is to the interest-rate environment. In lower-interest-rate environments, longer maturity has a larger influence on participation. However, participation appears to be equally sensitive to volatility at any given maturity.

LIQUIDITY AND VOLATILITY OF FUNDS OF FUNDS

While funds of funds tend to produce fairly low-volatility returns, implied volatility tends to be quite high. Once again, liquidity is to blame. When an issuer sells a call option to the end investor, the issuer will most likely want to hedge the resulting short position in the option. In the case of most "normal" underlying assets, such as a stock or an equity index, hedging is relatively easy because the underlying instrument is liquid and can to all intents and purposes be traded at will. The only problem the seller of the option faces is the trade-off between the frequency of rehedging and transaction costs.

Because a fund of funds can be traded only once a month or once a quarter, with asymmetry depending on the terms the issuer can negotiate with the fund, rehedging is far more complex. Not only that, but with the exception of the prescribed trading dates, the issuer is nearly always exposed to the risk of the underlying fund. The issuer can compensate for this only in the price of the option to the end investor. This problem was not envisaged by Black and Scholes when they developed their option pricing model. The Black-Scholes model assumes continuous liquidity. It is therefore not unusual for a call option on a fund of funds with quarterly liquidity and a realized volatility of around 6 percent to be priced by the issuer at an implied volatility of around 18 percent.

Structures on higher-volatility illiquid underlyings—for example, single-strategy hedge funds—are generally not regarded as good candidates for derivative underlyings because the combination of high volatility and low liquidity makes them virtually impossible to fully hedge. Some risk will always remain for the issuer. For this reason, the rest of this discussion is devoted to structures on relatively low-volatility fund of funds.

Fund of funds vary in terms of risk depending on various factors. Just as hedge funds can be broadly classified into styles, fund of funds can be also classified into styles, as Hedge Fund Research Inc. (HFRI) has done.

Table 28.1 shows realized volatility by FoF style. It is noteworthy that the conservative group appears to be of consistently lower volatility than the rest, including market-defensive funds.

Moreover, the volatility of conservative funds tends to have fewer and smaller spikes than the rest, as is apparent from Figures 28.9 to 28.12. These figures show also that not only do the strategic group of funds tend to be more volatile than the average fund of funds, but also that their volatility spikes more, and more frequently, than average. The overriding point is that, as mentioned earlier, not all fund of funds are created equal.

Increasing Participation

Many investors will want to achieve higher levels of participation than is possible with a bond-plus-vanilla-call structure. A number of variants have been devised to increase participation in structures on stock indices and mutual funds, but many of these do not work for funds of funds, either for liquidity reasons or because funds of funds do not pay a dividend.[3] However,

---

[3]The most common structure that does not work for these reasons is a S2MART certificate. In a S2MART (Safer Securities MAximizing ReTurn) certificate, the investor buys a zero-coupon bond as before. However, to make up the participation shortfall, the investor sells a geared out-of-the-money put option (e.g., 20 percent out-of-the-money). The investor is thus protected against the first 20 percent of losses, but begins to lose money below that threshold. However, in the case of hedge funds, this does not work because the hedge fund's dividend yield is zero, making the put option too cheap to make up the difference (UBS 2002b).

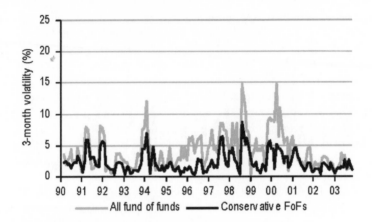

FIGURE 28.9   Three-Month Volatility: Conservative FoFs
Source: UBS (using Hedge Fund Research data).

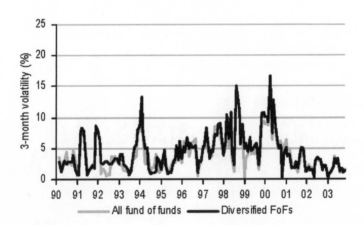

FIGURE 28.10   Three-Month Volatility: Diversified FoFs
Source: UBS (using Hedge Fund Research data).

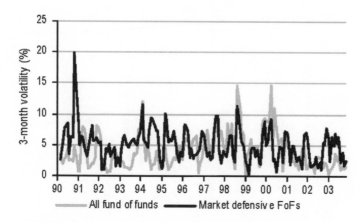

FIGURE 28.11 Three-Month Volatility: Market-Defensive FoFs
Source: UBS (using Hedge Fund Research data).

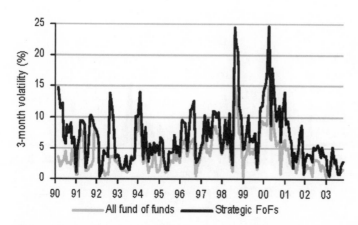

FIGURE 28.12 Three-Month Volatility: Strategic FoFs
Source: UBS (using Hedge Fund Research data).

TABLE 28.1 Realized Volatility of Funds of Funds, January 1990 to October 2003

	HFRI Fund of Funds: Composite Index	HFRI Fund of Funds: Conservative Index[a]	HFRI Fund of Funds: Diversified Index[a]	HFRI Fund of Funds: Market Defensive Index[a]	HFRI Fund of Funds: Strategic Index[a]
Volatility, Jan 90–Oct 03	5.74	3.31	6.17	5.97	9.34
Average 3-month volatility, Jan 90–Oct 03	4.09	2.32	4.37	5.11	6.88
Maximum 3-month volatility, Jan 90–Oct 03	14.78	8.64	16.60	19.88	24.69
Minimum 3-month volatility, Jan 90–Oct 03	0.32	0.30	0.10	0.33	0.39
Percentage of months when 3-month volatility >10%	3.66	0.00	7.32	3.66	22.56
Average 6-month volatility, Jan 90–Oct 03	4.73	2.65	5.10	5.55	7.74
Maximum 6-month volatility, Jan 90–Oct 03	13.37	7.11	15.21	13.96	21.18
Minimum 6-month volatility, Jan 90–Oct 03	0.96	0.83	1.07	2.13	2.26
Percentage of months when 6-month volatility >10%	5.59	0.00	8.70	2.48	18.01
Average 12-month volatility, Jan 90–Oct 03	5.12	2.91	5.53	5.70	8.31
Maximum 12-month volatility, Jan 90–Oct 03	10.61	5.93	11.91	10.74	16.82
Minimum 12-month volatility, Jan 90–Oct 03	1.98	1.01	1.83	3.22	3.13
Percentage of months when 12-month volatility >10%	10.32	0.00	12.90	5.81	19.35

Source: UBS (using Hedge Fund Research data).
[a]Hedge Fund Research's description of each index can be found at *www.hedgefundresearch.com*.

structures that work well include bond-plus-Asian-call option, fees/leverage (capital guarantee fee), bond-plus-call spread, also known as a GROI (guaranteed return on investment), and reduced protection.

For the purposes of this studzy, we ignore call spread structures because this strategy limits upside, and reduced protection structures since we are only concentrating on those structures that offer full protection of investor principal.

The concept of participation, and the idea that is possible to achieve higher participation by tweaking features of a structure, can be misunderstood. It is important to note that what the investor participates in is not necessarily the same as increasing exposure to the underlying. In other words, 90 percent participation in a structure based on a call with an Asian tail is not necessarily better in terms of final overall outcome than 80 percent participation in a structure with a vanilla call. We show how this works later.

Increased Participation: Asian Tails

In an Asian option, the payout depends on the average price of the underlying fund over some period leading up to expiry rather than the price of the fund at expiry. For example, a seven-year option with a one-year Asian tail has a payoff based on the average value of the underlying over the final year. This increases participation by effectively shortening the duration of the option. However, it also has the advantage of greatly reducing crash risk. As we show later, this can have a significant effect on the dispersion of possible final outcomes. In an ordinary call option, there is the risk that all of the upside can disappear if the price of the underlying crashes the day before expiry. Figure 28.13 illustrates the difference between participation that can be achieved by replacing the vanilla call option in a bond-plus-call structure with an Asian option.[4]

Despite its crash-protection advantage, an Asian option structure achieves higher participation rates than ordinary bond-plus-call. The reason is that the shortened effective duration of the option makes it cheaper.

Increased Participation: Capital Protection Fees

Capital protection fees are the most obvious way to increase participation, since they represent an extra payment for additional exposure to the option (i.e., leverage on the option). There are a myriad of ways to achieve this.

---

[4]Actually, this is known as an Asian "out" option, because the payout value is based on the average price of the underlying at the end of its life (i.e., a property of the option is calculated on the way out). The other possibility is an Asian "in" option, which has a payout based on a single price at the point of expiry, but which has a strike based on the average price of the underlying over some period at the start of the option's life (i.e., a property of the option is calculated on the way in). Both versions may be used in structures on hedge funds. However, an Asian "in" structure will not have the same partial crash protection feature as an Asian "out." An Asian "in" will also result in slightly lower participation than an Asian "out."

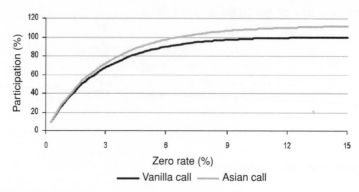

FIGURE 28.13   Participation at Different Interest Rates: Vanilla versus Asian Calls (Theoretical)
Source: UBS.
Note: This example prices seven-year structures using both vanilla and Asian calls assuming 18 percent implied volatility. The Asian has a one-year tail. This is illustrative only. Actual pricing depends on the characteristics of the underlying fund of funds and may deviate significantly from this illustration.

One way is to borrow the additional premium and amortize it over the life of the structure. Each month or quarter, depending on liquidity, the fee is deducted from the NAV of the underlying fund. While this method is simple to understand in principle, it may require the issuer to rehedge exposure more often than would be the case in a bond-plus-call structure without leverage or a capital guarantee fee since charging a fee on a monthly basis adds to the complexity of the return path of the derivative. The additional trading required by the issuer will add to the cost of the structure during its life. Issuers are therefore likely to try to pass this cost to the end investor.

A more cost-efficient method is to defer payment of the fee to the end of the life of the structure. The future value of the fee is then deducted from the final NAV of the fund before the call option payout is calculated. This means that the fee schedule does not interfere with the path of the underlying NAV. Because of its lower cost, this method tends to be more common.

DYNAMIC HEDGING PPNS

> *October. This is one of the peculiarly dangerous months to speculate in stocks in. The others are July, January, September, April, November, May, March, June, December, August, and February.*
> —Twain 1900, p. 166

A Potted History of Portfolio Insurance

September 11, 1976, might have passed unnoticed by students of financial history, but for one thing: That night, the financial product known as portfolio insurance[5] was invented (Luskin 1988). Three years earlier, Black and Scholes pointed out that, under risk neutrality, an option can be replicated by a zero-coupon bond and some amount of the underlying stock, and an option's value ought to depend on the price of these two elements (Black and Scholes 1973). The inventors Leland and Rubinstein (1988) reasoned that if the option position could be replicated in this way, the process could be reversed to create an option using a ZCB and the underlying stock, trading in and out of them as relative pricing changed.

However, it took another five years of development before the first portfolio insurance product was sold by Leland O'Brien Rubinstein Associates (now called LOR). This was a $500,000 account to be managed over six months. By the end of their first year of operations, Leland O'Brien Rubinstein had assets under management totaling $135 million, a notable sum at the time. The advent of the personal computer in 1983 allowed for the product to be licensed, and the simultaneous creation of Standard & Poor's (S&P) 500 index futures greatly reduced transaction costs, so growth was phenomenal. By mid-October 1987, equity market assets managed using some variant of portfolio insurance was estimated at the time to have been in the region of $60 billion to $80 billion, representing roughly 2 to 3 percent of U.S. market capitalization. Later estimates suggest that the total could have been as high as $100 billion. One insurance company alone is said to have had US$17 billion in portfolio insurance.

In hindsight, the pressure of portfolio insurance traders all leaning on their sell buttons at the same time, as they would if they were all insuring the same risky asset with the same insurance algorithm, should have been obvious. Unfortunately, it was not, and when the S&P 500 fell 5.16 percent on October 16, 1987, a Friday, a fair number had put so many sell orders into the market that the day closed with a backlog of unfilled sell orders. On the morning of October 19, the backlog was put into the market, which fell sharply, causing yet more sell orders to be put into the market. Key

---

[5] "Portfolio insurance" was the original name given to the product by its inventors. The term "insurance" is slightly misleading in that the product is not an insurance policy in the traditional sense of premiums paid and claims made in the event of some accident or disaster. Providers of the financial product known as portfolio insurance will not necessarily provide insurance cover for your property, car, or life. The product has subsequently been renamed by banks, which do not provide traditional insurance products, to avoid the accidental confusion of the two products.

stocks stopped trading, backing up the sell orders still further, and the S&P 500 closed 20.4 percent below the previous close, the largest one-day fall in its history. As a strategy, portfolio insurance failed that day.

However, it had worked quite well in normal markets up until that point, and the basic theory behind portfolio insurance is sound. The events of October 1987 do not invalidate portfolio insurance as a technique. They only serve to illustrate that portfolio insurance, poorly and slavishly applied to exactly the same asset by too many participants, can lead to disaster. Successful portfolio insurance requires that it be applied to truly uncorrelated assets, that is, to assets that have a tendency to behave differently in market shock conditions. Moreover, there is a limit to how much portfolio insurance can be written on similar products in a similar time frame.

In that regard, portfolio insurance is less risky for fund of funds. An S&P 500 future is different from an S&P 500 tracker fund in the same way that two slices of bread from the opposite end of a loaf are different. Funds of funds, however, tend to be much more diverse. Some funds of funds are more aggressive than others in terms of seeking geared directional exposure: others have large elements of nonequity exposure; and still others are strategic asset allocators, switching between asset types and styles according to the strategic asset allocator's view on relative performance.

Shocks that have historically affected a broad range of hedge funds simultaneously have spiked interest rates or liquidity shocks. Spiking interest rates make the bond element in portfolio insurance cheaper, and as is demonstrated later, this tends to reduce the need to trade out of the fund of funds to buy more zero-coupon bonds. Unfortunately, liquidity shocks tend to have the opposite effect. The Russian debt default led to falling interest rates as central banks worked to shore up liquidity.

In addition, the fact that one cannot trade in and out of fund of funds instantaneously is, ironically, an advantage. It means that, in all likelihood, any shock will be followed by a period where the issuer of portfolio insurance cannot rush for the sell button. Even if the fund of funds does not have time to recover by the time an issuer is required to make a portfolio insurance-related redemption, the fund of funds will still have some period of notice before any trade occurs. The fund of funds will then, in all likelihood, have a chance to trade out of its positions in a relatively orderly fashion and meet the issuer's redemption call.

We say "in all likelihood" because it could be that a shock will occur near one of the times when redemptions are possible. However, whether the fund of funds has monthly or quarterly redemption liquidity, the likelihood is still fairly small. Even then, fund of funds usually have a period of notification prior to redemption, which can cushion the blow somewhat. The only exception is when the issuer of portfolio insurance on the fund of funds has a managed account relationship with the fund of funds.

Finally, volatility of funds of funds, as we have already observed, is much lower than equity volatility. Asymmetric return distributions in funds of funds (the return distribution that are skewed upward) are very useful properties for holders of portfolio insurance structures on funds of funds. As is shown later, the likelihood is that it takes a relatively short period of time for a fund of funds to go up far enough to be safe, to all intents and purposes, from the need for the issuer to trade out of the fund of funds. Seen from the point of view of options, a portfolio insurance structure on a fund of funds should, in the absence of a shock early in its life, go deep in the money relative to volatility in a fairly short time frame. The same cannot be said of portfolio insurance on long-only equity products.

Figures 28.14 and 28.15 emphasize the differences in these characteristics. They show drawdowns in the S&P 500 (including 1987) and the HFRI Fund of Funds index on the same scale. The figures show index levels as a percentage of the prior peak and both have similarly scaled *y*-axes for easy comparison. Figure 28.14 plots daily closing S&P 500 prices, and Figure 28.15 plots monthly FoF closing prices. This might seem inconsistent, but we regard the figures as a fair comparison because they reflect the actual difference in trading liquidity.

The long time span during which the FoF index is at 100 in Figure 28.15 is in stark contrast to the length of time during which the S&P 500 is not at 100 in Figure 28.14. This is strong evidence of the much lower probability of having to sell a fund of funds as a result of portfolio insurance. In these figures, 100 means the asset is either flat or rising.

The relative choppiness of the two figures shows how much more likely it is that frequent trading has to occur in portfolio insurance on equity than

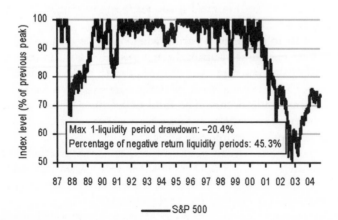

FIGURE 28.14 S&P 500 Drawdowns, Daily Liquidity
Source: UBS (using Thomson Financial Datastream data).

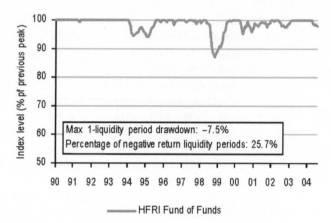

FIGURE 28.15 Fund of Funds Drawdowns, Monthly Liquidity
Source: UBS (using Hedge Fund Research data).

on a fund of funds. Daily versus monthly liquidity is naturally a contributor to this difference, but even if equity could only be traded monthly, the troughs would still be more frequent than for funds of funds. Moreover, routine drawdown troughs in equity are roughly the same size as the extreme drawdown troughs in funds of funds.

The 1987 crash in the S&P 500 is unusual, both because of its scale and severity. We have already noted the role of portfolio insurance as a contributing factor to the "suddenness" of the crash. But the most interesting feature of Figure 28.14 is that it reveals that the initial drawdown preceding the October 19 crash actually began on August 26—almost a full two months earlier. The initial drawdown was probably random, rather than directly related to portfolio insurance.

It is difficult to know what proportion of assets under FoF management is held via portfolio insurance structures. However, we estimate that portfolio insurance structures worth around $15 to $20 billion are currently in issue. This is roughly 2 percent of assets under management of around $1 trillion. While this may seem rather high at first glance when compared with the 2 to 3 percent figure for equities in 1987, we do not see great cause for concern about the systemic effects, for the reasons mentioned earlier. The diversity of funds of funds on which portfolio insurance is issued is relatively wide, and individual fund managers will seek to limit the amount of portfolio insurance products issued on them to a manageable amount.

Moreover, about $10 billion of the portfolio structures in issue are on managed accounts rather than direct investments in funds, which creates some time diversification in terms of the risk of all issuers needing to sell at once in the event of a shock. Managed accounts underlying portfolio insurance structures can be traded more frequently, whereas funds of funds underlying portfolio insurance structures cannot. Different terms of liquidity on the remaining constant proportion portfolio technique structures makes for additional time diversification of actual trades resulting from a shock.

Finally, as noted earlier, portfolio insurance structures on funds of funds tend to go into-the-money fairly rapidly. Roughly a third of the outstanding portfolio insurance structures currently in issue are sufficiently in the money as to pose relatively little systemic threat in the event of a shock.

CONSTANT PROPORTION PORTFOLIO TECHNIQUE

CPPT is the most common form of portfolio insurance structure issued on FoF underlyings. As with generic portfolio insurance, CPPT involves trading between a risky asset, in this case a fund of funds, and a riskless asset, in this case a zero-coupon bond. Minimum and maximum portfolio weightings that the risk asset can take in the portfolio need to be defined. However, unless specified otherwise, these are normally set at 0 percent and 100 percent, respectively, where 0 percent means nothing is invested in the risky asset and the portfolio consists only of a ZCB, and 100 percent means that the portfolio consists entirely of the risky asset with nothing invested in the ZCB.

The initial weight in the fund is between 0 percent (in theory) and 100 percent invested in the risky asset and is usually fairly high where fund of funds are concerned—normally much higher than the amount an issuer of call plus bond will place in a fund of funds as its initial trading hedge. As time passes, the portfolio is rebalanced at specified intervals to increase or reduce exposure to the risky asset, depending on whether the risky asset goes up or down in value.

The technique establishes a crash size, which depends partly on the volatility of the risky asset. The crash size is the maximum anticipated percentage fall in the risky asset between rebalancing points beyond which the issuer will suffer a loss. In some respects this is rather like a value-at-risk (VaR) calculation. Apart from volatility, other factors that affect the crash size are skewness and kurtosis, that is, asymmetry of the return distribution and the likelihood of extreme returns. Generally speaking, the likelihood of extreme negative returns is carefully weighed against volatility. Low volatility asset with some likelihood of extreme downside returns would result in a larger crash size than an asset with higher volatility but lower likelihood of extreme downside returns. In addition, since portfolio insurance generally involves trading into and out of bonds and risky assets, the liquidity of the risky asset will also be taken into account when setting the crash size. The last thing a CPPT issuer desires is the need to trade the risk asset and find no buyers or sellers in the market.

The next thing to be established is a bond floor, the lowest value the portfolio may take before the risky asset is liquidated completely and bonds bought with the proceeds to ensure that 100 percent of the initial principal is returned to the investor at maturity. The bond floor is set according to the prevailing interest rates at any point during the life of the structure. It is important to understand that the bond floor can shift around during the life of the trade. If interest rates rise, the bond floor falls. Conversely, if interest rates fall, the bond floor will rise.

The difference between the bond floor and the current value of the portfolio is referred to as the cushion, and the maximum supportable percentage fall in the risky asset within the portfolio is called the gap. In other words, the gap is the cushion divided by the value of the risky asset within the portfolio.

CPPT defines the perfectly balanced portfolio as one where the gap is equal to the crash size. So as the risky asset rises in value, increasing the cushion, the portfolio should ideally be rebalanced so that the proportion invested in the risky asset is larger, and the gap is reduced as far as the crash size. Conversely, if the risky asset falls in value and the cushion is reduced, exposure to the risky asset is reduced such that the gap is increased back to the crash size.

Investment professionals are in total agreement on very few things; one of them is that markets are constantly moving. In CPPT terms, this means that the gap is always fluctuating. It is both impractical and expensive, in terms of transaction costs, to rebalance the CPPT portfolio every time the price of the risky asset or ZCB ticks up or down. Moreover, if the risky asset is a fund of funds with the trading liquidity previously described, such rebalancing is impossible.

To resolve this, the final elements in CPPT are a band within which the gap is allowed to move before trading is triggered. In the case of fund of funds, where trading can occur only at certain intervals, the CPPT trading interval is usually set to the redemption interval. Asymmetric liquidity means that it is theoretically possible to relever the portfolio more often than it is possible to delever it. However, FoF structured products are usually difficult to deal with. This is why issuers of CPPT products on fund of funds usually specify a CPPT trading interval in line with the redemption liquidity of the fund of funds.

The nature of FoF liquidity brings out another point. Funds of funds normally require a notice period to subscribe or redeem funds. This means that there is an element of trading uncertainty in CPPT trading. The algorithm may indicate that a trade is required based on the closing price in the CPPT period, but the actual trade occurs at the next liquidity point (potentially three months later) and at a different price. The time gap means that the underlying fund of funds could have recovered to a price where trading would be unnecessary in the time between trade request and completion. The underlying fund may also have dropped still further in value, meaning that a larger trade would be required to rebalance the portfolio than was actually requested one liquidity cycle earlier.[6] This timing issue leaves open the possibility that the CPPT algorithm might not fully protect the investor's principal. In this circumstance, the issuer, who provides the guarantee, faces a loss, but not the end investor.

Another less well understood feature of CPPT worth noting is the fact that participation is variable and depends on the price path of the risky asset. A CPPT portfolio's natural starting point could be, say, 95 percent invested in the risky asset and 5 percent in bonds. If the risky asset drops 10 percent, then the portfolio might be rebalanced and some of the risky asset will be sold. The new portfolio may only be 70 percent invested in the risky asset at this point. Assuming the risky asset subsequently recovers, a new rebalancing point could be reached, which would take the weight of the risky asset up to, say, 97 percent. But in the meantime, the portfolio has only enjoyed 70 percent of the risky asset's upside, and when the risky asset is bought back, it will be more expensive relative to the portfolio's value. So it will never be possible to regain the previous performance in the risky asset once the portfolio has been delevered.

In Figure 28.16 we show a simulated CPPT note along with the value of the portfolio components. The simulation is based on HFRI Fund of Funds composite index returns. In this example, the initial weighting of the hypothetical fund of funds in the CPPT portfolio is 96.5 percent. However, our hypothetical fund trades down fairly early on in the CPPT note's life, triggering a deleverage event in June 2004. The fund of funds' weight in the CPPT portfolio falls from just under 97 to 61 percent. As the fund recovers, its weighting in the portfolio increases slightly until there is a sufficient gap between the bond floor and the hypothetical fund of funds to relever the CPPT portfolio. This occurs in September 2005, and the fund's new weighting in the portfolio rises from 65 to 88 percent. As the fund of funds continues to rise, its CPPT portfolio weight continues to rise organically

---

[6]This timing problem is not confined to portfolio insurance on hedge funds. The nature of trading hedge funds merely illustrates rather starkly a problem in all portfolio insurance—that prices can change faster than traders can trade, particularly if there is an imbalance in the market.

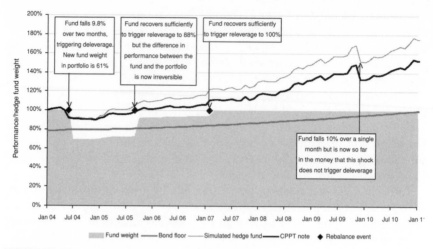

FIGURE 28.16   Simulated CPPT Note (Illustrative)
Source: UBS (using Hedge Fund Research data).
Note: The CPPT note has these parameters: minimum/maximum equity exposure is
0 percent/100 percent, the crash size is 20 percent and delever/relever triggers are
set at 15 percent/25 percent. A fee of 1.5 percent has been charged. The fee is
spread over the life of the note.

until the next rebalancing trigger relevers the fund to 100 percent, where it
remains until expiry.

No further events happen during the life of the fund except in November 2009, at which time the simulated fund suffers a downward shock that
is worse[7] than the one that occurred in June 2004. However, by November
2009, the hypothetical fund of funds has gained so much in value relative
to the bond floor that it has no effect on the portfolio. In fact, by this stage,
the simulated fund has risen so far off the bond floor that the shock would
have to drop by a staggering 23.9 percent before an immediate deleverage
event is triggered. This illustrates our earlier point that once a CPPT note
on an underlying fund of funds is sufficiently seasoned, it should be so deep
in-the-money as to pose very little systemic threat in the event of a shock
affecting hedge funds at once.

---

[7]We artificially introduced a 10 percent loss in November 2009. Note that this has
never happened in the history of the HFRI Fund of Funds composite index. This is
not to say it could not happen, either in the index or in an individual fund of funds.

As well as illustrating how a CPPT note might unfold, Figure 28.16 shows how a deleverage event erodes participation. Erosion typically tends to fall during the life of the CPPT note as long as there is an upward trend in the risky asset and that upward trend is steeper than the trend in the bond floor. Nevertheless, erosion means it is still possible to get locked out of the risky asset. Sometime during the life of the trade, the value of the risky asset could fall so that the portfolio hits the bond floor. In this case, the risky asset is liquidated completely and the entire portfolio becomes a ZCB. In order for the protection of principal to not be compromised from that point on, the portfolio must remain 100 percent invested in bonds no matter how much the risky asset rises in value afterward.

Fortunately, this is has been rare in the history of fund of funds CPPT structures. Should the worst occur, it may be possible for the investor to sell the note back to the issuer early if the investor prefers liquidity to the recovery of principal at maturity.

Figure 28.17 shows what happens if the simulated fund crashes through the bond floor. While the figure shows that the CPPT portfolio drops down to the bond floor, this is in fact what happens only from the investor's point of view. The portfolio value actually falls well below the

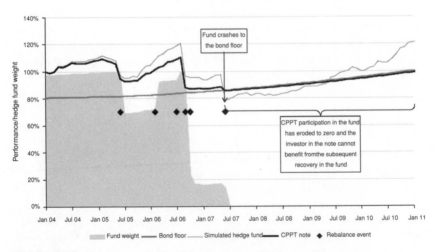

FIGURE 28.17 Simulated CPPT Note—Disaster Scenario (Illustrative)
Source: UBS (using Hedge Fund Research data).
Note: The CPPT note has these parameters: minimum/maximum equity exposure is 0 percent/100 percent, the crash size is 20 percent and delever/relever triggers are set at 15 percent/25 percent. A fee of 1.5 percent has been charged. The fee is spread over the life of the note.

bond floor. However, this should not affect the payout to investors, since the risk of this happening is usually borne by the issuer.

We had to modify the HFRI Fund of Funds composite index return distribution in order to achieve this. We introduced the possibility that returns of –20 percent, –15 percent and –10 percent, each with a probability of 0.6 percent, are added to the sample from which the simulation probabilities are drawn. This is not to say that in the world of fund of funds, large drawdowns are not likely to happen more frequently, especially if the choice of fund of funds is random.

CPPT VARIANTS

The construction of CPPT products on FoF underlyings is a fast-evolving business. Producing an exhaustive and detailed catalog of their variants would be a mammoth task. Instead, we concentrate on some of the parameters that can be varied and how their outcomes may differ from the basic CPPT note. Two popular variants are:

1. *Increased initial participation.* This trade is similar in all respects to a standard CPPT, except that here, 100 percent of the principal is invested in the fund of funds from the beginning. In the current environment this is not very different from the standard CPPT starting point: In the examples above, the initial weighting of the fund of funds in the portfolio is just under 97 percent. The variant that forces 100 percent or higher initial participation is the most common form in which CPPT notes are being issued today. Forcing higher initial participation is usually only a minor deviation from the "natural" CPPT portfolio.
2. *Leverage.* It is possible to introduce leverage in several ways. Leverage usually involves borrowing money to obtain more exposure to the underlying fund of funds. Within a CPPT structure, however, it is more common to use the trading features inherent in CPPT to achieve leverage. CPPT requires trading in and out of the risky asset, and it is assumed that the maximum weighting in either the bond or the stock is 100 percent. It is possible, however, to allow the weighting in the risky asset—in our case, the fund of funds—to increase beyond 100 percent. In order to achieve a weighting in the fund of funds of 125 percent, it is necessary in theory to have a –25 percent exposure to zero-coupon bonds. In other words, it is necessary to take a loan to finance the leveraged exposure. Leverage is usually financed at a floating rate (i.e., a spread to the London Interbank Offered Rate [LIBOR]) to reflect the issuer's funding costs and risks.

Achieving leverage through this route has two advantages that are not generally achievable in other structures without engaging in some fairly intricate and potentially expensive financial gymnastics.

1. Leveraged exposure to the fund of funds happens only if the fund of funds rises in value. In other words, the leverage is path-dependent and will occur only when it is judged safe by the CPPT algorithm.
2. Because leverage is path-dependent, so is the cost of leverage.

Issuers will normally charge an additional fee for leverage above and beyond the financing costs. This is because there is a slightly greater risk that the portfolio can, in the event of a serious shock, crash through the bond floor before the issuer has a chance to rebalance the portfolio. This additional fee seems fair since this gap risk is usually borne by the issuer.

A myriad of other CPPT variants exist, and more are being developed almost daily. It is possible to construct CPPTs that pay out fixed or variable coupons or with performance lock-ins. A CPPT with lock-ins captures positive performance over time and locks it in by either shifting the bond floor up or paying out the captured performance as a coupon. These more exotic variants are beyond the scope of this chapter. We only compare CPPT-based PPNs with option-based ones.

Comparison of PPNs

The products we have described are all designed to give the investor access to fund of funds without putting principal at risk. It may seem odd that so many variants exist that perform essentially the same function. But each variant has unique features that should make it preferable to different investors under different market conditions. The next section discusses some of the advantages and disadvantages of the basic types of capital protection structure.

METHODOLOGY AND DATA

We compare PPN performance by simulating investment in a set of structures on a number of different actual fund of funds. The structures we will compare are:

- ZCB plus vanilla call PPN.
- ZCB plus Asian call PPN. (Asian in this case means the option has a one-year Asian tail such that the final payout is based on the average of the last 13 NAVs of the underlying fund of funds.)

- ZCB plus vanilla call with a capital guarantee fee that raises participation to 100 percent.
- ZCB plus vanilla call with a capital guarantee fee that raises participation to 150 percent.
- Ordinary vanilla CPPT where initial exposure to the fund of funds is set to its natural level (so that initial exposure is less than 100 percent)
- CPPT with initial exposure set to its natural level (less than 100 percent) and maximum exposure set to 150 percent. A fee is charged for leverage whenever it is applied.
- CPPT with initial exposure set to 100 percent and maximum exposure set to 150 percent. A fee is charged for leverage whenever it is applied.
- CPPT with initial exposure set to its natural level (less than 100 percent) and maximum exposure set to 200 percent. A fee is charged for leverage whenever it is applied.

Each PPN has a five-year maturity and pricing assumptions are designed to be roughly comparable. All of these products are theoretical, and terms of actual PPNs may vary greatly. Some of the PPNs we have devised, especially the ones involving high leverage, are deliberately extreme to better underscore our observations. These terms are unlikely to be offered in the real world.

The data we use for our comparison consist of a selection of fund of funds reporting to the Altvest database. The number of fund of funds in the data set obtained that had reported returns for at least five years by April 2004 was 315. We used the returns from all of these funds to simulate the products just described.

The recent history of financial markets includes falling interest rates. Because of the way CPPT PPNs work, we felt this might prejudice their performance. Unfortunately, data for FoF performance during times when interest rates were rising are difficult to acquire. To simulate results in a rising rate environment, we have simply reversed the arrow of time. That is, we have simulated what would happen if yield curves had moved in reverse over time. Since many funds of funds benchmark themselves against cash (e.g., LIBOR), we have attempted to reflect this by also reversing the sequence of FoF returns.

We are aware that this is not a perfect approach. For example, it does not account for any short-term poor performance hedge funds could post in the immediate aftermath of an unexpected rate hike. We accept these limitations, with the caveat that models are useful but the real world is altogether more varied and interesting.

In both of these scenarios we apply no fund screening at all. Both samples therefore contain funds that would not be considered suitable for structuring. In our final scenario we apply rudimentary screening to the sample of funds such that only funds meeting these criteria were selected:

- The fund of funds must have reported returns for at least 24 months leading up to April 1999 (the start of PPNs maturing in April 2004).
- The fund of funds must have a good track record of results between inception and April 1999. We define this as posting positive returns at least 70 percent of the time.
- The fund of funds must be a relatively low-volatility fund. We define this as a fund of funds with a maximum volatility of 10 percent for returns posted prior to April 1999.

This is a relatively naive screening, which does not take into account any due diligence an issuer might perform in assessing the suitability of a fund of funds for structuring. Of the 315 funds of funds in the database on which five-year PPNs maturing in April 2004 are possible, 88 meet the criteria set out by the screening process.

RESULTS AND OBSERVATIONS

Our first scenario compares performance of PPNs on 315 fund of funds in normal time. The results are summarized in Table 28.2.

Among the option structures, the vanilla PPN pays out the highest final outcome on average with the second lowest dispersion of outcomes. The lowest dispersion is found in the Asian PPNs, which benefit from smoothing in the final year of its life. The PPNs where an additional cost is paid for additional option exposure by raising the strike feature much wider dispersion of outcomes. This is to be expected because introducing leverage generally amplifies volatility. More surprising is the fact that as more and more leverage is applied, the lower the average outcome. This suggests that leverage is not economically sound in option-based PPNs. Figure 28.18 shows that as leverage is increased via capital guarantee fees, the outcome distribution not only widens and becomes increasingly skewed to the left but also is slightly more likely to experience large positive outliers.

This is less surprising when we consider how leverage is achieved via capital guarantee fees. Recall that an additional option premium is purchased with a fee amortized over the life of the PPN and levied at the end. In other words, the strike of the option is effectively raised in order to achieve higher participation. As the strike is raised, only the most aggressive fund of funds are able to produce sufficient NAV growth to sig-

TABLE 28.2 Structures Expiring April 2004 in 315 Unscreened FoFs, Normal Direction of Time

	Vanilla	Asian	Vanilla with Capital Guarantee Fee to 100% Participation	Vanilla with Capital Guarantee Fee to 150% Participation	CPPT with Maximum Exposure of 100%	CPPT with Maximum Exposure of 150%	CPPT with 150% Max Exposure, 100% Initial Exposure	CPPT with Maximum Exposure of 200%	Underlying
Average outcome	151.38	150.25	151.05	144.93	149.22	159.36	161.26	163.89	159.29
Std dev of outcomes	29.32	27.75	33.65	48.34	34.88	53.21	54.07	76.70	34.11
Maximum outcome	340.24	321.98	369.27	470.38	368.46	556.65	556.65	820.61	377.77
Minimum outcome	100.00	100.00	100.00	100.00	100.00	100.00	100.00	100.00	87.36
Average return (%)	8.65	8.48	8.60	7.70	8.33	9.77	10.03	10.39	9.76
Maximum return (%)	27.75	26.35	29.86	36.30	29.80	40.97	40.97	52.34	30.45
Minimum return (%)	0.00	0.00	0.00	0.00	0.00	0.00	0.00	0.00	-2.67
Outcomes at par	5.0	4.0	7.0	34.0	4.0	6.0	11.0	8.0	0.0
As a % of trials	1.6%	1.3%	2.2%	10.8%	1.3%	1.9%	3.5%	2.5%	0.0%
Performs worse than vanilla		184.0	190.0	242.0	223.0	131.0	128.0	144.0	5.0
As a % of trials		58.4%	60.3%	76.8%	70.8%	41.6%	40.6%	45.7%	1.6%
Performs better than vanilla		127.0	120.0	68.0	90.0	180.0	182.0	168.0	310.0
As a % of trials		40.3%	38.1%	21.6%	28.6%	57.1%	57.8%	53.3%	98.4%

Source: UBS (using fund of funds returns data from Altvest).

Options are priced using Black-Scholes using an implied volatility of 18 percent. Parameters for all CPPT products are: 2 percent crash size, 15 percent/25 percent deleverage/releverage triggers. CPPT fees are 1.5 percent and leverage is charged at LIBOR + 90 basis points.

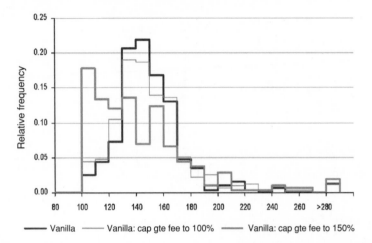

FIGURE 28.18   Outcome Distributions of Option-Based PPNs with Different Leverage
Source: UBS (using fund of funds returns data from Altvest).
Note: Options are priced using Black-Scholes using an implied volatility of 18 percent.

nificantly overcome the higher strike. Consequently, a higher and higher proportion of funds will fail to overcome the higher strike.

Among the CPPT-based PPNs, leverage behaves rather differently. As Table 28.2 and Figure 28.19 show, leverage in CPPT behaves much more as one would expect. More leverage in CPPTs produces a wider dispersion of outcomes, but it also significantly raises the average outcome. There is some tendency for outcome distributions to become more left skewed, so that there is a slightly higher likelihood of low positive returns, but not to the same extent as in leveraged-option PPNs. The fact that leverage is path dependent in CPPT means that it is selectively utilized when profitable and not used otherwise. This makes leverage much more cost effective in CPPT-based PPNs than in option-based ones.

It is popular these days to force initial exposure in CPPT PPNs upward toward 100 percent or even above that in cases where leverage is included. Table 28.2 shows that this tends to raise average final outcomes at the cost of wider dispersion. Moreover, the number of times when the PPN pays out just 100 rises dramatically when high initial exposure to the underlying is forced from the start. This is because high initial exposure to the underlying means early down moves in the underlying translate to more exaggerated down moves in the CPPT portfolio. In other words, the chance of being forced to delever by large amounts early on increases as a result of starting with higher early exposure.

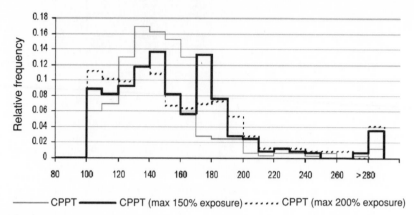

FIGURE 28.19 Outcome Distributions of CPPT-Based PPNs with Different
Leverage
Source: UBS (using fund of funds returns data from Altvest).
Note: Options are priced using Black-Scholes using an implied volatility of 18 percent.

In addition to modeling the 150 percent CPPT PPN with initial exposure of 100 percent, we have also modeled a 150 percent CPPT PPN that
forces initial exposure to start at 150 percent. The outcome distribution is
shown in Figure 28.20. Again, the average outcome rises and the distribution widens. However, while the probability of getting just 100 rises, the
difference between this statistic in CPPT starting at 100 percent versus 150
percent turned out to be insignificant. Moreover, since the problem is
caused by increased chances of early deleverage, this problem can potentially be circumvented by setting the deleverage/releverage triggers slightly
wider apart early in the life of the CPPT. Indeed, this feature is already
working its way into newer CPPT structures.

Leverage appears to us to be a key raison d'être for CPPT. When we
compare the unlevered CPPT PPN with the vanilla call PPN in Table 28.2,
we note that CPPT outcomes have more dispersion and are on average
lower than in the vanilla call PPN. This should not come as a surprise. The
CPPT algorithm is always effectively one step behind, trading in or out of
the fund of funds one liquidity cycle after the fund of funds has performed
well or badly.[8] This will produce wider dispersion and a degree of erosion

---

[8]Deming (1982) demonstrates that in systems that involve some random element,
attempting to compensate for error after the event is futile. He does this via an
experiment in which two people drop ball bearings through a funnel at a target. One

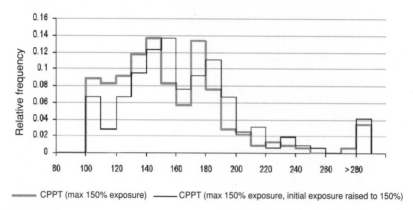

FIGURE 28.20　Outcome Distributions of CPPT-Based PPNs with Different Initial Exposure.
Source: UBS (using fund of funds returns data from Altvest).
Note: Options are priced using Black-Scholes using an implied volatility of 18 percent.

of exposure over time through trading in and out of the underlying will produce a lower average outcome.

But this could also be caused, or may be exaggerated, by the fact that the scenario we have devised here involves falling interest rates. We can say more about this by reversing the arrow of time. The results are summarized in Table 28.3.

When time is reversed, the environment changes to one where interest rates start from a lower point than in our first scenario. This means that option-based PPNs will have lower participation and CPPT-based PPNs will start with a smaller initial cushion to the bond floor. The effect on option-based PPNs is predictable: Average outcomes are a little lower, but so is outcome dispersion.

---

person is told to adjust the funnel's aim after every shot to compensate for any misses; the other is not. After several shots at the target, it becomes apparent that continually adjusting the aim of the funnel invariably produces a wider scatter of shots around the target. Deming's lesson is that it is best not to meddle with systems unless one has genuine predictive power over the next deviation from target. CPPT is an illustration of this principle. While we do not suggest that the CPPT algorithm should stop "meddling," we recognize that the CPPT algorithm by its very name *must* produce more widely dispersed results.

TABLE 28.3 Structures Expiring April 2004 in 315 Unscreened FoFs, Direction of Time Reversed

	Vanilla	Asian	Vanilla with Capital Guarantee Fee to 100% Participation	Vanilla with Capital Guarantee Fee to 150% Participation	CPPT with Maximum Exposure of 100%	CPPT with Maximum Exposure of 150%	CPPT with 150% Max Exposure, 100% Initial Exposure	CPPT with Maximum Exposure of 200%	Underlying
Average outcome	148.56	147.27	148.63	143.70	148.19	149.37	151.80	149.40	159.29
Std dev of outcomes	27.71	26.11	33.57	48.20	32.78	46.96	47.79	60.65	34.11
Maximum outcome	327.05	308.84	366.80	469.00	352.47	504.61	501.81	680.63	377.77
Minimum outcome	100.00	100.00	100.00	100.00	100.00	100.00	100.00	100.00	87.36
Average return (%)	8.24	8.05	8.25	7.52	8.18	8.36	8.71	8.36	9.76
Maximum return (%)	26.74	25.30	29.68	36.22	28.65	38.23	38.07	46.75	30.45
Minimum return (%)	0.00	0.00	0.00	0.00	0.00	0.00	0.00	0.00	-2.67
Outcomes at par as a % of trials	5 1.6%	4 1.3%	7 2.2%	34 10.8%	4 1.3%	6 1.9%	11 3.5%	8 2.5%	0 0.0%
Performs worse than vanilla as a % of trials		198 62.9%	179 56.8%	230 73.0%	173 54.9%	191 60.6%	170 54.0%	205 65.1%	5 1.6%
Performs better than vanilla as a % of trials		113 35.9%	131 41.6%	80 25.4%	137 43.5%	119 37.8%	140 44.4%	105 33.3%	310 98.4%

Source: UBS (using fund of funds returns data from Altvest).
Note: Options are prices using Black-Scholes using an implied volatility of 18 percent. Parameters for all CPPT products are: 20 percent crash size, 15 percent/25 percent deleverage/releverage triggers. CPPT fees are 1.5 percent and leverage is charged at LIBOR + 90 basis points.

In general, CPPT-based PPNs also show lower outcomes with lower dispersion. But the difference in performance of CPPT-based PPNs and option-based PPNs is surprising. In this artificial environment, CPPT-based products—even those that allow leverage—struggled to outperform option-based PPNs. Not only are average outcomes lower, but comparing the lower halves of Table 28.1 and Table 28.3, it is apparent that the number of instances when CPPT-based PPNs provided a better return than option-based PPNs was considerably lower in the time-reversed environment than in the normal environment.

One potential reason for this could be that a high bond floor early on leads to a greater chance of early deleverage. This in turn may lead to greater erosion of exposure, which would explain the lower average outcomes across the board. Indeed, the much smaller rise in average outcomes when leverage is allowed in CPPT PPNs in the time-reversed environment. It may also simply be a feature of the way we have reversed time. We have not assumed a timing difference between changes in interest rates and changes in hedge fund performance. If there is a delay in response in the real world— and this is almost certain to be the case—the result could be affected. However, the underlying logic that early trading in CPPT leads to greater erosion and therefore lower average outcomes would not be affected. We therefore believe that widening the trading band early in the life of a CPPT, especially one that allows leverage, is more important in a low-interest-rate environment, provided any additional costs do not make such a feature prohibitive.

In our final analysis we apply a simple screen to the FoF database to construct PPNs on only low-volatility fund of funds with a good track record, as described. The results are shown in Table 28.4.

It is unsurprising to us that when lower-volatility FoF with a good track record are chosen, higher average outcomes with lower dispersion are achieved in all the PPNs. But it is interesting that while option-based PPNs improved in this regard, CPPT-based PPNs appear to improve more. The differences in both average outcome and dispersion between the vanilla call PPN and the CPPT PPN without leverage are more or less halved in the case where we have screened fund of funds.

Leverage in CPPT PPNs also seems more efficient if screening is applied. In the unscreened sample, the average outcome for PPNs allowing up to 150 percent leverage was 6.7 percent higher than the average outcome for PPNs that do not allow leverage. The comparable number for the screened sample is 9.1 percent. However, the maximum return achieved in the screened sample for the 150 percent CPN was less than two-thirds of the value achieved in the unscreened sample. This is less surprising, since a sample of lower-volatility funds of funds is bound to produce less dispersion in final outcomes.

TABLE 28.4 Structures Expiring April 2004 in 88 Screened FoFs, Normal Direction of Time

	Vanilla	Asian	Vanilla with Capital Guarantee Fee to 100% Participation	Vanilla with Capital Guarantee Fee to 150% Participation	CPPT with Maximum Exposure of 100%	CPPT with Maximum Exposure of 150%	CPPT with 150% Max Exposure, 100% Initial Exposure	CPPT with Maximum Exposure of 200%	Underlying
Average outcome	152.39	152.27	152.17	146.06	151.24	165.04	164.95	172.21	160.57
Std dev of outcomes	21.11	20.98	24.19	34.12	24.61	37.69	37.47	52.78	24.44
Maximum outcome	47.76	243.62	262.34	309.99	270.66	359.90	360.45	480.90	270.84
Minimum outcome	100.00	100.00	100.00	100.00	100.00	100.00	100.00	100.00	99.00
Average return (%)	8.79	8.77	8.76	7.87	8.63	10.54	10.53	11.48	9.93
Maximum return (%)	19.90	19.49	21.28	25.39	22.03	29.19	29.23	36.90	22.0
Minimum return (%)	0.00	0.00	0.00	0.00	0.00	0.00	0.00	0.00	−0.20
Outcomes at par as a	1	1	1	6	1	1	1	1	0
% of trials	1.1%	1.1%	1.1%	6.8%	1.1%	1.1%	1.1%	1.1%	0.0%
Performs worse than vanilla as a	45	47	45	67	58	24	23	24	1
% of trials	51.1%	53.4%	51.1%	76.1%	65.9%	27.3%	26.1%	27.3%	1.1%
Performs better than vanilla as a	42	40	42	20	29	63	64	63	87
% of trials	47.7%	45.5%	47.7%	22.7%	33.0%	71.6%	72.7%	71.6%	98.9%

Source: UBS (using fund of funds returns data from Altvest).

Note: Options are prices using Black-Scholes using an implied volatility of 18 percent. Parameters for all CPPT products are: 20 percent crash size, 15 percent/25 percent deleverage/releverage triggers. CPPT fees are 1.5 percent and leverage is charged at LIBOR + 90 basis points.

CONCLUSION

Each of the types of PPN we describe can be useful for FoF underlyings. Option-based PPNs provide a relatively predictable return, particularly when the option is an Asian tailed one. For those willing to take a little extra risk in terms of predictability of outcome, CPPT might be a better choice. Superficially, CPPT structures can be complex and difficult to understand, and as we have shown, there are circumstances when they might not perform as well as expected. We have attempted to explain why CPPT might be disappointing under these circumstances by looking at the mechanics that underlie them.

We avoid hard and fast rules that dictate when CPPT PPNs might be good or bad, depending on the environment. This is an exercise in futility for two reasons:

1. They are still relatively new in the world of hedge funds. Their history is too short to assess how they behave under a variety of conditions. In short, the sample of CPPT PPN history is too small to be valid.
2. CPPT-based CPNs are evolving constantly and new variants are appearing all the time. These variants are often developed to suit changing conditions.

Instead of imposing strict rules, we recommend an analytical approach based on an understanding of the basic mechanics of CPPT PPN.

CHAPTER 29

Hedge Funds and the Stale Pricing Issue

Mohamed Gaber, Greg N. Gregoriou, and William Kelting

Most hedge funds commonly trade in illiquid securities, and, therefore, it is very difficult to obtain accurate monthly returns. The practice of stale pricing tends to intensify the scope of this problem. The only available alternative to hedge funds and fund of hedge funds (FoHF) managers is to smooth returns. In this chapter we investigate the advantages and disadvantages of stale pricing and offer a guide to evaluate the significance of stale pricing. This guide may help investors in hedge funds as well as FoHF managers to scrutinize the underpinning policies and procedures used in determining fair values of those funds. This guide is presented as a series of checklist questions.

INTRODUCTION

The issue of stale pricing refers to the practice of pricing a fund's shares based on prices of the stocks in the portfolio that do not present an accurate account of the fair value as a result of timing differences involved when trading illiquid stocks. Because of timing differences, a U.S. fund manager possessing Pacific Rim stocks will employ the closing prices of the foreign market to get the net asset value (NAV) of the fund. This is an incorrect method in fairly pricing stocks in the fund manager's portfolio because the manager is basing the NAV of the fund on stale (old) pricing information that is over a dozen hours (the approximate difference in hours between the United States and the Pacific Rim). Furthermore, events can arise throughout that time period that can considerably impact the value of the Pacific Rim stocks, resulting in an incorrect NAV that does not accurately reflect their fair value. Time zone differences can facilitate time zone arbitrage trading, because of mispricings in global stock markets. This may result in profits from stock purchased in one market and sold in the other, at a cost to shareholders of the fund. For example, an investor taking a position in a fund possessing foreign stocks will try to time the acquisition on a certain day when U.S. markets will display a broad increase. The investor's anticipation is that foreign stock markets will increase the next day, based on the broad movement of U.S. stock markets. For example, hedge funds (as well as other investors) may still take advantage of time zone differences through the use of futures contracts.

It is not unlawful to take an advantage of these timing differences; however, there is growing concern regarding fairness to the shareholders of the fund. The Securities and Exchange Commission (SEC) has a suggested that a redemption fee be made obligatory on investments that are kept for less than five business days.

Illiquid securities create a valuation problem because the last known market price for the stock may not reflect the present and fair market value. These valuation problems are further compounded in the case of hedge funds and funds of hedge funds (FoHF, a basket of hedge funds). Given that mutual funds report on a daily basis, the majority of hedge funds and FoHFs report their returns only on a monthly, net of all management and performance fees, and are generally not under the scrutiny of the SEC. Stale pricing in the hedge fund industry refers to artificially overvaluating international stocks that are part of the manager's portfolio. They are not regulated because they meet exceptions stipulated in acts enforced by the SEC regarding the limited number of shareholders, the type of investors, usually institutional and high-net-worth individuals, and because the offering of securities is not a public offering. Many hedge funds are also organized as offshore funds and thus do not fall under the SEC's jurisdiction.

The use of stale pricing to determine the NAV of a portfolio is not consistent with the position of both the accounting profession and the SEC, which require that investments be reported at fair value or "the amount at which the investment could be exchanged in a current transaction between willing parties, other than in a forced or liquidation sale" (Harrell and Spiegel 2004). In those cases, the fair value of an investment can be readily determined by accessing current market price data from various independent sources that price stocks. Illiquid stocks cause a problem in that no existing price may be currently available. Therefore, an attempt must be made to correctly estimate the current fair market value. In situations where foreign stock markets close prior to the U.S. markets, a market event that is expected to influence the value of a security may occur during the lag period. Therefore, rather than using the foreign market closing price, an attempt should be made to estimate the price of the security. Using these types of estimates can open the door for unwarranted manipulation. Because hedge funds charge a performance/incentive fee, there is a tendency to inflate the NAV. This has been the case for many of the recent frauds involving hedge funds. The International Organization of Securities Commissions (IOSCO 2003) states that "in order to make informed judgments, investors should be aware of hedge fund policies and procedures for the estimation of asset values." Furthermore, investors should make sure these policies and procedures are adhered to by hedge funds and FoHFs.

Hedge funds that are not registered with the SEC may or may not have their financial reports subject to the scrutiny of an independent auditor. Even if an independent auditor is appointed to audit an unregistered fund, the amount of work performed by the auditor may be less than for registered funds. Auditors of registered funds are required to test all portfolio valuations as of the date of the financial statements. In the case of unregistered funds, the extent of testing portfolio valuations is a matter of the auditor's judgment.

These issues are further compounded in funds of hedge funds. For example, certain hedge funds included in the fund may be registered, while others may be subject to independent auditing, and some may be neither registered nor subject to auditing. Moreover, the FoHF manager must wait for the hedge funds in the portfolio to report monthly net returns before determining the final return of the fund. If a hedge fund is late in reporting its monthly return, the manager will most probably use the hedge fund's prior net return to obtain an estimate for the current monthly net return. When new investors purchase shares in a fund of hedge funds that is late in reporting its monthly net returns, or if its monthly returns are not precise, they will be obtaining a better price because the fund may be undervalued. Investors selling their shares in such a fund, however, may be getting less than expected (Kazemi and Schneeweis 2004). We find that hedge funds smooth out returns, making them very attractive for allocation in stock and bond portfolios.

Funds of hedge funds may not always provide investors correct returns data, which may lead to an inaccurate analysis of statistical measures of their returns. As a result of returns smoothing, investors and academics may not be able to correctly assess a fund's true risk. Amenc, Malaise, Martellini, and Vaissié (2004) postulate that since hedge funds and funds of hedge funds are susceptible to skewness and kurtosis in their returns distribution, it may not be possible for the FoHF manager to predict drops in monthly returns and correctly assess the funds' net asset value.

Many hedge fund managers use their skills to identify and profit from price inefficiencies in stock and bond markets. Consequently, a majority of hedge fund managers are hesitant to disclose their trading strategies and are reticent about providing full disclosure of the stocks, bonds, and other investments in their portfolio.

Evaluating fund performance by using traditional measures, such as annualized returns, standard deviation, the modified Sharpe ratio, and the correlation coefficient, will likely lead to a misrepresentation of a fund's risk-reward profile (Amin and Kat 2003b). Furthermore, Murguia and Umemoto (2004) state that "although hedge fund managers may appear to provide returns in excess of their systematic risk exposures, they may be exposed to other risk factors not captured by traditional evaluation measures as stated in." Because hedge fund returns are nonnormal and as a result display skewness and kurtosis (the third and fourth moments of a distribution), measuring the actual performance of hedge funds and determining whether a FoHF manager is accurately reporting net returns is rather a difficult task. Many studies have documented that hedge funds exhibit a significant amount of excess returns, or alpha, even after adjusting for broad market exposure (Liang 2001). But these studies do not account for the illiquid stocks held by many hedge funds, which may drag down the returns.

In some cases, hedge funds may use stale pricing to artificially drive up their NAV because several emerging markets stocks may not provide daily or even monthly liquidity. Hedge fund managers investing in these foreign stocks will usually calculate the average of the latest returns to provide an estimate of the current monthly return.

While some hedge funds willingly report monthly returns net of all performance and management fees to database vendors, the data may not precisely reflect the exact and true value of a fund's NAV. Furthermore, information not available on illiquid stocks allows the hedge fund manager to price these stocks with whatever NAV he or she may decide to use. Often hedge fund managers may price these assets to reflect the holdings in their portfolio due to be reported to investors at the end of the month.

BACKGROUND INFORMATION

Since hedge funds are often used for portfolio diversification, managers have a strong incentive to report returns that are both consistent and uncorrelated to the market. This can artificially reduce the volatility and correlation of hedge funds to traditional indices (Asness, Krail, and Liew 2001). Kazemi and Schneeweis (2004) find that quarterly standard deviations are greater than monthly standard deviations, which is consistent with the stale pricing issue as a result of quarterly return adjustments. For example, if the market experiences an extreme drop, the hedge fund manager may not have certain illiquid stocks accurately priced for numerous months to reflect the new market value of the position. This would result in an overinflated NAV until the stocks in the portfolio accurately reflect their true market value. Thus, investors would have a false sense of the correct NAV, and therefore year-end returns would be inflated.

Some researchers have used lagged market betas to calculate the true market exposure of hedge funds. For example, Asness, Krail, and Liew (2001) use convertible arbitrage, fixed income arbitrage, and event-driven classifications to investigate this issue because these strategies maintain large quantities of international stocks that are very difficult to obtain a fair and accurate price for, especially if they are small or over-the-counter (OTC) stocks.

The issue of hedge funds adding alpha, as discussed in Schneeweis and Spurgin (1999), is refuted by Murguia and Umemoto (2004), who state that "hedge funds do not provide alpha but simply expand investment opportunities by including alternative investments into a stock and bonds portfolio." By manipulating the international stocks in a portfolio, the hedge fund manager can manipulate the alpha of the fund. Murguia and Umemoto (2004) affirm that hedge fund returns are overstated and investors must be able to recognize these warning signs. Doing so will allow investors a quicker exit before a catastrophic or extreme market event occurs.

RECENT DEVELOPMENTS

The Securities and Exchange Commission is moving ahead to regulate hedge funds, despite stiff opposition from critics both inside and outside the Commission. On October 27, 2004, the SEC adopted Rule 203(b)(3)–2, which will require most hedge fund advisors to register with the SEC under the Investment Advisers Act of 1940. The act currently applies to the managers of mutual funds, pension funds, corporate trusts, and endowments. Such a move would considerably extend the SEC's jurisdictional reach. Moreover, requiring hedge fund advisors to register would allow the SEC to find out more about how the industry operates and potentially uncover fraudulent behavior. Once registered with the SEC, fund advisors would be subject to regular examinations of their books and records, and would have to reveal to the SEC the number of funds they manage and the assets under management as well as information about their investors, employees, and the persons who control or are affiliated with the hedge fund advisor. In addition, as discussed earlier, the SEC (2004) has proposed to address the issue of time zone arbitrage by suggesting a 2 percent fee on fund shareholders who redeem their shares within five business days after purchase. The effectiveness of such an action is the subject of much controversy.

TABLE 29.1   Checklist of Questions

---

1. Has the board of directors (or equivalent) adopted a policy for valuation of securities?
2. Is there a committee (or individual) charged with responsibility for valuation?
3. Is the person or committee independent of those responsible for investment management functions?
4. Are independent pricing sources utilized wherever possible?
5. In cases where market prices are not available, how are valuations determined?
6. Are methods of valuation applied consistently over time?
7. Do those individuals determining fair value estimates have the appropriate expertise and experience?
8. Do the methods of valuation appear appropriate under the circumstances?
9. What models, if any, are used to estimate fair values?
10. If models are used, are they provided by an independent source?
11. Are model results compared to actual results on a regular basis?
12. Does the fund have an internal audit function?
13. Are security valuation policies and procedures subjected to the scrutiny of the internal auditors?
14. To whom does the internal audit function report?
15. Are internal audit reports filed on a regular bases and recommendations acted upon?
16. Is the fund registered with the SEC?
17. If registered, who are the independent auditors?
18. Did the independent auditors provide any comments regarding the fund's internal controls, particularly over the valuation of assets?
19. If unregistered, were the financial statements of the fund audited?
20. Who were the auditors?
21. Did the independent auditors provide any comments regarding the fund's internal controls, particularly over the valuation of assets?
22. If the fund is not audited, why?
23. If an FoF, does the manager scrutinize the funds in the portfolio as to their methods for valuation of assets and address questions similar to numbers 1 through 20?
24. Does the FoF have an established mechanism for regular monitoring of the hedge funds included in the portfolio, including periodic visits?

CHECKLIST OF QUESTIONS

Investors and potential investors in hedge funds need to gain an understanding of policies and procedures used by funds to value assets and should be particularly skeptical of cases where objective, independent pricing sources are not utilized. We have developed a checklist of 24 questions that might be used to assist in gaining that understanding. The checklist focuses only on issues of valuation and particularly valuation of assets where estimates are required. Investors must also be concerned with other issues and should raise other questions. For example, see the extensive checklist developed by the Investor Risk Committee of the International Association of Financial Engineers (2004). Our checklist appears in Table 29.1.

CONCLUSION

Under the direction of a board of directors, hedge fund management is responsible for making a good-faith effort to estimate fair market values. Uncertainty in estimating the fair market value of investments will result in somewhat larger incentive fees and may pose a potential and possible significant risk for hedge fund and FoHF investors. Stale pricing, though it may be objective, often does not provide a measure of fair market value and is inappropriate for decision-making purposes. Fair market value estimates may be less reliable but are more relevant. Investors in hedge funds and in funds of hedge funds and FoHF managers need to cautiously scrutinize the policies and procedures that hedge funds use to determine fair market value. A questionnaire approach such as that suggested in this chapter may be a useful tool in exercising this diligence.

References

Acito, C. J., and F. P. Fisher. (2002) "Fund of Hedge Funds: Rethinking Resource Requirements." *Journal of Alternative Investments*, Vol. 4, No. 4, pp. 25–35.

Ackermann, C., R. McEnally, and D. Ravenscraft. (1999) "The Performance of Hedge Funds: Risk, Return, and Incentives." *Journal of Finance*, Vol. 54, No. 3, pp. 833–874.

Adler, N., L. Friedman, and Z. Sinuany-Stern. (2002) "Review of Ranking Methods in the Data Envelopment Analysis Context." *European Journal of Operational Research,* Vol. 140, No. 2, pp. 86–102.

Agarwal, V., and N. Y. Naik. (2000a) "Generalized Style Analysis of Hedge Funds." *Journal of Asset Management*, Vol. 1, No. 1, pp. 93–109.

Agarwal, V., and N. Y. Naik. (2000b) "Multi-Period Performance Persistence Analysis of Hedge Funds." *Journal of Financial and Quantitative Analysis*, Vol. 35, No. 3, pp. 327–342.

Agarwal, V., and N. Y. Naik. (2000c) "On Taking the Alternative Route: Risks, Rewards and Performance Persistence of Hedge Funds." *Journal of Alternative Investment,* Vol. 2, No. 4, pp. 6–23.

Agarwal, V., and N. Y. Naik. (2004) "Risks and Portfolio Decisions Involving Hedge Funds." *Review of Financial Studies*, Vol. 17, No. 1, pp. 63–98.

Aigner, D. J., C. Hsiao, A. Kapteyn, and T. Wansbeek. (1984) "Latent Variable Models in Econometrics." In Z. Griliches and M. D. Intriligator, eds., *Handbook of Econometrics 2*. Amsterdam: North-Holland, pp. 1321–1393.

Ait-Sahalia, Y., J. Parker, and M. Yogo. (2001) "Luxury Goods and the Equity Premium." *Journal of Finance*, Vol. 59, No. 6, pp. 2959–3004.

Alexander, C. (1999) "Optimal Hedging Using Cointegration" *Philosophical Transactions of the Royal Society*, A 357, pp. 2039–2058.

Alexander, C., and A. Dimitriu. (2004a) "The Art of Investing in Hedge Funds." Discussion paper, ISMA Center, *www.ismacenter.rdg.ac.uk/dp*.

Alexander, C., and A. Dimitriu. (2004b) "Sources of Outperformance in Equity Markets: Mean Reversion, Common Trends and Herding." *Journal of Portfolio Management*, Vol. 30, No. 4, pp. 170–185.

Alexander, C., and A. Dimitriu. (2005) "Indexing and Statistical Arbitrage: Tracking Error or Cointegration?" *Journal of Portfolio Management*, Vol. 31, No. 2, pp. 1–15.

Ali, P. U. (2004) "Funds of Hedge Funds and Fiduciary Investors." *Australian Business Law Review*, Vol. 32, No. 7, pp. 362–366.

Ali, P. U., G. Stapledon, and M. Gold. (2003) *Corporate Governance and Investment Fiduciaries*. Rozelle, New South Wales: Lawbook Company.

Amenc, N., S. El Bied, and L. Martellini. (2002) "Evidence of Predictability in Hedge Fund Returns and Multi-Style Multi-Class Tactical Style Allocation Decisions." Working paper, EDHEC Risk and Asset Management Research Centre, Lille, France.

Amenc, N., S. El Bied, and L. Martellini. (2003) "Predictability in Hedge Fund Returns." *Financial Analysts Journal*, Vol. 5, No. 59, pp. 32–46.

Amenc, N., and L. Martellini. (2002) "Portfolio Optimization and Hedge Fund Style Allocation Decisions." *Journal of Alternative Investments*, Vol. 5, No. 2, pp. 7–20.

Amenc, N., and L. Martellini. (2003a) "The Alpha and Omega of Hedge Fund Performance Measurement." Discussion paper, EDHEC Business School, www.edhec-risk.com.

Amenc, N., and L. Martellini. (2003b) "The Brave New World of Hedge Fund Indices." Discussion paper, EDHEC Business School, *http://www. edhec-risk.com*.

Amenc, N., and L. Martellini. (2003c) "Optimal Mixing of Hedge Funds with Traditional Investment Vehicles." Discussion paper, EDHEC Business School, *www.edhec-risk.com*.

Amenc, N., L. Martellini,.and M. Vaissié. (2003d) "Benefits and Risk of Alternative Investment Strategies." *Journal of Asset Management*, Vol. 4, No. 2, pp. 96–118.

Amenc, N., P. Malaise, and L. Martellini. (2004) "Revisiting Core-Satellite Investing—A Dynamic Model of Relative Risk Management." *Journal of Portfolio Management*, Vol. 31, No.1, pp. 64–75.

Amenc, N., P. Malaise, L. Martellini, and M. Vaissié. (2004) "Fund of Hedge Fund Reporting: A Return-Based Approach to Fund of Hedge Fund Reporting." EDHEC Risk and Asset Management Research Centre, Lille, France.

American Institute of Certified Public Accountants. (2003) *AICPA Audit and Accounting Guide: Audits of Investment Companies*. New York: AICPA.

Amin, G. S., and H. M. Kat. (2002a) "Portfolios of Hedge Funds: What Investors Really Invest In." Working paper, ISMA Centre, University of Reading, Reading, U.K.

Amin, G. S., and H. M. Kat. (2002b) "Who Should Buy Hedge Funds? The Effects of Including Hedge Funds in Portfolios of Stocks and Bonds." ISMA Centre for Education & Research in Securities Markets, Working Paper Series.

Amin, G. S., and H. M. Kat. (2003a) "Hedge Fund Performance 1990–2000: Do the 'Money Machines' Really Add Value?" *Journal of Financial and Quantitative Analysis*, Vol. 38, No. 2, pp. 251–274.

Amin, G. S., and H. M. Kat. (2003b) "Stocks, Bonds and Hedge Funds: No Free Lunch!" *Journal of Portfolio Management*, Vol. 29, No. 4, pp. 113–120.

Amin, G. S., and H. M. Kat. (2003c) "Welcome to the Dark Side: Hedge Fund Attrition and Survivorship Bias Over the Period 1994–2001." *Journal of Alternative Investments*, Vol. 6, No. 1, pp. 57–73.

Anderson, T. R., K. B. Hollingsworth, and L. B. Inman. (2002) "The Fixed Weighting Nature of a Cross-Evaluation Model." *Journal of Productivity Analysis*, Vol. 17, No. 3, pp. 249–255.

Anjilvel, S., B. Boudreau, B. Johmann, M. Peskin, and M. Urias. (December 2001) "Hedge Funds—Strategy and Portfolio Insights." *Morgan Stanley Quantitative Strategies Research*, pp. 1–16.

Anson, M. (2001) "Hedge Fund Incentive Fees and the 'Free Option.'" *Journal of Alternative Investments*. Vol. 4, No. 2, pp. 43–48.

Anson, M. (2002a) "Symmetrical Performance Measures and Asymmetrical Trading Strategies: A Cautionary Example." *Journal of Alternative Investments*, Vol. 5, No. 1, pp. 81–85.

Anson, M. (2002b) "Financial Market Dislocations and Hedge Fund Returns." *Journal of Alternative Investments*, Vol. 5, No. 3, pp. 78–88.

Anson, M., and H. Ho. (2004) "Measuring the Long Volatility Strategies of Managed Futures." In G. N. Gregoriou, V. N. Karavas, F.-S. Lhabitant, and F. Rouah, eds., *Commodity Trading Advisors: Risk, Performance Analysis, and Selection*. Hoboken, NJ: John Wiley & Sons, pp. 183–202.

Artzner, P., F. Delbaen, J.-M. Eber, and D. Heath. (1999) "Coherent Risk Measures." *Mathematical Finance*, Vol. 9, No. 3, pp. 203–208.

Asness, C., R. Krail, and J. Liew. (2001) "Do Hedge Funds Hedge?" *Journal of Portfolio Management*, Vol. 1, No. 28, pp. 6–19.

Bacmann, J. F., and S. Pache. (2004) "Optimal Hedge Fund Style Allocation under Higher Moments." In B. Schachter, ed., *Intelligent Hedge Fund Investing*. London: Risk Books, pp. 393–421.

Bacmann, J. F., and S. Scholz. (June 2003) "Alternative Performance Measures for Hedge Funds." *Alternative Investment Management Journal* (London, U.K.) *http://www.aima.org/uploads/2003%5CJune%Crmf.pdf.*

Banker, R. D., A. Charnes, and W. W. Cooper. (1984) "Some Models for Estimating Technical and Scale Inefficiencies in Data Envelopment Analysis." *Management Science*, Vol. 30, No. 9, pp. 1078–1092.

Bansal, R., M. Dahlquist, and C. Harvey. (2004) "Dynamic Trading Strategies and Portfolio Choice." Working paper, Duke University, Chapel Hill, N.C.

Baquero, H., J. ter Horst, and M. Verbeek. (2002) "Survival, Look-Ahead Bias and the Performance of Hedge Funds." Working paper, Erasmus University, Rotterdam, Holland, and Tilburg University, Tilburg, Holland.

Barès, P. A., R. Gibson, and S. Gyger. (2001) "Style Consistency and Survival Probability in the Hedge Fund Industry." Working paper, Swiss Federal Institute of Technology and University of Zurich.

Barreto, S. L. (2004) "Hedge Fund Asset Flows Pass US $100 Billion Mark," *http://www.hedgeworld.com.*

Barry, R. (2002) "Hedge Funds: A Walk Through the Graveyard." Working paper, Applied Finance Centre, Macquarie University, Sydney, Australia.

Benjamin, J. (2003) "As Failure Rate Soars, Hedge Funds Bail Out," http://www.investment news.com.

Berényi, Z. (2003) *Risk and Performance Evaluation with Skewness and Kurtosis for Conventional and Alternative Investments*. Frankfurt: Peter Lang Publishers.

Bernardo, A. E., and O. Ledoit. (2000) "Gain, Loss and Asset Pricing." *Journal of Political Economy*, Vol. 108, No. 1, pp. 144–172.

Black, F., and M. Scholes. (1973) "The Pricing of Options and Corporate Liabilities." *Journal of Political Economy*, Vol. 81, No. 3, pp. 637–659.

Black, K. H. (2004) *Managing a Hedge Fund: A Complete Guide to Trading, Business Strategies, Risk Management and Regulations*. New York: McGraw-Hill.

Blum, P., M. Dacorogna, and L. Jaeger (2003) "Performance and Risk Measurement Challenges for Hedge Funds: Empirical Considerations." In L. Jaeger, ed., *The New Generation of Risk Management for Hedge Funds and Private Equity Investments*. London: Euromoney Books, pp. 412–433.

Bookstaber, R. (2000) "Understanding and Monitoring the Liquidity Crisis Cycle." *Financial Analysts Journal*, Vol. 56, No. 5, pp. 17–22.

Bookstaber, R., and R. Clarke. (1981) "Options Can Alter Portfolio Return Distributions." *Journal of Portfolio Management*. Vol. 7, No. 3, pp. 63–70.

Bowden, R. J. (1984) *Instrumental Variables*. Cambridge: Cambridge University Press.

Boyson, N. (2002) "How Are Hedge Fund Manager Characteristics Related to Performance, Volatility and Survival." Working paper, Columbus: Ohio State University.

Brandon, K. L. (2004) "The State of Hedge Funds: 2004." SIA Research Reports, New York: *http://www.sia.com.press*.

Brav, A., and P. A. Gompers. (1997) "Myth or Reality? The Long-Run Underperformance of Initial Public Offerings: Evidence from Venture and Non-Venture Capital-Backed Companies." *Journal of Finance*, Vol. 52, No. 4, pp. 1791–1821.

Brealey, R. A., and E. Kaplanis. (2001) "Hedge Funds and Financial Stability: An Analysis of Their Factor Exposures." *International Finance*, Vol. 4, No. 2, pp. 161–187.

Brooks, C., and H. M. Kat. (2002) "The Statistical Properties of Hedge Fund Index Returns and Their Implications for Investors." *Journal of Alternative Investments*, Vol. 5, No. 2, pp. 26–44.

Brown, S. J., and W. N. Goetzmann. (2003) "Hedge Funds with Style." *Journal of Portfolio Management*, Vol. 29, No. 2, pp. 101–112.

Brown, S. J., W. N. Goetzmann, and R. G. Ibbotson. (1999) "Offshore Hedge Funds: Survival and Performance 1989–1995." *Journal of Business*, Vol. 72, No. 1, pp. 91–117.

Brown, S. J., W. N. Goetzmann, and B. Liang. (2004) "Fees on Fees in Funds of Funds." *Journal of Investment Management*, Vol. 2, No. 4, pp. 39–56.

Brown, S. J., W. N. Goetzmann, and J. Park. (2001) "Careers and Survivals: Competition and Risk in the Hedge Fund and CTA Industry." *Journal of Finance*, Vol. 56, No. 5, pp. 1869–1886.

Brunel, J. L. P. (2003) "A New Perspective on Hedge Funds and Hedge Fund Allocations." AIMR Conference Proceeding, *Investment Counseling for Private Clients,* Vol. 4, No. 5, pp. 9–22.

Burghardt, G., R. Duncan, and L. Liu. (2003) "Understanding Drawdowns." Research note, Calyon Financial Research, Chicago: *http://www.calyonfinancial.com.*

Burghardt, G., R. Duncan, and L. Liu. (July 2004) "What You Should Expect from Trend Following." Research Note Calyon Financial, Chicago.

Bürki, V., and R. Larque. (2001) "Hedge Funds Returns and Their Drivers." Master's thesis in Banking and Finance, Ecole des HEC, University of Lausanne, Lausannne, Switzerland.

Campbell, J., and L. Viceira. (2002) *Strategic Asset Allocation: Portfolio Choice for Long-term Investors.* Oxford: Oxford University Press.

Capocci, D. (2003) "Convertible Arbitrage Funds in a Classical Portfolio." In G. N. Gregoriou, V. N. Karavas, and F. Rouah, eds., *Hedge Funds: Strategies, Risk Assessment, and Returns.* Washington, DC: Beard Books, pp. 71–98.

Capocci, D. (2004a) "CTA Performance, Survivorship Bias and Dissolution Frequencies," In G. N. Gregoriou, V. N. Karavas, F. S. Lhabitant, and F. Rouah, eds., *Commodity Trading Advisors: Risk, Performance, Analysis and Selection.* Hoboken, NJ: John Wiley & Sons, pp. 49–78.

Capocci, D. (2004b) "Neutrality of Market Neutral Funds." Working paper, University of Liège, Liège, Belgium.

Capocci, D., A. Corhay, and G. Hübner. (2005) "Hedge Fund Performance in Bull and Bear Markets." *European Journal of Finance* (forthcoming).

Capocci, D., and G. Hübner. (2004) "An Analysis of Hedge Fund Performance." *Journal of Empirical Finance,* Vol. 11, No. 1, pp. 55–89.

Carhart, M. (1997) "On Persistence in Mutual Fund Performance." *Journal of Finance,* Vol. 52, No. 1, pp. 57–82.

Carhart, M. M., J. N. Carpenter, A. W. Lynch, and D. K. Musto. (September 12, 2000) "Mutual Fund Survivorship." Working paper, *http://ssrn.com/abstract=238713.*

Chan, L. K. C., N. Jegadeesh, and J. Lakonishok. (1996) "Momentum Strategies." *Journal of Finance,* Vol. 51, No. 5, pp. 1681–1713.

Chance, D. M. (2003) "The Instability of the Relationship Between Stocks, Bonds and Managed Futures." *Journal of Applied Business Research,* Vol. 19, No. 1, pp. 75–93.

Charnes, A., W. W. Cooper, and E. Rhodes. (1978) "Measuring the Efficiency of Decision Making Units." *European Journal of Operational Research,* Vol. 2, No. 6, pp. 429–444.

Chopra, V. K., C. R. Hensel, and A. L. Turner. (1993) "Massaging Mean-Variance Inputs: Returns from Alternative Global Investment Strategies in the 1980s." *Management Science,* Vol. 39, No. 11, pp. 845–855.

Christie, W. G. (1990) "Dividend Yields and Expected Returns: The Zero Dividend Puzzle." *Journal of Financial Economics,* Vol. 28, No. 1–2, pp. 95–125.

Christie, W. G., and R. D. Huang. (1994) "The Changing Functional Relation Between Stock Returns and Dividend Yields." *Journal of Empirical Finance*, Vol. 1, No. 2, pp. 161–191.

Coën, A., and F. E. Racicot. (2004) "Higher Moment Estimators for Financial Regression Models with Errors in the Variables: The Cost of Equity Revisited." Working Paper, Université du Québec à Montréal (UQÀM).

Coleman, T. S., and L. B. Siegel. (1999) "Compensating Fund Managers for Risk-Adjusted Performance." *Journal of Alternative Investments*, Vol. 2, No. 3, pp. 9–22.

Coles, S., J. Heffernan, and J. Tawn. (1999) "Dependence Measures for Extreme Value Analyses," *Extremes*, Vol. 2, No. 4, pp. 339–365.

Collins, D. (August 2003) "Turning Asset Allocation on Its Head." *Futures Magazine*, pp. 64–66.

Dacorogna, M., U. Müller, O. Pictet, and C. De Vries. (2001) "The Distribution of Extremal Foreign Exchange Rate Returns in Extremely Large Data Sets." *Extremes*, Vol. 4, No. 2, p. 105–127.

Dagenais, M. G., and D. L. Dagenais. (1997) "Higher Moment Estimators for Linear Regression Models with Errors in the Variables." *Journal of Econometrics*, Vol. 76, No. 1–2, pp. 193–221.

Dagenais, M. G., and F. E. Racicot. (1993) "Estimation et Tests en Présence d'Erreurs de Mesure Sur les Variables Explicatives." Manuscript, C.R.D.E., University of Montreal.

Darling, G., K. Mukherjee, and K. Wilkens. (2004) "CTA Performance Evaluation with Data Envelopment Analysis." In G. N. Gregoriou, V. N. Karavas, F. S. Lhabitant, and F. Rouah, eds., *Commodity Trading Advisors: Risk, Performance Analysis, and Selection*, Hoboken, NJ: John Wiley & Sons, pp. 79–104.

Darst, D. (2003) *The Art of Asset Allocation*. New York: McGraw-Hill.

Davidson, R., and J. MacKinnon. (1993) *Estimation and Inference in Econometrics*. New York: Oxford University Press.

Davies, R. J., H. M. Kat, and S. Lu. (2004) "Fund of Hedge Funds Portfolio Selection: A Multiple Objective Approach." Working paper, ISMA Centre, University of Reading, Reading, U.K.

Davis, R. E. (2001) "Decision Policy Optimization Via Certain Equivalent Functions for Exponential Utility." In R. E. Davis, *Advances in Mathematical Programming and Financial Planning*. Greenwich: JAI Press, pp. 89–113.

Davison, A. C., and R. L. Smith. (1990) "Models for Exceedances over High Thresholds (with Discussion)." *Journal of the Royal Statistical Society*, Series B, Vol. 52, No.3, pp. 393–442.

DeBondt, W. F. M., and R. H. Thaler. (1985) "Does the Stock Market Overreact?" *Journal of Finance*, Vol. 40, No. 3, pp. 793–805.

de Melo, M., V. Beatriz and R. P. C. Leal. (2003) "Maximum Drawdown: Models and Applications." Coppead Working Paper Series, No. 359, *http://ssrn.com/abstract=477322*.

Deming, W. E. (1982) *Out of the Crisis*. Cambridge, MA: MIT Press International.

Dert, C., and B. Oldenkamp. (2000) "Optimal Guaranteed Return Portfolios and the Casino Effect." *Operations Research*, Vol. 48, No. 5, pp. 768–775.

Deutsche Bank. (March 31, 2003) "Institutional Alternative Investment Survey." Equity Prime Services Group of Deutschbank, New York.

Douglas, P. (2004) "Hedge Funds in Asia." *Journal of Financial Transformation*, Capco Institute, Vol. 10, pp. 97–105.

Dowd, K. (1998) *Beyond Value at Risk. The New Science of Risk Management*. New York: John Wiley & Sons.

Doyle, J., and R. Green. (1994) "Efficiency and Cross Efficiency in DEA: Derivations, Meanings and Uses." *Journal of the Operational Research Society*, Vol. 45, No. 5, pp. 567–578.

Durbin, J. (1954) "Errors in Variables." *International Statistical Review*, Vol. 22, pp. 23–32.

Edhec Business School. (2003) *Edhec European Alternative Multi-Management Practices Survey*. Research book, Lille, France.

Edwards, F. R., and M. O. Caglayan. (2001a) "Hedge Fund and Commodity Fund Investments in Bull and Bear Markets." *Journal of Portfolio Management*, Vol. 27, No. 4, pp. 97–108.

Edwards, F. R., and M. O. Caglayan. (2001b) "Hedge Fund Performance and Manager Skill." *Journal of Futures Markets*, Vol. 21, No. 11, pp. 1003–1028.

Edwards, F. R., and J. Liew. (1999) "Hedge Funds versus Managed Futures as Asset Classes." *Journal of Derivatives*, Vol. 6, No. 4, pp. 45–64.

Eichengreen, B., and D. Mathieson. (1998) *Hedge Funds and Financial Market Dynamics*. Washington, DC: International Monetary Fund.

El-Hassan, N., and P. Kofman. (2003) "Tracking Error and Active Portfolio Management." *Australian Journal of Management*, Vol. 28, No. 2, pp. 183–207.

Elton, E. J., and M. J. Gruber. (1995) *Modern Portfolio Theory and Investment Analysis*. New York: John Wiley & Sons.

Elton, E. J., M. J. Gruber, and C. R. Blake. (1996) "The Persistence of Risk-Adjusted Mutal Fund Performance." *Journal of Business*, Vol. 69, No. 2, pp. 133–157.

Embrechts, P., C. Klüppelberg, and T. Mikosch. (1997) *Modelling Extremal Events for Insurance and Finance*. Berlin: Springer-Verlag.

Ennis, R. M., and M. D. Sebastian. (2003) "Are Performance Fees Right for Your Fund? A Case Study." *Journal of Investing*, Vol. 12, No. 2, pp. 45–48.

Eurekahedge. (2003) "Trends in Asian Hedge Funds," *http://www.eurekahedge.com/news/archive_2003.asp*.

Fama, E. F., and K. R. French. (1993) "Common Risk Factors in the Returns on Stocks and Bonds." *Journal of Financial Economics*, Vol. 33, No. 1, pp. 3–56.

Fama, E. F., and K. R. French. (1998) "Value versus Growth: the International Evidence." *Journal of Finance*, Vol. 53, No. 6, pp. 1975–1999.

Favre, L., and J. Galeano. (2002) "Mean-Modified Value-at-Risk Optimization with Hedge Funds." *Journal of Alternative Investments*, Vol. 5, No. 2, pp. 21–25.

Feldman, B. (August 22, 2002) "Portfolio Construction with Alternative Investments." Ibbotson Associates, QWAFAFEW Seminar Presentation, Chicago.

Feldman, B. (2004) "Relative Importance and Valve," Chicago: Prism Analytics, *http://www.prismanalytics.com*.

Fitch Ratings. (2003) "Developments in Hedge Fund Securitisations." Credit Products Special Report, New York.

Focardi, S., and F. Fabozzi. (2003) "Fat Tails, Scaling and Stable Laws." *Journal of Risk Finance*, Vol. 5, No. 1, pp. 5–26.

Focardi, S., and F. Fabozzi. (2004) *The Mathematics of Financial Modeling and Investment Management*. Hoboken, NJ: John Wiley & Sons.

Fothergill, M., and C. Coke. (2001) "Funds of Hedge Funds: An Introduction to Multi-Manager Funds." *Journal of Alternative Investments*, Vol. 4, No. 2, pp. 7–16.

Fuller, W. A. (1987) *Measurement Error Models*. New York: John Wiley & Sons.

Fung, W., and D. A. Hsieh. (1997a) "Empirical Characteristics of Dynamic Trading Strategies: The Case of Hedge Funds." *Review of Financial Studies*, Vol. 10, No. 2, pp. 275–302.

Fung, W., and D. A. Hsieh. (1997b) "Survivorship Bias and Investment Style in the Returns of CTAs: The Information Content of Performance Track Records." *Journal of Portfolio Management*, Vol. 24, No. 1, pp. 30–41.

Fung, W., and D. A. Hsieh. (1999a) "Is Mean-Variance Analysis Applicable to Hedge Funds?" *Economic Letters*, Vol. 62, No. 1, pp. 53–58.

Fung, W., and D. A. Hsieh. (1999b) "A Primer on Hedge Funds." *Journal of Empirical Finance*, Vol. 6, No. 3, pp. 309–331.

Fung, W., and D. A. Hsieh. (2000) "Performance Characteristics of Hedge Funds and CTA Funds: Natural versus Spurious Biases." *Journal of Quantitative and Financial Analysis*, Vol. 35, No. 3, pp. 291–307.

Fung, W., and D. A. Hsieh. (2001) "The Risk in Hedge Fund Strategies: Theory and Evidence from Trend Followers." *Review of Financial Studies*, Vol. 14, No. 1, pp. 313–341.

Fung, W., and D. A. Hsieh. (2002a) "Asset-Based Hedge-Fund Styles and Portfolio Diversification." *Financial Analyst Journal*, Vol. 58, No. 5, pp. 16–27.

Fung, W., and D. A. Hsieh. (2002b) "Hedge-Fund Benchmarks: Information Content and Biases." *Financial Analysts Journal*, Vol. 58, No. 1, pp. 22–34.

Fung, W., and D. A. Hsieh. (2002c) "The Risk in Fixed-Income Hedge Fund Strategies." *Journal of Fixed Income*, Vol. 12, No. 2, pp. 1–22.

Fung, W., and D. A. Hsieh. (2003) "The Risk in Hedge Fund Strategies: Alternative Alphas and Alternative Betas." In L. Jaeger, ed., *The New Generation of Risk Management for Hedge Funds and Private Equity Investments*. London: Euromoney Books, pp. 72–87.

Fung, W., and D. A. Hsieh. (2004a) "Extracting Portable Alphas from Equity Long-Short Hedge Funds." *Journal of Investment Management*, Vol. 3, No. 4, pp. 57–75.

Fung, W., and D. A. Hsieh. (2004b) "Hedge Fund Benchmarks: A Risk Based Approach." *Financial Analysts Journal*, Vol. 60, No. 5, pp. 65–80.

Geltner, D. M. (1993) "Estimating Market Values from Appraised Values without Assuming an Efficient Market." *Journal of Real Estate Research*, Vol. 8, No. 3, pp. 325–345.

Getmansky, M., A. W. Lo, and I. Makarov. (2003) "An Econometric Model of Serial Correlation and Illiquidity in Hedge Fund Returns." Working paper, MIT Sloan School of Management, Boston.

Ghaleb-Harter, T. E., and R. McFall-Lamm. (2000) "Optimal Hedge Fund Portfolios." Deutsche Asset Management, mimeo., New York.

Glosten, L., and R. Jagannathan (1994) "A Contingent Claim Approach to Performance Evaluation." *Journal of Empirical Finance*, Vol. 1, No. 2, pp. 133–160.

Goetzmann, W. N., J. E. Ingersoll, and S. A. Ross. (2003) "High Water Marks and Hedge Fund Management Contracts." *Journal of Finance*, Vol. 58, No. 4, pp. 1685–1718.

Goetzmann, W. N., J. E. Ingersoll, M. Spiegel, and I. Welch. (2002) "Sharpening Sharpe Ratios." Working paper, Yale School of Management, New Haven, CT.

Goltz, F., L. Martellini, and M. Vaissié. (2004) "Hedge Fund Indexes from an Academic Perspective, Reconciling Investability and Representativity." Working paper, EDHEC, Lille, France.

Goodman, M., K. Shewer, and R. Horwitz. (December 2002) "Beware of Systematic Style Biases." *Risk Magazine*, pp. 17–19.

Gordon, R. N. (2004) "Making Hedge Funds More Tax-Efficient." *Journal of Wealth Management*, Vol. 7, No. 1, pp. 75–80.

Goyal, A., and I. Welch. (2003) "Predicting the Equity Premium with Dividend Ratios." *Management Science*, Vol. 49, No. 5, pp. 639–654.

Grauer, R. R., and N. H. Hakansson. (1985) "1934–1983 Returns on Levered, Actively Managed Long-Run Portfolios of Stocks, Bonds and Bills." *Financial Analysts Journal*, Vol. 41, No. 1, pp. 24–43.

Grauer, R. R., and N. H. Hakansson. (1986) "A Half-Century of Returns on Levered and Unlevered Portfolios of Stocks, Bonds and Bills, with and without Small Stocks." *Journal of Business*, Vol. 59, No. 2, pp. 387–318.

Grauer, R. R., and N. H. Hakansson. (1987) "Gains from International Diversification: 1968–1985 Returns on Portfolios of Stocks and Bonds." *Journal of Finance*, Vol. 42, No. 3, pp. 721–739.

Grauer, R. R., and N. H. Hakansson. (1993) "On the Use of Mean-Variance and Quadratic Approximations in Implementing Dynamic Investment Strategies: A Comparison of Returns and Investment Policies." *Management Science*, Vol. 39, No. 7, pp. 856–871.

Grauer, R. R., and N. H. Hakansson. (1995) "Gains from Diversifying into Real Estate: Three Decades of Portfolio Returns Based on the Dynamic Investment Model." *Real Estate Economics*, Vol. 23, No. 2, pp. 117–159.

Grauer, R. R., and N. H. Hakansson. (2001) "Applying Portfolio Change and Conditional Performance Measures: The Case of Industry Rotation via the Dynamic Investment Model." *Review of Quantitative Finance and Accounting*, Vol. 17, No. 3, pp. 237–265.

Greenwich Associates. (2003) "2003 U.S. Investment Mangement Survey." Greenwich,CT, *http://www.greenwich.com.*

Gregoriou, G. N. (2002) "Hedge Fund Survival Lifetimes." *Journal of Asset Management*, Vol. 2, No. 3, pp. 237–252.

Gregoriou, G. N. (2003a) "The Mortality of Funds of Hedge Funds." *Journal of Wealth Management*, Vol. 6, No. 1, pp. 42–53.

Gregoriou, G. N. (2003b) "Performance Appraisal of Hedge Funds Using Data Envelopment Analysis." *Journal of Wealth Management*, Vol. 5, No. 4, pp. 88–95.

Gregoriou, G. N. (2003c) "Performance Evaluation of Funds of Hedge Funds Using Conditional Alphas and Betas." *Derivatives Use, Trading & Regulation*, Vol. 8, No. 4, pp. 324–344.

Gregoriou, G. N., and F. Rouah. (2001) "Do Stock Market Indices Move the Ten Largest Hedge Funds? A Cointegration Approach." *Journal of Alternative Investments*, Vol. 4, No. 2, pp. 61–66.

Gregoriou, G. N., and F. Rouah. (2002) "Large versus Small Hedge Funds: Does Size Affect Performance?" *Journal of Alternative Investments*, Vol. 5, No. 3, pp. 75–77.

Gregoriou, G. N., and J. Zhu. (2005) *Evaluating Hedge Fund and CTA Performance: Data Envelopment Analysis Approach.* Hoboken, NJ: John Wiley & Sons.

Gregoriou, G. N., G. Hübner, N. Papageorgiou, and F. Rouah. (2005) "Survival of Commodity Trading Advisors: 1990–2003." *Journal of Futures Markets.*

Gregoriou, G. N., K. Sedzro, and J. Zhu. (2005) "Hedge Fund Performance Appraisal Using Data Envelopment Analysis." *European Journal of Operational Research*, Vol. 164, No. 2, pp. 555–571.

Grinold, R., and R. Kahn. (2000) *Active Portfolio Management: A Quantitative Approach to Providing Superior Returns and Controlling Risk.* New York: McGraw-Hill.

Gutpa, A., and B. Liang. (2003) "Risk Analysis and Capital Adequacy of Hedge Funds." Working paper, Centre for International Securities and Derivatives Markets, University of Massachusetts, Amherst, MA.

Hagelin, N., and B. Pramborg. (2004a) "Dynamic Investment Strategies with and without Emerging Equity Markets." *Emerging Markets Review*, Vol. 5, No. 2, pp. 193–215.

Hagelin, N., and B. Pramborg. (2004b) "Evaluating Gains from Diversifying into Hedge Funds Using Dynamic Investment Strategies." In B. Schachter, ed., *Intelligent Hedge Fund Investing.* London: Risk Books, pp. 423–445.

Hakansson, N. H. (1971) "On Optimal Myopic Portfolio Policies, with and without Serial Correlation of Yields." *Journal of Business*, Vol. 44, No. 3, pp. 324–334.

Hakansson, N. H. (1974) "Convergence to Isoelastic Utility and Policy in Multiperiod Choice." *Journal of Financial Economics*, Vol. 1, No. 3, pp. 201–224.

Hakansson, N. H., and W. T. Ziemba. (1995) "Capital Growth Theory." In R. Jarrow, V. Maksmovic, and W. T. Ziemba, eds., *Handbooks in Operations Research and Management Science: Finance*. Amsterdam: Elsevier Science, pp. 65–86.

Harrell, M. P., and J. A. Spiegel. (Spring 2004) "The Debevoise and Plimpton Private Equity Report," pp. 16–22.

Harri, A., and B. W. Brorsen. (2002) "Performance Persistence and the Source of Returns for Hedge Funds." Working paper, Department of Agricultural Economics, Oklahoma State University, Stillwater, OK.

Harvey, C. R., and A. Siddique. (2000) "Conditional Skewness in Asset Pricing Tests." *Journal of Finance*, Vol. 55, No. 3, pp. 1263–1296.

Harvey, C. R., J. C. Liechty, M. W. Liechty, and P. Müller. (2003) "Portfolio Selection with Higher Moments." Working paper, Drexel University, Philadelphia.

Hendricks, D., J. Patel, and R. Zeckhauser. (1993) "Hot Hands in Mutual Funds: Short-Run Persistence of Relative Performance, 1974–1988." *Journal of Finance*, Vol. 48, No. 2, pp. 93–130.

Henriksson, R. D. (2004) "Hedge Funds, Active Management, and the Asset Allocation Decision: A Descriptive Framework, Resolution Capital Management." Available from rhenriksson@rsolutioncap.com.

Herzberg, M., and H. Mozes. (2003) "The Persistence of Hedge Fund Risk: Evidence and Implications for Investors." *Journal of Alternative Investments*, Vol. 6, No. 2, pp. 22–42.

Hill, B. M. (1975) "A Simple General Approach to Inference about the Tail of a Distribution." *Annals of Statistics*, Vol. 35, No. 3, pp. 1163–1173.

Horvitz, J. E. (2000) "Asset Classes and Asset Allocation: Problems of Classification." *Journal of Private Portfolio Management*, Vol. 2, No. 4, pp. 27–32.

Horwitz, R. (2002) "Constructing a 'Risk-Efficient' Portfolio of Hedge Funds." Kenmar Global Investment, RiskInvest 2002 Conference Presentation, Boston. *www.qwafafew.org/chicago/handouts/feldman2august2002.pdf*.

Huang, C., and R. Litzenberger (1988) *Foundations for Financial Economics*. Upper Saddle River, NJ: Prentice-Hall.

Huberman, G., and S. Ross. (1983) "Portfolio Turnpike Theorems, Risk Aversion and Regularly Varying Utility Functions." *Econometrica*, Vol. 51, No. 5, pp. 1104–1119.

Hübner, G. (2004) "The Generalized Treynor Ratio." Working paper, Ecole d'Administration des Affaires, University of Liège, Liège, Belgium.

Ibbotson, R. G. (1975) "Price Performance of Common Stock New Issues." *Journal of Financial Economics*, Vol. 2, No. 3, pp. 235–272.

Indjic, D. (December, 2002) "Strategic Asset Allocation with Portfolios of Hedge Funds." *AIMA Journal* (London). *http://www.insightful.com/investors/aima_dec2002.pdf.*

Ineichen, A. (October 2000) "In Search of Alpha—Investing in Hedge Funds." UBS Warburg, London.

Ineichen, A. (2002a) "The Alpha in Fund of Hedge Funds—Do Fund of Hedge Funds Managers Add Value?" *Journal of Wealth Management*, Vol. 5, No. 1, pp. 8–25.

Ineichen, A. (2002b) "Funds of Hedge Funds: Industry Overview." *Journal of Wealth Management*, Vol. 4, No. 4, pp. 47–62.

Ineichen, A. (2003) *Absolute Returns: The Risk and Opportunities of Hedge Fund Investing.* Hoboken, NJ: John Wiley & Sons.

Ineichen, A. (2004) "Absolute Returns: The Future in Wealth Management?" *Journal of Wealth Management*, Vol. 7, No. 1, pp. 64–74.

Infovest21. (March 2004) "Investor Sentiment Survey" by Lois Peltz. New York.

Ingersoll, J. E. (1987) *Theory of Financial Decision Making.* Rowman & Littlefield Publishers, Inc. Lanham, MD.

Institutional Investor Hedge Fund 100 Institutional Investor. Study compiled under the direction of Lewis, K. and J. Kenney. (May 2004). "The Hedge Fund 100." *Institutional Investor,* New York, p. 73.

International Association of Financial Engineers Investor Risk Committee (IAFE). (June 2004) "Valuation Concepts for Investment Companies and Financial Institutions and Their Stakeholders," New York.

International Organization of Securities Commissions (IOSC). (February 2003) "Regulatory and Investor Protection Issues Arising from the Participation by Retail Investors in (Funds-of) Hedge Funds." Madrid, Spain.

Jacobs, B. I., K. N. Levy, and D. Starer. (1998) "On the Optimality of Long-Short Strategies." *Financial Analyst Journal,* Vol. 54, No. 2, pp. 40–51.

Jacobs, B. I., K. N. Levy, and D. Starer. (1999) "Long-Short Portfolio Management: An Integrated Approach." *Journal of Portfolio Management,* Vol. 25, No. 2, pp. 23–32.

Jaeger, L. (2002) *Managing Risk in Alternative Investment Strategies: Successful Investing in Hedge Funds and Managed Futures.* London: Financial Times/Prentice-Hall.

Jaffe, J. F. (1974) "Special Information and Insider Trading." *Journal of Business,* Vol. 47, No. 3, pp. 410–428.

Jagannathan R., and T. Ma. (2003) "Risk Reduction in Large Portfolios: Why Imposing the Wrong Constraints Helps." *Journal of Finance,* Vol. 54, No. 4, pp. 1651–1684.

Jegadeesh, N., and S. Titman. (1993) "Returns to Buying Winners and Selling Losers: Implications for Stock Market Efficiency." *Journal of Finance,* Vol. 48, No. 1, pp. 65–91.

Jegadeesh, N., and S. Titman. (2001) "Profitability of Momentum Strategies: An Evaluation of Alternative Explanations." *Journal of Finance,* Vol. 56, No. 2, pp. 699–720.

Jenkins, I. (2004) "Determining the Fees: Setting the Fees," *http://www.hedgefundintelligence.com.*

Jensen, M. (1968) "The Performance of Mutual Funds in the Period 1945–1964." *Journal of Finance*, Vol. 23, No. 2, pp. 389–416.

Jorion, P. (2000) "Risk Management Lessons from LTCM." *European Financial Management*, Vol. 6, No. 3, pp. 227–300.

Kahneman, D., and A. Tversky. (1979) "Prospect Theory: An Analysis of Decision Making under Risk." *Econometrica*, Vol. 47, No. 2, pp. 263–291.

Kat, H. M. (2003a) "Taking the Sting Out of Hedge Funds." *Journal of Wealth Management*, Vol. 6, No. 3, pp. 67–76.

Kat, H. M. (2003b) "Ten Things That Investors Should Know About Hedge Funds." *Journal of Wealth Management*, Vol. 5, No. 4, pp. 72–81.

Kat, H. M. (2003c) "The Dangers of Using Correlation to Measure Dependence." *Journal of Alternative Investment*, Vol. 6, No. 2, pp. 54–58.

Kat, H. M. (2004a) "Hedge Funds versus Common Sense: An Illustration of the Dangers of Mechanical Investment Decision Making." In B. Schachter, ed., *Intelligent Hedge Fund Investing*, London: Risk Books, pp. 9–26.

Kat, H. M. (2004b) "Managed Futures and Hedge Funds: A Match Made in Heaven." *Journal of Investment Management*, Vol. 2, No. 1, pp. 32–40.

Kat, H. M., and S. Lu. (2002) "An Excursion into the Statistical Properties of Hedge Fund Returns." Working paper, ISMA Centre, University of Reading, Reading, U.K.

Kazemi, H., M. Mahdavi, and T. Schneeweis. (2003) "Generalized Sharpe Ratio: A Defense Against Sharpened Sharpe Ratios." CISDM, Working paper, University of Massachusetts, Amherst, MA.

Kazemi, H., and T. Schneeweis. (2004) "Hedge Funds: Stale Prices Revisited." Working paper, CISDM, University of Massachusetts, Isenberg School of Management, Amherst, MA.

Kelly, J. L. (1956) "A New Interpretation of Information Rate." *Bell Systems Technical Journal*, Vol. 35, No. 3, pp. 917–926.

Kendall, M. G., and A. Stuart. (1963) *The Advanced Theory of Statistics*. New York: Harner Publishing Company.

Keynes, J. M. (1930) *A Treatise on Money, Volume Two.* New York: Macmillan & Company.

Kim, W., and S. J. Wei. (2001) "Offshore Investment Funds: Monsters in Emerging Markets?" Working paper, Brookings Institution, Washington, DC.

Klepper, S., and E. E. Leamer. (1984) "Consistent Sets of Estimates for Regressions with Errors in All Variables." *Econometrica*, Vol. 52, No. 1, pp. 163–184.

Koh, F., W. Koh, and M. Teo. (2003) "Hedge Fund Characteristics, Returns, and Style: An Asian Perspective." Working paper, Singapore Management University, Singapore.

Koopman, S. J., N. Shephard, and J. A. Doornik. (1999) "Statistical Algorithms for Models in State Space Form Using SSFPack 2.2." *Econometrics Journal*, Vol. 2, No. 1, pp. 113–166.

Kouwenberg, R. R. P., and W. T. Ziemba. (2004) "Incentives and Risk Taking in Hedge Funds," *http://ssrn.com/abstract=574186*.

Kraus, A., and H. Litzenberger. (1976) "Skewness Preference and the Valuation of Risk Assets." *Journal of Finance*, Vol. 31, No. 4, pp. 1085–1100.

Krokhmal, P., S. Uryasev, and G. Zrazhevsky (2002) "Risk Management for Hedge Fund Portfolios." *Journal of Alternative Investment*, Vol. 5, No. 1, pp. 10–30.

Kurdas, C. (2004) "Morgan Stanley Investment Chief: Hedge Funds Have Become Volatility-Shy," *http://www.hedgeworld.com*. ·

Lakonishok, J., A. Shleifer, and R. W. Vishny. (1994) "Contrarian Investment, Extrapolation, and Risk." *Journal of Finance*, Vol. 49, No. 5, pp. 1541–1578.

Larsen, G. A., and B. G. Resnick. (1998) "Empirical Insights on Indexing," *Journal of Portfolio Management,* Vol. 25, No. 1, pp. 51–60.

Lavinio, S. (2000) *The Hedge Fund Handbook*. Irwin Library of Investment & Finance. New York: McGraw-Hill.

Learned, M., and F. S. Lhabitant. (2002) "Hedge Fund Diversification: How Much Is Enough?" *Journal of Alternative Investment*, Vol. 5, No. 3, pp. 23–49.

Ledford, A., and J. Tawn. (1996) "Statistics for Near Independence in Multivariate Extreme Values." *Biometrika*, Vol. 83, No. 1, pp. 169–187.

Ledford, A., and J. Tawn. (1997) "Modeling Dependence within Joint Tail Regions." *Journal of the Royal Statistical Society*, Series B, Vol. 49, pp. 475–499.

Ledoit, O., and M. Wolf. (2003) "Improved Estimation of the Covariance Matrix of Stock Returns with an Application to Portfolio Selection." *Journal of Empirical Finance*, Vol. 10, No. 5, pp. 603–621.

Ledoit, O., and M. Wolf. (2004) "A Well-Conditioned Estimator for Large-Dimensional Covariance Matrices." *Journal of Multivariate Analysis*, Vol. 88, No. 2, pp. 365–411.

Lee, B., and Y. Lee. (2004) "The Alternative Sharpe Ratio." In B. Schachter, ed., *Intelligent Hedge Fund Investing*. London: Risk Books, pp. 143–177.

Lefèvre, E. (1994) *Reminiscences of a Stock Operator*. New York: John Wiley & Sons.

Lehman Brothers. (2000) *The Benefits of Hedge Funds: Asset Allocation for the Institutional Investors*. New York: Lehman Brothers.

Leland, H. (1972) "On Turnpike Portfolios." In K. Shell and G. P. Szego, eds., *Mathematical Methods in Investment and Finance*. Amsterdam: North-Holland, pp. 24–33.

Leland, H. (1999) "Beyond Mean-Variance: Performance Measurement in a Non-Symmetrical World." *Financial Analysts Journal*, Vol. 49, No. 1, pp. 27–36.

Leland, H., and M. Rubinstein. (1988) "Comments on the Market Crash: Six Months Later." *Journal of Economic Perspectives*, Vol. 2, No. 3, 1988, pp. 45–50.

Leung, E., P. A. Roffman, and J. Meziani. (May 2004) "Standard & Poor's Equity Long/Short Index, Structure, Methodology, Definitions, and Practices." Standard & Poor's. New York.

Lhabitant, F. S. (2001) "Assessing Market Risk for Hedge Funds and Hedge Funds Portfolios." *Journal of Risk Finance*, Vol. 3, No. 4, pp. 16–32.

Lhabitant, F. S. (2003) "Hedge Funds: A Look beyond the Sample." In G. N. Gregoriou, V.N. Karavas, and F. Rouah, eds. *Hedge Funds: Strategies, Risk Assessment, and Returns*. Washington, DC: Beard Books, pp. 209–234.

Lhabitant, F. S. (2004) *Hedge Funds: Quantitative Insights*. Hoboken, NJ: John Wiley & Sons.

Lhabitant, F. S., and M. L. De Piante Vicin. (2004) "Finding the Sweet Spot of Hedge Fund Diversification." Working paper, EDHEC Risk and Asset Management Research Centre, Nice, France.

Li, D. (1999) "Value at Risk Based on the Volatility, Skewness and Kurtosis." Riskmetrics Group, *http://www.riskmetrics.com/kurtovv.html*.

Liang, B. (1999) "On the Performance of Hedge Funds." *Financial Analysts Journal*, Vol. 55, No. 4, pp. 72–85.

Liang, B. (2000) "Hedge Funds: The Living and the Dead." *Journal of Financial and Quantitative Analysis*, Vol. 35, No. 3, pp. 309–326.

Liang, B. (2001) "Hedge Fund Performance: 1990-1999." *Financial Analysts Journal*, Vol. 57, No. 1, pp. 11–18.

Liang, B. (2003a) "The Accuracy of Hedge Fund Returns." *Journal of Portfolio Management*, Vol. 29, No. 3, pp. 111–122.

Liang, B. (2003b) "On the Performance of Alternative Investments: CTAs, Hedge Funds, and Funds-of-Funds." Working paper, Case Western Reserve University, Weatherhead School of Management, Cleveland, OH.

Liang, B. (2004) "Alternative Investments: CTAs, Hedge Funds, and Funds-of-Funds." *Journal of Investment Management*, Vol. 2, No. 4, pp. 76–93.

Liew, J. (2003) "Hedge Fund Index Investing Examined." *Journal of Portfolio Management*, Vol. 29, No. 2, pp. 113–123.

Lintner, J. (1965) "The Valuation of Risk Assets and the Selection of Risky Investments in Stock Portfolio and Capital Budgets." *Review of Economics and Statistics*, Vol. 47, No. 1, pp. 13–37.

Litzenberger, R. H., and K. Ramaswamy. (1979) "The Effect of Personal Taxes and Dividends on Capital Asset Prices: Theory and Empirical Evidence." *Journal of Financial Economics*, Vol. 7, No. 2, pp. 163–195.

Litzenberger, R. H., and K. Ramaswamy. (1982) "The Effects of Dividends on Common Stock Prices: Tax Effects or Information Effects?" *Journal of Finance*, Vol. 37, No. 2, pp. 429–443.

Lo, A. W. (1991) "Long-Term Memory in Stock Market Prices." *Econometrica*, Vol. 59, No. 5, pp. 1279–1313.

Lo, A. W. (2001) "Risk Management for Hedge Funds: Introduction and Overview." *Financial Analyst Journal*, Vol. 57, No. 6, pp. 16–33.

Lo, A. W. (2002) "The Statistics of Sharpe Ratios." *Financial Analysts Journal*, Vol. 58, No. 4, pp. 36–52.

Longin, F. and B. Solnik. (1995) "Is the Correlation in International Equity Returns Constant: 1960–1990?" *Journal of International Money and Finance*, Vol. 14, No. 2, pp. 3–23.

Lopez de Prado, M.M., and A. Peijan. (2004) "Measuring Loss Potential of Hedge Fund Strategies." *Journal of Alternative Investments*, Vol. 7, No. 1, pp. 7–31.

Loughran, T., and J. Ritter. (1995) "The New Issues Puzzle." *Journal of Finance*, Vol. 50, No. 1, pp. 23–52.

Lungarella, G. (2002) "Managed Futures: A Real Alternative." SwissHedge, Harcourt Investment Consulting, Zurich, Switzerland, pp. 9–13.

Luskin, D. (1988) *Portfolio Insurance: a Guide to Dynamic Hedging*. New York: John Wiley & Sons.

Lyon, J., B. Brad, and C. Tsai. (1999) "Improved Methods for Tests of Long-run Abnormal Stock Returns." *Journal of Finance*, Vol. 54, No. 1, pp. 165–201.

MacKinnon, J. (1992) "Model Specification Tests and Artificial Regressions." *Journal of Economic Literature*, Vol. 30. No. 1, pp. 102–146.

Madan, D., and G. S. McPhail. (2000) "Investing in Skews." Working paper, University of Maryland, Baltimore.

Malkiel, B., and A. Saha. (2004) *Hedge Funds: Risk and Return*, Working paper, Princeton Center for Economic Policy Research, Princeton University, Princeton, NJ.

Malinvaud, E. (1978) Methodes Statistiques de l'Econometrie, 3rd ed., Paris: Dunod.

Mandelker, G. (1974) "Risk and Return: The Case of Merging Firms." *Journal of Financial Economics*, Vol. 1, No. 4, pp. 303–335.

Markowitz, H. (1952) "Portfolio Selection." *Journal of Finance*, Vol. 7, No. 1, pp. 77–91.

Martellini, L., and V. Ziemann. (2004) "Higher Moment Betas." EDHEC working paper, EDHEC Business School, *http://www.edhec-risk.com*.

Martellini, L., M. Vaissie, and F. Goltz (2004) "Hedge Fund Indices from an Academic Perspective: Reconciling Investability and Representativity." Discussion paper, EDHEC Business School, *http://www.edhec-risk.com*.

Marx, G., and J. Thurber. (1994) *Groucho and Me*. London: Virgin Books.

McFall-Lamm Jr, R. (1999) "Portfolios of Alternative Assets: Why Not 100% Hedge Funds?" *Journal of Investing*, Vol. 8, No. 4, pp. 87–97.

McGuinness, S. (July, 2003) "Counting the Costs." *Hedge Funds Review*, pp. 32–33, *http://www.hedgefunds review.com*.

Merton, R. (1973) "An Intertemporal Capital Asset Pricing Model." *Econometrica*, Vol. 41, No. 1, pp. 867–888.

Michaud, R. (1998) *Efficient Asset Management*. Boston: Harvard Business School Press.

Mitchell, M, and T. Pulvino. (2001) "Characteristics of Risk and Return in Risk Arbitrage." *Journal of Finance*, Vol. 56, No. 6, pp. 2135–2175.

Molinero, R. (2003, April 10) "Rotella Capital Management" Seminar presenttion, Professional Risk Managers' International Association, Chicago, IL.

Moody's Investors Service. (2003) "Moody's Approach to Rating Collateralized Funds of Hedge Fund Obligations." Structured Finance Rating Methodology, New York.

Mossin, J. (1968) "Optimal Multiperiod Portfolio Policies." *Journal of Business*, Vol. 41, No. 2, pp. 215–229.

Muralidhar, A. (2000) "Risk-Adjusted Performance—The Correlation Correction." *Financial Analysts Journal*, Vol. 56, No. 5, pp. 63–71.

Muralidhar, A. (2001) "Skill, Horizon and Risk-Adjusted Performance." *Journal of Performance Measurement*. Vol. 6, No. 2. pp. 53–66.

Murguia, A., and D. Y. Umemoto (2004) "An Alternative Look at Hedge Funds." *Journal of Financial Planning*, Vol. 17, No. 1, pp. 42–49.

National Association of University Business Officers. (2003) NACUBO 2003 Endowment Study, *http://www.nacubo.org*.

Newey, W., and K. West. (1987) "A Simple Positive Semi-Definite, Heteroskedasticity and Autocorrelation Consistent Covariance Matrix." *Econometrica*, Vol. 55, No. 3, pp. 703–708.

Neyman, J. E., and S. Pearson. (1928) "On the Use and Interpretation of Certain Test Criteria for Purposes of Statistical Inference." *Biometrika*, Vol. 20A, No. 1, pp. 175–240.

Nicholas, J. G. (2004) *Hedge Fund of Funds Investing*. Princeton, NJ: Bloomberg Press.

Okunev, J., and D. White. (2004) "Hedge Fund Risk Factors and Value at Risk of Credit Trading Strategies." In B. Schachter, ed., *Intelligent Hedge Fund Investing*. London: Risk Books, pp. 303–364.

Osband, K. (2002) *Iceberg Risk*. New York: Texere.

Pal, M. (1980) "Consistent Moment Estimators of Regression Coefficients in the Presence of Errors in Variables." *Journal of Econometrics*, Vol. 14, No. 3, pp. 349–364.

Park, J. (1995) *Managed Futures as an Investment Set*. Doctoral dissertation, Columbia University, New York.

Park, J., and J. C. Staum. (1998) "Performance Persistence in Alternative Investment Industry." Working paper, Paradigm Capital Management, Inc., New York.

Pearson, E. S. (1929) "The Distribution of Frequency Constants in Small Samples from Non-normal Symmetrical and Skew Populations." *Biometrika*, Vol. 21, No. 1/4, pp. 259–286.

Phillips, M. K. (February 2003) "New Fans for Managed Futures." *Global Investor*, pp. 45–46.

Pickands, J. (1975) "Statistical Inference Using Extreme Order Statistics," *Annals of Statistics*, Vol. 3, No. 1, pp. 119–131.

Poon, S. H., M. Rockinger, and J. Tawn. (2004) "Extreme Value Dependency in International Stock Markets." *Review of Financial Studies*, Vol. 17, No. 2, pp. 581–610.

Posthuma, N., and P. L. Van der Sluis. (2004) "A Critical Examination of Historical Hedge Fund Returns." In B. Schachter, ed., *Intelligent Hedge Fund Investing*. London: Risk Books, pp. 365–386.

Pratt, J., and R. Zeckhauser. (1987) "Proper Risk Aversion." *Econometrica*, Vol. 55, No. 1, pp. 143–154.

Rockafellar, R. T., and S. Uryasev. (2002) "Conditional Value-at-Risk for General Loss Distributions." *Journal of Banking and Finance*, Vol. 26, No. 7, pp. 1443–1471.

Roll, R. (1978) "Ambiguity When Performance Is Measured by the Securities Market Line." *Journal of Finance*, Vol. 33, No. 4, pp. 1051–1069.

Roll, R. (1992) "A Mean/Variance Analysis of Tracking Error." *Journal of Portfolio Management*, Vol. 18, No. 4, pp. 13–22.

Ross, S. (1974) "Portfolio Turnpike Theorems for Constant Policies." *Journal of Financial Economics*, Vol. 1, No. 3, pp. 171–198.

Ross, S. (1976) "The Arbitrage Theory of Capital Asset Pricing." *Journal of Economic Theory*, Vol. 13, No. 2, pp. 341–360.

Rouwenhorst, K. G. (1998) "International Momentum Strategies." *Journal of Finance*, Vol. 53, No. 1, pp. 267–284.

Rubinstein, M. E. (1973) "The Fundamental Theorem of Parameter-preference Security Valuation." *Journal of Financial and Quantitative Analysis*, Vol. 8, No. 1, pp. 61–69.

Rudd, A. (1980) "Optimal Selection of Passive Portfolios." *Financial Management*, Vol. 9, No. 1, pp.57–66.

Rudd, A., and B. Rosenberg. (1980) "The 'Market Model' in Investment Management." *Journal of Finance*, Vol. 35, No. 2, pp. 597–606.

Rouwenhorst, K. G. (1998) "International Momentum Strategies." *Journal of Finance*, Vol. 53, No. 1, pp. 267–284.

Rudolf, M., H. Wolter, and H. Zimmermann. (1999) "A Linear Model for Tracking Error Minimization." *Journal of Banking and Finance*, Vol. 23, No. 1, pp. 85–103.

Rulle, M. (2003) "Trend-Following: Performance, Risk and Correlation Characteristics." Working paper, Graham Capital Management, Stamford, CT.

Schmidhuber, C., and P. Y. Moix. (September/December 2001) "Fat Tail Risk: The Case for Hedge Funds." *AIMA Newsletter* (London, U.K.), p. 22.

Schneeweis, T. (1998) "Evidence of Superior Performance in Hedge Funds: An Empirical Comment." *Journal of Alternative Investments*, Vol. 1, No. 2, pp. 76–79.

Schneeweis, T., and H. Kazemi. (2001) "The Creation of Alternative Tracking Portfolios for Hedge Fund Strategies." CISDM/SOM Working paper, University of Massachusetts, Amherst, MA.

Schneeweis, T., and G. Martin. (2001) "The Benefits of Hedge Funds: Asset Allocation for the Institutional Investor." *Journal of Alternative Investments*, Vol. 4, No. 3, pp. 7–26.

Schneeweis, T., and R. Spurgin. (1997) "Managed Futures, Hedge Funds and Mutual Fund Return Estimation: A Multifactor Approach." CISDM Working paper, University of Massachusetts, Amherst, MA.

Schneeweis, T., and R. Spurgin. (1998a) "Alternative Investments in the Institutional Portfolio." *AIMA Newsletter.* (London, U.K.), *http://www.aima.org/aima.asp?id=40.*

Schneeweis, T., and R. Spurgin. (1998b) "Multifactor Analysis of Hedge Funds, Managed Futures and Mutual Fund Return and Risk Characteristics." *Journal of Alternative Investment*, Vol. 1, No. 2, pp. 1–24.

Schneeweis, T., and R. Spurgin. (1999) "Alpha, Alpha...Who's Got the Alpha?" *Journal of Alternative Investments*, Vol. 2, No. 2, pp. 83–87.

Schneeweis, T., and R. Spurgin, R. (2000a) "Hedge Funds: Portfolio Risk Diversifiers, Risk Enhancers, or Both?" CISDM Working paper, University of Massachusetts, Amherst, MA.

Schneeweis, T., and R. Spurgin. (2000b) "Quantitative Analysis of Hedge Funds and Managed Futures Return and Risk Characteristics." CISDM, Working paper, University of Massachusetts, Amherst, MA.

Schneeweis, T., V. Karavas, and G. Georgiev. (2002) "Alternative Investments in the Institutional Portfolio." CISDM Working paper, University of Massachusetts, Amherst.

Scott, R. C., and P. A. Horvath. (1980) "On the Direction of Preference for Moments of Higher Order than Variance." *Journal of Finance*, Vol. 35, No. 4, pp. 915–919.

Securities and Exchange Commission. (September 2003) "Implications of the Growth of Hedge Funds: Staff Report to the United States Securities and Exchange Commission." Washington, DC.

Securities and Exchange Commission. (2004) "Mandatory Redemption Fees for Redeemable Fund Securities." Release No. IC-26375A. Washington, DC.

Sender, H., and J. Singer. (January 24, 2003) "Spectacularly Rapid Demise Strikes Tokyo Hedge Fund." *Wall Street Journal*.

Sexton, T. R., R. H. Silkman, and A. Hogan. (1986) "Data Envelopment Analysis: Critiques and Extensions," in R. H. Silkman, ed., *Measuring Efficiency and Assessment of Data Envelopment Analysis*. San Francisco: Jossey-Bass Publishers, pp. 73–105.

Shadwick, W., and C. Keating. (2002) "A Universal Performance Measure." *Journal of Performance Measurement*, Vol. 6, No. 3, pp. 59–84.

Sharma, M. (2004) "AIRAP—Alternative Views on Alternative Investments." In B. Schachter, ed., *Intelligent Hedge Fund Investing*. London: Risk Books, pp. 179–213.

Sharpe, M. (1999) "Constructing the Optimal Hedge Fund of Funds." *Journal of Wealth Management*, Vol. 2, No. 1, pp. 34–44.

Sharpe, W. F. (1964) "Capital Asset Prices: A Theory of Asset Equilibrium under Conditions of Risk." *Journal of Finance*, Vol. 19, No. 3, pp. 425–442.

Sharpe, W. F. (1992) "Asset Allocation: Management Style and Performance Measurement." *Journal of Portfolio Management*, Vol. 18, No. 2, pp. 7–19.

Sharpe, W. F. (1994) "The Sharpe Ratio." *Journal of Portfolio Management*, Vol. 21, No. 1, pp. 49–58.

Signer, A., and L. Favre. (2002) "The Difficulties of Measuring the Benefit of Hedge Funds." *Journal of Alternative Investments*, Vol. 5, No. 1, pp. 31–42.

Singer, B., R. Staub, and K. Terhaar. (2003) "Determining the Appropriate Allocation to Alternative Investments." *Journal of Portfolio Management*, Vol. 29, No.3, pp. 101–110.

Sortino, F. A., and L. N. Price. (1994) "Performance Measurement in a Downside Risk Framework." *Journal of Investing*, Vol. 3, No.3, pp. 59–65.

Spurgin, R. (2001) "How to Game Your Sharpe Ratio." *Journal of Alternative Investments*, Vol. 4, No. 3, pp. 38–46.

Spurgin, R., T. Schneeweis, and G. Georgiev. (2001) "Benchmarking Commodity Trading Advisory Performance with a Passive Futures-Based Index." CISDM Working Paper, Isenberg School of Management, University of Massachusetts, Amherst, MA.

Stadin, J. (2003) "Paying Now vs. Paying Later: A Financial Recruiter's Perspective on Compensation Packages." PerTrac Solutions Newsletter, Vol. 2, No. 4, pp. 1–5.

Strategic Financial Solutions LLC (2004) "Hedge Fund Database Survey," by Meredith Jones and Milt Baehr. November 2004, Memphis, TN.

Swinkels, L. A. P., and P. J. Van der Sluis. (2001) "Return-based Style Analysis with Time Varying Exposures." Center Discussion paper 2001-96, Tilburg University, Tilburg, Netherlands, http://www.ssrn.com.

Swinkels, L. A. P., P. J. Van der Sluis, and M. Verbeek. (2003) "Market Timing: A Decomposition of Mutual Fund Returns." ERIM Report Series Reference, No. ERS-2003-074-F&A. Available from *http://www.ssrn.com*.

Theil, H., and A. S. Goldberger. (1961) "On Pure and Mixed Statistical Estimation in Economics." *International Economic Review*, Vol. 2, No. 1, pp. 65–78.

Till, H. (September 2001a) "Life at Sharpe's End." *Risk & Reward*, pp. 39–43.

Till, H. (October 2001b) "Measure for Measure." *Risk & Reward*, pp.33–36.

Till, H. (2002) "How to Include Hedge Funds in a Risk Allocation Framework." *GARP Risk Review*, Vol. 2, No. 9, pp. 34–38.

Till, H. (2003a) "The Difficulties with Traditional Performance Measures When Applied to Hedge Funds." Premia Risk Consultancy, Inc, Chicago.

Till, H. (October, 2003b). "Risk Management for Alternative Investments." Risk-Invest Europe, London, U.K.

Till, H. (2004a) "On the Role of Hedge Funds in Institutional Portfolios." *Journal of Alternative Investments*, Vol. 6, No. 4, pp. 77–89.

Till, H. (2004b) "Risk Measurement of Investments in the Satellite Ring of a Core-Satellite Portfolio: Traditional versus Alternative Approaches." *Singapore Economic Review*, Vol. 49, No. 1, pp. 105–130.

Twain, M. (1900) *The Tragedy of Puddn'head and the Comedy Those Extraordinary Twins*. Hartford, CT: American Publishing Company.

UBS. (September 2001) "The Search for Alpha Continues—Do Fund of Hedge Fund Managers Add Value?" UBS Warburg Global Equity Research, London, England.

UBS. (September 2002a) "Asymmetric Returns." UBS Warburg Global Equity Research, London, England.

UBS. (February 2002b) "The S^2MART Certificate—Reduced Downside and High Participation." UBS Warburg Global Equity Research, London, England.

UBS. (May 2002c) "Return Expectations." UBS Warburg Global Equity Research, London, England.

UBS. (July 2004) "AIS Structuring: Tools for Alpha." UBS Global Equity Research, London, England.

Wachovia Securities. (2003) "Understanding Hedge Fund Linked Principal-Protected Securities." Structured Products Research, Charlotte, N.C.

Waring, B., D. Whitney, J. Pirone, and C. Castille. (2000) "Optimizing Manager Structure and Budgeting Manager Risk." *Journal of Portfolio Management*, Vol. 26, No. 3, pp. 90–104.

Waring, M. B., and L. B. Siegel. (2003) "The Dimensions of Active Management." *Journal of Portfolio Management*, Vol. 29, No. 3, pp. 35–51.

Weisman, A. B. (2002) "Informationless Investing and Hedge Fund Performance Measurement Bias." *Journal of Portfolio Management*, Vol. 28, No. 4, pp. 80–91.

Weisman, A., and J. Abernathy. (2000) "The Dangers of Historical Hedge Fund Data." In L. Rahl, ed., *Risk Budgeting*. London: Risk Books, pp. 65–81.

Wenner, F. (2002) "Determination of Risk Aversion and Moment-Preferences: A Comparison of Econometric Models." Dissertation 2606, St. Gallen University, St. Gallen, Switzerland.

Wilkens, K., and J. Zhu. (2003) "Classifying Hedge Funds Using Data Envelopment Analysis." In G. N. Gregoriou, V. N. Karavas, and F. Rouah, eds., *Hedge Funds: Strategies, Risk Assessment, and Returns*. Baltimore: Beard Books, pp. 161–175.

Wood, C. (August 26, 2004) "Argy sans Bargy." *CSLA Greed & Fear*, Singapore, pp. 1–7.

Zangari, P. (First quarter 1996) "A VaR Methodology for Portfolios that Include Options." *RiskMetrics Monitor*, pp. 4–12.

Zhu, J. (2003) *Quantitative Models for Performance Evaluation and Benchmarking*. Norwell, MA: Kluwer Academic Publishers.

Zivot, E., and Wang, J. (2002) *Modeling Financial Time Series with S-Plus*. New York, Springer-Verlag.

Index